Ultimate AWS Certified Advanced Networking (ANS-C01) Certification Guide

Master Advanced AWS Networking, Hybrid Architectures, and Security to Successfully Crack ANS-C01 Certification

Aishwarya. S

www.orangeava.com

First Published: May 2026

Published By: Orange Education Pvt Ltd, AVA®

Address: 9, Daryaganj, Delhi, 110002, India

275 New North Road Islington Suite 1314 London,
N1 7AA, United Kingdom

ISBN (PBK): 978-93-49887-01-5
ISBN (E-BOOK): 978-93-49887-40-4

Scan the QR code to explore our entire catalogue

www.orangeava.com

Get a Free eBook

We hope you're enjoying your recent book purchase! Your feedback is incredibly valuable to us and helps other readers discover books that truly make a difference.

If you found this book useful or enjoyable, we'd greatly appreciate it if you could leave a short review with a 5-star rating on Amazon. Your review supports our work and allows us to reach more learners worldwide.

As a thank-you, we're happy to offer you a **free digital copy of this book** plus a **30% discount code** for your next purchase on our official websites:

www.orangeava.com

www.orangeava.in (For the Indian Subcontinent).

☑ **How it works:**

Leave your review on Amazon, take a screenshot of the confirmation or use the following link to submit the claim and email it to **info@orangeava.com.** Once received the required detail, we will send your rewards within 24 hours, **along with one month free subcription to the book on AVA SkillShelf!**

Claim Form
https://rebrand.ly/4d2477

Thank you for your support—it truly means a lot to us.

Enjoy 1 Month of Free Access to AVA SkillShelf!

The future belongs to lifelong learners. With AVA SkillShelf, you go beyond reading books and start building real, job-ready skills curated by industry experts.

Your membership unlocks **200+ learning products** covering AI, Cloud, Python, Cybersecurity, Data Science, DevOps, and more—all in one platform. Our bestselling technical books are transformed into structured courses designed for practical, real-world application.

Learn directly from experienced professionals and published authors, with no filler—just actionable insights. Earn **verified digital certifications** to strengthen your CV, LinkedIn profile, and professional credibility.

Learn anytime, anywhere, on any device, at your own pace. Ideal for students, professionals, career switchers, and tech leaders.

For full access to all current and future courses, choose our **Annual Membership**. Simply scan the QR to get started!

For 1 month Free access, simply refer to the steps on the previous page titled: Get a Free ebook!

https://www.avaskillshelf.com/

Colored images

Please follow the links or scan the QR codes to download the ***Images*** of the book:

https://github.com/orgs/ava-orange-education/repositories

The code bundles and images of the book are also hosted on ***https://rebrand.ly/e157b2***

In case there's an update to the code, it will be updated on the existing GitHub repository.

Errata

We take immense pride in our work at **Orange Education Pvt Ltd,** and follow best practices to ensure the accuracy of our content to provide an indulging reading experience to our subscribers. Our readers are our mirrors, and we use their inputs to reflect and improve upon human errors, if any, that may have occurred during the publishing processes involved. To let us maintain the quality and help us reach out to any readers who might be having difficulties due to any unforeseen errors, please write to us at :

errata@orangeava.com

Your support, suggestions, and feedback are highly appreciated.

Dedicated to

Those who choose curiosity over comfort, and growth over fear.

To the quiet determination behind every long night, and the belief that learning never truly ends.

About the Author

Aishwarya. S is a Data Engineering, Analytics, and Governance specialist with nearly seven years of experience delivering enterprise-scale data and analytics solutions. She currently works at Accenture Solutions Pvt. Ltd., where she contributes to large, globally distributed programs focused on data governance, automation, and business intelligence. Her work centers on building reliable, scalable data systems that enable accurate reporting, operational efficiency, and informed decision-making.

Aishwarya's professional expertise spans data engineering, KPI standardization, data modeling, workflow automation, and advanced analytics. She has led enterprise data governance initiatives, standardized over 120 key performance indicators, and significantly improved data accuracy and compliance across complex organizational landscapes.

In addition to analytics and engineering, Aishwarya has extensive experience in intelligent automation. She has designed and implemented automated workflows using Microsoft Power Automate and Power Platform technologies, reducing manual effort, shortening reporting cycles, and improving overall productivity.

Aishwarya holds a Post Graduate degree in Data Science, a Master of Business Administration in Human Resources Management, and a Bachelor's degree in Electronics and Communication Engineering. She also holds multiple professional certifications across analytics, automation, governance, cybersecurity fundamentals, ServiceNow, and the Microsoft Power Platform.

Her professional excellence has been recognized through several prestigious awards, including the ATCI Americas Pinnacle Award – North Star, Accenture Celebrates Excellence (ACE) Awards, Automation Star Award, and multiple Rockstar and Zenith recognitions for performance, innovation, and leadership potential.

Aishwarya is passionate about practical, experience-driven learning. She focuses on bridging the gap between theoretical concepts and real-world implementation, helping professionals build confidence in applying complex technical skills. Through this book, she aims to equip readers with the clarity and practical understanding required to succeed in modern data and cloud-driven environments.

About the Technical Reviewer

Bhumika Gupta is a Platform Engineering professional at S&P Global, within the Market Intelligence division. She has nearly four years of experience in DevOps, automation, and cloud infrastructure, with a strong focus on building reliable, secure, and scalable cloud solutions that support critical business applications.

Her professional expertise spans AWS, Terraform, Kubernetes, Python, and CI/CD technologies. Throughout her career, she has contributed to developing and maintaining infrastructure-as-code frameworks, automating deployment pipelines, and optimizing cloud environments for performance and cost efficiency. Working in the fintech domain, Bhumika has been instrumental in projects involving cost optimization, infrastructure automation, and secure cloud architecture, ensuring that systems remain both robust and compliant with industry standards.

Bhumika holds two professional certifications from Amazon Web Services — AWS Certified Advanced Networking - Specialty and AWS Certified Solutions Architect - Associate — which validate her deep technical understanding of distributed systems, cloud networking, and architectural best practices. She earned her Bachelor of Technology degree in Computer Science and Engineering from Dr. A.P.J. Abdul Kalam Technical University.

Her current professional interests include cloud-native automation, infrastructure optimization, and secure infrastructure design. Beyond her professional commitments, she enjoys participating in sports, which helps her stay energized, focused, and motivated in her work.

Acknowledgments

This book would not have been possible without the guidance, support, and encouragement of many people along the way. I am deeply grateful to my mentors, managers, and colleagues for their trust, insights, and constant motivation, which played a crucial role in shaping my professional journey, and the practical perspectives shared in this book.

I would also like to thank the learners who challenged my thinking, and inspired me to keep improving. Special thanks to my teammates and collaborators whose insights and discussions helped shape the practical perspectives shared in this book.

On a personal note, heartfelt appreciation is also extended to my family and close friends for their unwavering belief, patience, and emotional support throughout this journey. Their encouragement during my long hours of learning, writing, and reflection made all the difference, and their constant support played a vital role in the completion of this work.

Preface

Cloud networking has evolved from a niche skill into a critical capability for modern IT professionals. As organizations increasingly migrate complex workloads to the cloud, the demand for engineers who can design, secure, and optimize scalable network architectures has grown exponentially. Amazon Web Services (AWS), as the leading cloud platform, offers a powerful and sophisticated networking ecosystem—but mastering it requires more than just theoretical knowledge.

This book was written to address a common challenge faced by many AWS professionals and network engineers, that is the gap between understanding concepts and applying them confidently in real-world environments. While documentation and training materials are abundant, they often lack the practical depth, architectural context, and exam-oriented clarity needed to truly master AWS advanced networking—or to succeed in the AWS Certified Advanced Networking - Specialty (ANS-C01) exam.

This guide takes a hands-on, scenario-driven approach to learning. Each chapter is designed not only to explain what a service does, but why it is used, when to choose it, and how to implement it effectively in production-grade architectures. Real-world scenarios, step-by-step labs, and troubleshooting insights ensure that the readers build practical skills alongside conceptual understanding.

The book follows a carefully structured learning path. It begins with core networking fundamentals to establish a strong foundation, then progresses into AWS networking services such as VPC design, Route 53, CloudFront, and Direct Connect. Advanced topics—including hybrid connectivity, multi-region architectures, security, automation, and high availability—are introduced gradually, making the content accessible to readers at different experience levels. Each section builds logically on the previous one, reinforcing concepts through practice and real-world examples.

A strong emphasis is placed on exam readiness throughout the book. Complex topics are broken down in alignment with the ANS-C01 exam blueprint, and each chapter includes targeted Q&A sections to reinforce key concepts. The final section is dedicated entirely to exam preparation, featuring mock questions, detailed explanations, and strategic guidance to help readers confidently approach even the most challenging scenarios.

Thus, whether you are an experienced network engineer transitioning to AWS, an AWS professional aiming to specialize in advanced networking, or a certification candidate seeking a focused and practical study resource, this book is designed to support your journey. In fact, this book is more than an exam guide—it is a practical companion for mastering AWS networking.

Chapter 1: Networking Fundamentals introduces core networking concepts, essential for understanding cloud and AWS environments. It covers networking models (OSI and TCP/IP), IPv4/IPv6 addressing, sub netting, and basic routing. Readers will learn how data flows between devices and how networks are structured to enable seamless communication. Practical examples illustrate concepts such as CIDR notation and static vs. dynamic routing, preparing readers to build and manage AWS networks effectively.

Chapter 2: Network Security Basics helps to learn the foundational principles of securing cloud networks. This chapter covers firewalls, ACLs, and AWS-specific features like Security Groups and NACLs. Readers will understand how to implement secure protocols such as HTTPS, TLS, and SSH to safeguard data in transit. Real-world examples demonstrate configuring access controls and protecting networks against unauthorized access.

Chapter 3: Network Design and High Availability focuses on designing scalable, high-availability architectures. It combines concepts such as load balancing, fault tolerance, and scalability. Readers will explore how to use AWS tools like Elastic Load Balancers (ELB) and Auto Scaling to design networks resilient to failure, ensuring minimal downtime and optimal performance.

Chapter 4: Network Monitoring and Troubleshooting explains how to monitor and troubleshoot networks effectively using AWS tools. The chapter also briefs the importance of metrics, logs, and alerts in identifying performance bottlenecks. Readers will use CloudWatch, VPC Flow Logs, and diagnostic commands such as traceroute to analyze network health, and resolve common issues like latency and dropped packets.

Chapter 5: Amazon VPC Basics introduces Amazon VPC, the foundation of AWS networking. Readers will learn to create isolated cloud environments, configure subnets, route tables, and gateways. Topics include NAT and Internet Gateways, enabling secure connectivity for workloads. Hands-on exercises guide the practical setup of VPCs, emphasizing traffic control and segmentation.

Chapter 6: Advanced VPC and Hybrid Connectivity dives into advanced VPC features and hybrid connectivity setups. Topics include VPC Peering, Transit Gateway, and inter-region connectivity. Readers will explore building scalable, multi-account architectures, while ensuring data security and optimal performance. Use cases demonstrate hybrid setups connecting on-premises data centers to AWS environments.

Chapter 7: Route 53 and DNS Traffic Management masters Amazon Route 53 to manage DNS and route traffic effectively. This chapter explains routing policies (simple, weighted, and geolocation) and failover strategies. Readers will gain hands-on experience configuring hosted zones and DNS records for fault tolerance and load distribution across AWS regions.

Chapter 8: CloudFront and Content Delivery covers how to deliver content globally with Amazon CloudFront. This chapter covers Content Delivery Networks (CDNs), caching strategies, and integration with S3 for static content. Readers will set up secure content delivery using HTTPS and TLS, ensuring low latency and high availability. Use cases include video streaming and web content optimization.

Chapter 9: VPN Connections and Direct Connect covers hybrid cloud setups using VPNs and AWS Direct Connect. Readers will configure Site-to-Site VPNs for secure connections and explore Direct Connect for low-latency, high-bandwidth links. Troubleshooting scenarios guide diagnosing and resolving connectivity issues in hybrid architectures.

Chapter 10: Network Optimization Techniques optimizes AWS networks for performance and cost. Topics include reducing latency, managing bandwidth, and using tools like Cost Explorer for monitoring. Readers will learn to identify bottlenecks, and implement solutions to enhance throughput, ensuring cost-effective, high-performing network operations.

Chapter 11: Network Security Services explores AWS WAF (Web Application Firewall) and Shield for protecting applications and network infrastructure from DDoS attacks. It explains the setup and configuration of WAF rules, how AWS Shield helps mitigate DDoS threats, and how to leverage Security Hub for centralized security monitoring. Readers will get hands-on experience creating protective measures and configuring alerting mechanisms.

Chapter 12: Disaster Recovery Strategies explores how to create disaster recovery plans for AWS infrastructure, covering the key concepts of backup, failover, and recovery. This chapter explores how to design fault-tolerant systems using multiple Availability Zones (AZs) and Regions, while adhering to Recovery Point Objective (RPO) and Recovery Time Objective (RTO). Practical exercises help in automating recovery processes, and verifying disaster recovery setups.

Chapter 13: Automating Network Deployments introduces Infrastructure as Code (IaC), and how it can automate network setups. Using AWS CloudFormation, readers will learn how to define network resources like VPCs, subnets, security groups, and route tables in templates. The chapter covers template creation, management, versioning, and testing, ensuring that readers can deploy entire networks automatically.

Chapter 14: Advanced Troubleshooting Techniques focuses on diagnosing and fixing advanced networking issues within AWS using AWS CLI, VPC Flow Logs, and CloudWatch Logs. It explains common pitfalls such as misconfigured route tables, improper security group settings, and connectivity issues between VPCs. Practical troubleshooting scenarios will guide the reader through diagnosing and resolving complex network problems.

Chapter 15: Exam Strategy and Tips contains strategies and tips for taking the AWS Certified Advanced Networking – Specialty (ANS-C01) exam. It focuses on time management, understanding the question formats, and tips for solving complex, scenario-based questions. Readers will learn how to identify key terms, and quickly analyze questions for accurate responses.

Chapter 16: Practice Questions on Realistic Scenarios provides practice questions designed to simulate real-world AWS networking challenges. The questions are aligned with the exam objectives, focusing on topics such as VPC configurations, security group management, and hybrid network setups. Each scenario has multiple-choice questions followed by detailed explanations to deepen the reader's understanding.

Chapter 17: Mock Tests with Detailed Explanations includes full-length mock tests designed to reflect the ANS-C01 exam. Each test is followed by a detailed explanation of the answers, clarifying why certain choices are correct or incorrect. This helps reinforce the understanding of key concepts, and improves exam-taking strategies. Mock tests are based on realistic scenarios and practice exam conditions.

Chapter 18: Final Q&A and Career Guidance provides a comprehensive review of key concepts, followed by a Q&A section to consolidate knowledge. It also offers career guidance on advancing in AWS networking roles, highlighting job opportunities, certifications and networking with industry professionals. This chapter includes additional resources like study groups, online forums, and AWS communities.

DID YOU KNOW

Did you know that Orange Education Pvt Ltd offers eBook versions of every book published, with PDF and ePub files available? You can upgrade to the eBook version at **www.orangeava.com** and as a print book customer, you are entitled to a discount on the eBook copy. Get in touch with us at: **info@orangeava.com** for more details.

At **www.orangeava.com**, you can also read a collection of free technical articles, sign up for a range of free newsletters, and receive exclusive discounts and offers on Print Books and eBooks.

PIRACY

If you come across any illegal copies of our works in any form on the internet, we would be grateful if you would provide us with the location address or website name. Please contact us at **info@orangeava.com** with a link to the material.

ARE YOU INTERESTED IN AUTHORING WITH US?

If there is a topic that you have expertise in, and you are interested in either writing or contributing to a book, please write to us at **business@orangeava.com**. We are on a journey to help developers and tech professionals to gain insights on the present technological advancements and innovations happening across the globe and build a community that believes Knowledge is best acquired by sharing and learning with others. Please reach out to us to learn what our audience demands and how you can be part of this educational reform. We also welcome ideas from tech experts and help them build learning and development content for their domains.

REVIEWS

Please leave a review. Once you have read and used this book, why not leave a review on the site that you purchased it from? Potential readers can then see and use your unbiased opinion to make purchase decisions. We at Orange Education would love to know what you think about our products, and our authors can learn from your feedback. Thank you!

For more information about Orange Education, please visit **www.orangeava.com**.

Table of Contents

Chapter 1
Networking Fundamentals

Introduction

Networking is the backbone of all modern computing systems, enabling communication, resource sharing, and data exchange between devices. In the context of cloud computing, networking takes on an even greater significance as it provides the underlying infrastructure for scalability, reliability, and connectivity. Whether it is enabling secure communication between geographically dispersed servers or ensuring the smooth delivery of services to users, networking is integral to cloud environments like AWS.

This chapter sets the stage for understanding the core principles of networking. It explores foundational topics such as the OSI and TCP/IP models, IP addressing, subnetting, and routing. These concepts form the building blocks of more complex networking topics and are crucial for configuring and managing cloud networks effectively.

Through a combination of theoretical insights and hands-on exercises, this chapter equips readers with the skills to analyze data flow, allocate IP addresses efficiently, and design basic network setups. By mastering these fundamentals, readers will be prepared to tackle the advanced networking topics and AWS-specific services introduced in later chapters.

This journey into networking begins with understanding how data travels from one device to another. It also involves learning about the protocols that govern these interactions and the mechanisms that ensure reliable communication. Let us dive in!

Structure

In this chapter, we will cover the following topics:

- Introduction to Networking
- OSI and TCP/IP Models
- IP Addressing, Subnetting and CIDR Notation
- Basics of Routing
- Problems and Exercises

Introduction to Networking

Networking is the process of connecting computers, devices, and systems to facilitate communication and resource sharing. Networks range from simple setups in homes to complex infrastructures in global enterprises.

Networking involves the transmission of data between devices over physical or wireless media. It allows for resource sharing, collaboration, and seamless communication between devices or users.

Key Characteristics:

- **Scalability**: Networks can grow to accommodate new devices.
    - Adding new computers or IoT devices to the LAN of a company without disrupting existing connections.
    - Cloud networks that automatically scale resources as user demand increases.
- **Reliability**: Redundancy mechanisms ensure continuous communication.
    - Using multiple routers or switches so that if one fails, traffic is rerouted through another path.
    - Data centers implementing redundant network links (such as dual Internet Service Providers) to prevent downtime.
- **Speed**: Data transfer happens rapidly across high-speed links.
    - Fiber-optic connections enabling gigabit or even terabit data transfers.
    - Content Delivery Networks (CDNs) that deliver web content faster by caching data closer to users.

Importance of Networking

Networking serves as the foundation for the digital age, enabling seamless communication, resource sharing, and connectivity across devices and systems. It plays a pivotal role in the efficient operation of modern technologies, from personal devices to enterprise-level IT infrastructures.

- **Facilitating Communication:** Networking allows devices to exchange information, forming the backbone of services like web browsing, email, and instant messaging. Without networking, the interconnected nature of our digital world would not exist.
- **Optimizing Resource Utilization:** By enabling shared access to printers, file systems, and applications, networks reduce redundancy and improve efficiency within organizations, making operations more cost-effective.
- **Empowering Cloud Platforms:** Networking is integral to cloud computing environments like AWS, Azure, GCP etc. It provides the connectivity required for virtual machines, containers, and services to work together, enabling on-demand scalability and flexibility for businesses.
- **Ensuring Security and Continuity:** Secure data transmission is achieved through technologies such as VPNs, encryption, and firewalls. Networking also supports redundancy and failover mechanisms, I.e., backup processes that automatically switch network operations to a standby system, server, or link when the primary one fails, ensuring that systems remain operational even during disruptions.
- **Advancing Technological Growth:** Networking drives innovation in areas like IoT, smart devices, and edge computing, opening new possibilities in industries ranging from healthcare to transportation.

In essence, networking is not just a technical foundation — it is the enabler of global connectivity and the catalyst for modern technological advancements.

USE CASE	DESCRIPTION
Communication	Enables messaging, voice calls, video conferencing, and email communication.
Resource Sharing	Allows multiple users to share printers, scanners, or storage devices.
Data Access	Permits access to remote databases, files, and cloud resources.
Collaboration	Facilitates team collaboration by enabling access to shared tools like Slack or Google Docs.
Internet Access	Provides global connectivity to websites, services, and online platforms.

Table 1.1: *Networking Use Cases and Description*

Types of Networks

Networks come in various forms, each designed to serve specific purposes based on scale, functionality, and connectivity. Understanding these types is crucial for designing efficient systems tailored to diverse needs.

- **Local Area Network (LAN):** A LAN connects devices within a limited area, such as an office, school, or home. It is characterized by high-speed connections and controlled environments. LANs are ideal for resource sharing, such as printers or file storage, and use technologies like Ethernet and Wi-Fi.
- **Wide Area Network (WAN):** WANs span large geographic areas, connecting multiple LANs. The internet is the most prominent illustration of a WAN. They rely on telecommunications links and are suitable for organizations with services in different locales.
- **Metropolitan Area Network (MAN):** A MAN covers a city or large campus, bridging the gap between LANs and WANs. It is frequently used by organizations for infrastructure management like traffic control or public Wi- Fi.
- **Wireless Local Area Network (WLAN):** WLANs extend LANs without physical cables, using wireless technologies like Wi-Fi. They are commonly found in homes, offices, and public spaces, enabling mobility for users.
- **Virtual Private Network (VPN):** A VPN provides secure access to private networks over public internet connections. It encrypts data, ensuring confidentiality and is widely used for remote work and secure communication.
- **Personal Area Network (PAN):** PANs connect personal devices within a short range, such as smartphones, laptops, or wearable devices, using technologies like Bluetooth. These networks are suitable for personal use and small-scale data sharing.
- **Storage Area Network (SAN):** A SAN connects storage devices to servers, optimizing data access for high-performance applications. These are commonly used in enterprise environments for managing large-scale storage systems.

In summary, the type of network chosen depends on the scope and requirements of the system, ranging from localized setups like LANs to expansive systems like WANs, each contributing uniquely to our interconnected world.

TYPE	SCALE	EXAMPLE
Local Area Network (LAN)	Small area (like a building)	Offices, schools, small businesses.
Wide Area Network (WAN)	Covers large geographical areas	The Internet, connecting cities or countries.
Metropolitan Area Network (MAN)	Medium-sized area (similar to that of a city)	City-wide government or university network.
Personal Area Network (PAN)	Very small, personal area	Bluetooth between phone and headphones.
Virtual Private Network (VPN)	Secure private network over public infrastructure	Remote access to corporate systems.

Table 1.2: *Networking Types, Its Scales and Examples*

Networking Devices

Networking devices are essential components that enable communication and data transfer across a network. Each device serves a specific function, ensuring that networks operate efficiently and securely.

- **Router:** A router determines the best path for data packets to reach their destination and can also provide firewall and network management capabilities.
- **Switch:** A switch operates within a Local Area Network (LAN), connecting multiple devices like computers, printers, and servers. It uses MAC addresses to forward data packets to the correct device, improving efficiency by reducing data collisions.
- **Hub:** A hub connects multiple devices in a network and broadcasts data to all connected devices. Unlike switches, hubs do not filter data, making them less efficient for modern networks.
- **Access Point (AP):** Access points extend wireless connectivity within a network, enabling devices like smartphones and laptops to connect via Wi-Fi. They are essential for creating Wireless Local Area Networks (WLANs).
- **Modem:** A modem modulates and demodulates data for transmission over communication lines like telephone or cable. It is commonly used to provide internet access by converting signals between digital devices and analog lines.
- **Firewall:** A firewall acts as a security barrier, monitoring and controlling incoming and outgoing network traffic based on predefined rules. It protects networks from unauthorized access and cyber threats.
- **Network Interface Card (NIC):** A NIC is a hardware component that enables bias to connect to a network. Modern NICs support both wired (Ethernet) and wireless (Wi- Fi) connections.
- **Gateway:** A gateway connects two different networks that may use different protocols, enabling data exchange. It often combines the functionalities of a router and a firewall.
- **Repeater:** A repeater amplifies and retransmits signals to extend the range of a network. It is used in scenarios where data must travel over long distances without losing integrity.
- **Bridge:** A bridge connects two LANs, enabling them to function as a single network. It helps reduce traffic congestion by segmenting the network and filtering data.

Each device plays a critical role in the design and operation of networks, from small home setups to complex enterprise systems. Together, they ensure seamless connectivity and robust performance.

DEVICE	FUNCTION	EXAMPLE
Router	Connects different networks and determines the best data path.	Internet routers in homes.
Switch	Connects devices within the same network and manages traffic flow.	Office switches managing workstations.
Access Point	Extends wireless connectivity to devices.	Wi-Fi access points in cafes.
Firewall	Secures the network by filtering unauthorized traffic.	Hardware or software firewalls.
Modem	Convert between digital formats or between digital and radio frequency signals.	DSL or fiber modems.

Table 1.3: *Networking Devices and Its Functions*

Network Architecture

Networking architectures define how data flows between devices.

Peer-to-Peer (P2P)

- All devices are equal and can act as both clients and servers.
- **Example:** File sharing among personal computers.

Client-Server

- Dedicated servers provide services to client devices.
- **Example:** Email servers handling user communication.

Types of Transmission Media

Some of the types of transmission media are provided as follows:

- **Wired Media:** Physical mediums like twisted-pair cables, coaxial cables, and fiber optics that transmit data through electrical signals or light. These offer high reliability and speed, often used in LANs. Types of wired media are as follows:
    - **Twisted Pair Cable**: Common for LANs.
    - **Coaxial Cable**: Used in cable TV networks.
    - **Fiber Optic Cable**: High-speed and long-distance data transmission.
- **Wireless Media:** Non-physical mediums such as radio waves, microwaves, and infrared signals that enable data transmission over the air, widely used in WLANs, mobile networks, and IoT. Types of wireless media are as follows:
    - **Radio Waves**: Used in Wi-Fi and Bluetooth.
    - **Microwaves**: Used in satellite communications.
    - **Infrared**: Used in remote controls and short-distance communication.

Real-Life Example of Networking

Imagine streaming your favorite show on a smart TV. The device connects to your home Wi-Fi, retrieves the video data from cloud servers via the internet, and seamlessly delivers it to your screen in real time — all powered by efficient networking.

Home Networking

- Devices like phones, laptops, and TVs connect to a home router.
- The router manages Internet access and enables resource sharing like printing.

Corporate Networking

- Employees access centralized databases via a LAN.
- VPNs secure remote employee access.

Key Networking Protocols

Networking protocols are standardized rules that govern data communication between devices in a network. They ensure that devices, regardless of their type or manufacturer, can exchange information efficiently and securely. The following is an overview of key networking protocols:

- **Transmission Control Protocol (TCP):** TCP is a reliable, connection-oriented protocol that ensures data is delivered accurately and in the correct order. TCP underlies applications like HTTP/HTTPS for web browsing and protocols like SMTP for email.
- **User Datagram Protocol (UDP):** UDP is a connectionless protocol that is ideal for applications like video streaming and online gaming, where minor data loss is acceptable.
- **Internet Protocol (IP):** IP is responsible for addressing and routing data packets between devices. IPv4 (32-bit addresses) and IPv6 (128-bit addresses) are its two main versions, with IPv6 designed to address the limitations of IPv4.
- **Hypertext Transfer Protocol (HTTP/HTTPS):** HTTP facilitates the transfer of web pages and other resources over the internet. HTTPS adds a layer of security by encrypting data, ensuring safe communication between browsers and servers.
- **Domain Name System (DNS):** DNS translates human-readable domain names into IP addresses. It acts as the phonebook of the internet, simplifying access to online resources.
- **Dynamic Host Configuration Protocol (DHCP):** DHCP automatically assigns IP addresses to devices in a network, simplifying network management and ensuring efficient IP address utilization.
- **Simple Mail Transfer Protocol (SMTP):** SMTP is used for sending emails between servers. It works in conjunction with protocols like IMAP and POP3, which handle email retrieval.
- **File Transfer Protocol (FTP):** FTP enables the file transfer between devices over a network. Secure variants, such as SFTP, add encryption for enhanced security.
- **Simple Network Management Protocol (SNMP):** SNMP monitors and manages network devices, providing administrators with real-time insights into network performance and issues.
- **Secure Shell (SSH):** SSH provides secure remote access to devices, encrypting commands and data transfers to prevent unauthorized access.
- **Border Gateway Protocol (BGP):** BGP is used for routing data between autonomous systems on the internet, ensuring efficient and reliable data transmission across large-scale networks.

Networking protocols are the foundation of all data communication, enabling seamless interaction between devices. Their diversity ensures that every type of network activity, from browsing to streaming, operates smoothly and securely.

The purpose and the uses of different networking protocols are tabulated as follows:

PROTOCOL	PURPOSE	EXAMPLE USE
HTTP/HTTPS	Facilitates web browsing and secure transactions.	Accessing websites.
FTP	Transfers files between client and server.	Uploading/downloading files.
SMTP	Sends emails between servers.	Sending corporate emails.
DNS	Resolves domain names to IP addresses.	Accessing google.com without needing to remember its IP address (such as 8.8.8.8)', since 8.8.8.8 is actually the public DNS server of Google and not the IP address of google.com.

Table 1.4: *Networking Protocols, Its Purposes, and Uses*

Figure 1.1 represents the setup of a network. This is a typical network setup that includes wireless points, switches, wifi, and so on.

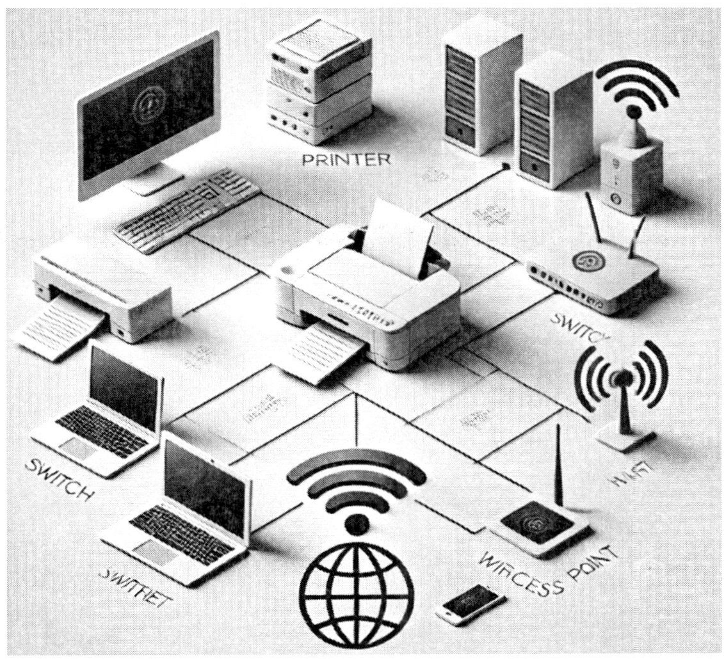

Figure 1.1: *A Typical Network Setup*

OSI and TCP/IP Models

The OSI (Open Systems Interconnection) and TCP/IP (Transmission Control Protocol/Internet Protocol) models are two frameworks that define how network communication occurs. They standardize protocols, enable interoperability, and ensure data transfer across diverse networks.

OSI Model

The **OSI model** divides the communication process into **seven layers**, each with a distinct role. It provides a clear framework for troubleshooting and understanding data flow.

LAYER	DESCRIPTION	REAL-WORLD EXAMPLES
Physical	Transmits raw data bits over physical media.	Ethernet cables, Wi-Fi signals.
Data Link	Manages error detection and device-to-device data transfer.	MAC addresses, switches, Wi-Fi frames.
Network	Handles routing and logical addressing of data packets.	Routers, IP addresses (like 192.168.1.1).
Transport	Ensures end-to-end communication and reliability (such as error checking).	TCP (emails) and UDP (video streaming).
Session	Establishes and manages communication sessions.	Session management for online meetings (like Zoom).
Presentation	Translates data formats and encrypts/decrypts data.	SSL/TLS encryption for secure websites.
Application	Provides network services to end-user applications.	HTTP (web browsing), SMTP (emails), FTP (file transfer).

Table 1.5: *Layers of OSI Model*

TCP/IP Model

The **TCP/IP model** simplifies networking into **four layers**, focusing on practical implementation. It forms the foundation of modern Internet communication.

Layers of the TCP/IP Model

LAYER	CORRESPONDS TO OSI LAYERS	FUNCTION	REAL-WORLD EXAMPLES
Network Access	Physical + Data Link	Manages hardware addressing and data transmission over media.	Ethernet, Wi-Fi, PPP (Point-to-Point Protocol), DSL
Internet	Network	Handles IP addressing and routing of data packets.	IP addresses (8.8.8.8), routers.
Transport	Transport	Provides reliable or fast data delivery between devices.	TCP (emails) and UDP (streaming).
Application	Session + Presentation + Application	Interfaces directly with user applications.	HTTP, HTTPS, FTP, DNS, SMTP (emails) or SSH (secure remote login)

Table 1.6: *Layers of TCP/IP Model*

Real-World Scenarios

The OSI and TCP/IP models are not just theoretical frameworks; they play a vital role in real-world networking by defining how data travels between devices. Each layer contributes a specific function, from establishing physical connections to ensuring reliable data delivery.

By examining practical scenarios, such as sending an email or loading a webpage, we can better understand how these models facilitate seamless communication and troubleshoot issues effectively.

Scenario 1: Sending an Email

- **Application Layer**: User writes an email in Gmail (SMTP protocol), IMAP/POP3 are used for retrieving the email.

- **Presentation Layer**: Email content is encrypted using TLS.
- **Session Layer**: Session is established with the mail server of the recipient.
- **Transport Layer**: Data is divided into packets (TCP ensures reliability).
- **Network Layer**: Packets are routed using IP addresses.
- **Data Link Layer**: Frames are transmitted over Ethernet.
- **Physical Layer**: Data is sent as electrical signals over a network cable.

Scenario 2: Watching a YouTube Video

- **Application Layer**: HTTP/HTTPS requests a video from the server of Youtube.
- **Transport Layer**: UDP streams video packets for real-time playback.
- **Network Layer**: Packets are routed across the Internet using IP.
- **Data Link Layer**: Frames are handled by the Wi-Fi network of the user.
- **Physical Layer**: Radio waves transmit data to the device of the user.

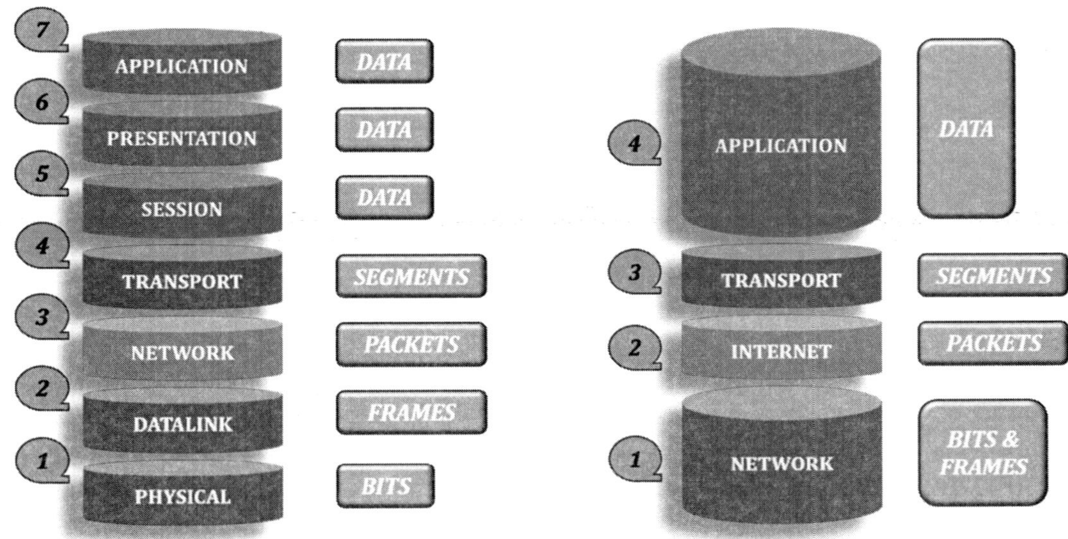

***Figure 1.2**: OSI and TCP/IP Comparison Diagram*

The OSI and TCP/IP models are critical for understanding how data travels across networks. While the OSI model provides theoretical insights, the TCP/IP model focuses on practical application, forming the backbone of modern networking. Together, these models enable seamless communication and robust network design.

IP Addressing and Subnetting

IP addressing and subnetting are foundational concepts in networking. They enable devices to identify and communicate over a network efficiently.

IP Address

An **IP address** is a unique identifier assigned to devices in a network to enable communication. It works like a postal address, ensuring that the data is sent to the correct device.

TYPE	DESCRIPTION	EXAMPLE
IPv4	32-bit address written in dotted decimal format. Due to its limited address space, IPv4 addresses are now largely exhausted.	192.168.1.1
IPv6	128-bit address written in hexadecimal format, introduced primarily to overcome IPv4 address exhaustion and to support large-scale networks.	2001:0db8:85a3::8a2e:0370:7334

Table 1.7: *Types of IP Addresses*

IPv4 Address Structure

- **4 Octets** (each ranging from 0 to 255).
- Example: 192.168.0.1

IPv6 Address Structure

An IPv6 address consists of 8 groups of hexadecimal numbers, separated by colons. Each group represents 16 bits, making IPv6 a 128-bit address in total.

Full format example:

2001:0db8:85a3:0000:0000:8a2e:0370:7334

Consecutive groups of zeros can be abbreviated using :: (only once per address).

Abbreviated example:

2001:0db8:85a3::8a2e:0370:7334

This abbreviation simplifies IPv6 addresses and makes them easier to read and write while maintaining the same address value.

Classes of IPv4 Addresses

IPv4 addresses are categorized into classes to define network size.

CLASS	RANGE (FIRST OCTET)	PURPOSE	DEFAULT SUBNET MASK	EXAMPLE
A	1-126	Large networks.	255.0.0.0	10.0.0.1
B	128-191	Medium-sized networks.	255.255.0.0	172.16.0.1
C	192-223	Small networks.	255.255.255.0	192.168.1.1
D	224-239	Multicasting.	N/A	224.0.0.1
E	240-255	Reserved for research.	N/A	No usable host addresses

Table 1.8: *Classes of IPv4 Addresses*

Note:

- *127.x.x.x is reserved for loopback testing (for example, 127.0.0.1) and is not assigned to networks, which is why Class A usable ranges stop at 126.*
- *255.255.255.255 is the limited broadcast address, not a valid Class E host address.*
- *Class E addresses are not used for normal host assignment, which is why an example is intentionally omitted.*

Subnetting

Subnetting divides a large network into smaller subnetworks to improve efficiency and security. Some of the purposes of subnetting are as follows:

- Reduces network congestion.
- Enhances security by isolating segments.
- Efficient utilization of IP addresses.

Subnet Mask

A **subnet mask** determines the division of an IP address into **network** and **host** portions.

SUBNET MASK	CIDR NOTATION	NUMBER OF SUBNETS	HOSTS PER SUBNET
255.255.255.0	/24	1	254
255.255.255.128	/25	2	126
255.255.255.192	/26	4	62
255.255.255.224	/27	8	30
255.255.255.240	/28	16	14

***Table 1.9**: Subnet Mask*

Importance of Subnetting

- **Efficient Resource Allocation**: Avoids wasting IP addresses.
- **Improved Security**: Isolates sensitive segments.
- **Reduced Traffic**: Minimizes broadcast traffic.

Real-Life Example of Subnetting

While often considered a theoretical concept, subnetting plays a key role in optimizing network performance, enhancing security, and maximizing the efficient use of IP addresses in real-world situations. From designing networks for organizations to managing traffic and ensuring secure communications, subnetting is fundamental to the infrastructure that powers modern digital services.

In this section, we will explore how subnetting applies in real-world scenarios, providing insight into its practical applications and the problems it helps to solve for network engineers and IT professionals.

Scenario:

- **Company XYZ** has a network 192.168.1.0/24.
- They want to create 4 departments, each needing its own subnet.

Solution:

- **Subnet Calculation**:
    - A /24 network provides 256 total IP addresses (254 usable).
    - To create 4 equal subnets, 2 bits are borrowed from the host portion:
        - New subnet prefix: /26
        - Each subnet contains 64 total addresses.
        - 62 usable host addresses per subnet.

- **Subnets**: | **Subnet** | **Range** | **Broadcast Address** |

  Subnet 1 (192.168.1.0/26)
  - Network address: 192.168.1.0 (not assignable)
  - Usable host range: 192.168.1.1 – 192.168.1.62
  - Broadcast address: 192.168.1.63 (not assignable)

  Subnet 2 (192.168.1.64/26)
  - Network address: 192.168.1.64 (not assignable)
  - Usable host range: 192.168.1.65 – 192.168.1.126
  - Broadcast address: 192.168.1.127 (not assignable)

  Subnet 3 (192.168.1.128/26)
  - Network address: 192.168.1.128 (not assignable)
  - Usable host range: 192.168.1.129 – 192.168.1.190
  - Broadcast address: 192.168.1.191 (not assignable)

  Subnet 4 (192.168.1.192/26)
  - Network address: 192.168.1.192 (not assignable)
  - Usable host range: 192.168.1.193 – 192.168.1.254
  - Broadcast address: 192.168.1.255 (not assignable)

By subnetting 192.168.1.0/24 into four /26 subnets, Company XYZ:

- Assigns one subnet per department.
- Ensures 62 usable IP addresses for each.
- Clearly separates network, usable, and broadcast addresses.
- Avoids common beginner mistakes.

Classless Inter-Domain Routing (CIDR)

CIDR uses **prefix notation** (like /24) to represent subnet masks.

CIDR NOTATION	SUBNET MASK	HOSTS PER SUBNET
/24	255.255.255.0	254
/25	255.255.255.128	126
/26	255.255.255.192	62

Table 1.10: *CIDR Notation*

Practical Exercises

In this section, we will explore hands-on exercises that will help you master subnetting techniques, from basic to advanced concepts. Through step-by-step examples and real-world applications, you will gain the confidence to design efficient and secure networks. Whether you are preparing for a certification or looking to refine your skills, these exercises are designed to enhance your understanding and application of subnetting principles.

Problem 1: Identify Network Details

Given IP: 192.168.10.34/28

Question: Identify the subnet range, broadcast address, and usable IP range.

Solution:

- **Subnet Mask**: /28 = 255.255.255.240 (16 addresses per subnet).
- **Block Size Calculation:**

  Block size = 256 – 240 = 16

  This means each /28 subnet spans 16 total IP addresses.
- **Subnet Range**: 192.168.10.32 - 192.168.10.47.
- **Broadcast Address**: 192.168.10.47.
- **Usable IP Range**: 192.168.10.33 - 192.168.10.46.

A /28 subnet provides 16 total IP addresses. After excluding the network address (192.168.10.32) and the broadcast address (192.168.10.47), there are 14 usable host addresses.

Problem 2: Subnetting a Larger Network

Company needs to divide 10.0.0.0/16 into 8 subnets.

Solution:

- **New CIDR**: /16 → /19 (8192 addresses per subnet).
- **Subnet Ranges:**

Subnet	**Range**	**Broadcast Address**
1	10.0.0.0 - 10.0.31.255	10.0.31.255
2	10.0.32.0 - 10.0.63.255	10.0.63.255

Note: *Each /19 subnet increases by 32 in the 3rd octet* (0, 32, 64, 96...).

CIDR Notation

Classless Inter-Domain Routing (CIDR) is a flexible way to allocate IP addresses and define subnets by using a **prefix length**. It replaces the rigid IP address classes (A, B, C) to optimize the use of available IP space.

CIDR notation represents an IP address with its associated **prefix length**.

The prefix length specifies the number of bits in the address used for the **network portion**.

Structure

IP Address / Prefix Length

- **IP Address**: Standard IPv4 or IPv6 address.
- **Prefix Length**: Number of bits used for the network.

Example:

- 192.168.1.0/24 → The first 24 bits are for the **network**, and the remaining 8 bits are for **hosts**.

Understanding CIDR Subnet Masks

Each prefix length corresponds to a **subnet mask**, which divides the IP address into **network** and **host** portions. As the prefix length increases, the number of hosts decreases, but the number of available subnets increases.

CIDR NOTATION	SUBNET MASK	HOSTS PER SUBNET	SUBNET BITS	HOST BITS
/24	255.255.255.0	254	24	8
/25	255.255.255.128	126	25	7
/26	255.255.255.192	62	26	6
/27	255.255.255.224	30	27	5
/28	255.255.255.240	14	28	4

Table 1.11: *CIDR Subnet Masks and Hosts*

Real-World Example of CIDR Notation

CIDR (Classless Inter-Domain Routing) notation plays a pivotal role in modern networking by offering a more efficient way to allocate and manage IP addresses. Unlike the older class-based system, CIDR enables network administrators to create more flexible and scalable IP address schemes, reducing waste and improving routing performance.

In real-world scenarios, CIDR is used in everything from configuring enterprise networks to optimizing cloud services, ensuring that resources are used efficiently. This notation simplifies network design and helps streamline traffic management, making it essential for anyone involved in network infrastructure, from internet service providers to large organizations.

Scenario:

A company has been assigned the block 192.168.0.0/22. This CIDR block includes **1024 IP addresses**.

Explanation:

- **Network Bits**: /22 (22 bits for network).
- **Host Bits**: 32 - 22 = 10 bits for host addresses.
- **Subnet Mask**: 255.255.252.0.

Subnet Ranges:

SUBNET	RANGE	BROADCAST ADDRESS
1	192.168.0.0 - 192.168.3.255	192.168.3.255

Table 1.12: *Subnet Ranges*

Benefits of CIDR Notation

By allowing for more precise and flexible subnetting, CIDR not only optimizes the use of IP address space but also enhances network scalability and efficiency. The ability to allocate Variable-Length Subnet Masks (VLSMs) ensures that IP addresses are distributed according to actual needs, reducing waste, and streamlining network performance.

In this section, we will explore the key benefits of CIDR notation and how it drives efficiency in modern networking, making it a crucial tool for both small-scale and large-scale network operations.

BENEFIT	EXPLANATION
Efficient IP Utilization	Prevents wastage of IPs by allowing variable-length subnet masks.
Scalability	Facilitates flexible subnetting for growing networks.
Simplified Routing	Reduces routing table size by grouping addresses with the same prefix.

Table 1.13: *CIDR Notation and Benefits*

CIDR in Routing

In networking, CIDR blocks aggregate multiple IP addresses into one routing entry, reducing complexity.

Example:

Instead of listing 192.168.0.0/24, 192.168.1.0/24, 192.168.2.0/24, CIDR aggregates them as 192.168.0.0/22.

CIDR notation simplifies IP addressing and routing by offering flexibility and efficiency. It is widely used for subnetting and optimizing routing tables, ensuring scalable and effective network management.

Basics of Routing

Routing is the process of determining the path data packets take to travel from a source to a destination across interconnected networks. Routers, the devices responsible for routing, ensure that data reaches the correct destination efficiently.

Routing involves:

- **Forwarding**: Sending packets from one network to another.
- **Path Selection**: Choosing the best path based on criteria like distance, speed, or cost.

TERM	DEFINITION
Router	A networking device that forwards data packets between networks.
Routing Table	A database in a router containing routes to various destinations.
Hop	A step or device a packet passes through enroute to its destination.

Table 1.14: *Key Terms of Routing*

Types of Routing

Routing can be classified into three main types:

TYPE	DESCRIPTION	EXAMPLE
Static Routing	Manually configured routes. Suitable for small, stable networks.	A small office with fixed routes.
Dynamic Routing	Automatically learns and updates routes using protocols like OSPF, RIP, or BGP.	ISPs using BGP for route updates.
Default Routing	Routes all packets to a specific gateway if no other route is known.	Home routers forwarding traffic to an ISP.

Table 1.15: *Classification of Routing*

Routing Process

Step-by-Step Routing:

1. **Packet Arrival**: A data packet arrives at a router.
2. **Header Inspection**: The router reads the destination IP address.
3. **Routing Table Lookup**: It searches for the best matching route.
4. **Forwarding Decision**: The packet is sent to the next hop or destination.

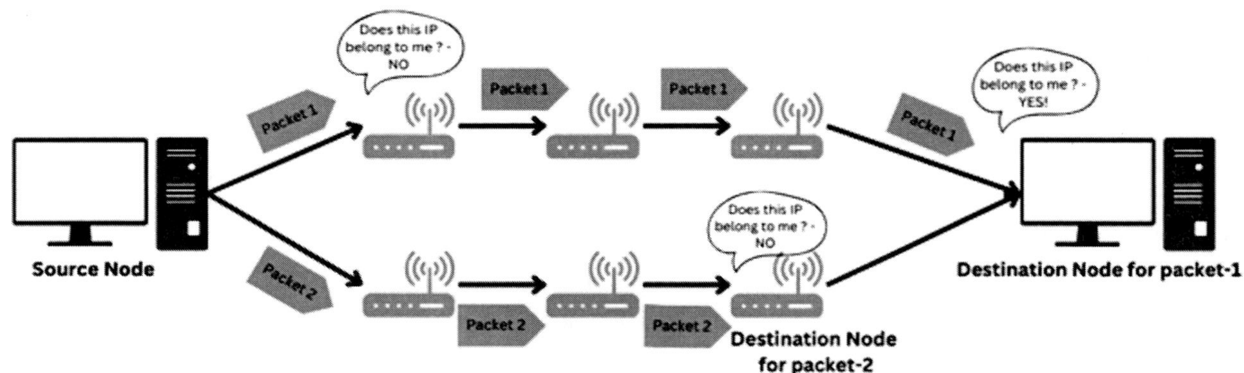

Figure 1.3: *Routing Process (Step-by-Step)*

Routing Tables

A routing table stores information about networks and paths.

DESTINATION	NEXT HOP	SUBNET MASK	METRIC	INTERFACE
192.168.1.0	192.168.0.1	255.255.255.0	1	eth0
10.0.0.0	10.0.0.1	255.0.0.0	2	eth1

Table 1.16: *Structure of a Routing Table*

Example:

- A packet destined for 192.168.1.50 matches 192.168.1.0/24 and is forwarded to 192.168.0.1 through eth0.

Dynamic Routing Protocols

Dynamic routing protocols enable routers to communicate and adapt to network changes.

PROTOCOL	TYPE	DESCRIPTION	METRIC
RIP (Routing Information Protocol)	Distance Vector	Uses hop count as the metric. Simple but slow.	Hop count (Max: 15).
OSPF (Open Shortest Path First)	Link State	Selects paths based on link state and speed.	Cost (Bandwidth-based).
BGP (Border Gateway Protocol)	Path Vector	Used for inter-domain routing (ISPs).	Path attributes.

Table 1.17: *Dynamic Routing Protocols*

Real-World Routing Example

Dynamic routing is a crucial component in modern networking, enabling routers to automatically adjust their routing tables based on real-time network conditions. In contrast to static routing, which requires manual configuration, dynamic routing adapts to network changes such as link failures or congestion, ensuring optimal data paths.

In real-world scenarios, dynamic routing protocols like OSPF (Open Shortest Path First) and BGP (Border Gateway Protocol) are widely used by internet service providers and large organizations to maintain robust, scalable, and efficient networks.

These protocols not only enhance network resilience but also simplify the management of complex infrastructures, making dynamic routing indispensable for businesses that rely on uninterrupted, high-performance connectivity.

Scenario:

A company has three branches: **HQ**, **Branch A**, and **Branch B**. Each branch has a unique subnet:

- HQ: 192.168.0.0/24
- Branch A: 192.168.1.0/24
- Branch B: 192.168.2.0/24

Routing Setup:

- Static routes are configured between HQ and the branches.
- A router at HQ has the following routing table:

DESTINATION	NEXT HOP	SUBNET MASK	INTERFACE
192.168.1.0	192.168.0.2	255.255.255.0	eth1
192.168.2.0	192.168.0.3	255.255.255.0	eth2

Table 1.18: *Routing Table of a Router at HQ*

Packet Flow:

1. A user at HQ (192.168.0.10) sends data to Branch A (192.168.1.20).
2. The HQ router forwards the packet to 192.168.0.2 (next hop for 192.168.1.0/24).

Static versus Dynamic Routing (Quick Contrast)

Static Routing:

Routes are manually configured. If the link between HQ and Branch A fails, traffic will stop until a network administrator manually updates the routes.

Dynamic Routing (such as OSPF):

Routers automatically detect link failures and recalculate paths. If the HQ–Branch A link goes down, traffic can be rerouted through another available path without manual intervention.

Routing Metrics

Routing protocols use metrics to select the best path.

Common Metrics:

METRIC	DESCRIPTION
Hop Count	Number of routers (hops) a packet passes through.
Bandwidth	Available bandwidth of the link.
Latency	Delay in transmitting data across the link.
Cost	Assigned value based on administrative preferences.

Table 1.19: *Common Routing Metrics*

Challenges in Routing

The following are a few of the challenges in routing:

- **Routing Loops**: Occur when data packets circle between routers endlessly.

  Example: A misconfigured network causes packets to bounce between two routers, slowing down all traffic.

- **Convergence Time**: Delay in updating routes across a network.

  Example: During a link failure, video calls may freeze until routers learn the new path.

- **Scalability**: Managing large routing tables in expansive networks.

  Example: A corporate WAN with hundreds of branches struggles if routers cannot efficiently store and process routes.

Solution to Loops:

- Use protocols with loop prevention mechanisms (like OSPF).

  Example: The SPF algorithm of OSPF ensures packets always follow a loop-free path.

- Apply **Split Horizon** or **Hold-Down Timers** in RIP.

  Example: Prevents routers from advertising incorrect routes back to the source, avoiding traffic loops during failures.

Exercises and Case Studies

Exercise 1: Analyse a Routing Table

Given the following routing table, identify the next hop for a packet destined for 10.1.2.5:

DESTINATION	NEXT HOP	SUBNET MASK	INTERFACE
10.1.0.0	10.1.0.1	255.255.0.0	eth0
192.168.1.0	192.168.0.1	255.255.255.0	eth1

***Table 1.20**: Routing Table for the Analysis*

Solution: The destination 10.1.2.5 matches 10.1.0.0/16. The next hop is 10.1.0.1 via eth0.

Dynamic Routing Process

1. Routers exchange route updates.
2. New routes are added to the routing table.
3. Data packets are forwarded based on updated tables.

Routing is the backbone of networking, enabling seamless data transfer across interconnected systems. Understanding routing basics, protocols, and configurations ensures efficient and secure communication in modern networks.

Problems and Exercises

When it comes to mastering network concepts, tackling real-world problems and exercises is essential for gaining practical experience and solidifying theoretical knowledge. Whether you are working with IP addressing, routing protocols, or network security, each challenge presents an opportunity to apply your skills in a dynamic environment.

These problems often mirror the complexities and nuances of actual network scenarios, allowing you to build critical problem-solving abilities. By engaging with a variety of exercises, you can test your understanding, identify potential gaps, and enhance your ability to navigate the evolving landscape of modern networking.

Problem 1: Network Routing Configuration

Scenario: You are the network administrator for a mid-sized company. You have two routers in your office setup, Router Alpha and Router Beta, which need to route traffic between two networks.

- **Router Alpha**: Connected to the network 10.1.1.0/24 with the IP address 10.1.1.1.
- **Router Beta**: Connected to the network 10.2.2.0/24 with the IP address 10.2.2.1.

Task:

- Configure static routes on both routers so that Router Alpha can reach 10.2.2.0/24, and Router Beta can reach 10.1.1.0/24.

Solution:

- **Router Alpha Configuration**:

  Router Alpha needs to forward traffic destined for LAN of Router Beta (10.2.2.0/24) to Router Beta via the transit link.

  - ip route 10.2.2.0 255.255.255.0 10.1.2.2
  - Destination network: 10.2.2.0/24
  - Next hop: 10.1.2.2 (The transit interface of Router Beta)

- **Router Beta Configuration**:

  Router Beta needs to forward traffic destined for the LAN (10.1.1.0/24) of Router Alpha to Router Alpha via the same transit link.

  - ip route 10.1.1.0 255.255.255.0 10.1.2.1
  - Destination network: 10.1.1.0/24
  - Next hop: 10.1.2.1 (The transit interface of Router Alpha)

Final Result

- Router Alpha can successfully route traffic to 10.2.2.0/24.
- Router Beta can successfully route traffic to 10.1.1.0/24.
- The transit network 10.1.2.0/30 provides a valid Layer-3 path for next-hop resolution.

Problem 2: Efficient IP Address Subnetting

Scenario: Your company has been assigned the IP block 192.168.10.0/24 and needs to create subnets for three departments:

- **Sales Department**: Needs 60 devices.
- **Engineering Department**: Needs 100 devices.
- **Support Department**: Needs 20 devices.

Task:

- Perform subnetting using the given IP block.
- Provide the subnet mask, usable IP ranges, and the CIDR notation for each department.

Solution:

Step 1: Sort Departments by Required Hosts (Largest First)

Using VLSM best practices, subnet allocation starts with the largest host requirement.

1. Engineering: 100 devices
2. Sales: 60 devices
3. Support: 20 devices

Step 2: Determine Required Subnet Sizes

The formula used is: $2^n - 2 \geq$ Required Hosts.

Engineering Department

- Required hosts: 100
- Smallest suitable subnet: /25
- Total IP addresses: 128
- Usable host addresses: 126

(**Note:** *The subnet provides more usable addresses than required, which is normal in subnetting.*)

- Subnet mask: 255.255.255.128

Sales Department

- Required hosts: 60
- Smallest suitable subnet: /26
- Total IP addresses: 64
- Usable host addresses: 62
- Subnet mask: 255.255.255.192

Support Department

- Required hosts: 20
- Smallest suitable subnet: /27
- Total IP addresses: 32
- Usable host addresses: 30
- Subnet mask: 255.255.255.224

Step 3: Subnet Allocation from 192.168.10.0/24

Subnets are assigned sequentially to avoid overlap.

Engineering Department

- Subnet: 192.168.10.0/25
- Network address: 192.168.10.0
- Usable IP range: 192.168.10.1 – 192.168.10.126
- Broadcast address: 192.168.10.127
- Usable hosts allocated: 126 (100 required)

Sales Department

- Subnet: 192.168.10.128/26
- Network address: 192.168.10.128

- Usable IP range: 192.168.10.129 – 192.168.10.190
- Broadcast address: 192.168.10.191
- Usable hosts allocated: 62 (60 required)

Support Department

- Subnet: 192.168.10.192/27
- Network address: 192.168.10.192
- Usable IP range: 192.168.10.193 – 192.168.10.222
- Broadcast address: 192.168.10.223
- Usable hosts allocated: 30 (20 required)

Step 4: Unused Subnet (Future Expansion)

After allocating all departments, the remaining unused address block is: 192.168.10.224/27

- Network address: 192.168.10.224
- Usable IP range: 192.168.10.225 – 192.168.10.254
- Broadcast address: 192.168.10.255
- Usable hosts available: 30

This unused subnet can be reserved for future departments, network growth, or infrastructure devices.

This subnetting design:

- Clearly distinguishes between required hosts and allocated usable IPs.
- Uses VLSM to efficiently divide the address space.
- Avoids subnet overlap.
- Minimizes IP wastage.
- Preserves address space for future expansion.

DEPARTMENT	SUBNET ADDRESS	USABLE IP RANGE	SUBNET MASK
Engineering Department	192.168.10.0/25	192.168.10.1 - 192.168.10.126	255.255.255.128
Sales Dept	192.168.10.64/26	192.168.10.129 - 192.168.10.190	255.255.255.192
Support Department	192.168.10.192/27	192.168.10.193 - 192.168.10.222	255.255.255.224

Table 1.21: *Solution Table for Efficient IP Address Subnetting*

Problem 3: Advanced Subnetting Using VLSM

Scenario: You are tasked with subnetting the 172.30.0.0/16 network for a company, and the following departments have specific requirements:

- **Accounting Department**: Needs 150 IP addresses.
- **Operations Department**: Needs 250 IP addresses.
- **HR Department**: Needs 50 IP addresses.

Task:

- Calculate the subnet mask and CIDR notation for each department.
- Provide the usable IP ranges for each subnet.

Solution:

Step 1: Sort the Departments by Host Requirement (Largest First)

VLSM allocation always starts with the largest subnet to avoid fragmentation.

a. Operations: 250 hosts
b. Accounting: 150 hosts
c. HR: 50 hosts

Step 2: Calculate Required Subnet Sizes

The formula used is: $2^n - 2 \geq$ Required Hosts.

Operations Department

a. Required hosts: 250
b. $2^8 - 2 = 254$ usable hosts
c. Subnet size: /24
d. Subnet mask: 255.255.255.0

Accounting Department

a. Required hosts: 150
b. $2^8 - 2 = 254$ usable hosts
c. Subnet size: /24
d. Subnet mask: 255.255.255.0

HR Department

a. Required hosts: 50
b. $2^6 - 2 = 62$ usable hosts
c. Subnet size: /26
d. Subnet mask: 255.255.255.192

Step 3: Allocate Subnets Sequentially from 172.30.0.0/16

Start allocating from the beginning of the address pool to ensure no overlap.

Operations Department

a. Subnet: 172.30.0.0/24
b. Network address: 172.30.0.0
c. Usable IP range: 172.30.0.1 – 172.30.0.254
d. Broadcast address: 172.30.0.255

Accounting Department

a. Subnet: 172.30.1.0/24
b. Network address: 172.30.1.0
c. Usable IP range: 172.30.1.1 – 172.30.1.254
d. Broadcast address: 172.30.1.255

HR Department

a. Subnet: 172.30.2.0/26
b. Network address: 172.30.2.0

c. Usable IP range: 172.30.2.1 – 172.30.2.62
d. Broadcast address: 172.30.2.63

Step 4: Remaining Address Space

After allocating the HR subnet, the next available IP address is: 172.30.2.64

All addresses from 172.30.2.64 to 172.30.255.255 remain unused and available for:

a. Future departments
b. Network expansion
c. Additional subnets of any size

This VLSM-based subnetting approach:

a. Allocates IP addresses efficiently based on real host needs.
b. Prevents overlapping subnets.
c. Minimizes wasted IP space.
d. Provides scalability for future growth.

Problem 4: Optimizing Routing with Dynamic Protocols

Scenario: Your network has three locations: New York, Berlin, and Sydney. The routers are running OSPF to exchange routing information.

- **New York Router** IP: 10.0.0.1, local network 192.168.10.0/24.
- **Berlin Router** IP: 10.1.0.1, local network 192.168.20.0/24.
- **Sydney Router** IP: 10.2.0.1, local network 192.168.30.0/24.

Task:

- Configure OSPF on each router so that all networks are reachable.
- Verify OSPF routing updates between the routers.

Solution:

- **Network Topology (Critical Prerequisite)**

OSPF neighbors must share a Layer-3 transit network. Therefore, we explicitly define WAN links between routers.

We will use a full-mesh topology so each site has direct redundancy.

Transit Subnets

Link	Subnet	Mask
New York ↔ Berlin	10.10.0.0/30	255.255.255.252
Berlin ↔ Sydney	10.10.0.4/30	255.255.255.252
New York ↔ Sydney	10.10.0.8/30	255.255.255.252

Table 1.22: *Transit Subnets*

LAN Subnets

Location	LAN
New York	192.168.10.0/24
Berlin	192.168.20.0/24
Sydney	192.168.30.0/24

Table 1.23: *LAN Subnets*

All OSPF routers will be in Area 0.

- **Interface IP Configuration**
  - **New York Router**

```
interface GigabitEthernet0/0
       description NY-LAN
      ip address 192.168.10.1 255.255.255.0
       no shutdown
interface GigabitEthernet0/1
       description NY-Berlin
      ip address 10.10.0.1 255.255.255.252
       no shutdown
interface GigabitEthernet0/2
       description NY-Sydney
      ip address 10.10.0.9 255.255.255.252
       no shutdown
interface Loopback0
      ip address 1.1.1.1 255.255.255.255
```

  - **Berlin Router**

```
interface GigabitEthernet0/0
       description Berlin-LAN
      ip address 192.168.20.1 255.255.255.0
       no shutdown
interface GigabitEthernet0/1
       description Berlin-NY
      ip address 10.10.0.2 255.255.255.252
       no shutdown
interface GigabitEthernet0/2
       description Berlin-Sydney
      ip address 10.10.0.5 255.255.255.252
       no shutdown
interface Loopback0
      ip address 2.2.2.2 255.255.255.255
```

  - **Sydney Router**

```
interface GigabitEthernet0/0
       description Sydney-LAN
      ip address 192.168.30.1 255.255.255.0
       no shutdown
```

```
interface GigabitEthernet0/1
  description Sydney-Berlin
      ip address 10.10.0.6 255.255.255.252
       no shutdown
interface GigabitEthernet0/2
       description Sydney-NY
      ip address 10.10.0.10 255.255.255.252
       no shutdown
interface Loopback0
      ip address 3.3.3.3 255.255.255.255
```

- **OSPF Configuration (Best Practice)**
  - **Design principles applied:**
    - Explicit router-id (loopback-based)
    - LAN interfaces passive
    - Correct wildcard masks
    - All routers in Area 0
  - **New York – OSPF**

    ```
    router ospf 1
     router-id 1.1.1.1

     network 10.10.0.0 0.0.0.3 area 0
     network 10.10.0.8 0.0.0.3 area 0
     network 192.168.10.0 0.0.0.255 area 0

     passive-interface GigabitEthernet0/0
    ```

  - **Berlin – OSPF**

    ```
    router ospf 1
     router-id 2.2.2.2

     network 10.10.0.0 0.0.0.3 area 0
     network 10.10.0.4 0.0.0.3 area 0
     network 192.168.20.0 0.0.0.255 area 0

     passive-interface GigabitEthernet0/0
    ```

  - **Sydney – OSPF**

    ```
    router ospf 1
     router-id 3.3.3.3

     network 10.10.0.4 0.0.0.3 area 0
     network 10.10.0.8 0.0.0.3 area 0
     network 192.168.30.0 0.0.0.255 area 0

     passive-interface GigabitEthernet0/0
    ```

- **Alternative (Recommended) Interface-Based OSPF**

  This avoids overly broad network statements:

  ```
  interface GigabitEthernet0/1
  ipospf 1 area 0
  ```

```
interface GigabitEthernet0/2
ipospf 1 area 0
```

LAN interfaces remain passive.

- **Verification Steps (Mandatory)**
  - **Verify Neighbor Adjacency**

    ```
    show ipospf neighbor
    ```

    Expected:

    All neighbors in FULL state
  - **Verify OSPF Routes**

    ```
    show ip route ospf
    ```

    Expected routes:
    - 192.168.10.0/24
    - 192.168.20.0/24
    - 192.168.30.0/24
  - **Verify LSDB**

    ```
    show ipospf database
    ```

    Expected:

    Router LSAs for 1.1.1.1, 2.2.2.2, 3.3.3.3
  - **End-to-End Connectivity**

    ping 192.168.20.1

    ping 192.168.30.1

    traceroute 192.168.30.1
- **OSPF Consistency Requirements (Important)**

  For neighbors to form, both ends must match:
  - Area ID
  - Hello / Dead timers
  - Authentication (if enabled)
  - Network type
  - MTU size

Optional authentication example:

ipospf authentication message-digest

ipospf message-digest-key 1 md5 OSPFKEY

Final Result

- OSPF neighbors successfully form.
- All LANs are reachable across sites.
- Design is secure, scalable, and realistic.

Problem 5: Efficient IP Addressing Strategy

Scenario: You have been given the IP block 192.168.100.0/24 and need to create subnets for four departments:

- **Admin Department**: Needs 100 IP addresses.
- **Sales Department**: Needs 50 IP addresses.
- **Tech Support**: Needs 30 IP addresses.
- **Marketing**: Needs 40 IP addresses.

Task:

- Perform subnetting to meet the requirements of each department.
- Provide the subnet masks, CIDR notations, and usable IP ranges for each department.

Solution:

- **Admin Department (100 IP addresses)**:
    - Required hosts: 100.
    - Formula: 2^7 - 2 = 126 → /25 subnet mask.
    - **Subnet**: 192.168.100.0/25, usable range: 192.168.100.1 - 192.168.100.126.
- **Sales Department (50 IP addresses)**:
    - Required hosts: 50.
    - Formula: 2^6 - 2 = 62 → /26 subnet mask.
    - **Subnet**: 192.168.100.128/26, usable range: 192.168.100.129 - 192.168.100.190.
- **Tech Support (30 IP addresses)**:
    - Required hosts: 30.
    - Formula: 2^5 - 2 = 30 → /27 subnet mask.
    - **Subnet**: 192.168.100.192/27, usable range: 192.168.100.193 - 192.168.100.222.
- **Marketing (40 IP addresses)**:
    - Required hosts: 40.
    - Formula: 2^6 - 2 = 62 → /26 subnet mask.
    - **Subnet**: 192.168.100.224/26, usable range: 192.168.100.225 - 192.168.100.254.

DEPARTMENT	SUBNET ADDRESS	CIDR NOTATION	USABLE IP RANGE	SUBNET MASK
Admin Dept	192.168.100.0/25	/25	192.168.100.1 - 192.168.100.126	255.255.255.128
Sales Dept	192.168.100.128/26	/26	192.168.100.129 - 192.168.100.190	255.255.255.192
Tech Support	192.168.100.192/27	/27	192.168.100.193 - 192.168.100.222	255.255.255.224
Marketing Dept	192.168.100.224/26	/26	192.168.100.225 - 192.168.100.254	255.255.255.192

***Table 1.24**: Solution Table for Efficient IP Addressing Strategy*

Conclusion

Chapter 1, Networking Fundamentals, laid the groundwork for understanding networking principles, focusing on key concepts like the OSI/TCP-IP models, IP addressing, CIDR notation, and routing fundamentals. By mastering these topics, readers gain the foundational knowledge needed to navigate and configure networks effectively.

The hands-on activities and exercises demonstrated practical implementations, bridging the gap between theory and real-world application. These skills are not only essential for passing AWS networking certification exams but also invaluable for managing cloud networks in professional environments.

As we transition to subsequent chapters, this foundation will enable readers to explore advanced topics such as AWS-specific networking services, security, and automation with confidence and clarity.

Points to Remember

- **Networking as the Backbone**
    - Networking is a critical component of modern IT, enabling communication and resource sharing across devices and systems. It plays a foundational role in cloud computing environments like AWS.
- **The OSI and TCP/IP Models**
    - The OSI model provides a conceptual framework for understanding data flow across seven layers, from Physical to Application.
    - The TCP/IP model simplifies this structure into four layers, making it more practical for real-world applications.
- **IPv4 and IPv6 Addressing**
    - IPv4 addresses are structured in a dotted-decimal format and classified into A, B, C, D, and E categories.
    - IPv6 offers an expanded address space with advanced features like built-in IPsec and Stateless Address Autoconfiguration (SLAAC).
- **CIDR Notation for Flexible Subnetting**
    - Classless Inter-Domain Routing (CIDR) enables efficient IP address allocation and allows for custom subnet sizes, addressing the limitations of traditional class-based addressing.
- **Routing Fundamentals**
    - Routing directs traffic between networks, with default gateways acting as exit points for non-local traffic.
    - Static routing is manually configured, while dynamic routing automates path selection using protocols like OSPF and BGP.

CHAPTER 2
Network Security Basics

Introduction

As businesses increasingly adopt cloud computing, ensuring network security becomes a critical challenge. Networks are often the first target for cyberattacks, making it essential to understand the principles and tools that keep them secure. This chapter focuses on foundational concepts like firewalls, Access Control Lists (ACLs), AWS-specific features like Security Groups, encryption protocols, and threat mitigation strategies. By combining theoretical knowledge with real-world examples, this chapter equips readers with the skills necessary to secure cloud networks effectively.

Structure

In this chapter, we will cover the following topics:

- Firewall Basics
- Access Control Lists (ACLs)
- Security Groups and Network Access Control Lists (NACLs)
- Secure Protocols: HTTPS, SSH, TLS

Firewall Basics

A firewall is a network security system designed to monitor and control incoming and outgoing network traffic grounded on destined security rules. It serves as a hedge between a trusted internal network and untrusted external networks, similar to the internet. Firewalls play a pivotal part in securing computer systems and sensitive data from cyber pitfalls like hacking, malware, and unauthorized access. By filtering business and administering security programs, firewalls help in maintaining network integrity and confidentiality.

Firewalls can be implemented in both hardware and software forms, with each having its distinct use cases and functionalities. With the increasing complexity of cyber threats and the rise of cloud computing, understanding firewall basics has become essential for both organizations and individual users.

The primary purpose of a firewall is to establish a defence mechanism to prevent unauthorized access to or from a private network. Depending on the rules set by the firewall, it can either allow or block data packets traveling through a network. The most common rule sets are based on IP addresses, domain names, protocols, ports, and specific applications.

In addition to basic traffic filtering, firewalls provide advanced functionalities, such as:

- **Packet Inspection:** Firewalls inspect incoming and outgoing packets to ensure that only those that meet the security criteria pass through.
- **Stateful Inspection:** This type of inspection tracks the state of active connections, allowing for more dynamic filtering based on the context of the communication.
- **Proxying:** Firewalls can act as an intermediary between two systems, relaying requests, and responses to obscure the internal network from the outside world.
- **NAT (Network Address Translation):** Firewalls can mask internal IP addresses, translating them into public-facing ones to enhance privacy and prevent direct exposure to external entities.

Types of Firewalls

There are several types of firewalls, each designed to cater to different networking needs and levels of complexity. These types include:

- **Packet-Filtering Firewalls:** This is the simplest form of firewall technology. It inspects network packets at the IP layer, checking source and destination addresses, ports, and the protocol. The firewall either permits or blocks the packet based on pre-configured rules. While efficient and fast, packet-filtering firewalls are limited in terms of security depth because they do not analyze the data payloads within the packets.
- **Stateful Inspection Firewalls:** Unlike packet-filtering firewalls, stateful inspection monitors the state of active connections, ensuring that packets are part of a legitimate ongoing session. They track the state of the connection and allow or block traffic based on whether the data matches expected parameters for a given connection.
- **Proxy Firewalls:** A proxy firewall operates at the application layer, acting as an intermediary between users and the services they want to access. It forwards requests from users to the service provider, filtering content, and masking the internal IP address of the user. Proxy firewalls can block harmful content and reduce the risk of direct attacks on internal networks.
- **Next-Generation Firewalls (NGFW):** NGFWs combine traditional firewall functionality with additional features like Intrusion Detection/Prevention Systems (IDS/IPS), application awareness, and deep packet inspection. They are designed to handle more complex and sophisticated threats, such as Advanced Persistent Threats (APTs), and offer more granular control over network traffic.
- **Web Application Firewalls (WAF):** WAFs specifically protect web applications from attacks such as SQL injection, cross-site scripting (XSS), and other vulnerabilities commonly exploited in web-based attacks. These firewalls operate at the application layer and inspect traffic specifically targeting web servers.
- **Cloud Firewalls:** As organizations increasingly migrate to cloud environments, cloud-based firewalls have emerged. These firewalls provide protection for cloud infrastructure by monitoring traffic and enforcing security policies in real-time. They can be scalable, offering protection for both public and private cloud resources.

OSI model reference:

- Packet filtering: Layer 3,
- Stateful inspection: Layer 4,
- Proxy/WAF: Layer 7

Key Firewall Concepts and Terminologies

Understanding key firewall concepts and terminologies is essential for effectively managing network security, as they define how traffic is filtered, monitored, and protected against potential threats.

- **Rule Sets:** Firewalls operate based on predefined rules, which define what traffic is allowed and what is blocked. These rules can be as simple as allowing traffic from specific IP addresses or as complex as analyzing the packet content for malware.
- **Access Control Lists (ACLs):** ACLs are the basic building blocks for rule sets. They define which users or systems can access certain resources and under what conditions. ACLs are typically associated with packet-filtering firewalls, as they help in filtering traffic based on various parameters such as IP address and port number.
- **Ports and Protocols:** Firewalls often filter traffic based on port numbers and protocols. Each network service (some of which includes HTTP, FTP, and DNS) uses specific ports (like port 80 for HTTP, port 443 for HTTPS). Firewalls can block or allow traffic based on the destination port number, helping to protect specific services from attacks.
- **Intrusion Detection and Prevention Systems (IDPS):** Firewalls integrated with IDPS technologies can detect and block malicious activities such as malware, buffer overflows, or Denial-of-Service (DoS) attacks. They analyze network traffic in real-time and take immediate action against suspicious activities.
- **Network Address Translation (NAT):** This technique is often used by firewalls to mask private internal IP addresses from public networks. NAT helps in conserving IP addresses and adds a layer of security by preventing external access to the internal network.
- **Logging and Monitoring:** Firewalls generate logs of traffic activity, which are essential for security monitoring, troubleshooting, and forensic analysis. Organizations typically monitor firewall logs to identify abnormal traffic patterns or potential security breaches.

Firewall Configurations

To maximize security, firewalls must be properly configured. A well-configured firewall provides a strong defence against unauthorized access, while an improperly configured one can leave systems vulnerable to attacks. Some common configurations include:

- **Default Deny:** A secure default configuration is one where all incoming and outgoing traffic is denied unless explicitly allowed by a firewall rule. This principle ensures that only necessary services and applications are exposed to the network.
- **Segmentation:** Firewalls can be used to segment different parts of a network, creating security zones with varying levels of trust. For example, a company might place its internal servers, financial systems, and customer databases in separate segments, each protected by different firewall rules.
- **VPN Integration:** Many firewalls support Virtual Private Networks (VPNs), enabling secure remote access to a network. VPNs encrypt the communication between the user and the firewall, ensuring that data remains secure as it travels over potentially untrusted networks like the internet.
- **Traffic Filtering:** Firewalls can be configured to block or allow traffic based on certain criteria. For instance, an organization might have geo-based IP restrictions or it might restrict access to certain ports, such as those commonly used for remote administration.

Firewall Performances and Challenges

In cloud-native environments, firewalls are often distributed/virtualized, so performance considerations differ from on-premises appliances. While firewalls provide essential protection, their implementation and management come with certain challenges:

- **Performance Impact:** Firewalls can introduce latency to network traffic due to the additional processing required for packet inspection. Next-generation firewalls, with their advanced security features, can be more resource-intensive, requiring higher throughput to handle large amounts of traffic.
- **Complexity in Configuration:** Configuring a firewall with the appropriate security policies can be complex, especially in large organizations. Misconfigurations, such as overly permissive rules or improperly segmented networks, can result in vulnerabilities that expose systems to attacks.
- **Evolving Threats:** As cyber threats evolve, firewalls need to be updated to address new types of attacks. Modern firewalls are designed to adapt to the changing landscape, but they must be regularly updated to remain effective against new Tactics, Techniques, and Procedures (TTPs) used by hackers.

In conclusion, firewalls are a cornerstone of network security, providing essential protection by controlling the flow of data between trusted and untrusted networks. By understanding the basics of firewall types, configuration, and key concepts, organizations can implement effective security measures to safeguard their data and resources. However, as cyber threats continue to evolve, firewalls require regular updates, continuous monitoring, and strict configuration management to remain effective against both known and emerging risks.

Access Control Lists (ACLs)

Access Control Lists (ACLs) are an essential aspect of network security, used to control the flow of traffic and manage permissions for different types of network resources. In computing, ACLs are used to specify which users/systems can access which resources and actions (read, write, execute). These lists serve as a method of implementing security policies by determining who can access what resources, and under what conditions. ACLs are widely used across various operating systems, networking devices, and applications to enforce security and manage permissions effectively.

An ACL is essentially a list of rules that specify the access control policy for a system or network. Each rule in an ACL identifies a subject (such as a user or system) and the permissions (such as read, write, or execute) granted to them on a given resource (such as files, directories, or network devices). These rules help ensure that only authorized entities can access sensitive data or systems, while also preventing unauthorized access and potential malicious activity.

Types of ACLs

ACLs can be categorized into different types based on their purpose and where they are applied. The two main types of ACLs in the context of network security are Standard ACLs and Extended ACLs.

CISCO numbering:

- Standard ACLs (1–99),
- Extended ACLs (100–199)

OSI layer mapping:

- Standard ACLs: Layer 3 (IP-based).
- Extended ACLs: Layers 3–4 (IP, protocol, ports).

Standard ACLs

Standard ACLs are used primarily to control traffic based on the source IP address of the packet. They are simple and provide basic filtering capabilities. With a standard ACL, you can permit or deny traffic from specific IP addresses to or from a network resource. These ACLs are often used in routers or switches to filter out unwanted traffic from entering or exiting a network.

For example, a standard ACL might allow traffic from a trusted IP address while denying access from all others. However, these ACLs are limited in their capabilities because they do not inspect the destination IP address, port numbers, or other advanced characteristics of network traffic.

Extended ACLs

Extended ACLs provide more granular control by allowing filtering based on both the source and destination IP addresses, along with other factors like protocols (TCP, UDP, and ICMP) and port numbers. This allows for more specific filtering rules and enables network administrators to control traffic in greater detail.

Extended ACLs are widely used in more complex network setups, where administrators need to differentiate between various types of traffic, such as allowing web traffic (HTTP) but blocking File Transfer Traffic (FTP) from specific hosts.

ACLs in File Systems

In the context of file systems, ACLs are used to define permissions for files and directories. Operating systems like Linux, Windows, and macOS implement ACLs to manage user access to the file system and other resources.

Windows ACLs

In Windows environments, ACLs are implemented as part of the security settings of files and folders. These ACLs define which users or groups can access a specific file or folder and what actions they can perform. Permissions in Windows ACLs include "Read," "Write," "Execute," and "Full Control." Administrators can assign permissions to individual users, groups, or special system accounts, thereby controlling access to sensitive information.

Each file or folder in Windows has a Discretionary Access Control List (DACL) that contains entries for users and groups along with their permissions. In addition, the system also has a System Access Control List (SACL), which is used for auditing access to objects.

Linux ACLs

Linux also supports ACLs for files and directories, providing more flexibility than the traditional Unix-based file permissions model (rwx for user, group, and others). Linux ACLs allow for more fine-grained control, where permissions can be assigned to individual users and groups beyond the file owner and group.

In Linux, the setfacl and getfacl commands are used to set and view ACLs, respectively. The ACLs define access for both users and groups and can specify permissions such as read, write, or execute.

ACLs in Networking Devices

In networking devices such as routers and firewalls, ACLs are used to manage traffic flow and enforce security policies. ACLs can control which packets are allowed or denied based on various criteria, including the source and destination IP address, protocol type, and port numbers.

ACLs in Routers

Routers commonly use ACLs to filter traffic between different networks or subnets. Network administrators define rules to control inbound and outbound traffic by specifying the allowed or denied IP addresses, port numbers, or even entire subnets. This allows routers to regulate traffic based on various parameters, improving the overall security and efficiency of the network.

For instance, an ACL might allow incoming traffic to a web server on port 80 but block incoming traffic on other ports. By using ACLs in this way, organizations can prevent unauthorized access to network resources and protect against various types of attacks.

ACLs in Firewalls

Firewalls are critical devices used to protect networks from external threats. They use ACLs to define which types of network traffic are allowed or blocked. By configuring ACLs on firewalls, administrators can specify rules that permit or deny traffic based on various attributes, such as source IP, destination IP, protocol, and port numbers.

For example, an organization might configure a firewall ACL to allow access to a web server from the public internet while denying access to other internal resources. Similarly, ACLs can be used to filter traffic based on the time of day, ensuring that only authorized users can access sensitive resources during specific hours.

Best Practices for ACL Implementation

While ACLs provide robust access control mechanisms, they need to be implemented and managed carefully to ensure that they are effective and secure. Here are some best practices for ACL implementation:

Principle of Least Privilege

This principle states that users should only have access to the resources they absolutely need to perform their job functions. ACLs should be configured to allow the minimum necessary permissions to users and systems, reducing the risk of accidental or malicious misuse.

Document ACL rules

In large enterprises and cloud infrastructures, undocumented ACLs often lead to troubleshooting and audit challenges. Administrators may struggle to understand why traffic is blocked or allowed if ACL rules are not properly recorded. Documenting ACL rules—including their purpose, scope, and change history—helps ensure clarity, simplifies maintenance, and supports compliance and security audits.

Regular Auditing

ACLs should be regularly audited to ensure they are still valid and in line with the security policies of the organization. Over time, the permissions and access control rules may change, and it is important to ensure that ACLs are updated accordingly to avoid potential security gaps.

Explicit Deny Statements

ACLs often process rules in a top-down order. Therefore, it is crucial to place explicit "deny" statements in the appropriate order to ensure that unauthorized traffic is blocked. In some cases, a "deny" rule placed after a "permit" rule might allow unwanted traffic, even if a deny rule is present.

Minimizing Complexity

Although extended ACLs offer more control, they can also become complex to manage. In highly dynamic environments, the sheer volume of ACL rules can become unmanageable. Therefore, ACLs should be designed in a way that keeps the rule sets as simple and clear as possible while still meeting the security requirements of the organization.

Testing ACLs

Before deploying in a live environment, it is important to test the rules in a controlled setting. This can prevent unintended access issues and ensure that the security configurations are functioning as expected.

Access Control Lists in Corporate Network

Imagine a large Multinational Corporation (MNC) that has a complex network infrastructure with various departments, including HR, IT, Finance, and Marketing. Each department has different security requirements, and sensitive data needs to be protected from unauthorized access. The MNC decides to implement Access Control Lists (ACLs) on their network devices and file systems to ensure that only authorized users and systems can access specific resources.

Scenario 1: ACLs in Networking Devices

An MNC uses several routers and firewalls to control traffic between the internal network and the outside world. The security team of the company configures ACLs on the router to filter incoming and outgoing traffic based on specific rules.

Note: *Routers/firewalls handle ACLs differently; firewalls often include stateful inspection, while router ACLs are typically stateless.*

For example:

The router is configured with a Standard ACL to restrict access to certain internal resources from external sources. This ACL ensures that only authorized users from trusted IP addresses can access the internal systems of the company. The security team defines rules that:

Allow traffic from the IP address range of the remote offices of the company to access certain servers in the headquarters, such as the email server and file server.

Deny all incoming traffic from any other external IP addresses to access these critical servers.

Additionally, the MNC uses an Extended ACL on their firewalls to provide more detailed filtering. The firewall is configured to allow web traffic (HTTP) to a public-facing web server while blocking other traffic types (such as FTP) from reaching the same server. This ensures that only legitimate users can access the public website of the company, while other potentially dangerous traffic is blocked.

Scenario 2: ACLs on File Systems

Within an MNC, sensitive data such as employee payroll information, financial reports, and proprietary business plans are stored on file servers. The IT team of the company configures Windows-based ACLs on these file systems to control access to this critical information.

For example:

- **HR Department:** Only HR managers and employees within the HR department are granted "Full Control" permissions to access employee payroll data and personal information. Employees outside of the HR department, including those in Marketing and IT, are denied access to this sensitive information.

- **Finance Department:** Only authorized finance team members have "Read/Write" permissions to access financial reports, which contain confidential information about the profits and losses of the company. Others, including managers from other departments, can only view the files but cannot make any changes.
- **Marketing Department:** Members of the marketing team have "Read" access to files containing market research and advertising campaigns but do not have permission to modify the files.

In modern enterprise environments, similar access control concepts apply to cloud storage platforms. For example, AWS S3 supports bucket policies and ACLs that define who can access buckets and individual objects, and what actions they can perform (read, write, or delete). By combining ACLs with identity and policy-based controls, organizations can enforce fine-grained access control across both on-premises file servers and cloud-based storage systems.

The Windows ACLs are configured using user groups to simplify permission management. Instead of assigning permissions to individual users, the IT team assigns access rights to groups such as "HR Managers," "Finance Team," and "Marketing Team." This approach makes it easier to manage permissions as new employees join the organization or when employees change roles—users can simply be added to or removed from the appropriate group.

A similar approach is followed on Linux-based file servers, where the IT team uses Linux ACLs for fine-grained access control. For example, using the setfacl command, the IT team grants read and write permissions to members of the Finance group on directories containing financial reports, while keeping payroll directories strictly restricted to HR users only. This ensures that sensitive payroll data remains protected while allowing authorized staff to perform their tasks efficiently.

By using group-based ACLs across both Windows and Linux systems, the company achieves consistent, scalable, and easily maintainable permission management in a heterogeneous enterprise environment.

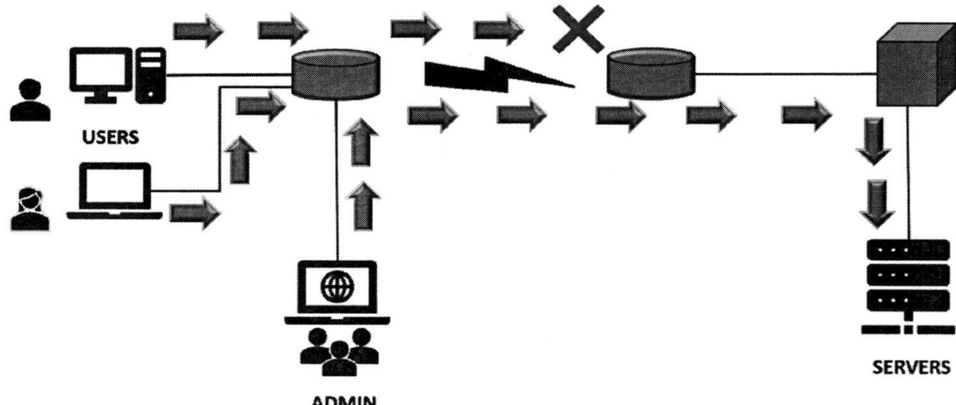

Figure 2.1: *ACLs in Network Security*

Scenario 3: ACLs in Remote Access Systems

The MNC also operates a Virtual Private Network (VPN) that allows employees to securely access company resources from remote locations. The VPN servers are configured with Access Control Lists (ACLs) to regulate access based on user identity, location, and time.

Access Examples

- **IT Team:** It has the highest level of access and can connect to the VPN from any location, 24/7, to manage servers, apply patches, and perform system maintenance.
- **HR Managers:** It can access the VPN only from approved office locations and during business hours, enabling secure access to employee records while reducing exposure risk.

- **Sales Team:** It has restricted VPN access limited to specific systems such as the Customer Relationship Management (CRM) platform, and is denied access to sensitive financial and payroll systems.
- **Additional Security Enhancement:** Modern VPN deployments often combine ACLs with strong identity verification mechanisms, such as Multi-Factor Authentication (MFA). By requiring an additional authentication factor (that includes a one-time password, mobile authenticator app, or hardware token), the company significantly reduces the risk of unauthorized access—even if user credentials are compromised.

By integrating ACLs, identity-based access controls, and MFA, the VPN ensures that employees have role-appropriate access while maintaining a strong security posture for remote connectivity.

Benefits of ACL Implementation at MNC

Implementing Access Control Lists (ACLs) enables an MNC to strengthen its network security posture while ensuring precise access management, regulatory compliance, and efficient operational control.

- **Security:** By implementing ACLs, MNC ensures that sensitive information is accessible only to authorized personnel, protecting the company from internal and external threats. Unauthorized users are blocked from accessing critical systems, thereby reducing the risk of data breaches.
- **Granular Control:** Extended ACLs provide granular control over network traffic, enabling MNC to allow or deny specific traffic types based on a variety of parameters such as IP address, protocol, and port number (like "deny TCP traffic from 10.0.0.0/8 to port 22 while allowing HTTP on port 80"). This allows for more fine-tuned security policies.
- **Compliance:** The MNC operates in multiple regions, and the company is subject to various data protection regulations, including GDPR and HIPAA. The ACLs help ensure that the company meets these compliance requirements by restricting access to sensitive data and maintaining proper auditing capabilities.
- **Operational Efficiency:** ACLs simplify the management of user access. Instead of manually managing access for each individual user, the company can use groups and roles, which streamlines the process of onboarding new employees or changing access levels for the existing ones. Group-based ACL assignment also reduces human error risk compared to individual user assignments.

Real-World Challenge: Managing ACLs in Large Networks

As the MNC continues to grow, managing Access Control Lists (ACLs) becomes increasingly complex due to the rising number of users, departments, applications, and network devices. The IT team faces significant challenges in maintaining consistent and secure ACL configurations, particularly when new devices are added or departments expand their operations.

Key challenges include:

- **Rule Conflicts:** As ACLs grow, overlapping or contradictory rules may be introduced, that might lead to unintended access being allowed or legitimate traffic being blocked. These conflicts increase the risk of security gaps and service disruptions.
- **Scalability Limitations:** Traditional ACLs are often difficult to scale in cloud and hybrid environments, where resources are dynamic and frequently change. In such scenarios, Policy-Based Access Control (PBAC) or role-based approaches provide greater flexibility and manageability.

- **Auditing and Change Tracking Difficulty:** Without a centralized management system, tracking historical ACL changes, identifying who made modifications, and verifying compliance becomes challenging. This makes security audits and troubleshooting more time-consuming and error-prone.

To address these issues, the company implements an automated, centralized ACL management and auditing tool that periodically reviews configurations, detects conflicts, enforces best practices, and updates ACLs as needed. This approach improves security posture, simplifies administration, and ensures ACLs remain accurate and effective as the organization scales.

In all, Access Control Lists (ACLs) are an essential component in securing computer systems, networks, and files by specifying which users or systems can access resources and the types of operations they can perform. ACLs play a significant role in maintaining security, and their use spans from simple network traffic filtering to detailed file system permissions. By properly implementing ACLs, organizations can reduce vulnerabilities and enhance the overall security posture of their infrastructure.

Whether applied in networking devices, file systems, or operating systems, ACLs help enforce security policies and prevent unauthorized access to sensitive information. As part of a larger security strategy, ACLs should be maintained and updated regularly, adhering to best practices like the principle of least privilege and regular auditing. When used correctly, ACLs provide a powerful and flexible mechanism for managing access control in modern IT environments.

Security Groups and Network Access Control Lists (NACLs)

In the realm of cloud computing and networking, security is a top priority to ensure that sensitive data and resources are protected from unauthorized access. Amazon Web Services (AWS), one of the leading cloud service providers, offers two primary tools for securing network resources: Security Groups and Network Access Control Lists (NACLs). Both are integral components of the Virtual Private Cloud (VPC) environment, designed to manage and control the flow of inbound and outbound traffic to and from instances, subnets, and other resources within the network.

While both Security Groups and NACLs function to regulate access, they differ in how they are applied and the level of granularity they offer. Security Groups provide instance-level security, while NACLs offer subnet-level control. Together, these tools create a layered defence strategy, helping administrators implement a robust security model for their cloud infrastructure.

Security Groups

A Security Group is a virtual firewall for Amazon EC2 instances that controls inbound and outbound traffic. Security Groups operate at the instance level, meaning they can be applied to individual EC2 instances or groups of instances. They are stateful, meaning that if an incoming request is allowed, the response is automatically allowed, regardless of the outbound rules.

Key Characteristics of Security Groups

- **Instance-level control:** Security Groups apply rules to individual instances or groups of instances.
- **Stateful:** If an inbound rule allows traffic from an IP address, the corresponding outbound traffic is automatically allowed, even if outbound rules do not explicitly permit it.
- **Allow-only rules:** Security Groups are designed to allow traffic but not block it. Administrators specify which traffic is allowed to reach instances, and all other traffic is implicitly denied.
- **Multiple Associations:** A single Security Group can be associated with multiple instances, allowing for easier management and scalability.

- **Dynamic Updates:** Changes to Security Group rules take effect immediately and do not require a restart of the instances or services.

Functioning of Security Groups

Security Groups consist of a set of rules that define which traffic is permitted to reach the associated instances. These rules are defined based on:

- Protocol (for instance, TCP, UDP, ICMP)
- Port range (such as, port 80 for HTTP, port 443 for HTTPS)
- Source IP address (like a specific IP address or a CIDR block)

For instance, a Security Group might allow inbound HTTP (port 80) traffic from any IP address (0.0.0.0/0), but only permit SSH (port 22) traffic from a specific trusted IP range. The rules are applied in a way that only allows the specified traffic, with everything else being implicitly denied.

Use Case for Security Groups

Consider a scenario where a web application is hosted on EC2 instances. The Security Group for these instances might allow inbound traffic on HTTP (port 80) and HTTPS (port 443) from any IP address but restrict SSH (port 22) access to a specific set of IP addresses belonging to the system administrators. This configuration ensures that the application is publicly accessible via web traffic while maintaining the security of the administrative access to the EC2 instances.

Example: AWS CLI Rule Entry

The following AWS CLI command allows HTTPS (TCP port 443) inbound traffic from any IP address (0.0.0.0/0) to a security group:

```
aws ec2 authorize-security-group-ingress \
  --group-id sg-0123456789abcdef0 \
  --protocol tcp \
  --port 443 \
  --cidr 0.0.0.0/0
```

Explanation:

- **`--group-id`** specifies the security group to modify
- **`--protocol tcp`** defines the transport protocol
- **`--port 443`** allows HTTPS traffic
- **`--cidr 0.0.0.0/0`** permits access from all IPv4 addresses.

This example demonstrates how security group rules can be configured programmatically in addition to using the AWS Management Console.

Network Access Control Lists (NACLs)

While Security Groups control traffic at the instance level, Network Access Control Lists (NACLs) provide a higher level of control at the subnet level. NACLs are designed to control traffic moving into and out of a subnet within a VPC. Unlike Security Groups, NACLs are stateless, meaning that if an inbound request is allowed, the response must also be explicitly allowed by the outbound rules. This gives administrators more fine-grained control over both directions of traffic flow.

Key Characteristics of NACLs

- **Subnet-level control:** NACLs apply rules to an entire subnet rather than to individual instances.

- **Stateless:** Both inbound and outbound rules must be configured separately, as responses to inbound traffic are not automatically allowed.
- **Allow and Deny rules:** Unlike Security Groups, which only allow traffic, NACLs can explicitly allow or deny traffic based on rules.
- **Ordered Rule Processing:** NACLs process rules in a sequential manner. Once a rule is matched, no further rules are evaluated.

  Like rule #100 allows HTTP, rule #110 denies all else.
- **Default NACL:** Each VPC comes with a default NACL that allows all inbound and outbound traffic. However, this can be modified to restrict access.

Functioning of NACLs

The ephemeral port range is (1024–65535 or AWS recommended 32768–65535). NACLs consist of a set of rules that allow or deny traffic based on:

- Protocol (like TCP, UDP)
- Port range (such as port 80 for HTTP)
- Source and destination IP addresses (including specific IP ranges)

The main difference between NACLs and Security Groups is that NACLs can have both Allow and Deny rules, whereas Security Groups only allow traffic and implicitly deny all others. This makes NACLs more flexible in certain use cases, such as when explicit blocking of certain traffic is required.

Use Case for NACLs

Consider a scenario where an MNC has multiple subnets in a VPC: one for web servers and one for database servers. The company wants to ensure that:

The web servers can communicate freely with the outside world (allowing HTTP/HTTPS traffic), but the database servers should only allow incoming traffic from the web servers and deny any direct inbound access from the internet.

To achieve this, the MNC configures NACLs on the database subnet with explicit Deny rules for all inbound traffic from external IPs, while allowing inbound traffic only from the IP range of the web server subset. In addition, the NACL on the web server subnet allows outbound HTTP and HTTPS traffic to any IP but ensures that only allowed inbound traffic from the internet reaches the servers.

Differences between Security Groups and NACLs

While both Security Groups and NACLs are used to control traffic, they differ significantly in scope, behavior, and use cases.

Security Groups:

- Operate at the instance level, meaning they control traffic to individual EC2 instances.
- Are stateful, meaning that if an incoming connection is allowed, the corresponding outgoing traffic is automatically permitted.
- Can only have Allow rules; there is no explicit ability to deny traffic.
- Allow multiple associations to instances, providing flexible management.
- Changes to rules take effect immediately, without needing to restart instances.

NACLs:

- Operate at the subnet level, controlling traffic entering and leaving entire subnets.
- Are stateless, meaning both inbound and outbound traffic must be explicitly allowed or denied.
- Can have both Allow and Deny rules, providing more control over traffic filtering.
- Rules are processed in sequential order, meaning the first matching rule is applied.
- Default NACL allows all traffic, which can be modified to restrict access as needed.

Best Practices for Using Security Groups and NACLs

To ensure optimal security and management of network resources, it is essential to follow some best practices when configuring Security Groups and NACLs.

Best Practices for Security Groups

- **Use descriptive names:** Clearly name Security Groups based on their intended purpose (such as "WebServerSG" or "DBServerSG") to avoid confusion.
- **Apply least privilege:** Only allow necessary traffic. For example, only allow SSH access from trusted IPs, and restrict HTTP access to specific IPs when appropriate.
- **Use multiple security groups:** Assign instances to multiple Security Groups based on their roles (like web server and database server), allowing more flexible management.
- **Regularly audit rules:** Review and update Security Group rules periodically to ensure that they align with the security policies of your organization.

Best Practices for NACLs

- **Minimize complexity:** Keep NACLs simple and avoid overly complex rule sets, as they can be difficult to manage and audit.
- **Use NACLs for explicit blocking:** NACLs are best used for explicit deny rules, particularly in scenarios where you want to block certain types of traffic entirely.
- **Apply a default NACL:** Ensure that the default NACL is configured to allow only the necessary traffic, or replace it with a custom NACL that provides more fine-grained control.
- **Regularly audit rules:** Like Security Groups, NACLs should be regularly audited to ensure that they are in line with the security posture of the organization.

Real-Life Scenario: Using Security Groups and NACLs in a Cloud-Based E-Commerce Platform

Let us consider an e-commerce company called **ABC**, which operates a cloud-based infrastructure for hosting its online shopping platform. The company has a large user base, and its cloud environment is hosted on Amazon Web Services (AWS).

ABC needs to ensure that their platform remains secure while still providing a seamless shopping experience for users. To manage the security of their cloud network, they implement Security Groups and Network Access Control Lists (NACLs) to control access to different resources, such as web servers, databases, and payment processing systems.

Scenario 1: Security Groups for Instance-Level Access Control

ABC hosts its website and user-facing application on a fleet of EC2 instances. These instances are organized into different tiers based on their function:

- **Web Servers:** Responsible for hosting the front-end of the website, processing user requests, and displaying product listings.
- **Application Servers:** Handle business logic, user authentication, and session management.
- **Database Servers:** Store customer data, product information, and transaction records.

  Each of these EC2 instances needs to be secured with Security Groups to control which types of traffic can reach them.

- **Web Server Security Group:** This Security Group allows incoming traffic on HTTP (port 80) and HTTPS (port 443) from any IP address, as the web servers need to be publicly accessible to customers browsing the platform. However, SSH (port 22) access is restricted to specific IP addresses belonging to the system administrators to ensure secure management.
- **Application Server Security Group:** The application servers interact with the web servers and the database servers. This Security Group allows inbound traffic on HTTP (port 80) from the web servers but blocks all inbound access from external sources. Outbound traffic is allowed for communication with external APIs for payment processing or shipping services.
- **Database Server Security Group:** The database servers are highly sensitive and need strict access controls. This Security Group allows inbound traffic only from the application servers (on a private subnet) and denies all other inbound traffic. Outbound traffic is also restricted to ensure the database only communicates with the application servers.

This setup ensures that only the right resources can communicate with each other. For instance, the web servers can receive traffic from the internet, but only the application servers can access the database servers. This minimizes the attack surface by preventing direct access to the sensitive database layer.

Scenario 2: NACLs for Subnet-Level Access Control

In addition to Security Groups, ABC also uses Network Access Control Lists (NACLs) to enforce additional layers of security at the subnet level. The infrastructure of the company is divided into multiple subnets based on the role of the resources, such as web-facing resources and internal resources.

ABC has two primary subnets:

- **Public Subnet:** Hosts the EC2 instances that need to be accessible from the internet (such as web servers, load balancers).
- **Private Subnet:** Hosts more sensitive resources that should not be directly accessible from the internet (some of which includes application servers, database servers).

ABC configures NACLs to control traffic between these subnets as follows:

- **Public Subnet NACL:** The NACL for the public subnet allows inbound traffic from the internet on ports 80 (HTTP) and 443 (HTTPS) to the web servers. It also allows outbound traffic for the web servers to fetch resources or communicate with external APIs. However, the NACL explicitly denies any inbound traffic on ports like 22 (SSH) and 3389 (RDP), ensuring that the web servers cannot be accessed via administrative protocols.
- **Private Subnet NACL:** The NACL for the private subnet controls traffic between the application servers and the database servers. It allows inbound traffic on the required application-specific ports (similar to HTTP on port 8080) from the public subnet but denies all inbound traffic from the internet. Additionally, the NACL denies any inbound traffic from external IP addresses to the database subnet, ensuring that only application servers can access the database servers.

The NACLs enforce these rules at the subnet level, meaning that even if an attacker gains access to the public subnet, they cannot directly communicate with or compromise the database servers, as the NACL for the private subnet blocks all such attempts.

Scenario 3: Combining Security Groups and NACLs for Layered Security

By combining Security Groups and NACLs, ABC creates a robust, layered security strategy that isolates sensitive resources and allows only authorized traffic to flow between them.

- **Web Traffic Management:** The Security Group for the web servers allows HTTP and HTTPS traffic from anywhere, while the NACL for the public subnet enforces additional rules, like denying SSH access from the internet. This dual layer ensures that only legitimate user traffic reaches the web servers while preventing malicious access attempts.
- **Application to Database Traffic:** Communication between the application servers and database servers is tightly controlled. The Security Group for the application servers allows outbound traffic to the database, but the database Security Group restricts inbound traffic to just those application servers. Simultaneously, the NACL for the private subnet blocks any other external traffic from reaching the database subnet.
- **Admin Access:** ABC restricts administrative access to EC2 instances by limiting SSH access. The Security Group for the web servers restricts SSH access to trusted admin IPs, while the NACL for the private subnet further restricts any unauthorized inbound traffic to the application and database subnets. This layered approach ensures that even if any vulnerability is discovered in one-layer, other security controls still prevent unauthorized access.

Scenario 4: Handling DDoS Attacks with Security Groups and NACLs

Given the high volume of traffic that an e-commerce platform like ABC might experience, protecting the platform against Distributed Denial-of-Service (DDoS) attacks is crucial. ABC uses a combination of Security Groups and NACLs to mitigate DDoS threats.

The Security Group is configured to only allow traffic from trusted IP ranges for administrative tasks such as SSH and RDP. It blocks all other unwanted connections.

The NACL for the public subnet contains additional rules to block known malicious IP ranges or traffic patterns, thereby reducing the risk of DDoS attacks. It can block traffic from specific IP ranges that appear to be the source of malicious requests or flooding.

Furthermore, ABC leverages the Shield of AWS and WAF (Web Application Firewall) services for more advanced DDoS protection, but the combination of Security Groups and NACLs forms a foundational security layer to reduce the attack surface. Here, SGs/NACLs are first-layer filtering, not substitutes for full DDoS protection.

The implementation by ABC of Security Groups and NACLs showcases how these two tools can work together to create a secure and scalable cloud infrastructure. Security Groups provide instance-level protection, ensuring that only authorized traffic reaches specific EC2 instances. NACLs offer subnet-level control, allowing ABC to implement more granular access policies and block unwanted traffic before it reaches critical resources.

By utilizing these two tools in tandem, ABC ensures that its cloud-based e-commerce platform is secure from various types of threats, including unauthorized access, malicious traffic, and DDoS attacks. This layered security approach not only secures sensitive data but also ensures smooth operation and customer satisfaction on the platform.

In all, both the Security Groups and Network Access Control Lists (NACLs) are critical components of cloud network security, offering powerful tools for controlling traffic and ensuring that only authorized entities can access sensitive resources. While Security Groups provide instance-level security and are stateful, NACLs operate at the subnet level and are stateless, offering more granular control over traffic flows.

Both tools complement each other in a multi-layered security architecture, where Security Groups handle fine-grained access to individual instances, and NACLs provide broader control over subnet-level traffic. By following best practices and understanding the unique characteristics of Security Groups and NACLs, organizations can enhance the security and manageability of their cloud infrastructure, safeguarding their data and applications from unauthorized access and potential threats.

Secure Protocols: HTTPS, SSH, TLS

In the increasingly digital world of today, security is one of the top concerns for users, businesses, and service providers. With the rapid growth of online activities, such as banking, shopping, and social media interactions, securing communications and data transmission is of paramount importance.

Secure protocols are the foundation of safe and private communication over the internet. Among the most widely used secure protocols are HTTPS, SSH, and TLS. These protocols play a crucial role in protecting the integrity, confidentiality, and authenticity of data exchanged between clients and servers.

- **HTTPS (Hypertext Transfer Protocol Secure):** Ensures that communications between a client (such as a web browser) and a server are encrypted and secure, preventing third parties from eavesdropping or tampering with the data.
- **SSH (Secure Shell):** Used for secure remote access to servers and devices, providing a way to manage systems and execute commands over unsecured networks.
- **TLS (Transport Layer Security):** It is the cryptographic protocol that underpins HTTPS, securing communication channels by encrypting data and ensuring its integrity.

These protocols, each in its own domain, contribute to creating a secure environment for various internet activities.

Let us dive deeper into the workings of these secure protocols, their features, use cases, and how they differ from one another.

HTTPS (Hypertext Transfer Protocol Secure)

HTTPS is an extension of HTTP, the protocol used for transferring data on the World Wide Web. While HTTP does not offer any encryption or security features, HTTPS provides a layer of protection by encrypting the data exchanged between a client (browser) and the server.

Working of HTTPS

Although HTTPS was originally secured by SSL, modern implementations exclusively use TLS (Transport Layer Security). When a user accesses a website that uses HTTPS, the server sends its SSL/TLS certificate, which contains a public key. The browser and server then perform a handshake -

- Browser verifies the certificate of the server against a trusted Certificate Authority (CA).
- Session key is established using asymmetric - symmetric encryption, to agree on encryption algorithms and keys. After the handshake, the communication becomes encrypted, ensuring that the data transferred between them is unreadable to eavesdroppers.

Key Features of HTTPS

HTTPS provides essential security features that protect web communications by ensuring confidentiality, authenticating servers, and maintaining the integrity of transmitted data.

- **Encryption:** HTTPS ensures that data exchanged between the client and the server is encrypted, protecting it from hackers and malicious third parties.
- **Authentication:** It verifies the identity of the server, ensuring that users are connecting to the correct website and not an imposter. Authentication relies on digital certificates signed by trusted CAs. This prevents Man-in-the-Middle (MITM) attacks.
- **Integrity:** HTTPS uses cryptographic hash functions (Authentication Codes (MACs) or HMAC) to ensure that data has not been tampered with during transmission.

HTTPS in Practice

Hypertext Transfer Protocol Secure (HTTPS) is essential for safeguarding sensitive online interactions by ensuring encrypted, authenticated, and tamper-proof communication between users and web services.

Online Banking: HTTPS is critical for secure online banking transactions, where sensitive data such as account numbers, passwords, and financial information need to be protected from cyber threats.

E-Commerce Websites: E-commerce platforms such as Amazon and eBay use HTTPS to secure customer transactions, credit card information, and personal details.

Feature	HTTPS
Integrity	Ensures transmitted data is not altered during transit.
Encryption	Yes, HTTPS encrypts data in transit using SSL/TLS protocols.
Authentication	Server authentication using SSL/TLS certificates issued by trusted Certificate Authorities (CAs).
Use Cases	Online banking, e-commerce, and social media.

Table 2.1: *HTTPS - Key Features and Use Cases*

SSH (Secure Shell)

SSH is a cryptographic network protocol used for secure remote administration of systems over an unsecured network. It is primarily used by system administrators to access and manage remote servers securely, but it can also be used for file transfers and tunnelling.

Working of SSH

When an administrator connects to a remote server using SSH, the server first provides its public host key, which the client validates to confirm the identity of the server. After this verification, the client and server perform a key exchange to establish an encrypted communication channel. This ensures that all data transferred (such as commands, files, and outputs) remains secure. Finally, the client authenticates itself (using a password or a private key), allowing secure access to the remote system.

SSH supports two types of authentications:

- **Password-based authentication:** The user provides a password to authenticate.
- **Public key-based authentication:** The private key of the user is used for authentication, making it more secure than passwords.

Key Features of SSH

Secure Shell (SSH) provides a comprehensive set of security features that enable safe remote access, efficient system management, and secure data transfer across networks.

- **Encryption:** SSH ensures that all data transferred between the client and server is encrypted, protecting it from eavesdropping and man-in-the-middle attacks.
- **Authentication:** SSH allows both password and key-based authentication for secure logins.
- **Command Execution:** SSH enables remote command execution, making it easier for administrators to manage systems and perform tasks like software installation or log checks.
- **File Transfer:** SSH supports secure file transfers using tools like SCP (Secure Copy Protocol) or SFTP (Secure File Transfer Protocol).

SSH in Practice

Secure Shell (SSH) is a fundamental protocol for securely managing remote systems and transferring data, offering strong encryption, authentication, and integrity protection across administrative and development workflows.

- **System Administration:** SSH is widely used by system administrators to remotely access servers, especially in environments where multiple systems need to be managed remotely, like web hosting companies or cloud service providers.
- **Git Repository Access:** Developers use SSH to access remote Git repositories, ensuring secure code transfer and version control.

Feature	SSH
Integrity	Protects against tampering using cryptographic hash-based MACs.
Encryption	Yes, data is encrypted using symmetric algorithms (after initial key exchange via public key cryptography).
Authentication	Password or public key authentication.
Use Cases	Remote server management, Git repository access, file transfers.

Table 2.2: *SSH - Key Features and Use Cases*

TLS (Transport Layer Security)

TLS is a cryptographic protocol designed to provide secure communication over a computer network. It is widely used in securing web traffic, email, messaging services, and more. TLS is the successor of SSL (Secure Sockets Layer), and although the term SSL is still commonly used, TLS is the protocol in use today.

Working of TLS

TLS operates by encrypting the communication between a client and a server using asymmetric encryption for the handshake and symmetric encryption for the data transfer (asymmetric encryption is used only for key exchange, and symmetric encryption handles actual data transfer). The TLS handshake involves the exchange of certificates and keys to establish a secure communication channel. Once the secure connection is established, both parties can transmit data with the assurance that it is protected from tampering, eavesdropping, and man-in-the-middle attacks.

Key Features of TLS

Some of the key features of TLS are as follows:

- **Encryption:** TLS ensures that data exchanged between a client and server is encrypted, safeguarding it from malicious entities.
- **Integrity:** TLS verifies the integrity of data, ensuring that it has not been altered during transit.
- **Authentication:** TLS authenticates the identity of the server using certificates, preventing impersonation attacks. Also, mutual TLS (mTLS) is where both client and server can authenticate each other (used in enterprises, APIs, and secure services).

TLS in Practice

Transport Layer Security (TLS) plays a critical role in securing modern digital communication by providing encryption, authentication, and data integrity across various applications such as web browsing, email, and real-time communication.

- **HTTPS:** TLS is used to encrypt the traffic in HTTPS, ensuring that web communications are secure.
- **Email Encryption:** TLS is used to secure email communication, protecting sensitive information sent via SMTP, IMAP, and POP3 protocols.

Feature	TLS
Encryption	Yes (via asymmetric and symmetric encryption)
Authentication	Server authentication via certificates
Use Cases	Web traffic, email communication, VoIP

Table 2.3: *TLS - Key Features and Use Cases*

Note: *Just like SSH and HTTPS, TLS uses Message Authentication Codes (MACs) or AEAD (Authenticated Encryption with Associated Data) to ensure that the data is not modified.*

Real-Life Example: Using Sequential Layers of Security in SaaS Platform

Consider an online platform that provides Software as a Service (SaaS) for businesses to manage their payroll. This platform requires robust security measures to protect sensitive data, such as employees' financial details, tax information, and payment histories.

- **HTTPS:** When customers access the payroll platform through their browsers, HTTPS is used to ensure secure communication between the browser and the web server. Any sensitive data, such as employee payment information, is transmitted over an encrypted channel, protecting it from hackers and ensuring that unauthorized parties cannot intercept the communication.
- **SSH:** The administrators of the platforms use SSH to securely log in to the backend servers to maintain the system. With SSH, they can remotely configure the servers, troubleshoot issues, and deploy updates while ensuring that all their commands are encrypted and cannot be intercepted by malicious actors.
- **TLS:** The payroll platform uses TLS to secure communications between the server of the application and the payment gateway. When users make a payment, TLS ensures that all payment data, including credit card numbers and transaction details, is encrypted, and protected from third-party eavesdropping or modification.

PROTOCOL	PURPOSE	USE CASE
HTTPS	Secure browsing and data transfer	Protecting customer information on a SaaS platform
SSH	Secure remote access and management	Administrators accessing backend systems
TLS	Secure communication between servers	Encrypting payment transactions between the server and payment gateway

Table 2.4: *Protocol, Its Purpose and Use Case*

In the age of digital communication, protocols such as HTTPS, SSH, and TLS are essential in ensuring the confidentiality, integrity, and authenticity of the data exchanged across the internet. HTTPS ensures secure browsing and online transactions, SSH facilitates secure remote server management, and TLS underpins the security of many internet services, from email to secure web traffic.

These protocols play a pivotal role in maintaining a secure and trustworthy online environment. As cyber threats evolve, understanding and implementing these protocols is crucial for safeguarding personal, corporate, and financial data across the globe.

Activities and Related Problems with Solutions

By engaging in these activities, learners not only gain hands-on experience with network security tools and configurations but also develop troubleshooting skills essential for real-world scenarios.

(Use commands like curl -v, telnet <ip> <port>, or browser developer tools to test connectivity)

Activity 1: Configuring Firewalls in AWS

Objective: Learn how to configure a virtual firewall in AWS using security groups to control inbound and outbound traffic for an EC2 instance.

Steps:

- **Access AWS Console:** Log into your AWS Management Console.
- **Launch EC2 Instance:** Go to the EC2 dashboard, launch an instance, and configure the instance details.

Create Security Group:

1. Navigate to the "Configure Security Group" step.
2. Add inbound rules for specific services (like HTTP on port 80, SSH on port 22).
3. Leave the default outbound rule to allow all traffic.
4. Apply Security Group: Attach the newly created security group to the instance.

Test Access:

Verify that only allowed traffic can reach the instance by trying to access services configured in the security group.

Problem: You configured a security group, but the EC2 instance remains inaccessible via SSH or HTTP.

Solution:

1. **Check Security Group Rules:** Ensure you added an inbound rule for SSH (port 22) or HTTP (port 80) with the correct source IP (such as 0.0.0.0/0 for open access or a specific IP for restricted access).

2. **Verify Network ACLs:** Ensure that the NACL of the subset allows inbound and outbound traffic for the respective ports.
3. **Test Internet Gateway:** If the instance is public, ensure the subnet is attached to a properly configured internet gateway.
4. **Instance Configuration:** Check the private IP of the instance and ensure that it is associated with the security group.

Activity 2: Setting up Security Groups

Objective: Learn to configure and manage security groups to control traffic for different services on an AWS EC2 instance.

Steps:

1. **Create Security Group:** In the AWS Console, navigate to the EC2 section and create a new security group.
2. Name the security group meaningfully (like "WebApp-SG").
3. Add inbound rules for HTTP (port 80), HTTPS (port 443), and custom rules for other services as required.
4. **Define Outbound Rules:** By default, AWS allows all outbound traffic. Customize this as necessary (such as block certain destinations).
5. **Attach Security Group:** Attach the security group to an instance or multiple instances.
6. **Test Traffic Flow:** Attempt to access the services configured in the security group to ensure they work as intended.

Problem: Despite creating the security group and attaching it to an instance, the web application is inaccessible from a browser.

Solution: If the web application is inaccessible despite correct security group configuration, check the following:

1. **Check Public IP:** Ensure the EC2 instance has a public IP address or is placed behind a properly configured Application or Network Load Balancer.
2. **Security Group Rules:**

   Verify that inbound rules allow:

   a. HTTP (port 80)
   b. HTTPS (port 443)

   from the appropriate source (such as **`0.0.0.0/0`** for public access or a restricted CIDR for security).
3. **Firewall Rules on the Instance:** Ensure the operating system firewall (such as iptables, firewalld, or ufw) allows inbound traffic on the required ports.
4. **Route Table Configuration:** Confirm that the route table of the subnet that includes a route to an Internet Gateway **`(0.0.0.0/0)`** for outbound and inbound internet traffic.
5. **Load Balancer Health Checks (If Used):**

   If the instance is behind a load balancer, verify that:

   a. The target instance is healthy.
   b. Health check ports and paths are correct.
   c. The instance security group allows traffic from the security group of the load balancer.

Activity 3: Using ACLs to Restrict Traffic

Objective: Set up Network ACLs (NACLs) to add an extra layer of security by restricting traffic at the subnet level.

Steps:

1. **Access NACLs in AWS Console:**
    a. Navigate to the VPC section and locate the NACLs.
2. Edit NACL Rules.
3. Add inbound rules to allow HTTP and HTTPS traffic.
4. Add outbound rules to permit responses for the same.
5. Block all other traffic explicitly by adding a deny rule.
6. **Associate NACL with Subnet:**
    a. Attach the NACL to the relevant subnet where your instances reside.
7. **Test Configuration:**

    Access the instances and verify the effectiveness of NACL rules by attempting blocked and allowed actions.

Problem: After applying NACL rules, legitimate traffic is blocked unexpectedly.

Solution:

1. **Rule Order:** NACL rules are evaluated in numerical order. Ensure that the allowed rules are preceded by the denied rules to avoid unintended blocking.
2. **Stateless Nature:** Unlike security groups, NACLs are stateless. Ensure outbound rules explicitly allow responses to the permitted inbound traffic.
3. **Subnet Association:** Verify the NACL is correctly associated with the subnet containing the instance.

Activity 4: Exploring Secure Protocols

Objective: Understand and implement secure protocols such as HTTPS, SSH, and TLS in network communication.

Steps:

1. Implement HTTPS.
2. Install an SSL/TLS certificate on your web server.
3. Configure the server to redirect HTTP traffic to HTTPS.
4. Set Up SSH.
5. Generate a key pair and configure your server to accept only key-based authentication.
6. Disable password-based logins for enhanced security.
7. **Enable TLS for Email:** Configure email services to use STARTTLS or implicit TLS for secure communication.

Problem: Your HTTPS website displays a "Not Secure" warning in the browser.

Solution:

- **Valid Certificate:** Ensure that your SSL/TLS certificate is valid and issued by a trusted Certificate Authority (CA).
- **DNS Settings:** Verify the domain name matches the one in the certificate.
- **Intermediate Certificates:** Install any missing intermediate certificates provided by the CA.
- **Server Configuration:** Check the HTTPS configuration of the server for errors, such as incorrect ports or cipher settings.

Conclusion

Network security serves as the backbone of modern digital infrastructure, ensuring the protection of sensitive data and systems from an ever-evolving array of threats. This chapter explored the fundamental principles and practical applications of network security, focusing on tools and strategies such as firewalls, Access Control Lists (ACLs), security groups, and secure protocols. By understanding and implementing these technologies, professionals can create robust defences against unauthorized access, data breaches, and cyberattacks.

The knowledge gained from this chapter equips readers with the skills needed to assess and enhance network security, whether in on-premises environments or cloud platforms. The practical activities provided a hands-on understanding of configuring and managing firewalls, security groups, and ACLs, ensuring learners are prepared to tackle real-world challenges. In the next chapter, let us focus on designing scalable, high-availability architecture, combining concepts like load balancing, fault tolerance, and scalability.

Points to Remember

Firewalls

- Act as a barrier between trusted and untrusted networks.
- Types include packet filtering, stateful inspection, proxy firewalls, and Next-Generation Firewalls (NGFWs).
- Essential for monitoring and controlling traffic flow based on predefined rules.

Access Control Lists (ACLs)

- Define rules to allow or deny network traffic based on IP addresses, protocols, or ports.
- Types: Standard ACLs (filter by source IP) and Extended ACLs (filter by multiple parameters).
- Applied to routers and firewalls for granular control.

Security Groups and NACLs

- **Security Groups:**

  Stateful, instance-level firewalls used in cloud environments like AWS to control inbound and outbound traffic.

- **NACLs:**

  Stateless, subnet-level controls that explicitly define both inbound and outbound traffic rules.

Secure Protocols

- **HTTPS:**

  Ensures encrypted communication between browsers and servers using SSL/TLS.

- **SSH:**

  Provides secure remote access to servers with public-key authentication.

- **TLS:**

  Encrypts communications in various applications, ensuring data confidentiality and integrity.

Best Practices

- Always follow the principle of least privilege: allow only necessary traffic.
- Regularly audit firewall rules, ACLs, and security group configurations.
- Keep software and protocols updated to protect against vulnerabilities.
- Combine multiple layers of security (like firewalls, NACLs, secure protocols) for comprehensive protection.

By mastering these concepts and practices, you can significantly enhance the security and resilience of any network, preparing for potential challenges in a constantly evolving cybersecurity landscape.

CHAPTER 3
Network Design and High Availability

Introduction

In the contemporary digital landscape, ensuring uninterrupted access to applications and services is critical for organizations. High availability and network design play a pivotal role in achieving resilient, scalable, and fault-tolerant systems. This chapter delves into designing networks that remain operational even during failures, leveraging Amazon Web Services (AWS) tools like Elastic Load Balancers (ELB) and Auto Scaling to provide robust solutions.

We will explore load balancing techniques, fault-tolerance mechanisms, and scalability strategies to equip readers with the knowledge to design AWS architectures that ensure minimal downtime and optimal performance. By the end of this chapter, readers will have a comprehensive understanding of designing highly available systems with AWS.

Structure

In this chapter, we will cover the following topics:

- Load Balancing Techniques
- Fault Tolerance Strategies
- Scalability
- Designing High Availability
- Case Studies

Load Balancing Techniques

In the current interconnected digital world, users expect applications and websites to be fast, reliable, and always accessible. Behind the scenes, load balancing is the silent hero ensuring smooth operations. Whether it is streaming a movie, shopping online, or accessing a cloud-based application, load balancers play a pivotal role in distributing traffic, preventing bottlenecks, and ensuring applications remain responsive even under heavy loads.

Cloud platforms like AWS provide powerful load-balancing solutions that adapt to different types of traffic and workloads.

These solutions are tailored to specific needs, from web-based content delivery to high-performance backend data processing. Understanding the nuances of load balancing and its various techniques is crucial for designing architectures that scale effortlessly, provide fault tolerance, and ensure uninterrupted availability.

Types of Load Balancing Techniques

Load balancing is the process of distributing incoming network traffic across multiple servers or resources to ensure no single server becomes overwhelmed. It improves application availability, fault tolerance, and overall performance by ensuring optimal use of resources and handling sudden traffic spikes.

In cloud environments like AWS, load balancers dynamically adjust traffic distribution, scaling up or down based on demand, thereby ensuring high availability and fault tolerance.

Different types of load balancing techniques are:

- Application Load Balancer (ALB),
- Network Load Balancer (NLB), and,
- Gateway Load Balancer (GWLB).

The different types of load balancing techniques are described as follows:

Application Load Balancers (ALBs)

Imagine a bustling e-commerce website that handles thousands of users browsing, adding items to their carts, and checking out simultaneously. Such an application involves multiple services, like product management, user authentication, and payment processing. Each service may reside on separate servers, yet users must experience the application as a cohesive whole. This is where an Application Load Balancer (ALB) excels, acting as the traffic director that ensures requests are routed to the correct service based on content.

ALBs are designed for applications operating at Layer 7 (the application layer) of the OSI model. They enable intelligent traffic distribution based on HTTP/HTTPS characteristics, such as URLs, headers, and query strings. This fine-grained control makes them ideal for modern, microservices-based architectures.

Key Features of ALBs

- **Host-Based Routing:** Direct traffic to specific servers based on hostnames (such as api.example.com versus www.example.com).
- **Path-Based Routing:** Send /images requests to a media server and /orders requests to a backend processing service.
- **WebSocket Support:** Ensure persistent connections for real-time applications.
- **SSL/ TLS termination:** Offloads SSL decryption from backend servers.

Figure 3.1 illustrates how an Application Load Balancer distributes traffic across target groups (EC2, Lambda, or IP addresses).

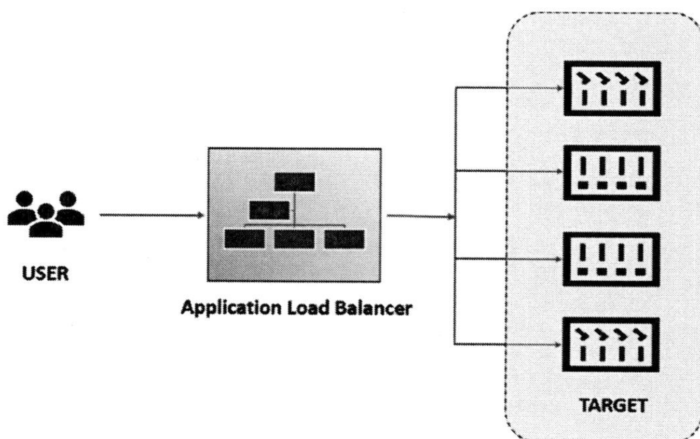

Figure 3.1: ALB *Workflow*

Use Cases

Some of the use cases of ALB are as follows.

- **E-commerce Website:** Routes /products traffic to one set of servers and /checkout traffic to another.
- **Microservices Architecture:** Routes traffic to specific services based on API endpoints.

  For Example, consider a retail application,
  - ALB routes requests for api.example.com/products to a "*product-service*" backend.
  - It routes requests for api.example.com/orders to an "*order-service*" backend.

Problem Statement

- **Challenge:** How can an application efficiently route requests for multiple subdomains and endpoints to the correct backend services?
- **Solution:** Use host-based and path-based routing in an ALB to direct traffic intelligently. For example:
  - api.example.com -> API backend
  - auth.example.com -> Authentication backend
  - www.example.com/orders -> Order-processing backend.

Network Load Balancers (NLBs)

Network Load Balancers operate at Layer 4 (transport layer) of the OSI model. They are optimized for handling millions of requests per second with ultra-low latency. NLBs are suitable for TCP, UDP, and TLS traffic and provide static IP addresses for predictable configurations.

Key Features of NLBs

- **High Performance:** It is ideal for latency-sensitive applications.
- **TLS offloading:**
  - Offloads encryption tasks from backend servers.
  - Should explicitly include TLS termination and certificate management on NLB.
- **Static IP addresses:** It simplifies DNS configurations.

The following is the diagrammatic representation of NLB Traffic flow. NLB distributes the incoming connections based on transport-layer protocols like TCP and UDP.

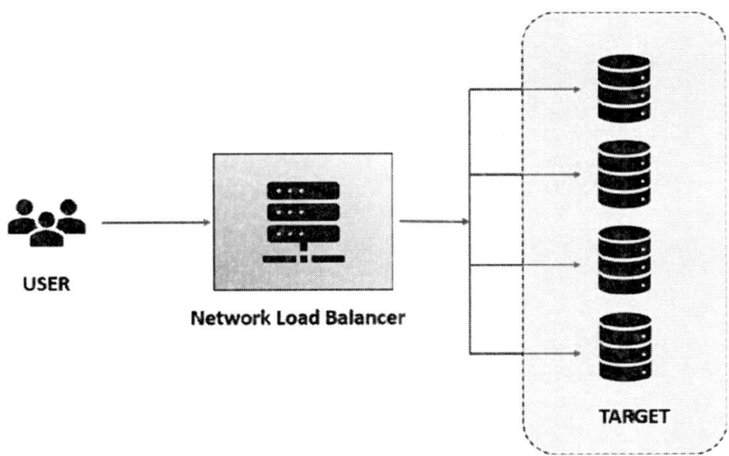

Figure 3.2: *NLB Traffic Flow*

Some of the use cases of NLB are as follows:

- **Financial Applications:** Low-latency stock trading platforms that rely on TCP connections.
- **Gaming Servers:** Supports millions of simultaneous connections with minimal delay.

  For Example, consider a trading platform.
- NLB handles secure, low-latency TCP traffic between traders and the server infrastructure.

Problem Statement

Challenge: How can a financial trading platform ensure ultra-low latency and high availability while handling millions of concurrent TCP connections between traders and backend trading systems?

Such platforms are highly sensitive to latency, packet loss, and downtime. Even small delays can result in financial loss, making performance and reliability critical.

Solution: Use a Network Load Balancer (NLB) configured with:

- TCP-based health checks to route traffic only to healthy backend servers
- TLS termination (if required) to ensure secure communication
- Static IP addresses for predictable and fast network routing

The NLB efficiently distributes traffic across backend servers while maintaining very low latency, high throughput, and fault tolerance.

Classic Load Balancers (CLBs)

Problem

A small startup or legacy application needs basic load balancing for a simple web application. The architecture does not require advanced routing rules, microservices support, or high-performance Layer 7 features. The team is unsure which type of load balancer to choose and wants a simple, straightforward option without complex configuration.

Solution

Classic Load Balancers operate at both Layer 4 and Layer 7 of the OSI model. While not as feature-rich as ALBs or NLBs, they provide basic load-balancing capabilities and are suited for simple architectures.

Key Features of CLBs

- Supports HTTP, HTTPS, and TCP protocols.
- Health checks for backend servers.

The following is the diagrammatic representation of CLB Traffic flow:

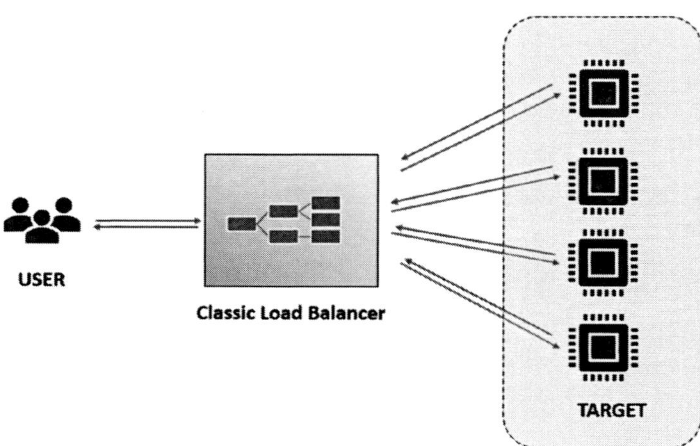

Figure 3.3: *CLB Traffic Flow*

Some of the use cases of CLB are as follows:

- Legacy applications still relying on older AWS configurations.
- Simple web applications with minimal routing requirements.

Gateway Load Balancers (GWLBs)

Problem

In large or complex cloud environments, organizations need to inspect and control network traffic (for example, using firewalls, intrusion detection/prevention systems, or deep packet inspection tools) without changing application architecture or routing logic. Managing and scaling these security appliances manually can be complex and error-prone.

Solution

Gateway Load Balancers allow transparent traffic inspection by combining a load balancer with third-party virtual appliances, such as firewalls or intrusion detection systems. They operate at Layer 3 (network layer) but use GENEVE (port 6081) tunneling protocol for traffic redirection.

Key Features of GWLBs

- Simplifies deployment of security appliances.
- Scales automatically with traffic and integrates with auto scaling group of appliances.
- Scales virtual appliances automatically.

The following diagram represents GWLB Traffic flow:

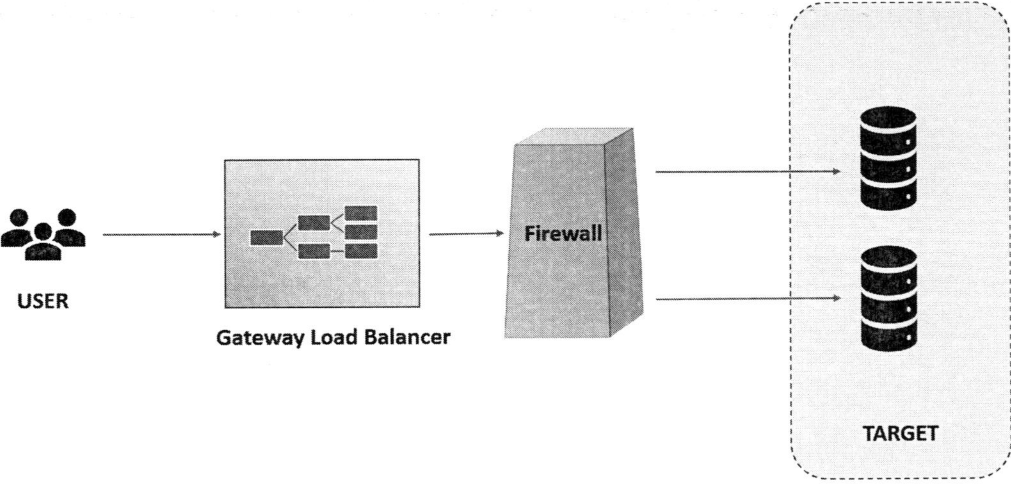

***Figure 3.4**: GWLB Traffic Flow*

Some of the use cases of GWLB are as follows:

- Security applications requiring inline traffic inspection.
- Centralized firewall management for multi-region deployments.

Elastic Load Balancing (ELB)

Elastic Load Balancing is an umbrella term for all AWS load balancers. It automatically distributes traffic and scales load balancers to handle varying workloads.

The following table provides the comparison of different AWS Load Balancers:

Feature	ALB	NLB	CLB	GWLB
Layer	7 (Application Layer)	4 (Transport Layer)	4 and 7	3 (Network Layer)
Protocols	HTTP, HTTPS, WebSocket	TCP, UDP, TLS	HTTP, HTTPS, TCP	All IP-based protocols. Encapsulated with GENEVE - Port 6081
Advanced Routing	Yes (Path, Host-based)	No	No	No
Latency	Higher than NLB due to Layer 7 processing	Ultra Low latency (single digit ms)	Higher than NLB due to Layer 7 processing	Similar to ALB (due to encapsulation overhead)
Use Case	Web apps, APIs	Financial, gaming apps	Legacy apps	Security appliances

Table 3.1: *Comparison of AWS Load Balancers*

Fault Tolerance Strategies

Fault tolerance ensures that a system remains operational even when one or more components fail. It is critical in designing resilient systems that provide continuous availability and minimize downtime. By employing strategies like redundancy, failover, and disaster recovery, organizations can safeguard their applications and data against hardware failures, software bugs, and even large-scale disasters.

This section provides an in-depth exploration of these strategies, complete with their principles, use cases, diagrams, and practical solutions to ensure high availability and business continuity.

Redundancy

Redundancy involves duplicating critical components or functions to prevent a single point of failure. Its goal is to reduce downtime and service disruption when a component fails.

In real-world systems, without disrupting operations, failover may not always be completely seamless—there can be brief switch-over delays depending on the redundancy model and system design.

Types of Redundancy

Redundancy strategies are essential for building resilient systems by ensuring continuous operation through the duplication of critical components across hardware, data, network, and application layers.

- **Hardware Redundancy:** Multiple physical devices (such as servers, storage units, or power supplies) operate in tandem so that if one component fails, another continues service without interruption.
- **Data Redundancy:** Data is replicated across multiple systems or locations to prevent data loss in case of hardware failure, corruption, or disasters.
- **Network Redundancy:** Multiple network paths or devices to avoid connectivity issues and single point of failure.
- **Application Redundancy:** Multiple instances of the same application run simultaneously, often across different Availability Zones or servers. If one application instance fails, traffic is automatically routed to healthy instances using load balancers, ensuring uninterrupted service.

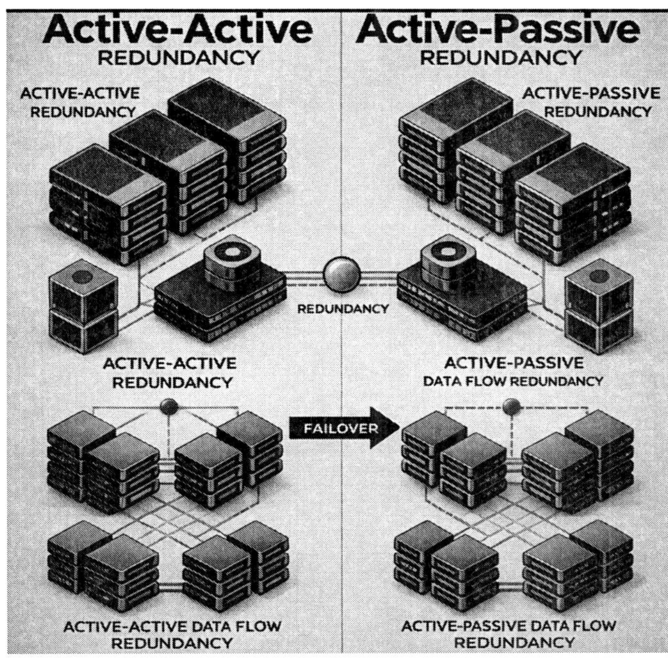

***Figure* 3.5:** *Active-Active and Active-Passive Redundancy*

Use Cases

Cloud Storage Services

- **Problem:** Ensuring that users can access their data even if a server fails.
- **Solution:** Use Amazon S3, which automatically replicates data across multiple Availability Zones within a region. This design provides high availability and extreme durability (99.999999999% – eleven nines), ensuring data remains accessible and protected even in the event of infrastructure failures.

Critical Business Applications

- **Problem:** A payment processing application must remain operational 24/7.
- **Solution:** Deploy the application across redundant servers and use a load balancer to distribute traffic.

Network Systems

- **Problem:** A network outage disrupts access to a corporate website.
- **Solution:** Configure redundant internet links and routers to ensure connectivity that is BGP with multiple ISPs.

Advantages

- Minimizes risk of downtime.
- Enhances reliability of systems.
- Reduces the impact of hardware failures.

Failover

Failover is the automatic transfer of operations to a backup system when the primary system fails. It is a dynamic process designed to maintain system availability without requiring manual intervention.

Failover typically works through the following steps:

1. **Monitoring**: The system continuously monitors the health of components using tools such as AWS CloudWatch, application health checks, or load balancer probes.
2. **Detection**: When a failure or degradation is detected, the failover mechanism is triggered based on predefined thresholds.
3. **Switching**: Traffic or workloads are redirected to a backup system, standby instance, or alternate region.
4. **Recovery / Validation**: The failed system is repaired, restarted, or rebuilt. Once validated as healthy, it may be reintegrated into production or kept as a standby resource.

Types of Failover

Failover mechanisms are critical for ensuring system resilience, with active–passive and active–active strategies providing different approaches to maintaining service continuity during failures.

Active–Passive Failover

- One system (primary) handles all traffic.
- A secondary system remains on standby.
- During failure, traffic switches to the passive system.
- Example: RDS Multi-AZ, DNS failover with a standby region.

Active–Active Failover

- Multiple systems handle traffic simultaneously.
- Load is distributed across regions or instances.
- If one system fails, traffic continues flowing to the remaining active systems.
- Example: Multi-region applications using load balancers or global databases.

Why This Matters

- Active–Passive is simpler and cost-effective but may have brief failover delays.
- Active–Active offers higher availability and performance but requires more complex design.
- Including a recovery step ensures long-term resilience and prevents repeated failures.

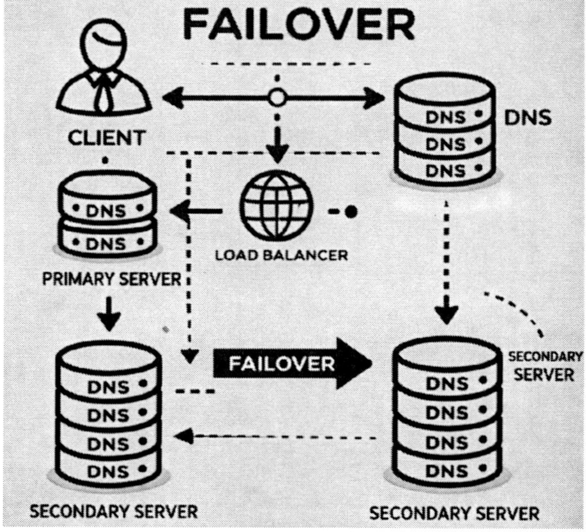

Figure 3.6: *Failover Mechanism*

Use Cases

High availability and failover strategies are essential for maintaining uninterrupted service by automatically detecting failures and redirecting traffic to healthy resources across infrastructure layers.

High Availability Databases

- **Problem:** A database crash leads to downtime for an e-commerce website.
- **Solution:** Use Amazon RDS Multi-AZ deployments. In this setup, a primary database instance is synchronously replicated to a standby instance in a different Availability Zone. If the primary database fails, the standby database automatically takes over, minimizing downtime and requiring no manual intervention.
- **Extended High-Availability Option (Cross-Region):** For applications that require regional disaster recovery in addition to high availability, Amazon Aurora Global Database can be used. Aurora Global Database replicates data across multiple AWS regions with low latency, enabling fast cross-region failover in the event of a regional outage.

DNS Failover

- **Problem:** A regional server becomes unreachable.
- **Solution:** Use AWS Route 53 with health checks configured on multiple endpoints. Route 53 continuously monitors the health of primary resources (such as load balancers or application endpoints) and automatically redirects traffic to a healthy backup region if a failure is detected.

Application Failover

- **Problem:** A server running an application goes offline due to hardware failure.
- **Solution:** Use Auto Scaling with ELB to monitor instance health and route traffic to healthy instances

Disaster Recovery

Disaster Recovery (DR) is the process of restoring operations and data after a catastrophic failure, such as natural disasters, cyberattacks, or regional outages. It focuses on reducing downtime and data loss.

Strategies for Disaster Recovery

Below is a comprehensive, in-depth explanation of commonly recognized Disaster Recovery (DR) strategies, emphasizing their structure, implementation, benefits, and challenges. These strategies are critical to ensuring minimal data loss and quick service restoration in the event of catastrophic failures such as natural disasters, cyberattacks, and major system outages.

AWS Services Mapping explicitly ties each strategy to AWS services.

- **Backup/Restore:** AWS Backup, S3 Glacier, EBS snapshots
- **Pilot Light:** CloudFormation, AWS Elastic Beanstalk, AMIs
- **Warm Standby:** RDS Multi-AZ, DynamoDB Global Tables, ELB + ASG
- **Multi-Site:** Route 53, Global Accelerator, Aurora Global DB, Active-Active VPC

Backup and Restore

Backup and Restore is often considered the baseline DR approach. It involves creating regular backups of data—usually stored offsite—and then restoring operations from these backups when a disaster occurs. Although this method can have longer restoration times, it is cost-effective and relatively simple to maintain.

The following are the key components of this strategy:

- **Backup Frequency:** Determines how often data snapshots are taken. Frequent backups reduce data loss but increase storage costs.
- **Storage Medium:** Backups can reside in object storage (such as AWS S3), tape archives, or cloud-based cold storage (like AWS Glacier).
- **Recovery Process:** Administrators retrieve backups from storage and restore them to new or existing infrastructure to resume operations.

Recovery Point Objective (RPO) and Recovery Time Objective (RTO)

- **RPO:** Moderate to high, depending on backup frequency.
- **RTO:** High, due to manual or semi-manual restoration processes.

Advantages

- **Low Cost:** Pay primarily for storage space.
- **Simplicity:** Straightforward to implement and manage.
- **Scalable:** Backups can grow in line with data volume.

Disadvantages

- **Longer Downtime:** Restoration from backups can take hours or even days.
- **Potential for Data Loss:** If the last backup was old, any changes since that point may be lost.

Use Case

- **Small Businesses or Dev/Test Environments:** It is applied where the cost of advanced DR solutions outweighs the impact of potential downtime.
- **Organizations with Low Uptime Requirements:** Suitable for applications that can afford extended downtime without significant revenue or data loss.

Pilot Light

Pilot Light is an approach where a minimal version of critical infrastructure and data is always active, but at a smaller scale. In case of a disaster, the pilot light can be "ignited" by scaling up or instantiating the rest of the environment using the existing core components.

The following are the key components of this strategy:

- **Core Database or Application Services:** Maintained in a running but lightweight state.
- **Automated Scaling Mechanisms:** Scripts and cloud capabilities that can quickly provision additional instances or resources.
- **Partial Redundancy:** Not all systems are fully active, but critical ones remain synced.

RPO and RTO

- **RPO:** Low to moderate, as data is continuously replicated to the pilot setup.
- **RTO:** Moderate, depending on how quickly you can scale your pilot to production-ready capacity.

Advantages

- **Reduced Costs:** Fewer resources are running continuously compared to a fully mirrored site.
- **Rapid Scaling:** With automation and scripts, the pilot light can be scaled to a live, production-level environment.

- **Easier Maintenance:** Since only core infrastructure is active, management overhead is reduced compared to larger DR solutions.

Disadvantages

- **Initial Scale-up Time:** Requires time to spin up additional resources, potentially causing short to moderate downtime.
- **Partial Redundancy:** Some system components might need reconfiguration or additional setup steps during a disaster event.

Use Case

- **Critical but Non-Continuous Workloads:** It is ideal for businesses that need a moderate level of availability but cannot justify the expense of a fully replicated environment.
- **Dynamic Environments:** Companies with automation pipelines that can provision infrastructure quickly benefit most from pilot light.

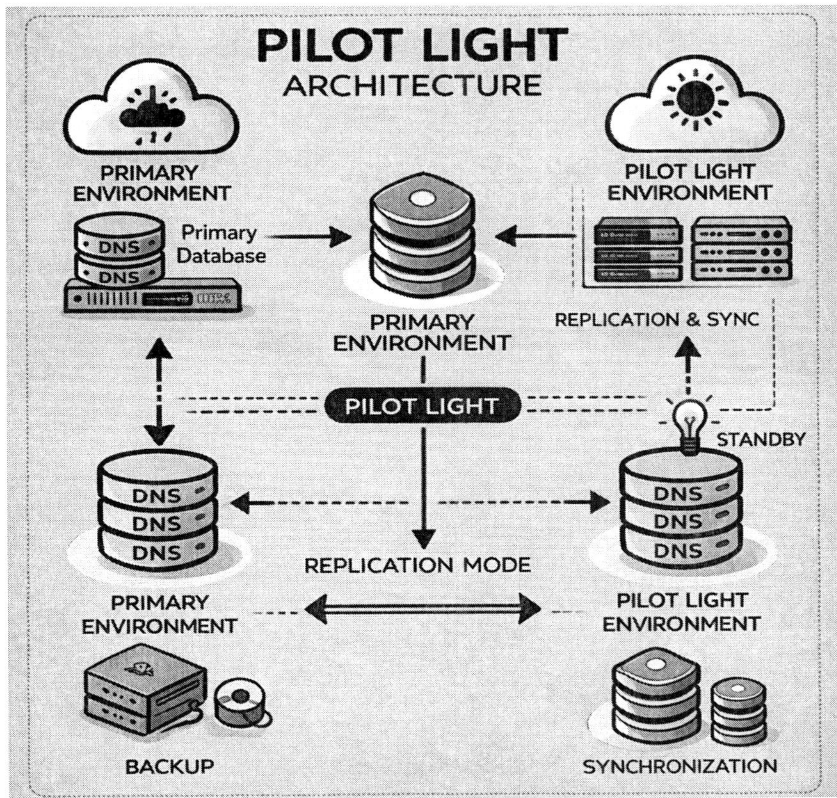

Figure 3.7: *Pilot Light – Disaster Recovery Architectures*

Warm Standby

Warm Standby is a disaster recovery strategy where a scaled-down version of a fully functional environment runs continuously, ready to take over operations quickly if the primary environment fails. This approach aims to balance cost and downtime, providing shorter recovery times than backup-only strategies without the expense of a fully active secondary site.

The key components of this strategy are as follows:

- **Partial Capacity in Secondary Site:** Continuous operation of essential services, but not at full production scale.
- **Real-Time Data Replication:** Ensures data consistency between primary and secondary sites.

- **Load Balancers and DNS Failover:** Switch user traffic from the primary site to the warm standby environment if needed.

RPO and RTO

- **RPO:** Typically low, due to ongoing data replication.
- **RTO:** Low to moderate, depending on how much additional capacity is required to handle full production load.

Advantages

- **Faster Recovery:** Since essential services are already running, downtime is limited.
- **Flexible Capacity:** You can dynamically scale the standby environment to handle full production traffic.
- **Consistent Data:** Real-time replication ensures minimal data loss.

Disadvantages

- **Increased Cost:** Maintaining an operational secondary environment can be costly, though still less than a fully active multi-site setup.
- **Complexity:** Requires careful coordination to ensure data and configurations match between the primary and secondary environments.

Use Cases

- **Financial or Healthcare Applications:** Warm Standby works well for industries that cannot tolerate extended downtime but must also consider cost constraints.
- **High-Value, Moderately Sensitive Workloads:** Balances the need for rapid recovery with budget limitations.

Multi-Site (Hot-Hot)

In a multi-site (also known as Hot-Hot) DR strategy, two or more fully operational and synchronized environments run simultaneously in different locations or regions. When one site fails, the other site(s) can continue serving traffic with minimal to zero downtime.

The following are the key components in this strategy:

- **Active-Active Architecture:** Both (or multiple) sites share the load during normal operations.
- **Global Traffic Management:** DNS-based routing (which includes AWS Route 53 latency routing) or load balancers distribute traffic between the sites.
- **Continuous Synchronization:** Data, applications, and configurations remain up-to-date across all active locations.

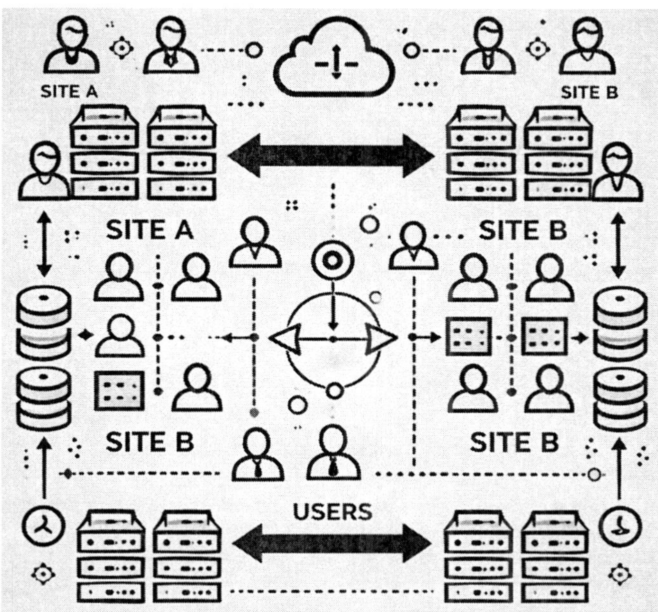

***Figure 3.8**: Multi-site – Disaster Recovery Architectures*

RPO and RTO

- **RPO:** Very low, as real-time replication ensures near-synchronous data updates.
- **RTO:** Nearly zero, since another site is already active.

Advantages

- **Minimal Downtime:** If one site fails, user traffic seamlessly switches to other active sites.
- **Improved User Experience:** Local or regional hosting can reduce latency and increase performance.
- **Excellent Data Consistency:** Real-time data synchronization keeps all sites in sync.

Disadvantages

- **High Cost:** Requires maintaining fully operational parallel infrastructures.
- **Operational Complexity:** Synchronizing multiple active sites demands more sophisticated monitoring and management.

Use Cases

- **Global E-Commerce and Streaming Services:** High-traffic platforms where any downtime is extremely costly and damaging to reputation.
- **Mission-Critical Applications:** Governments, stock exchanges, or large-scale SaaS providers that require continuous availability.

Additional Considerations

There are few considerations to be taken care of as we choose Disaster Recovery strategy. Some of them are as follows:

- **RTO and RPO Planning:** When choosing a DR strategy, it is vital to define acceptable thresholds for Recovery Time Objective (RTO)—how quickly systems must be restored—and Recovery Point Objective (RPO)—how much data loss is tolerable.
- **Security and Compliance:** Some of the security and compliance factors to be considered are:
    - **Encryption:** Sensitive data should be encrypted both in transit and at rest.

- **Access Control:** Implement least privilege principles for DR-related accounts.
- **Auditing:** Keep logs of any backup, restore, or replication processes for compliance and troubleshooting.

- **Testing and Drills:** Regularly test each DR strategy to ensure it functions as expected. Simulated failovers, backup restorations, and load testing can reveal issues before an actual disaster occurs.
- **Monitoring and Automation:** Use monitoring tools to track system health and automate failover or scaling procedures where possible. Services like Amazon CloudWatch, AWS Lambda, or third-party solutions can simplify orchestration.

Summary of DR Strategies

The following table gives the summarisation of the disaster recovery strategies that includes the complexity involved in implementation, its cost and the frequency of RTO and RPO:

STRATEGY	IMPLEMENTATION COMPLEXITY	COST	DOWNTIME (RTO)	DATA LOSS (RPO)
Backup and restore	Low	Low	High	Medium to high
Pilot light	Medium	Medium	Moderate	Low to moderate
Warm standby	High	High	Low to Moderate	Low
Multi-site	Very high	Very high	Minimal	Minimal

Table 3.2: *Summary of DR Strategies*

Use Cases

- **Natural Disasters**
  - **Problem:** A hurricane disrupts operations in a data center.
  - **Solution:** Use AWS S3 for data backup and deploy resources in another region for rapid recovery.
- **Cybersecurity Breaches**
  - **Problem:** A ransomware attack encrypts critical business data.
  - **Solution:** Implement regular backups and maintain an isolated backup copy in AWS Glacier.
- **Regional Outages**
  - **Problem:** A regional AWS outage causes service downtime.
  - **Solution:** Use AWS CloudFront and Route 53 to direct traffic to resources in another region.

Advantages

- Ensures business continuity during major disruptions.
- Protects against data loss.
- Supports compliance requirements for data recovery.

Selecting the right Disaster Recovery strategy depends on balancing business requirements (uptime, data protection) against budget and operational complexity. From the low-cost, higher-downtime model of Backup and Restore to the near-zero downtime Multi-Site approach, organizations have a range of options to protect their systems and data.

By carefully evaluating Recovery Time Objectives, Recovery Point Objectives, and long-term maintenance costs, teams can implement a robust disaster recovery plan tailored to their specific needs.

Comparison Table

Let us investigate the comparison of the three fault tolerance strategies via the table provided as follows:

FEATURE	REDUNDANCY	FAILOVER	DISASTER RECOVERY
PURPOSE	Prevent single point of failure	Automatically switch operations	Restore operations after major failures
COST	Medium to High	Medium to High	Varies by strategy
AUTOMATION	Usually manual scaling or configuration	Fully automated routing	Depends on automation setup (manual restore versus automated orchestration)
USE CASE	Continuous up time	Critical system health	Large-scale disruption

Table 3.3: *Comparison of Fault Tolerance Strategies*

Scalability

Scalability is the capacity of a system to handle an increasing amount of work by adding resources—either by enhancing existing components or by introducing additional ones. It is crucial for applications experiencing fluctuating traffic or continuous growth.

A scalable infrastructure can expand or contract based on demand, ensuring both high performance and cost efficiency.

Following are the key reasons why scalability is critical:

- **Performance under Load:** Prevents service degradation or downtime during traffic surges.
- **Cost Optimization:** Matches resource usage to actual demand, minimizing unnecessary expenditures.
- **User Experience:** Provides reliable response times and consistent uptime.

Vertical versus Horizontal Scaling

Vertical Scaling (Scaling Up/Down) enhances the capacity of a single server by upgrading its CPU, RAM, or storage, making it more powerful. It offers simplicity in management but has hardware limitations and higher costs as upgrades become more advanced.

Horizontal Scaling (Scaling out/in) expands capacity by adding multiple servers to distribute the workload, improving redundancy and fault tolerance. While it allows for near-infinite scaling, it requires more complex infrastructure management, such as load balancing and distributed computing.

Let us discuss them in detail.

Vertical Scaling (Scale up/down)

Vertical scaling means increasing or decreasing the capacity of a single resource (such as CPU, RAM) on a single machine or instance. Instead of distributing the workload across more machines, you make one machine more capable.

The mechanism of this scaling is done by upgrading the instance type (like from a medium to a large EC2 instance) or adjusting resources (more memory, faster CPU).

Advantages

- **Simple to Implement:** Often just a matter of changing instance sizes.
- **Easy Maintenance:** Fewer machines mean simpler monitoring and administration.

Disadvantages

- **Single Point of Failure:** Relying on one machine reduces fault tolerance.
- **Finite Limit:** Eventually, you hit a hardware or service limit (no infinite CPU/RAM).

For example, upgrading a database server from 8 GB to 16 GB of RAM can handle larger queries.

Increasing the CPU count in an application server to process more transactions.

Horizontal Scaling (Scale out/in)

Horizontal scaling expands resources by adding more machines (or nodes) to a system. Instead of making one machine more powerful, you spread the workload across multiple machines working in tandem.

The mechanism of the horizontal scaling is by spinning up additional instances—often automatically—behind a load balancer.

Advantages

- **High Fault Tolerance:** If one node fails, others can continue to operate.
- **Potentially Unlimited Growth:** You can keep adding more nodes as needed.

Disadvantages

- **Configuration Complexity:** Requires load balancing and distributed data handling.
- **Synchronization Overhead:** Maintaining consistency across multiple nodes can be challenging.

For example,

Deploying multiple EC2 instances behind an Amazon Elastic Load Balancer (ELB) to handle web traffic.

Creating a pool of servers for microservices, each scaling independently based on service-specific demand.

Comparison Table: Vertical versus Horizontal Scaling

Vertical and horizontal scaling represent two fundamental approaches to handling increased workload demands, each offering distinct advantages in terms of complexity, scalability, and fault tolerance.

Feature	Vertical Scaling	Horizontal Scaling
Definition	Increasing resources on a single node	Adding more nodes to share the load
Complexity	Lower (simpler to upgrade one node)	Higher (requires load balancing, orchestration)
Fault Tolerance	Lower (single point of failure)	Higher (multiple nodes, redundancy)
Scalability Limit	Limited by hardware constraints	Potentially very high
Typical Approach	Instance sizing changes (scale up/down)	Adding/removing servers (scale out/in)
Cost Implications	Incremental as resources increase	Pay for additional nodes as needed

Table 3.4: *Vertical versus Horizontal Scaling*

Auto Scaling Groups

An Auto Scaling Group (ASG) is a mechanism commonly provided by cloud providers (some of which includes, AWS, Azure, and GCP) to automatically adjust the number of running instances based on predefined policies or real-time metrics.

In AWS, you configure ASGs to maintain desired performance levels and handle variable traffic.

- **Desired Capacity:** The starting number of instances you want running.
- **Minimum Capacity:** The lowest acceptable number of instances for normal operation.
- **Maximum Capacity:** The upper limit to which the group can scale when traffic is high.

Key Features

- **Health Checks:** Automatically replaces unhealthy instances.
- **Integration with Monitoring:** Scales in or out based on metrics (like CPU usage, requests per second).
- **Notifications:** Sends alerts during scale events for auditing and operational insights.

Auto Scaling Operation

- **Monitoring:** CloudWatch (or equivalent) tracks performance metrics such as CPU utilization or memory usage.
- **Trigger Condition:** If CPU usage exceeds a threshold (such as 70%) for a specified duration, an "add instance" action is triggered. Conversely, if CPU usage falls below another threshold (for instance 30%), a "remove instance" action is triggered.
- **Scaling Activity:** The Auto Scaling Group adds or removes instances to match the desired state.
- **Load Balancing:** Additional or removed instances register or deregister with a load balancer (similar to Elastic Load Balancing in AWS), ensuring a smooth distribution of traffic.

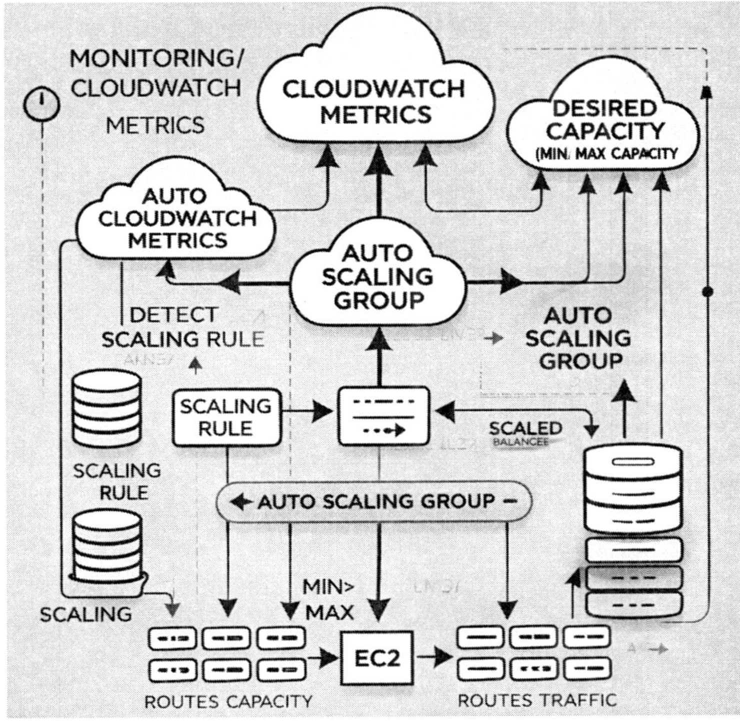

Figure 3.9: *Auto Scaling Workflow*

Explanation:

- Metrics are collected by CloudWatch (or similar service).
- Scaling rules assess metrics against thresholds.
- Auto Scaling Group adjusts the number of running instances accordingly.
- Instances are added or removed from the load balancer to manage traffic distribution.

Benefits of Using Auto Scaling

Auto Scaling enables dynamic resource management by automatically adjusting infrastructure capacity based on demand, ensuring high availability, cost efficiency, and improved system resilience.

- **Optimized Resource Usage:** Match the number of instances to current demand, avoiding over-provisioning.
- **High Availability:** Auto Scaling can replace failed instances automatically, enhancing reliability.
- **Cost-Effectiveness:** Scale down during low traffic to save costs, and scale up during peak times to maintain performance.
- **Flexible Policies:** Scale based on various metrics (CPU usage, network I/O, request latency) or based on custom business logic.

Also, multi-AZ placement as an indirect benefit of ASGs (if enabled), since this boosts resilience.

Advanced Auto Scaling Techniques

Advanced Auto Scaling techniques enhance system responsiveness and efficiency by enabling proactive, automated, and customizable scaling strategies based on predictable patterns and intelligent forecasting.

- **Scheduled Scaling:** Increase or decrease capacity at specific times (for example, predictable traffic spikes every weekday at noon).
- **Predictive Scaling:** Uses machine learning algorithms to forecast future demand and pre-emptively scale.
- **Lifecycle Hooks:** Run custom scripts or actions during instance launch or termination for final setup or data cleanup.

Common Use Cases

Auto Scaling and scaling strategies are widely applied across different workloads to address performance challenges, ensure reliability, and efficiently handle varying demand patterns.

- **E-Commerce Websites**
  - **Problem:** Traffic surges during promotions or holiday seasons cause slow loading times.
  - **Solution:** Horizontal scaling via Auto Scaling Groups adjusts the instance count to handle increased requests.
- **Batch Processing**
  - **Problem:** Large volumes of data need occasional intensive processing.
  - **Solution:** Temporarily scale out horizontally to multiple worker instances, then scale back when tasks complete.

- **API Services**
  - **Problem:** Inconsistent request volumes throughout the day.
  - **Solution:** A combination of horizontal scaling and a load balancer ensures consistent performance.
- **Database Servers**
  - **Problem:** Applications consistently outgrow the capacity of the current database.
  - **Solution:** Vertical scaling (upgrading the database instance) can be a straightforward option. For extremely large datasets, a horizontally scaled or sharded approach might be necessary.

For databases, vertical scaling via instance type upgrades is common. Horizontal scaling requires advanced techniques such as read replicas or sharding.

Best Practices

Adopting best practices for scaling ensures optimal performance, reliability, and cost efficiency by aligning infrastructure strategies with real-world application demands.

- **Combine Scaling Approaches:** Use vertical scaling for quick performance boosts but also employ horizontal scaling for better fault tolerance and near-limitless expansion.
- **Monitor Key Metrics:** Focus on application-centric metrics like request latency or queue length, not just CPU usage.
- **Regularly Review Limits:** Check AWS service limits (such as instance limits per region) to avoid hitting capacity ceilings.
- **Use Elastic Load Balancers:** Pair your Auto Scaling Group with an Application Load Balancer (ALB) or Network Load Balancer (NLB) to evenly distribute traffic.
- **Test and Tweak:** Continuously run load tests to validate scaling policies, ensuring a balance between performance and cost.

Summary

- **Vertical Scaling:** It is ideal for straightforward enhancements, where upgrading one instance is simpler than managing more instances. However, it is limited by hardware constraints and lacks resilience if the upgraded node fails.
- **Horizontal Scaling:** Allows almost unlimited growth and provides superior fault tolerance by distributing workloads across multiple nodes. The trade-off is more complex administration and the need for load balancing or clustering strategies.
- **Auto Scaling Groups:** Automate the process of scaling horizontally, adjusting the number of instances to meet real-time demand. This approach ensures applications remain responsive while optimizing costs.

By carefully selecting the right scaling method—or combining both—and leveraging Auto Scaling Groups, organizations can design systems that adapt to ever-changing workloads, maintain high availability, and operate with cost efficiency.

Designing High Availability (HA)

In the realm of cloud computing, High Availability (HA) denotes an infrastructure design that can tolerate diverse failures—ranging from component malfunctions to entire data center outages—without disrupting end-user experiences.

Systems architected for HA often incorporate multiple layers of redundancy, fault detection, and automated recovery processes to maintain consistent service levels.

Primary Goals of HA

- **Uninterrupted Service:** Users should not perceive significant downtime, even if individual resources fail.
- **Fault Isolation:** Issues should remain contained within localized components to prevent cascading failures.
- **Operational Resilience:** Routine tasks (patching, maintenance, scaling) should not impede system availability.

Multi-AZ (Multi-Availability Zone) Approach

Within many cloud platforms—AWS, for instance—regions are subdivided into Availability Zones (AZs), each operating as a distinct data center (or multiple data centers) with independent power, cooling, and network infrastructure.

Utilizing Multi-AZ means placing duplicate resources across at least two AZs in the same region to mitigate the impact of localized disruptions.

Architectural Considerations

- **Duplicate Servers:** Deploy the same set of application servers, containers, or virtual machines in at least two AZs. Auto Scaling Groups across AZs is the most common implementation.
- **Synchronized Databases:** Database services typically replicate data across AZs. For instance, Amazon RDS can conduct synchronous replication to maintain up-to-date copies.
- **Load Balancing:** Use a load balancer to distribute traffic among instances located in different AZs. If one AZ becomes unreachable, traffic is seamlessly rerouted.

Application Load Balancer (ALB) and Network Load Balancer (NLB) natively support cross-AZ balancing, while Classic LB does too but is legacy.

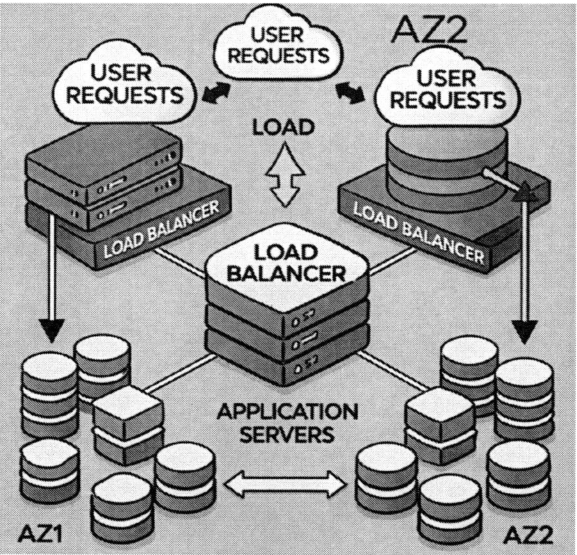

Figure 3.10: *Visual Representation of Multi-AZ Approach*

In the preceding image, one can understand that:

- **Load Balancer:** Acts as the entry point for all incoming requests.

- **AZ1 and AZ2:** Each holds identical or near-identical application stacks.
- **Data Replication:** Real-time or near-real-time synchronization ensures data integrity across zones.

Key Advantages

- **Local Failure Resistance:** If AZ1 encounters a major power disruption, AZ2 can continue serving traffic.
- **Automated Failover:** Managed services (like RDS) can switch from a primary to a standby database, typically without manual intervention.
- **Reduced Downtime:** User requests remain served by healthy AZs, minimizing interruptions.
- **Improved maintenance flexibility:** Patching instances in one AZ while traffic flows to another.

Potential Challenges

- **Higher Cost:** Operating multiple AZ environments can double certain infrastructure expenses.
- **Additional Complexity:** Configuration, health checks, and database replication require careful orchestration.
- **Latency Impact:** Although AZs are generally close, synchronous writes can incur a minor latency penalty for data-intensive tasks.

Multi-Region Strategy

A Multi-Region design involves deploying resources across geographically separate regions to guard against large-scale outages, natural disasters, or region-wide disruptions. Additionally, distributing workloads globally can reduce latency for end-users located far from a primary region.

Approaches to Multi-Region Deployments

- **Active-Active**
    - **Both Regions in Operation:** All regions actively handle user requests simultaneously.
    - **Load Distribution:** DNS-based routing (like latency or geolocation routing) directs users to the optimal region.
    - **Replication Strategy:** Asynchronous data replication is common, but near-real-time solutions exist depending on network connectivity and tolerance for eventual consistency.
    - **Real-World Examples (AWS)**
        - **Amazon DynamoDB Global Tables:** Enable fully managed, multi-region, active-active replication, allowing applications to read and write data locally in each region with automatic conflict resolution.
        - **Amazon Aurora Global Database:** Provides low-latency global reads and fast disaster recovery by replicating data across regions, thereby, supporting globally distributed applications.
- **Active-Passive:**
    - **Primary Region:** Handles all live traffic under normal conditions.
    - **Secondary Region:** Maintains replicas in a standby mode.
    - **Failover:** If the primary region becomes unavailable, traffic is redirected to the secondary region. Some solutions may require spinning up additional resources in the secondary location before it can fully handle production load.

- **Real-World Example (AWS)**: In AWS, this model is commonly implemented using Amazon S3 Cross-Region Replication (CRR) to keep data synchronized between regions, combined with Amazon Route 53 failover routing. Route 53 monitors application health and automatically redirects user traffic to the secondary region if the primary region fails.

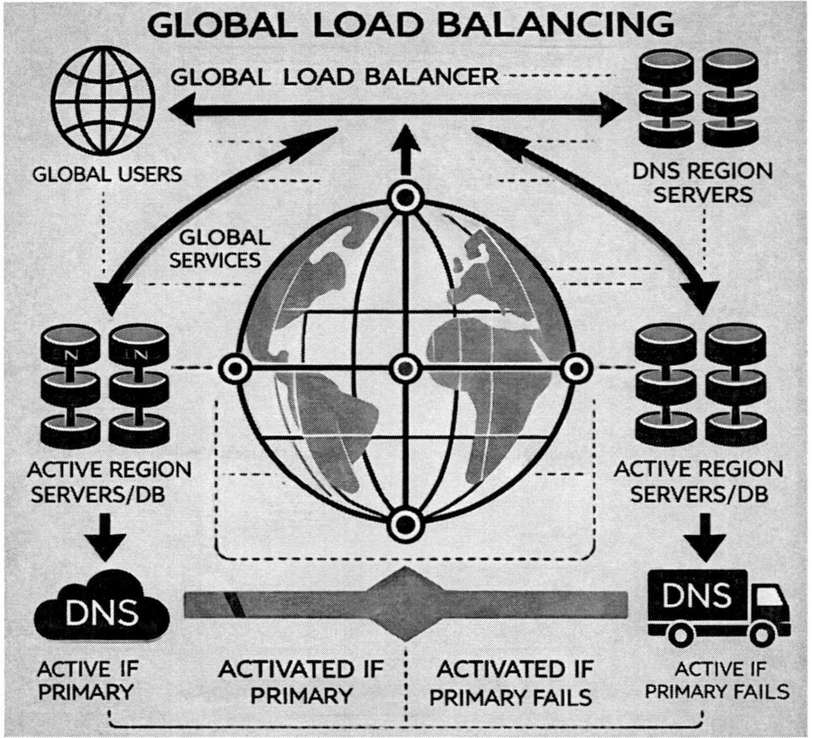

***Figure 3.11**: Illustrative Diagram of Multi-Region Deployment*

In the above illustrated figure,

- **DNS Service:** Could be AWS Route 53 or another global load balancing mechanism.
- **Active Region:** Fronts most or all traffic under standard operations.
- **Secondary Region:** Either remains idle (passive) or shares load (active-active).

Advantages of Multi-Region

- **Geographic Redundancy:** Even if an entire region is incapacitated, another region remains online.
- **Enhanced Performance:** Users connect to a closer region, reducing network latency.
- **Compliance and Data Residency:** Storing data in multiple regions can help meet various jurisdictional regulations.

Common Drawbacks

- **Complex Replication:** Maintaining data consistency across large distances poses challenges—especially with write-heavy workloads.
- **Significant Costs:** Running near-duplicate infrastructures in multiple locations demands larger budgets.
- **Orchestration Overhead:** Deployments, updates, and monitoring must be synchronized across regions.

Combining Multi-AZ and Multi-Region

Most organizations that seek a robust HA design often merge both strategies. Each region hosts a Multi-AZ setup, providing local high availability. Should that entire region fail, traffic can be shifted to a different region via DNS-based failover, ensuring global redundancy.

Example Scenario

- **Region A (Multi-AZ Setup):** This is the primary environment, handling the bulk of requests.
- **Region B (Multi-AZ Setup):** It maintains a consistent copy of the application and data. In an active-active design, Region B also serves some fraction of traffic. In an active-passive model, Region B is kept mostly idle, spinning up extra resources only if Region A fails.

Implementation Best Practices

- **Automation and Infrastructure as Code:** Tools like Terraform or AWS CloudFormation enable repeatable, consistent deployments across multiple AZs and regions.
- **Rigorous Health Checks:** Implement continuous monitoring (like CloudWatch in AWS) to quickly detect and isolate failed components. Also, Route 53 health checks (for DNS failover) and Application Load Balancer health checks (for AZ-level resilience).
- **Regular Failover Drills:** Simulate outages to confirm that failover processes work as expected, and refine runbooks when you detect bottlenecks. As a suggestion, using chaos engineering practices (such as AWS Fault Injection Simulator) can be used to go beyond manual drills.
- **Cost Analysis:** Evaluate the financial impact of operating multiple AZs and regions to ensure the investment aligns with business needs. AWS Cost Explorer / Trusted Advisor are used as tools to evaluate costs of HA strategies.
- **Network and Security Policies:** Set up secure cross-region connectivity (including VPC peering, VPN, or private links). VPC peering, VPN, or private links, consider explicitly naming AWS Transit Gateway as a scalable option for multi-region connectivity. Evaluate encryption, access controls, and compliance requirements at each stage.

Real-World Illustrations

Some of the illustrations of how and where the different strategies are applied are as follows.

Global Streaming Service

- **Challenge:** High volumes of concurrent traffic, with viewers spread across continents.
- **Solution:** Deploy edge servers in multiple regions using active-active routing. Each region also employs a Multi-AZ layout for local redundancy.
- **Outcome:** Consistently low latency, reduced risk of a complete outage, and the ability to handle sudden traffic spikes.

Financial Transactions Platform

- **Challenge:** System must remain online 24/7 for critical financial operations.
- **Solution:** Core transaction servers run in Multi-AZ mode within a primary region. A secondary region mirrors transactions asynchronously. If the primary region suffers a catastrophic event, the platform fails over to the secondary with minimal data loss.
- **Outcome:** Uninterrupted service continuity and compliance with stringent regulations.

In all, high availability hinges on eliminating single points of failure, whether at the AZ or regional level.

Multi-AZ strategies deliver resilience within a single region, offering protection from local data center incidents and streamlined failover.

Multi-Region designs bolster this further by spanning geographically diverse locations, mitigating full regional outages and improving global performance.

Organizations that prioritize uptime and fault tolerance often adopt a layered approach, incorporating both Multi-AZ and Multi-Region architectures. This not only safeguards mission-critical services against localized failures but also provides assurance against regional disruptions. Careful planning, rigorous testing, and ongoing optimization ensure that these strategies align with business objectives, performance requirements, and budget constraints.

Case Studies

The following are some of the case studies on the topics that are discussed in this *Chapter 3, Network Design and High Availability*:

These diverse scenarios underline the real-world applications of load balancing techniques, fault tolerance strategies (redundancy, failover, and disaster recovery) and scalability approaches (vertical, horizontal, and auto scaling), high availability strategies—ranging from simple Multi-AZ deployments to complex Multi-Region setups—can be adapted to various industries.

E-commerce Platform with ALB

Scenario

An online retail application needs to route traffic for /products and /cart to different microservices.

Solution

- Deploy ALB with path-based routing rules.
- Create target groups:
  - **Products Target Group:** Instances hosting product-service.
  - **Cart Target Group:** Instances hosting cart-service.

Outcome

- Smooth traffic routing between services.
- Better fault tolerance by spreading traffic across multiple instances.

Low-Latency Gaming with NLB

Scenario

A gaming company requires a low-latency solution to handle millions of concurrent players.

Solution

- Deploy NLB to manage TCP and UDP traffic.
- Use health checks to route players to healthy servers.
- Scale backend instances using Auto Scaling Groups.

Outcome

- High performance with minimal latency.
- Enhanced player experience during peak loads.

Redundancy for a Social Media Chat Service

Scenario

A fast-growing social media platform offers real-time chat functionality. Any server downtime leads to user dissatisfaction and public complaints on various review portals.

Challenges

- Single server dependency causes frequent slowdowns when user numbers spike.
- Limited capacity results in dropped chat messages, harming the user experience.

Solution

- **Duplicate Servers:** Two identical clusters across different availability zones handle chat traffic. If one server experiences high load or hardware failure, traffic automatically routes to the second cluster.
- **Database Mirroring:** Chat messages are simultaneously written to two separate storage systems. Should one storage system fail; the other remains immediately available.

Outcome

- **Continuous Availability:** Even with partial hardware failures, the chat service remains responsive.
- **Improved Reputation:** Fewer user complaints and higher ratings in app stores reflect the reliability of the platform.

Automatic Failover for a News Streaming App

Scenario

A digital news platform streams live video broadcasts. Frequent CDN issues can render the service offline, risking loss of critical viewer engagement, especially during breaking news events.

Challenges

- Single CDN providers occasionally face local outages, leading to abrupt service disruptions.
- Manual interventions are time-consuming, causing viewer frustration.

Solution

- **Secondary CDN:** The news company integrates a second content delivery network. DNS-level health checks detect outages in the primary CDN.
- **Automatic Switchover:** Once the primary CDN is deemed unavailable, viewers are silently redirected to the backup CDN, resuming broadcasts seamlessly.

Outcome

- **Minimal Downtime:** Automatic failover ensures live streams continue without end-user disruption.
- **Consistent User Base:** Retention rates improve as viewers trust the reliability of the service during critical news coverage.

Disaster Recovery (DR) for an E-Learning Platform

Scenario

An educational technology startup hosts interactive courses. Downtime is unacceptable during exam periods; losing student progress can result in reputational damage and refunds.

Challenges

- The primary data center is situated in a single region prone to seasonal storms.
- No existing fallback system to recover quickly if the entire data center is compromised.

Solution

- **Pilot Light Strategy:** A minimal version of the core database and application code runs continuously in a secondary location.
- **Scalable DR Environment:** If the primary site is damaged, the pilot setup scales up, cloning production configurations.
- **Regular DR Drills:** Monthly simulations confirm that restoring full functionality in the secondary site takes only minutes.

Outcome

- **Reduced Risk of Data Loss:** The exam submissions of the students remain secure even when the main location goes offline.
- **Faster Recovery:** Maintenance or natural disasters in the primary site cause less concern, as the backup site rapidly assumes full load.

Vertical Scaling for a Video Analytics Engine

Scenario

A marketing company develops an in-house video analytics system that collects and processes user-interaction data from millions of daily video plays.

Challenges

- Data processing tasks become increasingly CPU and memory-intensive as the user base expands.
- Under provisioned servers lead to backlogged analytics jobs and delayed insight reports.

Solution

- **Upgrade Server Instances:** The analytics engine moves from medium-tier to large-tier machines with more CPU cores and additional RAM.
- **Enhanced Storage I/O:** Faster SSDs reduce read/write bottlenecks when handling massive log files.

Outcome

- **Streamlined Data Processing:** The upgraded servers, process logs faster, thereby, minimizing report delays.
- **Simpler Management:** Maintaining a single powerful machine suits the skill set of the team, requiring fewer architectural changes than a fully distributed system.

Horizontal Scaling for an Online Gaming Platform

Scenario

A multiplayer online game receives significant player traffic during weekends and special in-game events. The load on servers spikes unpredictably, sometimes quadrupling during major updates.

Challenges

- One server cluster is insufficient, frequently hitting maximum CPU and memory limits.

- Latency rises sharply during events, forcing players to disconnect and fuelling negative reviews.

Solution

- **Multiple Server Clusters:** Deploy identical game servers behind a load balancer. New nodes can be launched on-demand.
- **Distributed Session Management:** Player sessions are stored in a central cache (like Redis), allowing seamless movement between servers without data loss.

Outcome

- **Superior Performance:** During promotions or new content releases, additional servers auto-provision, accommodating the surge without lag.
- **High Player Satisfaction:** Positive feedback grows as players experience smooth gameplay under heavy loads.

Auto Scaling Groups for an Event-Based Marketing Website

Scenario

A digital marketing agency hosts themed event websites that receive unpredictable traffic spikes tied to promotional campaigns or product launches.

Challenges

- Traffic can remain minimal for extended periods, suddenly spiking by tens of thousands of users when an event goes live.
- Over provisioning servers is expensive, while under provisioning risks downtime.

Solution

- **Policy-Driven Scaling:** CloudWatch monitors CPU utilization and concurrent sessions. Upon exceeding defined thresholds, additional instances automatically are online, distributing load.
- **Scheduled Scaling:** For known events, servers scale up ahead of the official launch to pre-empt performance bottlenecks.
- **Elastic Load Balancing:** As servers scale in or out, the load balancer updates target groups in real time.

Outcome

- **Cost Efficiency:** The site operates with minimal servers during off-peak periods, reducing overhead.
- **Reliable Event Launches:** High-traffic campaigns run smoothly, bolstering the reputation of the agency for delivering robust marketing solutions.

High-Traffic E-Commerce Platform

Scenario

An online retailer experiences massive traffic spikes during seasonal sales. Historically, sudden bursts of user traffic have caused server overloads and occasional outages.

To mitigate cart abandonment and lost revenue, the company seeks a robust High Availability solution.

Challenges

- **Unpredictable Traffic Surges:** The retailer cannot accurately forecast the timing and magnitude of traffic spikes.
- **Critical Data Integrity:** Transaction and inventory data must remain consistent to avoid double orders or mismatched stock counts.
- **Minimal Downtime:** Even a few minutes of downtime can lead to significant lost sales.

Solution

- **Multi-AZ Auto Scaling:** The frontend web servers are deployed across multiple Availability Zones within the same region. An Application Load Balancer (ALB) distributes incoming requests, ensuring no single AZ becomes a choke point.
- **Multi-AZ Database Replication:** The primary database runs in a Multi-AZ setup, providing a standby replica in another AZ. If the main database becomes unavailable, failover occurs seamlessly to the secondary replica.
- **Automated Scaling Policies:** Amazon EC2 Auto Scaling is configured to add or remove instances based on CPU and network usage. During heavy sales peaks, additional servers spin up across different AZs.

Outcome

- **Improved Uptime:** The retailer experiences near-zero downtime even during record-breaking holiday traffic.
- **Consistent Data:** Inventory and order data stay synchronized, reducing cart errors and order failures.
- **Cost Savings:** The retailer only scales out when necessary, optimizing infrastructure expenses while maintaining high performance.

FinTech Application with Regulatory Requirements

Scenario

A FinTech startup offers real-time payment processing for peer-to-peer transfers. Regulations mandate minimal service downtime, and data consistency is vital to meet compliance obligations.

The platform must also adhere to data residency rules in certain regions.

Challenges

- **Stringent SLA:** Financial institutions demand continuous availability and immediate transaction confirmations.
- **Data Residency:** The company must store certain transaction data within specific geographic boundaries.
- **Real-Time Processing:** Delayed or failed transactions can undermine customer trust and violate compliance standards.

Solution

- **Multi-Region Active-Passive Setup:** Two regions are utilized. The primary region processes all transactions, while the secondary region maintains synchronized replicas of the transaction database.
- **Compliance-Aware Routing:** Requests from certain jurisdictions are automatically routed to a compliant region, ensuring that the data stays in the correct location.

- **Automated Health Checks:** The DNS service (such as AWS Route 53) periodically checks the health of both the regions respectively. Upon detecting a major failure in the primary region, it initiates DNS failover to the secondary site.

Outcome

- **Continuous Operation:** The FinTech platform remains online under most failure scenarios, satisfying SLA requirements.
- **Regulatory Compliance:** Localized data storage across multiple regions meets or exceeds residency mandates.
- **User Trust:** Real-time transaction processing without significant downtime boosts client confidence in the reliability of the platform.

Global SaaS Analytics Platform

Scenario

A Software-as-a-Service (SaaS) provider offers analytical dashboards for enterprises worldwide. The service needs to provide consistent performance to users in various continents, which means latency must be minimal and uptime must be near 100%.

Challenges

- **Global User Base:** Clients spread across North America, Europe, and Asia expect similar response times.
- **Spiky Usage Patterns:** Different time zones lead to intermittent traffic peaks as each region starts its business day.
- **Data Synchronization:** Aggregated data is updated frequently, requiring real-time or near-real-time replication.

Solution

- **Multi-Region Active-Active:** The platform launches two primary clusters—one in North America and another in Europe—both actively serving their local user bases. A third region in Asia provides additional coverage for local customers.
- **Load Balancing with Latency Routing:** A global DNS load balancer detects user location and routes traffic to the nearest region for optimal performance.
- **Eventual Consistency Model:** Analytics data replicates asynchronously across all regions. While writes may incur minimal delays, read operations are served from the closest region to reduce latency.

Outcome

- **Enhanced User Experience:** Enterprises in North America, Europe, and Asia enjoy low-latency access to analytics dashboards.
- **Strong Resilience:** If one region encounters operational issues, traffic automatically shifts to another without significant downtime.
- **Scalable Growth:** Adding new regions becomes straightforward as customer bases expand in new markets.

Healthcare Data Management

Scenario

A healthcare organization stores and analyzes patient records for multiple hospitals. Government regulations demand secure data handling and continuous accessibility for medical staff, who might need immediate access to patient information at any time.

Challenges

- **Regulatory Compliance:** Patient data confidentiality and strict government oversight require secure storage and near-zero data loss.
- **Life-Critical Access:** Interruptions can delay patient care and potentially harm patients.
- **Complex Workflows:** Multiple departments—radiology, labs, outpatient services—depend on concurrent data access.

Solution

- **Multi-AZ VPC Configuration:** Infrastructure is hosted in a Virtual Private Cloud (VPC) spanning multiple Availability Zones. Each AZ contains mirrored servers and real-time replicated databases.
- **Failover Clustering:** A managed database service (such as Amazon RDS with Multi-AZ) ensures that if the primary database fails, a standby replica becomes active.
- **Highly Controlled Access:** Security groups and VPN tunnels connect hospital networks to the cloud environment, maintaining compliance with healthcare regulations like HIPAA.

Outcome

- **Uninterrupted Healthcare Services:** Doctors and nurses access critical patient data around the clock, even if one AZ experiences downtime.
- **Regulatory Assurance:** Through encryption, auditing, and resilient architecture, the organization meets mandatory data protection standards.
- **Reduces burdens:** Automated failover reduces administrative burdens and enables IT staff to focus on improvements rather than fire-fighting outages.

Conclusion

Designing networks for high availability is paramount in modern cloud environments, where downtime translates into both financial loss and diminished user trust. By employing techniques such as load balancing, fault tolerance, and scalability, organizations can create robust and cost-effective infrastructures capable of handling unpredictable traffic loads and unexpected failures. In this chapter, we explored how AWS services like Elastic Load Balancers (ELB) and Auto Scaling can reduce downtime and optimize performance. We also discussed the architectural patterns—Multi-AZ and Multi-Region—that further enhance resilience by distributing resources across distinct geographic or physical boundaries.

Whether your goal is to serve millions of users or ensure 24/7 operation for mission-critical applications, the strategies outlined here form the foundation of a forward-looking, scalable, and highly available architecture. In the next chapter, we shall learn how to monitor and troubleshoot networks effectively using AWS tools. The chapter explains the importance of metrics, logs, and alerts in identifying performance bottlenecks.

Points to Remember

- **Load Balancing Essentials**
  - Application Load Balancer (ALB) operates at Layer 7 with advanced routing (URL- or host-based).
  - Network Load Balancer (NLB) functions at Layer 4, emphasizing high throughput and low latency.
  - Efficient Resource Utilization: Balancers distribute traffic evenly, preventing server overload and enhancing fault tolerance.
- **Fault Tolerance Fundamentals**
  - **Redundancy:** Duplicating critical system components (servers, databases) to avoid single points of failure.
  - **Failover:** Seamlessly switching traffic to backup resources when the primary resource fails.
  - **Disaster Recovery:** Planning for catastrophic failures with backup strategies—ranging from simple backup/restore to multi-site deployments.
- **Scalability Approaches**
  - **Vertical Scaling:** Increasing the capacity of a single node (more CPU/RAM).
  - **Horizontal Scaling:** Adding more nodes to share the workload. This approach typically offers higher fault tolerance and near-limitless expansion.
  - **Auto Scaling Groups:** Automates the process of adding/removing instances in response to real-time demand, optimizing both performance and costs.
- **High Availability Architectures**
  - **Multi-AZ:** Deploying resources across multiple availability zones within a single region to protect against localized outages.
  - **Multi-Region:** Distributing workloads across geographically distinct regions to mitigate full regional failures and potentially reduce latency for global users.
- **Practical Considerations**
  - **Monitoring and Alarms:** Tools like Amazon CloudWatch or third-party solutions can detect anomalies early, triggering auto-healing or failover processes.
  - **Cost-Performance Balance:** While adding redundancy and multiple regions boosts resilience, it also incurs higher expenses— do evaluate ROI carefully.
  - **Testing and Drills:** Routine tests ensure failover and disaster recovery processes work as intended, minimizing surprises during real incidents.

By solidifying your grasp of these core concepts—load balancing, fault tolerance, scalability, and distributed architectures—you lay the groundwork for creating AWS networks that remain responsive and available under all conditions.

CHAPTER 4
Network Monitoring and Troubleshooting

Introduction

In the contemporary digital landscape, where businesses increasingly rely on cloud infrastructure for mission-critical applications, maintaining network health is of paramount importance. A well-functioning network forms the backbone of a seamless user experience, enabling fast, reliable, and secure communication between distributed resources. Modern cloud environments are inherently complex, consisting of interconnected components such as Virtual Private Clouds (VPCs), load balancers, NAT gateways, and internet gateways. Any disruption—whether caused by misconfiguration, latency spikes, packet loss, or security vulnerabilities—can quickly lead to degraded performance, service outages, or security breaches.

The importance of network monitoring has grown even further with the rise of emerging technologies such as Artificial Intelligence (AI) and the Internet of Things (IoT). For example, AI-driven applications used in real-time fraud detection or recommendation systems depend on low-latency, high-throughput networks to process data streams instantly. Similarly, IoT deployments in smart cities, healthcare monitoring, and industrial automation generate massive volumes of network traffic from distributed devices, making proactive monitoring essential to detect anomalies and prevent failures.

This chapter explores network monitoring and troubleshooting in AWS, equipping readers with the tools and techniques required to proactively detect, diagnose, and resolve network issues before they impact business operations. AWS provides a comprehensive set of monitoring services—including Amazon CloudWatch, VPC Flow Logs, AWS CloudTrail, AWS X-Ray, and Route 53 Health Checks—to deliver real-time visibility into network performance and behavior. In addition, traditional diagnostic utilities such as ping, traceroute, netstat, and tcpdump remain indispensable for deep-dive analysis and hands-on troubleshooting.

Structure

In this chapter, we will cover the following topics:

- AWS Network Monitoring Tools
- Common Network Issues in AWS
- Network Diagnostic Commands in AWS
- Proactive Monitoring in AWS
- Case Studies

Now, let us dive in and explore how to monitor, analyze, and troubleshoot AWS networks effectively!

AWS Network Monitoring Tools

In modern cloud environments, where applications are highly distributed and rely on interconnected services, real-time network monitoring is essential for ensuring seamless performance, security, and availability. Traditional monitoring focuses on static, manual oversight, while AWS-native monitoring is automated, scalable, and cloud-aware, making it better suited for modern distributed architectures. Traditional network monitoring methods are insufficient for cloud-based infrastructure, as cloud networks are dynamic, scalable, and often span multiple regions and availability zones. To address these complexities, AWS provides a suite of powerful monitoring tools designed to help administrators track network performance, detect anomalies, troubleshoot connectivity issues, and optimize resource usage.

Network monitoring is not just about identifying failures; it plays a crucial role in proactive management by predicting issues, preventing downtime, and securing data transmissions. AWS offers a range of tools that provide visibility into network traffic patterns, latency, security events, and resource utilization. These tools allow administrators to gather detailed insights, set up automated alerts, and take corrective actions before an issue escalates into a critical failure.

Importance of Network Monitoring

Network monitoring is not just about identifying issues when something goes wrong—it is about proactive network management to ensure consistent performance, security, and cost optimization.

For example:

Latency thresholds: Network latency consistently above 200 ms may indicate routing inefficiencies, congested links, or overloaded backend services.

Packet loss: Packet loss greater than 1–2% can significantly impact real-time applications such as video conferencing, VoIP, and online trading platforms.

Bandwidth utilization: Sustained bandwidth usage above 80% of link capacity can signal potential bottlenecks and the need for scaling or traffic optimization.

Security anomalies: Sudden spikes in rejected connections or unusual traffic patterns may indicate DDoS attacks or unauthorized access attempts.

Cost optimization: Monitoring NAT gateway or inter-AZ traffic can reveal unexpected data transfer costs, enabling organizations to optimize architecture and reduce cloud spend.

AWS offers a variety of network monitoring and troubleshooting tools that allow administrators to track key network metrics, analyze logs, set up alerts, and investigate network anomalies in real-time.

Common Network Issues in AWS

Before delving into AWS-specific monitoring tools, it is crucial to understand the common networking issues that organizations face in the cloud.

AWS Network Troubleshooting – Short Decision Flow

- App not reachable?

  → Check Route 53 / DNS.

- Traffic not reaching an instance?

  → Check Routes, Security Groups, NACLs (Reachability Analyzer).

- Connections dropped?

  → Check VPC Flow Logs.

- App slow / high latency?
  → Check CloudWatch, then X-Ray.
- Unexpected traffic spike?
  → Check CloudWatch, VPC Flow Logs, AWS Shield.
- Load balancer issues?
  → Check ELB target health and logs.

Some of the most prevalent network problems include:

- **High Latency:** Increased delay in data transmission, affecting application responsiveness and user experience.
- **Packet Loss:** Data packets getting dropped, leading to incomplete or slow-loading web pages and application failures.
- **Misconfigurations:** Incorrect route tables, security group rules, or ACL configurations that block intended network traffic.
- **DNS Resolution Failures:** Inability to resolve domain names to IP addresses, leading to application failures.
- **Cross-Region or Cross-VPC Connectivity Issues:** Problems arising from incorrect peering configurations, security group settings, or missing routes.
- **Unexpected Traffic Spikes:** Surges in inbound or outbound network traffic, potentially due to cyberattacks, faulty application behavior, or high user demand.
- **Load Balancer Failures:** Misconfigured or overloaded AWS Elastic Load Balancers (ELBs) leading to intermittent service disruptions.

To effectively monitor and resolve these issues, AWS provides an extensive set of monitoring and diagnostic tools.

Key AWS Network Monitoring Tools

AWS offers several services to help administrators track network performance, identify anomalies, and troubleshoot network-related issues. Some of the most essential tools covered in this chapter include:

- **Amazon CloudWatch → Metrics and Alerts**

  Acts as the central monitoring hub, collecting network metrics (latency, throughput, and errors), logs, and triggering alarms when thresholds are exceeded.

- **VPC Flow Logs → Traffic Visibility**

  Provides packet-level traffic data, showing which IPs are communicating, what is accepted or rejected, and helping diagnose connectivity or security issues.

- **AWS CloudTrail → Configuration and Access Tracking**

  Records API calls and configuration changes, helping identify whether network issues were caused by recent modifications to routes, security groups, or ACLs.

- **AWS X-Ray → Application-Level Latency**

  Traces requests across services to pinpoint where delays occur, distinguishing network issues from application bottlenecks.

- **Amazon Route 53 Health Checks → DNS and Endpoint Availability**

  Monitors DNS resolution and endpoint health, enabling detection of outages and automatic failover.

- **AWS Network Manager → Global Network Visibility**

  Provides a centralized view of AWS and on-premises networks, making it easier to monitor complex, hybrid, or multi-region architectures.

In addition to AWS-native tools, administrators can also use traditional network diagnostic commands such as:

- **Traceroute and MTR:** To analyze network paths and identify potential bottlenecks.
- **Ping and Netcat:** To test connectivity and diagnose latency issues.
- **TCPDump and Wireshark:** To capture and inspect network packets for deeper analysis.

Importance of AWS Network Monitoring Tools

The effectiveness of a cloud network depends on its ability to deliver consistent, secure, and high-performance communication between applications, users, and services. AWS network monitoring tools provide the following key benefits:

- **Real-Time Insights:** Track critical network metrics such as bandwidth utilization, request latency, packet loss, and error rates. Using Amazon CloudWatch, metrics are available at 5-minute default granularity or 1-minute granularity for more detailed and time-sensitive monitoring.

- **Log-Based Analysis:** Capture detailed inbound and outbound traffic logs to detect unusual behavior, unauthorized access attempts, or configuration issues. Integration with CloudWatch Logs enables centralized log analysis.

- **Proactive Alerting:** Configure automated alarms to notify administrators when thresholds are breached, such as sustained latency spikes or abnormal traffic patterns, allowing issues to be addressed before users are impacted.

- **Performance Optimization:** Identify network bottlenecks, inefficient routing paths, or uneven load distribution. When combined with the CloudWatch Agent, deeper system-level and network metrics can be collected from EC2 instances for more precise optimization.

- **Security and Compliance:** Monitor traffic patterns for unauthorized access, DDoS attacks, and policy violations, supporting security best practices and regulatory compliance.

- **Multi-Account Visibility:** In large environments, AWS supports centralized monitoring across multiple accounts using AWS Organizations together with CloudWatch cross-account dashboards, enabling a unified view of network health across the entire enterprise.

AWS provides a combination of metrics-based monitoring, log analysis, and traffic inspection tools to give administrators full control over their network. The most widely used AWS network monitoring tools include:

- **Amazon CloudWatch:** A centralized monitoring service that collects network and system performance metrics, generates logs, and triggers automated responses to network events.

- **VPC Flow Logs:** A logging tool that records information about network traffic flowing into, out of, and within an AWS Virtual Private Cloud (VPC), helping diagnose security and connectivity issues.

- **AWS Network Analyzer Tools:** A collection of diagnostic utilities, such as AWS Reachability Analyzer and AWS Network Manager, used to analyze connectivity issues and troubleshoot misconfigurations.

Each of these tools serves a unique purpose, but when combined, they provide a comprehensive monitoring solution that ensures network reliability, security, and efficiency.

In the following sections, we will explore these tools in detail, starting with Amazon CloudWatch, followed by VPC Flow Logs, and concluding with AWS Network Analyzer Tools.

Amazon CloudWatch: Network Monitoring and Performance Management

AWS provides Amazon CloudWatch, a fully managed observability and monitoring service, to track network performance metrics, system health, and resource utilization. CloudWatch enables administrators to collect, visualize, and analyze network and application data in real-time, ensuring proactive troubleshooting and operational efficiency.

Amazon CloudWatch plays a crucial role in detecting performance bottlenecks, tracking latency, monitoring bandwidth usage, and identifying security threats by analyzing logs and metrics. With automated alerts and customizable dashboards, administrators can respond to incidents before they cause system failures.

This section explores what Amazon CloudWatch is, how it works, and how it is used for network monitoring and troubleshooting in AWS.

Amazon CloudWatch

Amazon CloudWatch is a centralized monitoring service designed to provide real-time operational insights into AWS cloud resources, applications, and services. It enables users to collect metrics, logs, and events from AWS infrastructure and set up alarms to trigger automated responses when predefined thresholds are exceeded.

CloudWatch helps in:

- Tracking network health through real-time performance monitoring.
- Detecting anomalies and potential failures using logs and alerts.
- Optimizing resource utilization by analyzing traffic trends.
- Enhancing security by identifying unusual network activity.
- Automating incident response with CloudWatch alarms and AWS Lambda.

CloudWatch integrates seamlessly with AWS services such as EC2, RDS, Lambda, ELB, VPC, and API Gateway, ensuring end-to-end visibility across cloud applications.

Architecture Overview of Amazon CloudWatch

- Amazon CloudWatch is a fully managed monitoring service that collects metrics, logs, and events from AWS resources and applications.
- AWS services and custom applications publish data to CloudWatch automatically or via the CloudWatch Agent.
- Collected data is stored centrally and evaluated using alarms and anomaly detection.
- CloudWatch integrates with SNS, Lambda, Auto Scaling, and dashboards to trigger alerts and automated responses.

Key Features of Amazon CloudWatch

Amazon CloudWatch offers a robust set of features for network monitoring and performance analysis:

FEATURE	DESCRIPTION
CloudWatch Metrics	Collects real-time performance data from AWS services, tracking network activity such as bandwidth usage, request latency, and error rates.
CloudWatch Logs	Captures and stores log data from AWS services and applications, helping in troubleshooting and forensic analysis.
CloudWatch Alarms	Automatically triggers notifications or actions (such as Lambda functions, SNS alerts) when a specified metric exceeds a threshold.
CloudWatch Dashboards	Provides customizable visualizations of key network performance indicators using graphs and charts.
CloudWatch Events	Tracks system changes and automates responses based on predefined event rules.
CloudWatch Logs Insights	An interactive log analysis tool that enables users to run queries on log data for deep troubleshooting.
CloudWatch Contributor Insights	Identifies top contributors to high network traffic or error rates, enabling quick issue diagnosis.

Table 4.1: *Key Features of Amazon CloudWatch*

Monitoring by Amazon CloudWatch

Amazon CloudWatch is extensively used to monitor network performance, detect failures, and optimize connectivity across AWS environments. It allows administrators to proactively manage network health, analyze trends, and automate troubleshooting processes.

Note: *CloudWatch metrics for EC2 are available at 5-min intervals by default; 1-min requires detailed monitoring.*

Monitoring Network Performance Metrics

CloudWatch enables administrators to collect and visualize critical network metrics, such as:

- **Network In/Out:** Measures incoming and outgoing data transfer for EC2 instances.
- **Packet Loss and Latency:** Tracks delays and dropped packets between services.
- **Application Performance:** Monitors API Gateway latency, load balancer response times, and network request failures.
- **Network Bandwidth Usage:** Helps optimize resource allocation and cost management.

The following table is an example of CloudWatch Network Metrics for EC2:

METRIC NAME	DESCRIPTION
NetworkIn	The volume of incoming network traffic (bytes) to the instance.
NetworkOut	The volume of outgoing network traffic (bytes) from the instance.
NetworkPacketsIn	The number of packets received by the instance.
NetworkPacketsOut	The number of packets sent by the instance.
CPUUtilization	Tracks instance load to correlate with network spikes.

Table 4.2: *Example CloudWatch Network Metrics for EC2*

Analyzing VPC Flow Logs with CloudWatch

CloudWatch integrates with VPC Flow Logs to capture detailed information about network traffic within a Virtual Private Cloud (VPC).

These logs help:

- Identify security breaches by detecting unusual outbound requests.
- Troubleshoot connectivity issues between instances, services, or regions.
- Analyze network latency by measuring packet delays and dropped connections.

Administrators can stream VPC Flow Logs to Amazon CloudWatch Logs, where they can search, analyze, and set up alerts based on log data.

yaml

```
2 1234567890 eni-abcdef123456 192.168.1.10 54.239.26.1 443 8080 6 5 100 1622233345 1622233350 ACCEPT OK
```

Figure 4.1: *VPC Flow Log Entry*

This log entry provides:

- Source and destination IP addresses.
- Port numbers and protocols used.
- Action (ACCEPT/DENY).
- Packet count and bytes transferred.

Setting up CloudWatch Alarms for Network Health Monitoring

CloudWatch Alarms allow administrators to define thresholds for network metrics and trigger automated responses when those limits are exceeded.

For example:

- **Set an alarm for high latency:** Notify administrators if NetworkPacketsOut exceeds 1000 packets per second.
- **Trigger an automated action for dropped packets:** If NetworkPacketsDropped increases, launch a recovery instance.

Example CloudWatch Alarm Setup:

- **Metric:** NetworkOut
- **Threshold:** > 1 GB data transfer per minute.
- **Action:** Send an SNS notification to the network admin team.

Automating Incident Response with CloudWatch and AWS Lambda

CloudWatch integrates with AWS Lambda to automate self-healing network responses.

Use Case:

If CloudWatch detects high packet loss on an EC2 instance, it can automatically trigger a Lambda function to restart the instance or reroute traffic.

Example CloudWatch + Lambda Automation Flow:

- CloudWatch detects network failure (for instance, NetworkPacketsDropped is high).

- CloudWatch sends an event to AWS Lambda.
- Lambda function automatically fixes the issue by:
  - Restarting the affected EC2 instance.
  - Rerouting traffic using Route 53 failover policies.
  - Scaling up resources to handle high network load.

CloudWatch Dashboards for Real-Time Network Visualization

CloudWatch Dashboards provide an interactive view of real-time network performance, bottlenecks, and trends. These dashboards help:

- Monitor application and network health using graphs and charts.
- Correlate network issues with system events for faster troubleshooting.
- Provide centralized visibility across multiple AWS accounts and regions.

Example CloudWatch Dashboard Components:

GRAPH TYPE	MONITORED METRIC
Line Graph	EC2 instance NetworkIn and NetworkOut
Bar Chart	Top 5 contributors to high network traffic
Heatmap	Latency across different AWS regions

***Table* 4.3:** *CloudWatch Dashboard Components*

Finally, Amazon CloudWatch is an indispensable tool for monitoring, troubleshooting, and optimizing AWS network performance. With its ability to track real-time metrics, analyze logs, trigger automated alarms, and integrate with AWS Lambda for incident response, CloudWatch ensures that networks remain secure, resilient, and efficient.

In the next section, we will explore VPC Flow Logs, another critical AWS tool for analyzing and troubleshooting network traffic in cloud environments.

VPC Flow Logs: Network Traffic Analysis and Troubleshooting in AWS

In cloud-based environments, where network traffic flows dynamically between instances, services, and external networks, monitoring and analyzing network activity is critical for performance optimization and security. AWS provides VPC Flow Logs, a powerful tool that captures detailed information about incoming, outgoing, and internal traffic within a Virtual Private Cloud (VPC). By analyzing these logs, administrators can troubleshoot connectivity issues, detect security threats, and optimize network performance in real-time.

VPC Flow Logs help organizations gain deep visibility into network behavior, allowing them to identify latency issues, unauthorized access attempts, routing misconfigurations, and packet drops. These logs serve as a forensic tool for investigating anomalies, enforcing compliance, and securing AWS environments against potential threats.

This section provides a detailed overview of VPC Flow Logs, their features, use cases, implementation, and best practices for network monitoring and troubleshooting in AWS.

VPC Flow Logs

VPC Flow Logs is an AWS service that records metadata about network traffic flowing to and from network interfaces within a VPC. These logs do not capture the actual packet content but provide structured data on IP addresses, ports, protocols, and traffic accept/reject actions.

Note: VPC Flow Logs do not capture traffic to AWS DNS or 169.254.169.254 (metadata endpoint).

Key Characteristics of VPC Flow Logs:

- Captures detailed traffic metadata (source/destination IP, port, protocol, bytes transferred).
- Works at different levels: VPC-level, subnet-level, or network interface-level.
- Stores logs in CloudWatch Logs, S3, or Kinesis Firehose for further analysis.
- Supports filtering of logs to capture only relevant traffic patterns.
- Provides near real-time insights into traffic behavior and anomalies.

By leveraging VPC Flow Logs, administrators can track the flow of network packets, diagnose connection failures, and identify security vulnerabilities.

Key Features of VPC Flow Logs

The following are the key features and descriptions of VPC Flow Logs:

- **Granular Logging Levels:** Can capture logs at VPC, subnet, or network interface (ENI) levels.
- **Accept/Deny Traffic Analysis:** Identifies whether network packets were accepted or rejected based on security group and ACL rules.
- **Traffic Filtering:** Allows administrators to filter logs for specific IPs, ports, or protocols.
- **Multiple Storage Options:** Logs can be stored in CloudWatch, Amazon S3, or Kinesis Firehose for analysis.
- **Deep Security Insights:** Helps detect unauthorized access attempts, unusual traffic patterns, or DDoS activities.
- **Integration with AWS Services:** Works with Amazon GuardDuty, CloudWatch, and AWS Security Hub for threat detection.

Functioning of VPC Flow Logs

When VPC Flow Logs are enabled, AWS automatically captures metadata about network packets traversing the selected VPC, subnet, or ENI. These logs are then forwarded to the chosen storage destination (CloudWatch, S3, or Kinesis Firehose) for further processing and analysis.

Flow Log Lifecycle:

- Traffic is captured from a VPC, subnet, or network interface.
- Log entries are generated, containing traffic metadata (Refer to *Figure* 4.2).
- Logs are stored in CloudWatch, S3, or Kinesis for processing.
- Administrators analyze logs using AWS tools such as CloudWatch Insights, Athena, or SIEM solutions.

```yaml
2 1234567890 eni-abcdef123456 192.168.1.10 54.239.26.1 443 8080 6 5 100 1622233345 1622233350 ACCEPT OK
```

Figure 4.2: *VPC Flow Log Entry*

The fields and description of the fields from the VPC flow log entry are as follows:

- 2 → Log format version
- 1234567890 → AWS account ID
- eni-abcdef123456 → Elastic Network Interface (ENI) ID
- 192.168.1.10 → Source IP address
- 54.239.26.1 → Destination IP address
- 443 → Destination port (HTTPS)
- 8080 → Source port
- 6 → Protocol (TCP)
- 5 → Number of packets transferred
- 100 → Total bytes transferred
- 1622233345 → Start timestamp
- 1622233350 → End timestamp
- ACCEPT → Action (ACCEPT/DENY)
- OK → Logging status

This entry shows that a TCP connection was established between an internal instance and an external server on port 443 (HTTPS), and the traffic was accepted.

Use Cases of VPC Flow Logs

VPC Flow Logs provide deep network visibility and are used for performance monitoring, security analysis, and compliance auditing.

Network Performance Monitoring

VPC Flow Logs allow administrators to:

- Identify high-latency connections between AWS services.
- Detects bandwidth-intensive workloads causing congestion.
- Analyze dropped packets and network routing issues.
- Optimize data transfer costs by identifying unnecessary traffic.

Use Case:

If an application experiences high latency, administrators can analyze flow logs to identify slow network paths and troubleshoot performance bottlenecks.

Security and Threat Detection

By analyzing VPC Flow Logs, security teams can:

- Detect unauthorized access attempts from suspicious IP addresses.
- Identify DDoS attacks by monitoring excessive requests from a single source.
- Investigate data exfiltration attempts by tracking outbound traffic.
- Correlate network activity with AWS GuardDuty and Security Hub for real-time threat detection.

Use Case:

If a security team notices large outbound data transfers from an instance, they can use VPC Flow Logs to identify the source, destination, and potential security breach.

Troubleshooting Connectivity Issues

VPC Flow Logs help diagnose:

- Why cannot an EC2 instance connect to an RDS database?
- Why are external users unable to access a web server?
- Why does a Lambda function time out when connecting to an API?

Use Case:

If a web application fails to load, administrators can use VPC Flow Logs to determine if security group rules, NACLs, or misconfigured routes are blocking traffic.

Compliance and Auditing

VPC Flow Logs help organizations:

- Maintain audit trails of network traffic for regulatory compliance.
- Monitor data transfer logs to ensure security policies are enforced.
- Generate incident reports for forensic analysis.

Use Case:

A financial organization subject to PCI DSS compliance can use VPC Flow Logs to verify that sensitive data is not transmitted to unauthorized external locations.

Performance and Cost Consideration

While VPC Flow Logs are powerful, large volumes of flow logs can significantly increase CloudWatch Logs ingestion and storage costs in high-traffic environments.

To optimize performance and cost:

- Deliver VPC Flow Logs to Amazon S3 instead of CloudWatch Logs.
- Use Amazon Athena to query and analyze logs on demand.

This approach provides scalable, cost-effective analysis for large datasets while preserving long-term visibility.

Enabling VPC Flow Logs

Administrators can enable VPC Flow Logs using the AWS Management Console, CLI, or SDK.

Step-by-Step Guide (AWS Console):

1. Navigate to the VPC Dashboard in the AWS Management Console.
2. Select the VPC, Subnet, or Network Interface for which logs need to be enabled.
3. Click on "Create Flow Log."
4. Select Log Destination: CloudWatch Logs, S3, or Kinesis Firehose.
5. Define Log Format and Filtering: Choose to log all, accepted, or rejected traffic.
6. Click "Create" to enable VPC Flow Logs.

Best Practices for Using VPC Flow Logs

Some of the best practices for using VPC Flow logs and their benefits are as follows:

Caution Note: IAM *permissions are required for Flow Logs creation.*

- **Use Flow Logs at the ENI Level:**

  Captures granular traffic details, improving troubleshooting accuracy.

- **Filter out Unnecessary Logs:**
  Reduces storage costs and improves performance by logging only relevant traffic.
- **Integrate with SIEM Tools:**
  Enhances security monitoring by correlating logs with threat detection platforms.
- **Set up CloudWatch Alarms:**
  Automates detection of suspicious traffic patterns or high latency events.
- **Analyze Logs Using AWS Athena:**
  Queries large datasets efficiently for deep network insights.

In all, VPC Flow Logs provide unparalleled visibility into network activity, enabling real-time monitoring, security threat detection, and performance troubleshooting in AWS environments. By capturing and analyzing network metadata, administrators can proactively optimize network performance, enforce security policies, and ensure compliance.

In the next section, we will explore AWS Network Analyzer Tools, which provide additional diagnostic capabilities for network troubleshooting.

AWS Network Analyzer Tools

As cloud networks grow in complexity, managing and troubleshooting connectivity issues becomes a significant challenge. In AWS environments, multiple components—Virtual Private Clouds (VPCs), subnets, security groups, route tables, Elastic Load Balancers (ELBs), and private/public endpoints—work together to facilitate seamless communication. Any misconfiguration in these components can lead to latency, packet loss, unauthorized access, or complete network failure.

To help administrators troubleshoot connectivity issues, optimize routing, and enhance network security, AWS offers a suite of network analyzer tools. These tools provide automated diagnostics, real-time analysis, and visualization of network paths to help resolve connectivity issues efficiently.

In this section, we explore AWS Network Analyzer Tools, including:

- **AWS Reachability Analyzer:** It is for network path analysis.
- **AWS Network Manager:** It is for centralized monitoring of multi-region networks.
- **AWS Global Accelerator:** It is for optimizing application performance across regions.
- **AWS Route Analyzer (via Route 53):** It is for DNS troubleshooting.
- **AWS Firewall Manager:** It is for enforcing network security policies.

Each tool provides unique insights into network performance, routing efficiency, and security posture; thus, making them indispensable for maintaining a reliable cloud infrastructure.

Some of the key AWS Network Analyzer tools, their purpose and their best use case are given as follows.

TOOL NAME	PURPOSE	BEST USE CASE
AWS Reachability Analyzer	Analyzes connectivity paths between AWS resources	Troubleshooting misconfigured security groups, route tables, or ACLs
AWS Network Manager	Centralized visibility into global AWS networks	Managing multi-region VPC peering and hybrid cloud connectivity
AWS Global Accelerator	Improves latency and availability of applications across regions	Optimizing global traffic routing for high-performance applications

TOOL NAME	PURPOSE	BEST USE CASE
AWS Route Analyzer (Route 53 Resolver Query Logging)	Diagnoses DNS resolution issues using Route 53	Troubleshooting failed domain name lookups
AWS Firewall Manager	Enforces security policies across AWS accounts and VPCs	Preventing misconfigured firewalls and ensuring security compliance

Table 4.4: *Key AWS Network Analyzer Tools*

AWS Reachability Analyzer

AWS Reachability Analyzer is a network diagnostics tool that helps identify and troubleshoot connectivity issues between AWS resources. It performs path analysis to determine whether traffic can successfully flow between instances, VPCs, subnets, or internet gateways.

Working of AWS Reachability Analyzer:

- Specify the source and destination (such as EC2 instance to RDS, Lambda to API Gateway).
- Reachability Analyzer inspects route tables, security groups, network ACLs, and peering connections.
- It provides a visualization of the network path, highlighting any misconfigurations or blocked connections.

Use Cases:

- Diagnose connectivity failures between EC2 instances and databases.
- Identify misconfigured security group rules blocking network traffic.
- Verify network paths before deploying new applications.

Sample Output:

COMPONENT	STATUS
Security Group Rules	✅ Allows traffic
Route Table Entries	✅ Valid route
NACL Rules	❌ Blocked port detected
VPC Peering Connection	✅ Active

Table 4.5: *Sample Output of AWS Reachability Analyzer*

If an issue is found (like a missing route or blocked security group rule), Reachability Analyzer provides recommended fixes.

AWS Network Manager

AWS Network Manager is a centralized monitoring tool designed for organizations managing multiple VPCs, AWS Direct Connect links, and hybrid cloud networks.

The following are the key capabilities of the AWS network manager:

- **Unified Dashboard:** Provides a global view of network performance across AWS regions.
- **Real-Time Monitoring:** Tracks VPN, Direct Connect, and AWS Transit Gateway connections.
- **Policy-Based Automation:** Automatically detects and alerts on connectivity failures.

Use Cases:

- Monitor and troubleshoot hybrid cloud architectures (AWS + on-premises networks).
- Ensure high availability of VPN and Direct Connect links.
- Detect anomalies and optimize network routing for cost efficiency.

AWS Global Accelerator

AWS Global Accelerator is a traffic routing optimization service that improves latency, reliability, and security for global applications. It uses the AWS global network to direct user requests to the closest and healthiest application endpoint.

Working of AWS Global Accelerator:

- Reduces latency by routing traffic through the AWS backbone instead of the public internet.
- Provides automatic failover in case of regional failures.
- Optimizes multi-region workloads by directing users to the fastest available endpoint.

Use Cases:

- Improve website or API performance for global users.
- Ensure failover protection by rerouting traffic if an AWS region goes down.
- Optimize cross-region application performance for financial, gaming, and e-commerce platforms.

Sample Performance Improvement is shown in the following table:

WITHOUT GLOBAL ACCELERATOR	WITH GLOBAL ACCELERATOR
Traffic follows the **public internet**, leading to **high latency**	Traffic follows the **AWS global network**, reducing latency by **up to 60%**
Risk of regional failures affecting availability	**Built-in failover**, ensuring seamless redirection

Table 4.6: *Sample Performance Improvement of AWS Global Accelerator*

AWS Route Analyzer (via Route 53)

AWS Route 53 Resolver Query Logging and Route Analyzer helps troubleshoot DNS resolution failures and optimize domain name routing.

The key capabilities of the AWS route analyzer are as follows:

- Analyzes domain resolution failures to pinpoint DNS misconfigurations.
- Tracks request latency for faster troubleshooting.
- Verifies that domain records (A, CNAME, MX) are correctly configured.

Use Cases:

- Diagnose “Server Not Found” or “DNS Lookup Failed” errors.
- Optimize multi-region DNS failover configurations.
- Detect unauthorized changes to domain records.

Sample Troubleshooting Table:

DOMAIN NAME	RESOLUTION STATUS	ISSUE DETECTED
api.mycompany.com	✕ Failed	A record missing
login.mycompany.com	✅ Successful	No issues
db.internal.aws	✕ Timeout	Route 53 private hosted zone misconfigured

Table 4.7: *Sample Troubleshooting Table of AWS Route Analyzer*

If DNS records are misconfigured, Route Analyzer provides recommended fixes.

AWS Firewall Manager

AWS Firewall Manager is a security policy enforcement tool that helps organizations maintain consistent firewall rules, DDoS protection, and access controls across multiple AWS accounts.

The key capabilities of AWS Firewall Manager are as follows:

- Centralized security rule enforcement across AWS environments.
- Automatically applies firewall policies to new AWS accounts or VPCs.
- Integrates with AWS WAF and AWS Shield for enhanced security.

Use Cases:

- Ensure compliance by enforcing security rules organization-wide.
- Prevent accidental security misconfigurations across teams.
- Mitigate large-scale DDoS attacks before they impact infrastructure.

Thus, AWS provides a comprehensive set of network analyzer tools that help organizations monitor, troubleshoot, and optimize cloud networks. Each tool has a unique role in ensuring connectivity, security, and performance, making them essential for AWS network administrators.

By leveraging these tools, AWS users can proactively detect network failures, optimize performance, and strengthen cloud security.

Common Network Issues in AWS

A well-functioning network is the foundation of seamless cloud operations, ensuring fast, reliable, and secure communication between resources. However, as organizations scale their cloud infrastructure, network complexities increase, leading to performance bottlenecks, connectivity failures, and security vulnerabilities. In AWS environments, networking issues often arise due to misconfigurations, unexpected traffic patterns, or external influences such as internet congestion and cyber threats.

These issues can manifest as high latency, packet loss, misconfigured routing, DNS failures, or security-related access restrictions. If not identified and addressed promptly, they can lead to application downtime, degraded performance, and financial losses.

This section explores the most common network issues in AWS, including:

- **Latency (Network Delay):** When network communication slows down, affecting application performance.
- **Dropped Packets (Packet Loss):** When data fails to reach its destination, leading to incomplete or failed transactions.

- **Misconfigured Routing:** When incorrect route tables or security settings prevent proper connectivity.

Each of these issues impacts cloud-based applications, databases, and user experiences differently, making it crucial for AWS administrators to understand, diagnose, and resolve them effectively.

Network problems in AWS typically stem from one or more of the following factors:

CAUSE	IMPACT
Infrastructure Complexity	Multi-region setups, VPC peering, and hybrid cloud architectures increase troubleshooting difficulties.
Security Misconfigurations	Incorrect security groups, NACLs, or IAM policies can block intended traffic.
Internet Congestion	Variability in global traffic can introduce latency spikes.
Network Overutilization	High bandwidth consumption leads to slow response times and dropped packets.
DNS Failures	Incorrect or missing DNS records can cause domain resolution issues.
AWS Service Limits	Exceeding AWS bandwidth limits can degrade network performance.
Hardware or Software Failures	Malfunctioning network components (like AWS Transit Gateway misconfigurations) can cause connectivity disruptions.

Table 4.8: *Factors Causing AWS Network Problems*

The most common network issues in AWS are as follows:

Latency (Network Delay)

Latency refers to the time delay between a user request and the corresponding response in a network. In AWS, latency affects how quickly applications load, how fast databases process queries, and how efficiently services communicate across regions. High latency leads to slow application performance, degraded user experience, and potential revenue loss for businesses relying on cloud services.

Impact: High latency results in slow application response times, poor user experience, and database query delays.

Causes:

- **Long network paths:** Traffic routed through multiple regions.
- **Overloaded instances:** High CPU or memory utilization.
- **Internet congestion:** Public network variability.
- **Misconfigured load balancers:** Inefficient traffic distribution.

Example Scenario: A web application hosted on AWS EC2 in the US-East-1 region experiences high latency when accessed by users in Asia-Pacific due to inefficient routing.

Latency in AWS Services

Latency issues can arise in various AWS components, impacting:

- Web applications (slow page loads)
- APIs (delayed responses)
- Databases (slow query execution)
- Cross-region services (delayed communication)

AWS provides managed services to reduce latency and improve performance:

Amazon CloudFront

A global Content Delivery Network (CDN) that caches content at edge locations close to users, significantly reducing latency for static and dynamic web content.

AWS Global Accelerator

Improves application availability and performance by routing user traffic over the AWS global network to the nearest healthy endpoint, reducing network hops and internet congestion.

AWS provides low-latency infrastructure, but network congestion, suboptimal configurations, and inefficient routing can increase response times.

Understanding Network Latency

Network latency consists of multiple delay components:

TYPE OF LATENCY	DESCRIPTION	EXAMPLE IN AWS
Processing Delay	Time taken to **process a request**	EC2 instance processing an HTTP request
Queuing Delay	Time a packet waits in a queue before transmission	High traffic on an overloaded NAT Gateway
Transmission Delay	Time taken to **transmit data** based on bandwidth	Large files transferred over AWS Direct Connect
Propagation Delay	Time required for data to travel between locations	Data traveling between AWS **us-east-1 and ap-southeast-1**

Table 4.9: *Delay Components of Network Latency*

Network Latency in AWS Infrastructure

The following is a representation of how latency accumulates when a user accesses an AWS-hosted web application:

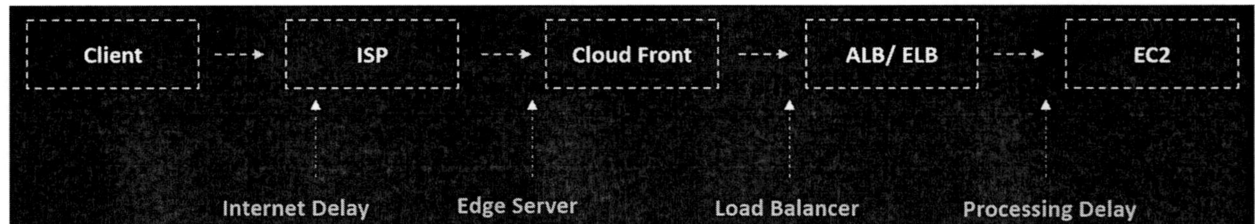

Figure 4.3: *End-to-End Latency in AWS*

Each stage adds latency, making optimization crucial.

Common Causes of Latency in AWS

Latency in AWS networks can be caused by multiple factors:

Suboptimal AWS Region Selection

- AWS operates in multiple geographic regions.
- Hosting applications in a distant region from users increases propagation delay.

Example: A user in India accessing an EC2 instance hosted in us-west-2 (Oregon) will experience significantly higher latency than if the application were hosted in ap-south-1 (Mumbai).

Fix:

- **Use AWS Global Accelerator:** Routes user traffic over the AWS global network to the nearest healthy endpoint, reducing internet congestion and latency.

- **Leverage AWS Local Zones:** Local Zones place AWS compute and storage closer to large population centers, enabling low-latency workloads such as media streaming, gaming, and real-time analytics.
- **Use AWS Wavelength Zones:** Designed for ultra-low latency (single-digit milliseconds) by embedding AWS infrastructure directly within 5G networks—ideal for AR/VR, IoT, and mobile edge applications.

Inefficient Load Balancing

- AWS Application Load Balancer (ALB) and Network Load Balancer (NLB) distribute traffic across instances.
- Overloaded or improperly configured load balancers increase response times.

Fix:

- Use Auto Scaling Groups to distribute workloads.
- Monitor ALB latency metrics in CloudWatch (TargetResponseTime).

High Network Traffic and Bandwidth Bottlenecks

- Large amounts of traffic can cause network congestion, increasing queueing delay.
- AWS NAT Gateway, Direct Connect, or VPNs may become overloaded.

Fix:

- Use AWS CloudFront CDN for caching content near users.
- Optimize VPC traffic flow using VPC Endpoints.

Cross-Region Latency

- Traffic between AWS regions takes longer to travel.
- Cross-region data replication (RDS, DynamoDB, S3) adds latency.

Fix:

- Enable Multi-AZ Replication for databases to reduce read latency.
- Use Amazon Route 53 latency-based routing.

Monitoring Latency with AWS Tools

AWS provides various tools to measure and troubleshoot latency effectively as shown in the following table:

METRIC	SERVICE	PURPOSE
TargetResponseTime	ALB/NLB	Measures load balancer latency
Latency	API Gateway	Tracks API request delays
ReadLatency / WriteLatency	RDS	Tracks database query speed
DeliveryTime	CloudFront	Measures edge server response time

Table 4.10: *CloudWatch Metrics for Latency*

The following figure depicts the latency Monitoring with AWS CloudWatch:

Figure 4.4: *Latency Monitoring with AWS CloudWatch*

Troubleshooting AWS Latency Issues

The step-by-step approach to reducing latency is as follows:

1. **Identify Latency Sources**
    a. Use **CloudWatch Metrics** to track delays in different components.
    b. Run ping and traceroute to test network paths.
2. **Optimize AWS Regions and Availability Zones**
    a. Deploy workloads in the **nearest AWS region** to reduce distance-related delays.
    b. Use **AWS Global Accelerator** to route traffic through AWS backbone.
3. **Improve Load Balancing and Scaling**
    a. Set up **Auto Scaling Groups** to prevent overloaded instances.
    b. Enable **ALB connection draining (deregistration delay)** to optimize traffic redirection.
4. **Use AWS Content Delivery Network (CDN)**
    a. Enable **AWS CloudFront** to serve cached content globally.
    b. Reduce database latency with **Amazon ElastiCache (Redis, Memcached)**.
5. **Optimize Network Routing and Traffic**
    a. Use **Amazon Route 53 latency-based routing** for faster DNS resolution.
    b. Configure **VPC Peering, Transit Gateway, and Direct Connect** for better routing.
6. **Monitor and Set Alerts**
    a. Enable **CloudWatch Alarms** for high Latency metrics.
    b. Use **AWS X-Ray** to analyze application performance.

In all, latency is a critical performance metric in AWS that directly affects user experience, database performance, and application responsiveness. Proactive monitoring, optimized architecture, and AWS services such as CloudFront, Route 53, and Global Accelerator help minimize latency and improve application performance.

Key Takeaways:

- Monitor latency with AWS CloudWatch and AWS X-Ray.
- Reduce network delays using Route 53 latency-based routing.
- Deploy workloads closer to users to minimize propagation delays.
- Use AWS Global Accelerator for low-latency traffic routing.
- Implement caching solutions (CloudFront, ElastiCache) to reduce load.

Dropped Packets (Packet Loss)

Dropped packets occur when network packets fail to reach their intended destination, resulting in failed transactions, slow application responses, or broken connections. In AWS environments, dropped packets can lead to disrupted communications between instances, load balancers, and databases, severely impacting performance and reliability.

Understanding why packets are lost, how to detect packet loss, and how to fix it is crucial for maintaining a stable cloud infrastructure. This section explores common causes, AWS monitoring tools, and troubleshooting techniques to minimize packet loss in AWS networks.

Impact: This leads to incomplete transactions, broken connections, and application timeouts.

Causes:

- **Network congestion:** Insufficient bandwidth causes packet drops.
- **Security group or ACL misconfigurations:** Unintentional blocking of critical traffic.
- **Unstable network paths:** AWS VPC peering or Direct Connect failures.
- **DDoS attacks:** Overwhelming incoming traffic causes legitimate packets to drop.

Example Scenario: A database hosted in AWS RDS intermittently drops connections due to excessive packet loss, affecting data integrity.

Packet loss in AWS Services

When data is transmitted over a network, packets travel between various AWS services (EC2, RDS, S3, Lambda) via VPCs, internet gateways, and peering connections. If a packet fails to reach its destination, it is considered "dropped."

The Packet Loss in AWS Services affects in the following ways:

- **Web Applications** → Slow or failed page loads.
- **APIs** → Delayed or incomplete responses.
- **Databases** → Connection timeouts or partial data transfer.
- **Load Balancers** → Increased request failures.

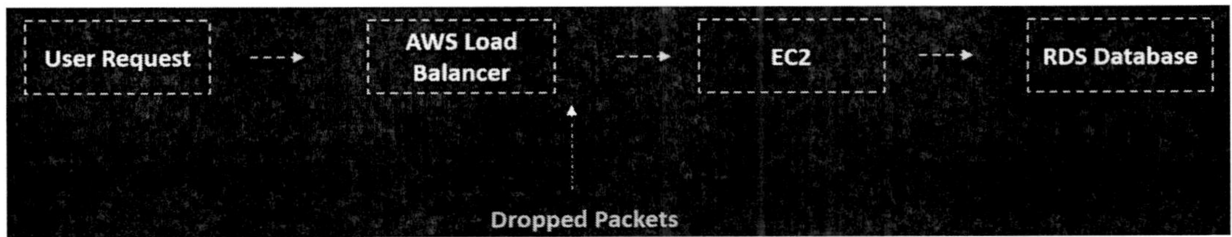

***Figure* 4.5:** *Network Packet Transmission in AWS*

Dropped packets can occur at any stage, causing failed connections.

Common Causes of Packet Loss in AWS:

- **Network Congestion**
    - If network interfaces (ENI), NAT Gateways, or VPNs become overloaded, packets are dropped.
    - High traffic in shared bandwidth environments (such as public internet or AWS Transit Gateway) increases packet loss.

  Fix:
    - Use AWS Direct Connect for dedicated bandwidth.
    - Optimize instance placement with proximity placement groups.
- **Security Group and Network ACL Misconfigurations**
    - Security groups or NACLs may block inbound or outbound packets, causing connectivity failures (Refer to *Figure* 4.6).
    - If security groups only allow HTTP (80) but block HTTPS (443), packets sent over HTTPS are dropped.

  Fix:
    - Use AWS Reachability Analyzer to verify allowed network paths.
    - Check VPC Flow Logs for REJECT entries.

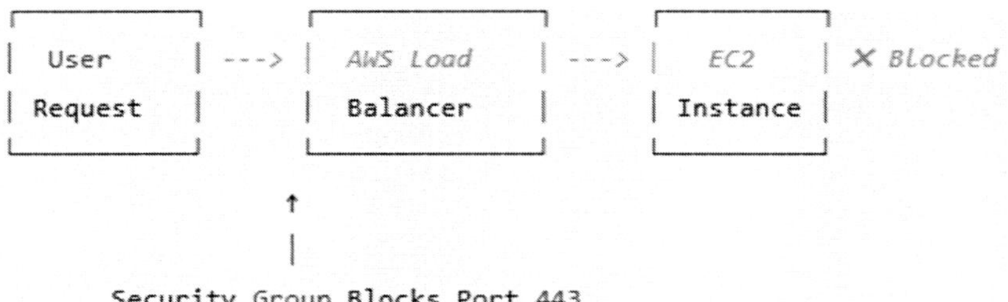

***Figure 4.6**: Security Group Blocking Packets*

Packets sent over blocked ports will be dropped.

- **Misconfigured Route Tables**
  - If route tables lack the correct entries, packets sent to external networks (such as the internet, peer VPCs, or on-premises networks) may be dropped or misrouted, leading to connectivity failures.

  Common Causes
  - Missing routes to an Internet Gateway, NAT Gateway, or VPC peering connection.
  - Incorrect next-hop targets.
  - Disabled or incorrect route propagation in centralized networking setups.

  Fix:
  - **Check AWS Route Tables:**

    Verify that route tables contain the correct destination CIDRs and next-hop targets.
  - **Use AWS VPC Peering:**

    Ensure routes are correctly added on both VPCs for inter-VPC communication.
  - **Validate AWS Transit Gateway Route Propagation:**

    In hub-and-spoke architectures, confirm that Transit Gateway route propagation is enabled and routes are correctly associated with the appropriate route tables. Missing or disabled propagation is a common cause of silent packet drops.
- **Unstable Network Paths and Cross-Region Connectivity Issues**
  - Packets traveling across regions, VPN tunnels, or Direct Connect links may experience high latency and packet loss.
  - AWS auto-healing network architecture ensures reliability, but misconfigured VPNs can drop packets due to encryption mismatches.

  Fix:
  - Use AWS Global Accelerator for optimized routing.
  - Enable CloudWatch Network Metrics for monitoring.

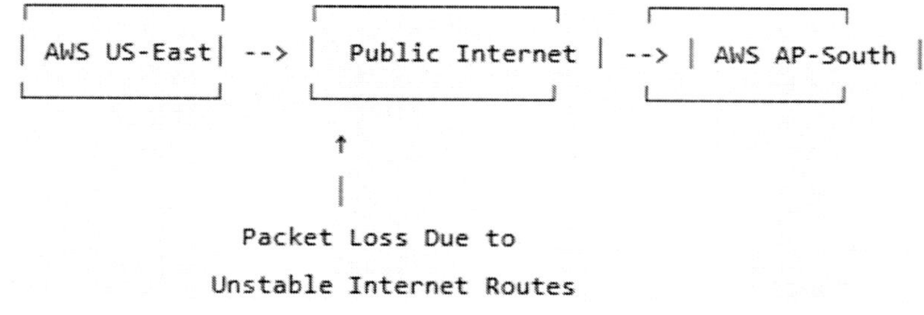

***Figure 4.7**: Cross-Region Packet Loss*

Using AWS Global Accelerator minimizes cross-region packet loss.

- **Load Balancer Connection Draining**
  - When load balancers remove unhealthy targets, in-flight requests may be dropped.

  Fix:

- Enable Connection Draining for ALB/NLB to allow requests to be completed before removing instances.

Detecting Packet Loss in AWS

AWS provides multiple tools to analyze network traffic and diagnose packet loss.

The following is the table for AWS CloudWatch Metrics for Network Monitoring:

METRIC	SERVICE	PURPOSE
NetworkPacketsIn	EC2	Tracks incoming packets
NetworkPacketsOut	EC2	Tracks outgoing packets
DroppedPackets	ALB	Shows lost requests
TCPResetCount	NLB	Identifies failed connections

***Table 4.11:** AWS CloudWatch Metrics for Network Monitoring*

Enable CloudWatch alarms to monitor packet drops.

Analyzing VPC Flow Logs for Packet Drops:

- VPC Flow Logs capture ACCEPT and REJECT entries, showing blocked traffic.
- Check for REJECT logs to identify which security group, NACL or route caused packet loss.

REJECT entries indicate NACL or SG blocks, whereas ACCEPT + TCP reset entries may indicate application-level packet drops.

Example VPC Flow Log Entry (Packet Dropped):

```
2 1234567890 eni-xyz123 192.168.1.5 35.200.10.1 443 6 5 100 1622233345 1622233350 REJECT OK
```

***Figure 4.8:** Log Entry for VPC Flow*

This log entry shows that a request to port 443 was rejected, causing packet loss.

Fixing Packet Loss in AWS

Troubleshooting Security Groups and ACLs:

- **Check Security Groups**
  - Run: **aws ec2 describe-security-groups**
  - Ensure the necessary ports and IP ranges are allowed.
- **Check Network ACLs**
  - Run: **aws ec2 describe-network-acls**
  - Verify that NACLs allow traffic on necessary ports.

Optimize AWS Routing:

- **Verify Route Table Entries**
  - Ensure correct routes for **internet gateways, NAT gateways, and VPC peering.**
  - Run: **aws ec2 describe-route-tables**

- **Enable Route 53 Health Checks**
  - Detects unreachable **endpoints** due to packet loss.

Reduce Cross-Region Latency and Packet Drops:

- **Use AWS Global Accelerator**
  - Routes traffic via **AWS backbone network** for reduced packet loss.
- **Enable VPC Peering or Transit Gateway**
  - Ensures **optimized VPC connectivity**.

Monitor and Automate Packet Loss Detection:

- **Set CloudWatch Alarms for High Packet Loss**
  - Example CloudWatch Alarm Rule:

```
{
  "Region": "us-east-1",
  "MetricName": "NetworkPacketsDropped",
  "Threshold": 10,
  "ComparisonOperator": "GreaterThanThreshold",
  "AlarmActions": ["arn:aws:sns:us-east-1:1234567890:NotifyAdmin"]
}
```

Use AWS Lambda for Auto-Remediation

- Automatically adjust security groups, route tables, or scaling policies.

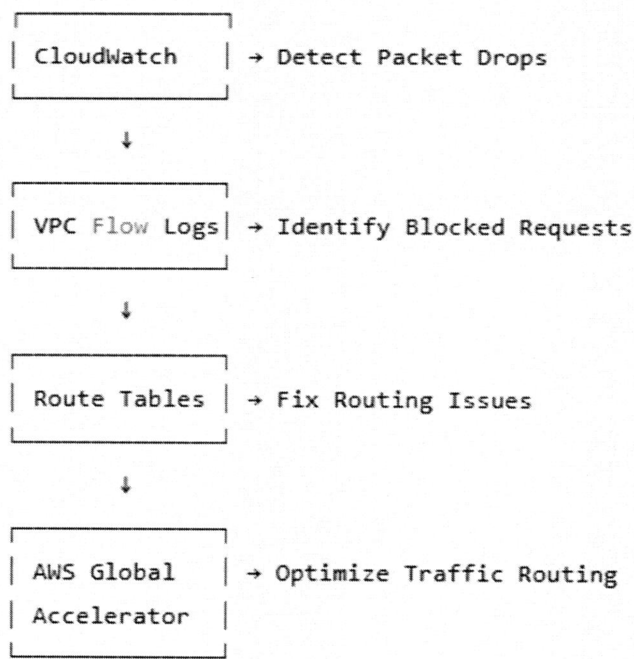

Figure 4.9: *AWS Troubleshooting Process for Packet Loss*

Follow this approach for efficient packet loss resolution.

Dropped packets can severely impact AWS network performance, leading to failed requests, slow applications, and broken connections. Using AWS CloudWatch, VPC Flow Logs, and Route 53 Health Checks, administrators can detect, diagnose, and fix packet loss issues efficiently.

Misconfigured Routing

Routing is the backbone of network communication in AWS, ensuring that packets travel between instances, services, VPCs, and external networks efficiently. When routing configurations are incorrect or missing, traffic may fail to reach its destination, leading to connectivity failures, application downtime, and security vulnerabilities.

Misconfigured routing in AWS can result from incorrect route table entries, missing NAT gateways, improper peering configurations, or VPC endpoint misconfigurations.

Impact: Causes connectivity failures, access restrictions, and broken application workflows.

Causes:

- Missing or incorrect route table entries.
- Improper NAT gateway or internet gateway configurations.
- Misconfigured VPN tunnels.
- VPC peering misconfigurations.

Example Scenario:

A private EC2 instance in VPC A (10.0.0.0/16) fails to communicate with a database hosted in VPC B (192.168.10.0/24) due to a missing VPC peering route entry.

Understanding common network issues in AWS is the first step toward effective monitoring, troubleshooting, and optimization. Each issue—latency, dropped packets, and misconfigured routing—can disrupt cloud operations if not addressed proactively.

Common Routing Issues in AWS:

- **Missing or Incorrect Route Table Entries**

  Note: *AWS automatically adds local routes (local) and only non-local CIDRs must be manually defined.*

  Cause:

  - The destination is not defined in the route table.
  - The route to an external CIDR block is missing.

  Impact:

  - Instances cannot communicate across subnets, VPCs, or the internet.

  Example:

  - An EC2 instance in a private subnet cannot access the internet because its route table lacks a NAT gateway route.

  Fix:

  - Check route tables using: **aws ec2 describe-route-tables**
  - Add the missing route entry:

    aws ec2 create-route --route-table-id rtb-abc123 --destination-cidr-block 0.0.0.0/0 --gateway-id igw-xyz789

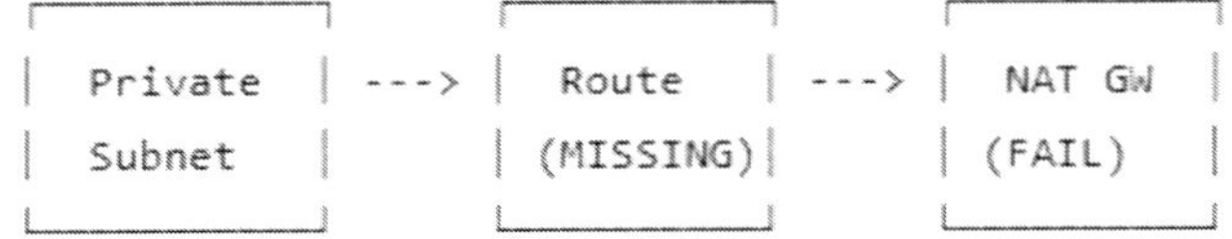

Figure 4.10: *Missing Route Entry*

Traffic is blocked because the route table lacks an outbound NAT gateway entry.

- **Misconfigured VPC Peering**

  Note: *VPC peering is non-transitive - missing routes between three or more peered VPCs won't propagate automatically.*

  Cause:

  - Missing or incorrect route table entries for peering connections.
  - Security groups or NACLs blocking cross-VPC traffic.

  Impact:

  - Two VPCs cannot communicate, even if peering is established.

  Example:

  - VPC A (10.0.0.0/16) and VPC B (192.168.1.0/24) are peered, but the route table of VPC A is missing an entry for VPC B.

  Fix:

  - Verify peering connections: **aws ec2 describe-vpc-peering-connections**
  - Add missing route entries in both VPCs.

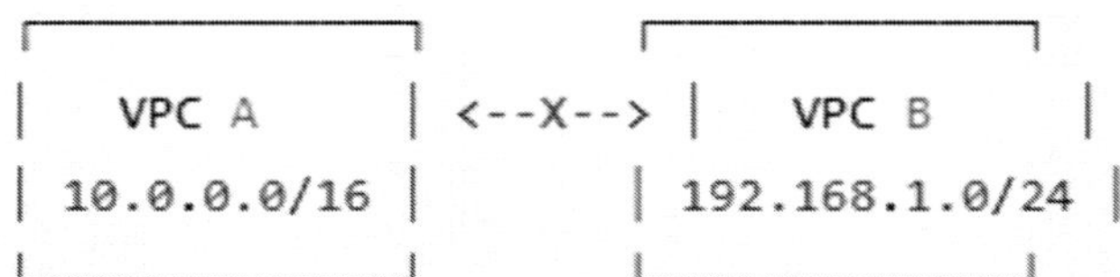

Figure 4.11: *Misconfigured VPC Peering*

Traffic is blocked because VPC A is missing a route for VPC B.

- **Private Subnets Lacking Internet Access**

  Cause:

  - No NAT gateway or internet gateway is configured.
  - Security groups or NACLs blocking outbound connections.

  Impact:

  - Private instances cannot download updates or communicate with external services.

  Fix:

  - Attach a NAT gateway for outbound traffic.
  - Add the correct route:

    aws ec2 create-route --route-table-id rtb-xyz789 --destination-cidr-block 0.0.0.0/0 --nat-gateway-id nat-abc123

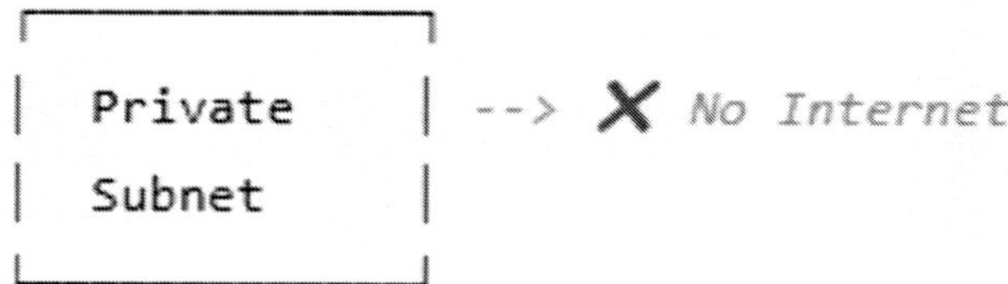

Figure 4.12: *No NAT Gateway for Private Subnet*

Traffic is dropped because there is no NAT gateway.

- **AWS Transit Gateway Misconfigurations**

  Cause:
  - Route tables for Transit Gateway do not contain the correct VPC routes.
  - Missing propagation settings.

  Impact:
  - Multi-VPC architectures cannot communicate properly.

  Fix:
  - Check Transit Gateway routes: **aws ec2 describe-transit-gateway-route-tables**
  - Ensure all VPCs are correctly associated.

  Associations and propagations can be verified under VPC -> Transit Gateway Route Tables -> Associations/Propagations tabs.

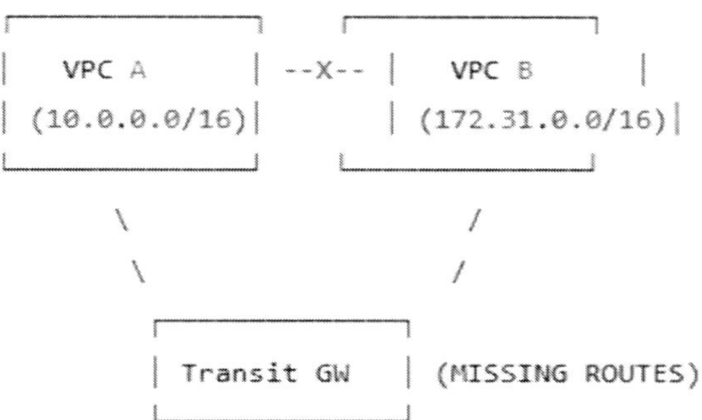

Figure 4.13: *Transit Gateway Routing Issue*

Traffic fails due to missing route propagation.

Troubleshoot Routing Issues in AWS:

- **Use AWS Reachability Analyzer**
  - Identifies missing routes, blocked security groups, or ACL misconfigurations.
  - Run the analysis: **`aws ec2 start-network-insights-analysis --network-insights-path-id nip-xyz123`**
- **Analyze VPC Flow Logs**
  - Detects dropped packets due to routing issues.
  - Enable logging: **`aws ec2 create-flow-logs --resource-id vpc-xyz123 --traffic-type REJECT`**

REJECT logs with reason = **`BLACKHOLE_ROUTE`** often indicate missing routes.

- **Verify Route Tables**
  - List all routes: **`aws ec2 describe-route-tables`**
  - Check if the correct gateway, NAT, or VPC Peering routes exist.

Misconfigured routing is a critical issue that can block communication, increase latency, and disrupt AWS services. By understanding route tables, VPC peering, NAT gateways, and AWS Transit Gateway, administrators can prevent and fix routing issues efficiently.

Key Takeaways:

- Use AWS Reachability Analyzer to detect misconfigured routes.

- Ensure correct VPC peering and Transit Gateway route propagation.
- Enable VPC Flow Logs to analyze rejected traffic.
- Monitor AWS CloudWatch for dropped packets and routing failures.

Proactive Recommendation: Regularly audit routing configurations using AWS Config and IAM Change Manager to prevent accidental misconfigurations

Network Diagnostic Commands in AWS

In cloud networking, where multiple components—such as EC2 instances, VPCs, security groups, NAT gateways, and load balancers—work together, network failures and performance issues can arise due to misconfigurations, latency, or external connectivity problems. Diagnosing these issues quickly and efficiently is critical to maintaining smooth network operations.

AWS provides powerful network monitoring tools such as CloudWatch, VPC Flow Logs, and AWS Network Analyzer Tools, but command-line diagnostic utilities remain essential for real-time troubleshooting of network connectivity. Diagnostic commands allow administrators to test connections, trace network paths, and capture traffic packets to pinpoint performance bottlenecks and security threats.

In this section, we introduce key network diagnostic commands, their importance in troubleshooting, and how they are used in AWS environments.

Network diagnostic commands are CLI-based tools used to analyze and troubleshoot network connectivity, latency, and packet transmission issues. These commands help AWS administrators and DevOps teams quickly identify the root cause of network failures, misconfigurations, and performance bottlenecks in cloud-based systems.

The significance of Network Diagnostic Commands is as follows:

- Quickly detect connectivity issues between AWS instances and external networks.
- Identify packet loss, high latency, and routing errors in real-time.
- Test firewall and security group configurations to ensure correct access controls.
- Capture and analyze network traffic to detect suspicious or unauthorized activity.
- Validate DNS resolution and IP reachability for troubleshooting domain-related issues.

Network Diagnostic Commands in AWS

Some diagnostic commands (like ping, traceroute) might require elevated privileges or specific VPC configurations in AWS.

AWS administrators commonly use the following three diagnostic commands for network troubleshooting:

COMMAND	PRIMARY FUNCTION	BEST USED FOR
Ping	Tests connectivity and packet loss between two hosts.	Checking if an instance can reach another server (internal or external).
Traceroute (Linux) / Tracert (Windows)	Maps the path that packets take from source to destination.	Identifying network latency and routing issues.
Packet Capture Tools (tcpdump, Wireshark, AWS VPC Traffic Mirroring)	Captures and analyzes network traffic at a granular level.	Deep inspection of network packets to detect anomalies or security threats.

Table 4.12: *Key Diagnostic Commands Used in AWS*

Each tool plays a unique role in troubleshooting different network-related problems, and they are often used together for a comprehensive network analysis.

AWS instances operate within a Virtual Private Cloud (VPC), meaning network connectivity depends on security groups, network ACLs, routing tables, and NAT gateways. Using diagnostic commands inside an AWS EC2 instance or from an on-premises system connecting to AWS helps administrators troubleshoot and resolve common network issues such as:

- **Instance Connectivity Failures** → Use ping to verify reachability.
- **Slow Network Performance** → Use traceroute to analyze routing paths.
- **Packet Loss and Unexpected Traffic** → Use tcpdump to capture and inspect packets.
- **Blocked Access by Security Groups or ACLs** → Use ping and traceroute to test firewall rules.
- **DNS Resolution Issues** → Use nslookup or dig (in addition to traceroute).

Network diagnostic commands are fundamental troubleshooting tools in AWS cloud networking. They provide immediate insights into network health, connectivity, and potential misconfigurations. By using ping, traceroute, and packet capture tools, AWS administrators can quickly identify and resolve network failures, optimize performance, and secure cloud environments.

Ping Command

Ping is a command-line utility used to test network connectivity between two devices by sending Internet Control Message Protocol (ICMP) Echo Request packets to a target host and measuring the response time.

Note: *ICMP is not a transport protocol but a control protocol.*

The ping command working is depicted as follows:

1. The sender executes the ping command with the IP address or hostname of the target.
2. ICMP Echo Request packets are sent to the target system.
3. If the target is reachable, it responds with an ICMP Echo Reply.
4. The sender calculates Round-Trip Time (RTT) and packet loss percentage to assess network performance.

Ping in AWS

AWS environments rely on security groups, network ACLs, and routing tables to manage network traffic. The Ping command helps identify network reachability issues caused by misconfigurations in these components. By default, ICMP Echo is blocked between VPCs unless explicitly allowed by security groups or NACLs.

The key benefits of Ping in AWS are given as follows:

- Verifies if an EC2 instance or database is reachable from another AWS resource or external network.
- Detects packet loss indicating network congestion or firewall restrictions.
- Measures latency (round-trip time, RTT) to evaluate network performance.
- Helps test connectivity before deploying applications to ensure proper routing.

The Ping command is available on Linux, Mac, and Windows systems and can be executed from:

- An AWS EC2 instance (Linux or Windows).
- An on-premises system connected to AWS.

- A third-party machine accessing AWS services.

The basic Ping syntax is as follows:

```
ping <destination-IP or hostname>
```

Example 1: Pinging an External Website from an AWS EC2 Instance

To check if an EC2 instance has internet access:

```
ping google.com (e.g., $ ping google.com)
```

Output:

PING google.com (142.250.182.238) 56(84) bytes of data.

64 bytes from 142.250.182.238: icmp_seq=1 ttl=115 time=32.5 ms

64 bytes from 142.250.182.238: icmp_seq=2 ttl=115 time=31.8 ms

- If responses are received, the EC2 instance has outbound internet access.
- If packets are lost, check if an internet gateway (IGW) is configured for the VPC.

Example 2: Pinging another EC2 Instance Within the Same VPC

```
ping 10.0.1.15
```

The following table provides the possible Outcomes and Interpretations:

PING OUTPUT	MEANING	POSSIBLE FIX
Reply received ✅	Instance is reachable	No issues detected
Request timed out ❌	Network ACL or security group blocking traffic	Allow inbound ICMP traffic
Destination host unreachable ❌	No route to the target system	Check route tables and VPC peering

Table 4.13: *Possible Outcomes and Interpretations*

Troubleshooting Network Issues

Some of the scenarios, ping commands, expected outcomes and possible fixes are listed in the following table:

SCENARIO	COMMAND	EXPECTED OUTCOME	POSSIBLE FIX
EC2 instance cannot access the internet	ping google.com	Request timed out	Attach an **Internet Gateway (IGW)**, update **NACLs**
EC2 instance cannot reach another EC2 in the same VPC	ping <target-private-IP>	Destination host unreachable	Allow **ICMP traffic** in **security groups**
High latency detected in API calls	ping api.example.com	RTT > 100ms	Optimize **Route 53 routing** or **use AWS Global Accelerator**

Table 4.14: *Troubleshooting Network Issues with Ping Command*

Limitations of Ping in AWS

- **Security Groups:**
  - Allow inbound ICMP Echo Request from the source IP.

```
aws ec2 authorize-security-group-ingress --group-id sg-12345678 --protocol
icmp --port -1 --cidr 0.0.0.0/0
```

  - If Ping fails, ensure that the security group of the destination allows ICMP traffic.
- **Network ACLs:**
  - Ensure that the Network ACL attached to the VPC subnet allows inbound and outbound ICMP traffic.
  - If ICMP is blocked at the NACL level, Ping will fail even if security groups allow it.
- **Route Tables:**
  - Check if a valid route exists between the source and destination. Use the AWS Reachability Analyzer to confirm network paths.

The port -1 in the CLI example allows all ICMP types - this might confuse beginners otherwise. Excessive Ping use for continuous monitoring can cause throttling or ICMP rate-limits in some AWS regions.

The Ping command remains one of the simplest yet most effective tools for verifying network connectivity, detecting packet loss, and measuring latency in AWS environments. While AWS blocks Ping by default, proper security groups and NACL configurations can allow ICMP for internal testing. However, for more advanced troubleshooting, administrators should complement Ping with other tools such as Traceroute, Netcat, and AWS Reachability Analyzer.

Traceroute Command: Analyzing Network Paths and Latency in AWS

In modern cloud environments, where applications span multiple regions, availability zones, and virtual networks, diagnosing connectivity issues and performance bottlenecks is essential. Unlike traditional data centers, AWS networks rely on security groups, network ACLs, private IP routing, and peering connections to manage traffic flows. When an instance or service experiences slow response times or intermittent failures, identifying the exact point of failure requires more than just basic connectivity tests.

The Traceroute command (tracert in Windows) is an advanced network diagnostic tool that maps the path data packets take from source to destination. It provides insights into each hop in the network, measuring latency and pinpointing network disruptions. In AWS, where traffic may traverse multiple internal and external network layers, Traceroute helps in diagnosing routing issues, firewall blocks, and high-latency connections. Traceroute uses ICMP (Windows) or UDP (Linux/macOS) by default.

This section explores the Traceroute command, its significance in AWS network troubleshooting, and real-world applications for performance analysis.

Understanding Traceroute

Traceroute is a command-line tool that traces the route packets take from a source system to a destination by identifying each intermediate router or network node along the way. Unlike the Ping command, which only verifies connectivity, Traceroute reveals the exact network path, helping administrators analyze network latency, bottlenecks, and misconfigured routes.

The Traceroute command works as follows:

- The command sends small data packets with a low Time-To-Live (TTL) value to the target destination.
- Each router in the path decreases the TTL value and, when it reaches zero, the router sends an ICMP “Time Exceeded” message back to the sender.

- The process repeats, increasing the TTL until the destination is reached, mapping all intermediate hops.
- TTL increments allow identifying the response time of each hop.
- Traceroute displays the IP address, hostname (if available), and response time (latency in milliseconds) of each hop.

Importance of Traceroute in AWS

AWS networks operate differently from traditional on-premises infrastructure, making Traceroute essential for troubleshooting cloud-based networking issues. Traceroute does not work with PrivateLink endpoints (traffic remains within AWS backbone, hops not exposed).

It helps in:

- Identifying network latency between EC2 instances, databases, and API endpoints.
- Diagnosing slow connections caused by inefficient routing or overloaded network paths.
- Detecting packet loss indicating possible firewall restrictions or misconfigured security groups.
- Validating VPC peering connections and private link routes.
- Analyzing external traffic flow from AWS to third-party services.

Traceroute can be executed from an AWS EC2 instance, an on-premises system, or a third-party network accessing AWS services. The command differs slightly between Linux/macOS (traceroute) and Windows (tracert).

Basic Syntax:

Linux/macOS: `traceroute <destination-IP or hostname>`

Windows: `tracert <destination-IP or hostname>`

Using Traceroute for AWS Network Troubleshooting

It is recommended to combine Traceroute results with VPC Flow Logs or Reachability Analyzer output for verification.

Example 1: Tracing a Route from an EC2 Instance to an External Website

To verify if an AWS instance has proper internet routing:

```
traceroute google.com
```

Expected Output:

```
1  ip-172-31-1-1.ec2.internal (172.31.1.1)  1.234 ms  1.567 ms  1.789 ms
2  * * * Request timed out
3  52.93.15.123 (52.93.15.123)  15.321 ms  14.890 ms  15.007 ms
4  142.251.45.1 (142.251.45.1)  30.123 ms  30.567 ms  31.456 ms
```

- The first hop (172.31.1.1) represents the private AWS VPC router.
- The third hop (52.93.15.123) is an AWS public network gateway.
- The final hop (142.251.45.1) is the network of Google, confirming successful connectivity.
- If the second hop times out, it may indicate an issue with outbound internet routing or security groups blocking ICMP traffic.

Example 2: Tracing the Route between Two EC2 Instances in Different VPCs

If an application running on EC2 in VPC-A cannot connect to EC2 in VPC-B, Traceroute can identify blocked routes or misconfigured VPC peering.

```
traceroute 10.0.2.15
```

Expected Output:

```
1  ip-10-0-1-1.ec2.internal (10.0.1.1)  1.123 ms  1.567 ms  1.789 ms
2  ip-10-0-2-1.ec2.internal (10.0.2.1)  12.345 ms  12.678 ms  13.001 ms
3  ip-10-0-2-15.ec2.internal (10.0.2.15)  14.123 ms  14.456 ms  14.678 ms
```

- If all hops respond, VPC peering and route tables are correctly configured.
- If the second hop times out, check if VPC peering, route tables, or security groups are blocking traffic.

Limitations of Traceroute in AWS

Ping confirms reachability, while Traceroute explains why reachability might fail. While Traceroute is effective for network path analysis, AWS-specific limitations can affect its accuracy:

- **ICMP Blocking in AWS Security Groups**
  - AWS blocks ICMP (Ping and Traceroute) by default.
  - To use Traceroute within a VPC, allow outbound ICMP traffic in security groups.
- **Private IP Routing in AWS**
  - Traceroute may not show all internal AWS hops because AWS optimizes internal routes.
  - Use VPC Flow Logs for deeper insight into intra-VPC network traffic.
- **Firewalls and Network ACLs Impacting Results**
  - If network ACLs block outbound traffic, Traceroute may show timeouts instead of real network hops.

Traceroute is a powerful diagnostic tool that helps AWS administrators analyze network paths, troubleshoot slow connections, and identify routing issues. While AWS-specific security restrictions can impact results, combining Traceroute with AWS tools such as VPC Flow Logs and Reachability Analyzer ensures a comprehensive approach to network troubleshooting.

Packet Capture Tools: Deep Network Traffic Analysis in AWS

Modern cloud environments rely on complex networking architectures where traffic flows between Virtual Private Clouds (VPCs), public endpoints, internal databases, and third-party APIs. When performance issues, security incidents, or unexpected network behaviors arise, basic diagnostic tools such as Ping and Traceroute may not provide enough detail. In such cases, administrators need packet capture tools to perform in-depth traffic analysis, detect anomalies, and troubleshoot connectivity issues at a granular level.

Packet capture tools provide real-time visibility into network traffic, allowing AWS administrators to inspect individual packets, analyze source-destination flows, and detect security threats such as unauthorized access or data exfiltration. In AWS, network packet capture can be achieved using built-in and third-party tools, including tcpdump, Wireshark, AWS VPC Traffic Mirroring, and AWS Network Firewall logging.

Understanding Packet Capture Tools

Packet capture tools intercept network packets in real-time and store them for analysis. Unlike Ping or Traceroute, which only provide connectivity and routing insights, packet capture tools examine actual data transmissions, including headers, payloads, and flags.

Significance of Packet Capture Tools:

- Detects unauthorized network activity, such as malware communication or data breaches.
- Troubleshoots performance bottlenecks by identifying dropped or delayed packets.
- Analyzes API traffic and application failures, ensuring requests and responses are correctly processed.
- Validates security policies by examining firewall and security group rule effectiveness.
- Provides forensic evidence in case of cybersecurity incidents or compliance audits.

Common Packet Capture Tools in AWS

Each tool provides a different level of packet analysis, ranging from real-time traffic sniffing (tcpdump and Wireshark) to automated security monitoring (VPC Traffic Mirroring and GuardDuty).

TOOL	PURPOSE	BEST USE CASE
Tcpdump	CLI-based network packet capture	Debugging network issues on EC2 instances
Wireshark	GUI-based deep packet inspection	Analyzing traffic patterns and security threats
AWS VPC Traffic Mirroring	Captures all network traffic from AWS instances	Monitoring unauthorized traffic and threat detection
AWS Network Firewall Logging	Logs and inspects traffic allowed or blocked by firewalls	Compliance auditing and security analysis
Amazon GuardDuty	Detects anomalies based on network flow data	Threat detection using machine learning

Table 4.15: *Common Packet Capture Tools*

Let us dive into how to use Packet Capture Tools in AWS.

Capturing Network Traffic with tcpdump on AWS EC2

tcpdump is a lightweight, command-line tool used to capture and analyze packets on Linux-based AWS instances. (Useful for debugging intra-VPC connectivity or SSL traffic).

Basic Syntax: `sudo tcpdump -i eth0`

- eth0 is the primary network interface for an AWS EC2 instance.
- Output shows captured packets in real-time.

Example Output:

```
12:34:56.789 IP 10.0.1.25.443 > 10.0.2.30.51000: Flags [P], seq 1:512, ack 1, win 1024
12:34:56.890 IP 10.0.2.30.51000 > 10.0.1.25.443: Flags [.] ack 512, win 8192
```

- Shows HTTPS communication (port 443) between two private IPs in AWS.
- Confirms data packets are successfully exchanged.

Saving Packets for Later Analysis -> `sudo tcpdump -i eth0 -w capture.pcap`

- Captures packets and saves them in PCAP format for Wireshark analysis.

Analyzing Packets with Wireshark

Wireshark is a GUI-based packet analysis tool used to visualize network traffic, filter specific packets, and detect anomalies.

Steps to Analyze AWS Traffic with Wireshark:

1. **Capture packets on an EC2 instance using tcpdump:** `sudo tcpdump -i eth0 -w /tmp/aws-traffic.pcap`
2. **Download the file to your local machine:** `scp -i mykey.pem ec2-user@your-aws-instance:/tmp/aws-traffic.pcap.`
3. Open the **`.pcap`** file in Wireshark for deep inspection.
4. **Use filters to analyze specific traffic (like show only failed TCP connections):** `tcp.flags.reset == 1`

Wireshark helps detect misconfigurations, application failures, and suspicious traffic patterns.

Do not capture sensitive production data unless compliant with company policies.

Capturing AWS Network Traffic with VPC Traffic Mirroring

- VPC Flow Logs capture traffic metadata (IP, ports, accept/reject) and are ideal for network troubleshooting, monitoring, and compliance.
- Traffic Mirroring captures full packet data (including payloads) and is used for deep packet inspection, threat detection, and forensic analysis.
- AWS VPC Traffic Mirroring allows administrators to mirror network traffic from EC2 instances to a monitoring tool for real-time analysis.

How It Works:

- **Select the Source Instance:** Choose an EC2 instance to monitor.
- **Configure a Target Destination:** Use an EC2-based traffic analysis tool (including Wireshark, security appliance).
- **Apply Filters:** Capture only relevant traffic (like only rejected packets).
- **Monitor and Analyze Traffic:** Detect security threats, unauthorized access, or misrouted packets.

VPC Traffic Mirroring is ideal for continuous security monitoring and compliance auditing.

Logging and Inspecting Firewall Traffic with AWS Network Firewall

AWS Network Firewall provides detailed logs of allowed and blocked traffic, enabling administrators to audit security policies and detect malicious activity.

Enabling Firewall Logging:

- Go to AWS Network Firewall Console.
- Enable Logging to send data to CloudWatch Logs or S3.
- Analyze Firewall Logs using AWS Athena or SIEM tools.

Useful for monitoring blocked requests, intrusion attempts, and compliance reporting.

Limitations of Packet Capture in AWS

While packet capture tools provide deep insights into network activity, they come with some challenges in AWS environments:

- **Limited Direct Access to AWS Infrastructure**
  - AWS does not provide direct access to underlying network hardware, which means packet capture is limited to EC2 instances.
  - To capture broader network traffic across multiple instances or subnets, AWS Traffic Mirroring must be used.
- **High Data Volumes Can be Costly**
  - Packet capture can generate very large data volumes. For example, capturing 1 Gbps of traffic continuously can produce over 10 TB of data per day, leading to significant S3 storage and processing costs.
  - To manage this, apply filters to capture only relevant protocols, ports, or traffic sources.
- **Security Groups and NACLs May Block Capture Attempts**
  - Security groups and network ACLs may block inbound or outbound traffic required for packet capture tools to function correctly.
  - Ensure that required ports and protocols are explicitly allowed for capture and analysis systems.

Proactive Monitoring in AWS

In modern cloud environments, where applications demand high availability, low latency, and seamless connectivity, reactive troubleshooting is not enough. Proactive monitoring is essential to prevent network failures before they occur, ensuring that businesses maintain uninterrupted operations and optimal performance.

AWS provides powerful monitoring tools that enable administrators to track critical network metrics, analyze real-time logs, and set automated alerts when predefined thresholds are breached. These tools allow organizations to detect anomalies, prevent outages, and optimize network resources in real-time.

This section explores the importance of proactive monitoring in AWS, key network metrics to track, and how automated alerting can help maintain a resilient cloud infrastructure.

Understanding Proactive Monitoring

Proactive monitoring involves continuous observation of network traffic, latency, packet loss, and system health to identify potential issues before they escalate into failures. By setting automated thresholds and alerts, administrators can respond to anomalies in real-time, reducing downtime and improving overall network efficiency.

Example Use Case: Detecting DNS latency before user complaints.

Significance of Proactive Monitoring in AWS

The significance of proactive monitoring in AWS is mentioned as follows:

- Prevents outages by detecting early warning signs of network failures.
- Optimizes performance by identifying high-latency routes and bandwidth constraints.
- Enhances security by flagging unusual traffic spikes or unauthorized access attempts.
- Reduces operational costs by detecting inefficient resource usage.
- Ensures compliance by continuously tracking network logs and policy violations.

Unlike reactive monitoring, where issues are addressed after they impact operations, proactive monitoring helps AWS teams mitigate risks before users experience disruptions.

Key Components of Proactive Network Monitoring in AWS

AWS provides a suite of monitoring and alerting tools that help track, analyze, and respond to network changes in real-time.

COMPONENT	PURPOSE	BEST USED FOR
Amazon CloudWatch	Collects and visualizes network performance metrics.	Monitoring bandwidth usage, latency, and network traffic trends.
AWS CloudTrail	Captures API activity and user actions.	Detecting unauthorized access and security incidents.
VPC Flow Logs	Logs network traffic at the VPC, subnet, and ENI levels.	Identifying blocked connections and analyzing packet loss.
AWS Network Firewall	Monitors and filters network traffic based on security policies.	Preventing unauthorized access and tracking firewall rule effectiveness.
AWS Security Hub	Aggregates and analyzes security-related data across AWS services.	Detecting threats, misconfigurations, and compliance violations.
Amazon Route 53 Health Checks	Monitors DNS resolution and endpoint availability.	Ensuring public and private applications remain accessible.

Table 4.16: *Components of Proactive Network Monitoring*

By combining these tools, AWS administrators can establish a proactive monitoring strategy that detects and mitigates network issues before they impact business operations.

Working of Proactive Monitoring in AWS

The working of Proactive Monitoring in AWS is as mentioned:

- **Define Critical Network Metrics:** Identify Key Performance Indicators (KPIs) such as latency, bandwidth utilization, packet loss, and error rates.
- **Set Thresholds and Alerts:** Configure CloudWatch Alarms, SNS Notifications, and AWS Lambda automation to trigger actions when thresholds are exceeded.
- **Analyze Traffic Logs:** Use VPC Flow Logs and CloudTrail to track traffic anomalies and security breaches.
- **Enable Automated Responses:** Integrate AWS Lambda with CloudWatch to execute self-healing actions, such as restarting instances or modifying routing tables.
- **Continuously Optimize Network Performance:** Regularly refine network security policies, routing rules, and firewall settings based on monitoring insights.

Proactive monitoring ensures continuous network visibility, allowing AWS teams to stay ahead of failures, optimize performance, and enhance security.

Proactive monitoring in AWS prevents failures before they disrupt business operations. By leveraging CloudWatch, VPC Flow Logs, AWS Firewall, and automated alerts, administrators can detect, diagnose, and resolve network issues in real-time.

The next section will explore how to set up alerts and thresholds for critical network metrics in AWS, ensuring automated responses to potential failures before they escalate.

Setting Alerts and Thresholds for Critical Network Metrics in AWS

Cloud networks must remain highly available, secure, and optimized for performance. Even a small misconfiguration or a sudden traffic surge can lead to latency issues, packet loss, service disruptions, or security vulnerabilities. To prevent such failures, AWS provides automated alerting and threshold-based monitoring, enabling administrators to respond to issues before they impact business operations.

By configuring CloudWatch Alarms, VPC Flow Logs, AWS Lambda automation, and SNS notifications, AWS administrators can track critical network metrics, detect anomalies, and take corrective actions in real-time.

Advanced Monitoring Capability: Anomaly Detection

Instead of relying solely on fixed thresholds, CloudWatch also supports Anomaly Detection, which uses machine learning models to establish dynamic baselines for metrics such as latency, packet drops, and traffic volume. This approach is especially useful in environments with fluctuating workloads, where static thresholds may generate false alarms or miss subtle issues.

Defining Critical Network Metrics and Thresholds

The first step in proactive monitoring is to identify key network performance indicators (KPIs) and establish thresholds that define acceptable limits. When a metric crosses its threshold, an alert is triggered, allowing administrators to investigate and take action immediately.

AWS provides several network performance indicators that should be continuously tracked.

Metric	Description	Recommended Threshold
NetworkIn / NetworkOut	Measures the volume of incoming/ outgoing traffic on an EC2 instance.	Alert when traffic exceeds **80% of available bandwidth.**
NetworkPacketsIn / NetworkPacketsOut	Tracks the number of packets sent and received.	Alert on **sudden packet drops or spikes.**
CPUUtilization	Measures how heavily an instance is processing requests.	Alert if CPU exceeds **90% for 5+ minutes** (could indicate a DDoS attack).
Latency (Amazon Route 53)	Tracks DNS response times and endpoint health.	Alert if response time exceeds **500ms** for public endpoints.
Flow Logs: ACCEPT/ DENY	Monitors traffic allowed or rejected by security groups.	Alert on **unusual denied requests from unknown IPs.**
VPC NAT Gateway Metrics	Tracks the utilization and throughput of NAT gateways.	Alert when **connections exceed the limit or latency spikes.**

Table 4.17: *Key Network Metrics to Monitor*

These metrics help AWS teams detect anomalies in real-time, ensuring that network failures and security threats are addressed immediately.

Configuring Alerts Using Amazon CloudWatch Alarms

Amazon CloudWatch allows administrators to set thresholds for network metrics and trigger alerts when values exceed predefined limits.

Steps to Create a CloudWatch Alarm for Network Latency:

1. Go to the CloudWatch Console in AWS.

2. Navigate to **`Alarms`** → Click **`Create Alarm`**.
3. Select a Network Metric (like "NetworkOut" for an EC2 instance).
4. Define the Threshold Condition (such as trigger an alarm when outgoing traffic exceeds 1 GB per minute).
5. Set Actions for the Alarm:
    a. Send an SNS Notification to alert administrators.
    b. Trigger an AWS Lambda function to mitigate the issue.
    c. Auto-scale instances if network congestion is detected.
6. Review and Create the Alarm.

Once activated, CloudWatch continuously monitors the metric and sends alerts if the threshold is exceeded.

CLI Example (For Automation and IaC Workflows)

```
aws cloudwatch put-metric-alarm \
  --alarm-name HighNetworkOut \
  --metric-name NetworkOut \
  --namespace AWS/EC2 \
  --statistic Average \
  --period 60 \
  --evaluation-periods 5 \
  --threshold 1000000000 \
  --comparison-operator GreaterThanThreshold \
  --alarm-actions arn:aws:sns:us-east-1:123456789012:NotifyAdmin \
  --dimensions Name=InstanceId,Value=i-0123456789abcdef0 \
  --region us-east-1
```

Explanation:

- period 60 → Metric checked every 60 seconds
- evaluation-periods 5 → Alarm triggers after 5 consecutive datapoints
- threshold 1000000000 → 1 GB network output
- alarm-actions → Sends notification via SNS

Setting up AWS SNS for Real-Time Notifications

AWS Simple Notification Service (SNS) sends alerts via email, SMS, or integration with third-party monitoring tools when a CloudWatch alarm is triggered.

Note: *IAM permissions required for CloudWatch -> SNS integration.*

How to Configure SNS for Network Alerts:

1. Go to the SNS Console → Click **`Create Topic`**.
2. Set Topic Name (say **`network-alerts-topic`**).
3. Create an SNS Subscription → Choose **`Email`** or **`SMS`** as the notification type.
4. Add Subscribers (Admins or DevOps Teams) to receive alerts.
5. Link SNS Topic to CloudWatch Alarm for automatic notifications.

Whenever network issues arise, SNS instantly notifies the responsible team, allowing for immediate action.

Automating Incident Response with AWS Lambda

Instead of just sending alerts, AWS can take automated corrective actions when a threshold is breached. AWS Lambda functions can be configured to respond to network failures without manual intervention.

Example: Automatically Restart an EC2 Instance on High Packet Loss

- CloudWatch detects excessive packet loss.
- Alarm triggers an SNS notification.
- SNS invokes an AWS Lambda function that restarts the instance.

AWS Lambda Function to Restart an EC2 Instance

```
import boto3

def lambda_handler(event, context):
    ec2 = boto3.client('ec2')
    instance_id = 'i-0abcd1234efgh5678'  # Replace with actual instance ID

    # Restart the instance
    ec2.reboot_instances(InstanceIds=[instance_id])

    return f"EC2 Instance {instance_id} restarted due to high packet loss"
```

This ensures the instance is automatically restarted before users experience connectivity issues.

Monitoring Traffic Logs with AWS VPC Flow Logs

AWS VPC Flow Logs capture detailed network traffic information, helping administrators detect suspicious activity, denied connections, and unusual traffic patterns. Flow Logs do not capture packet content (only metadata).

Enabling VPC Flow Logs for Security Monitoring:

1. Go to the VPC Console → Select the target VPC, Subnet, or Network Interface.
2. Click `Create Flow Log`.
3. Choose Log Destination (CloudWatch or S3).
4. Apply Filters (capture all, accepted, or rejected traffic).
5. Enable Logging and analyze data using AWS Athena or CloudWatch Logs Insights.

VPC Flow Logs provide deep insights into network behavior, enabling proactive security measures.

Best Practices for Setting up Alerts and Thresholds

The following are the best practices for setting up alerts and thresholds:

- Set alerts for critical metrics only to avoid unnecessary notifications.
- Use anomaly detection in CloudWatch to track unusual traffic spikes.
- Combine multiple monitoring tools (CloudTrail, VPC Flow Logs, and CloudWatch) for better insights.

- Regularly review and refine thresholds to adapt to evolving network conditions.
- Use automation (Lambda + SNS) to trigger self-healing actions and reduce manual intervention.

Proactive monitoring in AWS is only effective when paired with well-defined alerts and thresholds. By leveraging CloudWatch Alarms, VPC Flow Logs, AWS Lambda, and SNS notifications, administrators can automate responses, prevent downtime, and enhance security before issues escalate.

By continuously refining monitoring strategies and leveraging AWS automation, businesses can maintain high-performance cloud networks while ensuring security and reliability.

Case Studies

The following are real-world case studies demonstrating how AWS tools and diagnostic commands were used to monitor, troubleshoot, and optimize network performance across different environments.

Amazon CloudWatch for Proactive Network Monitoring

Case Study 1: Optimizing Network Performance for a Global E-commerce Platform

Challenge:

A global e-commerce company noticed intermittent slow page loads and checkout failures in different regions. Users reported high latency and unresponsive payment gateways, leading to cart abandonment and revenue loss.

Solution:

- Amazon CloudWatch was deployed to monitor key network metrics, including:
  - NetworkIn and NetworkOut to measure bandwidth consumption.
  - Latency metrics for API Gateway to track request delays.
  - CloudWatch Alarms configured to detect API response times exceeding 500ms.
- Route 53 Health Checks were enabled to monitor DNS resolution and endpoint health.
- CloudWatch Logs Insights was used to analyze historical trends and detect traffic surges.

Outcome:

- Detected API Gateway congestion during peak shopping hours.
- Enabled auto-scaling of API Gateway instances based on CloudWatch metrics.
- Reduced page load times from 1.2s to 400ms and checkout errors by 70%.

VPC Flow Logs for Network Security and Compliance

Case Study 2: Detecting Unauthorized Access Attempts in a Financial Institution

Challenge:

A financial services company detected suspicious login attempts on its AWS-hosted banking application. The security team needed to investigate if the attempts were from legitimate users or malicious actors.

Solution:

- VPC Flow Logs were enabled at the subnet level to track all inbound and outbound traffic.
- Logs were stored in CloudWatch Logs and analyzed using AWS Athena.

- CloudWatch Alarms were set up to trigger alerts on repeated failed login attempts.
- Security Hub and GuardDuty were integrated to correlate findings and detect anomalies.

Outcome:

- Identified multiple login attempts from an unknown IP address in a high-risk country.
- Blocked the IP address in AWS WAF, preventing further intrusion attempts.
- Enhanced security group rules to restrict access only to trusted IP ranges.
- Maintained compliance with banking regulations by logging and auditing security events.

Retention and Compliance Note

To meet banking and regulatory compliance requirements (such as PCI DSS and internal audit policies), VPC Flow Logs were archived to Amazon S3 and retained for 365 days. This ensured long-term auditability, forensic investigation capability, and compliance with data retention mandates.

AWS Network Analyzer Tools for Troubleshooting Connectivity Issues

Case Study 3: Diagnosing Cross-VPC Connection Failures in a SaaS Application

(Reachability Analyzer identifies both security group and route issues)

Challenge:

A SaaS company experienced frequent connection failures between EC2 instances in different VPCs. Users faced session timeouts when accessing multi-region application services.

Solution:

- AWS Reachability Analyzer was used to trace network paths between EC2 instances.
- AWS Network Manager was enabled to gain a centralized view of the multi-region AWS architecture of the company.
- CloudTrail logs were analyzed to check for unauthorized modifications to security groups or route tables.

Outcome:

- Identified missing route table entries for VPC peering connections.
- Updated route tables and verified successful packet transmission between instances.
- Reduced connection failure rates by 80%, improving user experience.

Diagnostic Commands: Ping, Traceroute, and Packet Capture

Case Study 4: Using Traceroute to Identify Latency Issues in a Video Streaming Service

Challenge:

A video streaming platform faced high buffering times and dropped connections, affecting user engagement.

Solution:

- Traceroute was executed from EC2 instances to analyze routing paths to content delivery endpoints.

- Wireshark and tcpdump were used to capture network packets and detect transmission delays.
- CloudWatch Network Latency Metrics were reviewed to identify spikes in response times.

Outcome:

- Found inefficient routing paths through non-optimal AWS regions.
- Implemented AWS Global Accelerator to route traffic through the lowest-latency path.
- Reduced buffering times by 50%, leading to improved user retention.

Proactive Monitoring: Setting Alerts and Thresholds

Case Study 5: Preventing Network Overloads in a Healthcare Cloud Application

Challenge:

A telemedicine platform experienced unpredictable traffic spikes, leading to network congestion and delayed video consultations.

Solution:

- CloudWatch Alarms were configured to detect high bandwidth usage exceeding 80%.
- SNS notifications were set up to alert DevOps teams on excessive traffic.
- AWS Lambda was integrated to dynamically scale network resources.

Outcome:

- Detected peak traffic patterns during specific consultation hours.
- Dynamically allocated additional EC2 and bandwidth resources during demand surges.
- Maintained 99.99% uptime, ensuring doctors and patients had uninterrupted consultations.

By continuously analyzing VPC Flow Logs and correlating them with security services, the organization shifted from reactive incident response after breaches occurred to a proactive security posture that detects and prevents threats before they impact operations.

These case studies demonstrate how AWS monitoring and troubleshooting tools help organizations maintain network performance, security, and availability. Whether it is proactively detecting latency issues, preventing security threats, or automating incident responses, AWS provides powerful solutions to optimize cloud networking.

Conclusion

Effective network monitoring and troubleshooting are essential for maintaining high performance, security, and reliability in AWS cloud environments. AWS provides a comprehensive set of tools and techniques to monitor, analyze, and optimize network traffic, detect anomalies, and automate responses to potential failures.

Some of the key topics covered include - Amazon CloudWatch for Real-Time Network Monitoring, VPC Flow Logs for Traffic Analysis and Security, AWS Network Analyzer Tools, Diagnostic Commands (Ping, Traceroute, Packet Capture), Proactive Monitoring with Alerts and Thresholds. By leveraging these tools and strategies, organizations can improve cloud network efficiency, prevent downtime, and secure AWS environments against evolving threats.

Points to Remember

- **Amazon CloudWatch – Proactive Network Monitoring**
  - Collects real-time network metrics (latency, packet loss, bandwidth utilization).
  - Configures CloudWatch Alarms to trigger alerts for unusual traffic patterns.
  - Automates incident response using AWS Lambda and SNS notifications.
  - Integrates with VPC Flow Logs and CloudTrail for complete network visibility.
- **VPC Flow Logs – Security and Traffic Analysis**
  - Captures network traffic metadata at VPC, subnet, or ENI levels.
  - Helps troubleshoot denied connections due to security group or ACL rules.
  - Detects unauthorized access attempts and unusual outbound data transfers.
  - Stores logs in CloudWatch, S3, or Kinesis Firehose for further analysis.
- **AWS Network Analyzer Tools – Diagnosing Routing and Connectivity Issues**
  - AWS Reachability Analyzer traces network paths to detect routing failures.
  - AWS Network Manager provides global visibility across multi-region AWS networks.
  - AWS Global Accelerator optimizes latency and failover handling for global applications.
  - Route 53 Resolver DNS Query Logging/ Route Analyzer troubleshoots DNS resolution failures and latency issues.
- **Diagnostic Commands – Troubleshooting Connectivity Issues**
  - Ping – Verifies basic network connectivity between AWS instances and external servers.
  - Traceroute – Maps network paths and identifies high-latency hops in AWS networking.
  - tcpdump/Wireshark – Captures live network packets for deep traffic analysis.
  - VPC Traffic Mirroring – Mirrors AWS network traffic for real-time monitoring and forensic analysis.
- **Proactive Monitoring – Setting Alerts and Automation**
  - Defines critical network thresholds for performance and security.
  - Uses CloudWatch Alarms to monitor bandwidth, latency, and packet drops.
  - Triggers AWS Lambda functions to auto-scale instances or modify routing rules.
  - Configures AWS SNS notifications to alert teams in case of security threats or failures.

By combining real-time monitoring, automated alerting, and deep traffic analysis, AWS administrators can ensure high availability, security, and optimal performance in cloud networks. Proactive monitoring, coupled with rapid troubleshooting, allows businesses to stay ahead of network failures, optimize resources, and enhance cloud security.

A strong AWS network monitoring strategy ultimately leads to improved reliability, reduced operational costs, and enhanced user experience. In the next chapter, we shall introduce Amazon VPC, the foundation of AWS networking. Also, you will learn to create isolated cloud environments and configure subnets, route tables, and gateways.

CHAPTER 5
Amazon VPC Basics

Introduction

In the modern cloud computing landscape, organizations demand highly secure, scalable, and efficient networking solutions. Amazon Virtual Private Cloud (Amazon VPC) is at the heart of AWS networking, providing users with the ability to create isolated, customizable cloud environments. As the foundation of AWS networking, VPC enables businesses to build robust architectures tailored to their security and performance needs.

With Amazon VPC, users gain complete control over their network configurations, including defining IP address ranges, subnet creation, route table management, and internet connectivity options. Whether deploying a simple web application or a complex multi-tier enterprise solution, VPC ensures seamless communication between resources while maintaining strict security measures.

This chapter aims to provide a comprehensive understanding of Amazon VPC, guiding readers through its core concepts, configurations, and best practices. Readers will learn how to set up isolated cloud networks, create subnets, configure route tables, and implement gateways to enable seamless and secure connectivity. Through step-by-step hands-on exercises, this chapter will empower users to build resilient network architectures, ensuring smooth and controlled traffic flow within their AWS environment.

By mastering the concepts in this chapter, readers will be well-equipped to design, implement, and manage cloud-based networking infrastructures that align with industry standards and organizational requirements. Whether you are an AWS beginner or an experienced cloud architect, this chapter will be a crucial stepping stone toward building a solid networking foundation on AWS.

Structure

In this chapter, we will discuss the following topics:

- VPC Overview
- Subnet Creation
- Route Tables in Amazon VPC
- Gateways in Amazon VPC
- Case Studies

VPC Overview

Amazon Virtual Private Cloud (Amazon VPC) is a fully configurable networking service that enables AWS users to establish a logically isolated virtual network within the AWS cloud. Acting as a dedicated, private section of AWS, a VPC provides users with complete control over their cloud networking infrastructure, including the configuration of subnets, IP address ranges, routing tables, and internet gateways.

With Amazon VPC, organizations can build secure, scalable, and highly available cloud environments tailored to their specific operational and security requirements. This isolation ensures that resources deployed within a VPC remain separate from other users in the AWS ecosystem while allowing seamless integration with other AWS services and on-premises data centers.

Unlike traditional on-premise networks, Amazon VPC removes the complexities of physical network management, enabling rapid provisioning, automation, and dynamic scalability. By using security groups, network Access Control Lists (ACLs), and VPN or Direct Connect integration, users can enforce strict security policies, control data flow, and facilitate hybrid cloud connectivity.

Key Characteristics of Amazon VPC

Here let us look into the key characteristics of Amazon VPC.

- **Complete Network Isolation:** Users have full control over their virtual networking environment, ensuring their resources remain private and secure.
- **Customizable Addressing:** VPC allows users to define their own IP address ranges, using IPv4 and optionally IPv6 addressing, to match organizational needs.
- **Flexible Connectivity Options:** VPCs can connect to the internet, other AWS VPCs, or on-premises networks via Internet Gateways, NAT Gateways, AWS Site-to-Site VPNs, AWS Direct Connect, and VPC Peering.
- **Granular Traffic Control:** Security groups and network ACLs provide precise control over inbound and outbound traffic, ensuring a highly secure cloud environment.
- **Highly Scalable and Fault-Tolerant:** Amazon VPC supports automatic failover mechanisms, load balancing, and multi-AZ deployment for enhanced reliability.
- **Seamless Integration with AWS Services:** VPC enables direct and secure access to AWS services like Amazon EC2, RDS, Lambda, and S3 while ensuring compliance and data security.

By leveraging Amazon VPC, businesses can deploy cloud-based applications with enterprise-grade security, high availability, and optimized performance while maintaining full control over their cloud networking environment.

Use Cases for Amazon VPC

Amazon VPC is widely used across various industries for different cloud computing scenarios. Some key use cases include:

Hosting Multi-Tier Applications

A common scenario in cloud deployments involves multi-tier applications, where different components require varied levels of security and accessibility.

- **Frontend Web Servers:** Placed in public subnets with access to the internet.
- **Application Servers:** Hosted in private subnets, accessible only by the frontend.

- **Database Servers:** Restricted to the private subnet, allowing only application-layer communication.

Benefit: It ensures better security by isolating database and application layers from direct internet access.

Example: An e-commerce website uses a VPC with three layers—public, private, and database subnets—to maintain security and efficiency.

Hybrid Cloud Networking

Organizations with on-premises infrastructure often extend their networks to AWS for scalability and cost-effectiveness.

- **AWS Site-to-Site VPN:** Securely connects an on-premises data center with AWS VPC.
- **AWS Direct Connect:** Establishes a dedicated high-speed connection for stable performance.
- **Peering between VPCs:** Enables secure communication between multiple AWS VPCs.

Benefit: It enables seamless expansion of on-premises networks into the cloud.

Example: A financial institution integrates its data center with AWS using Direct Connect to process high-volume transactions.

Data Analytics and Processing

Organizations leverage AWS for data analysis and large-scale processing while ensuring data security and segmentation.

- **Data Collection Nodes:** Deployed in public subnets for inbound data transfer.
- **Data Processing and Storage:** Hosted in private subnets with limited access.
- **S3 VPC Endpoints:** Used for secure storage without exposing data to the internet.

Benefit: Reduces costs by dynamically scaling analytics workloads within a private, controlled environment.

Example: A healthcare company processes patient records securely within a private VPC environment using AWS Glue and S3 endpoints.

Technical Note: AWS *Glue runs inside a* VPC *only when explicitly configured with* VPC *endpoints and subnet selection. Otherwise, Glue operates in an* AWS*-managed network outside the customer* VPC.

Basic Amazon VPC Architecture

Amazon Virtual Private Cloud (Amazon VPC) forms the foundational networking layer for AWS cloud environments. A well-designed VPC architecture enables users to deploy and manage cloud resources efficiently while ensuring security, scalability, and controlled traffic flow.

Key Components of Basic VPC Architecture

A basic Amazon VPC architecture consists of essential networking elements that define how resources communicate within AWS and with external networks. The following is a detailed breakdown of each component:

Virtual Private Cloud (VPC):

- The primary network container in which AWS resources operate.

- Users can define a CIDR block (for example, 10.0.0.0/16) to allocate private IP address space.
- Provides logical isolation, ensuring dedicated networking control for an AWS account.

Subnets:

- VPC is divided into multiple subnets, each residing in a specific AWS Availability Zone (AZ).
- **Two common types of subnets:**
  - **Public Subnets:** Connected to the internet, typically hosting web servers or bastion hosts.
  - **Private Subnets:** Isolated from direct internet access, used for sensitive workloads like databases.

Route Tables:

- Defines how traffic flows between subnets and external networks.
- Each subnet must be associated with a route table.
- Routes direct network traffic to destinations like internet gateways, NAT gateways, or VPN connections.

Internet Gateway (IGW):

- Provides direct internet connectivity to instances in a public subnet.
- It is attached to the VPC and enables traffic routing between public resources and external networks.

NAT Gateway / NAT Instance:

- Allows instances in a private subnet to access the internet for outbound traffic (for example, downloading software updates).
- Prevents direct inbound internet access to maintain security.

Security Groups & Network ACLs:

- **Security Groups (SGs):** Act as virtual firewalls at the instance level, allowing or blocking traffic based on user-defined rules.
- **Network ACLs (NACLs):** Provide an additional security layer at the subnet level, filtering traffic before it reaches security groups.

Elastic Load Balancer (ELB) (Optional):

Distributes incoming traffic evenly across multiple EC2 instances within a VPC to ensure high availability and scalability.

Virtual Private Gateway (VGW) and AWS Direct Connect (Optional):

- A Virtual Private Gateway (VGW) establishes a secure connection between AWS and an on-premises data center via AWS VPN.
- AWS Direct Connect provides dedicated network connections to AWS for low-latency and high-speed communication.

Basic VPC Architecture Diagram

The following is a simple architectural representation of a basic Amazon VPC setup:

```
+-----------------------------------------------------------+
|                    Amazon VPC (10.0.0.0/16)               |
|-----------------------------------------------------------/
|  +-----------------------+  +-----------------------+     /
|  |    Public Subnet      |  |   Private Subnet      |   |
|  | (10.0.1.0/24)        |  | (10.0.2.0/24)       |  |
|  | Web Servers, Bastion  |  | Database, App Servers |   |
|  +-----------------------+  +-----------------------+   /
|        | (IGW - Internet Access)       | (NAT - Private Access) |
+-----------------------------------------------------------+
```

***Figure 5.1**: Basic VPC Architecture*

Traffic Flow in a Basic VPC Architecture

In a cloud environment, efficient traffic flow management within a Virtual private Cloud (VPC) is essential for maintaining security, performance and connectivity. Understanding how traffic moves within a basic VPC helps in optimizing network design and ensuring seamless communication.

Public Subnet Communication:

Instances in public subnets use an Internet Gateway (IGW) for direct internet access.

Example: A web server hosting a public-facing website.

Private Subnet Communication:

- Instances in private subnets communicate internally within the VPC.
- They can access the internet only via a NAT Gateway/Instance (outbound only).

Example: A database storing confidential customer data.

Inter-Subnet Routing:

Public and private subnets communicate via the internal routing tables of VPC.

Example: A web application (public subnet) interacts with a backend database (private subnet).

Security Enforcement: Security Groups and Network ACLs restrict unauthorized traffic.

Example: A database in a private subnet can only receive queries from an application server in the same VPC.

The following is the table that shows the benefits of Using a Basic VPC Architecture:

BENEFIT	DESCRIPTION
Enhanced Security	Private subnets prevent direct internet access to critical workloads.
Scalability	Subnets and routing can be expanded as network requirements grow.
Custom Control	Users define their own IP ranges, subnet segmentation, and access policies.
High Availability	Multiple Availability Zones ensure redundancy and resilience.
Seamless AWS Integration	Native connectivity with services like EC2, RDS, Lambda, and ELB.

***Table 5.1**: Benefits of Basic VPC Architecture*

A Basic Amazon VPC Architecture provides the necessary foundation for cloud networking by enabling controlled, secure, and efficient connectivity within AWS. By understanding subnet segmentation, routing, security policies, and traffic control mechanisms, organizations can design robust and scalable cloud environments tailored to their operational needs.

Subnet Creation

Subnet creation in Amazon Virtual Private Cloud (VPC) is the process of dividing a VPC into multiple logical segments, known as subnets, to efficiently organize and manage cloud resources. Each subnet is assigned a specific range of IP addresses from the CIDR block of VPC and is associated with a particular AWS Availability Zone (AZ) to ensure redundancy and high availability.

Subnets help in traffic segmentation, network security, and controlled communication between different application components such as web servers, application servers, and databases. AWS enforces logical isolation between subnets, ensuring that resources are only accessible based on defined security policies.

AWS VPC supports two primary types of subnets, each designed to serve specific use cases:

Public Subnets

A public subnet is a subnet that has direct internet access via an Internet Gateway (IGW).

- **Purpose:** Used for public-facing services such as web servers, bastion hosts, and load balancers.
- **Configuration:** Must be associated with a Route Table that directs 0.0.0.0/0 traffic to an IGW.
- **Example Use Case:** Hosting a public-facing website accessible to users worldwide.

Private Subnets

A private subnet is an isolated subnet without direct internet access. It only allows outbound communication via a NAT Gateway or NAT Instance.

- **Purpose:** Used for backend services like databases, application servers, and internal APIs that requires security.
- **Configuration:** Uses a Route Table that directs traffic via a NAT Gateway (for outbound internet access) or stays entirely internal.
- **Example Use Case:** Hosting a database server that should only be accessed by an internal application.

Important Design Notes: CIDR Overlap and Subnet Sizing

- **CIDR Overlap Restrictions:** Subnet CIDR ranges must not overlap within a VPC. Additionally, VPC CIDR blocks must not overlap with on-premises networks or other VPCs if VPC peering, VPN, or Transit Gateway connectivity is planned.
- **Subnet Sizing Considerations:** Choose subnet sizes carefully to allow for future growth. For example, a /28 subnet provides only 16 IP addresses (11 usable for EC2), which may be insufficient for auto-scaling workloads. AWS also reserves 5 IP addresses per subnet, further reducing usable capacity.
- **Best Practice:** Allocate larger subnets (such as /24) for application tiers that may scale and smaller subnets for tightly controlled resources like databases.

Importance of Subnet Creation in AWS VPC

Creating subnets is a critical step in designing a well-structured and scalable cloud network. The following key aspects highlight its importance:

ASPECT	IMPORTANCE
Resource Segmentation	Allows logical separation of workloads (for example, public web servers versus private databases).
Security & Compliance	Public-facing and internal components can be isolated for better access control.
Efficient Traffic Management	Enables optimized routing between instances, reducing latency.
Availability & Fault Tolerance	Spanning subnets across multiple Availability Zones (AZs) ensures high availability.
Cost Optimization	Prevents unnecessary exposure to the internet, minimizing egress charges.
Hybrid Networking	Supports seamless connectivity between on-premises and AWS environments.

Table 5.2: *Importance of Subnet Creation*

Creating a Subnet in AWS VPC

The following is a step-by-step guide to creating a subnet within a VPC:

Step 1: Navigate to VPC Dashboard

1. Log in to the AWS Management Console.
2. Open the VPC Dashboard.
3. Click on **`"Subnets"`** in the navigation pane.
4. Click **`"Create Subnet"`**.

Step 2: Define Subnet Details

1. Select the VPC where the subnet will be created.
2. Choose an Availability Zone (AZ) (for example, us-east-1a).
3. Enter a Subnet Name (for example, Public-Subnet-1).
4. Assign a CIDR Block (for example, 10.0.1.0/24).

Step 3: Configure Routing and Internet Access

1. **For Public Subnets:**
    a. Associate the subnet with a Route Table that directs 0.0.0.0/0 to an Internet Gateway (IGW).
2. **For Private Subnets:**
    a. Ensure that no direct route to the internet is present.
    b. Optionally, configure a NAT Gateway for outbound internet access.

Step 4: Final Review and Creation

1. Click **`"Create Subnet"`** to finalize.
2. Verify the subnet details in the VPC Dashboard.

Some of the key use cases for creating subnets are listed in the following table:

USE CASE	SUBNET TYPE	DESCRIPTION
Hosting Web Applications	Public Subnet	Deploy web servers accessible to external users.
Secure Backend Systems	Private Subnet	Host databases and backend applications securely.
Load Balancing	Public Subnet	Place Elastic Load Balancers (ELB) for handling traffic.
Hybrid Cloud Connectivity	Private Subnet	Securely connect AWS with on-premises infrastructure.
Serverless & Containerized Workloads	Public & Private Subnets	AWS Lambda, ECS, and Kubernetes workloads use different subnet types.

Table 5.3: *Key Use Cases of Subnet Creation*

Let us dive deep into Public and Private subnets.

Public Subnet versus Private Subnet in Amazon VPC

In Amazon Virtual Private Cloud (VPC), subnets serve as smaller network segments within the IP address range of a VPC (CIDR block). Each subnet is associated with an AWS Availability Zone (AZ) and is categorized as either a Public Subnet or a Private Subnet based on its access to the internet.

This classification determines how AWS resources within the subnet communicate internally and interact with external networks. Proper subnet segmentation ensures security, scalability, and optimized traffic flow for cloud workloads.

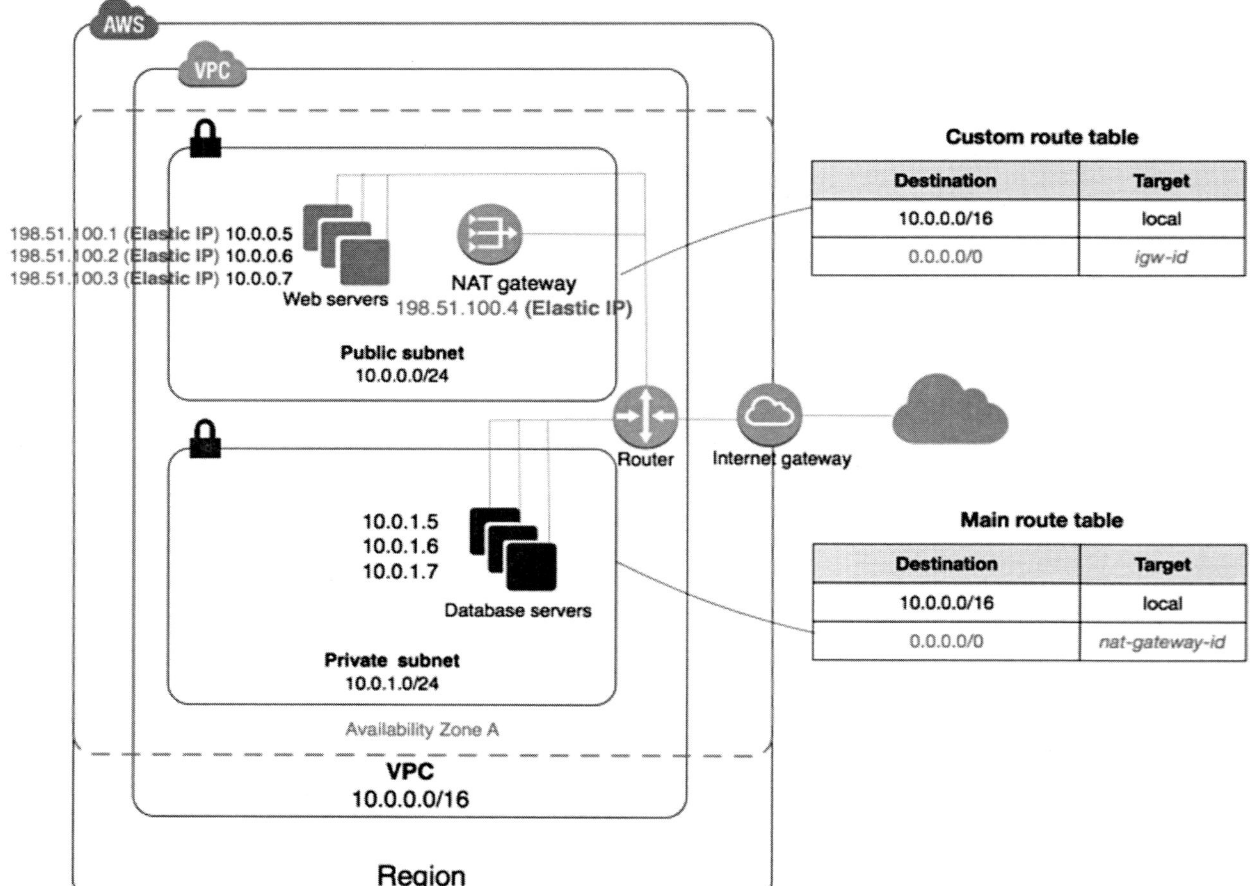

Figure 5.2: *Public versus Private Subnet Separation*

Public Subnet (Blue/Green zone)

- Connected to an Internet Gateway (IGW).
- Contains Web Servers / Load Balancers.
- Accepts incoming internet traffic.

Private Subnet (Orange/Red zone)

- No direct internet access.
- Contains Application Servers / Databases.
- Uses NAT Gateway only for outbound traffic.

Clear boundary lines show that:

- Internet traffic cannot directly reach private subnets.
- Access to private resources is controlled and layered.

Public Subnet

A public subnet is a subnet that has direct internet access, making it suitable for hosting publicly accessible applications, such as web servers and bastion hosts. It is considered "public" because its associated route table includes a route to an Internet Gateway (IGW), which enables communication with the external world.

The key characteristics of public subnet are given in the following table:

FEATURE	DESCRIPTION
Internet Accessibility	Public subnets can communicate with the internet through an Internet Gateway (IGW).
Use Case	Ideal for hosting web applications, API endpoints, and bastion hosts that need public access.
IP Addressing	Public subnets contain public IPv4 addresses or Elastic IPs (EIPs) for external connectivity.
Route Table Configuration	The route table includes a 0.0.0.0/0 entry pointing to an IGW.
Security Controls	AWS Security Groups and Network ACLs (NACLs) restrict inbound and outbound traffic.

***Table 5.4**: Key Characteristics of Public Subnet Creation*

Functioning of Public Subnets

- Outbound Communication:
  - When an EC2 instance in a public subnet sends traffic to the internet, the request routes through the Internet Gateway (IGW).
  - The IGW forwards the request to external networks, and the response returns through the same gateway.
- Inbound Communication:
  - Public-facing applications (for example, a website) can receive requests directly from the internet via the IGW.
  - AWS Security Groups and NACLs control which inbound connections are permitted.

Example Use Case: Hosting a public website, where users access an EC2 instance running Apache/ Nginx in a public subnet via HTTP/HTTPS.

Security Consideration: Avoid placing sensitive resources (for example, databases) in public subnets, as they could be exposed to security threats.

Private Subnet

A private subnet is a subnet that has no direct internet access and is designed for hosting backend workloads that require isolation from the public network. Unlike public subnets, private subnets do not have routes to an Internet Gateway (IGW), making them inaccessible from the internet.

The key characteristics of public subnet are given in the following table:

FEATURE	DESCRIPTION
Internet Accessibility	Private subnets do not have direct internet access.
Use Case	Best for hosting databases, internal application servers, and backend processing systems.
IP Addressing	Uses private IP addresses (for example, 10.0.2.0/24), not reachable from external networks.
Route Table Configuration	No direct 0.0.0.0/0 route to an IGW; instead, it can use a NAT Gateway for outbound access.
Security Controls	Network ACLs and Security Groups restrict unauthorized internal and external traffic.

Table 5.5: *Key Characteristics of Private Subnet Creation*

Functioning of Private Subnets

- Outbound Communication (via NAT Gateway):
  - Instances in a private subnet cannot access the internet directly.
  - If they need to communicate externally (for example, downloading OS updates), they must route traffic through a NAT Gateway or NAT Instance.
  - The NAT Gateway resides in a public subnet, acting as an intermediary.
- Inbound Communication (Restricted):
  - No direct inbound traffic is allowed from the internet.
  - Private subnet instances are accessible only from within the VPC (for example, from a public subnet via internal routing).

Example Use Case: Hosting an Amazon RDS (Relational Database Service) instance in a private subnet to store confidential customer data while restricting public access.

Security Consideration: Private subnets help minimize the attack surface by isolating sensitive workloads from external threats.

Public versus Private Subnet

The following is a simplified architecture illustrating how public and private subnets interact within an AWS VPC:

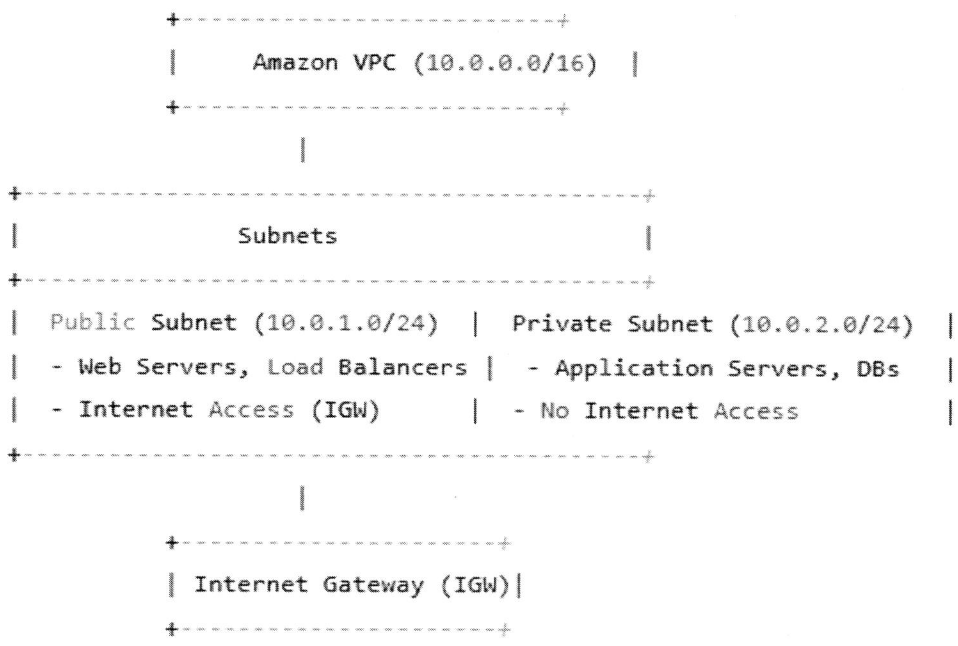

***Figure* 5.3:** *Public versus Private Subnet Architecture*

From the Diagram:

- Public Subnet (10.0.1.0/24) contains resources accessible from the internet via the Internet Gateway (IGW).
- Private Subnet (10.0.2.0/24) contains backend resources (for example, databases and application servers) with no direct internet access.
- Internet-bound requests from the private subnet must route through a NAT Gateway in the public subnet to access external services securely.

In Amazon VPC architecture, subnets play a crucial role in defining how cloud resources interact with each other and with external networks. The above high-level diagram illustrates the separation of public and private subnets within a single VPC, highlighting how network components are structured for efficient and secure operations.

Breakdown of the Architecture

This VPC architecture consists of three primary layers:

- Amazon VPC (Root Network Layer)
- Subnet Layer (Public and Private Segmentation)
- Connectivity Components (Internet Gateway for Public Access)

At the top of the diagram, we see the Amazon VPC (10.0.0.0/16).

Inference:

- This is the main virtual network that provides the foundation for deploying AWS resources.
- The CIDR block 10.0.0.0/16 defines the total IP address space allocated to this VPC.
- It acts as a private, logically isolated environment where users can create and manage multiple subnets.

Key Role:

The VPC is the main network container that houses all subnets, route tables, and security configurations.

- **Subnet Layer – Public and Private Subnets**

  The diagram then breaks the VPC into two subnets:

  - Public Subnet (10.0.1.0/24)
  - Private Subnet (10.0.2.0/24)

Each of these subnets has a specific role in managing the flow of traffic and maintaining security within the VPC.

Public Subnet (10.0.1.0/24)

Characteristics:

- Assigned an IP range of 10.0.1.0/24, which is a subset of the CIDR block of the main VPC.
- Directly accessible from the internet via an Internet Gateway (IGW).
- Used for hosting resources that need external exposure, such as:
  - Web Servers (for example, Apache, Nginx, or application frontends).
  - Load Balancers (for example, AWS Elastic Load Balancer) to manage traffic distribution.

Traffic Flow:

- **Inbound Traffic:** Users from the internet can access services hosted in the public subnet (for example, a web server).
- **Outbound Traffic:** Public subnet instances can send requests to the internet directly through the Internet Gateway (IGW).

Example Use Case: Hosting a publicly accessible website where users can interact with the application over the internet.

Private Subnet (10.0.2.0/24)

Characteristics:

- Assigned an IP range of **10.0.2.0/24**, ensuring logical separation from the public subnet.
- **Not directly connected to the internet**, meaning external users **cannot** access resources in this subnet.
- Typically used for **backend infrastructure**, such as:
  - **Application Servers** that process business logic.
  - **Database Servers** (for example, Amazon RDS, MySQL, PostgreSQL) that require a secure environment.

Traffic Flow:

- **Inbound Traffic:** Resources in the private subnet **only receive traffic from within the VPC** (for example, from the public subnet or other private subnets).
- **Outbound Traffic:** Private subnet instances **cannot access the internet directly** but can do so **via a NAT Gateway** (not shown in the diagram).

Example Use Case: Hosting an **internal API server or database** that should not be exposed to the public internet for security reasons.

- **Connectivity Components – Internet Gateway (IGW)**

At the bottom of the diagram, we see the Internet Gateway (IGW), which plays a crucial role in enabling internet access for the public subnet.

Purpose of the Internet Gateway (IGW):

- Provides external internet connectivity for instances in the public subnet.
- Outbound requests from public subnet instances (for example, web servers) are routed through this gateway.
- Inbound requests (for example, HTTP traffic from users) enter through the IGW and reach the public subnet.

Example Use Case: A user accesses a web application hosted in a public subnet through their browser, which routes the request via the **Internet Gateway**.

Security Consideration: Since the **private subnet does not have an Internet Gateway**, its resources remain isolated from the public internet.

Public and Private Subnet Interaction

In a real-world secure cloud deployment, public and private subnets interact in the following ways:

1. A user requests a webpage hosted on a web server in the public subnet.
2. The web server processes the request and queries the database, which resides in the private subnet.
3. The database server sends a response back to the web server.
4. The web server returns the requested data to the end-user via the Internet Gateway (IGW).

Example Scenario:

A retail e-commerce site where users browse products (hosted on a public subnet), but customer data and order processing occur securely in a private subnet.

The Public and Private Subnets of Amazon VPC allow users to logically segment cloud environments, improving security, scalability, and network management.

- Public Subnets are best suited for internet-facing applications like web servers.
- Private Subnets are essential for protecting sensitive workloads like databases and backend services.

By implementing proper security configurations, such as Security Groups, Network ACLs, and NAT Gateways, businesses can create a highly secure, scalable, and efficient cloud infrastructure in AWS.

Some of the Security Considerations for Public and Private Subnet Configurations are tabulated as follows:

SECURITY MEASURE	IMPLEMENTATION
Restricting Public Access	Ensure only required ports (for example, HTTP, HTTPS) are open for public subnet resources.
Isolating Database Instances	Always place database servers in private subnets to avoid direct internet exposure.
Using NAT Gateways	Private subnet instances requiring outbound internet access should use a NAT Gateway.
Applying Security Groups and NACLs	Define strict security rules for inbound and outbound traffic control.

Table 5.6: *Security Considerations for Public and Private Subnet Configurations*

The Public versus Private Subnet architecture is a fundamental networking design in AWS, ensuring both external accessibility and internal security. By structuring workloads into public and private segments, organizations can achieve high availability, security, and performance while minimizing security risks.

Some of the best practices for Subnet Design are given in the following table:

BEST PRACTICE	REASON
Distribute Subnets Across Multiple AZs	Ensures high availability and fault tolerance.
Follow CIDR Allocation Guidelines	Avoid IP conflicts and ensure efficient address allocation.
Use Private Subnets for Sensitive Data	Enhances security by limiting external exposure.
Leverage NAT Gateways for Outbound Access	Allows private subnet instances to access external resources securely.
Implement Security Groups and ACLs	Enforce granular security control over network traffic.

***Table* 5.7:** *Best Practices for Subnet Creation*

Subnet creation is an essential part of AWS VPC design, allowing users to segment workloads for optimized security, performance, and scalability. By strategically designing public and private subnets, businesses can deploy highly available, secure, and cost-efficient cloud architectures.

Routing between Subnets

Routing between subnets in Amazon Virtual Private Cloud (VPC) determines how network traffic moves from one subnet to another within the same VPC or to external networks. Each subnet in AWS VPC must be associated with a route table that defines traffic flow, ensuring controlled communication between resources. Understanding how routing works between public and private subnets is critical for designing secure and efficient cloud architectures. Properly configured routing enables secure communication, traffic isolation, and optimized network performance.

Route Table: A Route Table in Amazon VPC is a set of rules, called routes, that determine where network traffic should be directed. Each subnet in a VPC must be associated with a route table, which defines how it communicates with other subnets, VPCs, or external networks.

Key Functions of a Route Table

- Directs internal traffic between subnets.
- Routes outbound internet traffic through gateways (Internet Gateway or NAT).
- Allows private communication between VPCs using VPC Peering or Transit Gateway.
- Enables hybrid networking by routing on-premises traffic via VPN or Direct Connect.

AWS ensures that subnets within the same VPC can communicate by default, even without explicitly adding routes. However, external connectivity must be manually configured through proper routing entries.

Routing between Public and Private Subnets

In a typical VPC architecture, we divide subnets into public and private zones to optimize security and performance. Routing plays a crucial role in controlling traffic between these subnets.

Some of the routing components in a multi subnet VPC is tabulated as shown:

ROUTING COMPONENT	DESCRIPTION
Internet Gateway (IGW)	Enables direct internet access for public subnet instances.
NAT Gateway (NGW)	Allows private subnet instances to make outbound internet requests.
Route Table	Defines routing rules for each subnet.
Local Routes	Ensures private communication between subnets in the same VPC.

Table 5.8: *Routing Components in a Multi Subnet VPC*

The following is a simplified AWS VPC routing architecture, showing how public and private subnets communicate:

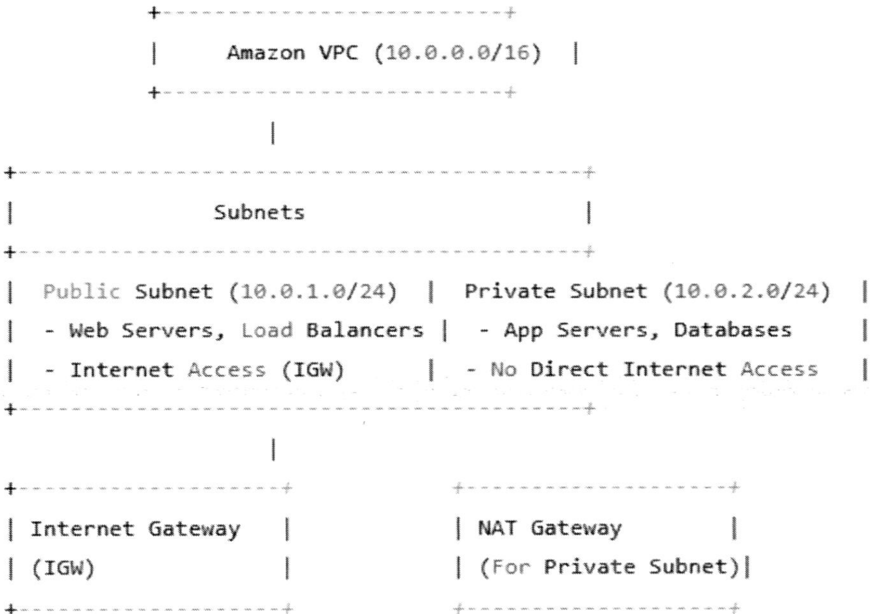

Figure 5.4: *Simplified AWS VPC Routing Architecture*

- The public subnet can directly access the internet through the Internet Gateway (IGW).
- The private subnet routes external requests through a NAT Gateway, ensuring security by blocking inbound connections.
- Both subnets communicate with each other using the local route of VPC.

Example Routing Scenarios

Scenario 1: Public Subnet Instance Accessing the Internet

1. A web server in the public subnet needs to fetch external updates.
2. The request follows the route table entry (0.0.0.0/0 → IGW).
3. The response is received directly from the internet.

Scenario 2: Private Subnet Instance Accessing External APIs

1. An application server in the private subnet needs to access a public API.
2. The request is routed through the NAT Gateway (0.0.0.0/0 → NGW).
3. The API server responds, and the reply returns via the NAT Gateway.
4. The application server remains inaccessible from the internet.

Scenario 3: Public Subnet Instance Communicating with Private Subnet Database

1. A web server in the public subnet queries an RDS database in the private subnet.
2. The request uses the local route (10.0.0.0/16 → local), ensuring secure internal traffic.
3. The database responds, allowing the web server to process user data.
4. No internet access is required for this communication.

Best Practices for Subnet Routing in Amazon VPC

To ensure secure, efficient, and well-optimized network communication within an AWS VPC, follow these best practices for subnet routing:

- **Use Separate Route Tables for Public and Private Subnets**
  - Maintain distinct route tables for public and private subnets to prevent misconfigurations.
  - Helps in isolating sensitive workloads from publicly exposed services.
- **Restrict Inbound Access to Private Subnets**
  - Private subnets should not have direct inbound internet access.
  - Use security groups and network ACLs to allow only internal VPC traffic.
  - If external connectivity is required, route traffic via a NAT Gateway instead of exposing the subnet.
- **Implement NAT Gateway for Secure Outbound Access from Private Subnets**
  - NAT Gateways allow private subnet instances to access the internet without exposing them to inbound threats.
  - Use AWS-managed NAT Gateways instead of manually configuring a NAT instance, as they provide higher availability and scalability.
- **Route Internal Traffic Efficiently Using VPC Peering or Transit Gateway**
  - When connecting multiple VPCs, prefer VPC Peering or AWS Transit Gateway for optimized routing.
  - Avoid unnecessary hops by ensuring that local routes between subnets are correctly configured.
- **Limit Public Subnet Access to Trusted Sources Only**
  - Only allow required ports (for example, HTTP/HTTPS for web servers) in public subnets.
  - Use Elastic Load Balancers (ELB) to manage traffic instead of exposing multiple instances.
  - Deny all unnecessary inbound requests using security groups and NACL rules.
- **Monitor and Analyze Network Traffic Using VPC Flow Logs**
  - Enable VPC Flow Logs to capture and analyze network traffic patterns.
  - Helps in detecting misconfigurations, unauthorized access attempts, and potential security breaches.
- **Optimize Routing Table Entries for Performance**
  - Avoid unnecessary long route chains that can slow down traffic processing.
  - Use summarized CIDR blocks instead of individual IP addresses when defining routes.
  - Regularly review and remove obsolete routes to prevent conflicts and redundancy.

- **Use PrivateLink or VPC Endpoints for Secure AWS Service Access**
    - Instead of routing AWS service traffic over the public internet, use VPC Endpoints or AWS PrivateLink.
    - Ensures low-latency, private communication with AWS services like S3, DynamoDB, and API Gateway.
- **Ensure High Availability by Distributing Subnets across Multiple Availability Zones (AZs)**
    - Deploy subnets across multiple AZs to prevent a single AZ failure from disrupting routing.
    - Configure Route 53 for DNS-based failover between AZs.
- **Regularly Audit and Update Security Rules**
    - Perform periodic security audits to ensure that routing tables, security groups, and NACLs are correctly configured.
    - Remove any unnecessary open routes to minimize attack exposure.

By following these best practices, organizations can design a highly secure, scalable, and resilient subnet routing strategy within AWS VPC.

Hence, Routing between subnets in Amazon VPC ensures secure, controlled, and optimized network traffic flow. By carefully configuring Route Tables, Internet Gateways, and NAT Gateways, organizations can maintain high security while enabling necessary connectivity.

- Public subnets enable direct internet access for front-facing applications.
- Private subnets provide isolated environments for backend services and databases.
- Routing tables manage traffic flow, ensuring that each subnet can only access authorized destinations.

Route Tables in Amazon VPC

A route table is a set of routing rules (routes) that control how traffic is forwarded within a VPC. Each subnet in a VPC must be associated with a route table, either explicitly or implicitly, to determine where its network traffic is directed.

Key Characteristics of a Route Table

- Each VPC automatically comes with a default route table.
- Route tables contain destination-target mappings for directing traffic.
- Multiple subnets can share the same route table.
- Subnets not explicitly associated with a custom route table use the main route table of the VPC.

The following diagram shows how route tables + gateways control whether EC2 instances can reach the internet, stay private, or communicate securely with an on-premises data center:

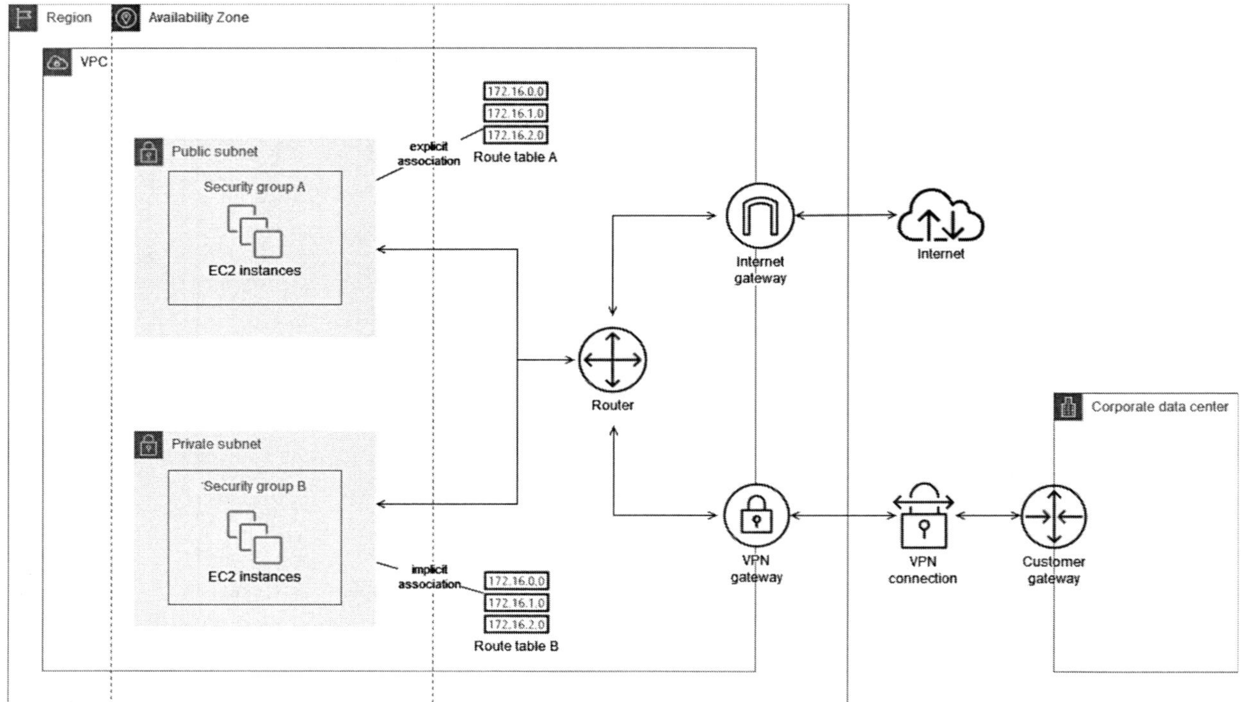

Figure 5.5: *Visual Example of a Route Table*

Components of a Route Table in Amazon VPC

A Route Table in Amazon VPC consists of several key components that determine how network traffic is directed within a VPC, between subnets, or to external networks. Below are the essential components of a route table, explained in a structured and detailed manner:

- **Destination (CIDR Block)**
    - Defines the range of IP addresses for which a specific route is applicable.
    - Can represent internal VPC communication (for example, 10.0.0.0/16 for VPC-wide traffic) or external destinations (for example, 0.0.0.0/0 for internet access).
    - Supports both IPv4 and IPv6 addressing to enable routing in dual-stack environments.

  Example:
    - 10.0.1.0/24 → local (Routes traffic within the VPC)
    - 0.0.0.0/0 → IGW (Routes all external traffic to the internet)
- **Target (Next-Hop Device)**
    - Specifies the next-hop network component that will handle the traffic.
    - Determines where the traffic is forwarded based on the destination CIDR.
    - Common targets include:
        - Local (for intra-VPC traffic).
        - Internet Gateway (IGW) (for internet access).
        - NAT Gateway (for private subnets needing outbound internet access).
        - Virtual Private Gateway (VGW) (for hybrid cloud networking).
        - VPC Peering Connection (for communication between different VPCs).

Example:

- 0.0.0.0/0 → igw-12345678 (Routes internet-bound traffic to an Internet Gateway).
- 192.168.1.0/24 → vgw-23456789 (Routes traffic to an on-premises network via a VPN Gateway).

- **Local Route (Default Entry in Every Route Table)**
  - A mandatory route that AWS automatically adds to every route table.
  - Allows communication between all subnets within the same VPC without requiring additional configurations.
  - The local route cannot be modified or deleted.

Example:

- 10.0.0.0/16 → local (Ensures all instances within the VPC can communicate).

Important Note: *Even though this route exists, security controls like Security Groups and Network ACLs must still be configured to allow subnet-to-subnet communication.*

- **Explicit (Custom) Routes**
  - Manually created routes that define traffic flow for external connectivity, multi-VPC communication, or hybrid networking.
  - Used for custom network architectures involving NAT Gateways, VPNs, or Peering Connections.

Example:

- 0.0.0.0/0 → nat-12345678 (Routes internet-bound traffic from a private subnet via a NAT Gateway).
- 172.31.0.0/16 → pcx-78901234 (Routes traffic to a different VPC using VPC Peering).

- **Route Table Associations**
  - Each subnet must be explicitly associated with a route table.
  - A subnet can be associated with only one route table at a time, but a route table can be shared among multiple subnets.
  - If a subnet is not explicitly associated with a custom route table, it defaults to the Main Route Table.

Example:

- Public subnets should be associated with a route table containing an Internet Gateway (IGW) route.
- Private subnets should be associated with a route table using a NAT Gateway for outbound internet access.

- **Main Route Table**
  - Every VPC has a default "Main Route Table" that automatically applies to all subnets unless explicitly overridden.
  - AWS assigns all newly created subnets to this table by default.
  - Users can modify the rules of the Main Route Table or create a custom route table for better subnet isolation.

Example:

- The Main Route Table may only contain local routes, ensuring internal VPC communication but no internet access unless modified.

Best Practice:

- Create separate custom route tables for public and private subnets to avoid accidental misrouting.

- **Edge Associations (For AWS Outposts and Local Zones)**
  - Edge Associations apply when using AWS Outposts or AWS Local Zones, which extend AWS infrastructure closer to on-premises locations.
  - This setting determines how Outposts or Local Zones route traffic back to AWS Regions.

Example: A Local Zone route table may have a default route to a parent AWS Region to enable full cloud integration.

Advanced Feature: Mostly used in hybrid or edge computing deployments.

COMPONENT	PURPOSE	EXAMPLE
Destination (CIDR Block)	Defines which IP range is covered by the route.	10.0.1.0/24, 0.0.0.0/0
Target (Next-Hop Device)	Specifies where traffic should be forwarded.	IGW, NAT, VGW, VPC Peering
Local Route	Ensures subnets in the same VPC can communicate.	10.0.0.0/16 → local
Explicit (Custom) Routes	Manually added routes for internet, VPNs, or peering.	0.0.0.0/0 → NAT Gateway
Route Table Associations	Links subnets to a specific route table.	Public Subnet → Public Route Table
Main Route Table	The default route table for unassociated subnets.	Automatically assigned by AWS
Edge Associations	Defines routing behavior for AWS Outposts or Local Zones.	Routes to an AWS Region

Table 5.9: *Components of a Route Table*

Route Table Configuration in Amazon VPC

Configuring a route table involves defining custom routes that enable secure communication between subnets, external networks, and AWS services.

Step 1: Creating a Custom Route Table

1. Go to the AWS Console → Navigate to the VPC Dashboard.
2. Click `Route Tables` → Click `Create Route Table`.
3. Provide a name (for example, "Private Subnet Route Table").
4. Select the VPC where the route table will be used.
5. Click `Create`.

Step 2: Adding Routes to the Route Table

1. Select the newly created Route Table.
2. Click Edit Routes and then Add Route.

3. Specify the destination CIDR block:
   a. 10.0.0.0/16 → local (For internal VPC communication).
   b. 0.0.0.0/0 → IGW (For public subnets to access the internet).
   c. 0.0.0.0/0 → NAT Gateway (For private subnets needing outbound internet access).
   d. 192.168.1.0/24 → VPN Gateway (For hybrid cloud integration).
4. Click `Save Routes`.

Step 3: Associating the Route Table with a Subnet

1. Go to the Route Table Associations tab.
2. Click `Edit Subnet Associations`.
3. Select the subnet(s) to associate with this route table.
4. Click `Save`.

Route Table Examples

The following are common route table configurations for different subnet types:

Public Subnet Route Table

A public subnet allows direct access to the internet using an Internet Gateway (IGW).

DESTINATION	TARGET	PURPOSE
10.0.0.0/16	Local	Internal VPC communication.
0.0.0.0/0	Internet Gateway (IGW)	Enables outbound/inbound internet access.

Table 5.10: *Public Subnet Route Table*

Example Use Case: Hosting a web server that needs to be publicly accessible.

Private Subnet Route Table

A private subnet does not allow direct internet access but can route outbound requests via a NAT Gateway.

DESTINATION	TARGET	PURPOSE
10.0.0.0/16	Local	Internal VPC communication.
0.0.0.0/0	NAT Gateway	Allows private subnet instances to access the internet.

Table 5.11: *Private Subnet Route Table*

Example Use Case: Hosting an internal database server that should not be exposed to the public internet.

VPN Route Table (For Hybrid Cloud Setup)

This configuration is used when connecting an on-premises data center to AWS via a VPN Gateway.

DESTINATION	TARGET	PURPOSE
10.0.0.0/16	Local	Internal VPC communication.
192.168.1.0/24	VPN Gateway (VGW)	Routes traffic to on-premises networks.

Table 5.12: *VPN Route Table*

Example Use Case: Secure hybrid cloud connectivity between AWS and an on-premises data center.

Best Practices for Configuring Route Tables

To ensure efficient and secure routing, follow these best practices:

- **Use Separate Route Tables for Public and Private Subnets**
  - Public subnets should route through an Internet Gateway.
  - Private subnets should never have a direct route to the internet.
- **Keep Route Tables Minimal and Well-Organized**
  - Avoid excessive custom routes that slow down routing decisions.
  - Use CIDR summarization to reduce unnecessary routing entries.
- **Implement Security Controls alongside Routing**
  - Security Groups and Network ACLs should complement route tables.
  - Use deny rules to prevent unauthorized traffic movement.
- **Regularly Audit and Monitor Routing Changes**
  - Enable VPC Flow Logs to detect anomalies.
  - Regularly review and update routes to match evolving architecture needs.
- **Optimize Hybrid Cloud Connectivity**
  - Use AWS Direct Connect or VPN Gateway for low-latency hybrid networking.
  - Ensure proper route propagation for hybrid cloud integration.

Configuring and associating route tables in Amazon VPC is essential for secure, scalable, and efficient cloud networking. By understanding how routes, gateways, and subnet associations work, organizations can optimize communication while maintaining security and performance.

Gateways in Amazon VPC

Gateways in Amazon Virtual Private Cloud (VPC) play a crucial role in enabling or restricting access to external networks, such as the public internet or on-premises data centers.

AWS provides multiple gateway types to control and route traffic, including the Internet Gateway (IGW) for public internet access, NAT Gateway for outbound-only internet access from private subnets, VPN Gateway for secure on-premises connectivity, and Transit Gateway for centralized routing between multiple VPCs and networks.

Among the different types of gateways available in AWS, NAT Gateway is particularly important for private subnet instances that need outbound internet access while remaining inaccessible from the public network.

NAT Gateway

A Network Address Translation (NAT) Gateway is an AWS-managed service that enables instances in private subnets to initiate outbound traffic to the internet while preventing inbound connections from external sources. This allows private instances to download updates, access external APIs, and communicate with public services securely.

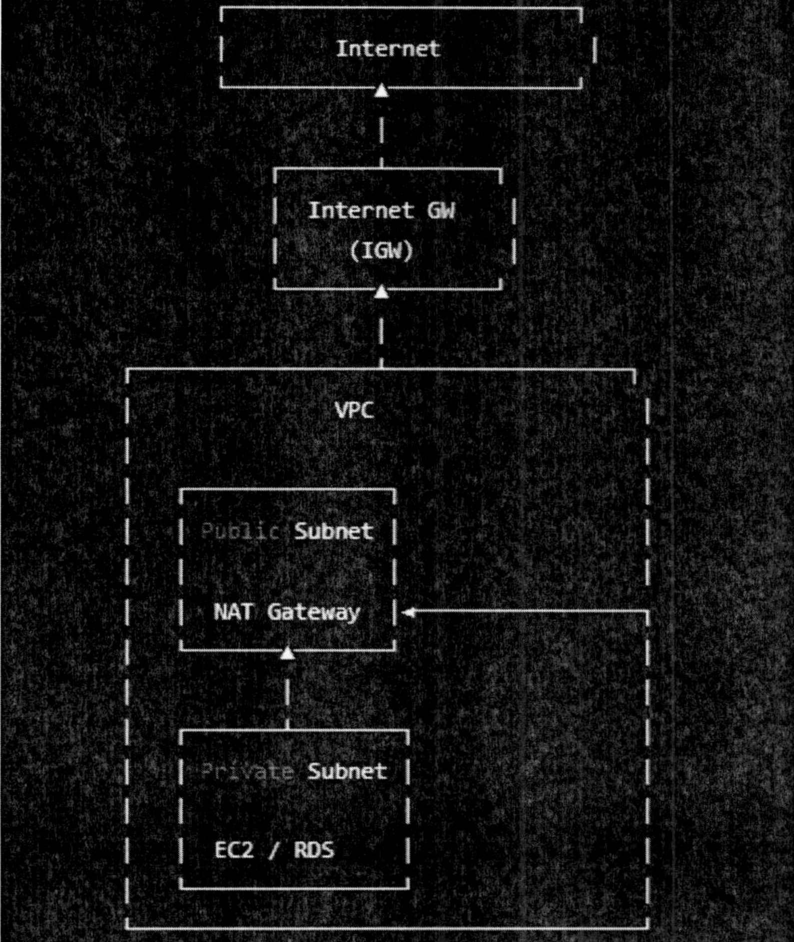

***Figure 5.6**: NAT Gateway in a Typical VPC Layout*

Key Features of NAT Gateway:

- Enables outbound internet access for private subnet instances.
- Prevents unsolicited inbound connections, ensuring security.
- NAT Gateways are zonal resources - you need one per AZ for high availability.
- Highly available and managed by AWS, reducing operational overhead.
- Automatically scales to handle varying levels of network traffic.
- Eliminates the need for a manually configured NAT instance, improving performance and reliability.

By default, private subnets in AWS do not have direct internet access, which prevents their resources from downloading software updates, accessing external services, or integrating with APIs.

A NAT Gateway allows only outbound internet traffic while maintaining the isolation of private subnet instances, ensuring security.

Example Use Case:

- A database server in a private subnet needs to download security patches from the internet.
- Since the private subnet has no direct internet access, routing outbound traffic through a NAT Gateway enables secure updates without exposing the database to external threats.

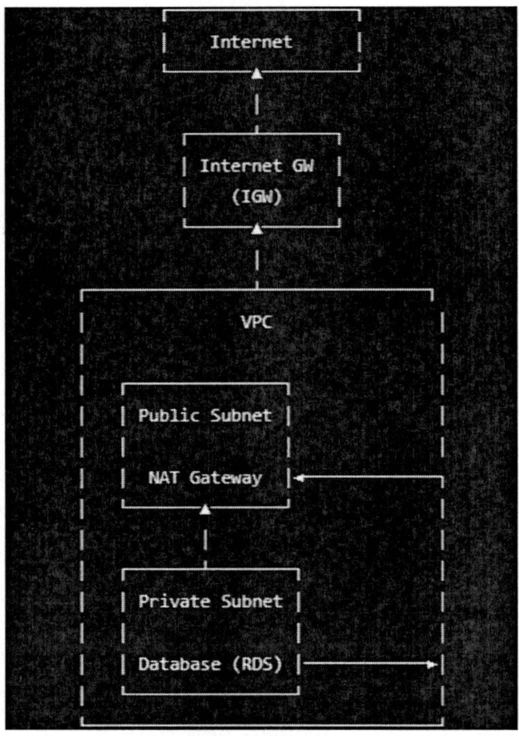

Figure 5.7: *Database in the Private Subnet Connecting via NAT Gateway*

A NAT Gateway acts as a proxy for private subnet instances, allowing them to communicate with the internet only for outbound requests.

Traffic Flow Using NAT Gateway

1. Instance in a Private Subnet (for example, 10.0.2.10) sends a request to an external service.
2. The request is routed to the NAT Gateway in the public subnet.
3. The NAT Gateway replaces the IP of the private instance with its own public IP.
4. The request reaches the internet, and the response is sent back to the NAT Gateway.
5. The NAT Gateway forwards the response to the original private instance.

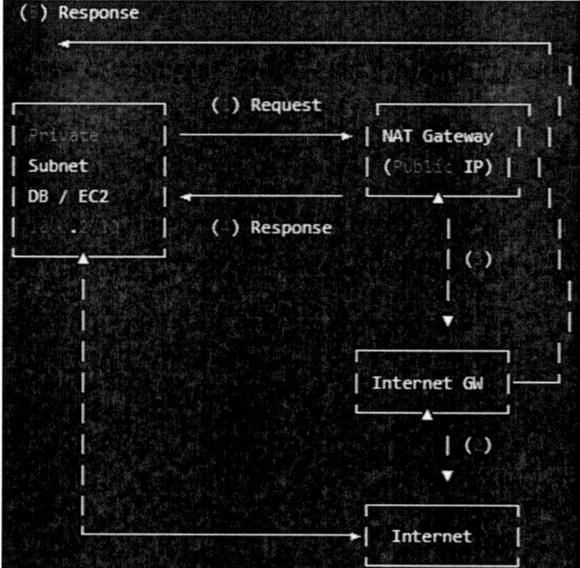

Figure 5.8: *Numbered Traffic Flow Diagram*

Security Benefit: The private instance remains hidden from direct external access, reducing attack risks.

Configuring a NAT Gateway in AWS

To set up a NAT Gateway for private subnet instances, follow these steps:

Step 1: Create a NAT Gateway

1. Navigate to AWS Console → VPC Dashboard
2. Click **`NAT Gateways`**
3. Click **`Create NAT Gateway`**
4. Configure the following:
   Subnet: Select a public subnet
   Elastic IP: Allocate or select an Elastic IP (EIP)
5. Click **`Create NAT Gateway`**

The NAT Gateway must always reside in a public subnet so that it can route traffic to the Internet Gateway.

Step 2: Update the Route Table for the Private Subnet

1. Go to VPC Dashboard → Route Tables.
2. Select the route table associated with the private subnet.
3. Click **`Edit Routes`**.
4. Add the following route:
   Destination: 0.0.0.0/0
   Target: NAT Gateway (e.g., nat-0abcd1234)
5. Click **`Save Routes`**.

This ensures all internet-bound traffic from private instances flows through the NAT Gateway.

Result:

- Instances in the private subnet can now send outbound traffic to the internet via the NAT Gateway.
- Inbound traffic is blocked, ensuring security and isolation.

Resulting Traffic Flow (Summary)

Private Instance → NAT Gateway → Internet Gateway → Internet

- Private instances initiate outbound access.
- Inbound access from the internet remains blocked.

Cost Implications

- NAT Gateways incur two types of charges:
  - Hourly charge (per NAT Gateway, per AZ)
  - Data processing charge (per GB of data processed)

Even if idle, the hourly cost continues as long as the NAT Gateway exists.

High outbound traffic = higher data processing cost.

NAT Gateway versus NAT Instance

Before AWS introduced NAT Gateways, users had to manually create NAT Instances (EC2 instances configured as routers). NAT Gateways provide a fully managed and scalable alternative.

Amazon VPC provides two methods for enabling outbound internet access from private subnets: NAT Gateway (AWS-managed) and NAT Instance (self-managed EC2 instance). The following is a detailed comparison between NAT Gateway versus NAT Instance to help you choose the right option for your AWS architecture.

- **Scalability**
  - **NAT Gateway:**
    - Fully managed by AWS and automatically scales based on network traffic.
    - Supports high throughput (up to 45 Gbps), making it suitable for large-scale applications.
  - **NAT Instance:**
    - Requires manual scaling; the performance depends on the chosen EC2 instance type.
    - Traffic capacity is limited by EC2 instance bandwidth, leading to performance bottlenecks under heavy load.

Best Choice: NAT Gateway is recommended for high-traffic applications due to its ability to scale automatically.

- **Availability and Fault Tolerance**
  - **NAT Gateway:**
    - Highly available by default, with AWS automatically handling failures.
    - Can be deployed in multiple Availability Zones (AZs) for redundancy.
  - **NAT Instance:**
    - Single point of failure unless manually configured with a secondary NAT Instance in another AZ.
    - Requires setting up Elastic Load Balancers (ELB) and failover mechanisms to ensure redundancy.

Best Choice: NAT Gateway is the superior option for fault tolerance and automatic failover.

- **Performance**
  - **NAT Gateway:**
    - Supports up to 45 Gbps of bandwidth, making it ideal for handling large data transfers.
    - Offers low latency and faster data processing due to AWS-managed optimization.
  - **NAT Instance:**
    - Performance is limited to the selected EC2 instance type.
    - If the instance cannot handle high traffic, it becomes a bottleneck, leading to slow responses.

Best Choice: NAT Gateway offers superior speed and efficiency for production environments.

- **Management and Maintenance**
  - **NAT Gateway:**
    - Fully managed by AWS, requiring no manual maintenance.
    - No need to configure updates, patches, or network interfaces.

- **NAT Instance:**
  - Requires manual setup, configuration, and ongoing maintenance.
  - The administrator is responsible for OS updates, security patches, and monitoring.

Best Choice: NAT Gateway eliminates operational overhead and reduces maintenance complexity.

- **Security**
  - **NAT Gateway:**
    - No need for SSH access, reducing attack risks.
    - Cannot be used as a bastion host, enhancing security by enforcing strict one-way traffic.
  - **NAT Instance:**
    - Requires manual security group and firewall configurations.
    - Can be accessed via SSH, increasing potential security vulnerabilities.

Best Choice: NAT Gateway provides built-in security features, making it the more secure option.

- **Cost Efficiency**
  - **NAT Gateway:**
    - Charged per hour (while provisioned).
    - Charged per GB of data processed.
    - Automatically scales with traffic.
    - Fully managed (no patching, no failover setup).

  Implication: Costs can rise quickly for workloads with frequent outbound traffic (patch downloads, APIs, external services).

  - **NAT Instance:**
    - Charged as an EC2 instance
      - Instance type (CPU/RAM)
      - EBS storage
    - Requires manual setup and management
      - Scaling
      - Patching
      - High availability (if needed)

  Implication: Can be more cost-effective for low traffic, especially with small instance types.

Example

Low-traffic workload (< 1 GB/hour outbound):

- A t3.nano NAT instance may be cheaper than a NAT Gateway because:
  - You pay only EC2 + minimal EBS.
  - No per-GB NAT processing charges.

High-traffic workload (tens or hundreds of GB/hour):

- NAT Gateway becomes more cost-effective, as:
  - No instance bottlenecks.

    - No scaling effort.
    - Better reliability under load.

Best Choice:

- **For large-scale workloads:** NAT Gateway is cost-effective due to automated scaling.
- **For small workloads:** NAT Instance may be cheaper, but requires manual management.
- **Ease of Deployment**
    - **NAT Gateway:**
        - Easy to set up via AWS Console, requiring just a public subnet and Elastic IP.
        - No manual configurations needed for high availability.
    - **NAT Instance:**
        - Requires manual creation, security group settings, and route table updates.
        - Need to disable source/destination checks and configure NAT functionality properly.

Best Choice: NAT Gateway is simpler to deploy and configure compared to NAT Instances.

- **Logging and Monitoring**
    - **NAT Gateway:**
        - Supports AWS CloudWatch metrics for real-time monitoring of bandwidth usage and packet drops.
    - **NAT Instance:**
        - Requires manual configuration of monitoring tools (for example, CloudWatch Agent, custom logs).
        - Logs must be manually exported and analyzed for troubleshooting.

Best Choice: NAT Gateway provides automatic logging and monitoring, making it easier to track performance.

- **Use Cases**
    - **NAT Gateway:**
        - Best for enterprise-grade applications with high traffic demands.
        - Suitable for production workloads that require automatic failover.
    - **NAT Instance:**
        - Useful for small-scale environments where traffic is low.
        - Preferred when custom routing or additional security features are needed.

Best Choice: NAT Gateway for high-traffic workloads; NAT Instance for small-scale or custom deployments.

Best Practices for Using NAT Gateways

Some of the best practices for using NAT Gateways are given below.

- **Deploy NAT Gateways in Highly Available Architectures**
    - Place one NAT Gateway per Availability Zone (AZ) to prevent single points of failure.
    - Distribute traffic across multiple NAT Gateways if using a multi-AZ setup.
- **Use Elastic IPs (EIP) for Persistent NAT Gateway Addresses**
    - Assign an Elastic IP to ensure a consistent public IP address for outbound traffic.

- **Monitor NAT Gateway Metrics Using CloudWatch**
    - Track bandwidth usage, packet drops, and latency metrics to identify potential performance bottlenecks.
- **Optimize Costs by Terminating Unused NAT Gateways**
    - NAT Gateways incur hourly costs, so delete unused ones to reduce expenses.
    - Consider VPC Endpoints or AWS PrivateLink for AWS service access to avoid NAT Gateway charges.
- **Secure Private Subnets with Security Groups and Network ACLs**
    - Even though private subnets are not directly exposed, apply strict security rules to prevent lateral movement in case of an internal security breach.

Common Pitfalls

- **Deleting a NAT Gateway without updating routes**
    - Private subnet route tables still point to the deleted NAT.
    - **Result:** Immediate outbound connectivity loss
- **Placing a NAT Gateway in a private subnet**
    - NAT Gateway must be in a public subnet with a route to an IGW.
- **Forgetting Elastic IP**
    - NAT Gateway requires an EIP; without it, internet access will not work.
- **Unexpected costs**
    - High outbound traffic can significantly increase per-GB charges.

NAT Gateways are zonal - cross-AZ failover requires multiple gateways. They are essential for secure outbound internet access from private subnets while preventing inbound threats. They offer better performance, high availability, and security compared to traditional NAT Instances.

By properly configuring NAT Gateways and route tables, AWS users can ensure efficient network connectivity, security, and scalability in their VPC architecture.

Feature	NAT Gateway (AWS-Managed)	NAT Instance (Self-Managed)
Scalability	Automatically scales with traffic	Requires manual resizing of EC2 instance
Availability	Highly available by default	Single point of failure unless configured with redundancy
Performance	Up to 45 Gbps throughput	Limited to EC2 instance bandwidth
Management	Fully managed by AWS	Manual setup, patching, and updates required
Security	No SSH access (more secure)	Can be accessed via SSH (potential risks)
Cost	Charges per hour and GB of data	Lower cost for low-traffic environments
Ease of Deployment	Simple setup via AWS Console	Requires manual configuration
Logging and Monitoring	AWS CloudWatch integration	Requires custom logging setup
Best Use Cases	High-traffic, production workloads	Low-traffic, custom routing needs

Table 5.13: *NAT Gateway versus NAT Instance*

Key Takeaway

- Choose NAT Gateway for scalability, automation, and security.
- Choose NAT Instance for small workloads or when cost savings outweigh management overhead.

While both NAT Gateway and NAT Instance serve the purpose of enabling outbound internet access from private subnets, NAT Gateway is the preferred choice for high availability, security, and minimal operational overhead.

Internet Gateway (IGW) in Amazon VPC

An Internet Gateway (IGW) is a key AWS networking component that enables direct internet access for resources hosted in a public subnet within an Amazon Virtual Private Cloud (VPC). It acts as the bridge between the VPC and the public internet, allowing inbound and outbound communication.

Understanding how an Internet Gateway works, its configuration, and its best practices is essential for building scalable and secure cloud architectures in AWS.

An Internet Gateway (IGW) is a horizontally scalable, highly available AWS-managed component that allows instances in public subnets to:

- Send outbound traffic to the internet.
- Receive inbound traffic from the internet.

Unlike a NAT Gateway, which only allows outbound traffic, an IGW supports both inbound and outbound internet access.

Internet Gateways are free. There is no hourly charge and no data processing cost for an IGW. You only pay for resources that use it (EC2, NAT Gateway, data transfer, and the like).

This is why architectures try to use IGW directly for public subnets and reserve NAT Gateways (paid) only for private ones.

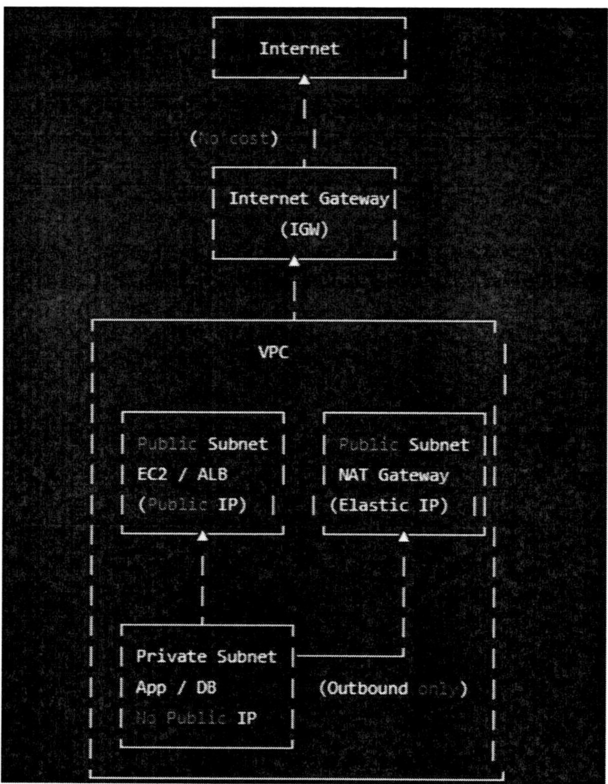

Figure 5.9: *Conceptual Flow Diagram*

Key Features of Internet Gateway (IGW)

- Fully managed by AWS (no manual setup or scaling required).
- High availability and fault tolerance across multiple Availability Zones (AZs).
- Bi-directional traffic support (allows both incoming and outgoing traffic).
- No additional cost—AWS provides IGWs for free.
- No bandwidth limitations, ensuring fast and efficient data transfer.
- IGW does not perform NAT for private IPs.
- IGW can be attached to only one VPC at a time.

By default, AWS VPCs are isolated from the internet for security reasons. An Internet Gateway is necessary to:

- Enable public-facing applications, such as web servers, APIs, and load balancers, to interact with external users.
- Allow resources in public subnets to access AWS services, external APIs, and software updates.
- Ensure high availability and low latency for internet traffic.

Example Use Case:

- A company hosts its website on EC2 instances in a public subnet.
- The Internet Gateway (IGW) enables users to access the website over the internet.
- The web server remains accessible while backend resources (for example, databases) stay protected in private subnets.

An IGW connects a VPC to the public internet, ensuring seamless bidirectional communication for public subnet resources.

Traffic Flow Using Internet Gateway

Effective traffic flow management is essential for maintaining security, performance, and connectivity. Understanding proper traffic moves is essential for optimizing network design and ensuring effective communication.

- **Outbound Traffic:**
  - An instance in a public subnet initiates a request to an external service.
  - The request is routed through the route table of the subnet, which directs it to the Internet Gateway (IGW).
  - The IGW translates the private IP address into a public IP (Elastic IP or assigned public IPv4 address).
  - The request reaches the destination website or service.
- **Inbound Traffic:**
  - A user sends a request to a web server hosted in a public subnet.
  - The request is directed to the Elastic IP (EIP) or public IPv4 address of the server.
  - The IGW translates the public IP back to the private IP of the instance.
  - The request is processed by the instance, and a response is sent back to the user.

Security Consideration:

- To prevent unauthorized access, Security Groups and Network ACLs (NACLs) must be properly configured to control inbound traffic.

Configuring an Internet Gateway in AWS

To set up an Internet Gateway (IGW) in AWS, follow these steps:

Step 1: Create an Internet Gateway

1. Navigate to AWS Console → VPC Dashboard.
2. Click `Internet Gateways` → Click `Create Internet Gateway`.
3. Provide a name for the IGW (for example, "MyIGW").
4. Click `Create`.

Step 2: Attach the IGW to a VPC

1. Select the newly created Internet Gateway.
2. Click `Actions` → Attach to VPC.
3. Choose the VPC where the IGW should be enabled.
4. Click `Attach Internet Gateway`.

Step 3: Configure the Route Table

1. Go to Route Tables in the VPC Dashboard.
2. Select the route table associated with the public subnet.
3. Click `Edit Routes` → Add Route.
4. Set:

    Destination: 0.0.0.0/0 (represents all external traffic).

    Target: The Internet Gateway ID (for example, igw-0123456789).
5. Click `Save Routes`.

Result:

- Instances in the public subnet can now access the internet.
- Private subnet instances remain isolated unless a NAT Gateway is used.

Best Practices for Using an Internet Gateway

Some of the best practices to follow while using an Internet Gateway are provided as follows:

- **Limit Public Internet Access to Necessary Resources:**
    - Assign public IPs only to resources that truly need internet access
    - Prefer Elastic Load Balancers (ALB/NLB) instead of exposing individual EC2 instances
    - Keep databases and backend services in private subnets

    Principle:

    - Fewer public endpoints = smaller attack surface
- **Apply Security Groups and Network ACLs**
    - **Security Groups (stateful):**
        - Allow inbound traffic only on required ports.
        - Common examples: 80 (HTTP), 443 (HTTPS).

  - **Network ACLs (stateless):**
    - Add an extra layer to restrict unnecessary inbound and outbound traffic.
    - Useful for coarse-grained subnet-level controls.
- **Monitor Traffic Using VPC Flow Logs**
  - **Enable VPC Flow Logs at:**
    - VPC level
    - Subnet level
    - ENI level
  - **Helps:**
    - Detect unauthorized access attempts.
    - Troubleshoot routing and security group issues.
    - Audit traffic flowing through the IGW.
- **Use PrivateLink or VPC Endpoints for AWS Services**
  - Avoid sending AWS service traffic over the public internet
  - **Use:**
    - Gateway VPC Endpoints (such as S3, DynamoDB)
    - Interface Endpoints / PrivateLink (like API Gateway, Secrets Manager)
  - **Benefits:**
    - Improved security.
    - Lower NAT Gateway data processing costs.
    - Reduced exposure to the internet.
- **Protect Public Endpoints with AWS Shield and WAF**
  - Enable AWS Shield (Standard) automatically for DDoS protection.
  - Use AWS WAF with ALB, API Gateway, or CloudFront to:
    - Block malicious IPs
    - Filter SQL injection / XSS attacks
    - Apply rate limiting

Best practice: Never expose a public endpoint without layered protection.

Common Mistakes (Internet Gateway)

- Assigning public IPs to all EC2 instances, even when they do not require internet access.
- Exposing individual EC2 instances directly instead of using an Elastic Load Balancer.
- Allowing overly permissive rules such as 0.0.0.0/0 on all ports in Security Groups.
- Forgetting to enable VPC Flow Logs, leading to poor visibility during incidents.
- Routing AWS service traffic (S3, DynamoDB, and so on) through the IGW or NAT Gateway instead of using VPC Endpoints.
- Not enabling AWS Shield or AWS WAF for publicly exposed applications.
- Placing sensitive resources (databases, internal services) in public subnets.
- Assuming IGW provides security filtering (it only provides connectivity, not protection).

Internet Gateway versus NAT Gateway: Key Differences

When designing AWS network architecture, choosing the right gateway type is critical for ensuring secure and efficient internet access. Both Internet Gateway (IGW) and NAT Gateway serve distinct purposes in Amazon VPC, but they cater to different networking needs.

- An Internet Gateway (IGW) enables public internet access for resources in a public subnet by allowing both inbound and outbound traffic.
- A NAT Gateway is designed for private subnet instances that need to initiate outbound internet connections while remaining inaccessible from the public internet.

The following table highlights the fundamental differences between these two AWS gateway services:

Feature	Internet Gateway (IGW)	NAT Gateway
Traffic Type	Supports both inbound and outbound traffic.	Supports only outbound traffic.
Subnet Type	Used for public subnets.	Used for private subnets.
Public IP Requirement	Requires a public IPv4 or Elastic IP.	Does not require public IPs for private instances.
Inbound Access	Allows internet users to access public subnet instances.	Blocks inbound connections from the internet.
Security Risk	Higher risk if misconfigured.	More secure as it prevents unsolicited inbound traffic.

Table 5.14: *Internet Gateway versus NAT Gateway*

Best Practice:

- Use an Internet Gateway (IGW) for web servers, APIs, and load balancers.
- Use a NAT Gateway for private subnet instances needing outbound access.

Case Studies

Let us look into an in-depth examination of real-world scenarios, to analyze key issues, challenges, and solutions.

Implementing a Secure and Scalable Network Architecture Using Amazon VPC

Case Study Overview

A leading e-commerce company is expanding its business and is also migrating its infrastructure to AWS. The company requires a secure, scalable, and a high-performance network architecture to support its web applications, customer databases, and backend processing systems. To achieve this, the company utilizes Amazon Virtual Private Cloud (VPC) to design an isolated cloud environment, ensuring security, high availability, and seamless internet connectivity.

This case study covers:

- **VPC Overview:** Creating an isolated cloud network.
- **Subnet Creation:** Setting up public and private subnets with controlled communication.
- **Route Tables:** Configuring routing policies for efficient traffic flow.
- **Gateways:** Implementing Internet Gateway (IGW) and NAT Gateway (NGW) for secure connectivity.

VPC Overview: Defining an Isolated Cloud Network

Challenge:

The company wants to isolate its cloud resources while ensuring controlled communication between internal applications and the internet. They need private networking for sensitive workloads and public accessibility for web services.

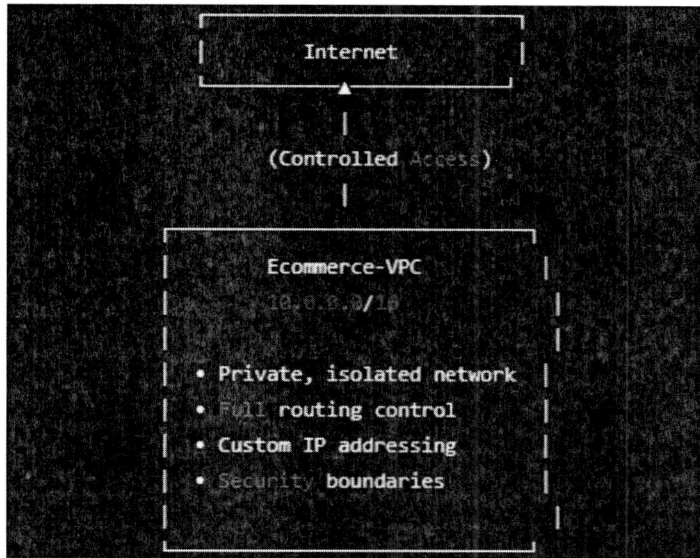

Figure 5.10: *Logical VPC Layout*

Solution:

The company creates an Amazon VPC named Ecommerce-VPC to establish a private, logically isolated cloud network with complete control over IP address ranges, routing, and internet access policies.

VPC Configuration Details:

The VPC Configuration details are provided as follows:

Component	Configuration
VPC Name	Ecommerce-VPC
CIDR Block	10.0.0.0/16
Region	us-east-1
Subnets	2 Public, 2 Private
Internet Access	Internet Gateway (IGW) for public subnets, NAT Gateway (NGW) for private subnets

Table 5.15: *VPC Configuration Details*

Outcome: The VPC serves as a secure networking foundation, providing network segmentation and controlled communication for workloads.

Subnet Creation: Public and Private Subnets and Routing between Subnets

Challenge:

The architecture of the company requires:

- Public subnets for hosting web applications and APIs.

- Private subnets for databases and backend processing, ensuring they remain isolated.
- Controlled communication between public and private subnets for application interaction.

Solution:

The company creates two public subnets and two private subnets across different Availability Zones (AZs) for high availability.

Subnet Type	Subnet Name	CIDR Block	Availability Zone	Purpose
Public Subnet 1	Public-Subnet-A	10.0.1.0/24	us-east-1a	Hosts web servers
Public Subnet 2	Public-Subnet-B	10.0.3.0/24	us-east-1b	Load balancers
Private Subnet 1	Private-Subnet-A	10.0.2.0/24	us-east-1a	Database servers
Private Subnet 2	Private-Subnet-B	10.0.4.0/24	us-east-1b	Application backend

Table 5.16: *Subnet Types, its Details and Purpose*

Subnet Routing Implementation:

- Public subnets have direct internet access via IGW.
- Private subnets route outbound traffic through NAT Gateway (NGW) in the public subnet.
- Internal communication between subnets occurs via local VPC routing.

Outcome: The company achieves clear network segmentation while ensuring controlled communication between the frontend (public) and backend (private) workloads.

By isolating databases and backend services in private subnets without direct internet access, the architecture significantly reduces the attack surface, ensuring that only controlled, application-level traffic from public subnets can reach sensitive workloads.

Route Tables: Configuring and Associating Routes

Challenge:

The company needs to ensure:

- Web applications (public subnets) can access the internet for serving customers.
- Database and application servers (private subnets) can access external services (for example, software updates) without being publicly exposed.
- Proper subnet-to-subnet communication within the VPC.

Reminder: Each subnet must be explicitly associated with a route table.

Solution:

The company configures two route tables:

A. Public Route Table (Associated with Public Subnets)

Destination	Target	Purpose
10.0.0.0/16	**local**	Ensures internal communication within the VPC
0.0.0.0/0	**Internet Gateway (IGW)**	Enables public internet access

Table 5.17: *Public Route Table*

Effect: Public-facing resources (for example, web servers) are accessible via the internet.

B. Private Route Table (Associated with Private Subnets)

Destination	Target	Purpose
10.0.0.0/16	**local**	Allows communication within the VPC
0.0.0.0/0	**NAT Gateway (NGW)**	Allows private subnets to send outbound traffic securely

Table 5.18: *Private Route Table*

Effect: Private instances can access external updates and APIs, but remain protected from unsolicited inbound internet traffic.

Gateways: Implementing Internet Gateway (IGW) and NAT Gateway (NGW)

Challenge:

- Web servers in the public subnet require full internet access.
- Database and application servers in private subnets should only initiate outbound connections (for example, software updates) while blocking inbound traffic.

Solution:

The company implements:

- Internet Gateway (IGW) for public subnets.
- NAT Gateway (NGW) in the public subnet for private subnet outbound access.

Internet Gateway Setup for Public Subnets

Steps Taken:

- Created an Internet Gateway (Ecommerce-IGW).
- Attached IGW to Ecommerce-VPC.
- Updated Public Route Table (0.0.0.0/0 → IGW).

Effect: Public subnet instances (for example, web servers) can now **serve external users**.

NAT Gateway Setup for Private Subnets

Steps Taken:

- Deployed a NAT Gateway (Ecommerce-NGW) in the public subnet.
- Attached an Elastic IP to ensure a static public IP.
- Updated Private Route Table (0.0.0.0/0 → NAT Gateway).

Effect: Private subnet instances can access the internet for updates but remain inaccessible from external sources.

Case Study Results

The following are the results provided based on the case study analysis:

Achieved a Secure, Scalable Cloud Network

- A fully isolated Amazon VPC provides strong security boundaries and granular network control.
- Public and private subnets enable clear workload segmentation, improving both security and performance.

- Architecture aligns with AWS Well-Architected Framework – Security Pillar by minimizing public exposure and enforcing least-privilege network access.

Seamless Routing and Traffic Flow

- Public-facing applications access the internet through the Internet Gateway (IGW).
- Private instances securely access external services using a NAT Gateway, without being directly exposed.
- All internal communication remains within the VPC, reinforcing trust boundaries and reducing attack vectors.

Aligns with Reliability Pillar through predictable routing and AZ-aware design.

Improved Performance and Cost Optimization

- Auto Scaling in public subnets ensures high availability during traffic spikes.
- Controlled outbound access from private subnets avoids unnecessary internet exposure and limits NAT traffic.
- Use of VPC endpoints (where applicable) reduces NAT Gateway data processing costs.

Aligns with Cost Optimization Pillar by balancing managed services with traffic control.

Security Compliance Achieved

- Security Groups and Network ACLs enforce strict inbound and outbound access controls.
- Private subnets block direct inbound internet traffic, protecting sensitive data and backend services.
- Architecture supports compliance with common security standards by enforcing network isolation.

Aligns with Security and Operational Excellence Pillars.

Measurable Business Impact

- Improved deployment time by ~40% after migrating to a standardized VPC architecture.
- Reduced manual network configuration errors through reusable subnet and routing patterns.
- Increased application availability due to multi-AZ subnet design.

This case study demonstrates a real-world implementation of Amazon VPC networking best practices, covering VPC setup, subnet design, route table configuration, and gateway usage.

By adopting this architecture, the e-commerce company successfully deployed a secure, reliable, scalable, and cost-optimized AWS environment aligned with the AWS Well-Architected Framework.

Conclusion

Amazon Virtual Private Cloud (VPC) is the backbone of AWS networking, enabling businesses to securely isolate, control, and manage their cloud environments. By strategically configuring subnets, route tables, and gateways, organizations can achieve scalability, security, and seamless connectivity.

Throughout this guide, we have covered:

- VPC Overview: Setting up an isolated cloud network.
- Subnet Creation: Dividing the network into public and private zones.
- Route Tables: Defining routing rules for efficient communication.
- Gateways: Implementing Internet Gateway (IGW) and NAT Gateway (NGW) for secure internet access.

In the real world, most enterprises start their AWS journey with this 2-tier VPC architecture (public + private subnets) because it strikes the right balance between security, scalability, and operational simplicity. It provides a proven baseline that can later be extended to multi-tier designs (web, app, and database), hybrid connectivity, and zero-trust networking models.

In the next chapter, we shall cover the Advanced Virtual Private Cloud (VPC) including VPC Peering, Transit Gateway, and inter-region connectivity.

Points to Remember

- **Amazon VPC: The Foundation of Cloud Networking**
  - Amazon VPC allows full control over network configurations, including IP addressing, subnet segmentation, and traffic routing.
  - A VPC operates in an isolated cloud environment, ensuring enhanced security and compliance.
  - Customizable components like subnets, route tables, and gateways make it scalable and flexible for various workloads.
- **Subnet Creation: Structuring Your Network Efficiently**
  - Subnets divide a VPC into smaller network segments to control access and resource placement.
  - Public subnets host resources that require direct internet access (for example, web servers).
  - Private subnets keep sensitive workloads isolated from external exposure (for example, databases, backend services).
  - Routing between subnets is managed via route tables, ensuring controlled communication.
- **Route Tables: Defining Network Traffic Flow**
  - Every subnet must be associated with a route table, which determines how traffic is forwarded.
  - Public route tables must include an Internet Gateway (IGW) route (0.0.0.0/0 → IGW) for outbound traffic.
  - Private route tables should route internet-bound traffic via a NAT Gateway to maintain outbound access while blocking inbound access.
  - Internal traffic remains within the VPC using local routes (10.0.0.0/16 → local).
- **Internet Gateway (IGW): Enabling Public Internet Access**
  - IGW allows public subnet instances to access the internet.
  - Supports inbound and outbound traffic, making it ideal for web servers, APIs, and load balancers.
  - Requires public IP addresses or Elastic IPs for external connectivity.
  - Security must be enforced using Security Groups and Network ACLs to prevent unauthorized access.
- **NAT Gateway (NGW): Secure Outbound Internet Access for Private Subnets**
  - NAT Gateway enables private subnet instances to access the internet for software updates, external API calls, and cloud services.

- Unlike IGW, NAT Gateway blocks inbound traffic, ensuring private subnet instances remain unreachable from the internet.
- Deployed in public subnets and associated with private subnet route tables (0.0.0.0/0 → NAT Gateway).
- Preferred over NAT Instances due to higher scalability, automatic failover, and lower maintenance overhead.

- **Best Practices for Amazon VPC Networking**
    - Use separate route tables for public and private subnets to enforce proper traffic control.
    - Deploy Internet Gateway (IGW) only where necessary, ensuring web-facing applications have controlled access.
    - Utilize NAT Gateway for private subnets to maintain security while allowing outbound traffic.
    - Enable VPC Flow Logs to monitor and audit network traffic for compliance and security analysis.
    - Implement AWS PrivateLink or VPC Endpoints to access AWS services securely without routing through the public internet.
    - Distribute workloads across multiple Availability Zones (AZs) for high availability and fault tolerance.
- **Common Mistakes to Avoid**
    - Placing or attaching a NAT Gateway to a private subnet
    - NAT Gateways must be deployed in a public subnet with a route to an Internet Gateway; placing them in a private subnet breaks outbound connectivity.
    - Using a single route table for both public and private subnets
    - This can accidentally expose private resources to the internet or block required access. Always use separate route tables to enforce proper traffic control.

By leveraging Amazon VPC and its networking components effectively, businesses can design robust cloud architectures that ensure high security, scalability, and efficient traffic management. In the next chapter, dive into advanced VPC features and hybrid connectivity setups. Topics include VPC Peering, Transit Gateway, and inter-region connectivity.

CHAPTER 6
Advanced VPC and Hybrid Connectivity

Introduction

As cloud architectures continue to evolve, businesses demand scalable, secure, and highly available network solutions. Virtual Private Cloud (VPC) in AWS serves as the foundation for creating isolated cloud environments, but as enterprises grow, their networking needs to extend beyond a single VPC.

This chapter explores advanced VPC features and hybrid connectivity strategies that enable organizations to interconnect multiple VPCs, AWS accounts, and even on-premises data centers. By implementing VPC Peering, AWS Transit Gateway, and inter-region connectivity, organizations can build efficient, secure, and globally distributed network architectures.

A hybrid cloud approach integrates on-premises infrastructure with cloud environments, allowing businesses to maintain low-latency connectivity, optimized security, and centralized network management. This chapter will guide you through the best practices, security considerations, and real-world use cases of hybrid networking.

Structure

In this chapter, we will walk through:

- VPC Peering
- AWS Transit Gateway
- Multi-Region Connectivity
- Security in Hybrid Networks
- Case Studies

VPC Peering

VPC Peering is an AWS service that allows direct, private connectivity between two Virtual Private Clouds (VPCs), enabling them to communicate using private IP addresses. This is a non-transitive, point-to-point networking connection and can be established between:

- VPCs within the same AWS account.
- VPCs across different AWS accounts.
- VPCs across different AWS regions (Cross-region peering).

Once peered, resources in both VPCs, such as EC2 instances, RDS databases, and Lambda functions, can communicate without traversing the public internet, providing low-latency, and secure communication.

In modern cloud architectures, applications are often distributed across multiple VPCs to enhance security, comply with organizational boundaries, or support different environments (for example, development, staging, and production). VPC Peering allows seamless communication between these isolated environments.

Common Scenarios Where VPC Peering is Beneficial:

- **Multi-Account Architectures:** Large organizations often use AWS Organizations to manage separate AWS accounts for security and billing. Peering enables these VPCs to share resources without exposing them to the public internet.
- **Environment Separation:** Companies might deploy production and development environments in separate VPCs for isolation. VPC Peering provides controlled communication between these environments.
- **Microservices Architecture:** In a microservices-based deployment, services might be deployed in different VPCs. Peering enables service-to-service communication without needing public endpoints.
- **Multi-Region Cloud Connectivity:** If a company has VPCs across multiple regions, VPC Peering ensures low-latency inter-region connectivity for global applications.

The following is a simple VPC Peering setup between two VPCs within the same AWS account:

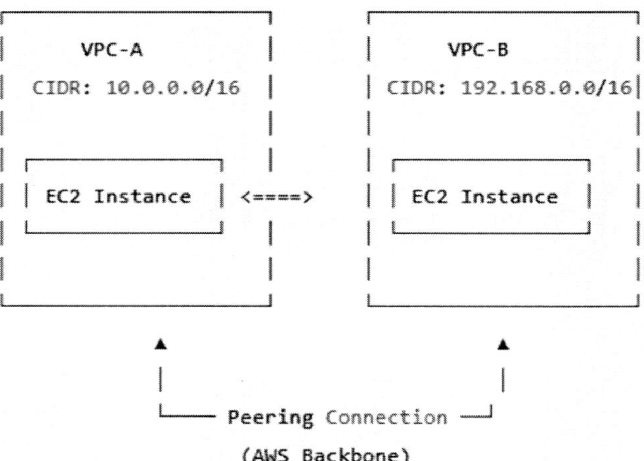

Figure 6.1: *VPC Peering Connection*

- `VPC-A (10.0.0.0/16)` and `VPC-B (192.168.0.0/16)` are peer reviewed.
- EC2 instances in VPC-A can communicate directly with instances in VPC-B using private IPs.
- The connection remains private, with no exposure to the internet.

Key Benefits of VPC Peering

- **Private and Secure Communication:** Traffic between peered VPCs does not traverse the public internet, enhancing security.
- **Low Latency and High Performance:** Uses the internal backbone network of AWS to ensure minimal latency.
- **Cross-Account Connectivity:** Peering allows connections between VPCs across different AWS accounts, making it ideal for multi-account architectures.

- **Cost-Efficient:** Unlike AWS Transit Gateway, VPC Peering has no additional bandwidth-based charges beyond standard data transfer costs.

Feature	VPC Peering	AWS Transit Gateway	AWS PrivateLink
Type of Connection	Point-to-Point	Hub-and-Spoke (Centralized)	Service Endpoint
Transitive Routing	✕ Not Supported	✓ Supported	✕ Not Supported
Cross-Account	✓ Yes	✓ Yes	✓ Yes
Cross-Region	✓ Yes	✓ Yes	✓ Yes
Cost**	No additional charge (only data transfer fees)	Transit Gateway pricing applies	PrivateLink pricing applies
Use Case	Simple VPC interconnectivity	Large-scale multi-VPC setups	Service-to-service connections

Table 6.1: *Comparison Table – VPC Peering versus Other AWS Networking Solutions*

**Peering itself has no hourly cost, but cross-region peering incurs standard inter-region data transfer charges (different from intra-region).

Limitations of VPC Peering

- **No Transitive Routing:**
  - If VPC-A is peered with VPC-B and VPC-B is peered with VPC-C, VPC-A cannot communicate with VPC-C through B.
  - This limitation requires manual peering connections between all VPCs that need direct communication, which can become complex in large environments.

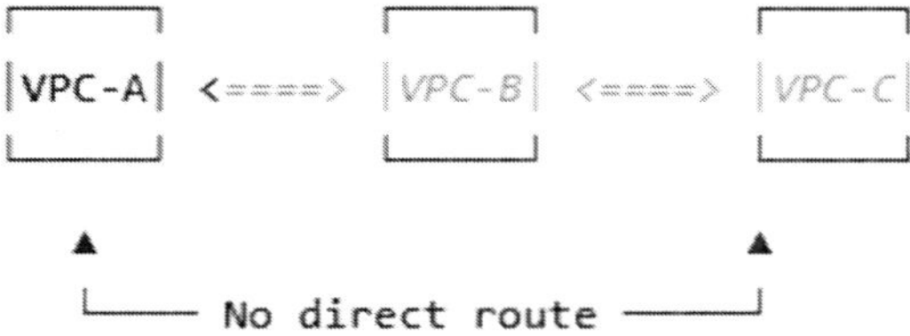

Figure 6.2: *Transitive Routing Limitation*

- **Manual Route Management:** Routes must be manually configured in the route table of each VPC, making management complex in large-scale environments.
- **Overlapping CIDR Blocks that are Not Supported:** If the CIDR blocks of two VPCs overlap, peering cannot be established, which may require re-planning IP ranges.
- **DNS Resolution Configuration:** Private DNS resolution must be explicitly enabled for cross-VPC name resolution.

The maximum number of active peering connections per VPC is limited (125 as of now, but confirm AWS limits).

Setting up VPC Peering

Setting up a VPC Peering connection involves several carefully coordinated steps to ensure secure, private, and efficient communication between two Virtual Private Clouds (VPCs). This section provides a step-by-step guide, complete with best practices, diagrams, and detailed configurations to successfully establish and manage VPC peering connections.

To establish a VPC peering connection, the following high-level steps are required:

- **Create a VPC Peering Connection:** Initiate the peering request from the requesting VPC.
- **Accept the Peering Connection:** The owner of the peer VPC must accept the request.
- **Update Route Tables:** Modify route tables in both VPCs to enable traffic flow.
- **Update Security Groups and Network ACLs:** Configure security groups and ACLs for permitted traffic.
- **Enable Private DNS Resolution (Optional):** Allow DNS name resolution across peered VPCs.

Step 1: Initiating a VPC Peering Request

1. Navigate to AWS VPC Console → Select Peering Connections → Click **`Create Peering Connection`**.
2. Choose Requester VPC and specify the Peer VPC (same or another AWS account).
3. Select the AWS region (same or cross-region peering).

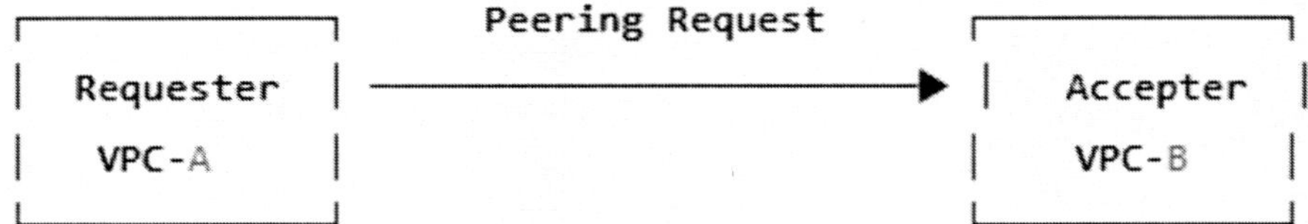

Figure 6.3: *Peering Request Flow*

Step 2: Accepting the Peering Request

1. The owner of the Peer VPC must accept the request via the VPC Peering Console.
2. If it is a cross-account request, the accepting user must have permissions for accepting peering connections.

Even after establishing the peering connection, traffic will not flow between VPCs until route tables are updated.

Route tables define how traffic is routed within and across VPCs. Without adding routes, VPCs remain isolated despite the active peering connection.

Step 3: Configuring Route Tables

1. Go to Route Tables in both VPCs.
2. Add a new route pointing to the CIDR block of the Peer VPC, specifying the VPC Peering Connection as the target.

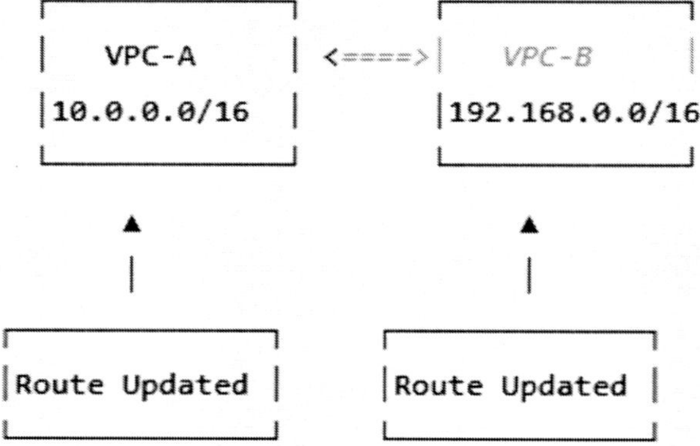

Figure 6.4: *Traffic Flow Post Route Configuration*

Even with route tables configured, traffic will be blocked unless Security Groups (SGs) and Network Access Control Lists (NACLs) are properly set up.

Step 4: Updating Security Groups and Network ACLs

1. Modify Security Groups to allow traffic from the Peer VPC CIDR block.
2. Adjust Network ACLs to ensure traffic is permitted between both VPCs.

Step 5: Enabling Private DNS Resolution (Optional)

If applications need to communicate via private domain names, enable DNS resolution for peering connections using the AWS CLI or console.

Issue	Possible Cause	Solution
Peering connection is active, but no traffic	Route tables not updated	Add proper routes to both VPCs
Ping/SSH failing despite route updates	Security groups or NACLs blocking traffic	Allow inbound/outbound traffic for peer CIDR
Intermittent or hanging connections	MTU mismatch (jumbo frames)	Ensure MTU is consistent (typically 1500) across instances, VPNs, and on-prem devices; disable jumbo frames if needed
DNS names not resolving	DNS resolution not enabled	Enable private DNS resolution for peering
Peering request rejected	Overlapping CIDR blocks or permissions	Use unique CIDR ranges; check IAM roles

Table 6.2: *Troubleshooting Common Issues*

Best Practices for VPC Peering

While setting up a VPC Peering connection may seem straightforward, maintaining an efficient, secure, and scalable network architecture requires adherence to several best practices. This section covers strategic guidelines, architectural tips, and security considerations to optimize VPC peering in AWS environments.

- **Optimize Route Management**
  - **Use a Consistent CIDR Strategy:** Avoid overlapping CIDR blocks to prevent routing conflicts.
  - **Automate Route Updates:** In large environments, use AWS Lambda with SDK/API calls to manage routes dynamically.
- **Scale for Multi-Account Environments**
  - **Use AWS Organizations and Service Control Policies (SCPs):** Prevent unauthorized users from creating unnecessary peering connections.
  - **Implement a Naming Convention:** Define a structured naming convention for easier management (like peer-us-east-1-vpc1-vpc2).
- **Monitor and Secure Peering Connections**
  - **Use AWS VPC Flow Logs:** Capture traffic patterns and detect unauthorized access attempts.
  - **Apply Principle of Least Privilege:** Restrict security group rules to only required ports/IPs.

- **Consider Alternatives for Large-Scale Networking**

  For large multi-VPC architectures, VPC Peering may become difficult to scale. Consider:

  - **AWS Transit Gateway:** Enables centralized VPC connectivity with transitive routing.
  - **AWS PrivateLink:** Provides service-to-service private connectivity without exposing VPCs to each other.

Consider a scenario in which a **media streaming company** operates three environments:

- **Production VPC:** Hosts customer-facing applications.
- **Staging VPC:** Used for testing new features before deployment.
- **Analytics VPC:** Runs machine learning workloads on user data.

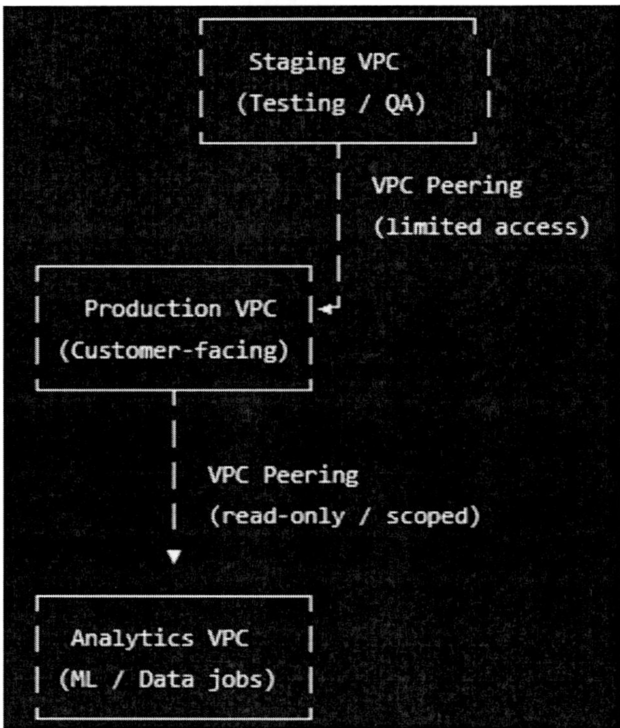

Figure 6.5: *Media Streaming Company – VPC Peering Design*

VPC peering is not transitive.

If Staging needed Analytics access later, it would require explicit peering — or a hub-and-spoke design using Transit Gateway.

Challenge:

They need secure, low-latency connectivity between Production ↔ Staging and Production ↔ Analytics while preventing direct Staging ↔ Analytics communication for security reasons.

Solution with VPC Peering:

1. **Established two VPC Peering connections:**
   a. Production ↔ Staging
   b. Production ↔ Analytics
2. Configured route tables and security groups to control traffic flow.
3. Enabled DNS resolution for seamless communication between environments.

Outcome:

- Achieved **low-latency communication** for real-time analytics.
- Improved **testing workflows** by enabling direct Staging-Production connectivity.
- Enhanced **security controls** by restricting unnecessary communications.

VPC Peering provides private, low-latency connectivity between AWS VPCs, making it ideal for small to medium-sized architectures that require simple, secure, and direct communication.

However, VPC Peering is limited by its lack of transitive routing and manual management overhead in large-scale environments. For complex architectures, consider using AWS Transit Gateway or PrivateLink.

Multi-Region VPC Peering

In an increasingly globalized digital landscape, organizations often deploy applications across multiple AWS regions to achieve high availability, disaster recovery, and lower latency for global users. Multi-region VPC Peering enables private, secure communication between VPCs located in different AWS regions, ensuring that applications can seamlessly communicate without routing traffic over the public internet.

This section explores how multi-region VPC peering works, its benefits, limitations, use cases, and best practices to leverage global AWS infrastructure efficiently.

Multi-region VPC Peering is a feature that allows direct, private connectivity between VPCs in different AWS regions. Similar to same-region peering, it uses the global network backbone of AWS, providing low-latency, and encrypted communication between cross-region resources.

Key Benefits of Multi-Region VPC Peering

- **Global Low-Latency Communication:** Establish private connections between VPCs in different geographical regions without relying on public internet routes.
- **Enhanced Disaster Recovery:** Multi-region peering enables quick failover and redundancy, ensuring applications remain available even if a region experiences downtime.
- **Improved User Experience:** By serving users from VPCs closest to their location, you can reduce latency and improve responsiveness.
- **Simplified Global Network Architecture:** Connect applications deployed in various regions without complex VPN configurations.
- **Cost-Effective Alternative:** Compared to third-party network providers, the backbone of AWS offers competitive pricing and reliable performance.

When you peer two VPCs across AWS regions, AWS establishes a private network tunnel between them using its global fiber network. This connection allows bidirectional communication between instances, databases, and services in both VPCs.

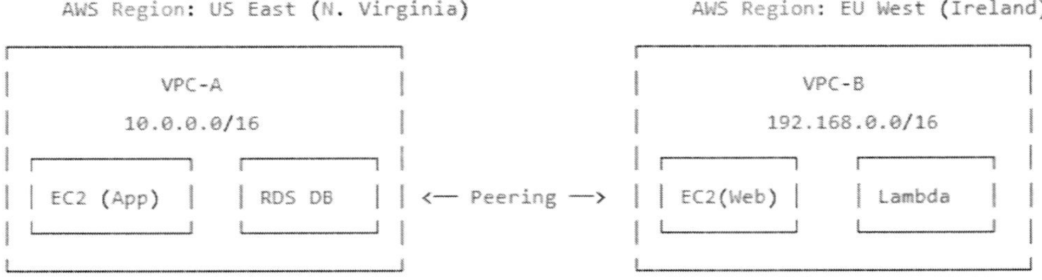

Figure 6.6: *VPC Peering across AWS Regions*

- VPC-A (in us-east-1) and VPC-B (in eu-west-1) are connected via a multi-region VPC peering connection.
- Resources such as EC2 instances, RDS databases, and Lambda functions communicate directly over the secure backbone of AWS.
- Traffic never leaves the AWS network, ensuring privacy and reducing latency.

Use Cases for Multi-Region VPC Peering

Disaster Recovery and High Availability

- **Scenario:** A financial services company runs its primary infrastructure in us-east-1 and maintains a secondary infrastructure in eu-west-1 for disaster recovery.
- **Solution:**
    - Multi-region peering ensures real-time replication of critical data between both VPCs.
    - In case of failure in us-east-1, traffic reroutes to eu-west-1.
- **Benefit:** Achieves High Availability (HA) and Disaster Recovery (DR) compliance.

Global Application Deployment

- **Scenario:** A global e-commerce platform serves customers in North America and Europe.
- **Solution:**
    - Deploys applications in us-east-1 (for US customers) and eu-west-1 (for European customers).
    - Peered VPCs enable centralized data access while maintaining regional deployments.
- **Benefit:** Provides low-latency access and regionally compliant data processing.

Hybrid Cloud Solutions across Regions

- **Scenario:** A healthcare provider needs to securely share patient data between its on-premises data center and AWS VPCs across multiple regions.
- **Solution:**
    - Establishes multi-region VPC peering for secure data synchronization.
    - Integrates with AWS Direct Connect for on-premises connectivity.
- **Benefit:** Ensures HIPAA compliance and fast, secure data access.

Mergers and Acquisitions Integration

- **Scenario:** Two companies operating in different AWS regions merge and need to integrate their applications.
- **Solution:**
    - Peered VPCs allow both environments to communicate directly during integration.
    - Gradual consolidation occurs without service disruption.
- **Benefit:** Facilitates smooth transition and collaborative operations.

Challenges and Considerations in Multi-Region Peering

While multi-region VPC peering is powerful, certain challenges must be considered:

- **Data Transfer Costs:**
  - Cross-region data transfer incurs charges.
  - Evaluate cost implications for high-volume data replication.
- **No Transitive Routing:**
  - If VPC-A ↔ VPC-B and VPC-B ↔ VPC-C are peered, VPC-A cannot communicate with VPC-C through B.
  - **Solution:** Create direct peering connections between all necessary VPCs or use AWS Transit Gateway.
- **Latency Considerations:**
  - Despite the global backbone of AWS, cross-region latency may still affect real-time applications.
  - Use latency monitoring tools to assess suitability.

Best Practices for Multi-Region VPC Peering

- **Use Unique CIDR Blocks:** Prevents routing conflicts.
- **Implement IAM Policies:** Restrict peering modifications to authorized users.
- **Monitor Peering Traffic:** Use VPC Flow Logs for auditing and security analysis.
- **Plan for Costs:** Budget for cross-region data transfer fees.
- **Consider AWS Transit Gateway for Complex Setups:** Offers simplified, scalable multi-region connectivity.

Case Study: Global SaaS Application Deployment

Scenario: A SaaS company provides a **video conferencing platform** with users in the **US, Europe, and Asia**.

Challenges:

- Need for low-latency communication between global data centers.
- Compliance with regional data regulations.

Solution:

- Deployed VPCs in us-east-1, eu-central-1, and ap-southeast-1.
- Established multi-region VPC peering connections between all regions.
- Enabled private DNS resolution for seamless service discovery.

Outcome:

- **Reduced latency by 30%** for global users.
- **Improved customer experience** with faster data retrieval.
- **Compliance achieved** with regional data processing regulations.

Multi-region VPC peering is an essential tool for organizations seeking global scalability, high availability, and disaster recovery in their cloud architectures. While it offers direct, secure connectivity across regions, careful planning around costs, latency, and network complexity is crucial for successful deployment.

AWS Transit Gateway

As organizations scale their cloud infrastructure, managing connectivity between multiple Virtual Private Clouds (VPCs), on-premises networks, and remote offices becomes increasingly complex. While VPC Peering provides direct connections between VPCs, it becomes unmanageable in large-scale environments due to its point-to-point nature and lack of transitive routing.

AWS Transit Gateway (TGW) addresses these challenges by acting as a central hub to connect multiple VPCs, AWS accounts, on-premises data centers, and remote networks. With a hub-and-spoke architecture, Transit Gateway simplifies network topology, improves scalability, and provides transitive routing—enabling connected VPCs to communicate through the gateway without requiring direct peering between each VPC.

While VPC Peering works well for small-scale environments, it does not scale efficiently when you need to connect dozens or hundreds of VPCs. AWS Transit Gateway resolves this by:

- Centralizing network management through a single gateway.
- Supporting transitive routing, enabling VPCs to communicate through the TGW.
- Reducing the complexity of maintaining multiple peering connections.
- Enhancing security and compliance through route segmentation and policies.
- Providing scalability to connect thousands of VPCs and on-premises networks.

Key Features of AWS Transit Gateway

AWS Transit Gateway offers a robust set of features that enable centralized, scalable, and secure network connectivity across diverse cloud and hybrid environments.

- **Centralized Connectivity:** Transit Gateway acts as a central router for your entire network, allowing VPCs, VPNs, Direct Connect, and AWS services to connect through a single point.
- **Transitive Routing Support:** Unlike VPC Peering, TGW allows VPC-A ↔ VPC-B ↔ VPC-C communication through one central hub.
- **Multi-Region Support:** Establish inter-region peering between Transit Gateways in different AWS regions for global network architectures.
- **Security and Segmentation:** Use route tables to segment traffic and control connectivity between VPCs, enhancing security.
- **High Scalability and Performance:**
    - Supports up to 5,000 VPC attachments per Transit Gateway (AWS-published limit as of 2024).
    - Handles multi-gigabit per second throughput.
    - Scales automatically with traffic demand, eliminating the need for manual bandwidth provisioning.
- **Simplified Management:** Manage network connections through a single interface using the AWS Management Console, CLI, or Infrastructure-as-Code (IaC) tools.

The following is a table that compares the Transit Gateway with VPC Peering:

Feature	AWS Transit Gateway	VPC Peering
Routing Type	Hub-and-Spoke (Centralized)	Point-to-Point
Transitive Routing	✅ Supported	❌ Not Supported
Scalability	Thousands of VPCs	Limited & Complex
Cost Efficiency (Large Scale)	✅ More efficient	❌ Costly at scale
Multi-Region Support	✅ Yes (via TGW Peering)	✅ Limited
Management Complexity	Simplified (One TGW)	Complex (Full Mesh)
Use Case	Large, complex networks	Simple connections

***Table 6.3**: Transit Gateway versus VPC Peering*

Transit Gateway functions as a central router, enabling connected networks (VPCs, VPNs, Direct Connect, and so on) to communicate with one another through the gateway. This eliminates the need for complex peering relationships.

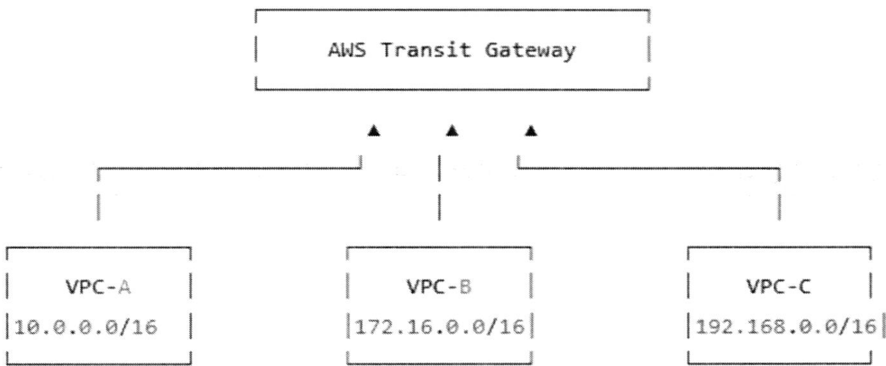

***Figure 6.7**: Hub-and-Spoke Architecture Using AWS Transit Gateway*

- Each VPC attaches to the TGW, forming a spoke connection.
- VPC-A can communicate with VPC-B and VPC-C through the Transit Gateway.
- No direct peering between VPCs is required, reducing complexity.

Use Cases for AWS Transit Gateway

AWS Transit Gateway is widely used in complex cloud architectures to simplify connectivity, enable hybrid networking, and support multi-region resilience at scale.

Large-Scale Multi-VPC Architectures

- **Scenario:** A global e-commerce company operates 50+ VPCs across multiple AWS accounts.
- **Solution:**
  - Implemented Transit Gateway to centralize VPC connectivity.
  - Used separate route tables for production and development environments.
- **Benefit:** Reduced complexity from 1,225 peering connections (for 50 VPCs in a full mesh) to one centralized TGW.

Hybrid Cloud Connectivity

- **Scenario:** A financial services company needs secure, low-latency connectivity between its on-premises data center and AWS environment.
- **Solution:**
    - Connected on-premises network to TGW via AWS Direct Connect and IPSec VPN.
    - Enabled multi-region connectivity using Transit Gateway inter-region peering.
- **Benefit:** Achieved high-speed, private connectivity with failover capabilities.

Multi-Region Disaster Recovery

- **Scenario:** A healthcare provider requires business continuity with cross-region failover.
- **Solution:**
    - Deployed Transit Gateways in us-east-1 and us-west-2.
    - Established inter-region peering for seamless VPC-to-VPC communication.
- **Benefit:** Ensured 99.99% uptime with automatic disaster recovery.

Key Components of AWS Transit Gateway

AWS Transit Gateway consists of key components that enable scalable, flexible, and high-performance connectivity across VPCs, on-premises networks, and multiple regions.

- **Attachments:**
    - **VPC Attachments:** Connect VPCs directly to the TGW.
    - **VPN Attachments:** Securely connect on-premises networks.
    - **Direct Connect Attachments:** High-bandwidth, private network connections.
    - **Peering Attachments:** Connect TGWs across AWS regions.
- **Transit Gateway Route Tables:**
    - Define how traffic flows between attachments.
    - Support multiple route tables for traffic segmentation (such as isolate production and development environments).

  The default route table association and propagation can be disabled for granular segmentation - otherwise, new attachments might accidentally inherit unwanted routes.
- **Bandwidth Management:**
    - Elastic scaling to handle multi-gigabit throughput.
    - Supports thousands of connections without performance degradation.

Advantages of AWS Transit Gateway

AWS Transit Gateway provides a scalable and centralized networking solution that simplifies connectivity, enhances availability, and optimizes costs for complex cloud architectures.

- **Simplified Network Management:** Single hub for all connectivity.
- **Cost-Effective at Scale:** Eliminates full-mesh peering complexities.
- **Supports Transitive Routing:** Enables communication between connected VPCs through the TGW.

- **High Availability:** Built-in redundancy ensures uptime.
- **Global Reach:** Seamless inter-region connectivity via TGW peering.

Limitations and Considerations

While AWS Transit Gateway offers powerful networking capabilities, it is important to consider its limitations related to cost, complexity, and evolving feature support when designing architectures.

- **Additional Cost:** Transit Gateway has per-hour and per-GB data transfer charges.
- **Complex Route Management:** Requires careful planning to avoid misrouted traffic.
- **No IPv6 Support for Inter-Region Peering (as of now):** IPv6 support is limited in certain configurations. IPv6 support is evolving - check AWS docs for the latest status

Best Practices for AWS Transit Gateway Deployment

Implementing best practices for AWS Transit Gateway deployment ensures efficient network segmentation, enhanced security, and scalable connectivity across multiple VPCs and accounts.

- **Segment Traffic Using Multiple Route Tables:** Isolate sensitive workloads (like separate tables for dev and prod).
- **Monitor Traffic Flow with VPC Flow Logs:** Track and audit network activity.
- Use AWS RAM (Resource Access Manager) to share TGWs across accounts.
- Tag attachments and route tables consistently.
- **Leverage AWS Organizations:** Simplify multi-account VPC attachments.
- **Implement Security Controls:** Use AWS Firewall Manager for added protection.
- **Plan for High Availability:** Deploy TGW attachments in multiple Availability Zones.

Setting up AWS Transit Gateway

Setting up an **AWS Transit Gateway (TGW)** enables you to **centralize network management** and establish **efficient connectivity** across multiple VPCs, on-premises networks, and even other AWS Transit Gateways in different regions. This section provides a **comprehensive, step-by-step guide** on how to set up, configure, and manage AWS Transit Gateway, ensuring **optimal performance, security, and scalability**.

Overview of the Setup Process

The process of setting up AWS Transit Gateway involves the following key steps:

1. Create the Transit Gateway.
2. Create and Attach VPCs to the Transit Gateway.
3. Configure Transit Gateway Route Tables.
4. Update VPC Route Tables.
5. Verify Connectivity and Monitor Traffic.
6. (Optional) Attach On-Premises Networks via VPN or Direct Connect.
7. (Optional) Establish Inter-Region Transit Gateway Peering.

Step 1: Create the Transit Gateway

Using the AWS Management Console

1. **Navigate to the AWS Console:**
    a. Open the VPC Dashboard.
    b. Click `Transit Gateways` under the Transit Gateway section.
2. **Create Transit Gateway:**
    a. Click `Create Transit Gateway`.
    b. Fill in the required details:
        i. **Name:** centralized-tgw
        ii. **Description:** Central hub for multi-VPC connectivity
        iii. **Amazon ASN (Autonomous System Number):** (Default is 64512; modify if needed for BGP connections)
        iv. **DNS Support:** Enabled (Allows private DNS resolution between VPCs)
        v. **VPN ECMP Support:** Enabled (For load balancing VPN connections)
        vi. **Default Route Table Association and Propagation:** Choose based on your network segmentation plan.
3. **Create and Save:**
    a. Click `Create Transit Gateway`.
    b. Note the Transit Gateway ID (such as tgw-0a1b2c3d4e5f6g7h).

Step 2: Create and Attach VPCs to the Transit Gateway

Attaching VPCs allows them to communicate with other VPCs and on-premises networks through the Transit Gateway.

Using the AWS Console

1. Go to the VPC Dashboard → Transit Gateway Attachments.
2. Click `Create Transit Gateway Attachment`.
3. Select Attachment Type:
    i. Choose `VPC` from the dropdown.
4. Configure Attachment:
    i. **Transit Gateway ID:** Select your TGW (tgw-0a1b2c3d4e5f6g7h).
    ii. **VPC:** Select the VPC you want to attach (for example, VPC-A).
    iii. **Subnets:** Choose at least one subnet per Availability Zone for high availability.
5. Click `Create Attachment`.

    Repeat the process for all VPCs you want to attach.
6. Check Attachment Status:

    The attachment state will show `"pendingAcceptance"` if cross-account attachments are created. The peer account must accept the attachment.

Step 3: Configure Transit Gateway Route Tables.

Route tables in the Transit Gateway define how traffic is directed between attachments. Each attachment can associate with one route table and propagate routes to it.

Create a Transit Gateway Route Table:

1. Go to **`Transit Gateway Route Tables`** in the AWS Console.
2. Click **`Create Route Table`**.
3. Assign a name (like tgw-prod-route-table) and select your Transit Gateway.
4. Click **`Create`**.

Associate Attachments with Route Tables:

1. Select the newly created route table.
2. Click **`Associations`** → **`Create Association`**.
3. Choose the VPC attachment (such as VPC-A-attachment).

Propagate Routes to the TGW Route Table:

1. Click **`Propagations`** → **`Create Propagation`**.
2. Select the VPC attachment to automatically add its CIDR block to the route table.

Using AWS CLI for Route Table Management

Step 4: Update VPC Route Tables.

Even after configuring the Transit Gateway, **VPC route tables must be updated** to direct traffic towards the TGW.

Steps:

1. Navigate to Route Tables in the VPC console.
2. Select the route table associated with your VPC subnets.
3. Click **`Edit Routes`** → Add Route
4. Destination: Peer VPC's CIDR block (such as 172.16.0.0/16)
5. Target: Select the Transit Gateway ID (tgw-0a1b2c3d4e5f6g7h)
6. Click **Save Routes**.

Repeat for all VPCs involved in the architecture.

Step 5: Verify Connectivity and Monitor Traffic.

Testing Communication between VPCs:

1. Launch EC2 instances in both VPCs (like VPC-A and VPC-B).
2. Connect via SSH and ping the private IP of the other EC2 instance.
3. Successful ping indicates correct routing and security configurations.

Step 6: (Optional) Attach On-Premises Networks via VPN or Direct Connect.

VPN Attachment Setup:

1. Create a Customer Gateway (CGW) representing your on-premises network.
2. Establish a VPN connection to the TGW.
3. Download and configure the VPN device.

Direct Connect Attachment Setup:

For high-bandwidth, low-latency connections:

1. Create a Direct Connect Gateway.

2. Attach the TGW to the Direct Connect Gateway.
3. Establish connectivity with on-premises routers.

Use Case: Ideal for hybrid cloud architectures requiring consistent performance.

Step 7: (Optional) Establish Inter-Region Transit Gateway Peering

To enable global connectivity:

1. Create a peering connection between Transit Gateways in different regions:
2. Accept the peering request in the target region.
3. Update route tables to direct cross-region traffic.

Result: Global VPC communication across multiple AWS regions.

The following is the figure describing the complete transit gateway architecture:

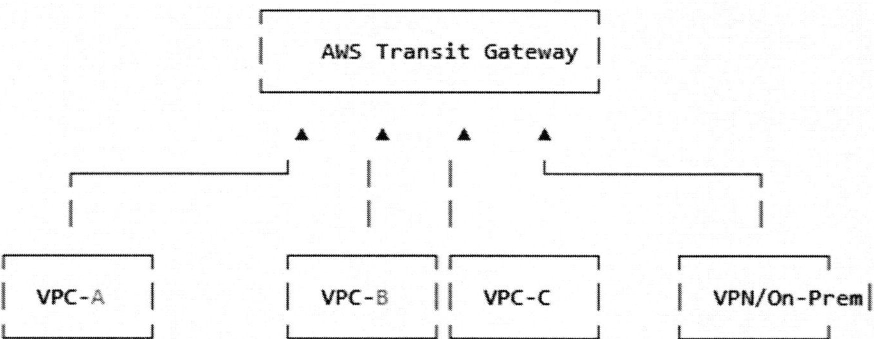

Figure 6.8: *Multi-VPC, Multi-Region, and On-Premises Connectivity with TGW*

- VPCs communicate through TGW without direct peering.
- On-premises network connected via VPN/Direct Connect.

Setting up AWS Transit Gateway transforms how organizations manage their network connectivity. By following this step-by-step guide, you can establish scalable, secure, and efficient connections across VPCs, AWS accounts, on-premises data centers, and even global AWS regions.

AWS TGW reduces complexity, enhances performance, and centralizes network management, making it an essential component of modern cloud architectures.

Multi-Region Connectivity

In the interconnected digital world of today, organizations increasingly operate across multiple geographic locations to meet customer demands for high availability, low latency, and global scalability. As businesses expand globally, multi-region connectivity becomes crucial to ensure seamless communication between cloud environments, on-premises data centers, and distributed applications.

Multi-region is not always required. Some businesses mistakenly assume "multi-region = best practice." It is useful to clarify trade-offs early (cost, complexity vs. actual business need).

Multi-region connectivity enables organizations to interconnect AWS resources deployed in different AWS regions, facilitating resilient, secure, and high-performance architectures. This approach is essential for companies aiming to:

- Serve global users with minimal latency.
- Achieve robust disaster recovery and business continuity.

- Comply with data residency and sovereignty requirements.
- Maintain redundancy and fault tolerance across regions.

This chapter explores the strategies, tools, and best practices for implementing multi-region connectivity using AWS Transit Gateway, VPC Peering, Direct Connect, and VPN solutions. We will dive into real-world use cases, illustrating how organizations can build hybrid architectures that seamlessly connect on-premises data centers with AWS environments across multiple regions.

Importance of Multi-Region Connectivity

Multi-region connectivity is a key architectural strategy for delivering globally distributed applications with improved performance, resilience, and regulatory compliance.

- **Global Reach with Low Latency:** By deploying resources across multiple AWS regions, organizations can serve users from the nearest region, improving application responsiveness and reducing latency.
- **Disaster Recovery and High Availability:** Multi-region architectures enable failover mechanisms that minimize downtime in case of regional failures or outages.
- **Regulatory Compliance:** Certain jurisdictions require data to reside within specific regions. Multi-region setups ensure compliance while maintaining global operations.
- **Hybrid Cloud Enablement:** Businesses running on-premises workloads can leverage multi-region AWS connectivity for backup, replication, and hybrid application deployments.

Key Connectivity Options for Multi-Region Setups

AWS provides several solutions for establishing multi-region connectivity:

- **AWS Transit Gateway Inter-Region Peering:**
  - Connects Transit Gateways across different AWS regions.
  - Enables transitive routing between VPCs in different regions.
  - Low-latency communication over the AWS global backbone.
- **VPC Peering (Cross-Region):**
  - Direct, point-to-point connections between VPCs in different regions.
  - Best suited for simple architectures with few VPCs.
  - No transitive routing, requiring separate connections for each VPC pair.
- **AWS Direct Connect (DX) with Multi-Region Access:**
  - Provides dedicated private connections to AWS from on-premises environments.
  - Reduced latency and increased bandwidth compared to VPNs.
  - Supports multi-region VPC connectivity through Direct Connect Gateway.
- **AWS Cloud WAN:**
  - It is a newer AWS service for global connectivity
  - It could be mentioned as an alternative for enterprise-scale networking.
- **VPN Connections across Regions:**
  - Secure IPSec tunnels for encrypted communication.
  - Useful for quick, cost-effective cross-region connectivity.
  - May experience higher latency compared to Direct Connect.

Challenges in Multi-Region Connectivity

While multi-region architectures offer significant benefits, they come with certain challenges:

- **Increased Complexity:** Managing multiple regions requires careful planning and configuration.
- **Higher Costs:** Cross-region data transfer and infrastructure duplication may incur additional expenses.
- Monitoring and troubleshooting multi-region traffic.
- IAM/scoping complexities when managing cross-region resources.
- Security policies differ across jurisdictions.
- **Latency Considerations:** Despite the backbone network of AWS, latency can still be a factor, especially over long distances.
- **Routing Conflicts:** Misconfigured route tables can lead to traffic blackholing or overlapping CIDR conflicts.

Multi-region connectivity is a vital component of modern cloud architectures, allowing organizations to serve global customers, enhance availability, and meet compliance requirements. AWS offers robust solutions that cater to various connectivity needs, whether you are connecting VPCs, integrating on-premises environments, or building global applications.

In the following sections, we will explore design considerations, technical configurations, and real-world use cases to help you build effective, secure, and scalable multi-region architectures.

Multi-Region VPC Design Considerations

Designing a multi-region Virtual Private Cloud (VPC) architecture requires careful planning to ensure optimal performance, high availability, compliance, and cost-efficiency. With AWS offering a global infrastructure spanning multiple regions, organizations can strategically deploy applications to reduce latency, enhance fault tolerance, and meet data residency requirements.

Key Considerations for Multi-Region VPC Design

This section explores the key considerations and best practices for architecting robust multi-region VPC networks. We will address factors like latency, redundancy, data compliance, security, and how to choose between different connectivity options such as AWS Transit Gateway Inter-Region Peering and VPC Cross-Region Peering.

Latency and Network Performance

Low latency is critical for real-time applications, global user experiences, and cross-region data replication.

Considerations:

- Inter-region latency varies depending on the geographical distance between AWS regions.
- Use AWS Global Accelerator or Amazon CloudFront to reduce latency for user-facing applications.
- For backend VPC communications, use AWS Transit Gateway Inter-Region Peering to leverage the private global network of AWS for lower latency.

Redundancy and High Availability

Natural disasters, regional outages, or unexpected failures can disrupt services. Redundancy ensures continuous availability.

Considerations:

- Deploy applications in multiple AWS regions for geo-redundancy.
- Use multi-region active-active or active-passive architectures for failover.
- Implement Amazon Route 53 health checks to automatically route traffic to healthy regions.
- Ensure multi-AZ (Availability Zone) deployments within each region for added resilience.

Data Residency and Compliance

Laws like GDPR and HIPAA require data storage and processing within specific geographic boundaries.

Considerations:

- Deploy VPCs in regions that comply with local data regulations.
- Use AWS Organizations Service Control Policies (SCPs) to restrict resource deployment to specific regions.
- Ensure cross-region data transfers comply with regulatory requirements.

Connectivity Options: Transit Gateway versus VPC Peering

Choosing the right connectivity method affects scalability, cost, and network complexity.

Option A: AWS Transit Gateway Inter-Region Peering

Pros:

- The centralized hub-and-spoke model reduces complexity.
- Transitive routing allows VPC-A to communicate with VPC-B through the TGW.
- High scalability for large multi-account environments.
- Encrypted, low-latency communication via AWS backbone.

Cons:

- Additional per-hour and per-GB data transfer charges.
- Requires careful route table management to avoid conflicts.

Option B: VPC Cross-Region Peering

Pros:

- Direct, private connectivity between two VPCs.
- Cost-effective for small architectures with few VPCs.
- No Transit Gateway overhead costs.

Cons:

- No transitive routing – each VPC pair requires its own peering connection.
- Scalability issues with more than a few VPCs.
- Complex management as the number of VPCs increases.

Security and Access Control

Multi-region architectures increase the attack surface and require robust security measures.

Considerations:

- Use Security Groups and Network ACLs to restrict traffic between VPCs.
- Enable AWS Identity and Access Management (IAM) policies for fine-grained control over VPC and TGW configurations.

- TGW inter-region peering traffic is automatically encrypted on AWS backbone, but some customers still use VPN/IPSec for compliance.
- Implement AWS Key Management Service (KMS) for encrypting data in transit and at rest.
- Use VPC Flow Logs to monitor and audit cross-region traffic.

Cost Optimization

Cross-region data transfers can significantly increase AWS costs.

Considerations:

- Use cost calculators to estimate cross-region traffic expenses.
- Minimize unnecessary data replication and only transfer essential data.
- Leverage Direct Connect for high-volume, cost-effective cross-region communication.
- Enable cost allocation tags to monitor and attribute expenses accurately.

DNS and Traffic Management

Efficient traffic routing and DNS management ensure that users access the nearest, healthiest region.

Considerations:

- Use Amazon Route 53 for geo-based routing and health checks.
- Enable private DNS resolution for seamless VPC-to-VPC communication.
- Implement latency-based routing policies to direct users to the closest region.

Data Replication and Synchronization

Cross-region replication ensures data availability but may introduce latency and consistency challenges.

Considerations:

- Use Amazon S3 Cross-Region Replication (CRR) for object storage.
- For databases, use Amazon RDS Global Databases, Amazon Aurora Global Database, or DynamoDB Global Tables depending on workload and consistency needs.
- Evaluate latency, consistency, and cost trade-offs
- Strongly consistent replication increases write latency, while eventual consistency offers lower latency at the cost of temporary data divergence.

Multi-Region VPC Design Patterns

Active-Active Architecture

Description: Both regions handle traffic simultaneously, improving latency and availability. Global consistency across databases is challenging; recommend DynamoDB Global Tables or Aurora Global DB depending on workload.

Use Cases:

- Global applications require continuous uptime.
- Load-balanced workloads across continents.

Active-Passive Architecture

Description: The primary region handles traffic; the secondary serves as a failover site.

Use Cases:

- Disaster recovery solutions with lower operational costs.

- Applications where active redundancy is not required.

Hub-and-Spoke Model with Transit Gateway

Description: Transit Gateway serves as the central hub connecting multiple regional VPCs. Transit Gateway inter-region peering is non-transitive.

Use Cases:

- Large enterprises with multi-account environments.
- Organizations needing centralized network management.

The following is the diagram to represent Multi-Region VPC Architecture:

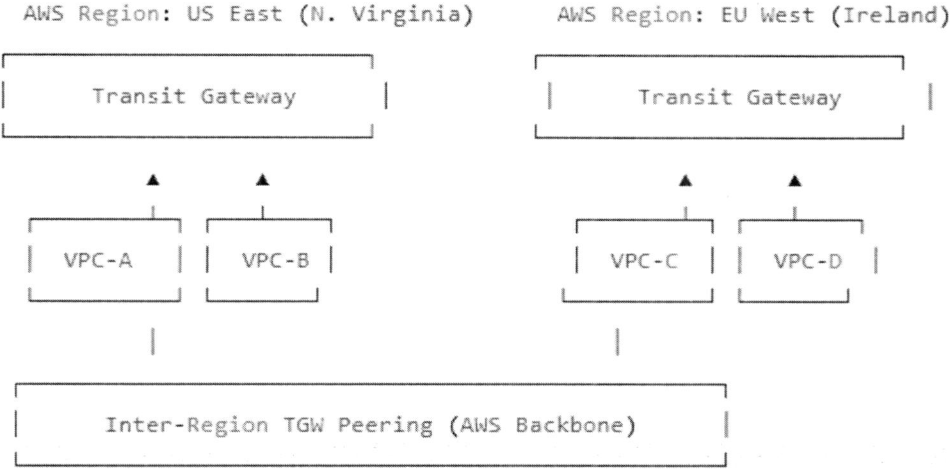

Figure 6.9: *Multi-Region Connectivity Using AWS Transit Gateway Peering*

- VPCs communicate seamlessly across regions using Transit Gateway peering.
- AWS backbone ensures low-latency, secure communication.

Best Practices for Multi-Region VPC Design

Designing a multi-region VPC architecture requires adopting best practices that ensure scalability, security, high availability, and efficient traffic management across distributed cloud environments.

- **Plan CIDR ranges carefully:** Avoid overlapping networks to enable seamless peering, Transit Gateway, and hybrid connectivity.
- **Enable VPC Flow Logs:** Monitor and troubleshoot cross-region traffic patterns and unexpected routing behavior.
- **Use AWS Organizations:** Centralize account governance, billing, and security guardrails across regions.
- **Segment traffic with multiple Transit Gateway route tables:** Enforce isolation between environments (prod, non-prod, shared services).
- **Share Transit Gateways using AWS Resource Access Manager (RAM):** Enable centralized TGW ownership while allowing controlled multi-account attachments.
- **Implement DNS failover with Amazon Route 53 policies:** Use health checks and failover routing to improve application availability.

- **Secure hybrid connectivity:** Use IPSec VPNs or Direct Connect for encrypted, reliable on-premises integration.
- **Consider AWS Cloud WAN at large scale:** Simplify operations when managing multiple Transit Gateways across dozens of regions and accounts.
- **Test disaster recovery regularly:** Run game days to validate routing, failover behavior, and operational readiness before real outages occur.

Designing an effective multi-region VPC architecture requires balancing performance, cost, security, and compliance considerations. By carefully selecting connectivity methods, optimizing route management, and implementing robust failover mechanisms, organizations can deliver seamless global services while maintaining resilience and efficiency.

Cross-Region Peering versus AWS Transit Gateway Inter-Region Peering

When designing multi-region AWS architectures, establishing secure, efficient, and cost-effective connectivity between VPCs across regions is critical. AWS provides two primary solutions for cross-region connectivity:

- **VPC Cross-Region Peering:** A direct, point-to-point connection between two VPCs in different AWS regions.
- **AWS Transit Gateway (TGW) Inter-Region Peering:** A centralized, hub-and-spoke solution that connects multiple VPCs and on-premises networks through Transit Gateways in different regions.

Both options enable private communication across the global backbone network of AWS, ensuring low latency and secure data transfer without traversing the public internet. However, the choice between them depends on factors like network complexity, scalability, cost, and management overhead.

In this section, we shall compare these two solutions in detail, providing use cases, architectural diagrams, benefits, drawbacks, and decision-making criteria to help you choose the right approach for your multi-region connectivity needs.

Overview of Cross-Region Connectivity Options

VPC Cross-Region Peering

- Direct connection between two VPCs in different AWS regions.
- Suitable for simple architectures requiring low-latency connectivity between two VPCs.
- No transitive routing – VPC-A cannot communicate with VPC-C through VPC-B.
- Cost-effective for small-scale environments.

No bandwidth bottleneck is imposed by AWS (data is limited by instance/network interface bandwidth, not the peering link itself).

AWS Transit Gateway Inter-Region Peering

- Connects Transit Gateways (TGWs) in different AWS regions.
- Hub-and-spoke architecture supports transitive routing.
- Ideal for large-scale, multi-account, and multi-region environments.
- Higher setup complexity and costs compared to VPC Peering.

Inter-region TGW peering is non-transitive. The following is the architecture comparison of VPC Cross-Region Peering and AWS Transit Gateway Inter-Region Peering:

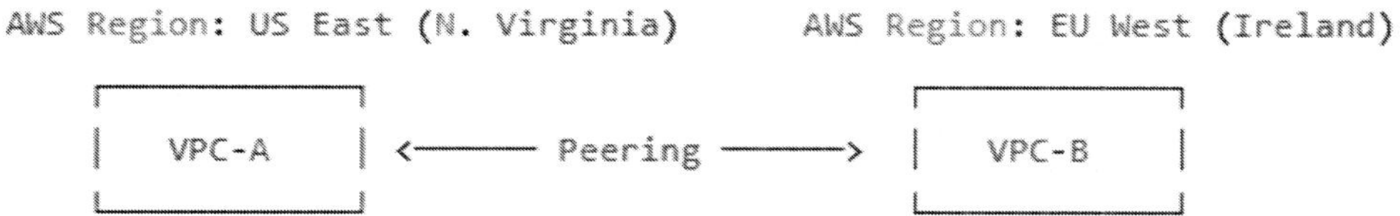

Figure 6.10: *VPC Cross-Region Peering*

- Direct connection between two VPCs.
- Requires separate peering connections for each VPC pair.

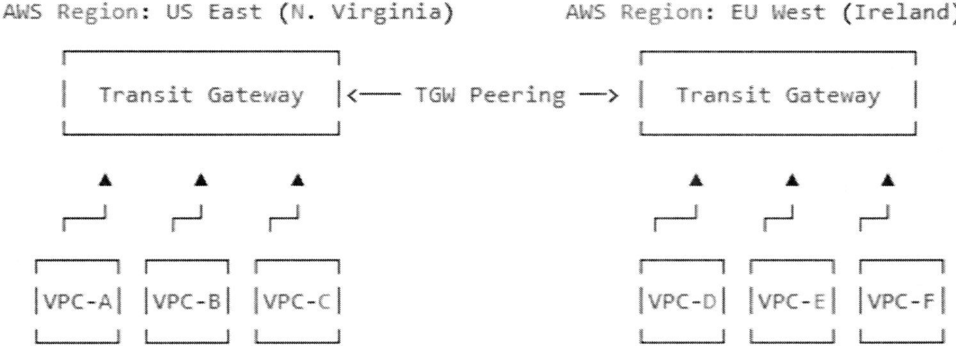

Figure 6.11: *AWS Transit Gateway Inter-Region Peering*

- Centralized connectivity for multiple VPCs.
- Transitive routing simplifies VPC-to-VPC communication.

The following is the table to show the feature-to-feature comparison:

Feature	VPC Cross-Region Peering	AWS Transit Gateway Inter-Region Peering
Architecture Type	Point-to-Point	Hub-and-Spoke (Centralized)
Transitive Routing	✕ Not Supported	✓ Supported
Scalability	Limited	Highly Scalable (1000s of VPCs)
Latency	Low	Low (AWS Backbone)
Cost	Lower for few connections	Cost-effective at large scale
Management Complexity	Simple for 1-2 VPCs	Simplified for large environments
Cross-Account Support	✓ Yes	✓ Yes
Multi-Region Support	✓ Yes	✓ Yes
Failover & High Availability	Manual	Built-In with TGW Peering **
Use Cases	Simple, direct VPC connections	Complex, large-scale, multi-region networks

Table 6.4: *Feature-to-Feature Comparison*

TGW peering does not automatically do cross-region failover - it supports redundant, highly available peering connections, but failover between regions still requires DNS.

Decision-Making Framework

Question	Recommended Solution
Do you need to connect only two VPCs across regions?	✅ **VPC Cross-Region Peering**
Is transitive routing between multiple VPCs required?	✅ **AWS Transit Gateway Inter-Region Peering**
Are you managing a large, multi-account AWS environment?	✅ **Transit Gateway**
Is cost the primary concern with minimal VPC connections?	✅ **VPC Peering**
Do you need centralized network management?	✅ **Transit Gateway**

Table 6.5: *Decision Making Framework*

Do you require interconnection with on-premises via Direct Connect/VPN?"

Answer: Transit Gateway, since peering does not support VPN/DX attachments.

Case Study: Global Retail Enterprise

Scenario:

A retail company operates regional AWS environments across North America, Europe, and Asia with over 30 VPCs across multiple accounts.

Challenges:

- High network complexity with existing VPC peering connections.
- Need for transitive routing between regions and accounts.
- Compliance with regional data privacy laws.

Solution:

- Implemented AWS Transit Gateway Inter-Region Peering.
- Consolidated VPCs under a hub-and-spoke model.
- Used Route 53 for global DNS failover.

Outcome:

- Reduced network complexity by 80%.
- Improved latency by 30% for global users.
- Achieved 99.99% availability with redundant architectures.

Choosing between VPC Cross-Region Peering and AWS Transit Gateway Inter-Region Peering depends on the size, architecture complexity, scalability requirements, and budget of your organization.

- Use VPC Peering for simple, low-cost direct connections between two VPCs.
- Use Transit Gateway for large-scale, multi-region networks requiring transitive routing and centralized management.

Making the right choice ensures optimal performance, reduced costs, and simplified network management for your multi-region architecture.

High Availability and Disaster Recovery Strategies

In the currently always-on digital landscape, High Availability (HA) and Disaster Recovery (DR) are critical components of any enterprise-grade cloud architecture. Customers expect services to be available around the clock, while regulatory compliance often demands effective disaster recovery solutions. The global infrastructure of AWS offers robust tools to build resilient architectures capable of withstanding failures, whether due to hardware issues, software bugs, human errors, or regional outages.

HA = resilience to localized failures (AZ, node, or service level).

DR = recovery from large-scale outages (region or catastrophic failure).

This section explores strategies, architectures, and best practices for implementing multi-region high availability and disaster recovery using AWS Transit Gateway, VPC Peering, Route 53, and other AWS services. We'll also cover common deployment patterns, cost considerations, and real-world use cases to help you design systems that balance resilience, performance, and cost-effectiveness.

Importance of High Availability and Disaster Recovery

High Availability (HA) and Disaster Recovery (DR) are critical components of modern system design, ensuring continuous operations, regulatory compliance, and resilience against infrastructure failures.

- **Business Continuity:** Downtime can lead to lost revenue, damaged reputation, and customer dissatisfaction. HA and DR architectures minimize service interruptions.
- **Compliance Requirements:** Industries like finance and healthcare often require robust DR plans to comply with regulations.
- **Global User Expectations:** Users demand fast, uninterrupted service regardless of location or infrastructure failures.
- **Protection against Regional Outages:** Even with the resilient infrastructure of AWS, regional failures can occur. Multi-region architectures ensure service continuity.

AWS Services Enabling High Availability and Disaster Recovery

AWS Transit Gateway (TGW):

- Enables transitive routing between VPCs across regions.
- Facilitates fast, private communication for HA and DR setups.

VPC Peering (Cross-Region):

- Direct connectivity for simple DR solutions.
- Ideal for low-cost backup environments.

Amazon Route 53:

- DNS failover and traffic routing for multi-region deployments.
- Supports latency-based routing and health checks.

AWS Direct Connect and VPN:

- Reliable, low-latency connectivity to on-premises environments.
- Redundant connections ensure network resilience.

AWS Storage and Database Solutions:

- **Amazon S3 Cross-Region Replication:** Ensures durable, distributed storage.
- **RDS Global Databases:** Provides multi-region failover for relational databases.
- **DynamoDB Global Tables:** Facilitates active-active database replication across regions.

High-Availability Deployment Patterns

- **Active-Active:** Global e-commerce, SaaS apps.
- **Active-Passive:** internal applications, regional workloads.

Multi-AZ versus Multi-Region Deployments

- **Multi-AZ (Within a Region)**
  - Protects against Availability Zone failures.
  - Not sufficient for regional outages.
- **Multi-Region (Across Regions)**
  - Protects against entire region failures.
  - Enables geographically distributed workloads.
  - Higher complexity and cost compared to single-region setups.

Active-Active Multi-Region Architecture

Description:

- Deploys identical environments in two or more AWS regions.
- Both regions handle production traffic simultaneously.

Benefits:

- Zero downtime during regional failures.
- Improved latency for global users.
- Built-in redundancy with balanced workloads.

Challenges:

- Requires data synchronization across regions.
- Higher costs due to duplicated resources.

The following architecture diagram shows the Active-Active setup:

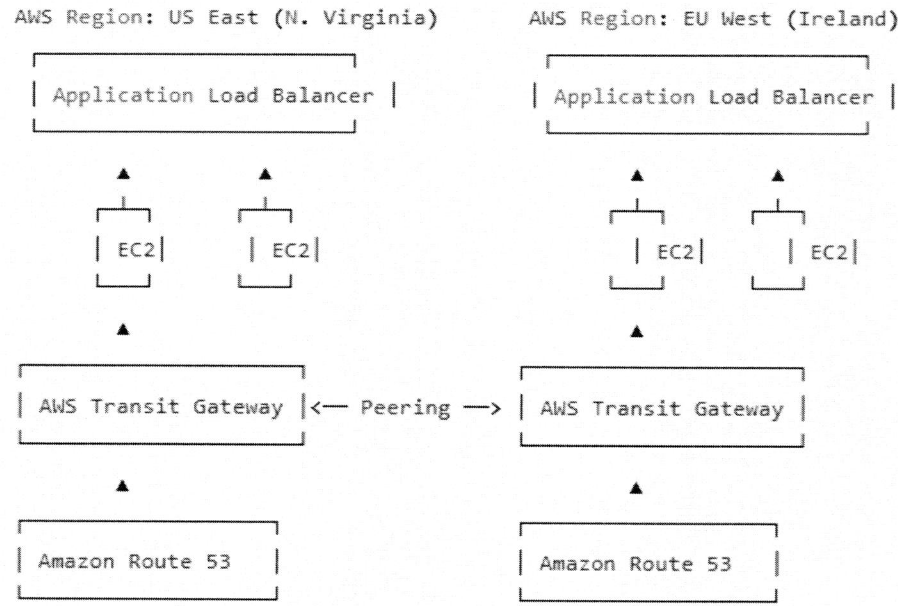

Figure 6.12: *Active – Active Setup*

- Route 53 manages traffic routing between regions.
- Transit Gateways ensure seamless VPC communication across regions.

Active-Passive Multi-Region Architecture

Description:

- Primary region handles all traffic.
- Secondary region remains on standby, activated during failovers.

Benefits:

- Lower operational costs compared to active-active.
- Quick recovery with Route 53 failover policies.

Challenges:

- Higher RTO/RPO compared to active-active.
- Potential for cold-start latency during failover.

The following architecture diagram shows the Active-Passive setup:

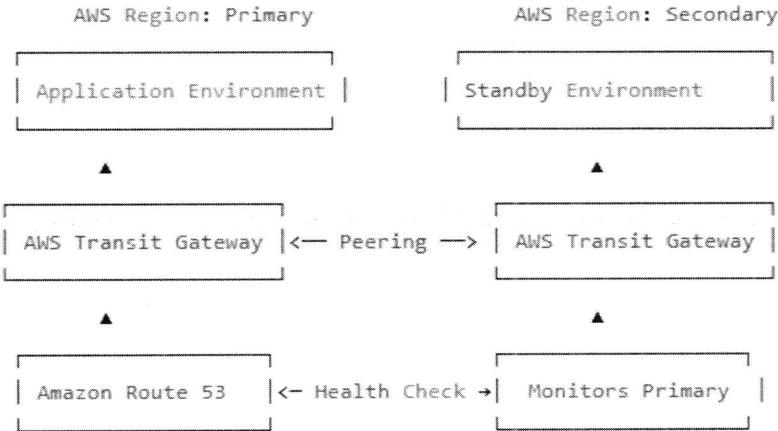

Figure 6.13: *Active-Passive Setup*

- Failover triggers Route 53 DNS updates.
- Transit Gateway handles inter-region communication.

Disaster Recovery (DR) Strategies

Some of the Disaster Recovery (DR) Strategies are provided as follows.

Backup and Restore

Description:

- Regular backups stored in Amazon S3 with Cross-Region Replication.
- DR site is provisioned on-demand during disaster recovery.

Benefits:

- Lowest cost DR option.
- Ideal for non-critical applications.

Challenges:

- High RTO/RPO (longer recovery times).

- Requires manual restoration of services.

Pilot Light

Description:

- Minimal infrastructure (such as databases, core services) runs in the DR region.
- Full infrastructure scaled up during failover.

Benefits:

- Faster recovery than backup-restore methods.
- Cost-effective with critical services always available.

Challenges:

Requires scaling procedures during failover.

Warm Standby

Description:

- Smaller-scale version of production runs continuously in DR region.
- Quickly scaled up during a disaster.

Benefits:

- Low RTO and RPO.
- Faster recovery than pilot light.

Challenges:

Higher operational costs due to active resources.

Multi-Region Active-Active (Full DR)

Description:

- Fully operational environments in both primary and secondary regions.
- Load balancing manages traffic between regions.

Benefits:

- Instant failover with zero downtime.
- Maximized availability and resilience.

Challenges:

- Highest cost DR solution.
- Complex data synchronization requirements.

Implementing High Availability with AWS Transit Gateway

AWS Transit Gateway plays a critical role in ensuring network resilience:

- **Inter-region TGW Peering:** Enables low-latency communication between regions.
- **Route Propagation and Associations:** Automatically updates routing for faster failover.
- **Hybrid Cloud Integration:** Supports on-premises-to-AWS failover strategies.

Building highly available and resilient multi-region architectures is essential for organizations seeking business continuity, customer trust, and regulatory compliance. AWS provides a robust toolkit—Transit Gateway, VPC Peering, Route 53, and global data services—to design, implement, and manage HA and DR strategies tailored to your needs.

By carefully considering cost, complexity, and application requirements, you can build architectures that ensure uptime, protect data integrity, and deliver seamless global experiences.

Security in Hybrid Networks

As organizations adopt hybrid cloud architectures, security becomes a critical challenge in ensuring seamless, secure connectivity between on-premises data centers and AWS cloud environments. A hybrid network introduces multiple attack surfaces, requiring robust security controls to protect data, applications, and network traffic across both cloud and traditional infrastructure.

Hybrid environments must defend against threats such as unauthorized access, data breaches, man-in-the-middle attacks, and misconfigurations while maintaining scalability, compliance, and operational efficiency. To address these risks, AWS provides a suite of security services and best practices for encrypting data, securing traffic, and enforcing access controls in hybrid network deployments.

Here, let us explore essential security strategies for hybrid networks, including IPsec VPNs, encryption mechanisms, secure routing policies, identity management, and AWS security tools. It also highlights real-world use cases, industry best practices, and compliance considerations to help enterprises build resilient and protected hybrid cloud architecture. Security in Hybrid Networks is crucial due to the following factors.

Expanding Attack Surface

Hybrid networks connect on-premises infrastructure, cloud services, and remote users, increasing potential vulnerabilities. Misconfigured firewalls, unprotected endpoints, or unencrypted data transfers can expose sensitive assets to cyber threats.

Compliance and Regulatory Requirements

Industries like finance, healthcare, and government require strict security measures to comply with GDPR, HIPAA, PCI-DSS, and SOC 2.

Example:

- HIPAA: Encrypt PHI using S3 + KMS + CloudHSM.
- PCI-DSS: Use Network Firewall + TLS 1.2+ for payment traffic.
- GDPR: Route 53 geolocation routing to enforce EU-only data residency.

Hybrid architectures must implement data residency, encryption, and logging policies to meet regional and global compliance standards.

Preventing Unauthorized Access

Hybrid environments often integrate multiple identity and access management (IAM) systems, creating risks of privilege escalation or unauthorized data access. Organizations must enforce strong authentication, least privilege policies, and zero-trust security models.

Ensuring Secure Interconnectivity

Hybrid networks rely on VPNs, Direct Connect, and Transit Gateway to enable communication between cloud and on-premises resources. Without proper encryption and secure routing policies, data transmissions can be intercepted or compromised.

AWS Security Tools for Hybrid Networks

Some of the AWS Security Tools for Hybrid Networks are provided as follows:

AWS Identity and Access Management (IAM)

- Defines fine-grained access controls to AWS services and hybrid resources.

- Implements least privilege access, Multi-Factor Authentication (MFA), and IAM roles for secure API access.

AWS VPN (IPsec) and AWS Direct Connect

- Secures hybrid connections between on-premises and AWS using IPsec encryption.
- Ensures private, dedicated connections for low-latency, encrypted communications.

AWS Shield and AWS Web Application Firewall (WAF)

- AWS Shield Advanced protects against DDoS attacks on hybrid cloud services.
- AWS WAF safeguards hybrid applications from SQL injection, XSS, and other web threats.

AWS CloudTrail and Amazon GuardDuty

- AWS CloudTrail logs all API activities across AWS accounts and hybrid environments.
- GuardDuty provides AI-driven threat detection for hybrid network anomalies.

AWS Security Hub and AWS Network Firewall

- AWS Security Hub aggregates threat intelligence and security best practices.
- AWS Network Firewall enforces deep packet inspection and intrusion detection for hybrid cloud traffic.

IPsec VPNs for Hybrid Cloud Security

As organizations adopt hybrid cloud environments, ensuring secure and encrypted communication between on-premises data centers and AWS becomes a top priority. IPsec (Internet Protocol Security) VPNs offer a cost-effective, scalable, and encrypted solution to establish secure tunnels between on-premises networks, branch offices, and AWS Virtual Private Clouds (VPCs).

An IPsec VPN encrypts network traffic at the IP layer, preventing unauthorized access and data interception during transmission. It plays a crucial role in hybrid cloud security, particularly when AWS Direct Connect is not an option or when organizations need redundancy in secure connections.

This section explores how IPsec VPNs work, their architecture, key security features, implementation steps, and best practices to ensure a robust and resilient hybrid cloud setup.

IPsec VPN Overview

An IPsec VPN (Internet Protocol Security Virtual Private Network) is a tunnelling protocol that encrypts data transmitted between networks to ensure secure communication over public or private networks.

Some of the Key Features of IPsec VPNs in Hybrid Cloud are as follows.

- **End-to-end encryption:** Prevents data exposure during transit.
- **Authentication mechanisms:** Ensures only authorized entities can establish connections.
- **Data integrity protection:** Prevents data tampering or modification.
- **Flexible connectivity:** Supports hybrid environments with cloud and on-premises systems.
- **Cost-effective security:** Eliminates the need for expensive private leased lines.

IPsec VPN Architecture for Hybrid Cloud

Components of an AWS Hybrid IPsec VPN Setup

An AWS IPsec Site-to-Site VPN typically consists of the following components:

Component	Description
Customer Gateway (CGW)	A physical or software VPN device in an on-premises data center that initiates the secure connection.
AWS Virtual Private Gateway (VGW)	A managed VPN endpoint on AWS that connects to the VPC.
IPsec Tunnel	The encrypted connection that secures data exchange.
Routing Policies	Defines how traffic flows between the cloud and on-premises.

Table 6.6: *Components of an AWS Hybrid IPsec VPN Setup*

IPsec VPN Deployment Architecture

The following is a typical AWS Site-to-Site VPN architecture connecting an on-premises data center to an AWS VPC using IPsec encryption:

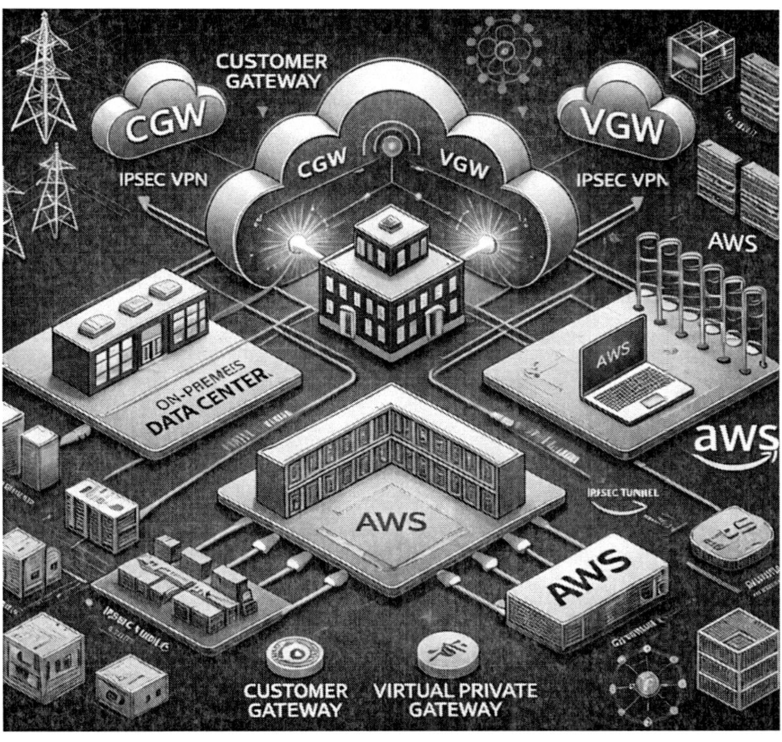

Figure 6.14: *IPsec VPN Architecture Diagram*

- The Customer Gateway (CGW) resides in the on-premises data center and establishes an encrypted connection.
- The AWS Virtual Private Gateway (VGW) serves as the endpoint in AWS to handle VPN traffic.
- An IPsec Tunnel is created between CGW and VGW, encrypting all traffic.
- Routing rules and security groups are configured to control inbound and outbound traffic.
- Data is transmitted securely between AWS and the on-premises network.

Setting up an AWS IPsec VPN

The following are the steps to be followed while setting up an AWS IPsec VPN:

Step 1: Configure the Customer Gateway (CGW)

1. Identify the public IP address of your on-premises VPN device.

2. Set up routing policies to ensure secure communication with AWS.

Step 2: Create a Virtual Private Gateway (VGW) in AWS

1. Attach the VGW to your AWS VPC.
2. Define the BGP ASN (Autonomous System Number) if using dynamic routing.

Step 3: Establish the Site-to-Site VPN Connection

1. Navigate to AWS VPN Console → Create VPN Connection.
2. Specify the Customer Gateway details and VPN settings.
3. Configure static or dynamic routing (BGP).

Step 4: Configure IPsec Policies

1. **Phase 1 (IKE Negotiation):**
    a. Authentication method (pre-shared key or certificate-based).
    b. Encryption algorithms (AES-256 for strong security).
    c. Key exchange protocol (Diffie-Hellman groups).
2. **Phase 2 (Data Encryption):**
    a. Integrity verification (SHA-256).
    b. Perfect Forward Secrecy (PFS) for additional protection.

Step 5: Test and Monitor the VPN

1. Ping AWS instances from on-premises to verify connectivity.
2. Enable AWS CloudWatch for VPN monitoring.
3. Use VPC Flow Logs to analyze traffic patterns.

Security Best Practices for IxPsec VPNs

Some of the best security practices for IPsec VPNs are as follows:

Use Strong Encryption Standards

- Enforce AES-256 for data encryption.
- Use SHA-256 for message authentication.
- Enable Perfect Forward Secrecy (PFS) to generate new encryption keys periodically.

Implement Multi-Factor Authentication (MFA)

- Use certificate-based authentication instead of pre-shared keys.
- Restrict access using IAM policies and roles.

Enable Redundancy and High Availability

- Deploy multiple VPN tunnels for failover protection.
- Consider AWS Direct Connect as a backup for critical workloads.

Monitor VPN Traffic with AWS Security Tools

- Use AWS CloudTrail to log API activities.
- Enable AWS GuardDuty for threat detection.
- Deploy AWS Network Firewall to inspect VPN traffic.

Optimize Performance and Latency

- Use BGP dynamic routing for automatic failover.
- Avoid routing asymmetric traffic across multiple VPN tunnels.
- Implement local egress points for hybrid applications.

IPsec VPNs play a crucial role in hybrid cloud security, providing end-to-end encrypted communication between on-premises data centers and AWS VPCs. By implementing strong encryption policies, authentication mechanisms, and continuous monitoring, organizations can securely extend their network to the cloud while ensuring high availability and compliance.

Encryption Mechanisms for Hybrid Cloud Security

In hybrid cloud environments, encryption is a fundamental security measure to protect data in transit and at rest. As organizations move workloads between on-premises infrastructure and AWS, they must ensure confidentiality, integrity, and compliance with security standards.

This section explores various encryption mechanisms, their implementation in AWS hybrid cloud architecture, and best practices for securing sensitive information across different environments.

Types of Encryption in Hybrid Cloud

Encryption can be categorized into three primary types based on when and how data is encrypted:

Encryption at Rest

Protects data stored in databases, file systems, or object storage from unauthorized access.

- **AWS Services:** Amazon S3, RDS, EBS, and DynamoDB support encryption at rest using AWS Key Management Service (AWS KMS).
- **On-Premises Storage:** Uses BitLocker (Windows), LUKS (Linux), or hardware-based encryption.

Encryption in Transit

Ensures secure communication between on-premises networks and AWS services.

- **IPsec VPN:** Encrypts data packets before transmission over a hybrid network.
- **TLS/SSL:** Used for securing HTTP-based communications between clients and AWS services.

End-to-End Encryption

Protects data throughout its lifecycle—from creation to storage and transmission.

- **Client-Side Encryption:** Encrypts data before sending it to the cloud.
- **Zero Trust Security Models:** Ensures continuous encryption across all network layers.

To secure hybrid cloud environments, encryption mechanisms must be applied at various levels:

Encryption Layer	Technology	Use Case
Storage Layer	AES-256	Encrypts EBS, RDS, S3, and on-prem disks
Network Layer	IPsec VPN, TLS/SSL	Secures AWS and on-premises communication
Application Layer	End-to-End Encryption (E2EE)	Encrypts API and database queries
Data Layer	AWS KMS, HSM	Encrypts secrets, API keys, and sensitive data

Table 6.7: *Encryption in Hybrid Cloud Architecture*

Key AWS Encryption Mechanisms

Some of the Key AWS Encryption Mechanisms are as follows:

AWS Key Management Service (AWS KMS)

- A centralized encryption key management service.
- Supports automatic key rotation for enhanced security.
- Integrates with AWS services like S3, EBS, and RDS for seamless encryption.

AWS CloudHSM (Hardware Security Module)

- A dedicated hardware encryption device for high-security workloads.
- Meets compliance standards like FIPS 140-2 for regulatory environments.

AWS Certificate Manager (ACM)

- Automates TLS/SSL certificate provisioning for web applications.
- Helps secure custom domains, APIs, and AWS services with managed certificates.
- Encryption Implementation in a Hybrid Cloud

Scenario: Securing Hybrid Data Transfer between On-Prem and AWS

Use Case: A company needs to securely transfer customer records between its on-premises data center and AWS S3 storage.

Solution:

- **Encrypt Data on-Premises:**
    - Use AES-256 encryption to encrypt customer records before upload.
    - Store encryption keys in on-prem Key Management Systems (KMS).
- **Secure Data Transfer:**
    - Use an IPsec VPN tunnel to protect data in transit.
    - Use TLS 1.2 encryption when transferring files via AWS Transfer Family.
- **Encrypt Data at Rest in AWS:**
    - Enable S3 default encryption using AWS KMS.
    - Use AWS CloudHSM for highly regulated workloads requiring dedicated encryption.

Encryption Best Practices for Hybrid Cloud

Some of the best practices of Encryption for Hybrid Cloud are as follows:

Use Strong Encryption Algorithms

- Enforce AES-256 encryption for all storage and data transfers.
- Ensure TLS 1.2+ or IPsec VPN tunnels for secure communication.

Centralized Key Management

- Use AWS KMS for cloud-based key management.
- Implement on-premises HSM for regulated industries requiring dedicated hardware security.

Implement Role-Based Access Control (RBAC)

- Use AWS IAM roles and fine-grained permissions to limit key access.
- Enable Multi-Factor Authentication (MFA) for administrative controls.

Enable Data Loss Prevention (DLP)

- Monitor AWS CloudTrail logs for encryption key usage.
- Use AWS Macie for automated sensitive data discovery in S3.

Automate Key Rotation

- Configure automatic key rotation in AWS KMS and on-prem HSM.
- Rotate TLS/SSL certificates using AWS Certificate Manager.

Encryption is a critical component of hybrid cloud security, protecting data at every stage—from storage to transmission. By implementing AWS KMS, IPsec VPNs, CloudHSM, and TLS-based encryption, organizations can ensure compliance, data confidentiality, and end-to-end security.

In the next section, we will explore secure routing policies to further enhance hybrid cloud security.

Secure Routing Policies for Hybrid Networks

In a hybrid cloud environment, secure routing policies play a critical role in ensuring safe, efficient, and controlled network traffic flow between on-premises infrastructure and AWS cloud services. Organizations must implement routing strategies that prevent unauthorized access, optimize performance, and enforce network segmentation to protect sensitive workloads.

This section explores routing techniques, security best practices, and AWS-specific solutions for building a robust and resilient hybrid network.

Some of the Key Routing Challenges in Hybrid Cloud are as follows.

- **Latency and Performance Issues:** Managing delays when routing traffic between data centers and cloud environments.
- **Security Risks:** Preventing unauthorized access, man-in-the-middle attacks, and routing misconfigurations.
- **Multi-Path Conflicts:** Ensuring traffic follows optimized and redundant paths without unnecessary loops.
- **Compliance and Governance:** Enforcing geolocation-based routing for regulatory compliance.

To address these challenges, hybrid cloud architectures must adopt secure routing policies with encryption, redundancy, and strict access controls.

Hybrid Cloud Routing Strategies

Hybrid cloud routing strategies are essential for enabling secure, scalable, and efficient communication between on-premises infrastructure and cloud environments, leveraging a combination of routing methods and connectivity options.

Static vs. Dynamic Routing

- **Static Routing:**
    - Manually configured routes with fixed paths.
    - Suitable for small hybrid networks with minimal routing changes.
    - **Security risk:** Requires manual updates, which can lead to misconfigurations.
- **Dynamic Routing (BGP – Border Gateway Protocol):**
    - Routes are automatically updated based on network conditions.
    - Used in large hybrid architectures where traffic loads change dynamically.

- **Security risk:** Requires route filtering and authentication to prevent hijacking attacks.

AWS Hybrid Cloud Environments Prefer Dynamic Routing (BGP) for Scalability and Security.

Secure Routing via VPN (IPsec VPN)

- Establishes an encrypted tunnel between on-premises and AWS networks.
- Ensures confidentiality and integrity of data in transit.
- **Security best practices:**
  - Use IKEv2 and AES-256 encryption.
  - Enable Perfect Forward Secrecy (PFS) to protect against key compromise.
  - Apply route filtering to limit VPN access to authorized IPs only.

Secure Routing via AWS Direct Connect

- Provides a private, dedicated connection between on-premises data centers and AWS.
- Reduces latency and enhances security by avoiding the public internet.
- **Security best practices:**
  - Use Virtual Private Gateway (VGW) to control traffic between AWS and on-premises networks.
  - Enforce access controls using AWS Identity and Access Management (IAM).
  - Implement redundant Direct Connect links for failover protection.

Secure Routing via AWS Transit Gateway (TGW)

- Acts as a central hub to interconnect multiple VPCs and on-premises networks.
- Simplifies hybrid cloud management by eliminating complex peering relationships.
- **Security best practices:**
  - Define separate route tables for different departments or applications.
  - Use traffic segmentation to prevent unauthorized cross-network access.
  - Monitor traffic using AWS CloudWatch and VPC Flow Logs.

AWS Route 53 for Secure DNS-Based Routing

- AWS Route 53 provides DNS-based traffic routing across hybrid environments.
- Supports geolocation-based routing for compliance with data localization laws.

Latency-based routing combined with DNS failover is often used in DR + compliance scenarios.

- **Security best practices:**
  - Enable DNSSEC (Domain Name System Security Extensions) to prevent DNS spoofing attacks.
  - Use AWS WAF (Web Application Firewall) to protect against DNS-based DDoS attacks.
  - Configure failover routing policies to redirect traffic in case of a network outage.

Best Practices for Secure Routing in Hybrid Networks

Some of the best practices for Secure Routing in Hybrid Networks are as follows.

- Enforce Least Privilege Routing.
- Implement Route Filtering and Firewalls
- Enable Redundant Routing for High Availability
- Monitor and Audit Routing Policies

Case Study: Secure Hybrid Routing for a Financial Institution

Scenario

A global financial firm needs a secure hybrid network that:

- Ensures low-latency connections for high-speed trading.
- Restricts sensitive banking data from being exposed to the public internet.
- Implements automatic failover for disaster recovery.

Solution

- **AWS Direct Connect for Private Network Routing**
    - A dedicated Direct Connect link between the on-premises data center and AWS.
    - Uses BGP dynamic routing to automatically update routes based on network availability.
- **Transit Gateway for Centralized Routing**
    - Acts as a single control point for managing routing across multiple AWS VPCs.
    - Implements segmented route tables to enforce strict access control.
- **IPsec VPN as a Backup Connection**
    - Configured as a failover path in case the Direct Connect link fails.
    - Uses AES-256 encryption to secure banking transactions in transit.
- **Route 53 for Secure DNS Resolution**
    - Directs customer traffic to the nearest AWS region for optimal performance.
    - Uses geolocation-based routing to comply with regional data residency laws.

Outcome

- 99.99% uptime with multi-path failover.
- No unauthorized access due to strict routing security policies.
- Improved transaction speed using low-latency Direct Connect routes.

Secure routing policies are essential for protecting hybrid cloud environments against cyber threats, misconfigurations, and unauthorized access. Organizations must adopt a multi-layered approach, leveraging VPNs, Direct Connect, Transit Gateway, and Route 53 to create a secure, high-performance hybrid network.

By implementing route filtering, traffic segmentation, redundancy, and continuous monitoring, businesses can enhance security, optimize performance, and ensure compliance in their hybrid cloud architecture.

Case Studies

Hybrid connectivity plays a crucial role in modern IT architectures, enabling organizations to integrate on-premises infrastructure with AWS cloud environments. It facilitates seamless data exchange, high availability, and secure network communication, allowing businesses to scale operations without fully migrating to the cloud.

This section explores real-world use cases and case studies that demonstrate the importance of hybrid cloud networking in various industries.

Connecting On-Premises Data Centers to AWS

Use Case Overview

Many enterprises maintain on-premises data centers for regulatory, security, or performance reasons but need AWS cloud resources for scalability and redundancy. Hybrid connectivity solutions enable:

- Secure data transfer between on-prem and AWS.
- Seamless application integration across both environments.
- Disaster recovery and backup solutions using AWS cloud.

Hybrid Connectivity Methods

- AWS Direct Connect: Dedicated private connection with low latency and high bandwidth.
- IPsec VPN: Secure encrypted tunnel over the internet.
- AWS Transit Gateway: Centralized connectivity management.
- AWS Storage Gateway: Hybrid storage integration.

Example: Large Financial Institution

A global banking enterprise connects its on-premises data centers to AWS for real-time fraud detection and risk management.

Solution: Used AWS Direct Connect + VPN backup for high availability.

Result: Reduced latency by 50% and ensured compliance with financial regulations.

Hybrid Network Design for Enterprises

Use Case Overview

Enterprises require a secure, high-performance network that integrates on-prem infrastructure, multiple AWS VPCs, and remote offices while maintaining centralized control.

Key Components of Hybrid Enterprise Networks

- Multi-Region AWS VPCs: Connecting regional offices with AWS cloud.
- Transit Gateway: Managing connectivity across multiple VPCs and data centers.
- Secure Routing Policies: Implementing firewalls and traffic segmentation.
- Global Load Balancing: Distributing workloads across on-prem and AWS cloud.

Example: Global Retail Chain

A multinational retail company needed to synchronize inventory management across 300+ stores and AWS cloud.

Solution: Used Transit Gateway + Route 53 DNS-based routing to ensure optimal performance.

Result: Achieved 99.99% uptime and reduced operational costs.

Disaster Recovery and Business Continuity in Hybrid Environments

Use Case Overview

Hybrid connectivity provides a resilient disaster recovery strategy, ensuring:

- Data backup and replication across on-premises and AWS storage.

- Failover mechanisms to redirect traffic in case of network failures.
- Minimal downtime with automated recovery processes.

Hybrid Disaster Recovery Strategies

- Pilot Light Model: Critical applications run in AWS on standby.
- Warm Standby: A scaled-down version of the production environment runs in AWS.
- Full-Scale Failover: Instant switch to AWS in case of failure.
- AWS Elastic Disaster Recovery (EDR): Automates failover and failback.

Example: Healthcare Provider

A hospital chain needed disaster recovery for its patient record systems.

Solution: Used AWS Elastic Disaster Recovery + S3 storage replication.

Result: Achieved RTO (Recovery Time Objective) of under 10 minutes with zero data loss.

Compliance and Regulatory Challenges in Hybrid Networks

Use Case Overview

Industries such as finance, healthcare, and government require strict data compliance when integrating on-premises and cloud networks.

Compliance Considerations for Hybrid Cloud

- Data Localization Laws: Ensuring sensitive data remains in specific regions.
- Encryption Requirements: End-to-end encryption using TLS, AES-256.
- Access Controls: IAM policies, multi-factor authentication (MFA).
- Auditing and Monitoring: AWS CloudTrail, VPC Flow Logs for security.

Example: Government Agency

A federal agency needed a hybrid cloud while complying with GDPR and HIPAA.

Solution: Used AWS GovCloud + PrivateLink for secure data access.

Result: Achieved full regulatory compliance while maintaining hybrid connectivity.

Finally,

- Hybrid connectivity enables secure, scalable, and compliant integration of on-premises and AWS cloud resources.
- AWS Direct Connect, VPN, Transit Gateway, and security policies play a crucial role in optimizing hybrid networks.
- Real-world implementations across finance, healthcare, retail, and government showcase the importance of robust hybrid network designs.

Conclusion

Throughout this document, we explored Advanced VPC and Hybrid Connectivity, detailing how organizations can seamlessly integrate on-premises infrastructure with AWS cloud environments. Also, few real-world use cases for examining how enterprises, financial institutions, healthcare providers, and government agencies implement hybrid networking for scalability, security, and compliance.

With the rapid expansion of cloud computing, hybrid connectivity has become a strategic necessity for businesses. Organizations must balance cost-efficiency, security, and performance while ensuring seamless communication between their on-prem and cloud environments. AWS provides robust solutions for hybrid architectures, enabling businesses to build scalable, resilient, and secure networks.

In the next chapter, we shall look into how to master Amazon Route 53 to manage DNS and route traffic effectively and an explanation of routing policies (simple, weighted, and geolocation) and failover strategies.

Points to Remember

AWS Virtual Private Cloud (VPC) enables users to create isolated network environments within AWS. Hybrid connectivity bridges the gap between on-premises data centers and AWS cloud environments. Security, scalability, and performance are key factors in designing hybrid architectures.

- **VPC Peering: Connecting VPCs within and across AWS Accounts**
  - VPC Peering enables private connectivity between two VPCs, eliminating the need for internet gateways or VPNs.
  - Peering connections can be intra-region or inter-region, but they do not support transitive routing.
  - Routing tables must be updated manually to allow communication between peered VPCs.
- **AWS Transit Gateway: Centralized Network Management**
  - Unlike VPC Peering, Transit Gateway supports transitive routing, simplifying complex network architectures.
  - Enables multi-region connectivity, centralized monitoring, and policy-based routing.
  - Ideal for large enterprises managing multiple AWS accounts and on-premises connections.
- **Multi-Region Connectivity: Expanding across AWS Regions**
  - Inter-region VPC Peering allows private connectivity across AWS regions with low latency and encrypted links.
  - Hybrid architectures must factor in data transfer costs, regulatory compliance, and failover strategies.
  - Ensures high availability for distributed applications and disaster recovery.
- **Security in Hybrid Networks: Protecting Cloud and On-Premises Environments**
  - AWS Security Groups and Network ACLs enforce traffic restrictions at different levels.
  - AWS Firewall Manager and AWS Shield help protect against DDoS attacks and unauthorized access.
  - Zero Trust principles should be applied—ensuring identity-based access control and least privilege policies.

In all, Hybrid cloud adoption is growing, with AWS offering various solutions for seamless integration. Businesses must prioritize security, cost efficiency, and performance optimization in hybrid architectures. Automation, Zero Trust models, and AI-driven network management are the future of hybrid networking. Continuous monitoring and optimization are the key to maintaining network reliability and security.

CHAPTER 7
Route 53 and DNS Traffic Management

Introduction

Amazon Route 53 is a highly scalable and reliable Domain Name System (DNS) web service designed to route user requests to AWS resources efficiently. It acts as a domain registrar and DNS resolver, ensuring that internet traffic is directed to the correct endpoints, whether they are hosted on AWS, on-premises, or other cloud providers.

For example, "If a user in India types "www.example.com", Route 53 can route them to the nearest AWS region for low latency.

The Domain Name System (DNS) acts as the phonebook of the internet, translating human-readable domain names (for example, www.example.com) into IP addresses that computers use to communicate. Route 53 enhances this by offering intelligent routing and automated failover mechanisms to optimize performance and availability.

DNS traffic management plays a critical role in delivering low latency, effective load balancing, and high availability for applications. Inefficient routing can lead to real-world consequences such as increased costs and misdirected traffic across regions. Poor DNS configuration may result in slow website performance due to suboptimal routing paths, service downtime if failover mechanisms are not properly implemented, and potential security vulnerabilities caused by misconfigured records.

This chapter explores key DNS concepts, including hosted zones, routing policies, and health checks. It covers the fundamentals of managing public and private hosted zones and DNS records, explains how routing policies such as weighted, geolocation, latency-based, and failover routing can be used to control traffic flow, and highlights the importance of DNS health checks in maintaining continuous monitoring and enabling reliable failover strategies for high availability.

By the end of this chapter, you will have a strong understanding of the capabilities of Route 53 and how to configure it for scalability, reliability, and security.

Structure

In this chapter, we will look into:

- Hosted Zones
- Routing Policies
- DNS Health Checks
- Case Studies

Hosted Zones

A hosted zone in Amazon Route 53 is a container for DNS records that define how internet traffic is routed for a specific domain or subdomain. Hosted zones allow users to manage DNS configurations efficiently within AWS while maintaining high availability and low latency.

There are two primary types of hosted zones in Route 53:

- **Public Hosted Zones:** Used for domains accessible over the internet.
- **Private Hosted Zones:** Used for internal networking within AWS Virtual Private Clouds (VPCs).

Public Hosted Zones

Amazon Route 53 allows users to manage DNS records efficiently using hosted zones, which act as containers for DNS configurations. Public hosted zones specifically handle domain name resolutions for resources accessible over the internet. They enable businesses and developers to map domain names to AWS services such as EC2 instances, Elastic Load Balancers (ELB), CloudFront distributions, and S3 buckets.

In this section, we will explore the concept, functionality, setup, and best practices for public hosted zones in Route 53. Understanding these elements will help users configure domain names effectively, ensuring high availability and performance for their online applications.

Before configuring a public hosted zone, it's essential to understand its purpose and functionality. A public hosted zone is directly linked to a registered domain and serves as the authoritative DNS provider, ensuring that internet users can access AWS-hosted resources seamlessly.

A public hosted zone in Amazon Route 53 is a DNS configuration that enables internet-facing domain names to be resolved into IP addresses. This ensures that when users type a domain (for example, www.example.com) in a browser, Route 53 provides the correct IP address for the web server, load balancer, or any AWS service associated with the domain.

Public hosted zones allow users to:

- Map custom domains to AWS resources (such as EC2, S3, API Gateway).
- Manage multiple DNS records such as A, CNAME, MX, and TXT records.
- Ensure fault tolerance with failover routing.
- Distribute traffic efficiently across multiple AWS regions using routing policies.

Once a public hosted zone is created in Route 53, it becomes the authoritative DNS provider for the domain, meaning all queries regarding that domain will be resolved using the Route 53 name servers assigned to it.

Working of Public Hosted Zones

Understanding the working mechanism of public hosted zones is crucial for managing domain name resolution. This process involves multiple steps, starting from domain registration to DNS queries being resolved by Route 53.

A public hosted zone works as follows:

- **Domain Registration**
    - A user registers a domain via Route 53 or an external registrar like GoDaddy, Namecheap, or Google Domains.

 - The registrar assigns default name servers, which can be updated to Route 53's authoritative name servers.

- **Hosted Zone Creation**
  - The user creates a public hosted zone for the domain in Route 53.
  - AWS assigns a set of four name servers, which must be updated in the domain registrar's settings.
- **DNS Record Configuration**
  - The user creates A records, CNAME records, and MX records to define how tra ffic is directed.
  - Alias records can be used to map domains to AWS services like S3 or CloudFront.
- **Query Resolution**
  - When a user enters the domain in a browser, the request is forwarded to Route 53's name servers.
  - Route 53 resolves the request based on the DNS records and returns the appropriate IP address.
  - The browser uses the IP address to establish a connection with the server hosting the website or application.

Example

If a public hosted zone is set up for www.example.com with an A record pointing to an EC2 instance's IP (54.123.45.67):

- A user enters www.example.com in a browser.
- The browser contacts Route 53 to resolve the domain name.
- Route 53 returns 54.123.45.67 as the IP address.
- The browser connects to the server, displaying the website.

Configuring a Public Hosted Zone in Route 53

Setting up a public hosted zone in Route 53 involves multiple steps, including domain registration, hosted zone creation, and DNS record configuration. These steps ensure seamless domain name resolution for AWS-hosted applications.

Step 1: Register a Domain (If Not Already Registered).

1. Register a domain through Amazon Route 53 or any external domain registrar.
2. If using an external registrar, update the Name Server (NS) records to Route 53's assigned servers.

Step 2: Create a Public Hosted Zone.

1. Navigate to the AWS Management Console → Route 53.
2. Click **`Hosted Zones`** → **`Create Hosted Zone`**.
3. Enter the domain name (like example.com).
4. Select **`Public Hosted Zone`** and click **`Create`**.

Step 3: Configure DNS Records.

Once the public hosted zone is created, add necessary DNS records:

1. **A Record** maps the domain to an IPv4 address.
2. **AAAA Record** maps the domain to an IPv6 address.
3. **CNAME Record** maps one sphere to another (for instance, www.example.com → example.com).
4. **MX Record:** Configures email routing.
5. **TXT Record:** Stores additional information for security and validation (including SPF records).

Step 4: Validate and Test the Configuration.

1. Use nslookup or dig commands to check if Route 53 resolves the domain correctly.
2. Test the domain in a browser to ensure proper functionality.

Use Cases for Public Hosted Zones

Public hosted zones provide scalable, high-performance DNS management for businesses and individuals. They are widely used for various purposes, including website hosting, API management, and load balancing.

- **Hosting Websites on AWS**
    - Use Route 53 to map a domain name to an EC2 instance, S3 bucket, or CloudFront distribution.
    - Ensure low-latency access by using latency-based routing.
- **Managing Subdomains for Microservices**
    - Assign different subdomains to API endpoints and microservices.
    - Example: api.example.com for API requests, dashboard.example.com for the admin portal.
- **Load Balancing and Fault Tolerance**
    - Distribute traffic across multiple AWS regions with weighted routing policies.
    - Implement failover configurations for high availability.
- **Custom Email Hosting with MX Records**
    - Configure MX records to route emails through Amazon WorkMail or third-party email providers like Google Workspace.
- **Domain Aliases for Branding**
    - Use CNAME records to deflect users from one domain to another (for example, store.example.com → shop.example.com).

Best Practices for Public Hosted Zones

To optimize performance, security, and scalability, one should follow best practices when configuring public hosted zones.

- **Use Alias Records for AWS Services:** Alias records simplify routing to S3, CloudFront, and ALB, reducing query costs.
- **Implement TTL Optimization:** Set short TTLs for frequently changing records and longer TTLs for static records.

- **Enable DNSSEC:** Protect against DNS spoofing and man-in-the-middle attacks.
- **Monitor DNS Traffic:** Use Route 53 Query Logging to track DNS queries and troubleshoot issues.
- Avoid hardcoding IPs (always use ELB/ALB/CloudFront alias instead).
- Use multiple routing policies (weighted, latency-based) to optimize performance.
- **Implement Failover Configurations:** Set up health checks and failover routing to ensure high availability.

Public hosted zones in Amazon Route 53 provide a robust DNS solution for managing domain names, ensuring reliable access to internet-facing applications. By understanding their functionality, configuration, use cases, and best practices, users can optimize DNS management for high availability and performance.

Private Hosted Zones

Amazon Route 53 Private Hosted Zones (PHZs) allow organizations to create and manage domain name resolutions within their private AWS environments. Unlike public hosted zones, which serve domains accessible over the internet, private hosted zones are used within AWS VPCs to resolve domain names for internal resources. This ensures secure and efficient communication between services within an AWS Virtual Private Cloud (VPC).

PHZs do not require a registered domain - they can use custom/internal-only domains (such as .internal).

In this section, we will explore the concept, functionality, setup, and best practices for private hosted zones in Route 53. Understanding these topics will enable users to configure internal domain names efficiently, ensuring security, scalability, and reliability for AWS-based applications and services.

Private hosted zones are an essential component of AWS networking, providing custom DNS resolution for internal AWS services. These zones ensure that applications running within a VPC can use friendly domain names instead of IP addresses for communication.

A private hosted zone (PHZ) in Amazon Route 53 is a DNS configuration that allows internal domain resolution for AWS resources within one or more VPCs. Unlike public hosted zones, which provide DNS services over the internet, private hosted zones are restricted to specific VPCs, ensuring secure name resolution.

Key Features of Private Hosted Zones:

- **Internal Domain Resolution:** Provides DNS name resolution for AWS resources within private networks.
- **Secure Access:** Limits DNS queries to authorized AWS VPCs, preventing external exposure.
- **Custom Domain Names:** Users can create internal domain names like db.internal.example.com.
- **Multi-VPC Association:** A single PHZ can be linked to multiple AWS VPCs for centralized management.

Private hosted zones eliminate the need for hardcoding IP addresses, enabling dynamic and scalable internal networking for AWS-based applications.

Working of Private Hosted Zones

To fully utilize private hosted zones, it is essential to understand how they resolve DNS queries within AWS environments. This involves domain name registration, DNS query resolution, and VPC integration.

A private hosted zone functions as follows:

- **Domain Name Definition:**
    - The user defines an internal domain (such as example.internal) in Route 53 under a private hosted zone.
    - This domain is only accessible within the specified VPC(s).
- **VPC Association:**
    - The private hosted zone is associated with one or more AWS VPCs.
    - Only resources within these linked VPCs can resolve the domain names.
- **DNS Query Resolution:**
    - When an AWS resource (like EC2 instance) queries a domain name within the private hosted zone, the request is directed to the private DNS service of Route53.
    - Route 53 resolves the domain name to the associated private IP address of the resource.
- **Security and Access Control:**
    - External queries from the internet or other VPCs cannot resolve the records of the private hosted zone, ensuring secure internal traffic management.

Consider an internal database running in a private subnet of an AWS VPC:

- The database server has an internal IP (such as 10.0.1.5).
- Instead of accessing it using an IP address, a private hosted zone allows users to refer to it as db.internal.example.com.
- Any EC2 instance within the same VPC can resolve db.internal.example.com to its private IP (10.0.1.5) without exposing the database to the internet.

This setup improves security, manageability, and flexibility in AWS-based architectures.

Configuring a Private Hosted Zone in Route 53

Setting up a private hosted zone in Route 53 involves multiple steps, including creating the hosted zone, associating it with VPCs, and configuring DNS records. These steps ensure secure and efficient domain name resolution within AWS environments.

Step-by-Step Configuration:

Step 1: Create a Private Hosted Zone.

1. Open the AWS Management Console → Navigate to Route 53.
2. Click `Hosted Zones → Create Hosted Zone`.
3. Enter the domain name (like example.internal).
4. Select Private Hosted Zone for Amazon VPC and choose the VPC(s) to associate.
5. Click `Create Hosted Zone`.

Step 2: Configure DNS Records.

1. Within the newly created private hosted zone, click `Create Record Set`.
2. Define A records, CNAME records, or MX records to map domain names to private IPs.

Example: Create an A record for db.internal.example.com pointing to 10.0.1.5.

Step 3: Test Internal Domain Resolution.

1. Connect to an EC2 instance within the associated VPC.
2. Run the command: `nslookup db.internal.example.com`
    a. If configured correctly, the private IP address (10.0.1.5) will be returned.

Step 4: Ensure VPC DNS Support is Enabled.

1. Navigate to the VPC Dashboard → Select the VPC associated with the PHZ.
2. Ensure Enable DNS Resolution and Enable DNS Hostnames options are checked.

Best Practices for Private Hosted Zones

To maximize the effectiveness of private hosted zones, users should follow best practices that enhance security, reliability, and maintainability within AWS environments.

- **Use Meaningful Domain Names:** Structure private domains logically, such as dev.internal.example.com, prod.internal.example.com.
- **Enable Route 53 Resolver for Hybrid Environments:** For hybrid cloud setups (AWS + On-Premises), configure Route 53 Resolver to enable cross-network DNS resolution.
- **Limit Access Using IAM Policies:** Restrict Route 53 management permissions to authorized users using AWS Identity and Access Management (IAM).
- **Monitor DNS Resolution Performance:** Use AWS CloudWatch Logs and Route 53 query logging to track DNS performance and troubleshoot failures.
- **Avoid Overlapping Domains across VPCs:** Ensure unique domain naming conventions to prevent DNS conflicts in multi-VPC environments.
- **Use Private Hosted Zones for Internal Applications Only:** Never expose private hosted zone records to the public internet for security reasons.
- **Integrate with AWS Services for Enhanced Security:** Use AWS PrivateLink and VPC Peering to extend private DNS resolution across AWS accounts securely.

Amazon Route 53 Private Hosted Zones are essential for managing internal DNS resolution in AWS environments. They enable organizations to create custom domain names for internal services while ensuring secure and efficient communication within AWS VPCs. By implementing these best practices, users can maximize reliability, security, and scalability in their private networks.

This concludes the detailed exploration of private hosted zones in Route 53. Next, we will discuss routing policies and their role in DNS traffic management.

Managing DNS Records in Route 53

Amazon Route 53 provides a robust and flexible way to manage DNS records, allowing users to map domain names to resources both inside and outside AWS. Managing DNS records efficiently is crucial for ensuring availability, optimizing performance, and implementing failover strategies.

In this section, we will explore the different types of DNS records, their functions, how to create and manage them in Route 53, and the best practices to follow.

Types of DNS Records in Route 53

DNS records serve as the foundation for domain name resolution. Each type of record plays a specific role in directing traffic, ensuring security, and managing failover strategies.

Route 53 supports multiple DNS record types, each serving a different purpose. The following are the most commonly used record types:

- **A Record (Address Record)**
    - Maps a domain name to an IPv4 address (like www.example.com → 192.0.2.1).
    - Essential for directing traffic to web servers and other network resources.
- **AAAA Record**
    - Similar to an A record but maps a domain name to an IPv6 address.
    - Example: www.example.com → 2606:4700:4700::1111.
- **CNAME Record (Canonical Name Record)**
    - Creates an alias for a domain name, redirecting traffic to another domain.
    - Example: blog.example.com → example.com.
    - CNAME cannot be created at the root/apex of a domain (for example, you can't set example.com as a CNAME).
    - Instead, Route 53 supports alias records for this use case.
- **MX Record (Mail Exchange Record)**
    - Directs email traffic to the appropriate mail servers.
    - Example: mail.example.com → Google or AWS WorkMail servers.
- **TXT Record (Text Record)**
    - Stores text-based information used for domain verification, SPF, DKIM, and security purposes.
    - Example: SPF records define which servers can send emails on behalf of a domain.
- **SRV Record (Service Record)**
    - Specifies hostnames and ports for services such as SIP or XMPP.
    - Example: _sip._tcp.example.com → 10 5 5060 sipserver.example.com.
- **PTR Record (Pointer Record)**
    - Used for reverse DNS lookups, mapping an IP address back to a domain name.
    - Example: 192.0.2.1 → example.com.
    - PTRs are typically managed by the IP address owner (for example, ISP, AWS for Elastic IPs), not by the domain owner in Route 53.
- **NS Record (Name Server Record)**
    - Identifies the authoritative name servers responsible for a domain.
    - Example: example.com → ns-123.awsdns-45.net.
- **SOA Record (Start of Authority Record)**
    - Defines key domain settings, including the primary name server, admin email, and refresh intervals.
    - Example: Provides DNS hierarchy and replication details.
    - SOA records are automatically created by Route 53 and not usually modified by users.

Understanding these record types is crucial for setting up scalable and secure domain configurations in Route 53.

Creating and Managing DNS Records in Route 53

Once you understand the different record types, the next step is creating, modifying, and deleting records in Route 53. AWS provides an intuitive console, CLI, and SDK options for managing records efficiently.

Step-by-Step Guide to Creating a DNS Record

Step 1: Access Hosted Zones.

1. Open the AWS Management Console → Navigate to Route 53.
2. Click **`Hosted Zones`** → Select the hosted zone where you want to add records.

Step 2: Create a New Record.

1. Click **`Create Record`** → Enter the subdomain or root domain (example.com or www.example.com).
2. Select the record type (A, CNAME, MX, and so on).
3. Enter the IP address, alias, or target domain.
4. Configure the TTL (Time to Live) to define cache duration.

Step 3: Configure Routing Policy.

1. Choose from Simple, Weighted, Latency-based, Geolocation, or Failover Routing.
2. Define additional settings as per the chosen routing policy.

Step 4: Save and Apply Changes.

1. Click **`Create Record`** to save the new entry.
2. Changes propagate across the DNS system within the defined TTL period.

Modifying and Deleting DNS Records

Domain configurations may need changes over time due to infrastructure upgrades, traffic shifts, or security updates. Modifying or deleting records ensures dynamic and optimized traffic management.

Modifying DNS Records in Route 53:

- Access Hosted Zones → Locate the existing record.
- Click **`Edit`** → Modify record value, TTL, or routing policy.
- Click **`Save`** to apply changes.

Deleting DNS Records in Route 53:

- Navigate to the Route 53 console → Open the desired hosted zone.
- Select the record → Click **`Delete`**.
- Confirm deletion.

Note: *Deleting a critical record (for example, NS or A record) may cause service disruptions.*

Best Practices for Managing DNS Records

To maintain a highly available, secure, and efficient DNS configuration, AWS recommends the following best practices for managing DNS records:

- **Use Alias Records for AWS Services:**
  - Route 53 supports alias records for AWS services like CloudFront, S3, and Elastic Load Balancing (ELB).
  - This improves resolution speed and eliminates the need for static IPs.
- **Implement Failover and Health Checks:**
  - Configure failover records with Route 53 health checks to redirect traffic during outages.
- **Leverage TTL for Performance Optimization:**
  - Short TTL values improve agility for dynamic infrastructure.

    Short TTL = faster failover but more queries.
  - Long TTL values reduce DNS query load and improve caching efficiency.

    Long TTL = better performance but slower propagation of changes.
- **Secure Sensitive DNS Records:**
  - Use AWS IAM policies to control Route 53 record modifications.
  - Route 53 DNS Firewall (with Resolver rules) as an additional layer of DNS security for advanced use cases.
  - Avoid exposing internal records via public hosted zones.
- **Regularly Audit DNS Records:**
  - Periodically review and update DNS records to align with infrastructure changes.

Managing DNS records in Route 53 is critical for controlling domain resolution, optimizing performance, and ensuring fault tolerance. By understanding the different DNS record types, how to create and modify them, and implementing best practices, organizations can effectively manage their cloud-based DNS infrastructure.

Routing Policies

Amazon Route 53 provides routing policies that determine how DNS queries are handled. These policies allow organizations to distribute traffic efficiently across multiple endpoints, ensuring fault tolerance, optimal performance, and improved availability. By selecting the right routing policy, businesses can control traffic distribution based on factors such as latency, geography, load balancing, and failover mechanisms.

Importance of Routing Policies in AWS

Effective DNS routing is critical in cloud architectures, as it enhances application performance, supports global user bases, and mitigates failures. The routing policies of Route 53 help organizations:

- Optimize traffic flow based on user location and network conditions.
- Enhance redundancy and failover capabilities, reducing downtime risks.
- Distribute workload efficiently to balance performance across multiple servers.
- Ensure compliance with geographic regulations by directing traffic based on user location.
- Implement dynamic scaling strategies for cloud-based applications.

By leveraging the routing policies of Route 53, businesses can design resilient, high-performance architectures that deliver seamless user experiences.

This section covers the different routing policies available in Amazon Route 53. Each policy serves a unique purpose and is designed for specific use cases. The following is a structured breakdown:

- **Simple Routing Policy:** Directs all traffic to a single resource without additional logic.
- **Weighted Routing Policy:** Distributes traffic across multiple endpoints based on assigned weights.
- **Latency-Based Routing Policy:** Routes users to the endpoint with the lowest network latency.
- **Geolocation Routing Policy:** Routes traffic based on the geographical location of the user.
- **Geoproximity Routing Policy:** Routes traffic based on location bias and shifting traffic dynamically.
- **Failover Routing Policy:** Ensures high availability by redirecting traffic to backup resources in case of failure.
- **Multivalue Answer Routing Policy:** Returns multiple records for a domain to enable DNS-based load balancing.

Each routing policy plays a crucial role in traffic management, enabling organizations to design customized routing strategies for various application needs. In the next sections, we will explore these policies in detail.

Simple Routing Policy

The Simple Routing Policy in Amazon Route 53 is the most straightforward and commonly used DNS routing strategy. It is primarily used when a domain needs to resolve to a single resource without any advanced traffic management rules. Unlike other policies that involve load balancing, failover, or geographic-based routing, Simple Routing ensures that all users querying a domain receive the same IP address or endpoint.

This policy is ideal for small-scale applications, static websites, or single-instance deployments, where there is no need for distributing traffic across multiple endpoints.

Importance of Simple Routing Policy

The Simple Routing Policy is useful in scenarios where:

- A domain or subdomain should always resolve to one specific IP address or resource.
- No traffic balancing or failover mechanisms are required.
- The architecture is simple, such as single-instance web applications or standalone S3-hosted websites.
- The same DNS response should be provided to every user, regardless of their location.

Working of Simple Routing

To effectively use Simple Routing, it is important to understand how Route 53 processes DNS queries when this policy is applied.

- When a DNS query is made to a domain (such as example.com), Route 53 looks up the record and returns the single IP address or endpoint associated with that domain.
- There is no logic for traffic distribution, failover, or geographic optimization—every request gets the same response.
- Route 53 stores these mappings in hosted zones, which contain DNS records like A, AAAA, CNAME, and others.

- If multiple values are assigned to a record (like multiple IPs), Route 53 randomly returns one without any traffic weighting.

Example: If www.example.com is mapped to an EC2 instance IP (192.168.1.10), every user who queries www.example.com will receive this same IP address.

Configuring Simple Routing in Route 53

Setting up Simple Routing in Route 53 involves creating a hosted zone, defining DNS records, and assigning an endpoint.

To configure Simple Routing in Route 53:

1. **Create a Hosted Zone.**
   a. Go to the AWS Route 53 console and select **`Hosted Zones`**.
   b. Click **`Create Hosted Zone`** and enter your domain name (like example.com).
   c. Choose the type: Public Hosted Zone (for external access) or Private Hosted Zone (for VPC-specific routing).
2. **Add a DNS Record.**
   a. Select the newly created hosted zone.
   b. Click **`Create Record Set`** and configure:
   c. **Record Name:** (like www.example.com).
   d. **Record Type:** A (IPv4), AAAA (IPv6), CNAME (alias), and so on.
   e. **Value:** The target IP address or AWS resource (like 192.168.1.10).
3. **Save and Deploy.**
   a. Once saved, Route 53 propagates the record across DNS servers.
   b. Now, any DNS query to www.example.com will resolve to the specified IP.

Use Cases of Simple Routing

Simple Routing is best suited for scenarios where only one endpoint is required without the need for load balancing or failover mechanisms.

Some key use cases include:

- **Static Websites:** Websites hosted on a single Amazon S3 bucket or a single EC2 instance.
- **Internal Applications:** Private DNS records for internal systems, such as an on-premises database.
- **Basic Web Servers:** Small-scale applications that do not require traffic distribution across multiple regions.
- **Single-Region APIs:** APIs with a single endpoint that do not require latency-based routing.

Example: A startup launches a web application on an EC2 instance in us-east-1. Using Simple Routing, they map app.example.com to this single EC2 instance, ensuring all users receive the same endpoint.

Limitations of Simple Routing

Despite its simplicity, Simple Routing has several limitations, making it unsuitable for highly available and distributed architectures. Some key limitations include:

- **No Load Balancing:** All traffic is routed to a single resource, leading to potential performance bottlenecks.
- **No Failover Support:** If the assigned endpoint fails, Route 53 does not redirect traffic to a backup resource.
- **No Geographic Optimization:** Users may experience higher latency if they are far from the hosted resource.
- **Scalability Issues:** As traffic grows, a single instance or endpoint may become overwhelmed.

Example: A company hosts an application in North America, but users from Asia experience high latency. Simple Routing does not redirect users to a closer AWS region, leading to a poor user experience.

In all, Simple Routing directs all DNS queries to a single endpoint without advanced traffic management. It is easy to configure and best suited for small applications, static websites, and internal DNS records. The setup involves creating a hosted zone and adding an A, CNAME, or other DNS record types. The limitations include lack of load balancing, failover, and geographic optimization. Also, more advanced architectures require Weighted, Failover, or Latency-Based Routing to optimize performance and availability.

By understanding Simple Routing, users can decide whether it meets their application's requirements or if they need a more advanced routing strategy.

Weighted Routing Policy

The Weighted Routing Policy in Amazon Route 53 allows administrators to distribute traffic among multiple resources based on assigned weight values. This approach is beneficial for load balancing, traffic testing, and gradual migrations, providing a mechanism to control the proportion of requests directed to each resource.

Unlike Simple Routing, which always returns the same DNS response, Weighted Routing distributes traffic dynamically according to predefined percentages.

Traffic percentages are approximate due to DNS caching.

Importance of Weighted Routing Policy

The Weighted Routing Policy is crucial in scenarios such as:

- **Gradual Migrations:** Shifting traffic from an old system to a new system without causing downtime.
- **Canary Deployments:** Testing a new version of an application by sending a small percentage of traffic before full deployment.
- **Load Distribution:** Spreading requests across multiple AWS resources to prevent overloading a single instance.

Working of Weighted Routing

To effectively use Weighted Routing, it is important to understand how Route 53 assigns weights to different endpoints and distributes traffic accordingly.

- Traffic is distributed based on assigned weights for each record in Route 53.
- A higher weight means more traffic is directed to that endpoint.
- The total weight across all records determines the percentage of traffic each resource receives.

Example:

If you have two servers with the following weights:

- Server A – Weight 80
- Server B – Weight 20

Route 53 will route 80% of traffic to Server A and 20% to Server B.

Configuring Weighted Routing in Route 53

Setting up Weighted Routing in Route 53 requires defining multiple DNS records for the same domain and assigning different weights to each resource.

To configure Weighted Routing in Route 53:

1. **Create a Hosted Zone.**
   a. In the Route 53 console, navigate to Hosted Zones and create/select a domain (e.g., example.com).
2. **Create Weighted Records.**
   a. Click `Create Record Set` and configure:
   b. **Record Name:** (such as www.example.com).
   c. **Record Type:** A (IPv4), AAAA (IPv6), CNAME, and the like.
   d. **Value:** IP address or AWS resource (for example, EC2, ALB, S3).
   e. **Routing Policy:** Select Weighted Routing.
   f. **Set Weight:** Assign weight values based on the desired traffic distribution.
3. **Repeat for Additional Endpoints.**
   a. Create another record for a second server or resource with a different weight.
4. **Test and Validate.**
   a. Use nslookup or dig to verify DNS resolution behavior.

Use Cases of Weighted Routing

Weighted Routing is an essential DNS strategy in various real-world applications. Some common use cases include:

- **Blue-Green Deployments:** Shift traffic from an old application version to a new one incrementally.
- **A/B Testing:** Test different versions of an application by directing traffic to different environments.
- **Failover Testing:** Send a portion of traffic to a backup system to verify reliability.
- **Regional Load Distribution:** Balance user requests across AWS regions.

Example: An e-commerce company deploys a new API version. To test it safely, they configure:

- 90% traffic to the old API.
- 10% traffic to the new API.

Once validated, they gradually shift all users to the new API.

Limitations of Weighted Routing

Despite its flexibility, Weighted Routing has certain limitations.

- **Not real-time:** DNS caches can delay traffic shifts.
- **No automatic failover:** If one endpoint fails, traffic is still routed according to weight.
- **Client-side caching:** Some DNS resolvers store responses, leading to inconsistent results.

To overcome these, Route 53 can be combined with health checks and failover routing.

Weighted Routing is a powerful DNS-based traffic management strategy that enables load balancing, phased deployments, and controlled traffic distribution. While it offers great flexibility, administrators must account for DNS caching, failover handling, and traffic validation to ensure smooth operations.

Latency-Based Routing (LBR)

Latency-Based Routing (LBR) in Amazon Route 53 is designed to direct user requests to the AWS region with the lowest latency. It improves application performance by reducing delays in network responses, ensuring that end-users connect to the closest and fastest resource.

When a user initiates a request, Route 53 evaluates the latency between their DNS resolver and AWS regions where application instances are hosted. The request is then routed to the resource with the shortest response time, optimizing performance.

Importance of Latency-Based Routing

Latency-Based Routing is crucial for:

- Enhancing user experience by minimizing network delays.
- Serving a global audience efficiently by utilizing the distributed infrastructure of AWS.
- Reducing congestion and optimizing resource utilization across multiple regions.
- Ensuring seamless failover by dynamically selecting the fastest available endpoint.

Working of Latency-Based Routing

To effectively use LBR, it is important to understand how Route 53 determines the optimal endpoint for user requests based on network latency measurements.

- AWS continuously measures network latency between different AWS regions and internet users.
- When a user queries a domain using LBR, Route 53 selects the endpoint with the lowest measured latency from the location of the user.
- The decision is based on historical latency data, rather than real-time network conditions.

Example: The company has application servers in US-East (Virginia) and Asia-Pacific (Singapore).

- A user from New York is routed to the Virginia server due to lower latency.
- A user from Tokyo is routed to the Singapore server, as it offers a faster response time.

Configuring Latency-Based Routing in Route 53

To use LBR in Route 53, administrators must configure multiple records in a hosted zone, each corresponding to different AWS regions.

To set up Latency-Based Routing:

1. **Create a Hosted Zone.**
    a. In the Route 53 console, navigate to Hosted Zones and select or create a domain (e.g., example.com).
2. **Create Latency-Based Records.**
    a. Click `Create Record Set` and configure:
        i. **Record Name:** (such as www.example.com).
        ii. **Record Type:** A (IPv4), AAAA (IPv6), CNAME, and the like.
        iii. **Value:** IP address of an EC2 instance, Load Balancer, or S3 bucket in one AWS region.
        iv. **Routing Policy:** Select Latency-Based Routing.
        v. **Region:** Choose the AWS region where this resource is deployed.
3. **Repeat for Other AWS Regions.**
    a. Add additional records for other AWS regions where the application is hosted.
4. **Test and Validate.**
    a. Use dig or nslookup to verify DNS responses based on location.

Use Cases of Latency-Based Routing

LBR is widely used for global applications where performance and responsiveness are critical. Some common scenarios include:

- **Global Content Delivery:** Serving users from the nearest AWS region to improve website loading speeds.
- **Multi-Region Disaster Recovery:** Ensuring users are routed to the fastest available region during a failure.
- **Gaming Applications:** Reducing lag for players by connecting them to the closest game server.
- **API Optimization:** Distributing API requests to the lowest-latency backend service.

Example: A video streaming platform operates in three AWS regions (US, Europe, Asia).

- Viewers from Los Angeles connect to US servers.
- Viewers from London connect to Europe servers.
- Viewers from Tokyo connect to Asia servers.

This ensures minimal buffering and optimal streaming quality.

Limitations of Latency-Based Routing

Despite its advantages, LBR has certain limitations that must be considered.

- **Latency-based decisions are not real-time:** Route 53 relies on pre-measured latency data, which may not reflect sudden network changes.
- **No automatic failover:** If the lowest-latency endpoint becomes unavailable, traffic is not automatically rerouted unless Failover Routing is combined.
- **Client-side caching:** Some DNS resolvers cache responses, which may not always reflect the latest latency conditions.
- **Regional availability:** LBR only works if resources are deployed in multiple AWS regions.

To mitigate these, organizations often combine LBR with health checks and failover mechanisms for improved resilience.

Latency-Based Routing is a powerful strategy for improving performance and optimizing traffic distribution. By directing users to the lowest-latency AWS region, applications can provide faster response times and a better user experience. However, it should be carefully configured with failover mechanisms to handle regional failures effectively.

Geolocation Routing

Geolocation Routing in Amazon Route 53 allows administrators to direct traffic based on the geographical location of users making DNS queries. This ensures that users are served by region-specific resources, improving content localization, compliance, and regulatory adherence. Unlike Latency-Based Routing, which selects the fastest route, Geolocation Routing ensures that users from specific locations are always routed to designated endpoints—regardless of latency.

For example, a business with data centers in the United States, Europe, and Asia can use Geolocation Routing to send:

- U.S. users to an application hosted in AWS US-East (N. Virginia).
- European users to AWS EU (Frankfurt).
- Asian users to AWS APAC (Singapore).

This method provides control over user traffic flow, allowing businesses to customize experiences based on geography.

Importance of Geolocation Routing

Geolocation Routing is critical for:

- **Content localization:** Delivering region-specific versions of applications.
- **Regulatory compliance:** Directing users to in-region servers to meet data residency laws.
- **Optimized user experience:** Providing geographically relevant services and features.
- **Security and access control:** Restricting access to applications from unauthorized regions.

Working of Geolocation Routing

Understanding the mechanics of Geolocation Routing helps in designing an effective DNS architecture for global applications.

- When a user makes a DNS query, Route 53 checks the originating IP address of the resolver.
- The system determines the user's location at the continent, country, or state level (if available).
- Route 53 then directs the query to the predefined resource assigned for that location.
- If no specific routing rule exists for the user's location, Route 53 sends them to a default endpoint (configured by the administrator).

Example: A financial services company must comply with GDPR laws by ensuring that European users only access servers within the EU. By implementing Geolocation Routing:

- Users in Germany, France, and Spain are directed to AWS EU (Frankfurt).
- U.S. users connect to AWS US-East (N. Virginia).
- Asian users are routed to AWS APAC (Tokyo).

This setup guarantees that user data stays within legally compliant regions.

Configuring Geolocation Routing in Route 53

Setting up Geolocation Routing in Route 53 involves defining traffic flow rules based on geographic locations.

To configure Geolocation Routing:

1. **Create a Hosted Zone.**
    a. Open the Route 53 console and navigate to Hosted Zones.
    b. Select or create a domain (like example.com).
2. **Create Geolocation-Based Records.**
    a. Click `Create Record Set` and configure:
        i. **Record Name:** (such as www.example.com).
        ii. **Record Type:** A (IPv4), AAAA (IPv6), CNAME, and the like.
        iii. **Value:** The IP address of an AWS resource (including EC2 instance, Load Balancer, and so forth).
        iv. **Routing Policy:** Select Geolocation Routing.
        v. **Location:** Choose the continent, country, or state where this rule applies.
3. **Define a Default Record (Failsafe Route).**
    a. If the location of a user does not match any configured rule, Route 53 falls back to the default record.
    b. Create a record without a geolocation setting to serve as a global catch-all.
4. **Test and Validate Configuration.**
    a. Use tools like dig or nslookup to check DNS resolution based on different geographic locations.

Use Cases of Geolocation Routing

Geolocation Routing is widely used across industries to optimize service delivery, enhance security, and comply with regulations. Some common use cases include:

- **Content Localization:** Directing users to region-specific websites or applications.
- **Compliance with Data Residency Laws:** Ensuring customer data stays within legal boundaries.
- **Regional Load Balancing:** Spreading traffic across multiple AWS regions based on user location.
- **Security and Access Restrictions:** Blocking or allowing access from specific countries.

Example: A media streaming platform provides different content in different regions.

- Users in the U.S. get access to Hollywood movies.
- Users in India receive Bollywood content.
- Users in China are blocked due to government restrictions.

This ensures that the content is tailored to the audience while meeting regulatory requirements.

Limitations of Geolocation Routing

While Geolocation Routing is powerful, it has certain limitations that should be considered before implementation.

- **Accuracy of IP-Based Location**
  - Route 53 relies on IP databases, which may not always be accurate.
  - Some users behind VPNs or proxies might be misrouted.
- **No Real-Time Latency Considerations**
  - Unlike Latency-Based Routing, Geolocation Routing does not prioritize fastest response times.
  - Users might be directed to a region with higher latency if that is their designated endpoint.
- **Complexity in Global DNS Management**
  - Managing hundreds of geolocation rules can be cumbersome for large-scale applications.
- **Default Routing Challenges**
  - If no specific rule exists for the location of a user, they are directed to the default record, which may not always be ideal.

Example: A company operating in Africa may find that some users from smaller countries do not match any predefined rule. These users will be directed to the default region, potentially causing performance issues.

Geolocation Routing in Amazon Route 53 is a powerful tool for directing user traffic based on location, ensuring compliance, localized experiences, and regional optimizations. However, it should be carefully planned to account for limitations in IP-based geolocation accuracy and performance trade-offs. When implemented correctly, Geolocation Routing significantly improves service delivery, security, and user experience across global AWS deployments.

Failover Routing

Failover Routing in Amazon Route 53 is designed to ensure high availability and automatic recovery of applications by redirecting traffic when a primary resource fails. It is a crucial mechanism for businesses that require minimal downtime, such as e-commerce platforms, banking systems, and enterprise applications.

Unlike other routing policies that distribute traffic based on performance or geography, Failover Routing focuses on resilience, ensuring that if a primary endpoint (server, database, or load balancer) becomes unavailable, traffic is immediately redirected to a healthy secondary resource.

For example, a web application deployed in AWS US-East (N. Virginia) can be set up with:

- A primary resource (EC2 instance, ALB, or CloudFront) in US-East.
- A secondary (backup) resource in AWS US-West (Oregon).

If Route 53 detects that the primary instance is unhealthy, it automatically fails over to the backup resource, maintaining service availability.

Importance of Failover Routing

Failover Routing is critical for:

- **Minimizing downtime:** Ensuring users experience uninterrupted service.
- **Enhancing disaster recovery:** Providing a secondary failover mechanism.
- **Protecting against regional failures:** Redirecting traffic in case of AWS region-wide issues.
- **Optimizing cost and performance:** Using standby resources only when necessary.

Working of Failover Routing

Failover Routing operates based on health checks and predefined failover rules to ensure uninterrupted service.

- Route 53 continuously monitors the health of primary resources using AWS Health Checks.
- If the primary resource becomes unresponsive, Route 53 automatically reroutes traffic to the secondary (backup) resource.
- Failover can be either:
    - **Active-Passive:** Traffic flows to the primary resource until it fails, and then switches to the secondary resource.
    - **Active-Active:** Traffic is distributed across multiple healthy endpoints, with automatic reallocation if one fails.

Example: A financial service provider hosts a banking app in AWS US-East, with a backup in AWS US-West. If the primary app server crashes, Route 53 detects the failure and instantly redirects traffic to the backup server in US-West.

Primary and Secondary Endpoints

Failover Routing requires defining a primary endpoint (active resource) and a secondary endpoint (standby resource).

- **Primary Endpoint:** The main resource that handles user traffic under normal conditions.
- **Secondary Endpoint:** A backup resource that remains idle until failover occurs.

Route 53 determines failover based on:

- Health status of the primary endpoint.
- Configured failover rules (failover threshold, health check settings).
- Response time from both endpoints.

Example: A multi-region online store has a primary load balancer in US-East, with a backup in EU-West. If Route 53 detects downtime, traffic is redirected to EU-West to keep the store operational.

Configuring Failover Routing in Route 53

Setting up Failover Routing involves creating health checks and configuring failover policies.

To configure Failover Routing:

- **Create a Hosted Zone**
    - Open the Route 53 console and select Hosted Zones.
    - Choose or create a domain (such as example.com).
- **Create a Health Check**
    - Navigate to Health Checks in Route 53.
    - Click Create Health Check and configure:
        - **Endpoint Type:** Choose HTTP, TCP, or HTTPS.
        - **Endpoint Target:** Enter the IP of the primary resource or DNS name.
        - **Failure Threshold:** Define how many failed attempts trigger a failover.

- **Create Failover Records**
  - Under the hosted zone, click `Create Record Set`.
  - Configure a record for the primary resource:
    - **Name:** www.example.com
    - **Type:** A (IPv4) or CNAME
    - **Routing Policy:** Select Failover
    - **Failover Type:** Primary
    - Associate Health Check
  - Configure a record for the secondary resource:
    - **Failover Type:** Secondary
    - Associate Health Check
- **Test and Validate**
  - Simulate a failure on the primary endpoint and check if Route 53 redirects traffic.

Use Cases of Failover Routing

Failover Routing is widely used to enhance application resilience and disaster recovery strategies. Some common use cases include:

- **Disaster Recovery (DR) Sites:** Redirecting traffic to secondary locations in case of failure.
- **Multi-Region Deployments:** Ensuring applications remain available during regional outages.
- **Business Continuity Planning:** Providing uninterrupted service in the event of infrastructure failure.

Example: A global SaaS provider hosts its API services in AWS US-East but has a backup in AWS APAC (Singapore). If Route 53 detects downtime in US-East, traffic is instantly rerouted to the APAC servers, ensuring zero disruption.

Limitations and Considerations

While Failover Routing improves availability, it has certain limitations and best practices that must be considered.

DNS TTL Delays

- Route 53 changes propagate based on TTL values.
- For critical applications, set TTL to 30–60 seconds for faster failover.
- Lower TTL improves recovery time but increases DNS query load and cost.

Health Check Configuration

- Incorrect health check thresholds can cause false positives or delayed failover.
- Use string matching for application-level validation, enable CloudWatch alarm integration for metric-based health checks, and rely on Route 53 health checkers from multiple AWS regions to detect regional failures accurately.

Cost Considerations

- Running redundant secondary resources incurs additional AWS costs.

Cross-Region Latency

- Failing over between geographically distant regions can impact performance.

Failover Routing is an essential tool for ensuring high availability in AWS environments. By monitoring primary resources and automatically redirecting traffic, organizations can minimize downtime, improve disaster recovery, and enhance user experience. However, careful planning is required to balance cost, latency, and reliability.

DNS Health Checks

Ensuring the availability and reliability of web applications and network resources is a fundamental requirement for modern businesses. DNS health checks and failover strategies in Amazon Route 53 provide an automated mechanism to monitor the health of endpoints and redirect traffic when failures occur. These mechanisms enhance resilience, ensuring that users are always directed to a functional resource, even in the event of infrastructure failures.

The health checks of Amazon Route 53 continuously evaluate the availability of servers, load balancers, and other endpoints by sending periodic requests and monitoring responses. If a primary resource becomes unresponsive, Route 53 can trigger failover mechanisms to redirect traffic to a backup or alternative endpoint, thereby minimizing downtime.

DNS health checks and failover strategies are critical for:

- **High Availability:** Ensuring users always reach an operational service, even if an outage occurs.
- **Disaster Recovery:** Providing seamless traffic redirection to backup infrastructure in case of failures.
- **Performance Optimization:** Directing users to the healthiest and most responsive endpoints.
- **Cost Efficiency:** Avoiding unnecessary infrastructure costs by activating backup resources only when needed.
- **Global Resilience:** Allowing businesses to maintain operations across multiple geographical locations.

For instance, an e-commerce website serving global customers can use DNS failover strategies to ensure uninterrupted shopping experiences, even if one data center goes offline.

Route 53 Health Checks

Amazon Route 53 health checks play a crucial role in ensuring the availability and reliability of web applications and network resources. These health checks actively monitor the status of endpoints—such as web servers, databases, and load balancers—and determine whether they are healthy or unhealthy based on predefined criteria.

When an endpoint fails a health check, Route 53 can automatically trigger failover mechanisms to redirect traffic to a backup resource, preventing service disruption. By continuously evaluating system health, businesses can achieve high availability, improved fault tolerance, and enhanced disaster recovery capabilities.

Working of Route 53 Health Checks

Route 53 health checks function by sending periodic requests to an endpoint and analyzing the response. If the endpoint does not respond as expected, Route 53 considers it unhealthy and can reroute traffic to a backup endpoint or an alternate AWS region.

The way Health Checks Operate in Route 53 is given as follows:

1. **Defining the Endpoint:** The health check is configured with an IP address or domain name to monitor.
2. **Selecting the Monitoring Method:** Route 53 uses HTTP, HTTPS, or TCP requests to verify availability.
3. **Performing Regular Checks:** Route 53 sends periodic requests and waits for a response.
4. **Evaluating the Response:** If the endpoint responds within a specified time frame, it is considered healthy. If it fails multiple consecutive checks, it is deemed unhealthy.
5. **Triggering Failover Actions:** When an endpoint is marked unhealthy, Route 53 reroutes traffic based on predefined failover routing policies.

Route 53 Health Checks are Essential as it:

- Prevents traffic from being sent to unreachable or failed servers.
- Enables automated failover, minimizing downtime.
- Integrates with Amazon CloudWatch for performance insights and alerts.

Monitoring Methods Used in Route 53 Health Checks

Some of the monitoring methods used in Route 53 Health Checks are:

HTTP and HTTPS Health Checks

1. Route 53 sends an HTTP(S) GET request to the target endpoint.
2. If the server responds with HTTP 2xx or 3xx status codes, it is considered healthy.
3. If the response includes HTTP 4xx or 5xx errors, the endpoint is marked unhealthy.

Use Cases:

- Monitoring web applications hosted on Amazon EC2 or on-premises servers.
- Ensuring availability of REST APIs and microservices.

TCP Health Checks

1. Route 53 establishes a TCP connection with the target endpoint.
2. If the connection is successfully opened, the endpoint is marked healthy.
3. If the TCP handshake fails, the endpoint is considered unhealthy.

Use Cases:

- Checking database connectivity (for example, Amazon RDS).
- Monitoring non-HTTP services such as FTP servers and messaging queues.

Calculated Health Checks

1. Aggregates results from multiple health checks to determine overall system health.
2. If a majority of checks fail, the entire system is marked unhealthy.

Use Cases:

- Large-scale applications with multiple redundant endpoints.
- Distributed services spanning multiple AWS regions.

Latency-Based Health Checks

1. Measures response time from multiple AWS regions.

2. Routes traffic to the endpoint with the lowest latency.

Use Case:

- Optimizing performance for global users by directing them to the nearest healthy endpoint.

Route 53 Determining Endpoint Health

Health Check Evaluation Criteria

Route 53 determines endpoint health using failure thresholds and response times:

- If an endpoint fails multiple consecutive checks, it is marked unhealthy.
- Route 53 waits for a specified number of successful checks before restoring the status to healthy.

Integration with AWS Services

- **Amazon CloudWatch:** Generates alarms when health checks fail.
- **AWS Lambda:** Automates remediation actions (such as restarting an EC2 instance).
- **Elastic Load Balancing (ELB):** Distributes traffic to only healthy backend instances.

Route 53 health checks provide a robust monitoring solution that helps organizations maintain high availability and fault tolerance. By proactively detecting failures and triggering automated failover actions, businesses can ensure their applications remain operational even in the event of infrastructure issues.

Types of Health Checks

Amazon Route 53 provides various types of health checks to monitor the status of network resources and ensure seamless failover in case of endpoint failure. These health checks proactively assess the availability and performance of resources such as web servers, APIs, databases, and load balancers.

Selecting the right type of health check is crucial for ensuring uptime, reducing response latency, and implementing intelligent failover strategies. Route 53 supports different types of health checks to meet diverse application needs, including endpoint-based monitoring, calculated health checks, and state-of-origin checks.

Endpoint Health Checks

Endpoint health checks are the most commonly used type in Route 53. These checks determine whether a specific web server, API, or database endpoint is available and responsive.

Route 53 continuously sends requests to the endpoint and monitors the responses. If the endpoint fails to respond as expected, it is marked unhealthy, and traffic is rerouted to a backup resource using failover routing.

Working of Endpoint Health Checks

1. Route 53 sends an HTTP, HTTPS, or TCP request to the endpoint.
2. The response is analyzed based on status codes and response time.
3. If the endpoint fails multiple consecutive checks, it is marked unhealthy.
4. If it later meets the success criteria, it is restored to healthy status.

Use Cases:

- Monitoring web applications to ensure availability.
- Ensuring database servers are responsive.
- Detecting failures in API endpoints.

Latency-Based Health Checks

Latency-based health checks measure the response time of an endpoint from multiple AWS regions and help Route 53 direct users to the endpoint with the lowest latency.

This type of health check is essential for global applications, ensuring that users receive the fastest response times by directing them to the nearest and fastest responding server.

Route 53 in itself does not route traffic purely based on latency metrics; it provides latency data that informs latency-based routing decisions.

Working of Latency-Based Health Checks

1. Route 53 health checkers in different AWS regions send requests to the endpoint.
2. The system measures the time taken to receive a response.
3. Traffic is dynamically routed to the region with the lowest latency.

Use Cases:

- CDNs (Content Delivery Networks) to optimize load times.
- E-commerce platforms serving customers worldwide.
- Gaming applications requiring low-latency interactions.

TCP Health Checks

Unlike HTTP-based checks that inspect the response content, TCP health checks only establish a connection to a target endpoint without inspecting application-level responses.

TCP checks are useful for monitoring databases, FTP servers, and non-HTTP services where an active network connection determines availability.

Working of TCP Health Checks

1. Route 53 attempts to establish a TCP connection on a specified port (like 3306 for MySQL).
2. If the connection is successfully established, the endpoint is healthy.
3. If the connection fails or times out, the endpoint is unhealthy.

Use Cases:

- Ensuring database servers (Amazon RDS, MySQL, PostgreSQL) are reachable.
- Monitoring FTP or mail servers that do not use HTTP-based communication.
- Checking connectivity to custom applications running on specific ports.

Calculated Health Checks

Calculated health checks aggregate the results of multiple individual health checks and determine system health based on a logical condition.

Instead of monitoring a single endpoint, these checks combine the status of multiple health checks and return an overall healthy/unhealthy status based on a predefined threshold.

Working of Calculated Health Checks

1. Route 53 groups multiple health checks into a calculated check.
2. A logical condition is applied (such as at least 2 out of 3 endpoints must be healthy).
3. If the condition fails, the calculated check is marked unhealthy.

Use Cases:

- Ensuring that at least one regional data center is available.
- Verifying multi-region failover readiness.
- Aggregating multiple API health checks into a single metric.

CloudWatch-Linked Health Checks

AWS CloudWatch-linked health checks allow Route 53 to monitor custom application metrics and alarms instead of network-level health signals.

For example, rather than just checking if a web server is online, these checks can monitor application-specific metrics such as CPU utilization, memory usage, or error rates.

Working of CloudWatch-Linked Health Checks

1. Route 53 integrates with Amazon CloudWatch Alarms.
2. If the CloudWatch alarm triggers, Route 53 marks the endpoint as unhealthy.
3. The system reroutes traffic based on failover policies.

Use Cases:

- Detecting high CPU usage and diverting traffic before a server crashes.
- Monitoring memory leaks in microservices.
- Implementing custom health indicators beyond standard HTTP/TCP checks.

Selecting the appropriate Route 53 health check type depends on the specific requirements of your application, traffic distribution, and failover strategy.

- Endpoint health checks monitor web servers, APIs, and databases.
- Latency-based checks optimize performance by routing users to the fastest endpoint.
- TCP health checks validate connectivity to non-HTTP services.
- Calculated health checks aggregate multiple status signals for complex architectures.
- CloudWatch-linked health checks extend monitoring beyond basic availability checks.

By using a combination of these health checks, businesses can maximize uptime, prevent outages, and provide seamless user experiences even in high-availability and multi-region architectures.

Automated Failover Mechanisms

Automated failover mechanisms in Amazon Route 53 ensure high availability and reliability by automatically rerouting traffic to healthy resources when a failure is detected. These mechanisms use health checks and routing policies to identify unresponsive endpoints and redirect users to backup servers, ensuring minimal downtime and optimal performance.

Failover automation is critical for businesses running mission-critical applications, global services, and real-time platforms where uninterrupted service is essential. Route 53 provides various failover strategies that integrate seamlessly with AWS services like ELB (Elastic Load Balancing), CloudFront, and AWS Global Accelerator.

Primary-Backup Failover

Primary-backup failover is the most common failover strategy, where traffic is directed to a primary resource by default, and in case of failure, it is automatically switched to a backup resource.

Route 53 continuously monitors the health of the primary endpoint using health checks. If the primary resource becomes unhealthy or unreachable, Route 53 routes traffic to the backup instance to maintain availability.

Working of Primary-Backup Failover

1. A primary endpoint (such as primary web server) is configured as the default route for traffic.
2. A backup endpoint (similar to a secondary server in another AWS region) is designated as the failover option.
3. Route 53 monitors the health of the primary endpoint using a health check.
4. If the primary fails, Route 53 automatically redirects traffic to the backup.
5. Once the primary endpoint recovers, traffic is restored to the original route.

Use Cases:

- Disaster recovery solutions to ensure uptime.
- E-commerce websites requiring continuous availability.
- Enterprise applications with secondary data centers as failover.

Active-Active Failover

Unlike primary-backup failover, active-active failover distributes traffic simultaneously across multiple healthy endpoints. This approach improves performance, load balancing, and redundancy.

Route 53 does not natively load-balance traffic - this is achieved via multiple healthy records, not a traditional load balancer.

All configured endpoints remain active, and if one fails, Route 53 simply removes it from traffic distribution and continues routing requests to the remaining healthy endpoints.

Working of Active-Active Failover

1. Multiple resources (such as web servers, databases) are designated as active endpoints.
2. Route 53 distributes traffic evenly across all active endpoints.
3. Health checks continuously monitor each endpoint.
4. If one endpoint becomes unhealthy, Route 53 removes it from traffic routing.
5. Traffic is automatically redirected to the remaining healthy endpoints.

Use Cases:

- Global applications needing high availability across multiple regions.
- Load-balanced applications distributing traffic dynamically.
- High-performance content delivery systems (like video streaming).

Latency-Based Failover

Latency-based failover enhances performance and user experience by directing traffic to the endpoint with the lowest response time. Latency-based health checks measure endpoint responsiveness; latency-based failover uses those results to reroute traffic dynamically.

This method ensures that users are always connected to the fastest, nearest resource and minimizes disruptions caused by slow or unresponsive servers.

Working of Latency-Based Failover

1. Route 53 continuously measures the response time of each endpoint from different geographic locations.
2. Traffic is routed to the server with the lowest latency.
3. If the fastest endpoint fails, traffic is automatically redirected to the next fastest available endpoint.
4. When the failed endpoint recovers, it is reintroduced into the routing pool.

Use Cases:

- Multi-region applications ensuring optimal performance.
- Gaming services requiring low-latency connections.
- Real-time financial trading platforms.

Geolocation-Based Failover

Geolocation-based failover ensures users are routed to region-specific endpoints based on their physical location. This approach is useful for compliance, content localization, and regional failover strategies.

If an endpoint assigned to a region fails, Route 53 can redirect traffic to an alternate endpoint in a nearby region, ensuring continued service.

Working of Geolocation-Based Failover

1. Users are mapped to a specific endpoint based on their location.
2. Route 53 health checks monitor each regional endpoint.
3. If a regional endpoint fails, traffic is redirected to a predefined backup endpoint.
4. Once the primary regional endpoint is restored, traffic is redirected back.

Use Cases:

- Regulatory compliance (including European users accessing EU-hosted servers).
- Content localization (for example, showing region-specific product catalogs).
- Failover strategies where primary data centers are tied to specific regions.

Failover with AWS Services (ELB, CloudFront, Global Accelerator)

Route 53 integrates seamlessly with other AWS services to provide robust failover and load balancing capabilities.

- **Elastic Load Balancer (ELB):** Distributes traffic between multiple backend servers, reducing downtime.
- **CloudFront:** Ensures failover for Content Delivery Networks (CDNs) by dynamically switching edge locations.
- **AWS Global Accelerator:** Provides multi-region failover and intelligent traffic routing.

Enhancing AWS Services Failover

1. **ELB Failover:** Traffic is distributed across multiple backend instances, and Route 53 reroutes requests if an entire region fails.
2. **CloudFront Failover:** Edge locations dynamically detect failures and serve content from alternate locations.

3. **Global Accelerator Failover:** Provides automatic regional failover for latency-sensitive applications.

Use Cases:

- High-traffic websites needing scalable failover.
- Multi-region applications using Global Accelerator.
- Media streaming and content delivery with CloudFront failover.

Automated failover mechanisms in Route 53 ensure continuous service availability by dynamically detecting failures and rerouting traffic. From primary-backup failover for disaster recovery to latency-based failover for performance optimization, each method serves a specific business need.

Integrating failover with AWS services like ELB, CloudFront, and Global Accelerator further enhances resilience, making Route 53 a powerful DNS and traffic management solution for modern cloud applications.

Case Studies

Understanding theoretical concepts is crucial, but applying them in real-world scenarios is what truly enhances learning. This section explores case studies and real-time examples demonstrating how the DNS management, routing policies, and health checks of Amazon Route 53 are used in practical situations.

By examining real-world implementations, readers can:

- Gain insights into industry best practices for DNS and traffic management.
- Understand how failover mechanisms improve service availability.
- Learn how businesses optimize performance using Route 53's routing policies.

This section covers three key areas:

- Managing Hosted Zones (Public and Private DNS Zones)
- Routing Policies in Action
- Automated Failover and Health Checks

Managing Hosted Zones for a Global E-Commerce Platform

A leading global e-commerce company faced DNS challenges in handling millions of daily visitors across multiple continents. They needed a highly scalable, secure, and globally distributed DNS infrastructure to ensure customers accessed the nearest data center.

Solution Using Route 53 Hosted Zones

1. Public Hosted Zones were created to manage domain names for different regions (particularly
2. us.shop.com, eu.shop.com).
3. Private Hosted Zones were used within AWS VPCs to securely resolve internal service communications.
4. DNS records (A, CNAME, MX, TXT, and so on) were configured to support web traffic, emails, and authentication.
5. Multi-region redundancy was implemented by associating private hosted zones with multiple AWS accounts.

Outcome

- Improved website availability and load balancing across global markets.

- Enhanced internal service communication with private DNS resolution.
- Reduced latency for users by directing them to the closest servers.

Key Takeaway: Hosted zones play a critical role in managing public and private DNS infrastructure efficiently.

Optimizing Routing Policies for a Video Streaming Service

A global video streaming company wanted to enhance user experience by ensuring low latency content delivery. They needed a smart routing strategy to reduce buffering and optimize traffic flow across different regions.

Solution Using Route 53 Routing Policies

1. Latency-Based Routing was implemented to route users to the nearest AWS CloudFront edge locations.
2. Weighted Routing was used to gradually roll out new streaming servers, ensuring a seamless transition without overloading resources.
3. Geolocation Routing helped comply with content licensing by restricting access to certain regions while offering alternate content.
4. Failover Routing ensured backup servers were available in case of regional failures.

Outcome

- 30% reduction in video buffering time and improved streaming speed.
- Automatic traffic distribution to healthy servers, minimizing downtime.
- Legal compliance by restricting and directing traffic based on geographical location.

Key Takeaway: The routing policies of Route 53 help optimize performance, balance traffic, and ensure content availability.

Real-Time Example: Using Automated Failover for a Financial Trading Platform

A real-time financial trading platform needed to maintain 99.99% uptime since downtime could result in millions of dollars in losses. They required a failover mechanism that could instantly switch to backup servers in case of system failures.

Solution Using Route 53 Failover and Health Checks

1. Primary-Backup Failover was configured with primary trading servers in the US and backup servers in Europe.
2. Route 53 Health Checks continuously monitored the latency and availability of the primary servers.
3. If a failure was detected, automated failover routing rapidly redirected, typically within seconds depending on DNS TTL settings.
4. Failover testing was conducted periodically to ensure a seamless switchover in case of real-world outages.

Outcome

- Achieved 99.99% uptime by instantly rerouting traffic to healthy servers.

- Reduced financial risks by preventing trading disruptions.
- Seamless failover experience for traders, ensuring zero downtime.

Key Takeaway: Automated failover mechanisms in Route 53 are critical for high-availability applications that cannot afford downtime.

Through these case studies and real-time examples, we see how Route 53 enables scalable, fault-tolerant, and optimized DNS and traffic management. Whether it's an e-commerce business, streaming service, or financial platform, Route 53 provides powerful solutions to enhance availability, security, and performance.

Conclusion

In this chapter, we explored Amazon Route 53, a highly scalable and reliable Domain Name System (DNS) web service designed to provide domain registration, DNS routing, and health checking capabilities. By leveraging Route 53, organizations can improve the availability, performance, and security of their applications across global AWS regions.

In the next chapter, we shall learn to deliver content globally with Amazon CloudFront. It also covers Content Delivery Networks (CDNs), caching strategies, and integration with S3 for static content.

Points to Remember

This section highlights the essential takeaways from *Chapter 7, Route 53 and DNS Traffic Management* to reinforce your understanding of Amazon Route 53, hosted zones, DNS routing policies, health checks, and failover mechanisms.

Amazon Route 53 Overview

- Amazon Route 53 is a highly available, scalable, and secure DNS web service designed to route end-user requests to AWS resources and external domains.
- It supports domain registration, DNS resolution, traffic management, and health checking, making it a crucial component for cloud-based architectures.
- Route 53 integrates seamlessly with AWS services like CloudFront, Elastic Load Balancer (ELB), and S3 to enhance application availability and performance.

Hosted Zones and DNS Records

- Hosted zones are the DNS namespaces managed within Route 53 and come in two types:
    - **Public Hosted Zones:** Used for domains accessible over the internet.
    - **Private Hosted Zones:** Used for internal DNS resolution within AWS VPCs.
- Route 53 supports various DNS record types to map domain names to AWS resources, including:
    - **A (Address) Record:** Maps a domain to an IPv4 address.
    - **AAAA Record:** Maps a domain to an IPv6 address.
    - **CNAME (Canonical Name) Record:** Redirects one domain name to another.
    - **MX (Mail Exchange) Record:** Directs email traffic.
    - **TXT (Text) Record:** Used for security and verification purposes.

DNS Routing Policies in Route 53

Route 53 provides multiple routing policies to manage traffic distribution effectively:

- **Simple Routing:** Directs traffic to a single endpoint, suitable for basic applications.
- **Weighted Routing:** Distributes traffic across multiple resources based on assigned weights, useful for load balancing and testing.
- **Latency-Based Routing:** Routes users to the closest AWS region to minimize latency and enhance performance.
- **Geolocation Routing:** Directs traffic based on the geographical location of the user, helping with localized content delivery.
- **Failover Routing:** Ensures high availability by redirecting traffic to a backup endpoint if the primary resource fails.

Health Checks and Automated Failover

Route 53 Health Checks monitor the availability and performance of applications by checking endpoints at regular intervals.

Types of Health Checks:

- **Endpoint Health Checks:** Monitor the response of a specific web server or IP.
- **Calculated Health Checks:** Aggregate multiple health checks for a combined status.
- **Latency-Based Health Checks:** Track the response time from different AWS regions.

Failover Mechanisms automatically redirect traffic to backup resources in case of failure, ensuring business continuity and minimal downtime.

Real-World Applications of Route 53

- E-commerce platforms use Route 53's failover routing to prevent service disruptions.
- Global SaaS applications implement latency-based routing to provide a seamless user experience worldwide.
- Media streaming services utilize geolocation routing to optimize content delivery based on user regions.
- Financial and banking applications rely on health checks to maintain high availability and operational stability.

Best Practices for Using Route 53

- Always configure redundant failover routing to prevent single points of failure.
- Use weighted routing to gradually shift traffic between different application versions.
- Enable DNSSEC (Domain Name System Security Extensions) for enhanced security and protection against spoofing.
- Use calculated health checks to minimize redundant checks.
- Leverage CloudWatch alarms for DNS health visibility.
- Regularly test and update health check configurations to reflect the latest infrastructure changes.
- Implement private hosted zones for secure internal DNS resolution within AWS VPCs.

Mastering Route 53 and DNS traffic management allows businesses to build resilient, scalable, and efficient cloud architectures. By leveraging intelligent routing policies, health checks, and failover mechanisms, organizations can enhance uptime, improve performance, and optimize user experiences across global AWS regions.

Chapter 8
CloudFront and Content Delivery

Introduction

In the present-day digital landscape, users expect fast and seamless access to web content, whether it is a static website, high-definition video, or dynamic application data. However, delivering content efficiently across different geographical locations presents significant challenges. Latency, bandwidth constraints, and security vulnerabilities can all degrade user experience and impact business performance.

To address these challenges, Content Delivery Networks (CDNs) play a crucial role in optimizing web performance by distributing content across multiple edge locations worldwide. Amazon CloudFront, CDN service by AWS, ensures low-latency, high-availability, and secure content delivery by caching content closer to users and dynamically optimizing content retrieval.

This chapter delves into the fundamentals of Amazon CloudFront, its integration with AWS services like Amazon S3, and essential configurations for secure content delivery. By the end of this chapter, readers will have a thorough understanding of caching strategies, HTTPS/TLS configurations, and real-world use cases like video streaming and website acceleration.

Structure

In this chapter, we will walk through:

- CloudFront Overview
- Caching Strategies
- Integration with Amazon S3
- HTTPS and TLS Configurations
- Case Studies

CloudFront Overview

In the contemporary digital world, users expect fast and seamless access to web content, whether it is a website, video, or software application. Slow-loading websites and buffering videos can lead to poor user experience, reduced engagement, and even financial losses for businesses. To address this challenge, Content Delivery Networks (CDNs) have emerged as a powerful solution, enabling efficient and high-performance content delivery across the globe.

Content Delivery Network (CDN)

Imagine an online store with one big warehouse located in one city. If customers from all over the world place orders, deliveries will take longer for people who live far away. Now imagine the same store has many small warehouses spread across different cities, each stocked with the same popular products. Orders are delivered from the nearest warehouse, making delivery much faster.

A Content Delivery Network (CDN) works in a very similar way.

Instead of serving website content—such as images, videos, or web pages—from a single central server, a CDN stores copies of this content in multiple locations around the world, closer to users. When someone opens a website, the content is delivered from the nearest location, resulting in faster load times and a smoother experience.

Amazon CloudFront is AWS's CDN service that follows this exact model, using a global network of servers (called edge locations) to deliver content quickly, securely, and reliably.

Amazon CloudFront is designed to optimize the distribution of static and dynamic content with minimal latency. By leveraging a globally distributed network of edge locations, CloudFront ensures that users receive content from the nearest data center, significantly reducing load times and improving reliability. This chapter explores how CloudFront functions, its integration with AWS services like Amazon S3, and key caching strategies to enhance performance.

Before diving into the technical capabilities of CloudFront, it is essential to understand the role of CDNs in modern web applications and how they help in latency reduction, bandwidth optimization, and security enhancement.

Understanding Content Delivery Networks (CDNs)

CDNs play a crucial role in modern internet infrastructure by distributing content across multiple locations to enhance speed, availability, and security. These networks cache content closer to end users, reducing the distance data needs to travel and optimizing web performance.

CDN and Its Working

A Content Delivery Network (CDN) is a globally distributed network of servers that work together to deliver web content efficiently. Instead of relying on a single origin server, CDNs store copies of frequently requested files in multiple locations, known as edge locations or PoPs (Points of Presence).

- **User Request:** When a user requests a webpage, video, or image, the CDN determines the nearest edge location.
- **Cache Lookup:** If the content is already cached at the edge location, it is served immediately, minimizing the load on the origin server.
- **Origin Fetch (if needed):** If the requested content is not available in the cache, the CDN fetches it from the origin server and delivers it to the user.
- **Content Caching:** The CDN stores the retrieved content for future requests, reducing the need to access the origin server repeatedly.

By decentralizing content distribution, CDNs reduce latency, improve load balancing, and enhance reliability.

Benefits of Using a CDN for Web Applications

CDNs offer multiple advantages for websites, applications, and media platforms. Some key benefits include:

- **Improved Website Performance and Load Times**
  - CDNs serve content from edge locations that are physically closer to users, reducing latency and page load times.
  - Reduced dependence on the origin server prevents slowdowns during high traffic periods.
- **Reduced Bandwidth and Infrastructure Costs**
  - By caching static content such as images, videos, and scripts, CDNs decrease the number of direct requests to the origin server.
  - This lowers bandwidth consumption, leading to significant cost savings, especially for high-traffic websites.
- **Increased Availability and Scalability**
  - CDNs distribute network traffic across multiple servers, preventing overload on any single system.
  - In the event of a server failure, content can be served from alternative edge locations, ensuring high availability.
- **Enhanced Security and DDoS Protection**
  - CDNs act as a shield between users and the origin server, reducing exposure to cyber threats.
  - Built-in DDoS protection, Web Application Firewalls (WAF), and TLS/SSL encryption help secure content delivery.

Fitting CloudFront into the AWS Ecosystem

Amazon CloudFront is AWS's managed CDN service, seamlessly integrating with other AWS products for a scalable, secure, and high-performance content delivery solution.

- **Deep Integration with AWS Services**
  - **Amazon S3:** CloudFront can be used to deliver static content stored in S3 buckets efficiently.
  - **AWS Lambda@Edge:** Enables execution of serverless functions at edge locations for dynamic content personalization.
  - **AWS Shield and AWS WAF:** Provides advanced security features to defend against attacks.
- **Flexible Caching and Performance Optimization**
  - CloudFront allows custom cache policies, TTL (Time-to-Live) settings, and real-time logs to fine-tune content delivery.
  - CloudFront also improves performance through compression. It supports gzip and Brotli compression to optimize file transfer speeds.
    - **Gzip** offers wide compatibility and efficient compression for most browsers.
    - **Brotli** provides higher compression ratios for modern browsers, resulting in smaller file sizes and faster load times.
    - CloudFront automatically selects the best option supported by the device of the user.

- **Secure and Low-Latency Content Delivery**
  - CloudFront enforces HTTPS and TLS encryption to ensure secure data transmission.
  - The global network infrastructure of AWS guarantees low latency and high availability for worldwide users.

With its cost-effective, scalable, and highly secure architecture, CloudFront is the ideal choice for businesses seeking to enhance their web performance, media streaming, and application delivery.

CDNs have revolutionized the way content is distributed online, enabling faster, secure, and highly scalable web applications. Amazon CloudFront, as part of AWS, provides a robust CDN solution that integrates seamlessly with other cloud services, allowing businesses to optimize performance while reducing infrastructure costs.

Key Features of Amazon CloudFront

Amazon CloudFront is a globally distributed Content Delivery Network (CDN) that enhances the speed, security, and efficiency of content delivery. By leveraging edge locations, advanced caching mechanisms, and seamless integration with AWS services, CloudFront ensures low-latency performance for users worldwide.

The core capabilities of CloudFront revolve around global distribution, intelligent request routing, and deep AWS integration. These features make it an ideal choice for delivering static assets, dynamic content, APIs, and live media streaming. In this section, we will explore the key functionalities that empower CloudFront to optimize content delivery and reduce server load.

Global Edge Locations and Latency Reduction

One of the primary advantages of CloudFront is its extensive network of globally distributed edge locations. These locations, often referred to as Points of Presence (PoPs), play a critical role in minimizing latency and enhancing performance.

Working of Global Edge Locations

CloudFront strategically places edge locations in major cities and network hubs worldwide. When a user requests content, the request is routed to the nearest edge location, rather than traveling all the way to the origin server. This significantly reduces response time and improves the user experience.

Latency Reduction Mechanisms

- **Proximity-Based Request Handling**
  - CloudFront automatically detects the geographic location of the user and directs the request to the closest available edge location.
  - This minimizes network travel time, ensuring faster content delivery.
- **Content Caching at Edge Locations**
  - Frequently accessed files (images, videos, stylesheets, and scripts) are cached at edge locations, reducing redundant requests to the origin server.
  - Cached content is served instantly, lowering latency and reducing bandwidth costs.
- **Real-Time Network Optimization**
  - CloudFront leverages the high-speed backbone network of AWS to dynamically route traffic through the most efficient pathways.
  - This ensures optimal network performance even under high traffic loads.

- CloudFront routes traffic over the AWS backbone (transit) network, a private, high-speed global network connecting AWS edge locations and regions.
- Unlike standard internet routing that depends on congested public paths, this backbone avoids unpredictable routes.
- This enables CloudFront to deliver low-latency, reliable performance, even during high traffic loads.

By utilizing over hundreds of edge locations globally (as of 2026), CloudFront ensures faster page loads, smoother video streaming, and reduced server congestion.

Cache Behaviors and Request Routing

The caching system of Amazon CloudFront is designed to balance performance with flexibility. CloudFront allows users to define custom caching policies and control how requests are routed to different backend origins.

Cache Behaviors in CloudFront

Cache behaviors define how CloudFront decides what to cache, how long to cache it, and when to fetch fresh content from the origin. By configuring cache behaviors, you control the balance between performance, cost efficiency, and content freshness for different types of requests. The following mechanisms—TTL settings, object versioning, and cache key customization—work together to ensure content is delivered quickly while remaining accurate and up to date.

- **Time-to-Live (TTL) Settings**
    - Determines how long content is stored at edge locations before refreshing from the origin.
    - Shorter TTL ensures up-to-date content, while longer TTL improves caching efficiency.
- **Object Versioning for Cache Invalidation**
    - Uses unique URLs (such as image-v2.png) to ensure updated files are fetched without relying on cache expiration.
- **Cache Key Customization**
    - CloudFront allows fine-tuning of cache keys based on headers, cookies, or query parameters to optimize delivery for dynamic content.

Cache key customization is especially useful for e-commerce websites, where query strings or cookies determine product variations (such as size, color, or user location), ensuring that CloudFront serves the correct cached response to each user.

Intelligent Request Routing

CloudFront employs smart request routing to direct user requests efficiently:

- **Geographic Routing**
    - Requests are sent to the nearest edge location for optimal latency.
    - If content is not cached, CloudFront retrieves it from the origin and stores it for future requests.
- **Multi-Origin Support**
    - CloudFront can route requests to different AWS services, such as Amazon S3, EC2, or an on-premises server.
    - This enables dynamic and hybrid content delivery strategies.

- **Origin Failover Mechanism**
    - In case of primary origin failure, CloudFront can automatically switch to a backup origin, ensuring high availability.

If an S3 bucket in us-east-1 fails, CloudFront can automatically switch traffic to a backup bucket in another region.

By providing granular cache control and intelligent request routing, CloudFront optimizes content delivery while minimizing redundant origin fetches.

Integration with AWS Services

One of the most powerful aspects of CloudFront is its deep integration with AWS services, enabling seamless content delivery across the AWS ecosystem.

- **Amazon S3 – Static Content Delivery**
    - CloudFront can directly serve static assets (which include, images, videos, JavaScript, CSS) from Amazon S3.
    - Enhances security by allowing private content access with signed URLs and OAI (Origin Access Identity).
- **AWS Lambda@Edge – Dynamic Content Processing**
    - CloudFront supports serverless edge computing using Lambda@Edge, allowing developers to modify requests and responses in real time.
    - Examples include image resizing, A/B testing, and security authentication at the edge.
- **AWS Shield and AWS WAF – Security Protection**
    - CloudFront integrates with AWS Shield (DDoS protection) and AWS WAF (Web Application Firewall) to mitigate cyber threats.
    - Protects against malicious bot attacks, SQL injections, and unauthorized access.
- **Amazon Route 53 – Domain Name System (DNS) Integration**
    - CloudFront integrates with Route 53 for low-latency DNS resolution, ensuring that requests are directed to the best-performing edge location.

  Amazon CloudWatch – Performance Monitoring
    - CloudFront logs can be analyzed using CloudWatch, enabling real-time performance monitoring and troubleshooting.

By leveraging AWS-native integrations, CloudFront provides a scalable, secure, and highly optimized content delivery solution for businesses of all sizes. The key features of Amazon CloudFront revolve around global distribution, caching intelligence, and AWS integration, making it a robust and high-performance CDN. By leveraging edge locations, CloudFront accelerates content delivery, reduces latency, and ensures scalability.

With custom cache settings, request routing optimizations, and security integrations, CloudFront provides a cost-effective and reliable solution for modern content distribution needs.

CloudFront Request Flow and Performance Optimization

Amazon CloudFront is designed to optimize content delivery by leveraging a distributed network of edge locations and intelligent caching mechanisms. Understanding how CloudFront processes requests is crucial for maximizing its performance benefits, minimizing latency, and ensuring efficient content delivery.

In this section, we will explore the request flow within CloudFront, the difference between cache hits and cache misses, and the role of signed URLs and signed cookies in securing content. These concepts are essential for fine-tuning performance and ensuring controlled access to sensitive resources.

CloudFront Request Flow

When user requests content through CloudFront, the request follows a structured path designed to enhance performance, security, and scalability.

- **User Request Initiation**
    - A user accesses a website, application, or API through a CloudFront-distributed domain (like https://d123xyz.cloudfront.net/image.jpg).
    - The request is automatically routed to the nearest edge location based on the user's geographic location.
- **Edge Location Processing**
    - CloudFront checks whether the requested content is already cached at the edge location.
    - If the content is available (cache hit), it is served instantly to the user.
    - If the content is not cached (cache miss), CloudFront forwards the request to the origin server (such as Amazon S3, EC2, or an on-premises server).
- **Origin Server Interaction**
    - If the edge location does not have the requested content, it retrieves it from the designated origin server.
    - The origin processes the request and sends the content back to the CloudFront edge location.
- **Content Caching at Edge Locations**
    - The retrieved content is cached at the edge location based on predefined caching policies and Time-to-Live (TTL) settings.
    - Future requests for the same content will be served directly from the edge location, reducing load on the origin server.
- **Response Delivery to User**
    - CloudFront returns the content to the end user with optimized performance, reduced latency, and security measures applied (such as HTTPS encryption and access control).

This request flow ensures fast, secure, and scalable content delivery, improving user experience and offloading infrastructure resources.

Cache Hit versus Cache Miss and Performance Impact

Caching is at the heart of the performance optimization strategy at CloudFront. Cache hits and cache misses determine how efficiently content is delivered and how often requests reach the origin server.

Cache Hit

A cache hit occurs when the requested content is already stored at the CloudFront edge location, allowing it to be served immediately without contacting the origin server.

Benefits of Cache Hits:

- **Reduced Latency:** Content is delivered from the nearest edge location instead of traveling to the origin.
- **Lower Server Load:** Fewer requests reach the origin, improving scalability and reducing infrastructure costs.
- **Faster Response Times:** Cached content is served almost instantly to users.

Cache Miss

A cache miss occurs when the requested content is not stored at the CloudFront edge location. In this case, CloudFront must fetch the content from the origin, increasing response time.

Performance Impact of Cache Misses:

Increased Latency: Requests take longer as they must travel to the origin and back.

For example, a cache hit may serve content in ~20–30 ms from a nearby edge location, whereas a cache miss can increase latency to 150–300 ms or more, depending on the user's distance from the origin.

Higher Server Load: More requests reach the origin, increasing processing overhead.

Potential Bottlenecks: If too many requests bypass the cache, the origin server may struggle with high traffic.

Optimizing Cache Hit Ratios

To maximize cache hits and reduce unnecessary origin requests, implement the following strategies:

- **Set Appropriate TTL (Time-to-Live) Values.**
  - Configure longer TTLs for static content (such as images, CSS, and JavaScript) to improve performance.
  - Use shorter TTLs for dynamic or frequently updated content to maintain freshness.
  - **Common pitfall:** Overly aggressive TTLs can cause stale content to be served, so TTL values should balance performance with update frequency.
- **Use Object Versioning.**
  - Append version numbers or timestamps to URLs (for instance style-v2.css) to ensure users receive updated content while keeping older versions cached.
- **Enable Origin Shield.**
  - The Origin Shield of CloudFront adds a centralized regional cache layer between edge locations and the origin, ensuring that cache misses are consolidated and fewer direct requests reach the origin.

By improving cache hit ratios, CloudFront reduces latency, enhances scalability, and delivers a smoother user experience.

Using Signed URLs and Signed Cookies for Secure Access

CloudFront provides robust security mechanisms to restrict access to private content. Using signed URLs and signed cookies, you can ensure that only authorized users can access specific resources.

Signed URLs

A signed URL is a pre-authenticated URL that grants temporary access to specific content. It includes custom policies, expiration times, and user-specific access controls.

Working:

1. The application generates a signed URL with embedded authentication parameters.
2. The user accesses the signed URL, and CloudFront verifies its validity.
3. If the URL is valid, the content is delivered; otherwise, access is denied.

Use Cases for Signed URLs

- **Paywall-Protected Content:** Secure premium videos, courses, or digital downloads.
- **Time-Limited Access:** Ensure temporary access to resources without exposing public URLs.
- **Per-User Authorization:** Restrict access based on user identity or role.

Signed Cookies

Unlike signed URLs, signed cookies provide secure access to multiple restricted resources without modifying individual URLs. They are ideal for users who need to access an entire section of content without signing each URL separately.

Working:

1. The application generates a signed cookie containing authentication details.
2. The cookie is sent to the user's browser and automatically included in subsequent requests.
3. CloudFront verifies the cookie before granting access to restricted resources.

Use Cases for Signed Cookies

- **Subscription-Based Content:** Allow logged-in users to access a library of videos or documents.
- **Multi-File Access:** Ideal when users need access to multiple files without modifying URLs.

Feature	Signed URLs	Signed Cookies
Best for	Individual file access	Access to multiple files
URL Modification	Required	Not required
Session-Based Access	No	Yes
Use Case	Expiring downloads, single-use links	Membership portals, streaming services

***Table 8.1:** Choosing between Signed URLs and Signed Cookies*

By implementing signed URLs and signed cookies, CloudFront enables fine-grained access control while ensuring content security.

Understanding the CloudFront request flow and performance optimization techniques is essential for building a scalable and efficient content delivery strategy. CloudFront processes user requests through a network of edge locations, caching content to reduce latency.

Cache hits improve performance, while cache misses can impact response times and increase origin load. Security measures such as signed URLs and signed cookies help protect sensitive content and enforce user-based access restrictions.

By leveraging these features, organizations can enhance website speed, reliability, and security, delivering seamless experiences to global users.

While signed URLs and signed cookies protect private content, caching strategies ensure that both secure and public content are delivered efficiently.

Caching Strategies

Efficient content delivery relies heavily on caching mechanisms that store and serve frequently requested data from edge locations rather than repeatedly fetching it from the origin server. Amazon CloudFront uses advanced caching strategies to reduce latency, improve load times, and optimize resource utilization.

This section explores key caching concepts, including cache behaviors, TTL (Time-to-Live) settings, cache invalidation, and versioning techniques. By fine-tuning these configurations, organizations can enhance website performance, lower infrastructure costs, and deliver a seamless user experience.

Cache Behavior and Optimization

The caching system of CloudFront determines how, when, and for how long content is stored at edge locations. By understanding cache behaviors and applying optimization techniques, businesses can significantly improve performance and reduce the need for frequent origin requests.

This subsection covers the fundamentals of Cache-Control headers, TTL configurations, and cache invalidation methods that help fine-tune content delivery based on application requirements.

Understanding Cache-Control Headers and Time-to-Live (TTL)

Caching policies in CloudFront are controlled using HTTP headers, specifically Cache-Control and Expires headers, which define how long content remains cached at the edge locations before it needs to be refreshed from the origin server.

Cache-Control Headers Explained:

- Cache-Control: `max-age=<seconds>`
  - Defines the duration (in seconds) that content should be cached.
  - Example: Cache-Control: max-age=3600 caches the content for one hour.
- Cache-Control: no-cache
  - Forces the client or intermediary caches to validate content with the origin before serving it.
- Cache-Control: no-store
  - Prevents caching altogether, ensuring content is always fetched from the origin.

Time-to-Live (TTL) in CloudFront

TTL defines how long CloudFront caches objects at edge locations before revalidating them with the origin. It consists of three configurable settings:

- **Minimum TTL:** The shortest duration an object remains cached.
- **Maximum TTL:** The longest duration an object remains cached before it must be refreshed.
- **Default TTL:** The standard cache duration when no explicit Cache-Control headers are set.

By fine-tuning these TTL settings, organizations can balance content freshness with performance efficiency.

Configuring Cache Policies for Static and Dynamic Content

Not all content types require the same caching strategy. Static content, such as images, CSS, and JavaScript files, can be cached for longer durations, while dynamic content (e.g., user-generated content, personalized pages) requires frequent updates.

Best Practices for Caching Static Content

- Set a high TTL (days or weeks) for static assets that rarely change.
- Use object versioning (for example, style-v2.css) to manage updates without overriding cache settings.
- Enable compression (Gzip/Brotli) to reduce file size and load times.

Optimizing Dynamic Content Caching

- Use short TTL values (seconds or minutes) to ensure fresh content delivery.
- Leverage Lambda@Edge to personalize and manipulate cached responses dynamically.
- Configure Origin Shield to reduce load on the backend when dynamic requests bypass caching.

Effective cache policies ensure optimal performance while maintaining up-to-date content delivery.

Handling Cache Invalidation and Versioning

Caching is powerful, but it also introduces challenges in content updates. When new versions of assets are deployed, cached copies must be updated or invalidated to prevent serving outdated content.

Cache Invalidation Methods:

Manual Invalidation:

- CloudFront allows users to manually invalidate specific cached objects.
- Example: Running an invalidation request for index.html to update homepage content.

Wildcard Invalidation:

- Invalidate multiple objects using wildcards (like /* to clear all cached files).

Automatic Invalidation via CI/CD Pipelines:

- Integrate cache invalidation with deployment pipelines for seamless updates.

Using Object Versioning to Avoid Invalidation Costs

Instead of frequent cache invalidations, object versioning is a cost-effective alternative:

- Append version numbers to file names (such as logo-v2.png instead of logo.png).
- Use query string parameters (similar to script.js?v=2.0) to force browsers to fetch the latest version.

By combining cache invalidation and versioning strategies, organizations can efficiently manage content updates while reducing unnecessary invalidation costs.

Trade-offs: Invalidation vs. Object Versioning

- **Wildcard Invalidation (/*):** Simple to use and immediately clears cached content, but it can be expensive at scale and may cause a temporary spike in origin load.
- **Object Versioning:** Avoids invalidation costs and preserves cache efficiency, but requires code, configuration, or deployment updates to reference new object versions.

In practice, many organizations use object versioning for routine updates and reserve invalidation for urgent fixes or rare exceptions.

Optimizing caching strategies in CloudFront is crucial for delivering high-performance web applications. By configuring cache behaviors, fine-tuning TTL settings, and implementing intelligent invalidation methods, businesses can achieve faster load times, reduced origin traffic, and lower operational costs.

Performance Tuning for CloudFront Caching

Optimizing CloudFront caching is not just about setting TTL values and cache policies. Performance tuning extends beyond cache policies - it includes compression, error handling, and monitoring for resilience and speed. Effective performance tuning ensures that content loads faster, error responses are handled gracefully, and administrators can proactively monitor caching behavior for continuous improvement.

This section covers essential performance optimization techniques, including Gzip and Brotli compression, custom error responses, failover strategies, and real-time logging. By implementing these strategies, organizations can enhance page load speeds, improve fault tolerance, and monitor key metrics for optimized content delivery.

Compression Techniques: Gzip and Brotli

Compression plays a crucial role in reducing file size and improving content delivery speeds. By using modern compression techniques, CloudFront can transmit files more efficiently, reducing bandwidth consumption and improving user experience.

Brotli is not supported by Internet Explorer, and some CDNs selectively serve Brotli only over HTTPS.

Enhancing Performance using Compression

When a user requests a file, CloudFront can compress the response before sending it. This reduces the amount of data transmitted over the network, leading to faster page load times and reduced latency. Compression is particularly beneficial for:

- HTML, CSS, and JavaScript files
- JSON and XML data
- Text-based assets

Gzip vs. Brotli Compression

CloudFront supports two widely used compression algorithms:

- **Gzip Compression**
    - A well-established compression standard supported by all modern browsers.
    - Best suited for compressing text-based files, such as HTML, CSS, and JavaScript.
    - Reduces file sizes by 60-80%, significantly improving performance.
    - Example: A 200 KB HTML file can be compressed to around 50 KB.
- **Brotli Compression**
    - A newer compression algorithm developed by Google, offering better compression ratios than Gzip.
    - Particularly effective for smaller files, reducing them by up to 30% more than Gzip.
    - Supported by most modern browsers but not as universally compatible as Gzip.

Configuring Compression in CloudFront

To enable compression in CloudFront:

1. Navigate to CloudFront Distribution Settings.
2. Enable the **`"Compress Objects Automatically"`** option.
3. CloudFront will then serve compressed files when the requesting browser supports it.

By using both Gzip and Brotli, organizations can ensure faster data transfer, improved page load speeds, and an overall enhanced user experience.

Custom Error Responses and Failover Strategies

Even with optimized caching and delivery mechanisms, errors can still occur due to server issues, network failures, or invalid requests. Handling these errors efficiently prevents poor user experience and ensures high availability.

Custom Error Responses in CloudFront

By default, CloudFront returns standard HTTP error codes (for instance 404, 503) when an issue arises. However, organizations can customize these error responses to provide meaningful feedback to users.

Key Benefits of Custom Error Responses:

- **Improved User Experience:** Display branded error pages instead of generic messages.
- **Reduced Latency:** Serve cached error pages instead of requesting them from the origin.
- **SEO Optimization:** Prevent search engines from penalizing websites due to excessive error responses. Search engines handle custom 404 pages better when coded properly.

Configuring Custom Error Responses in CloudFront:

1. Navigate to Error Pages in the CloudFront distribution settings.
2. Define custom responses for specific HTTP error codes (such as 404, 500, or 503).
3. Set a TTL value for how long CloudFront should cache the error response.

Failover Strategies in CloudFront

Failover ensures that users continue to receive content even when the primary origin is unavailable.

Methods to Implement Failover:

- **Using a Secondary Origin**
  - CloudFront can be configured with multiple origins (including primary and backup servers).
  - If the primary origin fails, CloudFront automatically switches to the backup.
- **Origin Shield for Load Balancing (Performance/ Load Protection)**
  - AWS Origin Shield acts as an additional caching layer between CloudFront and the origin.
  - It reduces traffic to the origin, preventing failures due to high request loads.
- **Using Route 53 for DNS Failover**
  - Amazon Route 53 health checks can detect origin failures.
  - Requests are redirected to an alternate origin when failures occur.

By implementing custom error responses and failover mechanisms, organizations can improve resilience, maintain high availability, and minimize disruptions in content delivery.

Using CloudFront Real-Time Logs for Performance Monitoring

Monitoring the performance of CloudFront in real-time is crucial for troubleshooting issues, optimizing cache behavior, and ensuring seamless content delivery. CloudFront provides detailed real-time logs that help administrators analyze traffic patterns, cache efficiency, and request processing times.

CloudWatch Metrics versus Real-Time Logs Distinction:

- CloudWatch = aggregated/periodic,
- Real-Time Logs = granular, per-request.

Key Benefits of Real-Time Logging:

- **Immediate Insights:** Detect performance issues as they occur.
- **Cache Hit/Miss Analysis:** Understand how frequently CloudFront serves content from the cache versus the origin.
- **Security Monitoring:** Identify and mitigate potential threats, such as unusual request patterns or DDoS attacks.

Setting up CloudFront Real-Time Logs:

1. **Enable Real-Time Logging in CloudFront**
    a. Navigate to CloudFront distribution settings.
    b. Select Real-Time Logs under the monitoring section.
2. **Configure Log Destination**
    a. CloudFront supports Amazon Kinesis Data Streams, which can be used to process logs in real-time.
    b. Logs can be analyzed using AWS Lambda, Amazon S3, or Amazon CloudWatch.
3. **Analyze Log Data for Performance Insights**
    a. Monitor latency metrics to identify slow response times.
    b. Evaluate error rates to detect backend failures.
    c. Track cache hit ratios to optimize caching strategies.

By leveraging CloudFront real-time logs, organizations can proactively monitor, troubleshoot, and optimize content delivery to provide a seamless user experience.

Performance tuning in CloudFront is essential for delivering fast, reliable, and optimized content to users worldwide. By implementing compression techniques (Gzip and Brotli), customizing error responses, configuring failover mechanisms, and utilizing real-time logs, businesses can achieve lower latency, reduced bandwidth consumption, and enhanced fault tolerance.

Cost Optimization Strategies for CloudFront Caching

Optimization of costs while delivering content efficiently is one of the key priorities for businesses that use Amazon CloudFront. Although CloudFront significantly reduces latency and enhances user experience, ineffective caching strategies and frequent origin requests can lead to higher data transfer costs.

By implementing smart cost optimization strategies, organizations can minimize expenses without compromising performance. This section explores key techniques such as leveraging Regional Edge Caches, using Lambda@Edge for intelligent caching, and managing origin requests efficiently to lower costs while maintaining high-speed content delivery.

Reducing Data Transfer Costs with Regional Edge Caches

Amazon CloudFront uses Regional Edge Caches (RECs) as an intermediate caching layer between the primary CloudFront edge locations and the origin server. These caches serve as additional layers that store frequently requested content closer to end-users, reducing the number of direct origin fetches.

To be more clear,

- RECs = automatically part of CloudFront.
- Origin Shield = optional centralized layer you enable for further cost reduction.

Regional Edge Caches Reduce Costs

Let us look into how the regional edge caches reduce the costs.

- **Minimizes Origin Requests:** Requests that would otherwise reach the origin are served from Regional Edge Caches, reducing the load on the origin server.
- **Decreases Data Transfer Fees:** AWS charges for data transfer between CloudFront and the origin. Since Regional Edge Caches reduce these fetches, they help lower overall data transfer **costs.**
- **Enhances Cache Efficiency:** Content that expires quickly in edge locations can still be available in Regional Edge Caches, preventing unnecessary origin retrievals.

Configuring Regional Edge Caches for Cost Savings

1. Enable origin shield in CloudFront settings to use Regional Edge Caches efficiently.
2. Increase cache TTL (Time-to-Live) values to maximize cached content availability.
3. Monitor cache hit ratios to determine if content is being effectively served from caches instead of the origin.

By leveraging Regional Edge Caches, businesses can reduce expenses while improving performance by ensuring that cached content is retained longer before requiring a request to the origin.

Using Lambda@Edge for Intelligent Caching Decisions

AWS Lambda@Edge is a serverless compute service that allows organizations to execute custom logic at CloudFront edge locations. It enables dynamic decision-making, helping optimize caching strategies based on real-time user requests.

Lambda@Edge Helps Reduce Costs

- **Modifies HTTP Headers for Better Caching**
  - Lambda@Edge can alter cache-control headers dynamically based on user location, device type, or request patterns, ensuring that frequently accessed content remains cached longer.
- **Implements Content Personalization Without Fetching from the Origin**
  - Instead of fetching personalized content from the origin for every request, Lambda@Edge can serve different cached versions of content based on user attributes.

- **Reduces Unnecessary Origin Requests**
  - It enables conditional requests, meaning content is fetched from the origin only when necessary, saving bandwidth costs.

Use Cases for Cost Optimization

- **Cache Optimization:** Adjust TTL values dynamically to extend cache lifespan for different users.
- **Intelligent Redirections:** Redirect users to cached content based on geolocation or device type.
- **Security Enhancements:** Block unauthorized requests before they reach the origin, reducing load and costs.

By implementing Lambda@Edge, organizations can reduce origin fetches, optimize caching policies, and deliver personalized experiences while keeping expenses under control.

Managing Origin Requests to Minimize Costs

Every request sent from CloudFront to the origin incurs data transfer and compute costs. Inefficient cache policies, frequent content invalidation, and unnecessary dynamic requests can drastically increase AWS costs.

Best Practices for Reducing Origin Requests

- **Optimize Cache Key Settings.**
  - CloudFront caches content based on the cache key, which may include elements such as query strings, headers, and cookies.
  - Reducing unnecessary cache variations ensures that content is efficiently reused instead of fetching from the origin.
- **Use Origin Shield for Request Consolidation.**
  - Origin Shield acts as a centralized caching layer, ensuring that multiple edge locations do not send redundant requests to the origin.
  - This consolidation significantly reduces the number of requests reaching the origin, cutting down data transfer fees.
- **Implement Stale-While-Revalidate Strategy.**
  - Instead of invalidating cache frequently, CloudFront can serve stale content while asynchronously revalidating it in the background.
  - This approach ensures faster load times while reducing the frequency of origin requests.
  - For critical real-time data, stale responses may cause consistency issues if TTLs are too long
- **Set Up API Caching for Dynamic Content.**
  - CloudFront can cache responses from API endpoints, reducing the number of requests made to backend servers.
  - API caching is especially useful for high-traffic applications where data doesn't change frequently.

By managing origin requests strategically, businesses can significantly lower operational costs while ensuring users receive a seamless experience with minimal latency.

Cost optimization is a critical aspect of using Amazon CloudFront effectively. By implementing strategies such as leveraging Regional Edge Caches, utilizing Lambda@Edge for dynamic caching decisions, and minimizing origin requests, businesses can reduce AWS expenses while maintaining high-performance content delivery.

Organizations must continuously monitor cache efficiency, request patterns, and data transfer costs to ensure they are making the most of the caching capabilities of CloudFront. By fine-tuning these cost-saving techniques, companies can strike the right balance between performance and affordability.

Integration with Amazon S3

Amazon CloudFront seamlessly integrates with Amazon S3 (Simple Storage Service) to deliver static and dynamic content globally with high availability, security, and performance. By using CloudFront as a Content Delivery Network (CDN) in front of an S3 bucket, businesses can reduce latency, offload traffic from origins, and enhance security through access controls and encryption.

This chapter explores how to configure CloudFront with an S3 origin, ensuring efficient caching, cost optimization, and secure content delivery. It also covers strategies to enhance performance by tuning cache policies and access settings to optimize the content delivery experience.

Setting Up CloudFront with an S3 Origin

To leverage CloudFront with S3, an S3 bucket must first be configured as the origin. CloudFront then serves cached content from global edge locations, ensuring that users receive data with minimal latency. This section details the step-by-step process of creating an S3 bucket, configuring CloudFront to serve static content, and optimizing caching strategies.

Creating an S3 Bucket for CloudFront Distribution

Setting up an S3 Bucket:

1. Sign in to AWS Console → Navigate to Amazon S3.
2. Create a New Bucket.
    a. Choose a unique bucket name.
    b. Select a region closest to your primary users.
3. Configure Permissions.
    a. Block public access (CloudFront will handle secure distribution).
    b. Enable S3 bucket policies for controlled access.
4. Enable Versioning and Logging *(optional but recommended)*.
    a. Versioning allows rollback in case of unintended changes.
    b. Logging provides insights into requests made to the bucket.

The following are the pros of using S3 with CloudFront:

- **Scalability:** Handles unlimited storage for static content.
- **Security:** Supports encryption, IAM policies, and signed URLs.
- **Reliability:** Redundant storage ensures data durability.

By setting up an S3 bucket correctly, CloudFront can serve content efficiently while maintaining security and scalability.

Configuring CloudFront to Deliver Static Content from S3

Once the S3 bucket is ready, the next step is to configure CloudFront as a CDN for content distribution.

Steps to Create a CloudFront Distribution for S3 Content

1. Go to the `AWS CloudFront Console` → Click `Create Distribution`.
2. Set the Origin.
    a. Choose S3 bucket as the origin type.
    b. Select the S3 bucket name.
    c. Enable Origin Access Control (OAC) to restrict direct S3 access.
3. Configure Default Cache Behavior.
    a. Choose GET, HEAD requests (for static content like images, videos, and HTML files).
    b. Enable gzip or Brotli compression for better performance.
    c. Set cache policies (covered in 3.1.3).
4. Enable HTTPS for Secure Delivery.
    a. Choose TLS certificates for secure connections.
5. Deploy and Test.
    a. Create the distribution and wait for deployment (~10–15 minutes).
    b. Use the CloudFront domain URL to access content.

Benefits of CloudFront for Static Content

- **Reduces Latency:** Caches files at global edge locations for faster delivery.
- **Minimizes Origin Load:** Serves requests without fetching from S3 frequently.
- **Ensures Security:** Prevents direct access to S3, reducing attack risks.

By properly configuring CloudFront for S3, organizations can achieve low-latency, secure content delivery while offloading S3 traffic.

Optimizing Performance with Cache Policies

CloudFront caching is the key to reducing costs and improving speed. Configuring cache policies ensures that frequently accessed content stays at edge locations for faster delivery.

Key Cache Policy Settings

- **TTL (Time-to-Live) Configuration**
    - **Short TTL (1–5 minutes):** For **dynamic** or frequently changing content.
    - **Long TTL (24 hours+):** For **static** content like images, videos, and stylesheets.
- **Cache Key Customization**
    - Define which parts of the request (headers, query strings, cookies) determine unique cache entries.
    - Avoid unnecessary variations to maximize cache reuse.
- **Origin Shield (For Reducing Origin Requests)**
    - Helps reduce S3 origin traffic by serving from an intermediate caching layer.
    - Enhances performance during high-traffic events.

- **Compression Settings**
  - Enable Gzip and Brotli to serve smaller, optimized content.

Improving Performance with Optimized Caching

- **Speeds Up Content Delivery:** Users receive cached content instantly.
- **Reduces AWS Costs:** Minimizes origin fetches, lowering data transfer fees.
- **Handles High Traffic Efficiently:** Edge locations take the load off the origin.

Integrating Amazon CloudFront with S3 allows businesses to deliver static content with high performance, low latency, and strong security. By:

- Creating a well-configured S3 bucket for content storage.
- Setting up CloudFront distribution with the right security and caching policies.
- Optimizing cache behaviors to reduce costs and improve speed.

Organizations can effectively scale content delivery while ensuring security, cost efficiency, and performance optimization.

Securing S3 Content with CloudFront

Security is a critical aspect of content delivery, especially when distributing sensitive or restricted content. By default, Amazon S3 allows direct access to stored objects, which can expose content to unauthorized users. To mitigate this risk, CloudFront provides multiple security features to control access to S3 content while ensuring efficient distribution.

This section explores various security mechanisms, including Origin Access Control (OAC) to prevent direct access to S3, access control policies, and signed URLs and cookies for granting temporary access to specific users. These techniques ensure only authorized users can retrieve content while maintaining high performance and scalability.

Using Origin Access Control (OAC) to Restrict Direct S3 Access

By default, Amazon S3 objects can be accessed through public URLs, which may unintentionally expose sensitive content. Origin Access Control (OAC) is the recommended and current method for securely connecting Amazon CloudFront to S3. It ensures that only CloudFront distributions can access S3 objects, preventing direct public access.

Working of OAC:

1. **CloudFront Uses Signed Requests:** CloudFront signs requests to S3 using AWS Signature Version 4.
2. **S3 Verifies the Request:** The S3 bucket policy allows access only from the authorized CloudFront distribution.
3. **Direct S3 Access Is Blocked:** Public access to the bucket is disabled, ensuring all traffic flows through CloudFront.

Steps to Enable OAC in CloudFront:

1. Navigate to the AWS CloudFront Console and select the distribution.
2. Edit `Origin Settings` and choose `Amazon S3` as the origin.
3. Enable Origin Access Control (OAC) and create or select an OAC.

4. Update the S3 bucket policy to allow access from the CloudFront distribution.
5. Block public access to the S3 bucket.
6. Deploy changes and verify that direct S3 URLs are inaccessible.

Benefits of OAC:

- Stronger security using SigV4-signed requests.
- No need for legacy virtual users or ACL-based access.
- Recommended by AWS for new and existing distributions.
- Improves security without changing application logic.

Use OAC as the default and future-proof approach for securing S3 origins with CloudFront. OAI should only be used for maintaining existing legacy setups, not for new designs.

Note on Origin Access Identity (OAI): *Origin Access Identity (OAI) is a legacy mechanism that uses a virtual CloudFront user to access S3. While it is still supported for older distributions, AWS recommends Origin Access Control (OAC) for all new implementations due to its improved security model and tighter AWS integration.*

Preventing Unauthorized Access to S3 Content

Restricting direct access is only one part of securing content. Additional security measures ensure only authenticated users can access specific objects.

Key Security Measures for S3 and CloudFront:

- **Restricting Bucket Access with IAM Policies**
    - Define IAM roles and permissions to control who can access content.
    - Use least privilege principles to limit unnecessary permissions.
- **Blocking Public Access to S3 Objects**
    - Enable S3 Block Public Access settings to prevent unauthorized public access.
    - Regularly audit permissions to ensure no misconfigurations.
- **Encrypting S3 Objects for Enhanced Security**
    - Use Server-Side Encryption (SSE) for automatic encryption at rest.
    - Enable AWS Key Management Service (KMS) for advanced encryption control.
- **Enforcing HTTPS for Secure Transfers**
    - CloudFront supports HTTPS enforcement for encrypting data in transit.
    - Redirect all HTTP requests to HTTPS to prevent data interception.

By combining these techniques, organizations can prevent data leaks, unauthorized access, and security vulnerabilities while distributing content securely.

Implementing Signed URLs and Cookies for Access Control

Sometimes, businesses need to serve private content to specific users for a limited time or under specific conditions. CloudFront enables this by using signed URLs and signed cookies to grant temporary access.

Signed URLs and Signed Cookies:

- **Signed URLs:** Provide temporary access to a specific **single file**.
- **Signed Cookies:** Grant access to **multiple restricted files** for a session.

Steps to Configure Signed URLs:

1. **Create a CloudFront Key Pair.**
   a. Go to the AWS Management Console → Create an `RSA key pair`.
2. **Associate the Public Key with CloudFront.**
   a. Add the public key to CloudFront Trusted Key Groups.
3. **Generate a Signed URL Using a Private Key.**
   a. The application uses the private key to sign requests.
4. **Users Access Content via the Signed URL.**
   a. The URL expires after a predefined time.

Steps to Configure Signed Cookies:

1. Enable Signed Cookies in CloudFront Settings.
2. Generate Signed Cookies in the Application Backend.
3. Users Receive Authentication Tokens and access multiple restricted objects.

Advantages of Using Signed URLs and Cookies:

- **Granular Access Control:** Restrict access based on time, location, or IP.
- **Enhanced Security:** Prevent unauthorized sharing of links.
- **Efficient for Large-Scale Applications:** Allows flexible authentication across multiple files.

Real-world use cases include:

- Pay-per-view or subscription video streaming, where access is granted only for a limited viewing window.
- Secure software downloads, ensuring installers or updates are accessible only to licensed users.
- Time-limited business reports or invoices, allowing temporary access to sensitive documents.
- Online learning platforms, where course materials are unlocked only for enrolled students.

By implementing signed URLs and cookies, organizations can enforce temporary, conditional access to sensitive content while leveraging the caching and distribution capabilities of CloudFront.

Security is an essential part of delivering content via CloudFront and S3. By using Origin Access Control (OAC), organizations can prevent unauthorized direct access to S3 objects while ensuring CloudFront manages content retrieval. IAM policies, HTTPS enforcement, and encryption provide additional layers of protection.

Note: *CloudFront Key Pairs (root account) are deprecated; AWS now recommends Trusted Key Groups with KMS-backed keys.*

For applications that require restricted content access, signed URLs and signed cookies enable precise control over who can access content and for how long. These security mechanisms help businesses achieve both performance and security in content delivery, ensuring that only authorized users can retrieve critical data.

Versioning and Content Expiry in S3 with CloudFront

Managing content updates efficiently is critical in Content Delivery Networks (CDNs) to ensure users receive the latest content without compromising performance. CloudFront caches objects for improved latency and load reduction, but this introduces a challenge—how to update or expire content properly when changes occur in the S3 origin.

To address this, Amazon S3 offers versioning, lifecycle policies, and cache invalidation techniques that work in conjunction with CloudFront. These strategies help manage content freshness, automatic expiry, and efficient updates while optimizing costs.

This section explores S3 versioning, automated content expiry, and cache invalidation, ensuring content is always up to date while maintaining high performance and minimal latency.

Using S3 Versioning for Better Cache Management

Amazon S3 versioning is a feature that allows multiple versions of an object to be stored in a bucket. Instead of overwriting existing files, S3 retains previous versions, making it possible to retrieve older copies when needed.

When CloudFront caches an object, it serves the same version until the cache expires or is invalidated. S3 versioning enables better cache control by:

- Appending version IDs to object URLs (such as image.jpg?v=2).
- Ensuring older versions remain accessible if needed.
- Reducing cache conflicts when updating files—CloudFront treats each version as a unique file.

Steps to Enable Versioning in S3

1. Go to the **`Amazon S3 console`** → Select the S3 bucket.
2. Navigate to **`Properties`** → Find **`Bucket Versioning`**.
3. Enable versioning at bucket level.
4. Once active, all objects can maintain historical versions.

Best Practices for Using Versioning with CloudFront

- Append version identifiers to URLs (logo.png?v=3) to prevent stale content.
- Automate version changes via CI/CD pipelines for smooth deployments.
- Set lifecycle rules to delete old versions and optimize storage costs.

By leveraging S3 versioning, organizations can ensure seamless content updates, reduce cache invalidation needs, and enhance overall content management efficiency.

Automating Content Expiry with Lifecycle Policies

Not all content needs to be stored indefinitely. Stale or outdated files can consume storage and affect cache efficiency. Amazon S3 lifecycle policies automate the deletion or archival of objects, ensuring storage is optimized and costs remain under control.

Common S3 Lifecycle Policy Use Cases

- **Access logs:** Automatically delete after ~30 days to reduce storage costs for short-lived operational data.
- **Marketing images:** Transition to S3 Glacier after ~90 days once campaigns end and access becomes rare.

- **Application backups:** Move to Glacier after ~30 days for long-term, low-cost retention.
- **Temporary reports:** Delete after 7–14 days to automatically clean up short-lived business documents.
- **Unused or draft media uploads:** Remove after ~30 days to eliminate abandoned or unused files.

Key Benefits of Lifecycle Policies

- Automatically remove outdated files from S3 to prevent unnecessary cache buildup.
- Reduce storage costs by transitioning older content to Amazon S3 Glacier.
- Ensure fresh content delivery by defining expiry rules for temporary objects.

Configuring Lifecycle Policies in S3

1. Open the Amazon S3 console → Select a bucket.
2. Go to `Management` → Click `Create Lifecycle Rule`.
3. Set Expiry Conditions
    a. Delete files after X days (such as, expire logs after 30 days).
    b. Move older versions to cheaper storage tiers.
4. Enable the policy → CloudFront automatically removes expired content.

Lifecycle expiry in S3 does not auto-purge CloudFront cache. Instead, CloudFront will return 404 once the origin is deleted.

Best Practices for Lifecycle Policies

- Set shorter retention periods for temporary or frequently updated content.
- Use object tagging to categorize files and apply policies selectively.
- Combine lifecycle policies with CloudFront caching rules to optimize storage and CDN efficiency.

By implementing automated expiry policies, businesses can enhance storage efficiency, ensure content freshness, and control costs seamlessly.

Handling Content Updates Efficiently with Cache Invalidation

CloudFront caches objects at edge locations to reduce latency. However, when content change; outdated versions may persist in the cache. Cache invalidation ensures users receive the latest content without waiting for TTL expiration.

Methods to Update Cached Content

- **Versioning (Recommended):**
    - Appends version numbers to URLs (like style.css?v=2).
    - Best used for static assets such as CSS, JS, and images.
- **Cache Invalidation:**
    - Manually removes cached content from CloudFront edge locations.
    - Best for immediate updates, such as critical fixes.

- **Shorter TTL Settings:**
    - Reduces the cache expiration time to refresh content faster.
    - Ideal for frequently updated content that changes often.

Performing Cache Invalidation in CloudFront

1. Go to AWS CloudFront Console → Select the distribution.
2. Navigate to the `Invalidations` tab → Click `Create Invalidation`.
3. Enter Object Paths.
    a. Use exact paths (`/images/logo.png`).
    b. Use wildcards (`/images/*`) to remove multiple files.
4. Submit Invalidation Request → Changes propagate across CloudFront edge locations.

Best Practices for Efficient Cache Invalidation

- Use versioning instead of frequent invalidations to reduce costs.
- Group invalidations efficiently (avoid unnecessary wildcard requests).
- Monitor cache hit ratios and adjust TTL settings accordingly.

Cache invalidation is a powerful tool for ensuring that users always receive fresh, updated content while maintaining optimal performance and cost-efficiency.

Effectively managing content updates in CloudFront and S3 is essential for optimizing performance, reducing costs, and ensuring content accuracy. S3 versioning helps prevent cache conflicts, lifecycle policies automate content expiry, and cache invalidation ensures immediate updates when necessary.

By combining these strategies, businesses can maintain a highly responsive, cost-efficient, and secure content delivery system that meets evolving user demands.

HTTPS and TLS Configurations

Security is a fundamental aspect of content delivery, ensuring that data transmitted over the internet remains confidential and protected from malicious attacks. Amazon CloudFront supports HTTPS and Transport Layer Security (TLS) configurations to provide secure content delivery, protecting both users and websites from potential threats. By implementing SSL/TLS certificates, organizations can establish trust with their users, encrypt sensitive information, and comply with industry security standards. In this section, we will explore the importance of HTTPS, how CloudFront ensures secure transmission, and the impact of HTTPS on performance and search engine rankings.

Importance of Secure Content Delivery

As cyber threats continue to evolve, securing content delivery has become a top priority for businesses worldwide. HTTPS not only protects sensitive data from being intercepted but also establishes authenticity, ensuring that users interact with a legitimate website. Secure content delivery through CloudFront enhances website security, builds user trust, and optimizes performance by leveraging encryption technologies.

Importance of HTTPS for Web Security

- HTTPS (HyperText Transfer Protocol Secure) encrypts data between the client and the server, preventing eavesdropping and data tampering.
- It protects sensitive user information, such as login credentials, payment details, and personal data, from cybercriminals.

- HTTPS ensures that users connect to an authentic website which reduces the risk of phishing and Man-in-the-Middle (MitM) attacks.
- Many modern browsers flag non-HTTPS sites as insecure, discouraging users from accessing them.

Ensuring End-to-End Encryption with CloudFront

- CloudFront supports SSL/TLS certificates to encrypt data transmission between clients and CloudFront edge locations.
- TLS ensures that content remains protected not only between the user and CloudFront but also between CloudFront and the origin server.
- Users can configure CloudFront to use HTTPS for both viewer and origin requests, ensuring end-to-end encryption.
- AWS Certificate Manager (ACM) allows for easy management and automatic renewal of SSL/TLS certificates.

Impact of HTTPS on Performance and SEO

- Search engines, such as Google, prioritize HTTPS-enabled websites in search rankings, improving their visibility and credibility.
- HTTPS enhances performance by enabling HTTP/2, which allows multiplexing and header compression, reducing latency.
- Secure sites load faster on modern browsers, leading to a better user experience and higher retention rates.
- Compliance with security standards (including PCI-DSS for payment processing) is easier with HTTPS, making it a necessity for e-commerce and financial services.

By securing content delivery with HTTPS and TLS, CloudFront ensures that organizations can provide fast, encrypted, and trusted experiences for users across the globe. In the next sections, we will explore how to configure HTTPS and TLS certificates within CloudFront for optimal security and performance.

Enabling HTTPS on CloudFront

To ensure secure content delivery and compliance with modern web security standards, enabling HTTPS on Amazon CloudFront is essential. HTTPS protects data in transit by encrypting communications between users and CloudFront edge locations, as well as between CloudFront and the origin servers. CloudFront offers seamless integration with AWS Certificate Manager (ACM) for managing SSL/TLS certificates, simplifying the process of securing content.

In this section, we will explore the different ways to enable HTTPS on CloudFront, including setting up SSL/TLS certificates, configuring HTTPS for distributions, and enforcing secure connections for all requests.

Using AWS Certificate Manager (ACM) for SSL/TLS Certificates

AWS Certificate Manager (ACM) is a managed service that helps users provision, manage, and deploy SSL/TLS certificates for secure applications. ACM simplifies the process of obtaining and renewing certificates without requiring manual intervention.

- **Automated Certificate Provisioning:** ACM provides free SSL/TLS certificates for use with CloudFront, eliminating the need for third-party purchases.

- **Seamless Integration with CloudFront:** ACM certificates can be directly attached to CloudFront distributions, securing all requests automatically.
- **Automatic Renewal:** ACM handles certificate renewals, ensuring that HTTPS remains enabled without downtime.
- **Wildcard and Multi-Domain Support:** ACM allows organizations to secure multiple subdomains with a single certificate.
- **No Additional Cost:** SSL/TLS certificates issued by ACM are free when used with AWS services like CloudFront and Elastic Load Balancing.

Configuring HTTPS for CloudFront Distributions

Once an SSL/TLS certificate is available in ACM, it must be configured for use with a CloudFront distribution to enable secure content delivery.

- **Attaching an SSL/TLS Certificate:** Users can associate an ACM-managed certificate with their CloudFront distribution through the AWS Management Console or CLI.
- **Choosing the Right Security Policy:** CloudFront supports multiple TLS security policies, allowing users to select the best encryption strength for their needs.
- **Enabling HTTPS for Viewer Requests:** CloudFront can be configured to accept HTTPS-only connections, ensuring secure communication with users.
- **Configuring HTTPS for Origin Requests:** Secure connections between CloudFront and origin servers (such as Amazon S3, EC2, or a custom origin) protect sensitive data from interception.
- **Redirecting HTTP to HTTPS:** CloudFront offers an option to automatically redirect all HTTP requests to HTTPS, ensuring users always access content securely.

Enforcing HTTPS for All CloudFront Requests

To maintain a strict security posture, it is important to enforce HTTPS for all incoming and outgoing requests within a CloudFront distribution.

- **Using Viewer Protocol Policy of CloudFront:** This setting ensures that all client requests use HTTPS, rejecting unsecured HTTP traffic.
- **Redirecting HTTP Requests Automatically:** CloudFront can be configured to return an HTTP 301 or 302 redirect to upgrade non-secure requests to HTTPS.
- **Configuring Origin Protocol Policy:** CloudFront can be set to communicate with the origin server exclusively over HTTPS, preventing unencrypted data transmission.
- **Using HSTS (HTTP Strict Transport Security):** HSTS enforces HTTPS by instructing web browsers to only load content securely, even if users manually type an HTTP URL.
- **Monitoring HTTPS Usage with CloudFront Logs:** Real-time logging and AWS CloudTrail integration help track HTTPS request compliance and identify potential security issues.

By properly configuring HTTPS within CloudFront, organizations can ensure secure, encrypted communication across all content delivery touchpoints. The next section will discuss best practices for maintaining strong TLS configurations and optimizing security settings for CloudFront distributions.

Advanced Security Configurations

Implementing HTTPS is a fundamental step in securing content delivery through CloudFront, but advanced security configurations are necessary to enhance protection against cyber threats and ensure optimal performance. Organizations must fine-tune their TLS settings, configure custom SSL certificates for specific business needs, and monitor security logs for vulnerabilities or suspicious activity.

In this section, we will explore critical aspects of advanced security configurations, including TLS version selection, the use of custom SSL certificates for enterprises, and the importance of monitoring SSL/TLS security logs.

TLS Version Selection and Security Policies

Transport Layer Security (TLS) is the cryptographic protocol used to secure HTTPS connections. Selecting the appropriate TLS version and security policies is crucial for maintaining a strong security posture while ensuring compatibility with user devices and applications.

- **Supported TLS Versions:** CloudFront requires TLS 1.2 or higher by default. TLS 1.3 offers lower latency and should be used unless compatibility demands TLS 1.2.
- **Choosing the Right TLS Security Policy:** AWS offers predefined TLS security policies that dictate the allowed cipher suites and protocols. Organizations can select policies that align with their compliance and security requirements.
- **Enforcing Strong Encryption:** CloudFront enables users to mandate TLS 1.2 or higher, reducing vulnerabilities associated with older encryption standards.
- **Performance Benefits of TLS 1.3:** TLS 1.3 includes improvements such as faster handshake processes and reduced latency, making it a preferred choice for high-performance applications.
- **Backward Compatibility Considerations:** While enforcing higher security standards, businesses must ensure that their chosen TLS version remains accessible to their user base without causing compatibility issues.

Custom SSL Certificates for Enterprise Use

While AWS Certificate Manager (ACM) provides free SSL/TLS certificates for CloudFront, some enterprises may require custom certificates to meet specific security policies or branding requirements.

- **Using Third-Party SSL Certificates:** Businesses can import SSL certificates from external Certificate Authorities (CAs) into AWS for use with CloudFront distributions.
- **Dedicated IP Custom SSL Support:** Most enterprises should use SNI-based SSL (default). Dedicated IP SSL is only required for legacy clients that don't support SNI.
- **Wildcard and Multi-Domain Certificates:** Custom SSL certificates allow organizations to secure multiple domains or subdomains under a single certificate, improving manageability.
- **Certificate Rotation and Management:** Managing SSL certificate renewal, revocation, and rotation is critical for maintaining security and preventing expired certificate issues.
- **Compliance with Industry Standards:** Custom SSL configurations allow organizations to meet specific compliance requirements such as PCI DSS (for payment security) and HIPAA (for healthcare data security).

Monitoring SSL/TLS Performance and Security Logs

Continuous monitoring of SSL/TLS performance and security logs is essential to detect vulnerabilities, optimize response times, and ensure compliance with security standards.

CloudFront exposes TLS metrics in CloudWatch (handshake time, error counts). Combine with Real-Time Logs for deep analysis.

- **Using AWS CloudTrail for Auditing:** CloudTrail logs all CloudFront API requests, helping administrators track SSL/TLS configuration changes and identify potential misconfigurations.
- **CloudFront Real-Time Logs:** These logs provide detailed insights into HTTPS request performance, including TLS handshake times, cipher usage, and session resumption rates.
- **Threat Detection with AWS WAF:** Integrating AWS Web Application Firewall (WAF) with CloudFront enhances protection against malicious attacks, such as DDoS and SQL injection.
- **Certificate Expiry and Renewal Alerts:** AWS provides automated notifications for expiring certificates, helping organizations avoid downtime due to expired SSL/TLS certificates.
- **Performance Optimization through Log Analysis:** By analyzing SSL/TLS handshake latency and failure rates, organizations can fine-tune their security policies while maintaining fast content delivery.

By implementing these advanced security configurations, organizations can enhance the security, reliability, and efficiency of their CloudFront distributions. In the next section, we will explore real-world case studies that demonstrate the effectiveness of these strategies in securing content delivery.

Case Studies

Amazon CloudFront has proven to be an essential tool for businesses across various industries, offering reduced latency, improved performance, enhanced security, and cost-efficient content delivery. Organizations ranging from e-commerce platforms to media companies have leveraged CloudFront to optimize their content distribution strategies.

This section presents three real-world case studies demonstrating how CloudFront has been successfully utilized for different purposes:

- Enhancing the speed and scalability of a global e-commerce website.
- Optimizing and securing video streaming using CloudFront and Amazon S3.
- Strengthening web security by enforcing HTTPS and mitigating cyber threats.

By analyzing these use cases, we gain practical insights into the impact of the caching, security, and performance-enhancing features of CloudFront.

Accelerating a Global E-commerce Website Using CloudFront

Let us look into a real time scenario for Improving Latency and Scaling to Handle High Traffic.

Improving Latency and Scaling to Handle High Traffic

A multinational e-commerce platform faced challenges in delivering fast-loading web pages and handling high traffic volumes, especially during seasonal sales and promotional events. The company needed a robust content delivery strategy to:

- Reduce website latency for global customers.
- Scale dynamically to accommodate traffic spikes.
- Improve the overall user experience and conversion rates.

Solution

By integrating CloudFront as a global CDN, the e-commerce company leveraged:

- CloudFront edge locations to serve cached content closer to users, reducing page load times.

- Regional Edge Caches to optimize content delivery by further reducing latency.
- The built-in DDoS protection of CloudFront (AWS Shield) to maintain availability during high-traffic events.

Implementing Caching Strategies to Reduce Origin Requests

To optimize performance and reduce backend load, the company implemented an intelligent caching strategy:

- Configuring cache behaviors for static assets (images, CSS, and JavaScript) to be cached longer.
- Setting up short TTL values for dynamic content like product availability and pricing, ensuring real-time updates.
- Using Lambda@Edge functions to personalize cached responses without frequently hitting the origin.

Results

- 50% faster page load times due to edge caching.
- 80% reduction in origin requests, reducing server costs.
- Improved scalability, allowing the platform to handle millions of users without performance degradation.

Secure Video Streaming Using CloudFront and S3

This case study views on a leading Media Company that requires a secure solution for optimizing Video Delivery with CloudFront.

Media Company Optimizing Video Delivery with CloudFront

A leading media company required a secure and scalable solution to deliver high-quality on-demand video streaming while ensuring content security. Their key challenges included:

- Efficiently delivering high-resolution videos with minimal buffering.
- Preventing unauthorized access and content piracy.
- Reducing operational costs by optimizing data transfer.

Solution

- Configured CloudFront with an S3 origin to serve video files efficiently.
- Enabled adaptive bitrate streaming (HLS and DASH), allowing videos to dynamically adjust quality based on user bandwidth.
- Utilized CloudFront edge caching to minimize latency and deliver a seamless viewing experience worldwide.

Implementing Signed URLs for Access Control

To prevent unauthorized sharing of premium content, the company implemented CloudFront Signed URLs for access control:

- Generated time-limited signed URLs that allowed only authenticated users to access videos.
- Integrated AWS Lambda to dynamically generate signed URLs based on user subscriptions.
- Restricted access to specific IP ranges to prevent content theft.

Results

- 35% reduction in bandwidth costs due to caching at CloudFront edge locations.

- Enhanced security, preventing unauthorized downloads and stream theft.
- Seamless streaming experience, increasing customer retention and satisfaction.

Enhancing Web Security Using CloudFront with HTTPS

Using AWS Certificate Manager to Secure Content Delivery

A financial services company needed to secure its web applications and API endpoints while ensuring high availability and low latency. Their primary concerns were:

- Encrypting sensitive user data during transit.
- Preventing security threats such as MITM (Man-in-the-Middle) attacks.
- Ensuring regulatory compliance with security standards.

Solution

- Enabled HTTPS across all CloudFront distributions using AWS Certificate Manager (ACM).
- Configured TLS 1.2 and 1.3 for strong encryption and performance optimization.
- Implemented HTTP to HTTPS redirects to enforce secure connections for all requests.

Protecting Against DDoS and Bot Attacks

The company also required protection against DDoS attacks and malicious bot traffic. To mitigate threats, they:

- Activated AWS Shield Standard, providing automatic DDoS mitigation for CloudFront.
- Configured AWS WAF (Web Application Firewall) with custom rules to block malicious requests.
- Enabled rate limiting to prevent brute-force login attempts.

Results

- 100% HTTPS adoption, ensuring encrypted communication for all users.
- DDoS mitigation with zero downtime during traffic spikes.
- Increased customer trust due to improved security measures.

These case studies highlight how businesses leverage CloudFront for enhanced content delivery, performance, and security. Whether optimizing latency for an e-commerce platform, securing media streaming, or enforcing HTTPS for financial applications, CloudFront provides a robust, scalable, and cost-effective solution.

In the next section, we will summarize the key takeaways from our exploration of the features and best practices of CloudFront.

Conclusion

Amazon CloudFront is a powerful Content Delivery Network (CDN) that enhances web performance, reduces latency, and ensures secure content distribution across the globe. Throughout this guide, we explored its key aspects, including caching strategies, integration with Amazon S3, HTTPS configurations, and advanced security measures. By implementing effective caching techniques, businesses can reduce origin load and optimize content delivery, while security features such as Origin Access Control (OAC), signed URLs, and TLS encryption help safeguard data. Additionally, enforcing HTTPS, leveraging AWS Certificate Manager for SSL/TLS configurations, and using the monitoring tools of CloudFront can further enhance both security and performance. These strategies collectively improve user experience, lower infrastructure costs, and strengthen web application security.

As technology evolves, CloudFront continues to play a crucial role in modern content delivery, with trends like AI-driven caching, edge computing, and 5G integration shaping its future. Organizations must stay ahead by adopting best practices such as optimizing TTL settings, leveraging real-time logging, and securing content with the built-in features of CloudFront. With the increasing demand for high-speed and secure web experiences, businesses that effectively utilize CloudFront can ensure seamless content distribution while maintaining cost efficiency. By continuously monitoring and optimizing CloudFront configurations, organizations can build scalable, resilient, and future-ready digital infrastructure, thereby, keeping pace with evolving user expectations and cybersecurity challenges.

In the next chapter, we shall look into hybrid cloud setups using VPNs and AWS Direct Connect. Readers will configure Site-to-Site VPNs for secure connections and explore Direct Connect for low-latency, high-bandwidth links.

Points to Remember

Performance and Cost

- **CloudFront Enhances Performance:** By caching content at global edge locations, CloudFront reduces latency and improves load times for users worldwide.
- **Effective Caching Strategies:** Configuring cache behaviors, TTL settings, and cache invalidation ensures optimized content delivery while minimizing origin requests.
- **Cost Optimization Strategies:** Using regional edge caches, Lambda@Edge for intelligent caching, and optimizing origin requests can significantly lower data transfer costs.
- **Customizing Cache Policies:** Implementing versioning, short TTL settings, and cache invalidation helps manage content updates efficiently.

Security

- **Seamless Integration with S3:** CloudFront can securely deliver both static and dynamic content stored in Amazon S3 using features like Origin Access Identity (OAI).
- **HTTPS for Secure Content Delivery:** Enabling HTTPS with AWS Certificate Manager (ACM) ensures end-to-end encryption, protecting data from unauthorized access.
- **TLS Security Configurations:** Selecting the right TLS versions and enforcing security policies strengthens the protection of data transmitted over CloudFront.
- **Advanced Security Measures:** Signed URLs, signed cookies, and AWS WAF help control access and protect against unauthorized users and cyber threats.

Monitoring and Future

- **Real-Time Monitoring and Logging:** Utilizing CloudFront real-time logs and AWS CloudWatch enables proactive performance optimization and security monitoring.
- **Future Trends in CDN Technology:** AI-driven caching, edge computing, and 5G integration are shaping the evolution of CloudFront and content delivery networks.

CHAPTER 9
VPN Connections and Direct Connect

Introduction

As organizations increasingly adopt hybrid cloud architectures, establishing secure and reliable network connectivity between on-premises infrastructure and AWS is critical. VPN (Virtual Private Network) connections and AWS Direct Connect offer two primary solutions to achieve seamless integration, each catering to different performance, security, and bandwidth requirements.

This chapter explores Site-to-Site VPNs, which enable secure, encrypted tunnels between an on-premises network and AWS. It also delves into AWS Client VPN, a scalable solution for remote users to securely access AWS resources. Additionally, the chapter covers AWS Direct Connect, a dedicated high-bandwidth networking option that enhances performance by reducing latency and improving reliability. Finally, troubleshooting strategies for diagnosing and resolving common VPN connectivity issues are discussed to ensure a resilient hybrid cloud environment.

Structure

In this chapter, we will walk through:

- Site-to-Site VPNs
- Client VPNs
- AWS Direct Connect
- Troubleshooting VPN Issues
- Case Studies

Site-to-Site VPNs

As organizations move towards hybrid cloud environments, ensuring secure and seamless connectivity between on-premises infrastructure and AWS becomes a top priority. Site-to-Site VPNs (Virtual Private Networks) provide an encrypted tunnel that allows organizations to extend their private network to AWS securely. This enables seamless communication between cloud-based and on-premises resources, facilitating hybrid workloads, disaster recovery solutions, and secure data transfers.

AWS Site-to-Site VPN leverages IPsec (Internet Protocol Security) to establish encrypted connections between an on-premises data center or office network and an AWS Virtual Private Cloud (VPC). This ensures that all transmitted data remains protected from unauthorized access and interception. Compared to traditional networking solutions, Site-to-Site VPNs are cost-effective, easy to deploy, and flexible, making them ideal for organizations looking to integrate AWS with their existing IT infrastructure without requiring dedicated physical connections.

This section explores how Site-to-Site VPNs work, their key benefits, and a step-by-step approach to setting up a secure tunnel between AWS and on-premises networks. Additionally, it covers best practices for optimizing performance and security to ensure reliable hybrid cloud connectivity.

Understanding Site-to-Site VPNs and Their Use Cases

In the contemporary interconnected digital landscape, businesses often require a secure and efficient way to link their on-premises infrastructure with cloud environments. Site-to-Site VPNs (Virtual Private Networks) serve as a critical solution by providing a secure, encrypted tunnel between the private network and AWS of an organization. This approach enables seamless hybrid cloud deployments, ensuring that cloud-based applications and services can communicate with on-premises resources as if they were part of the same local network.

By leveraging AWS Site-to-Site VPN, businesses can establish a cost-effective and scalable hybrid network without the need for dedicated leased lines. This section delves into the core concepts of Site-to-Site VPNs, their architectural components, and real-world use cases where they play a vital role in secure cloud connectivity.

Site-to-Site VPN

A Site-to-Site VPN is a secure, encrypted connection that allows two networks to communicate over the public internet as if they were directly connected. In AWS, this is achieved by establishing an IPsec (Internet Protocol Security) tunnel between an on-premises network (or another cloud provider) and an AWS Virtual Private Cloud (VPC).

The VPN connection is fully managed by AWS and terminates at either a Virtual Private Gateway (VGW) or a Transit Gateway (TGW) within the AWS network. All traffic passing through the tunnel is encrypted in transit, ensuring confidentiality and integrity of sensitive data.

AWS Site-to-Site VPN supports both — static routing and dynamic routing (BGP), giving organizations flexibility in how routes are advertised and maintained between on-premises and cloud environments. This makes it suitable for a wide range of hybrid connectivity use cases—from simple single-VPC setups to large-scale, multi-VPC architectures.

Feature / Aspect	Virtual Private Gateway (VGW)	Transit Gateway (TGW)
Primary Use Case	Simple hybrid connectivity for a single VPC	Centralized hub for connecting multiple VPCs and on-premises networks
Scalability	Limited - one VGW per VPC	Highly scalable - supports thousands of VPC and VPN attachments
Architecture	Point-to-site (VPC-centric)	Hub-and-spoke or mesh architecture
Routing	Static routes or BGP with a single VPC	Advanced routing with route tables per attachment
Multi-VPC Connectivity	Requires VPC peering or multiple VPNs	Native multi-VPC connectivity
Operational Overhead	Lower, simpler to configure	Higher, but much more flexible
Best For	Small or medium environments	Large enterprises and complex network topologies

Table 9.1: *Virtual Private Gateway (VGW) versus Transit Gateway (TGW)*

- Choose VGW if you need quick, cost-effective hybrid connectivity for a single VPC.
- Choose TGW if you are designing a scalable, enterprise-grade network with multiple VPCs, regions, or on-premises locations.

Key Use Cases of Site-to-Site VPNs

Site-to-Site VPNs provide a versatile solution for businesses across various industries. Some of the most common use cases include:

- **Hybrid Cloud Deployments**
    - Organizations with on-premises data centers can use Site-to-Site VPNs to securely connect their infrastructure to AWS. This enables them to run applications across both environments, leveraging AWS for scalability while maintaining critical workloads on-premises.
- **Disaster Recovery and Backup**
    - Businesses can use Site-to-Site VPNs to replicate data to AWS for disaster recovery. In the event of an on-premises failure, critical applications and services can quickly switch to AWS resources, ensuring business continuity.
- **Secure Remote Office Connectivity**
    - Companies with multiple branch offices can use VPN tunnels to securely connect remote sites to a central AWS environment. This allows employees to access cloud-based applications and services securely from any location.
- **Extending Corporate Networks to the Cloud**
    - Site-to-Site VPNs enable organizations to treat AWS as an extension of their corporate network. This allows them to use AWS resources without exposing internal systems to the public internet, improving security and control.
- **Migrations and Cloud Adoption**
    - Businesses migrating workloads to AWS can use Site-to-Site VPNs as a temporary solution for secure connectivity before transitioning to more permanent networking solutions like AWS Direct Connect.

By understanding the fundamentals of Site-to-Site VPNs and their practical applications, organizations can effectively leverage this technology to build secure and resilient hybrid cloud architectures. The next section will explore the step-by-step process of setting up a Site-to-Site VPN connection in AWS.

Configuring an AWS Site-to-Site VPN

Setting up an AWS Site-to-Site VPN is a crucial step in establishing a secure and reliable connection between an on-premises network and an AWS Virtual Private Cloud (VPC). By configuring a Site-to-Site VPN, organizations can ensure encrypted communication over the public internet while integrating their existing infrastructure with AWS services. This process involves setting up a Virtual Private Gateway (VGW) or Transit Gateway (TGW), creating a VPN connection, and configuring the on-premises customer gateway to establish a secure tunnel.

In this section, we will walk through the essential steps to configure an AWS Site-to-Site VPN, covering the necessary components, network settings, and routing configurations. By following these steps, businesses can create a stable and secure hybrid cloud environment.

Step 1: Setting up the AWS Virtual Private Gateway (VGW) or Transit Gateway (TGW)

Choosing the Right Gateway

AWS provides two options for terminating VPN connections:

- **Virtual Private Gateway (VGW):** Used when connecting a single VPC to an on-premises network.
- **Transit Gateway (TGW):** Used for more complex architectures, allowing multiple VPCs and on-premises networks to communicate through a centralized hub.

For organizations with a simple hybrid cloud setup, a **VGW** is often sufficient. However, for enterprises managing multiple VPCs or locations, a **TGW** provides better scalability and routing control.

Creating a Virtual Private Gateway (VGW)

1. Navigate to the AWS Management Console → VPC Dashboard.
2. Click `Virtual Private Gateways` → `Create Virtual Private Gateway`.
3. Provide a name for the gateway and select Autonomous System Number (ASN) (default AWS ASN or a custom ASN).
4. Click `Create Virtual Private Gateway`.
5. Attach the VGW to the required VPC to establish connectivity.

Creating a Transit Gateway (TGW) (If Required)

1. Navigate to `AWS Management Console` → `VPC Dashboard` → `Transit Gateways`.
2. Click `Create Transit Gateway` and enter the required details.
3. Configure routing settings for multiple VPC and on-premises connectivity.
4. Attach the Transit Gateway to the VPCs and external networks as needed.

Step 2: Creating a Customer Gateway (CGW)

A Customer Gateway (CGW) represents the on-premises router or firewall that will establish the VPN tunnel to AWS. This must be configured to match the settings defined in AWS.

1. Go to `AWS Management Console` → `VPC Dashboard` → `Customer Gateways`.
2. Click `Create Customer Gateway` and enter the following:
    a. **Name:** Assign a meaningful identifier.
    b. **Routing Type:** Choose **Static** or **Dynamic (BGP)**.
    c. **IP Address:** Enter the public IP address of the on-premises router.
    d. **Device Information (Optional):** Provide vendor details for reference.
3. Click `Create Customer Gateway`.

Step 3: Creating the Site-to-Site VPN Connection

With the VGW/TGW and CGW configured, the next step is to create the VPN connection.

1. Navigate to `AWS Management Console` → `VPC Dashboard` → `VPN Connections`.
2. Click `Create VPN Connection` and enter:
    a. **Name:** Assign a meaningful name.

   b. **Target Gateway:** Select either Virtual Private Gateway (VGW) or Transit Gateway (TGW).
   c. **Customer Gateway:** Choose the previously created CGW.
   d. **Routing Options:**
      i. **Static Routing** (manually define CIDR ranges)
      ii. **Dynamic Routing (BGP)** (allows automatic route propagation)
3. Click `Create VPN Connection`.

After creation, AWS provides two IPsec tunnel details. These tunnels should be configured on the on-premises router/firewall to establish the VPN connection.

Step 4: Configuring the On-Premises VPN Device

To complete the setup, the on-premises router or firewall must be configured to establish the VPN tunnel with AWS. The configuration depends on the network hardware (Cisco, Juniper, Palo Alto, and so on).

1. **Download the AWS VPN Configuration File**:
   a. After creating the VPN connection, navigate to `VPN Connections`.
   b. Select the newly created VPN and click `Download Configuration`.
   c. Choose the appropriate vendor and model for your firewall/router.
2. **Apply the Configuration on the On-Premises Router**:
   a. Use the downloaded configuration file to set up the IPsec tunnel.
   b. Define IKE Phase 1 and Phase 2 settings, encryption methods, and authentication parameters.
   c. Enable Border Gateway Protocol (BGP) if using dynamic routing.
   d. Set up static routes if BGP is not used.
3. **Test the Connection**:
   a. Ping AWS resources to verify connectivity.
   b. Use AWS VPN CloudWatch metrics to monitor tunnel status.

Step 5: Configuring Routing for Site-to-Site VPN

Proper routing is essential for directing traffic between AWS and the on-premises network. Depending on the VPN setup, routing can be configured in multiple ways:

- **Static Routing**: Manually define the CIDR blocks for on-premises and AWS resources.
- **Dynamic Routing (BGP)**: Allows AWS and on-premises routers to exchange routes automatically.

To configure routing in AWS:

1. Navigate to `AWS Management Console` → `VPC Dashboard` → `Route Tables`.
2. Select the relevant VPC Route Table.
3. Add a new route:
   a. **Destination**: On-premises CIDR block.
   b. **Target**: Virtual Private Gateway (VGW) or Transit Gateway (TGW).
4. Save the configuration.

Step 6: Verifying and Monitoring VPN Connection

Once all configurations are complete, it is essential to verify the VPN connection and monitor its performance.

1. **Testing the VPN Connection**
   a. Use traceroute or ping from on-premises devices to AWS instances.
   b. Check AWS VPN Tunnel Status (should show UP/Connected).
   c. Verify that applications can communicate across the VPN tunnel.
2. **Monitoring with CloudWatch Metrics**

   AWS provides CloudWatch metrics to track VPN health and performance, including:
   a. **Tunnel State**: Indicates if the VPN tunnel is active or down.
   b. **Bytes In/Out**: Measures data transfer over the VPN tunnel.
   c. **Tunnel Data Loss and Latency**: Identifies potential performance bottlenecks.

To monitor the VPN:

1. Go to **`AWS Management Console`** → **`CloudWatch Dashboard`**.
2. Select **`VPN Metrics`** under Networking.
3. Set up CloudWatch Alarms for tunnel failure notifications.

Configuring an AWS Site-to-Site VPN is an essential step for businesses seeking a secure hybrid cloud environment. By establishing an encrypted tunnel between AWS and on-premises infrastructure, organizations can ensure seamless communication while maintaining high security and control. Following best practices in routing, encryption, and monitoring helps in maintaining a reliable VPN connection.

Security Best Practices for Site-to-Site VPNs

Ensuring the security of a Site-to-Site VPN is essential for protecting sensitive data as it traverses public networks. Although AWS provides strong encryption and security measures for VPN connections, organizations must implement additional safeguards to mitigate risks such as unauthorized access, data interception, and misconfigurations.

In this section, we will explore the key security best practices for AWS Site-to-Site VPNs, including encryption protocols, authentication mechanisms, access control policies, and continuous monitoring. Implementing these strategies will help organizations maintain a secure and resilient hybrid cloud environment.

Implement Strong Encryption and Authentication

Using robust encryption and authentication methods is critical to preventing unauthorized access and ensuring data confidentiality.

Use Strong Encryption Protocols (AES-256, SHA-2)

- Configure AES-256 encryption for VPN tunnels to secure data in transit.
- Use SHA-2 (SHA-256 or SHA-384) for data integrity verification, ensuring transmitted data has not been altered.
- Avoid using deprecated encryption algorithms such as MD5 or SHA-1, as they are vulnerable to attacks.

Leverage Internet Key Exchange Version 2 (IKEv2)

- IKEv2 provides enhanced security, faster rekeying, and improved resilience against connection failures compared to IKEv1.
- It supports modern cryptographic suites, making it the preferred choice for secure VPN tunnels.

Enable Multi-Factor Authentication (MFA) for VPN Management

- Restrict access to AWS VPN configurations by requiring MFA for administrative users.
- Implement IAM policies that enforce MFA for VPN-related actions, reducing the risk of unauthorized modifications.

Enforce Strict Access Controls and Least Privilege

Restricting VPN access to only authorized systems and users minimizes the attack surface and prevents unauthorized connections.

Define Specific Source and Destination CIDR Blocks

- Configure route-based VPNs with specific CIDR blocks to control which network segments can communicate.
- Avoid using overly broad CIDR ranges (such as 0.0.0.0/0) in VPN configurations, as this increases security risks.

Use Security Groups and Network ACLs

- Apply AWS Security Groups to limit which instances can receive traffic from the VPN.
- Configure Network ACLs (NACLs) to enforce additional security restrictions at the subnet level.

Restrict VPN Access Based on Roles and Policies

- Use AWS Identity and Access Management (IAM) to define permissions for VPN creation, modification, and deletion.
- Apply the principle of least privilege to ensure that only necessary users have access to VPN configurations.

Protect Against Man-in-the-Middle (MitM) and Spoofing Attacks

MitM and spoofing attacks can compromise VPN security by intercepting or modifying network traffic.

Enable Perfect Forward Secrecy (PFS)

- Configure Diffie-Hellman (DH) Group 14 or higher to establish unique session keys for each VPN session.
- PFS ensures that even if one encryption key is compromised, past and future communications remain secure.

Use Digital Certificates Instead of Pre-Shared Keys (PSK)

- Pre-Shared Keys (PSK) are vulnerable to brute-force attacks if not properly managed.
- Digital certificates provide stronger authentication and reduce the risk of unauthorized access.

Monitor VPN Connection Logs for Anomalous Activity

- Enable AWS CloudWatch Logs and VPC Flow Logs to detect unusual traffic patterns.
- Set up AWS CloudTrail to log all VPN configuration changes and identify unauthorized modifications.

Implement Automated Monitoring and Alerts

Continuous monitoring helps detect and respond to security threats in real-time.

Use AWS GuardDuty for Threat Detection

- Enable AWS GuardDuty to detect suspicious activity in VPN traffic.
- GuardDuty can identify unauthorized access attempts, port scanning, and unusual data transfers.

Set up AWS CloudWatch Alarms for VPN Health Monitoring

- Monitor tunnel status and set up CloudWatch alarms for VPN disconnections or latency spikes.
- Automate alerts for failed authentication attempts or excessive rekeying events.

Enable Logging and Audit Trails with AWS CloudTrail

- Use CloudTrail to track administrative actions related to VPN setup and modifications.
- Regularly review logs to identify potential security threats and compliance violations.

Regularly Test and Update VPN Configurations

Routine testing and updates ensure that VPN security settings remain effective against evolving threats.

Conduct Penetration Testing on VPN Connections

- Perform regular security assessments to identify vulnerabilities in VPN configurations.
- Simulate attack scenarios to test VPN resilience against brute-force attacks, MitM attacks, and traffic interception.

Update VPN Firmware and Security Patches

- Ensure that on-premises VPN devices and AWS VPN configurations are running the latest security updates.
- Patch known vulnerabilities in network hardware, operating systems, and VPN software.

Review and Rotate Encryption Keys Periodically

- Regularly update IPsec keys and authentication credentials to reduce the risk of key compromise.
- Automate key rotation policies for IKEv2 rekeying to maintain strong encryption.

Securing an AWS Site-to-Site VPN requires a multi-layered approach that includes encryption, authentication, access control, monitoring, and continuous updates. By implementing these security best practices, organizations can protect their hybrid cloud connections from unauthorized access, data breaches, and cyber threats. Regular testing, automated monitoring, and proactive security measures ensure that VPN connections remain reliable and secure in an ever-evolving threat landscape.

Client VPNs

In an increasingly remote and distributed work environment, organizations need secure, scalable, and reliable methods for employees and stakeholders to access AWS resources. AWS Client VPN provides a fully managed, secure connection for remote users to access cloud and on-premises networks without the need for complex infrastructure setups. Unlike Site-to-Site VPNs, which connect entire networks, Client VPNs are designed for individual users who need secure access from any location.

This section explores AWS Client VPN, its architecture, and how it enables businesses to provide secure remote access. We will cover the process of configuring an AWS Client VPN, authentication and authorization mechanisms, and key security best practices to ensure robust access control. By implementing Client VPN solutions effectively, organizations can maintain productivity while enforcing security and compliance policies.

Overview of AWS Client VPN and Its Benefits

With the rise of remote work and global business operations, secure access to cloud environments has become essential. AWS Client VPN provides a fully managed solution for remote users to securely connect to AWS and on-premises networks. Unlike traditional VPNs, AWS Client VPN eliminates the need for physical infrastructure, offering a scalable, cloud-native approach to remote connectivity.

This section delves into the fundamentals of AWS Client VPN, explaining how it works and the advantages it provides to businesses. By leveraging AWS Client VPN, organizations can enhance security, ensure compliance, and offer a seamless user experience for employees accessing cloud resources remotely.

Understanding AWS Client VPN

AWS Client VPN is a managed VPN service that allows remote users to securely access AWS resources and on-premises networks over an encrypted connection. It supports OpenVPN-based clients and integrates with AWS Identity and Access Management (IAM) for authentication and authorization.

Key components of AWS Client VPN include:

- **VPN Endpoint:** The primary access point for client connections.
- **Authentication Methods:** Supports Active Directory, mutual authentication, and federated authentication with SAML-based providers.
- **Authorization Rules:** Define access permissions for different user groups.
- **Target Networks:** Specify AWS VPCs or on-premises resources accessible via the VPN.
- **Logging and Monitoring:** Integrates with AWS CloudWatch and AWS CloudTrail for visibility and auditing.

By understanding these components, organizations can implement a secure, flexible, and scalable remote access solution that meets their operational needs.

Key Benefits of AWS Client VPN

AWS Client VPN offers multiple advantages over traditional VPN solutions, making it an ideal choice for businesses requiring secure remote access.

- **Fully Managed Service:** AWS handles the infrastructure, scaling, and maintenance, reducing operational overhead. This allows IT teams to focus on business-critical tasks rather than VPN management.

- **Scalable and Elastic:** Unlike traditional VPNs that require manual scaling, AWS Client VPN automatically adjusts to support thousands of concurrent users based on demand.
- **Secure and Compliant:** AWS Client VPN enforces robust security with TLS encryption, authentication mechanisms, and integration with IAM policies. This ensures compliance with industry regulations such as GDPR, HIPAA, and SOC 2.
- **Seamless Integration with AWS Services:** Client VPN integrates natively with AWS services such as Amazon VPC, AWS Directory Service, and AWS CloudWatch, allowing organizations to manage access control and monitor activity efficiently.
- **Multi-Platform Compatibility:** AWS Client VPN supports multiple operating systems, including Windows, macOS, and Linux, ensuring users can connect securely from various devices.

By leveraging AWS Client VPN, businesses can enhance security, improve user experience, and provide employees with a seamless way to access corporate resources from anywhere.

Setting up AWS Client VPN for Secure Remote Access

As remote work and distributed teams become more common, organizations need secure and efficient ways to connect users to cloud and on-premises resources. AWS Client VPN provides a scalable, fully managed VPN solution that enables remote employees to access AWS resources securely. By leveraging encryption, authentication, and network policies, businesses can ensure that only authorized users connect to their environments.

This section provides a step-by-step guide to setting up AWS Client VPN, covering configuration, authentication options, and best practices for secure remote access.

Configuring an AWS Client VPN Endpoint

The first step in enabling remote access is to create an AWS Client VPN endpoint, which acts as the gateway for users connecting to AWS resources.

Step 1: Define the VPN Endpoint

1. Navigate to the AWS Client VPN console.
2. Click `Create Client VPN Endpoint` and configure the following:
    a. **Client IPv4 CIDR Range:** Defines the IP address range assigned to VPN clients.
    b. **Server Certificate:** Required for encrypting VPN traffic using TLS.
    c. **Authentication Method:** Choose from AWS Directory Service, mutual authentication, or SAML-based authentication.
    d. **Logging Options:** Enable CloudWatch logs for monitoring and auditing VPN activity.
3. Click `Create VPN Endpoint` and wait for AWS to provision it.

Step 2: Associate a Target Network

1. Once the VPN endpoint is created, associate it with an Amazon VPC subnet where users will connect.
2. Go to the Target Network Associations section, click `Associate`, and select the appropriate subnet.

Step 3: Configure Authorization Rules

1. Define authorization rules to control user access to AWS resources.
2. Set rules based on user groups, IP addresses, or AWS IAM policies.

By following these steps, organizations can establish a secure AWS Client VPN endpoint that serves as the access point for remote users.

Security Note: TLS and Certificate Management

AWS Client VPN requires TLS to secure all client connections. Server certificates must be managed through AWS Certificate Manager, ensuring encrypted communication and protection against interception or tampering. Proper certificate rotation and lifecycle management are critical for maintaining long-term VPN security.

Configuring Authentication for AWS Client VPN

Authentication is a crucial component of VPN security, ensuring that only authorized users gain access. AWS Client VPN supports multiple authentication methods, allowing organizations to choose based on their security requirements.

Option 1: Active Directory Authentication

- Integrates with AWS Directory Service or an existing on-premises Active Directory.
- Enables seamless access control based on user roles and permissions.

Option 2: Mutual Authentication (Certificate-Based)

- Uses client certificates issued by AWS Certificate Manager (ACM) or a third-party certificate authority.
- Ensures that only devices with valid certificates can connect.

Option 3: Federated Authentication (SAML-Based)

- Allows Single Sign-On (SSO) with identity providers like Okta, Azure AD, or Ping Identity.
- Ideal for organizations that require centralized user authentication.

Use Case / Requirement	Recommended Authentication Method	Reason
Existing on-premises or managed AD	Active Directory Authentication	Leverages existing users, groups, and policies
Device-based or automated access	Mutual (Certificate-Based) Authentication	Strong device identity without user credentials
Enterprise SSO with MFA	Federated (SAML-Based) Authentication	Centralized identity, MFA, and conditional access
Minimal user management overhead	Federated (SAML-Based) Authentication	Identity handled entirely by external IdP
High-security, locked-down environments	Mutual Authentication	Eliminates password-based access
Hybrid workforce with multiple IdPs	Federated Authentication	Scales easily across identity platforms

Table 9.2: *Authentication Method Decision Table*

Selecting the right authentication method enhances security while providing a seamless login experience for users.

Connecting Clients to the VPN

After setting up the VPN endpoint and authentication, users need to connect their devices to AWS Client VPN.

Step 1: Download VPN Configuration

1. Navigate to the **`AWS Client VPN console`**.
2. Select the VPN endpoint and download the configuration file.

Step 2: Install an OpenVPN-Compatible Client

1. AWS Client VPN is compatible with OpenVPN clients on Windows, macOS, and Linux.
2. Install the OpenVPN client and import the configuration file.

Step 3: Establish a VPN Connection

1. Launch the VPN client and connect using the provided credentials.
2. Verify connectivity by accessing AWS resources or running a traceroute command.

Once connected, users can securely access AWS applications, databases, and services as if they were on an internal corporate network.

Best Practices for Secure Remote Access

To ensure the security and efficiency of AWS Client VPN, organizations should follow best practices:

- **Implement Least Privilege Access:** Use authorization rules to restrict user access to only necessary resources.
- **Enforce Multi-Factor Authentication (MFA):** Combine VPN authentication with MFA for an added layer of security.
- **Monitor VPN Usage:** Enable AWS CloudWatch logs to track VPN connections and detect unusual activity.
- **Optimize Performance:** Use split tunneling to direct only AWS-bound traffic through the VPN, reducing network congestion.

By following these steps and best practices, organizations can securely configure AWS Client VPN to provide remote users with reliable, encrypted access to AWS resources.

Authentication and Authorization Mechanisms for Client VPN

Ensuring secure access to AWS resources through Client VPN requires robust authentication and authorization mechanisms. Authentication verifies the identity of users attempting to connect, while authorization determines their level of access within the network. AWS Client VPN offers multiple authentication methods, including Active Directory, mutual certificate authentication, and SAML-based federated authentication. Additionally, authorization rules help enforce access controls based on user roles and network policies.

This section explores the authentication and authorization options available in AWS Client VPN, guiding organizations in selecting and implementing the right approach for their security needs.

Authentication Mechanisms in AWS Client VPN

Authentication is the first step in securing VPN access, ensuring that only verified users and devices can establish connections. AWS Client VPN supports three primary authentication methods:

- **Active Directory (AD) Authentication**
    - Integrates AWS Client VPN with AWS Directory Service or an existing on-premises Active Directory.

  - Enables centralized user management using existing AD credentials.
  - Supports group-based access controls, allowing administrators to define VPN permissions per user group.

  Implementation Steps:

  1. Deploy AWS Directory Service (or connect an existing AD).
  2. Enable AD authentication in the Client VPN endpoint settings.
  3. Define security group rules to manage access control.

  Best Used For: Organizations that rely on Microsoft Active Directory for identity management.

- **Mutual Certificate Authentication**
  - Uses TLS-based authentication, requiring both client and server certificates.
  - Certificates are issued using AWS Certificate Manager (ACM) or a third-party Certificate Authority (CA).
  - Ensures that only devices with a valid client certificate can establish a VPN session.

  Implementation Steps:

  1. Generate client and server certificates using ACM or OpenVPN.
  2. Upload certificates to AWS and configure them in the Client VPN endpoint.
  3. Distribute client certificates to authorized users.

  Best Used For: Scenarios where device-level authentication is required, such as contractor access or BYOD (Bring Your Own Device) environments.

- **Federated Authentication (SAML 2.0)**
  - Enables Single Sign-On (SSO) using identity providers (IdPs) like Okta, Azure AD, or Ping Identity.
  - Eliminates the need for managing VPN-specific credentials.
  - Allows multi-factor authentication (MFA) enforcement through the IdP.

  Implementation Steps:

  1. Configure a SAML-based IdP and create a VPN application.
  2. Set up AWS IAM roles and policies to map users to VPN access permissions.
  3. Enable SAML authentication in AWS Client VPN.

  Best Used For: Organizations that use cloud-based IdPs and require seamless, scalable authentication with MFA capabilities.

Authorization Mechanisms in AWS Client VPN

Once authentication is complete, authorization mechanisms define which resources and services users can access over the VPN. AWS Client VPN enforces access controls through authorization rules and network security policies.

Defining Authorization Rules

- Authorization rules control which users or groups can access specific AWS resources.
- Administrators define rules based on Active Directory groups, client IP addresses, or IAM roles.

Source (User Group)	Destination Network	Action
Developers	10.0.1.0/24 (VPC Subnet)	Allow
Contractors	10.0.2.0/24 (Restricted Subnet)	Deny

Table 9.3: *Example Authorization Rule*

Implementation Steps:

1. Go to the AWS Client VPN console.
2. Define an authorization rule based on user groups or specific CIDR ranges.
3. Apply the rule to the VPN endpoint and test connectivity.

Enforcing Security Groups and Network ACLs

- AWS security groups and network ACLs (NACLs) provide an additional layer of authorization.
- Security groups restrict traffic at the instance level, while NACLs apply to entire subnets.

Best Practices:

- Allow VPN traffic only to required resources (such as application servers, databases).
- Implement deny-by-default policies to prevent unauthorized access.
- Monitor access logs using AWS CloudWatch and AWS CloudTrail for auditing.

Best Practices for Authentication and Authorization in AWS Client VPN

To maintain a secure and well-managed Client VPN, organizations should follow these best practices:

- **Use Multi-Factor Authentication (MFA)**
  - Enforce MFA for all VPN users to prevent unauthorized access.
  - If using SAML authentication, integrate MFA policies at the IdP level.
- **Implement Role-Based Access Control (RBAC)**
  - Assign VPN access based on user roles (for example, developers, administrators, contractors).
  - Use Active Directory groups or IAM policies to enforce least privilege access.
- **Regularly Rotate Certificates and Credentials**
  - Periodically renew client and server certificates to prevent expired authentication.
  - For AD authentication, enforce password rotation policies.
- **Monitor VPN Logs and Access Patterns**
  - Enable AWS CloudWatch Logs for real-time tracking of VPN connections.
  - Use AWS GuardDuty to detect suspicious VPN activity.

By carefully configuring authentication and authorization mechanisms, businesses can ensure that their AWS Client VPN remains secure, scalable, and resilient against unauthorized access attempts.

AWS Direct Connect

In the digital landscape of today, organizations require fast, secure, and reliable network connectivity to efficiently integrate on-premises data centers with cloud environments. While VPN solutions provide secure connections over the public internet, they often suffer from latency fluctuations, bandwidth limitations, and potential security risks. To address these challenges, AWS Direct Connect offers a dedicated, high-bandwidth connection that bypasses the public internet, providing consistent performance, enhanced security, and reduced data transfer costs.

AWS Direct Connect is an enterprise-grade networking solution that enables organizations to establish a private link between their on-premises infrastructure and AWS resources. By leveraging Direct Connect, businesses can achieve low-latency data transfer, higher throughput, and more predictable network performance. This chapter explores the fundamentals of AWS Direct Connect, its benefits, setup process, and best practices for ensuring a seamless hybrid cloud infrastructure.

By the end of this section, readers will have a comprehensive understanding of AWS Direct Connect, how to deploy it for high-performance hybrid cloud architectures, and strategies to enhance security, scalability, and cost efficiency.

Introduction to AWS Direct Connect and When to Use

As businesses increasingly migrate workloads to the cloud, the need for fast, reliable, and secure connectivity between on-premises environments and AWS becomes critical. Traditional VPN connections, which rely on the public internet, are often susceptible to latency fluctuations, bandwidth limitations, and security vulnerabilities. To overcome these challenges, AWS Direct Connect provides a dedicated private network connection to AWS, ensuring low-latency, high-bandwidth, and secure data transfer.

AWS Direct Connect establishes a dedicated fiber-optic connection between the data center or corporate network and AWS of an organization, bypassing the public internet. This enhances performance, improves security, and optimizes costs by reducing data transfer charges compared to standard internet-based connections. Organizations using Direct Connect can seamlessly extend their on-premises networks to AWS, ensuring consistent application performance and robust hybrid cloud architectures. This section explores the fundamentals of AWS Direct Connect, its key advantages, and the ideal use cases where it provides the most value.

By understanding the advantages and ideal use cases of AWS Direct Connect, organizations can make informed decisions about deploying a dedicated network connection to enhance cloud performance, security, and cost efficiency.

In cloud computing, network connectivity plays a crucial role in determining performance, security, and cost efficiency. Organizations often rely on internet-based VPNs to connect their on-premises infrastructure to AWS, but these connections are subject to latency fluctuations, security risks, and bandwidth limitations. AWS Direct Connect is a dedicated, private network solution that provides a secure and consistent connection between the data center, office, or colocation facility and AWS of an organization.

By bypassing the public internet, Direct Connect offers predictable performance, reduced data transfer costs, and enhanced security. This makes it ideal for enterprises needing high-bandwidth, low-latency access to AWS resources for mission-critical applications, hybrid cloud deployments, and large-scale data transfers.

Working of AWS Direct Connect

AWS Direct Connect establishes a dedicated physical connection between the network of an organization and an AWS Direct Connect location. The process involves the following key components:

- **Direct Connect Locations**
  - AWS has Direct Connect locations in data centers worldwide, where customers can establish a dedicated connection to AWS.

  - These locations serve as entry points to the global infrastructure of AWS.
- **Physical Network Link**
  - The connection is made using fiber-optic cables, providing a dedicated 1 Gbps, 10 Gbps, or higher-speed link.
  - Customers can either connect directly to AWS or use a partner network provider to establish the link.
- **Virtual Interfaces (VIFs)**
  - Direct Connect supports multiple Virtual Interfaces (VIFs) that allow segmented network traffic to AWS services.
  - A Private VIF is used for connecting to an Amazon VPC, while a Public VIF allows access to AWS public services like S3, DynamoDB, and SNS.
- **Redundant Connections for High Availability**
  - To ensure fault tolerance, AWS recommends establishing multiple Direct Connect connections in different locations.
  - Customers can use AWS Direct Connect Gateway to connect multiple VPCs across AWS regions via a single Direct Connect link.

Feature	AWS Direct Connect	Internet-Based VPN
Latency	Low, predictable latency	High, fluctuating latency
Security	Private, dedicated link	Exposed to public internet threats
Performance	Consistent and reliable	Affected by congestion and ISP routing
Data Transfer Cost	Lower outbound transfer costs	Higher egress charges

***Table 9.4**: AWS Direct Connect versus VPN-Based Internet Connections*

AWS Direct Connect is a powerful solution for businesses requiring high-speed, secure, and cost-effective connectivity to AWS. By establishing a dedicated physical link, organizations can bypass the internet, improve performance, reduce costs, and enhance security. Understanding how Direct Connect works and its core components is essential for businesses seeking seamless hybrid cloud integration and optimized AWS access.

Key Use Cases of AWS Direct Connect

Choosing the right network connectivity option is critical for ensuring optimal performance, security, and cost efficiency in cloud environments. While traditional VPN connections over the internet provide flexibility, they may not meet the needs of enterprises requiring high-bandwidth, low-latency, and secure connections to AWS. AWS Direct Connect is designed for organizations that demand consistent network performance, lower data transfer costs, and enhanced security.

This section explores when AWS Direct Connect is the right choice, highlighting scenarios where it provides significant advantages over internet-based VPNs.

High-Performance Hybrid Cloud Architectures

Organizations that operate hybrid cloud infrastructures—where workloads are distributed across on-premises data centers and AWS—require seamless connectivity to ensure efficient communication between environments. AWS Direct Connect:

- Enables fast, dedicated network links between on-premises infrastructure and AWS.
- Reduces network congestion and improves application responsiveness for hybrid deployments.

- Provides low-latency, high-bandwidth connectivity critical for running distributed applications.

Example: A financial services company using AWS for real-time market data analysis can leverage Direct Connect to ensure ultra-low-latency data transfers between its on-premises trading systems and AWS analytics workloads.

Large-Scale Data Transfers with Reduced Costs

Transferring large volumes of data between AWS and an on-premises data center over the internet can result in high costs and unpredictable transfer speeds. AWS Direct Connect helps:

- Reduce outbound data transfer costs by leveraging dedicated pricing instead of public internet-based rates.
- Ensure faster and more consistent data transfers for backup, disaster recovery, and big data processing.
- Enable predictable throughput for high-bandwidth applications like media streaming and genomic research.

Example: A media company needing to transfer terabytes of video content daily from AWS S3 to its on-premises editing suite benefits from the high-speed, cost-effective data transfer capabilities of Direct Connect.

Compliance and Security Requirements

For industries handling sensitive data (such as healthcare, finance, and government organizations), AWS Direct Connect provides a private, dedicated link that enhances security by:

- Bypassing the public internet, reducing exposure to cyber threats.
- Meeting strict compliance regulations (like HIPAA, PCI DSS, and FedRAMP).
- Offering greater control over network security policies compared to standard VPN connections.

Example: A healthcare provider storing patient records in AWS can use Direct Connect to ensure HIPAA-compliant secure access without exposing data to the public internet.

Low-Latency Access for Latency-Sensitive Applications

Applications that rely on real-time processing and minimal latency—such as high-frequency trading, VoIP services, or gaming platforms—need a predictable and optimized network connection. AWS Direct Connect ensures:

- Ultra-low-latency access to AWS services.
- Reduced packet loss and jitter, improving application performance.
- Seamless user experience for globally distributed applications.

Example: An online multiplayer gaming company requiring sub-10ms latency for its game servers can use Direct Connect to maintain a stable and lag-free experience for players worldwide.

Multi-Region AWS Deployments with Direct Connect Gateway

Enterprises operating in multiple AWS regions often need to connect their on-premises networks to multiple VPCs across different regions. AWS Direct Connect Gateway provides:

- Single Direct Connect link to connect multiple AWS regions.
- Reduced operational complexity by consolidating network architecture.
- Efficient workload distribution across AWS environments.

Example: A multinational corporation with AWS workloads in North America, Europe, and Asia can use Direct Connect Gateway to connect all regions with a single high-speed connection instead of managing multiple VPN tunnels.

AWS Direct Connect is the ideal solution for organizations requiring high-performance, secure, and cost-efficient connectivity to AWS. Whether for hybrid cloud deployments, large-scale data transfers, regulatory compliance, low-latency applications, or multi-region connectivity, Direct Connect provides significant advantages over standard internet-based VPNs. Understanding when to use Direct Connect helps businesses make strategic networking decisions to enhance their cloud operations effectively.

Key Benefits of AWS Direct Connect

As organizations increasingly adopt cloud-first and hybrid cloud strategies, reliable network connectivity becomes a crucial factor in ensuring seamless operations. AWS Direct Connect offers a dedicated, private network connection between the on-premises infrastructure and AWS of an organization, providing significant advantages over traditional internet-based connections. This section explores the key benefits of AWS Direct Connect, highlighting how it enhances performance, security, and cost efficiency for businesses with demanding network requirements.

High-Performance and Low-Latency Connectivity

One of the primary advantages of AWS Direct Connect is its ability to provide low-latency, high-bandwidth network connections to AWS services. Unlike traditional VPNs that rely on the unpredictability of public internet traffic, Direct Connect offers:

- Consistent and predictable performance for mission-critical applications.
- Lower network latency, ensuring faster response times for real-time applications.
- Reduced packet loss, making it ideal for high-speed data transfers, live video streaming, and financial transactions.

Example: A financial institution using Direct Connect for high-frequency trading benefits from sub-millisecond latency, ensuring faster order execution.

Reduced Data Transfer Costs

AWS Direct Connect helps organizations lower their overall cloud networking costs by providing dedicated pricing for data transfer. Compared to standard internet-based data transfers, Direct Connect:

- Reduces outbound data transfer charges significantly.
- Provides predictable pricing for network traffic.
- Enables cost-effective high-volume data transfers, which is especially beneficial for media, healthcare, and big data applications.

Example: A video streaming platform transferring petabytes of content between AWS S3 and its on-premises data center can reduce data transfer costs by using Direct Connect instead of a standard internet connection.

Enhanced Security and Compliance

Security is a major concern for organizations handling sensitive or regulated data. AWS Direct Connect enhances security by:

- Bypassing the public internet, reducing exposure to cyber threats such as DDoS attacks and data breaches.
- Providing private, dedicated connections that offer better data integrity and confidentiality.

- Helping meet compliance standards such as HIPAA (healthcare), PCI DSS (financial services), and FedRAMP (government).

Example: A healthcare organization can use AWS Direct Connect to securely transfer Electronic Health Records (EHRs) between AWS and its on-premises data centers while ensuring HIPAA compliance.

Reliable and Scalable Network Infrastructure

AWS Direct Connect is designed to scale with business needs, offering:

- Multiple connection speeds, ranging from 50 Mbps to 100 Gbps, to accommodate different workloads.
- Dedicated network paths that improve connection stability.
- Resilience through redundant connections, ensuring high availability.

Example: A multinational corporation can deploy multiple Direct Connect links to increase redundancy and failover protection, maintaining business continuity even in case of a network failure.

Seamless Hybrid Cloud Integration

For businesses operating in a hybrid cloud environment, AWS Direct Connect enables seamless connectivity between on-premises infrastructure and AWS services. It supports:

- Hybrid cloud architectures by integrating on-premises workloads with AWS.
- Direct access to AWS services such as Amazon EC2, S3, RDS, and VPCs.
- Integration with Direct Connect Gateway, allowing access to multiple AWS regions from a single connection.

Example: A global enterprise running data analytics workloads on AWS while storing proprietary data on-premises can use Direct Connect for high-speed, secure access between both environments.

AWS Direct Connect offers numerous benefits that make it an ideal solution for businesses requiring high-performance, secure, and cost-efficient cloud connectivity. Its ability to reduce latency, lower data transfer costs, enhance security, ensure reliability, and support hybrid cloud integration makes it a preferred choice for enterprises with mission-critical workloads. By leveraging Direct Connect, organizations can streamline cloud operations, enhance user experiences, and achieve greater efficiency in cloud networking.

Provisioning a Direct Connect Connection and Virtual Interfaces

Setting up AWS Direct Connect involves more than just establishing a physical connection—it requires careful provisioning of Virtual Interfaces (VIFs) to ensure seamless and secure data transfer between an on-premises network and AWS. A well-provisioned Direct Connect connection enhances network performance, security, and reliability by enabling organizations to efficiently route their traffic based on workload requirements.

This section provides a step-by-step approach to provisioning AWS Direct Connect, explaining the different types of VIFs, how they function, and the best practices for ensuring an optimized configuration.

Setting up a Direct Connect Connection

Setting up a Direct Connect connection involves establishing a dedicated, private network link between your on-premises data center and AWS. This provides lower latency, higher bandwidth, and more consistent network performance compared to public internet connections.

1. **Choosing the Right Direct Connect Location**

   AWS Direct Connect is available through AWS Direct Connect locations, which serve as network access points for establishing private connectivity. Organizations must:

   a. Select the closest AWS Direct Connect location to minimize latency.

   b. Determine whether to establish a dedicated or hosted connection based on bandwidth needs.

   c. Work with AWS Direct Connect partners if they do not have direct access to AWS locations.

   Example: A business headquartered in London should select an AWS Direct Connect location within the same geographical region to reduce latency and optimize performance.

2. **Ordering and Establishing the Physical Connection**

   Once an AWS Direct Connect location is selected, the next step is to order a Direct Connect connection via the AWS Management Console. This involves:

   a. Specifying the port speed (ranging from 50 Mbps to 100 Gbps).

   b. Requesting a Letter of Authorization and Connecting Facility Assignment (LOA-CFA) from AWS to initiate the connection.

   c. Working with a network provider to establish a physical fiber connection between the on-premises data center and the AWS Direct Connect location.

   Best Practice: Ensure that the on-premises network equipment (routers and switches) supports the bandwidth and redundancy requirements before proceeding with the physical setup.

3. **Testing the Physical Link**

   Before configuring virtual interfaces, it is essential to validate the physical connectivity by:

   a. Conducting loopback tests to confirm signal integrity.

   b. Checking for proper link light status on network equipment.

   c. Ensuring that the network provider has completed all necessary configurations.

   Once the physical connection is operational, the next step is to configure VIFs for routing traffic.

Configuring Virtual Interfaces (VIFs)

Configuring Virtual Interfaces (VIFs) involves setting up logical connections on an AWS Direct Connect link to route network traffic between your on-premises environment and AWS. VIFs enable dedicated paths for either public AWS services or private VPC resources, ensuring secure and efficient data transfer.

Understanding Virtual Interfaces (VIFs)

Virtual interfaces (VIFs) determine how traffic flows between AWS and an on-premises network. AWS Direct Connect supports three types of VIFs:

- **Private VIF:** Used for accessing AWS resources inside a Virtual Private Cloud (VPC), such as EC2 instances, RDS databases, and private subnets.
- **Public VIF:** Enables direct access to AWS public services such as Amazon S3, DynamoDB, and CloudFront over a dedicated network path.

- **Transit VIF:** Used in conjunction with AWS Transit Gateway to establish connectivity across multiple VPCs and AWS Regions.

Example: A business needing private connectivity to its AWS-hosted applications would configure a Private VIF, while a content delivery company accessing Amazon S3 would use a Public VIF.

Creating a Virtual Interface in AWS

To create a VIF, follow these steps in the AWS Management Console:

1. Navigate to **`AWS Direct Connect`** > **`Virtual Interfaces`** > **`Create Virtual Interface`**.
2. Select the appropriate VIF type (Private, Public, or Transit).
3. Choose the Direct Connect connection to associate with the VIF.
4. Configure the BGP (Border Gateway Protocol) settings to establish dynamic routing.
5. Specify the VLAN ID (for Private and Transit VIFs) to segregate traffic.
6. Assign an AWS-side and customer-side IP address for the interface.
7. Confirm and create the VIF, then associate it with the appropriate AWS resources.

Best Practice: Use multiple VIFs to segment traffic based on security, compliance, and performance needs, ensuring optimal routing and load balancing.

Validating and Optimizing the Connection

Testing the Virtual Interface Configuration

Once the virtual interface is configured, it is critical to verify connectivity and routing behavior by:

- Checking BGP session status to confirm active peering between AWS and the on-premises router.

  BGP Validation

  ```
  show ip bgp summary
  ```

- Performing latency tests to measure network performance.

  Connectivity Test

  ```
  ping 10.0.1.10
  ```

- Ensuring data transfer works correctly based on predefined routing policies.

  Routing Path Verification

  Linux / macOS

  ```
  traceroute 10.0.1.10
  ```

  Windows

  ```
  tracert 10.0.1.10
  ```

Optimizing Performance and Redundancy

To improve reliability and efficiency:

- Deploy multiple Direct Connect connections for high availability and failover support.
- Use AWS Direct Connect Gateway to enable connectivity across multiple AWS regions.
- Implement network monitoring tools to proactively detect performance issues.

Provisioning a Direct Connect connection and virtual interfaces is a critical step in establishing a reliable, high-performance, and secure network link to AWS. By following the best practices for VIF configuration, testing, and optimization, organizations can enhance connectivity, reduce latency, and streamline hybrid cloud operations.

Direct Connect Redundancy and High-Availability Considerations

While AWS Direct Connect provides a dedicated, high-bandwidth connection between on-premises environments and AWS, ensuring redundancy and high availability is critical to maintaining continuous, fault-tolerant connectivity. Without proper redundancy strategies, a failure in the physical connection or misconfigured routing policies can lead to downtime, increased latency, or complete service disruption.

This section explores the best practices for implementing redundancy, ensuring fault tolerance, and leveraging AWS services to maximize availability and network resilience when using Direct Connect.

Designing a Redundant Direct Connect Architecture

Designing a redundant Direct Connect architecture involves establishing multiple AWS Direct Connect connections across different locations or devices to ensure continuous network availability. This setup helps eliminate single points of failure and provides high availability and failover capabilities for critical workloads.

The Need for Redundancy

AWS Direct Connect relies on physical network links, making it susceptible to failures caused by:

- Hardware malfunctions in network devices or fiber optics.
- Link failures due to provider outages.
- Congestion or routing issues affecting performance.
- Human errors in configuration or maintenance.

To mitigate these risks, businesses must design redundant Direct Connect connections that can seamlessly take over in case of failures.

Single versus Multiple Direct Connect Connections

AWS recommends at least two independent Direct Connect connections for critical workloads. Organizations can choose from:

- **Single Direct Connect (No Redundancy):** Risky, as any failure results in complete downtime.
- **Multiple Direct Connects in the Same Location:** Improves reliability but is vulnerable to regional outages.
- **Multiple Direct Connects in Different Locations:** Best for disaster recovery and maximum uptime.

Best Practice: For mission-critical applications, deploy Direct Connect connections in at least two geographically separated AWS locations to ensure resilience.

Leveraging Virtual Interfaces (VIFs) for High Availability

Using multiple Virtual Interfaces (VIFs) allows organizations to optimize traffic flow across redundant connections:

- **Active/Passive Setup:** One Direct Connect remains primary, while the other acts as a backup.

  Routing policies used:

  - **BGP Local Preference**

    Assign a higher local preference to routes learned via the primary Direct Connect link.

  - **AS Path Prepending**

    Prepend the on-premises ASN multiple times on the backup link to make it less preferred.

  Outcome: Traffic normally flows through the primary link and automatically shifts to the secondary link during failures.

- **Active/Active Setup:** Both Direct Connects share traffic load, providing higher bandwidth and load balancing.

  Routing policies used:

  - **Equal BGP Local Preference**

    Advertise routes with the same local preference on both links.

  - **Minimal AS Path Length**

    Avoid AS path prepending to allow equal-cost path selection.

  - **ECMP (Equal-Cost Multi-Path)**

    Enables load sharing across both Direct Connect connections where supported.

  Outcome: Traffic is dynamically distributed across both links, providing load balancing and resiliency.

- **AWS Direct Connect Gateway:** Enables multi-region connectivity, allowing traffic to route through the most optimal Direct Connect link.

  Routing optimization techniques:

  - Advertise region-specific prefixes to control traffic locality.
  - Use BGP attributes to prefer the geographically closest Direct Connect location.
  - Apply selective route propagation to prevent unnecessary cross-region traffic.

  Outcome: Traffic is routed through the most optimal Direct Connect link based on region and policy.

Example: A financial institution using Active/Active Direct Connect links ensures uninterrupted trading operations by dynamically distributing network traffic.

Configuring Backup Connectivity with VPN Failover

Configuring Backup Connectivity with VPN Failover involves setting up a secondary VPN connection that automatically activates if the primary VPN fails. This ensures continuous secure connectivity between on-premises infrastructure and AWS, minimizing downtime during network disruptions.

Using AWS Site-to-Site VPN as a Backup

In the event of a Direct Connect failure, an AWS Site-to-Site VPN can serve as a backup to ensure continuous network availability. This involves:

- Establishing an IPsec VPN connection between the on-premises data center and AWS.
- Configuring automatic failover using BGP (Border Gateway Protocol).
- Ensuring VPN routes have higher AS path costs than Direct Connect routes, so they are used only when Direct Connect is down.

Best Practice: A well-configured AWS VPN failover provides automatic recovery during Direct Connect disruptions, ensuring business continuity.

Implementing BGP Routing for Seamless Failover

BGP enables dynamic routing adjustments by:

- Detecting Direct Connect failures and switching traffic to the VPN backup.
- Prioritizing Direct Connect routes with a lower BGP preference to ensure VPN is only used as a last resort.
- Preventing routing loops by correctly advertising prefixes and AS path lengths.

Example: A global e-commerce platform uses BGP failover policies to ensure customers can always access their website, even if a Direct Connect link goes down.

Monitoring and Optimizing Direct Connect Availability

Monitoring and Optimizing Direct Connect Availability refers to the continuous tracking of AWS Direct Connect connections to ensure high uptime and performance. It involves using tools like CloudWatch and Network Manager to detect issues, balance traffic, and implement failover strategies for reliable connectivity between on-premises infrastructure and AWS.

AWS Direct Connect Resiliency Toolkit

AWS provides built-in monitoring tools for ensuring Direct Connect uptime and performance:

- **AWS CloudWatch:** Tracks metrics such as latency, packet loss, and link health.
- **AWS Direct Connect Resiliency Toolkit:** Automates failover testing and connection validation.
- **AWS Trusted Advisor:** Offers recommendations for high availability and redundancy improvements.

Best Practice: Configure CloudWatch alarms for early detection of latency spikes or degraded performance in Direct Connect connections.

- **Periodic Failover Testing**

  Even with redundancy, regular failover testing ensures systems can switch seamlessly when failures occur. Recommended best practices include:

  - Simulating Direct Connect outages to verify failover mechanisms.
  - Testing BGP route propagation to confirm automatic switching between primary and backup paths.
  - Validating VPN backup configurations to ensure uninterrupted access.

- **Quarterly Failover Testing Checklist**
  - Simulate Direct Connect Outage
    - Disable the primary Direct Connect interface or virtual interface (VIF).
    - Confirm traffic stops flowing through the primary path.
    - Verify no manual intervention is required to trigger failover.
  - Validate BGP Route Switching
    - Confirm BGP sessions on the primary link move to an Idle or Down state.
    - Verify routes are withdrawn from the primary path.
    - Ensure backup Direct Connect or VPN routes are automatically preferred.
    - Check BGP attributes (local preference / AS path) behave as expected.

  - Confirm VPN Backup Routing
    - Verify Site-to-Site VPN tunnels transition to UP and become active.
    - Confirm route tables prefer VPN paths when Direct Connect is unavailable.
    - Validate latency and throughput remain within acceptable thresholds.
- Application-Level Validation
  - Test access to critical applications and databases.
  - Confirm no session drops for stateful workloads where possible.
  - Validate logging and monitoring capture the failover event.
- Restore Primary Connectivity
  - Re-enable the primary Direct Connect link.
  - Confirm traffic returns to the preferred path.
  - Verify BGP convergence time meets operational SLAs.

Example: A healthcare provider performs quarterly Direct Connect failover testing by simulating link failures, validating BGP route convergence, and confirming VPN backup connectivity. This proactive approach ensures uninterrupted access to patient data and compliance with availability and reliability requirements.

Optimizing Network Performance for Redundancy

To further enhance reliability and performance in hybrid network architectures, organizations should adopt the following optimization strategies:

- **Use Jumbo Frames (9001 MTU)**

  Enable jumbo frames on Direct Connect interfaces to reduce packet fragmentation and improve throughput for large data transfers.

- **Deploy Multiple Virtual Interfaces (VIFs)**

  Use multiple VIFs to separate traffic types (for example, production, backup, and management), enabling optimized routing, better fault isolation, and granular traffic control.

- **Implement Direct Connect Gateway for Multi-Region High Availability**

  Leverage Direct Connect Gateway to extend a single Direct Connect connection across multiple AWS regions, improving resilience and simplifying multi-region architectures.

Performance Monitoring and Analytics

Continuous visibility into network behavior is essential for maintaining optimal performance and redundancy. Organizations can use native AWS services such as AWS Network Manager to gain centralized visibility into global network health, monitor routing changes, and identify connectivity issues across Direct Connect, VPN, and VPC resources.

For deeper performance analytics, path visualization, and user-experience monitoring, third-party tools such as ThousandEyes or SolarWinds can be integrated to detect latency spikes, packet loss, and routing anomalies across hybrid and internet paths.

Best Practice

Continuously analyze network traffic patterns using AWS-native and third-party monitoring tools, and proactively adjust routing policies (such as BGP local preference and AS path prepending) to maintain optimal performance, resilience, and predictable failover behavior.

Troubleshooting VPN Issues

In hybrid cloud architectures, Virtual Private Network (VPN) connections play a crucial role in ensuring secure and seamless communication between on-premises networks and AWS environments. However, VPNs are prone to issues such as connectivity failures, high latency, misconfigurations, and performance bottlenecks, which can disrupt business operations and degrade user experience.

To maintain a stable and high-performing VPN connection, it is essential to identify, diagnose, and resolve common problems efficiently. This section provides a comprehensive approach to troubleshooting VPN issues, covering network connectivity problems, latency concerns, and common misconfigurations. By following best practices and using AWS-provided monitoring tools, organizations can ensure optimal VPN reliability and performance.

Diagnosing Common Site-to-Site and Client VPN Issues

VPN connections serve as a critical link between on-premises networks and AWS environments, facilitating secure data transmission and remote access to cloud resources. However, network disruptions, configuration errors, or performance bottlenecks can impact VPN availability and efficiency. Identifying the root cause of issues requires a structured troubleshooting approach that includes analyzing logs, verifying configurations, and testing network connectivity.

Step 1: Check connectivity

Step 2: Logs

Step 3: Configuration

Step 4: Authentication

This section covers common VPN-related problems and provides guidance on diagnosing them effectively. Whether dealing with a Site-to-Site VPN or an AWS Client VPN, understanding the primary causes of failures can help organizations quickly restore connectivity and maintain a secure network.

Site-to-Site VPN Connectivity Issues

Understanding common connectivity challenges in AWS Site-to-Site VPNs is crucial for ensuring reliable hybrid cloud operations. Some of the frequent connectivity problems include:

- **Phase 1 and Phase 2 Negotiation Failures:** Misconfigured encryption settings or mismatched policies between AWS and the on-premises VPN gateway can prevent successful VPN establishment.
- **Incorrect Security Group or NACL Rules:** If AWS security groups or network ACLs block VPN traffic, it can result in dropped connections.
- **ISP or Network Provider Issues:** External factors such as ISP outages or bandwidth limitations can impact VPN stability.
- **Routing Configuration Errors:** If the correct static or dynamic routes are not configured in AWS or on-premises devices, VPN traffic might not flow correctly.

Diagnosing these issues involves analyzing VPN logs, checking route tables, and verifying encryption parameters to ensure both sides of the connection align properly.

Client VPN Access Problems

AWS Client VPN allows remote users to securely connect to AWS resources, but several factors can disrupt access. Common issues include:

- **Authentication Failures:** Users may experience login issues due to incorrect credentials, misconfigured IAM policies, or authentication server problems.
- **IP Address Assignment Conflicts:** Overlapping IP ranges or incorrect CIDR block allocations can prevent clients from connecting successfully.
- **Certificate and TLS Configuration Errors:** If TLS certificates are expired or improperly configured, the VPN handshake process can fail.
- **DNS Resolution Issues:** Clients may connect but fail to reach AWS services due to misconfigured DNS settings.

To diagnose Client VPN problems, it is essential to review CloudWatch logs, check identity provider settings, and verify client-side configurations.

High Latency and Packet Loss in VPN Connections

Even when a VPN connection is established, slow performance or intermittent packet loss can significantly affect productivity. Causes of latency and packet loss include:

- **Congested Network Paths:** High traffic loads or suboptimal routing between AWS and the on-premises network can introduce latency.
- **MTU (Maximum Transmission Unit) Mismatches:** If MTU settings are not optimized, packet fragmentation and retransmissions can degrade performance.
- **Inefficient Routing Policies:** Misconfigured BGP (Border Gateway Protocol) settings or improper route prioritization can cause delays in data transmission.
- **Encryption Overhead:** While encryption enhances security, improper cipher suite configurations can add processing delays.

Troubleshooting latency requires packet analysis, route optimization, and network performance monitoring using AWS tools like VPC Flow Logs and CloudWatch metrics.

By following structured diagnostic techniques, organizations can resolve VPN connectivity and performance issues efficiently, ensuring seamless hybrid cloud operations.

Resolving AWS Direct Connect Performance and Routing Challenges

AWS Direct Connect offers a dedicated, high-bandwidth connection between on-premises data centers and AWS, reducing reliance on the public internet. However, organizations using Direct Connect may encounter performance bottlenecks, suboptimal routing configurations, and connectivity issues that impact network efficiency. Addressing these challenges requires careful analysis of network paths, bandwidth allocation, and routing policies to ensure smooth and high-performing data transfer.

This section provides practical strategies for diagnosing and resolving Direct Connect performance issues, focusing on latency reduction, efficient routing, and optimizing network throughput.

Diagnosing Bandwidth and Throughput Issues

Even with a dedicated link, bandwidth limitations and unexpected traffic bottlenecks can degrade performance. Common causes include:

- **Oversubscription of the Direct Connect Link:** If network traffic exceeds the provisioned bandwidth, packet loss and high latency can occur.
- **Congestion in the Network of the Customer:** Bottlenecks on the enterprise side, such as poor internal network design or firewall limitations, can impact throughput.

- **Suboptimal TCP Window Sizes:** Inefficient TCP configurations may restrict data flow, especially for long-distance Direct Connect links.

Resolution Strategies

- Use AWS CloudWatch and NetFlow analytics to monitor traffic patterns and identify congestion points.
- Adjust TCP window scaling settings for long-distance data transfers.
- Consider provisioning multiple Direct Connect connections or using Link Aggregation Groups (LAG) for increased capacity.

Troubleshooting Latency and Packet Loss

Latency-sensitive applications require consistent network performance, but issues like packet loss and fluctuating latency can disrupt operations. Common reasons for these problems include:

- **Suboptimal Peering Points:** Traffic may take inefficient routes, increasing round-trip times.
- **Jitter and Packet Reordering:** Variability in packet arrival times can cause application instability.
- **Encryption Overhead in Hybrid Setups:** Using IPsec VPN over Direct Connect for security can introduce additional latency.

Resolution Strategies

- Perform traceroutes and latency tests to pinpoint delays along the network path.
- Optimize BGP route advertisements to ensure Direct Connect is the preferred route.
- Evaluate whether encryption is necessary and, if so, use optimized cryptographic settings to minimize overhead.

Addressing Routing Misconfigurations

Routing issues can disrupt traffic flow between AWS and on-premises environments, leading to intermittent connectivity or inefficient path selection. Some frequent routing misconfigurations include:

- **Asymmetric Routing:** Traffic flows through Direct Connect in one direction but returns via the internet, causing latency spikes and security concerns.
- **Incorrect BGP Path Selection:** Improper BGP weight and local preference settings can result in suboptimal route choices.
- **Misconfigured Route Tables and VPC Associations:** Missing or incorrect route entries in AWS VPC route tables can prevent Direct Connect traffic from reaching its intended destination.

Resolution Strategies

- Use BGP attributes (such as AS path prepending and local preference) to control route selection.
- Verify that on-premises and AWS routing policies align, avoiding asymmetric paths.
- Regularly review VPC route tables and Direct Connect gateway configurations to ensure consistency.

AWS Direct Connect provides a high-speed, low-latency network link to AWS, but performance and routing challenges can arise without proper configuration. By diagnosing bandwidth issues, optimizing routing policies, and minimizing latency, organizations can ensure seamless and efficient hybrid cloud connectivity.

Best Practices for Monitoring and Maintaining Hybrid Network Connectivity

In hybrid cloud architecture, ensuring consistent network performance and security is critical for seamless operations between on-premises infrastructure and AWS. Proactive monitoring and maintenance help identify issues early, optimize connectivity, and prevent downtime. Without proper visibility, problems such as latency spikes, bandwidth saturation, and misconfigurations can degrade application performance.

This section outlines the best practices for monitoring hybrid network environments, leveraging AWS-native tools and industry standards to maintain high availability, security, and optimal performance in Site-to-Site VPN and Direct Connect setups.

Implementing Comprehensive Network Monitoring

To maintain a stable hybrid network, organizations must deploy real-time monitoring solutions that track network health, traffic patterns, and potential bottlenecks. Key considerations include:

- **End-to-End Visibility:** Monitoring both AWS and on-premises network components ensure a complete understanding of latency, packet loss, and jitter.
- **Traffic Pattern Analysis:** Identifying unexpected traffic spikes or congestion helps in proactive bandwidth adjustments.
- **Anomaly Detection:** Using AI-driven analytics or machine learning to spot deviations from normal network behavior.

Recommended Tools

- **AWS CloudWatch:** Monitors VPN and Direct Connect metrics such as tunnel status, throughput, and packet drops. For example: latency > 150 ms triggers CloudWatch alarm.
- **AWS CloudTrail:** Tracks network configuration changes and detects unauthorized modifications.
- **VPC Flow Logs:** Captures IP traffic flow, helping diagnose connectivity and security issues.
- **Third-Party NMS (Network Monitoring Systems):** Tools like Nagios, Zabbix, and SolarWinds provide deeper insights into network health.

Ensuring High Availability and Redundancy

Network failures can disrupt business operations, making redundancy and failover strategies essential for maintaining connectivity. Key considerations include:

- **Multiple VPN Tunnels:** Deploying redundant Site-to-Site VPN connections across different AWS Regions and Availability Zones enhances fault tolerance.
- **Direct Connect Failover Planning:** Using multiple Direct Connect links or combining Direct Connect with VPN as a backup ensures resilient connectivity.
- **Automated Failover Mechanisms:** Leveraging AWS Route 53, BGP failover settings, and health checks for automatic route switching during failures.

Best Practices

- Implement Diverse ISP Connections: Ensures failover paths in case of a provider outage.
- Configure BGP Multi-Path Routing: Allows load balancing across multiple Direct Connect links.

- Enable Cloud WAN or Transit Gateway: Simplifies multi-region and multi-account networking for hybrid architectures.

Security Hardening for Hybrid Cloud Connectivity

Securing hybrid network connections prevents data breaches, unauthorized access, and traffic interception. Organizations must enforce strong encryption, strict access controls, and continuous security monitoring.

Key Security Measures

- **Use Strong Encryption:** VPN tunnels should use AES-256 encryption with SHA-2 hashing for data protection.
- **Implement Role-Based Access Control (RBAC):** Restrict access to Direct Connect and VPN configurations based on least privilege principles.
- **Enable AWS Shield and AWS WAF:** Protects against DDoS attacks and malicious traffic.
- **Rotate BGP Authentication Keys:** Regularly updating BGP session keys enhances routing security.

Monitoring Security Logs

- **AWS Security Hub:** Provides a unified security posture with automated compliance checks.
- **Amazon GuardDuty:** Detects suspicious network activity in VPN and Direct Connect traffic.
- **AWS Config:** Monitors changes in VPC route tables, VPN configurations, and Direct Connect settings for compliance.

Maintaining hybrid network connectivity requires a combination of real-time monitoring, redundancy planning, and robust security measures. By leveraging AWS-native tools and industry best practices, organizations can ensure high availability, optimal performance, and a secure hybrid cloud infrastructure. Regular audits, proactive issue resolution, and continuous network optimization are the key to a resilient hybrid networking strategy.

Case Studies

As organizations increasingly adopt hybrid cloud architectures, the need for secure, reliable, and high-performance connectivity between on-premises environments and AWS cloud resources becomes critical. AWS provides multiple networking solutions, including Site-to-Site VPN, Client VPN, and Direct Connect, to enable seamless integration while maintaining security, compliance, and scalability. However, implementing these solutions effectively requires a deep understanding of configuration best practices, security policies, and troubleshooting methodologies.

The following case studies illustrate practical implementations of AWS networking solutions across various industries, showcasing how organizations have leveraged AWS VPNs and Direct Connect to overcome challenges related to latency, security, scalability, and performance. These real-world scenarios provide insights into best practices, problem-solving approaches, and key considerations for designing robust hybrid cloud networks.

Case Study 1: Implementing a Site-to-Site VPN for a Global Logistics Company

Objective: Securely extend the on-premises network of the company to AWS for real-time shipment tracking and analytics.

Challenges

- The company operated multiple data centers worldwide but needed a secure and cost-effective way to connect them to AWS.
- Intermittent connectivity issues between regional offices caused delays in data synchronization.
- Compliance requirements mandated encrypted communications for sensitive shipment data.

Solution

- AWS Site-to-Site VPN was deployed to establish secure tunnels between data centers and AWS VPCs.
- AWS Transit Gateway was configured to manage multiple VPN connections efficiently.
- CloudWatch Logs and VPC Flow Logs were used to monitor traffic patterns and diagnose connection drops.

Results

- Improved data consistency and real-time tracking across all logistics hubs.
- Reduced latency by 35% through optimized routing and BGP configurations.
- Met compliance requirements by encrypting data in transit using AES-256.

Case Study 2: Deploying AWS Client VPN for a Remote Workforce in a Financial Institution

Objective: Enable secure remote access to AWS-hosted financial applications for a distributed workforce.

Challenges

- Employees and third-party vendors required secure access to AWS resources from different geographic locations.
- The company had strict compliance and security policies, requiring Multi-Factor Authentication (MFA) and IP-based access restrictions.
- Scaling issues with legacy VPN solutions caused slow access speeds for remote users.

Solution

- AWS Client VPN was deployed with Active Directory-based authentication to enforce access policies.
- MFA and AWS Identity and Access Management (IAM) policies were implemented to enhance security.
- Split tunneling was enabled to optimize bandwidth usage for remote employees.
- AWS WAF and GuardDuty were configured to monitor for unusual login attempts and potential security threats.

Results

- 100% compliance with financial data security regulations.
- Seamless remote access with improved authentication security.
- 20% faster VPN connection speeds due to the scalable infrastructure of AWS.

Case Study 3: AWS Direct Connect for a High-Traffic E-Commerce Platform

Objective: Improve network reliability and performance for an e-commerce platform experiencing high traffic spikes during sales events.

Challenges

- VPN-based connectivity was causing high latency and inconsistent performance.
- Traffic surges during major sales events resulted in network congestion.
- AWS-hosted databases needed a low-latency, dedicated connection to on-premises data centers.

Solution

- AWS Direct Connect was provisioned to establish a private, high-bandwidth link between on-premises data centers and AWS.
- Multiple Direct Connect links were deployed with BGP failover mechanisms to ensure redundancy.
- CloudWatch monitoring was set up to track network performance and proactively address bottlenecks.

Results

- 50% reduction in latency, significantly improving customer experience during peak traffic.
- 99.99% uptime with redundant Direct Connect links.
- Secure and fast data transfer, reducing reliance on public internet connections.

Case Study 4: Troubleshooting VPN and Direct Connect Issues in a Hybrid Cloud Architecture

Objective: Resolve connectivity, latency, and misconfiguration issues affecting a multi-region hybrid cloud setup.

Challenges

- Site-to-Site VPN connections were frequently dropping due to incorrect MTU settings.
- Direct Connect link was experiencing asymmetric routing issues, causing packet loss and high latency.
- Security logs indicated potential unauthorized access attempts via VPN.

Solution

- Packet capture and VPC Flow Logs identified MTU mismatches, which were corrected to ensure stable VPN tunnels.
- BGP route optimization was implemented to eliminate asymmetric routing in Direct Connect.
- AWS Security Hub and GuardDuty were used to detect and block unauthorized VPN login attempts.

Results

- Stable VPN connectivity with 99.9% uptime after MTU adjustments.
- 40% lower latency through Direct Connect route optimization.
- Enhanced security posture, preventing unauthorized access attempts.

Key AWS Metrics and Logs Used for Monitoring

VPN Monitoring

- CloudWatch metrics:
  - TunnelState
  - TunnelDataIn
  - TunnelDataOut
- CloudWatch Logs:
  - Client VPN connection logs
  - Site-to-Site VPN tunnel status logs

Traffic and MTU Validation

- VPC Flow Logs fields:
  - srcaddr, dstaddr
  - packets, bytes
  - action (ACCEPT / REJECT)
- Used to identify fragmentation patterns and dropped packets

Direct Connect Monitoring

- CloudWatch metrics:
  - ConnectionState
  - VirtualInterfaceState
  - BGPStatus
  - PacketDropCount
- Router-side BGP logs for convergence and flap detection

Security Monitoring

- GuardDuty findings:
  - UnauthorizedAccess:EC2/VPN
  - Credential reconnaissance alerts
- Security Hub aggregated findings across accounts and regions

These case studies demonstrate how AWS Site-to-Site VPN, Client VPN, and Direct Connect can be used to create secure, high-performance hybrid cloud architectures. By leveraging AWS-native tools for monitoring, security, and automation, organizations can ensure scalable, reliable, and optimized network connectivity.

In the next section, we will summarize the key takeaways from our exploration of VPNs, its features and best practices.

Conclusion

This chapter explored the essential components of hybrid cloud networking using AWS Site-to-Site VPN, Client VPN, and Direct Connect. These services enable organizations to establish secure, high-performance connectivity between their on-premises infrastructure and AWS cloud resources. By understanding configuration, security best practices, redundancy strategies, and troubleshooting techniques, businesses can ensure seamless, resilient, and scalable network integration. A well-architected hybrid network enhances performance, reduces costs, and strengthens security, making it a crucial element in cloud adoption.

In the next chapter, we shall look into how we shall optimize AWS networks for performance and cost that include reducing latency, managing bandwidth, and using tools like Cost Explorer for monitoring.

Points to Remember

- Site-to-Site VPN provides secure encrypted tunnels between on-premises data centers and AWS, ensuring data confidentiality and integrity.
- Client VPN allows remote users to securely access AWS resources, with flexible authentication and authorization mechanisms.
- AWS Direct Connect offers low-latency, high-bandwidth dedicated connections, reducing network congestion and improving performance for hybrid architectures.
- Redundancy and high availability are critical for ensuring continuous connectivity—leveraging multiple VPN tunnels or Direct Connect connections prevents disruptions.
- Effective troubleshooting of VPN and Direct Connect issues involves diagnosing latency, misconfigurations, and routing problems using AWS monitoring tools.
- Security best practices, such as encryption, multi-factor authentication, and access control policies, help protect network traffic and prevent unauthorized access.
- Hybrid cloud connectivity must be continuously monitored using AWS tools like CloudWatch, VPC Flow Logs, and AWS Network Manager to maintain optimal performance and security.

By implementing these best practices and strategies, organizations can build robust, scalable, and secure hybrid cloud networks that align with business goals and compliance requirements.

CHAPTER 10
Network Optimization Techniques

Introduction

As businesses scale their cloud infrastructure, optimizing network performance and cost becomes essential for efficient operations. AWS offers a range of network optimization techniques to improve latency, bandwidth management, and cost control, ensuring a high-performing and cost-effective environment. Organizations must balance performance and expenses by strategically monitoring network usage, managing bandwidth allocation, and prioritizing critical traffic.

This chapter explores the key strategies for network optimization in AWS, including bandwidth management, latency reduction, traffic shaping, and cost monitoring. Readers will learn how to identify network bottlenecks, implement performance-enhancing solutions, and leverage AWS tools like Cost Explorer and Budgets to maintain cost efficiency while ensuring seamless connectivity.

Structure

In this chapter, we will walk through:

- Bandwidth Management
- Latency Optimization
- Traffic Shaping Techniques
- Cost Monitoring
- Case Studies

Bandwidth Management

Efficient bandwidth management is a critical component of optimizing network performance in AWS environments. As cloud workloads grow, businesses must ensure that available network bandwidth is effectively monitored, allocated, and optimized to prevent congestion, reduce costs, and maintain high availability for mission-critical applications. Without proper bandwidth management, networks can experience bottlenecks, increased latency, and unpredictable costs, leading to degraded application performance.

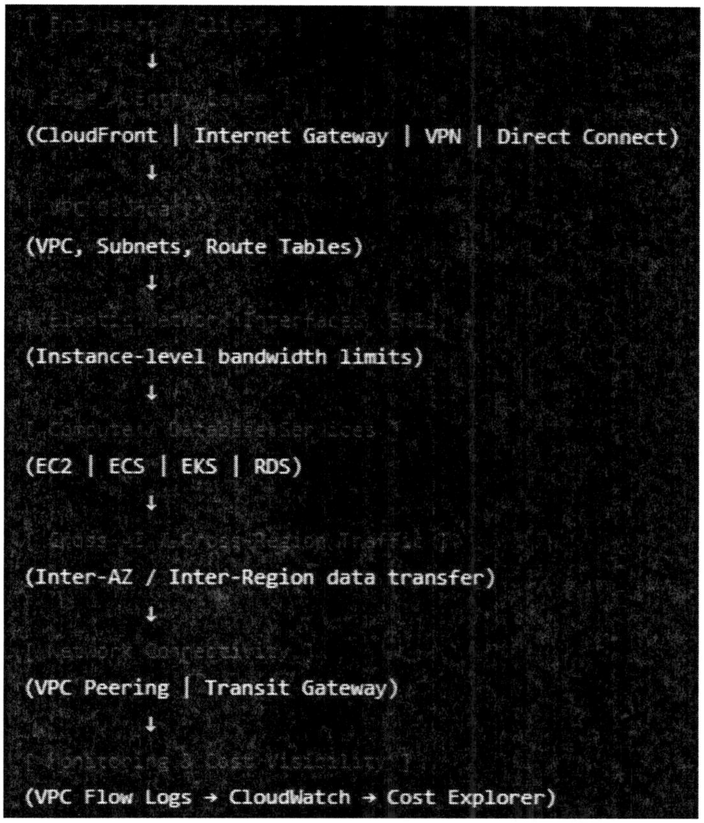

```
        ↓
(CloudFront | Internet Gateway | VPN | Direct Connect)
        ↓
(VPC, Subnets, Route Tables)
        ↓
(Instance-level bandwidth limits)
        ↓
(EC2 | ECS | EKS | RDS)
        ↓
(Inter-AZ / Inter-Region data transfer)
        ↓
(VPC Peering | Transit Gateway)
        ↓
(VPC Flow Logs → CloudWatch → Cost Explorer)
```

Figure 10.1: *Bandwidth Monitoring and Optimization Flow*

This section explores key strategies for monitoring and allocating bandwidth across AWS services. Readers will learn how to identify bandwidth usage patterns, detect potential congestion points, and implement AWS tools to maintain a balanced and cost-effective network infrastructure. By leveraging AWS-native solutions such as Amazon CloudWatch, AWS Cost Explorer, and VPC Flow Logs, organizations can proactively track bandwidth consumption and optimize resource allocation to enhance overall network efficiency.

Bandwidth Cost Visibility with Cost Explorer

AWS Cost Explorer provides clear visibility into bandwidth-related spending by breaking down data transfer costs by service, region, and usage type. By filtering for inter-AZ and inter-Region traffic, teams can quickly identify high-cost network paths, track trends, and detect unexpected spikes. These insights help correlate architecture decisions with cost impact and guide targeted bandwidth optimization efforts.

Understanding Bandwidth Utilization and Network Congestion

Managing bandwidth effectively starts with understanding how it is utilized across an AWS network. Bandwidth utilization refers to the amount of available network capacity being used at any given time, while network congestion occurs when demand exceeds the available bandwidth, leading to performance degradation, packet loss, and increased latency.

This section explores the factors influencing bandwidth consumption, the impact of network congestion on AWS workloads, and strategies to analyze usage trends. By leveraging AWS monitoring tools, organizations can identify traffic patterns, optimize data flow, and mitigate congestion issues to ensure seamless network performance.

Factors Affecting Bandwidth Utilization

Efficient bandwidth management is essential for maintaining network performance, reducing costs, and preventing congestion in AWS environments. Various factors impact bandwidth utilization, including the nature of workloads, the number of active connections, protocol efficiency, and traffic distribution across AWS regions and services. Understanding these factors allows organizations to optimize data flow, allocate resources effectively, and enhance network reliability.

Following are the primary elements that influence bandwidth consumption in AWS networks.

Key Factors Influencing Bandwidth Utilization

- **Workload Type and Size**

  The type and scale of workloads running in AWS directly impact bandwidth usage. Data-intensive applications, such as big data analytics, media streaming, and real-time processing, require significant network throughput. Workloads generating frequent or large data transfers consume more bandwidth compared to smaller, intermittent processes.

  - **Example:** Video streaming platforms utilizing Amazon CloudFront for content delivery require high bandwidth to ensure smooth playback.
  - **Optimization Tip:** Implement caching strategies, compression techniques, and edge computing to reduce data transfer volumes.

- **Number of Active Connections**

  The more users and services actively transmitting data, the greater the bandwidth demand. Applications with multiple concurrent users, APIs serving millions of requests, or interconnected microservices can strain network capacity.

  - **Example:** An e-commerce website experiencing a traffic surge during sales events may face bandwidth saturation due to high simultaneous user sessions.
  - **Optimization Tip:** Use AWS Auto Scaling, Elastic Load Balancing (ELB), and content caching (Amazon CloudFront) to distribute load efficiently.

- **Protocol Overhead and Data Transfer Efficiency**

  The choice of communication protocols affects how efficiently data is transmitted across networks. Some protocols introduce additional overhead, increasing bandwidth consumption.

  - **TCP versus UDP:** TCP ensures reliable data delivery but adds overhead due to acknowledgments and retransmissions. UDP is lightweight but lacks error correction, making it suitable for low-latency applications like VoIP or online gaming.
  - **HTTP versus HTTPS:** Secure HTTPS traffic incurs encryption overhead, impacting bandwidth usage compared to unencrypted HTTP traffic.
  - **Example:** A financial institution running secure transactions over HTTPS will experience higher bandwidth demand than a basic web application.
  - **Optimization Tip:** Use protocol tuning, compression (gzip, Brotli), and connection pooling (keep-alive settings) to improve data transfer efficiency.

- **AWS Service-Specific Traffic**

  Different AWS services consume bandwidth differently based on their usage patterns. Some AWS services generate more internal and external traffic, affecting overall network utilization.

  - **Amazon S3:** Data retrieval from S3 buckets, especially across regions, increases bandwidth consumption.

  - **Amazon RDS:** Database replication and query execution generate network traffic between application servers and database instances.
  - **AWS Lambda:** Invoking functions frequently, especially across VPCs, can lead to increased data transfer costs.
  - **Example:** A company hosting machine learning models in Amazon S3 will incur significant bandwidth usage when frequently accessing large datasets.
  - **Optimization Tip:** Leverage AWS PrivateLink, AWS Global Accelerator, and VPC Endpoints to optimize service-specific traffic.

- **Cross-Region and Cross-AZ Data Transfers**

  Transferring data between AWS regions and availability zones (AZs) significantly impacts bandwidth costs and performance. AWS charges for data movement between regions and AZs, making inefficient traffic patterns costly.

  - **Example:** A global enterprise replicating databases between AWS regions for disaster recovery may face unexpected bandwidth expenses.
  - **Optimization Tip:** Reduce unnecessary inter-region traffic by using Amazon CloudFront, AWS Direct Connect, and region-specific storage strategies.

The following table helps to enable quick comparison of causes versus impact, highlighting cost-sensitive traffic patterns and reinforcing optimization levers tied to each factor:

Factor	What Drives Bandwidth Usage	Typical Impact	Optimization Focus
Workload Type and Size	Data-intensive workloads (analytics, streaming, real-time processing)	High sustained throughput	Caching, compression, edge delivery (such as Amazon CloudFront)
Number of Active Connections	Concurrent users, APIs, microservices	Bandwidth spikes and congestion	Auto Scaling, Elastic Load Balancing, content caching
Protocol Overhead	TCP/HTTPS acknowledgments, encryption, retransmissions	Increased bandwidth consumption	Protocol tuning, gzip/Brotli compression, keep-alive
AWS Service-Specific Traffic	Service interactions (S3 access, DB replication, Lambda invocations)	Internal and external data transfer costs	VPC Endpoints, AWS PrivateLink, traffic localization
Cross-Region and Cross-AZ Transfers	Inter-Region replication, multi-AZ architectures	Higher latency and transfer charges	Regional data locality, AWS Direct Connect, CDN usage

Table 10.1: *Factors Influencing Bandwidth Utilization in AWS*

Bandwidth utilization in AWS environments depends on multiple factors, including workload size, connection density, protocol efficiency, service-specific traffic, and cross-region data transfers. Organizations must actively monitor and optimize these factors to prevent network congestion, reduce costs, and enhance application performance. Implementing AWS-native networking tools, caching mechanisms, and efficient data routing strategies helps maintain a balanced and scalable cloud network.

Identifying Network Congestion in AWS

Network congestion occurs when data traffic exceeds the available bandwidth, leading to slow performance, increased latency, and potential service disruptions. In AWS environments, congestion can arise from high-demand applications, inefficient routing, misconfigured network resources, or unexpected traffic spikes. Identifying congestion early is essential for maintaining high availability, low-latency connections, and cost efficiency.

Once network congestion is detected, mitigation should be prioritized based on impact and traffic criticality. Latency-sensitive or customer-facing workloads should be addressed first by scaling out resources (such as increasing instance counts or throughput capacity), followed by reducing repeated data transfers through caching and content delivery optimization using Amazon CloudFront. For sustained congestion, routing adjustments—such as rebalancing traffic across Availability Zones, optimizing route tables, or leveraging managed connectivity services—help distribute load more evenly. Combining short-term scale-out actions with longer-term traffic optimization ensures performance stability while preventing recurring congestion and unnecessary bandwidth costs.

This section explores common indicators of network congestion in AWS, along with tools and techniques to detect and resolve these issues effectively.

Indicators of Network Congestion in AWS

- **Increased Latency and Slow Application Response Times**

  One of the primary signs of network congestion is increased latency, causing applications to load slower or respond with delays. High-latency connections can severely impact real-time applications, database queries, and API responsiveness.

  - **Example:** An e-commerce platform experiencing slow checkout processing due to network congestion between its web servers and database instances.
  - **Detection Method:** Use AWS CloudWatch metrics (Latency, RequestCount, 5XXErrorRate) to monitor response times.

- **High Network Interface Utilization**

  When AWS Elastic Network Interfaces (ENIs) or Elastic Load Balancers (ELBs) approach their bandwidth limits, congestion occurs, leading to dropped packets and delays.

  - **Example:** A web application using AWS ALB (Application Load Balancer) facing high inbound traffic, causing performance degradation.
  - **Detection Method:** Monitor Amazon CloudWatch metrics for NetworkIn, NetworkOut, and Load Balancer Capacity Units (LCUs).

- **Increased Packet Loss and Retransmissions**

  Congestion often leads to packet loss, where data packets fail to reach their destination, triggering retransmissions. This issue wastes bandwidth, slows performance, and increases cloud costs.

  - **Example:** A VoIP service hosted on AWS experiencing voice distortions and call drops due to packet loss.
  - **Detection Method:** Use AWS VPC Flow Logs, AWS CloudWatch, and AWS Reachability Analyzer to track dropped packets and TCP retransmissions.

- **Unexpected Spikes in Data Transfer Costs**

  AWS charges for data transfer across regions, availability zones, and the internet. Unexpected increases in transfer costs can indicate inefficient routing or congestion-driven traffic rerouting.

  - **Example:** A media streaming company facing high AWS data transfer charges due to frequent cross-region requests instead of using cached CloudFront distributions.
  - **Detection Method:** Analyze AWS Cost Explorer and AWS Trusted Advisor for unusual data transfer patterns.

- **Underperforming Direct Connect or VPN Links**

  AWS Direct Connect and Site-to-Site VPNs provide dedicated network connections to AWS resources. If these connections experience degradation, it may indicate bandwidth overutilization or misconfigurations.

  - **Example:** A financial firm using AWS Direct Connect notices delays in stock market data retrieval due to congestion in their dedicated link.
  - **Detection Method:** Use AWS Direct Connect Monitoring in CloudWatch to assess link health and throughput.

AWS Tools for Detecting Network Congestion

AWS provides several tools and services to identify, analyze, and mitigate network congestion:

- **Amazon CloudWatch:** Monitors network traffic, latency, and throughput metrics.
- **AWS VPC Flow Logs:** Captures details about IP traffic for troubleshooting and security analysis.
- **AWS CloudTrail:** Tracks API calls and network configuration changes that may affect bandwidth.
- **AWS Reachability Analyzer:** Diagnoses network connectivity issues and potential bottlenecks.
- **AWS Cost Explorer:** Identifies unexpected data transfer costs due to inefficient routing.

The following table maps tool → purpose → insight in seconds. It separates performance metrics versus traffic records versus cost data and also helps readers choose the right tool first during congestion incidents.

Tool	Primary Use	Metric Focus	Data Type
Amazon CloudWatch	Real-time monitoring and alerting	Throughput, latency, packet drops	Time-series metrics
AWS VPC Flow Logs	Traffic analysis and congestion diagnosis	Source/destination IPs, bytes, accept/reject	Network flow records
AWS CloudTrail	Audit configuration changes impacting bandwidth	Network-related API calls	Event logs
AWS Reachability Analyzer	Identify routing issues and blocked paths	Path availability, misconfigurations	Network path analysis
AWS Cost Explorer	Detect abnormal data transfer spending	Data transfer usage and cost trends	Billing and usage data

Table 10.2: *AWS Tools for Detecting Network Congestion – Comparison*

Detecting network congestion in AWS requires proactive monitoring, traffic analysis, and performance benchmarking. Key indicators such as high latency, packet loss, interface saturation, and increased data transfer costs signal congestion issues. Leveraging AWS-native tools like CloudWatch, VPC Flow Logs, and Reachability Analyzer enables organizations to diagnose, optimize, and prevent network slowdowns, ensuring seamless connectivity and cost-effective cloud operations.

Allocating Bandwidth Efficiently across AWS Services

Efficient bandwidth allocation is essential for maintaining optimal application performance, reducing costs, and preventing network congestion in AWS environments. Organizations must distribute bandwidth strategically across compute, storage, database, and networking services to meet performance requirements while avoiding over-provisioning or underutilization.

This section explores techniques for allocating bandwidth effectively across AWS services, optimizing resource usage, and leveraging AWS-native tools to enhance network efficiency.

Understanding Bandwidth Allocation in AWS

Bandwidth allocation in AWS involves distributing available network capacity across different workloads, services, and regions based on traffic demands.

- AWS provides elastic networking capabilities, allowing organizations to scale bandwidth dynamically.
- Misallocation can result in bottlenecks, increased latency, and higher data transfer costs.
- Understanding AWS networking limits, pricing models, and service-specific requirements helps in making informed bandwidth allocation decisions.

Example: Misallocated Bandwidth in CloudWatch Metrics

A compute-heavy application running on undersized EC2 instances may show consistently high NetworkIn and NetworkOut metrics in Amazon CloudWatch, frequently approaching the maximum throughput of the instance. At the same time, NetworkPacketsDropped may spike, indicating congestion at the interface level. This pattern signals bandwidth misallocation—where workload demand exceeds allocated network capacity—prompting corrective actions such as scaling out instances, selecting higher-bandwidth instance types, or redistributing traffic across Availability Zones.

Prioritizing Bandwidth for Critical Applications

Bandwidth prioritization in AWS is typically implemented through architecture and configuration controls rather than traditional packet-level QoS. For multi-VPC environments, AWS Transit Gateway allows bandwidth governance by controlling attachment throughput and routing paths, ensuring critical VPCs use optimized routes. Dedicated connectivity via AWS Direct Connect provides predictable bandwidth and lower latency for high-priority workloads. Traffic shaping is further achieved by restricting or isolating non-critical flows using Network ACLs, security groups, and traffic segmentation.

Some workloads require higher bandwidth and lower latency than others. AWS enables traffic prioritization through:

- **Quality of Service (QoS) Policies:** Ensuring high-priority applications (such as video streaming, VoIP, database replication) receive sufficient bandwidth.
- **AWS Transit Gateway Bandwidth Controls:** Allocating bandwidth per VPC attachment to optimize multi-VPC traffic.
- **Traffic Mirroring and Network ACLs:** Restricting non-essential traffic to reduce network congestion.

Example: A financial firm prioritizing AWS Direct Connect bandwidth for real-time stock trading applications while limiting bandwidth for background data transfers.

Use Case	AWS Feature	Benefit
Real-time trading / financial apps	**AWS Direct Connect**	Low-latency, guaranteed bandwidth
Multi-VPC critical workloads	**AWS Transit Gateway**	Controlled routing and optimized throughput
Video streaming / media delivery	**Amazon CloudFront**	Reduced backbone bandwidth usage
Microservices traffic isolation	Network ACLs / Security Groups	Limits noisy neighbor impact
Traffic analysis and enforcement	Traffic Mirroring	Visibility into non-essential traffic

Table 10.3: *Bandwidth Prioritization – Use Case Mapping*

Caution: Avoid Bandwidth Starvation

Over-prioritizing critical traffic without defined limits can unintentionally starve lower-tier workloads, causing cascading delays or failures in background processes such as logging, backups, or batch jobs. Effective bandwidth prioritization should balance guarantees for critical paths with minimum throughput baselines for secondary services to maintain overall system stability.

Bandwidth Optimization for AWS Compute Services

AWS compute services, such as EC2, Lambda, and ECS, rely on network bandwidth to handle requests, communicate with databases, and serve users. Optimizing bandwidth allocation across these services includes:

- **Using Instance Types with Higher Network Performance:** Selecting EC2 instances with enhanced networking (Elastic Network Adapter - ENA) or EFA (Elastic Fabric Adapter) for high-throughput workloads.
- **Implementing Load Balancers:** Distributing traffic efficiently using Application Load Balancer (ALB) or Network Load Balancer (NLB) to prevent overloading a single instance.
- **Optimizing Auto Scaling Groups:** Ensuring bandwidth is evenly distributed as instances scale up or down.

Cost Consideration:

Enhanced networking options such as Elastic Network Adapter (ENA) and Elastic Fabric Adapter (EFA) do not carry a separate hourly charge, but they are available only on higher-tier EC2 instance types, which have a higher per-hour cost. While these instances increase compute spend, they can reduce overall costs by improving throughput, lowering job runtimes, and minimizing the need for over-provisioning or excessive horizontal scaling.

Example: An AI-powered analytics platform selecting EC2 instances with 100 Gbps networking to process large datasets efficiently.

Bandwidth scaling is closely linked to application architecture choices, particularly whether workloads are stateless or stateful. Stateless applications scale horizontally with ease—when paired with services like Amazon EC2 Auto Scaling and load balancers, bandwidth demand is naturally distributed across multiple instances, reducing the risk of network saturation. In contrast, stateful applications concentrate traffic on fewer nodes (such as databases or session-bound services), making them more susceptible to bandwidth bottlenecks and requiring higher per-instance network capacity. Designing applications to be as stateless as possible enables more efficient bandwidth utilization, smoother scaling behavior, and better resilience under high traffic conditions.

Managing Bandwidth for Storage and Database Services

AWS storage (S3, EBS, FSx) and database services (RDS, DynamoDB, Aurora) consume bandwidth for data transfers, replication, and backups. Effective allocation strategies include:

- **Using S3 Transfer Acceleration:** Enhancing data transfer speeds over long distances.
- **Optimizing Cross-Region Replication:** Minimizing bandwidth usage by enabling only necessary replications.
- **Configuring Read Replicas for Databases:** Reducing bandwidth strain on primary instances by distributing read traffic across replicas.

Example: A global SaaS provider reduced inter-region bandwidth costs by using Amazon S3 Transfer Acceleration for cross-border file uploads, while also achieving significant latency improvements by routing traffic through AWS edge locations. Upload times for users in distant regions dropped noticeably, resulting in faster data availability, improved user experience, and reduced retry-related network overhead

Leveraging AWS Direct Connect and VPN for Dedicated Bandwidth

For enterprise workloads, hybrid cloud setups, and on-premises connectivity, AWS offers Direct Connect and Site-to-Site VPN to allocate dedicated bandwidth:

- **AWS Direct Connect:** Provides a private, high-bandwidth, and low-latency link between on-premises and AWS resources.

  For resilience, AWS Direct Connect should be deployed with redundant links across separate locations or devices, along with a Site-to-Site VPN as a backup. BGP routing enables automatic failover to the VPN if Direct Connect becomes unavailable, preserving connectivity with minimal operational impact.

- **AWS Site-to-Site VPN:** Secures bandwidth for remote offices connecting to AWS via an IPSec VPN tunnel.
- **Traffic Engineering with BGP Routing:** Allocates bandwidth efficiently by defining custom route priorities.

Example: A healthcare organization using AWS Direct Connect to securely transmit large medical imaging files without bandwidth contention.

Using AWS Cost Management Tools for Bandwidth Allocation

AWS provides tools to track, analyze, and optimize bandwidth usage across services:

- **AWS Cost Explorer:** Identifies high-bandwidth services and regions to optimize costs.
- **AWS Trusted Advisor:** Flags inefficient bandwidth usage and suggests network optimization recommendations.
- **Amazon VPC Traffic Mirroring:** Analyzes real-time network traffic to detect misallocations or security risks.

Example: A gaming company analyzing AWS Cost Explorer reports to reduce unnecessary cross-region traffic.

Allocating bandwidth efficiently across AWS services ensures optimal performance, cost savings, and reduced network congestion. By prioritizing critical applications, leveraging AWS-native tools, and implementing best practices for compute, storage, and hybrid networking, organizations can enhance their cloud network efficiency while maintaining scalability and security.

Implementing AWS Tools for Bandwidth Monitoring and Optimization

Efficient network management in AWS requires continuous monitoring, analysis, and optimization of bandwidth usage. Without proper monitoring, organizations risk network congestion, increased latency, and unnecessary costs. AWS offers a suite of tools that enable users to track bandwidth consumption, detect anomalies, and implement proactive optimizations.

In practice, reactive optimization relies on responding to congestion after performance degrades, while proactive optimization uses continuous insights from tools like Amazon CloudWatch and AWS Cost Explorer to anticipate bandwidth issues, adjust capacity early, and prevent disruptions before users are impacted.

This section explores how AWS-native tools such as Amazon CloudWatch, AWS Cost Explorer, AWS Trusted Advisor, VPC Flow Logs, and Network Manager can be leveraged to monitor and optimize bandwidth allocation for enhanced performance and cost efficiency.

Using Amazon CloudWatch for Network Performance Insights

Amazon CloudWatch provides real-time metrics and logs to monitor AWS network performance, including bandwidth usage. Key functionalities include:

- **Tracking Data Transfer Rates:** Monitor network in/out metrics for EC2 instances, load balancers, and databases.
- **Setting Alarms for Anomalous Bandwidth Spikes:** Identify sudden increases in data transfer and take preventive measures.
- **Analyzing Traffic Patterns:** Use CloudWatch Logs Insights to detect inefficient bandwidth utilization.

Common CloudWatch Metrics Used

- NetworkIn / NetworkOut (EC2 instance throughput)
- ProcessedBytes (Application Load Balancer)
- ActiveConnectionCount (Load Balancer traffic intensity)
- NetworkPacketsDropped (early congestion indicator)

Sample CloudWatch Alarm (JSON – simplified)

```
{
  "MetricName": "NetworkOut",
  "Namespace": "AWS/EC2",
  "Statistic": "Average",
  "Period": 300,
  "EvaluationPeriods": 2,
  "Threshold": 800000000,
  "ComparisonOperator": "GreaterThanThreshold",
  "AlarmDescription": "Alert when outbound traffic exceeds ~800 Mbps"
}
```

Example: A streaming company uses Amazon CloudWatch alarms to detect outbound traffic spikes exceeding 800 Mbps for 10 consecutive minutes, enabling rapid optimization of caching and bitrate delivery before user experience degrades.

Leveraging AWS Cost Explorer for Bandwidth Cost Analysis

AWS Cost Explorer helps organizations analyze and forecast bandwidth-related expenses. Key capabilities include:

- **Identifying High-Cost Data Transfers:** Breakdown of inter-region, intra-region, and internet-facing bandwidth usage.
- **Predicting Future Costs:** Estimate bandwidth expenditures based on historical usage trends.
- **Optimizing Traffic Flow:** Identify excessive data movement between AWS regions and optimize for cost savings.

Example: A multinational enterprise reduces AWS data transfer costs by rerouting workloads to a single-region architecture after analyzing Cost Explorer reports.

Utilizing AWS Trusted Advisor for Bandwidth Optimization Recommendations

AWS Trusted Advisor provides real-time recommendations to enhance network efficiency and reduce unnecessary bandwidth costs. Key features include:

- **Detecting Inefficient Data Transfers:** Flags unoptimized cross-region traffic driving up costs.
- **Identifying Underutilized Resources:** Suggests scaling down bandwidth-heavy instances if they are over-provisioned.
- **Ensuring Compliance with Best Practices:** Helps enforce network security and performance optimizations.

Example: A finance company leverages AWS Trusted Advisor to identify costly inter-region data replication, leading them to implement in-region storage for better efficiency. As a result, the organization reduced cross-region data transfer charges by approximately 30% and improved application response times by eliminating unnecessary long-distance data flows.

Monitoring Network Traffic with Amazon VPC Flow Logs

Amazon VPC Flow Logs capture detailed network traffic metadata, helping administrators analyze and optimize bandwidth usage. Benefits include:

- **Identifying High-Traffic Workloads:** Detect which instances, subnets, or services are consuming excessive bandwidth.
- **Detecting Latency and Packet Loss Issues:** Pinpoint network bottlenecks affecting application performance.
- **Improving Security and Compliance:** Monitor suspicious traffic flows that could indicate data leaks.

Example: A cybersecurity firm uses VPC Flow Logs to detect unauthorized outbound traffic and optimize internal bandwidth allocation.

Enhancing Network Visibility with AWS Network Manager

AWS Network Manager provides a centralized view of global AWS networks, allowing businesses to monitor and optimize bandwidth allocation efficiently. Key functionalities include:

- **Real-Time Network Topology Visualization:** Displays traffic flows across AWS regions, Direct Connect links, and VPN tunnels.
- **Automated Performance Monitoring:** Detects bandwidth saturation points and suggests corrective actions.
- **Multi-Region Optimization:** Helps orchestrate traffic routing strategies across multiple AWS locations.

Example: A logistics company with multiple AWS regions utilizes AWS Network Manager to identify and reduce unnecessary cross-region data transfers.

Implementing AWS Auto Scaling for Bandwidth Optimization

AWS Auto Scaling ensures that bandwidth-intensive applications adjust dynamically based on demand. Strategies include:

- **Scaling Load Balancers Dynamically:** Adjusting ALB/NLB capacity based on real-time traffic volume.
- **Optimizing Data Transfer with S3 Intelligent Tiering:** Reducing bandwidth costs by automatically shifting less frequently accessed data to lower-cost storage tiers.
- **Dynamically Adjusting EC2 Instances:** Ensuring network resources scale up/down as required.

Example: A cloud gaming provider leverages Auto Scaling to expand bandwidth during peak hours and reduce costs during off-peak times.

Implementing AWS-native tools for bandwidth monitoring and optimization ensures organizations maintain high network performance, cost efficiency, and scalability. By leveraging Amazon CloudWatch, AWS Cost Explorer, Trusted Advisor, VPC Flow Logs, and Network Manager, businesses can proactively detect bandwidth inefficiencies, prevent congestion, and reduce costs while maintaining seamless operations.

Latency Optimization

In the current scenario of digital landscape, low-latency network performance is crucial for delivering responsive applications, real-time communication, and seamless user experiences. Whether hosting a web application, database, or global enterprise network, reducing latency ensures that data travels efficiently between users and cloud resources.

AWS provides a variety of solutions to optimize network latency, including intelligent routing strategies, caching mechanisms, and edge networking services. By leveraging AWS Global Accelerator, Route 53 latency-based routing, Amazon CloudFront, and Amazon ElastiCache, businesses can significantly enhance data delivery speeds and application responsiveness.

It is important to distinguish network latency from application latency. Network latency refers to the time taken for data packets to travel between clients and AWS infrastructure, influenced by distance, routing paths, and network congestion. Application latency, on the other hand, includes processing delays within the application itself—such as database queries, compute execution, or inefficient code paths. While application optimization improves processing speed, AWS networking services primarily target network latency reduction by shortening data paths and bringing content closer to users.

This section explores best practices and AWS tools for reducing latency, optimizing data routing, and leveraging caching to improve overall network performance and efficiency.

Identifying Sources of Network Latency in AWS Environments

Network latency is a critical factor that impacts the performance of applications and services in the cloud. High latency can lead to slower load times, reduced user satisfaction, and inefficient resource utilization. Identifying the root causes of latency within an AWS environment is the first step toward optimizing network performance.

AWS environments experience latency due to various factors, including physical distance, routing inefficiencies, network congestion, and under-optimized application architectures. By understanding these sources, businesses can implement targeted solutions to enhance responsiveness and improve data transmission efficiency.

This section explores the primary sources of network latency in AWS, how to measure them, and best practices for minimizing their impact.

Network Latency Factors in AWS

Several factors contribute to network latency in AWS environments, including:

- **Geographical Distance**: Data must travel across multiple regions or Availability Zones (AZs), increasing latency.
- **Routing Inefficiencies**: Suboptimal routing paths may introduce unnecessary network hops and delays.
- **Congestion at Network Gateways**: High traffic loads on NAT gateways, internet gateways, or VPN connections can slow data transfer.
- **DNS Resolution Delays**: Inefficient Domain Name System (DNS) queries can increase response times.
- **Compute and Storage Bottlenecks**: Slow application servers, overloaded databases, or high I/O operations can add processing delays.

Understanding these factors helps in implementing solutions such as AWS Global Accelerator, Route 53 latency-based routing, and optimized traffic routing policies.

Tools for Measuring Latency in AWS

To effectively address latency, businesses need tools to measure and monitor network performance. AWS offers several built-in services for analyzing latency, including:

- **AWS CloudWatch**: Provides network latency metrics for EC2 instances, load balancers, and VPCs.
- **AWS X-Ray**: Helps track request traces across applications to identify bottlenecks.
- **Amazon CloudFront Reports**: Analyzes edge location performance and caching efficiency.
- **VPC Flow Logs**: Monitors traffic patterns to identify delays in data transmission.
- **Third-Party Tools**: Solutions like ThousandEyes, Datadog, or New Relic offer additional network insights.

By leveraging these tools, organizations can pinpoint latency issues, implement data-driven optimizations, and enhance overall network efficiency.

Optimizing Route 53 and VPC Peering for Faster Connectivity

Efficient network performance in AWS depends on how traffic is routed across regions, Availability Zones (AZs), and Virtual Private Clouds (VPCs). Poor routing strategies can introduce unnecessary latency, increasing response times for applications and services. Amazon Route 53 and VPC Peering are key AWS solutions that help optimize connectivity by ensuring traffic follows the most efficient path.

Route 53 is a highly available and scalable Domain Name System (DNS) web service of AWS, which enables intelligent traffic routing based on latency, geographic location, and failover mechanisms. On the other hand, VPC Peering allows direct private connectivity between two VPCs, reducing reliance on slower internet-based traffic.

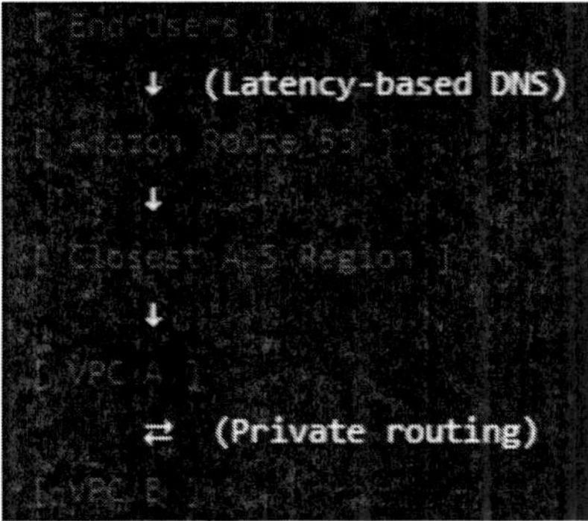

Figure 10.2: *Architectural View – Optimized Routing with Route 53 and VPC Peering*

This section explores how to optimize Route 53 settings and configure VPC Peering to improve network latency and ensure seamless communication between AWS resources.

Enhancing Traffic Routing with Amazon Route 53

Amazon Route 53 provides several routing policies that help reduce latency and improve application responsiveness. Some key optimizations include:

- **Latency-Based Routing (LBR)**: Directs users to the lowest-latency AWS region based on their location.
- **Geolocation Routing**: Ensures users connect to the closest AWS region for improved speed and compliance.
- **Failover Routing**: Enhances availability by automatically rerouting traffic to a backup endpoint if the primary one fails.
- **Multi-Value Answer Routing**: Distributes traffic across multiple healthy endpoints, reducing congestion.
- **Weighted Routing**: Allocates traffic between resources based on predefined weight values, useful for load balancing and gradual deployments.

By strategically implementing Route 53 routing policies, businesses can optimize traffic flow, minimize latency, and provide faster, more reliable user experiences.

Improving Inter-VPC Communication with VPC Peering

AWS VPC Peering allows private, high-speed communication between VPCs within the same or different AWS regions without requiring an internet gateway, VPN, or NAT device. Some best practices for optimizing VPC Peering include:

- **Using Direct VPC Peering Instead of NAT Gateways**: NAT gateways introduce additional hops, increasing latency. Direct peering removes the need for intermediate devices.
- **Optimizing Route Tables**: Ensure route tables are correctly configured to direct traffic efficiently between peered VPCs.
- **Enabling DNS Resolution for Peered VPCs**: By default, AWS does not resolve private DNS names across VPC peers. Enabling DNS resolution in Peering Connections allows seamless cross-VPC communication.
- **Using AWS Transit Gateway for Scalable Peering**: For environments with multiple interconnected VPCs, AWS Transit Gateway provides a more scalable alternative to one-to-one peering.

By leveraging the intelligent traffic management of Route 53 and the direct connectivity of VPC Peering, businesses can achieve low-latency, high-performance networking in AWS.

Leveraging AWS Global Accelerator and CloudFront for Low-Latency Performance

In global and latency-sensitive applications, reducing network delays is crucial to ensuring a seamless user experience. AWS Global Accelerator and Amazon CloudFront are two powerful AWS services designed to enhance performance, improve availability, and minimize latency for internet-facing applications.

AWS Global Accelerator uses a global network of AWS to route user requests to the nearest available AWS endpoint, bypassing congested internet paths and improving response times. Amazon CloudFront, the Content Delivery Network (CDN) of AWS, caches static and dynamic content at edge locations worldwide, reducing the need to fetch data from distant origin servers.

By leveraging Global Accelerator and CloudFront, businesses can optimize network performance, reduce round-trip times, and deliver content efficiently to users across the globe.

Optimizing Application Performance with AWS Global Accelerator

AWS Global Accelerator improves the speed and reliability of applications by using the low-latency global network infrastructure of AWS instead of the public internet. Key features and benefits include:

- **Intelligent Traffic Routing:** Routes user traffic to the optimal AWS Region or endpoint based on health, geography, and congestion levels.
- **Static Anycast IPs:** Provides two static IP addresses that serve as a fixed entry point for applications, reducing the need for frequent DNS resolution and preventing disruptions.
- **Automatic Failover:** Detects unhealthy endpoints and instantly redirects traffic to the nearest healthy resource, enhancing availability.
- **Performance-Based Routing:** Optimizes network paths dynamically to ensure minimal packet loss, jitter, and latency.

Using AWS Global Accelerator ensures that traffic reaches AWS infrastructure through the fastest, most reliable routes, significantly improving performance for global applications.

Enhancing Content Delivery with Amazon CloudFront

Amazon CloudFront is a highly distributed CDN that accelerates content delivery by caching data at edge locations around the world. Some key optimizations include:

- **Edge Caching for Reduced Latency:** Stores static and dynamic content closer to users, minimizing origin fetch times.
- **Dynamic Content Optimization:** Uses Lambda@Edge to execute custom logic at AWS edge locations, reducing processing delays.
- **HTTPS and TLS Optimizations:** Ensures secure, encrypted connections with minimal overhead.
- **Compression and Caching Policies:** Supports Gzip and Brotli compression for smaller payloads and faster transfers.

By integrating AWS Global Accelerator for routing optimization and CloudFront for content acceleration, businesses can significantly reduce network latency, improve user experience, and optimize global application performance.

Traffic Shaping Techniques

In modern cloud environments, network traffic can fluctuate based on user demand, application workload, and data transfer requirements. Without proper management, high-priority applications may experience performance degradation due to network congestion or bandwidth contention. To address this, organizations leverage traffic shaping techniques to regulate, prioritize, and optimize network traffic for better performance and cost efficiency.

Traffic shaping involves controlling the flow of data packets based on predefined rules, ensuring that mission-critical applications receive the required bandwidth while preventing lower-priority traffic from overwhelming the network. AWS offers various tools and services, such as AWS Quality of Service (QoS), Elastic Load Balancing (ELB), and AWS Transit Gateway, to help organizations implement effective traffic shaping strategies.

This section explores how businesses can classify, prioritize, and manage traffic flows to maintain low-latency, high-performance, and cost-effective network operations in AWS environments.

Using Quality of Service (QoS) Policies for Network Traffic Control

In cloud-based networks, different types of traffic compete for bandwidth, and not all traffic holds the same level of priority. Quality of Service (QoS) policies enable organizations to control and optimize network traffic by assigning different priority levels to various types of data. By implementing QoS, businesses can ensure smooth operation for latency-sensitive applications, such as real-time video streaming, VoIP calls, and financial transactions, while deprioritizing less critical traffic like software updates or background data transfers.

QoS at Layer 3 is largely outside the native control of AWS, so most enforcement happens at the network edge or via appliances.

AWS does not provide native QoS settings at the instance level, but network administrators can apply QoS policies through AWS services such as AWS Transit Gateway, AWS Direct Connect, and Elastic Load Balancing (ELB). These tools help regulate bandwidth usage, reduce network congestion, and enhance overall performance by allocating resources based on business-critical needs.

Understanding QoS and Traffic Prioritization

Quality of Service (QoS) works by classifying network traffic into multiple priority levels based on factors like packet type, application, or source/destination. The key components of QoS include:

- **Traffic classification:** Identifying different types of data packets, such as voice, video, or file transfers.
- **Bandwidth allocation:** Assigning a specific portion of network resources to high-priority applications.
- **Traffic policing:** Limiting the data rate for lower-priority traffic to avoid network congestion.
- **Latency management:** Reducing packet delays by ensuring high-priority traffic is processed first.

AWS QoS implementation is more policy-based than packet-marking-based.

By leveraging QoS, businesses can prevent network slowdowns and optimize performance for mission-critical applications.

Implementing QoS in AWS with Transit Gateway and Direct Connect

AWS offers multiple solutions for organizations looking to implement QoS policies at a network level. Two of the most effective methods include:

- **AWS Transit Gateway:**
  - Provides centralized management of traffic flows between VPCs and on-premises networks.
  - Supports route-based traffic prioritization to ensure critical workloads receive priority over less important traffic.
  - Helps reduce congestion by efficiently distributing network load.
- **AWS Direct Connect:**
  - Establishes dedicated, private connections between AWS and on-premises environments.
  - Allows customers to define traffic classes and allocate bandwidth accordingly.
  - Reduces latency and improves network predictability, especially for hybrid cloud environments.

By leveraging these AWS services, organizations can prioritize business-critical applications, enhance user experience, and ensure network efficiency.

Implementing AWS Network Firewall and Security Groups for Traffic Prioritization

In cloud-based environments, ensuring secure and optimized traffic flow is critical for performance and security. AWS provides AWS Network Firewall and Security Groups as key components for managing and prioritizing network traffic effectively. These tools help organizations filter, inspect, and control inbound and outbound traffic while ensuring that high-priority applications receive the necessary network resources.

By properly implementing firewall rules and security group configurations, organizations can create a structured network policy that prioritizes mission-critical workloads, prevents unauthorized access, and minimizes latency. These measures contribute to better network performance and enhanced security in AWS environments.

Example: Traffic Prioritization Using Firewall Rules

An enterprise configures AWS Network Firewall and Security Groups to explicitly allow high-priority traffic on port 443 (HTTPS) for customer-facing applications and port 22 (SSH) only from trusted administrative IP ranges. At the same time, non-essential background services—such as internal batch processing ports or unused legacy protocols—are restricted or rate-limited. This approach ensures that critical application traffic remains responsive while preventing low-priority or noisy traffic from consuming unnecessary bandwidth.

Using AWS Network Firewall for Traffic Filtering and Prioritization

AWS Network Firewall is a managed security service that provides stateful, deep packet inspection to monitor and control traffic flow between VPCs and external networks. It allows businesses to:

- Define firewall rules that prioritize essential services while restricting or limiting lower-priority traffic.
- Enforce traffic inspection policies for applications requiring higher security, such as financial transactions and healthcare data.
- Apply network-based intrusion prevention to detect and block malicious traffic while allowing legitimate, high-priority requests.

Prioritization in AWS Firewall is achieved through rule order and traffic handling actions.

By implementing AWS Network Firewall, organizations can enhance traffic control, prevent security threats, and improve overall network efficiency.

Configuring Security Groups for Controlled Access and Traffic Flow

Security Groups act as virtual firewalls for AWS resources, controlling inbound and outbound traffic at the instance level. When used effectively, Security Groups can help prioritize and optimize network traffic by:

- Allowing high-priority applications (such as VoIP, live streaming, database access) to communicate without latency issues.
- Restricting non-essential traffic from consuming bandwidth and causing congestion.
- Defining port-based access rules to ensure only authorized services and users can interact with critical resources.

By carefully configuring AWS Security Groups, businesses can reduce network bottlenecks, enforce security policies, and maintain a well-structured network that prioritizes essential services.

Combining AWS Network Firewall and Security Groups for Optimized Traffic Flow

To maximize network efficiency and security, organizations should implement a layered approach by combining AWS Network Firewall and Security Groups:

- AWS Network Firewall ensures that global traffic filtering rules are applied across entire VPCs, prioritizing essential services while blocking unwanted traffic.
- Security Groups provide fine-grained control at the instance level, restricting unauthorized access and ensuring that resources receive the necessary bandwidth.

- Both tools work together to prevent network congestion, reduce attack surfaces, and optimize traffic routing for mission-critical applications.

By integrating AWS Network Firewall with Security Groups, businesses can enforce advanced security policies while maintaining optimal traffic flow, resulting in higher availability, lower latency, and improved protection against threats.

Best Practice: When integrating AWS Network Firewall with Security Groups, keep rule sets minimal and purpose-driven. Avoid overlapping or overly granular rules that increase inspection complexity and can introduce unnecessary latency in traffic paths. Periodically review and consolidate rules to ensure that only essential traffic is inspected, maintaining both performance and security efficiency.

Managing Data Transfer Priorities with AWS Transit Gateway

In complex AWS environments, efficiently managing data transfer between multiple VPCs, on-premises networks, and AWS services is crucial for maintaining performance and cost-effectiveness. AWS Transit Gateway serves as a centralized hub for routing traffic between these networks, simplifying management while enhancing security and scalability.

One of the key advantages of AWS Transit Gateway is its ability to prioritize critical data flows, ensuring that essential applications and workloads receive the necessary bandwidth. By implementing optimized routing policies and bandwidth controls, organizations can reduce congestion, improve application performance, and minimize unnecessary data transfer costs.

Understanding AWS Transit Gateway and Its Role in Traffic Management

AWS Transit Gateway acts as a high-performance cloud router, enabling seamless connectivity between multiple AWS environments and external networks. Its primary functions in traffic management include:

- Centralizing network traffic from multiple VPCs, Direct Connect links, and Site-to-Site VPNs.
- Reducing network complexity by eliminating the need for multiple VPC peering connections.
- Enhancing security and control by applying routing rules and access policies for specific traffic flows.

By utilizing AWS Transit Gateway, businesses can effectively manage traffic between multiple AWS resources while optimizing data transfer priorities.

Implementing Routing Policies for Optimized Data Flow

Proper routing policy configuration within AWS Transit Gateway is essential for ensuring critical workloads receive priority network access. Some key strategies include:

- Defining route tables for different workload types (like separating production, development, and testing traffic).
- Prioritizing mission-critical applications by directing them through lower-latency connections such as AWS Direct Connect.
- Restricting non-essential traffic from consuming excessive bandwidth, preventing performance degradation.

By implementing optimized routing policies, businesses can ensure that important workloads maintain high availability and low latency, even during peak network usage.

Using AWS Transit Gateway Bandwidth Controls to Prevent Congestion

AWS doesn't natively enforce "hard" bandwidth caps but allows design-based control via route segmentation and QoS-like prioritization. AWS Transit Gateway allows administrators to allocate bandwidth efficiently across connected networks, preventing congestion and ensuring smooth data flow. Some methods for effective bandwidth control include:

- Applying bandwidth limits on non-essential traffic to prevent it from interfering with high-priority applications.
- Leveraging AWS Cost Allocation Tags to monitor data transfer usage and optimize cost management.
- Using AWS Transit Gateway Network Manager to analyze traffic patterns and adjust bandwidth allocations dynamically.

By actively managing data transfer priorities with AWS Transit Gateway, organizations can maintain a high-performance network, reduce costs, and ensure seamless connectivity across their cloud and hybrid infrastructure.

Cost Monitoring

In cloud networking, cost management is as critical as performance optimization. Without proper monitoring, network-related expenses—such as data transfer costs, bandwidth usage, and AWS service consumption—can quickly escalate. AWS provides powerful cost management tools like AWS Cost Explorer and AWS Budgets to help organizations track, analyze, and control their cloud spending.

By leveraging these tools, businesses can gain visibility into their network costs, set budget limits, and proactively manage expenses. This ensures that network optimizations not only improve performance but also remain cost-efficient and aligned with business goals.

Example: By using AWS Cost Explorer and AWS Budgets to track data transfer trends, a mid-sized SaaS company discovered that cross-Availability Zone traffic was driving unnecessary network costs. After re-architecting traffic flows and setting budget alerts, the company reduced network-related spending by approximately 30% while maintaining the same application performance.

Analyzing Network Cost Drivers and Reducing Unnecessary Expenses

Effective cost management in AWS requires a deep understanding of the key factors driving network expenses. Organizations often incur high costs due to excessive data transfer, inefficient resource allocation, and suboptimal routing. Without proper analysis and optimization, these expenses can quickly spiral out of control.

By leveraging AWS Cost Explorer and other cost monitoring tools, businesses can identify the primary cost drivers, analyze trends, and implement strategies to reduce unnecessary expenses. Optimizing network architecture, minimizing data transfer costs, and implementing cost-aware policies can lead to significant savings while maintaining high performance.

Identifying Key Network Cost Drivers in AWS

Understanding the key cost drivers behind network expenses in AWS is essential for budget optimization and cost efficiency. AWS networking costs are primarily influenced by data transfer charges, inter-region communication, traffic between AWS services, and inefficient routing configurations. Businesses that fail to monitor and optimize these factors may encounter unexpected cost spikes that impact overall cloud expenditure.

By identifying and analyzing these cost drivers, organizations can make informed decisions on resource allocation, traffic management, and network architecture optimization. This ensures cost-effective operations without compromising performance.

Strategies to Reduce Network Costs in AWS

Reducing AWS network costs requires a proactive approach that balances performance, security, and cost efficiency. Organizations can optimize data transfer, use cost-effective AWS services, and implement traffic management best practices to minimize unnecessary expenses. By leveraging AWS-native tools and adopting efficient network architectures, businesses can significantly lower their operational costs while maintaining high availability and performance.

Key Strategies for Reducing AWS Network Costs

- **Optimize Data Transfer across AWS Services**
    - Use AWS PrivateLink for communication between services to avoid expensive public internet traffic.
    - Prefer VPC Peering or AWS Transit Gateway for inter-VPC communication instead of routing through public endpoints.
- **Leverage AWS Free Tier and Cost-Effective Pricing Plans**
    - Take advantage of AWS Free Tier limits for network services to minimize costs for development and testing environments.
    - Use AWS Savings Plans or Reserved Instances for predictable workloads to reduce on-demand pricing.
- **Reduce Inter-Region and Outbound Data Transfer Costs**
    - Minimize cross-region replication unless necessary by using regionalized architectures.
    - Use CloudFront caching and edge locations to distribute content closer to users, reducing outbound data transfer costs.
- **Monitor and Control Unnecessary Traffic**
    - Implement AWS Cost Explorer and AWS Budgets to analyze high-cost network traffic patterns.
    - Set up VPC Flow Logs to monitor unexpected data transfers and detect costly misconfigurations.
- **Use Compression and Data Optimization Techniques**
    - Enable gzip compression for web traffic to reduce data transfer costs.
    - Optimize large dataset transfers with AWS Snowball or AWS DataSync instead of using public internet connections.

By implementing these strategies, businesses can effectively manage network costs while maintaining high-performance connectivity in AWS environments. Continuous monitoring and optimization using AWS-native tools will further help organizations prevent unnecessary expenses and ensure cost-efficient network operations.

Setting up AWS Budgets for Proactive Cost Monitoring

AWS Budgets provides budget visualization, real-time alerts, and automation hooks that allow organizations to track network-related spending, receive notifications when thresholds are approached, and trigger corrective actions before costs exceed planned limits.

Managing AWS network costs efficiently requires a proactive approach rather than reactive cost control. AWS Budgets enables organizations to set spending limits, track usage trends, and receive alerts when costs exceed predefined thresholds. By leveraging AWS Budgets, businesses can avoid unexpected expenses, optimize resource allocation, and maintain financial control over their AWS network infrastructure.

Key Steps for Setting up AWS Budgets

1. **Defining Cost and Usage Budgets**
    a. Identify network cost categories such as data transfer, VPC, and Direct Connect expenses.
    b. Create separate budgets for total spend, service-specific costs, and linked accounts.
    c. Set forecast-based budgets to anticipate future expenses based on historical trends.
2. **Configuring Budget Thresholds and Alerts**
    a. Establish spending thresholds at different percentages (like 50%, 75%, or 90% of the budget).
    b. Enable automated notifications via email, Amazon SNS, or AWS Chatbot for budget breaches.
    c. Set up alerts for anomalous network cost spikes, ensuring quick corrective actions.
3. **Integrating AWS Budgets with AWS Cost Explorer**
    a. Use AWS Cost Explorer to analyze historical usage patterns and adjust budgets accordingly.
    b. Visualize network cost trends and identify cost-saving opportunities based on real-time data.
    c. Optimize budgets based on seasonal traffic patterns or workload scaling needs.
4. **Automating Cost Controls with AWS Budgets Actions**
    a. Configure AWS Budgets Actions to trigger automatic responses when thresholds are exceeded.
    b. Implement resource throttling, termination, or rightsizing for cost-heavy services.
    c. Use AWS Lambda to enforce policies, such as restricting non-essential network services.

Setting up AWS Budgets provides a structured approach to proactively managing network expenses while ensuring cost efficiency in AWS environments. By leveraging budget thresholds, real-time alerts, and automated cost controls, organizations can prevent overspending and optimize network costs effectively.

Leveraging AWS Cost Explorer for Optimized Network Spend Management

Effective cost management is a critical component of maintaining an optimized AWS network infrastructure. AWS Cost Explorer is a powerful visualization and analysis tool that helps businesses track, analyze, and optimize their network-related expenses. By using detailed cost breakdowns, historical trends, and forecast capabilities, organizations can gain insights into network spend patterns and implement cost-saving measures without compromising performance.

Key Strategies for Optimized Network Spend Management

1. **Analyzing Cost and Usage Trends**
    a. Utilize filtering and grouping features of AWS Cost Explorer to break down network costs by service, region, linked accounts, or specific AWS resources.
    b. Identify high-cost areas, such as excessive data transfer fees or inefficient routing configurations.
    c. Leverage historical spending data to predict future costs and adjust budgets proactively.
2. **Identifying Cost Anomalies and Unexpected Expenses**
    a. Enable daily and monthly cost reports to detect sudden spikes in network usage or unusual billing patterns.
    b. Set up custom reports for AWS networking services such as AWS Direct Connect, VPC, NAT Gateway, and CloudFront.
    c. Use anomaly detection features to receive alerts when network spend deviates significantly from normal usage patterns.
3. **Optimizing Data Transfer Costs**
    a. Assess AWS inter-region and intra-region data transfer charges and optimize workloads accordingly.
    b. Identify opportunities to reduce NAT Gateway costs by replacing unnecessary outbound traffic routes.
    c. Optimize network architecture by leveraging AWS Global Accelerator and CloudFront for efficient content delivery.
4. **Forecasting and Planning for Future Network Expenses**
    a. Use the forecasting tools of AWS Cost Explorer to estimate future network costs based on historical trends.
    b. Plan cost-efficient scaling strategies by analyzing expected workload growth and adjusting network configurations accordingly.
    c. Implement a reserved or savings plan approach for predictable network usage patterns to lower long-term costs.

AWS Cost Explorer empowers organizations to analyze, monitor, and optimize network expenses with data-driven insights. By leveraging cost trend analysis, anomaly detection, and forecasting tools, businesses can ensure cost-efficient network operations while maintaining high performance. Implementing strategic cost controls allows organizations to maximize AWS network efficiency while keeping expenses under control.

Case Studies

Optimizing AWS networks for performance and cost efficiency requires a strategic approach to bandwidth management, latency reduction, traffic shaping, and cost monitoring. The following case studies illustrate real-world scenarios where organizations successfully implemented AWS networking best practices to enhance efficiency and reduce operational costs.

Case Study 1: Enhancing Performance with Bandwidth Management

A global e-commerce company experienced network congestion due to fluctuating traffic patterns, especially during peak shopping seasons. This resulted in slow page loads, degraded user experience, and increased cart abandonment rates.

Challenges

- Unpredictable bandwidth consumption across AWS services.
- High NAT Gateway data transfer costs.
- Difficulty in allocating bandwidth efficiently between critical and non-essential workloads.

Solution

- Implemented Amazon CloudWatch to monitor bandwidth utilization in real time.
- Analyzed Amazon VPC Flow Logs to pinpoint inefficient subnets and traffic paths contributing to unnecessary data transfer.
- Reconfigured AWS Transit Gateway to prioritize e-commerce transaction traffic over background data processing.
- Reduced NAT Gateway dependency by leveraging AWS PrivateLink for internal service communication.

Results

- 30% reduction in data transfer costs.
- Enhanced application responsiveness during high-traffic events.
- More predictable bandwidth allocation for critical workloads.

Case Study 2: Reducing Latency with Route 53 and AWS Global Accelerator

A global SaaS provider struggled with high latency and inconsistent application performance for international users. Customers in Asia and South America experienced delayed API responses, leading to customer dissatisfaction.

Latency Measurement Approach

Latency improvements were measured using Amazon CloudWatch metrics (such as API response time and network latency) combined with synthetic health checks to simulate user requests from different geographic regions. This provided consistent before-and-after benchmarks for evaluating routing and acceleration improvements.

Challenges

- High latency in cross-region communication.
- Suboptimal DNS resolution for international users.

- Inefficient content delivery routing.

Solution

- Implemented AWS Global Accelerator to reduce routing hops and provide users with low-latency access points.
- Used Amazon Route 53 latency-based routing to direct users to the nearest AWS region.
- Cached static content with Amazon CloudFront to offload traffic from origin servers.

Results

- 50% improvement in API response times for global customers.
- Reduced inter-region data transfer costs by optimizing traffic routes.
- Enhanced user experience and higher customer retention rates.

Case Study 3: Implementing Traffic Shaping for Business-Critical Workloads

A financial services firm relied on AWS for real-time trading applications, but network congestion affected latency-sensitive transactions. Large-scale data transfers impacted trading speed, resulting in financial losses due to delayed execution.

Challenges

- Network congestion during high-volume trading hours.
- Lack of traffic prioritization for critical transactions.
- Unpredictable latency spikes affecting trade execution speeds.

Solution

- Configured AWS Network Firewall to enforce traffic shaping policies.
- Used Quality of Service (QoS) policies to prioritize low-latency trading transactions over background data transfers.
- Deployed AWS Transit Gateway to streamline traffic between on-premises data centers and AWS.

Results

- 95% reduction in latency spikes during peak trading hours.
- Seamless execution of financial transactions with minimal delays.
- Better bandwidth utilization, ensuring critical services always had the highest priority.

Case Study 4: Optimizing Network Costs with AWS Cost Explorer and Budgets

A media streaming company faced unexpected AWS network costs due to high inter-region data transfers and unmonitored bandwidth consumption.

Challenges

- Uncontrolled data transfer costs between AWS regions.
- Lack of real-time cost tracking and forecasting tools.
- Inefficient caching strategies, leading to excessive origin server requests.

Solution

- Used AWS Cost Explorer to identify cost spikes and break down network expenses.
- Configured AWS Budgets to set alerts for unexpected cost increases.
- Optimized CloudFront caching policies to reduce origin fetches and minimize bandwidth costs.
- Enabled Amazon S3 Transfer Acceleration for faster and cost-efficient data transfers.

Results

- 40% reduction in monthly network costs.
- Predictable budgeting with proactive cost monitoring.
- Improved content delivery speed without additional expenses.

Implementation Notes

The cost optimization improvements were achieved within 4–6 weeks through close collaboration between the DevOps and Finance teams. DevOps engineers focused on traffic analysis and caching optimization, while Finance teams used AWS Cost Explorer and AWS Budgets to track trends, validate savings, and enforce budget controls.

These case studies highlight real-world applications of AWS networking best practices. By implementing efficient bandwidth management, latency optimization, traffic shaping, and cost control measures, organizations can enhance network performance while reducing operational costs. AWS offers a comprehensive suite of tools that, when used strategically, can transform network efficiency and business operations.

In the next section, we will summarize the key takeaways from our exploration of VPNs, its features and best practices.

Conclusion

Optimizing network performance and cost efficiency in AWS requires a strategic blend of monitoring, traffic prioritization, and proactive cost management. This chapter explored best practices for bandwidth allocation, latency reduction, traffic shaping, and cost monitoring, ensuring that AWS networks remain high-performing and cost-effective. By leveraging AWS tools such as Cost Explorer, CloudFront, Route 53, and AWS Global Accelerator, organizations can significantly enhance network throughput, reduce congestion, and optimize spending.

In the next chapter, we shall explore AWS WAF (Web Application Firewall) and Shield for protecting applications and network infrastructure from DDoS attacks. Also, let us explore the setup and configuration of WAF rules, how AWS Shield helps mitigate DDoS threats, and how to leverage Security Hub for centralized security monitoring.

Points to Remember

- **Effective Bandwidth Management is Essential**
  - Monitoring **network usage patterns** prevents bottlenecks and optimizes performance.
  - **AWS CloudWatch and VPC Flow Logs** help track and analyze bandwidth consumption.
  - **Traffic segmentation** using AWS Transit Gateway improves efficiency across multiple VPCs.

- **Latency Optimization Boosts Performance**
    - AWS Global Accelerator reduces cross-region latency by routing traffic to the nearest AWS edge location.
    - Route 53 latency-based routing ensures users are directed to the fastest available resource.
    - CloudFront caching minimizes request delays and reduces data transfer costs.
- **Traffic Shaping Enhances Network Efficiency**
    - Quality of Service (QoS) policies allow prioritization of critical workloads.
    - AWS Network Firewall and Security Groups help control inbound and outbound traffic effectively.
    - AWS Transit Gateway optimizes data transfer priorities, ensuring mission-critical applications run smoothly.
- **Cost Monitoring Prevents Unexpected Expenses**
    - AWS Cost Explorer helps break down network costs and identify unnecessary expenses.
    - AWS Budgets enable proactive cost alerts and spending limits for better financial control.
    - Optimizing inter-region data transfers and using S3 Transfer Acceleration reduces data transfer fees.

By implementing the techniques outlined in this chapter, businesses can maximize AWS network performance while keeping operational costs under control. A well-optimized network not only ensures seamless user experiences but also contributes to business scalability and long-term cost savings.

CHAPTER 11
Network Security Services

Introduction

As cloud adoption continues to grow, network security remains a top priority for organizations leveraging AWS infrastructure. Ensuring robust security measures is essential to protect applications, data, and networks from cyber threats such as DDoS attacks, unauthorized access, and security misconfigurations. AWS provides specialized security services—including AWS WAF, AWS Shield, and AWS Security Hub—that work together to deliver layered, defense-in-depth protection.

AWS WAF operates at the application layer (Layer 7) to inspect and filter HTTP/S traffic, blocking common web exploits and malicious requests before they reach applications. AWS Shield provides always-on protection at the network and transport layers (Layers 3 and 4), defending workloads against large-scale and sophisticated DDoS attacks. Complementing these preventive controls, AWS Security Hub acts as a centralized security management service; aggregating findings from AWS security services and third-party tools to deliver continuous visibility, compliance insights, and actionable remediation guidance.

This chapter explores how to configure AWS WAF to filter malicious traffic, leverage AWS Shield for DDoS protection, and utilize AWS Security Hub for centralized security monitoring. Additionally, it covers vulnerability management strategies to protect applications from common security risks and ensure compliance with security best practices. By implementing these AWS security solutions in tandem, organizations can build resilient cloud environments that balance strong security, high availability, and optimal performance.

Structure

In this chapter, we will walk through:

- AWS WAF Configuration
- AWS Shield
- Security Hub
- Vulnerability Management

AWS WAF Configuration

Web applications are constantly exposed to cyber threats, including SQL injection, cross-site scripting (XSS), and bot attacks. Without proper security measures, these threats can compromise sensitive data, disrupt services, and impact business operations. AWS Web Application Firewall (AWS WAF) provides a powerful and flexible solution to protect web applications from malicious traffic by filtering requests based on custom rules and predefined security policies.

AWS WAF allows organizations to define Web Access Control Lists (ACLs) that enforce security policies tailored to their specific needs. These ACLs enable filtering of malicious IP addresses, blocking known attack patterns, and preventing unauthorized access. Additionally, AWS WAF integrates with Amazon CloudFront, Application Load Balancer (ALB), and API Gateway, offering scalable and low-latency protection for web applications.

Example Attack Scenario: Blocking an SQL Injection Attempt

Consider a public-facing e-commerce application hosted behind an Application Load Balancer. An attacker attempts to exploit a vulnerable login form by submitting a malicious SQL payload such as:

' OR 1=1 --

This input is designed to manipulate backend database queries and bypass authentication. When AWS WAF Managed Rules for SQL injection (SQLi)—such as the AWSManagedRulesSQLiRuleSet—are associated with the Web ACL of the application, the request is automatically inspected at Layer 7. AWS WAF detects the SQL injection pattern in the request parameters and immediately blocks the request before it reaches the application, returning an HTTP 403 response and logging the event for further analysis.

This proactive filtering prevents unauthorized access without requiring any changes to the application code, significantly reducing the attack surface.

This section explores how AWS WAF operates, the process of creating Web ACLs, and defining custom security rules to safeguard applications. By mastering AWS WAF configuration, organizations can effectively mitigate threats while maintaining high availability and performance.

Understanding AWS WAF and Its Role in Network Security

In the digital landscape of today, web applications are prime targets for cyber threats, ranging from automated bot attacks to sophisticated SQL injection and cross-site scripting (XSS) exploits. Traditional firewalls provide basic perimeter protection, but they often lack the granularity required to inspect and control application-layer (Layer 7) traffic. This is where AWS Web Application Firewall (AWS WAF) plays a critical role in strengthening network security.

AWS WAF is a fully managed security service that enables organizations to monitor, inspect, and control HTTP and HTTPS requests directed at their web applications. It uses Web Access Control Lists (Web ACLs) to evaluate incoming requests against defined security rules, allowing malicious traffic to be blocked while legitimate traffic continues uninterrupted. AWS WAF supports custom rules, managed rule groups, and rate-based controls, providing a flexible and scalable approach to application-layer security without degrading performance.

Match-Based Rules versus Rate-Based Rules

AWS WAF rules generally fall into two categories, each designed to address different threat patterns:

- **Match-Based Rules:** Match-based rules evaluate individual requests against specific conditions such as request headers, query strings, URI paths, IP addresses, or known attack signatures. These rules are ideal for detecting known, repeatable attack patterns.

  Example: A match-based rule blocks requests containing SQL injection patterns (for example, UNION SELECT or ' OR 1=1). If a single request matches the defined pattern, AWS WAF immediately blocks it—regardless of how frequently the request occurs.

- **Rate-Based Rules:** Rate-based rules track the number of requests from a single IP address over a defined time window (typically five minutes). These rules are designed to mitigate high-volume or abusive traffic patterns rather than individual malicious payloads.

  Example: A rate-based rule blocks an IP address that sends more than 2,000 requests in five minutes to a login endpoint. This is effective against brute-force login attempts or bot-driven scraping, even if each individual request appears legitimate.

When to Use Each Rule Type

- Use match-based rules to stop well-known attack signatures such as SQL injection and XSS.
- Use rate-based rules to control traffic floods, credential stuffing, and bot abuse.
- Combine both rule types within a single Web ACL for layered protection.

This section delves into the core functionalities of AWS WAF, its role in protecting cloud-based applications, and how organizations can leverage its capabilities to enforce security best practices and meet compliance requirements. By applying the right mix of match-based and rate-based rules, organizations can significantly reduce their attack surface while maintaining application availability and performance.

Core Functions of AWS WAF

AWS WAF is designed to protect applications by filtering, monitoring, and managing web traffic. It achieves this through several key functions:

- **Request Filtering and Traffic Control:** AWS WAF allows users to define rules that block, allow, or monitor traffic based on request attributes such as IP addresses, HTTP headers, query strings, and request body content.

  Applied example: Block all requests containing suspicious query strings such as ../ to prevent directory traversal attacks, while allowing normal application traffic to pass through.

- **Rate-Based Rules:** It can limit the number of requests from a particular IP address within a specified time window, preventing brute-force attacks and bot-based traffic surges.

  Applied example: Limit login requests to 100 requests per minute per IP address. If the threshold is exceeded, AWS WAF temporarily blocks the IP to prevent credential stuffing attacks.

- **Integration with AWS Services:** AWS WAF seamlessly integrates with Amazon CloudFront, API Gateway, and Application Load Balancer, ensuring security at the edge locations and entry points of applications.

  Applied example: Attach a Web ACL to a CloudFront distribution so malicious requests are blocked at the edge before reaching the backend application hosted on Amazon EC2.

- **Custom and Managed Rule Sets:** Users can define custom rules or use AWS Managed Rules, which provide preconfigured protections against common threats like OWASP Top 10 vulnerabilities.

  Applied example: Enable the AWSManagedRulesCommonRuleSet to automatically block common attack patterns, while adding a custom rule to allow only specific IP ranges to access an internal admin portal.

By leveraging these capabilities, AWS WAF enhances security without impacting latency or application performance.

Advantages of Using AWS WAF in Cloud Security

Implementing AWS WAF offers several benefits in securing web applications:

- **Scalability and Elastic Protection:** AWS WAF automatically scales to handle fluctuating traffic volumes, ensuring consistent protection during traffic spikes such as product launches, seasonal sales, or flash events.

  Example Metric: During peak traffic events, organizations can continue inspecting millions of requests per minute without pre-provisioning capacity, while maintaining stable application performance.

- **Real-Time Threat Mitigation:** AWS WAF evaluates requests in real time and enforces rules instantly, allowing security teams to block malicious traffic as soon as suspicious behavior is detected.

  Example Outcome: After enabling AWS Managed Rules, many organizations observe a significant reduction in common web attacks, such as SQL injection and XSS attempts, within the first few days of deployment—often before any application-level impact occurs.

- **Cost-Effective Security Solution:** AWS WAF follows a pay-as-you-go pricing model, charging only for the number of Web ACLs, rules, and inspected requests. This eliminates the need for expensive on-premises firewalls, licensing fees, and manual scaling.

  Example Comparison: Instead of maintaining dedicated hardware appliances sized for peak load, organizations pay only for actual traffic inspected—often resulting in lower operational costs during normal traffic periods.

- **Improved Compliance and Regulatory Adherence:** AWS WAF helps organizations meet regulatory and security requirements by enforcing consistent traffic inspection and blocking known attack vectors.

  Example Use Case: For PCI DSS-regulated applications, AWS WAF managed rules can automatically block malicious input targeting payment forms, while logging blocked requests to support audit and compliance reporting.

AWS WAF is a powerful defense mechanism that enables organizations to proactively mitigate web-based attacks, ensuring secure and high-performing applications.

Creating Web Access Control Lists (ACLs) for Traffic Filtering

A Web Access Control List (Web ACL) is a fundamental component of AWS WAF (Web Application Firewall), allowing organizations to define security rules that filter, monitor, and control web traffic to their applications. Web ACLs are critical in preventing unauthorized access, mitigating attacks, and ensuring compliance with security policies.

By creating custom rule sets, organizations can specify which requests to allow, block, or count based on multiple attributes, such as IP addresses, HTTP headers, request body contents, and geographic origin. AWS WAF Web ACLs provide a layered defense strategy, offering fine-grained control over incoming traffic to Amazon CloudFront, API Gateway, and Application Load Balancer (ALB).

This section explores the process of creating and managing Web ACLs, detailing the steps to define security rules, set priority levels, and ensure effective traffic filtering.

Defining Web ACL Rules and Conditions

To effectively filter traffic, organizations must define Web ACL rules based on specific conditions that match potential threats. These conditions include:

- **IP-Based Filtering:** Block or allow requests from specific IP addresses or CIDR blocks to prevent access from malicious sources.
- **Geographic Restrictions:** Use Geo Match Conditions to block traffic from high-risk locations or enforce region-specific security policies.
- **Rate-Based Rules:** Mitigate DDoS and bot attacks by limiting the number of requests an IP address can make within a given time frame.
- **String Matching Conditions:** Inspect URL paths, query strings, and HTTP headers to filter traffic based on patterns associated with common exploits.
- **SQL Injection and XSS Protection:** Leverage the built-in detection capabilities of AWS WAF to block requests containing SQL injection or cross-site scripting (XSS) attempts.

By defining these rules, AWS WAF enables precise traffic filtering, reducing the risk of unauthorized access and malicious activities.

How Rule Evaluation Works

- Rules in a Web ACL are evaluated in ascending priority order (lower number = higher priority).
- AWS WAF processes one rule at a time for each request.
- As soon as a rule matches and performs an action (ALLOW or BLOCK), rule evaluation stops.
- If no rules match, the default Web ACL action (allow or block) is applied.

This means a poorly ordered rule can unintentionally allow malicious traffic or block legitimate users.

Best Practice: Priority-Based Rule Design

A commonly recommended evaluation order is:

- Explicit ALLOW rules (trusted IPs, internal users)
- Explicit BLOCK rules (known bad IPs, blocked countries)
- Rate-based rules (traffic abuse control)
- Managed rule groups (SQLi, XSS, OWASP protections)
- Default action (typically ALLOW)

Designing Web ACLs with this layered priority structure ensures accurate filtering, reduces unnecessary inspection overhead, and minimizes the risk of misconfiguration.

Creating and Configuring Web ACLs in AWS WAF

The process of creating and configuring a Web ACL in AWS WAF involves several key steps:

Step 1: Accessing AWS WAF

1. Log into the AWS Management Console.
2. Navigate to AWS WAF and Shield from the Security Services menu.
3. Select Web ACLs and click `Create Web ACL`.

AWS CLI – List existing Web ACLs (to verify scope):

```
aws wafv2 list-web-acls \
  --scope REGIONAL \
  --region ap-south-1
```

Note:

- Use REGIONAL for ALB and API Gateway.
- Use CLOUDFRONT for CloudFront (always created in us-east-1).

Step 2: Defining Basic Web ACL Settings

1. Enter a Web ACL name for easy identification.
2. Choose the AWS resource to associate with the Web ACL (CloudFront, ALB, or API Gateway).
3. Select the region where the Web ACL will be deployed.

AWS CLI – Create a basic Web ACL:

```
aws wafv2 create-web-acl \
  --name MyWebACL \
  --scope REGIONAL \
  --default-action Allow={} \
  --visibility-config \
    SampledRequestsEnabled=true,\
    CloudWatchMetricsEnabled=true,\
    MetricName=MyWebACLMetric \
  --region ap-south-1
```

Key configuration points:

- Default action is usually ALLOW.
- CloudWatch metrics enable traffic visibility and alerts.

Step 3: Adding Rules and Rule Groups

1. Choose from AWS Managed Rules or create custom rules to define filtering criteria.
2. Add conditions such as IP filtering, rate limits, string matching, and geo restrictions.
3. Set a priority order for rules to ensure proper execution.

Example: Add an AWS Managed SQL Injection rule group

```
{
  "Name": "SQLiProtection",
  "Priority": 10,
  "Statement": {
    "ManagedRuleGroupStatement": {
      "VendorName": "AWS",
      "Name": "AWSManagedRulesSQLiRuleSet"
    }
  },
  "OverrideAction": {
    "None": {}
  },
```

```
    "VisibilityConfig": {
      "SampledRequestsEnabled": true,
      "CloudWatchMetricsEnabled": true,
      "MetricName": "SQLiProtection"
    }
  }
```

Rule placement insight: Managed rules are typically placed after IP allow/block rules but before the default action.

Step 4: Defining Actions for Rule Matches

1. Choose Allow, Block, or Count for requests that match a rule.
2. Configure AWS WAF logging and monitoring for real-time traffic analysis.

   Example: Rate-based rule to limit login attempts

```
{
  "Name": "RateLimitLogin",
  "Priority": 5,
  "Statement": {
    "RateBasedStatement": {
      "Limit": 100,
      "AggregateKeyType": "IP"
    }
  },
  "Action": {
    "Block": {}
  },
  "VisibilityConfig": {
    "SampledRequestsEnabled": true,
    "CloudWatchMetricsEnabled": true,
    "MetricName": "RateLimitLogin"
  }
}
```

   Use case: Blocks IPs exceeding 100 requests in 5 minutes, preventing brute-force login attacks.

Step 5: Enabling Logging and Monitoring

AWS WAF logs can be streamed to Amazon CloudWatch Logs, S3, or Kinesis Data Firehose.

AWS CLI – Enable logging:

```
aws wafv2 put-logging-configuration \
  --logging-configuration '{
    "ResourceArn":"<WEB_ACL_ARN>",
    "LogDestinationConfigs":["<CLOUDWATCH_LOG_GROUP_ARN>"]
  }'
```

This enables:

- Real-time traffic inspection
- Attack pattern analysis
- Compliance and audit support

Step 6: Deploying the Web ACL

1. Review the Web ACL configuration.
2. Click **Save** and Deploy to apply security policies to the selected AWS resources.

   Example: Associate Web ACL with an ALB

   ```
   aws wafv2 associate-web-acl \
     --web-acl-arn <WEB_ACL_ARN> \
     --resource-arn <ALB_ARN>
   ```

After deployment, AWS WAF immediately begins inspecting incoming requests based on rule priority and defined actions.

By following this structured configuration process—defining scope, ordering rules correctly, testing with COUNT, and enabling logging—organizations can deploy AWS WAF safely and effectively. A well-designed Web ACL ensures that legitimate traffic flows uninterrupted while malicious requests are blocked in real time, strengthening application security without impacting performance.

Managing and Updating Web ACLs for Continuous Protection

Security threats evolve over time, requiring organizations to regularly update and optimize their Web ACLs. AWS provides tools to monitor, analyze, and refine Web ACL rules based on real-time threat intelligence.

- **Monitoring with AWS WAF Logs:** Enable logging to Amazon S3 or AWS CloudWatch to track request activity and identify potential attack patterns.
- **Analyzing Traffic Trends:** Use AWS WAF metrics and dashboards to assess the effectiveness of the existing rules and adjust them as needed.
- **Automating Updates:** Integrate AWS WAF with AWS Lambda to dynamically update rule sets in response to emerging threats.
- **Testing Rule Changes:** Before enforcing new rules, use the "Count" action to simulate how changes will impact traffic flow.

By continuously managing Web ACLs, organizations enhance their security posture and ensure proactive protection against evolving cyber threats.

Creating and managing Web ACLs in AWS WAF is a vital step in securing web applications against a variety of threat vectors. By implementing custom rule sets, leveraging real-time monitoring, and continuously optimizing security policies, organizations can effectively filter traffic and mitigate attacks before they reach their infrastructure.

Defining Custom WAF Rules to Protect Web Applications

While AWS provides a set of managed rules for web application security, many organizations require customized protection tailored to their specific needs. Custom AWS WAF rules enable businesses to define precise filtering criteria, ensuring that only legitimate traffic reaches their applications while blocking malicious requests.

By creating custom WAF rules, organizations can strengthen their security posture against SQL injection, cross-site scripting (XSS), bot attacks, and unauthorized access attempts. These rules help businesses implement fine-grained control over web traffic, ensuring compliance with security policies and regulatory requirements.

This section covers the process of creating, configuring, and optimizing custom WAF rules to enhance the security of AWS-hosted web applications.

Identifying Security Risks and Attack Patterns

Before defining custom AWS WAF rules, it is essential to identify the security risks and attack patterns that could compromise web applications. Understanding how each threat manifests — and which AWS WAF capability addresses it — enables more precise and effective rule design.

- **SQL Injection (SQLi):** Attackers inject malicious SQL statements into input fields or query parameters to manipulate backend databases and extract or modify sensitive data.
    - **AWS WAF mitigation:**
        - AWS Managed Rules (SQLi Rule Set)
        - String matching and regex pattern rules on query strings and request bodies
    - **Example:** Block requests containing SQL keywords such as UNION SELECT or ' OR 1=1.
- **Cross-Site Scripting (XSS):** Malicious scripts are injected into web pages and executed in the browsers of the users, potentially leading to session hijacking or data theft.
    - **AWS WAF mitigation:**
        - AWS Managed Rules (XSS Rule Set)
        - String match rules on headers, query parameters, and request bodies
    - **Example:** Block requests containing <script> tags or encoded JavaScript payloads.
- **Bot Attacks:** Automated bots perform activities such as credential stuffing, content scraping, or automated form submissions.
    - **AWS WAF mitigation:**
        - Rate-based rules to limit requests per IP.
        - AWS Managed Bot Control rules (if enabled).
    - **Example:** Throttle login attempts to 50–100 requests per IP per minute to prevent brute-force attacks.
- **DDoS Traffic Spikes:** Attackers flood applications with excessive traffic, degrading performance or causing service outages.
    - **AWS WAF mitigation:**
        - Rate-based rules to block high-volume request sources.
        - Integration with AWS Shield for network- and transport-layer DDoS protection.
    - **Example:** Automatically block IPs exceeding 2,000 requests in five minutes, while Shield absorbs volumetric floods.
- **Unauthorized API Access:** Malicious users exploit exposed or poorly secured APIs to access backend services or sensitive data.
    - **AWS WAF mitigation:**
        - IP allow lists for trusted clients.
        - Header and string matching rules to enforce API keys or custom headers.
        - Rate-based rules to limit API abuse.

- **Example:** Allow API requests only if a specific authorization header is present and originates from trusted CIDR ranges.

By analyzing application logs, AWS WAF logs, CloudWatch metrics, and historical security incidents, organizations can identify recurring attack patterns and map them to the appropriate AWS WAF controls. This targeted approach ensures that custom rules are both effective and efficient, reducing false positives while strengthening application-layer security.

Creating Custom AWS WAF Rules for Threat Mitigation

Once security risks are identified, organizations can define custom rules in AWS WAF to protect web applications from threats. These rules can be configured based on specific attack patterns, request attributes, and user behavior.

Step 1: Access AWS WAF and Create a Custom Rule

1. Navigate to the AWS WAF console.
2. Select an existing Web ACL or create a new one.
3. Click `Add Rules` and choose `Create Custom Rule`.

Step 2: Define Rule Criteria and Matching Conditions

Organizations can configure rules based on multiple conditions:

1. **IP Filtering Rules:**
   a. Block or allow traffic from specific IP addresses or CIDR ranges.
   b. **Example:** Restrict access to administrative panels from known IPs only.
2. **Geographic Restriction Rules:**
   a. Use Geo Match Conditions to block requests from high-risk countries.
   b. **Example:** Prevent unauthorized login attempts from unapproved locations.
3. **Rate-Based Rules:**
   a. Define limits on the number of requests allowed from a single IP within a specified time frame.
   b. **Example:** Mitigate brute-force attacks by limiting login attempts per IP.
4. **String Match Rules (Header and Body Filtering):**
   a. Inspect HTTP headers, query strings, and request bodies for malicious content.
   b. **Example:** Block requests containing common SQL injection payloads.
5. **Bot Mitigation Rules:**
   a. Identify and block traffic from automated bots and scrapers.
   b. **Example:** Challenge all requests lacking a valid User-Agent header.

Step 3: Assign Actions to the Rule

Once the rule conditions are set, define the action for matching requests:

1. **Allow:** Permit the request to proceed to the web application.
2. **Block:** Deny the request, preventing it from reaching the backend.
3. **Count:** Log the request for analysis without blocking it (useful for testing new rules).

Step 4: Prioritize Rule Execution Order

Rules within a Web ACL execute based on priority. Arrange high-risk filtering rules at the top, followed by general security rules to ensure that the most critical threats are mitigated first.

Step 5: Deploy the Custom Rule

1. Review the rule configuration.
2. Click **Save** and Apply Changes.
3. Monitor rule performance using AWS WAF logs and CloudWatch metrics.

Testing and Fine-Tuning Custom WAF Rules

After deploying custom WAF rules, continuous testing and optimization are crucial to minimize false positives and enhance security effectiveness.

Testing Custom Rules

- Use "Count" mode of AWS WAF to track how many requests match a rule without blocking traffic.
- Simulate attack scenarios using penetration testing tools like OWASP ZAP or Burp Suite.
- Validate rule performance using AWS CloudWatch metrics and AWS WAF logs.

Fine-Tuning Rules for Improved Accuracy

- **Reduce False Positives:** Modify thresholds and conditions for rules that block legitimate traffic.
- **Refine IP Reputation Lists:** Regularly update IP blocklists and allowlists based on traffic patterns.
- **Adjust Rate-Based Rules:** Tune rate limits to balance security and application availability.
- **Automate Rule Updates:** Use AWS Lambda functions to dynamically adjust WAF rules based on real-time threats.

Defining custom AWS WAF rules allows organizations to proactively mitigate security threats while maintaining application performance and availability. By analyzing attack patterns, configuring targeted security policies, and continuously optimizing rule sets, businesses can enhance web application security and minimize exposure to cyber threats.

Implementing AWS WAF is a critical step in securing web applications against evolving threats such as SQL injection, cross-site scripting (XSS), bot attacks, and DDoS attempts. By strategically configuring Web Access Control Lists (ACLs) and custom rules, organizations can establish a robust security perimeter that prevents unauthorized access while allowing legitimate traffic to flow smoothly.

A well-defined WAF implementation requires continuous monitoring, fine-tuning of rules, and regular updates to keep pace with new attack vectors. Organizations should leverage AWS CloudWatch logs, AWS Shield, and Security Hub to gain real-time insights into potential threats and take proactive measures.

Ultimately, an optimized AWS WAF deployment enhances both security and performance, ensuring that web applications remain resilient, compliant, and available while providing a seamless user experience. By integrating automated threat intelligence, rate-based filtering, and customized security policies, businesses can safeguard their digital assets and minimize operational risks in the cloud.

AWS Shield

As cyber threats continue to evolve, Distributed Denial-of-Service (DDoS) attacks remain one of the most disruptive and damaging threats to modern cloud applications. AWS Shield provides a managed, always-on DDoS protection service designed to detect, absorb, and mitigate attacks before they impact business operations. By leveraging real-time threat intelligence, network traffic analysis, and automated mitigation techniques, AWS Shield ensures that applications remain available and responsive even under attack.

AWS Shield is available in two tiers: AWS Shield Standard, which offers basic, free DDoS protection, and AWS Shield Advanced, which provides enhanced defenses, deeper insights, and financial protections against large-scale attacks. Shield integrates seamlessly with AWS WAF, CloudFront, Route 53, and Elastic Load Balancing (ELB) to provide a multi-layered security approach.

This section explores how AWS Shield works, its key features, and best practices for enabling automatic mitigation. Readers will gain a comprehensive understanding of configuring AWS Shield, monitoring attack patterns, and leveraging AWS services to enhance resilience against sophisticated DDoS threats. By the end of this section, organizations will be equipped with the knowledge to proactively protect their cloud environments from service disruptions and costly downtime.

Introduction to AWS Shield: Standard versus Advanced

In an era where cyber threats are increasingly sophisticated, organizations must adopt proactive defense mechanisms to safeguard their cloud infrastructure. AWS Shield is a managed Distributed Denial-of-Service (DDoS) protection service that defends AWS applications from malicious traffic, ensuring high availability and resilience against disruptions. AWS Shield operates in two service tiers—Shield Standard and Shield Advanced—each offering different levels of protection based on security needs and risk tolerance.

Understanding the differences between AWS Shield Standard and AWS Shield Advanced is critical for organizations to determine which level of security best suits their applications. This section provides an in-depth comparison of both tiers, explaining their capabilities, benefits, and key use cases.

AWS Shield Standard: Built-in DDoS Protection for All AWS Customers

AWS Shield Standard is automatically enabled for all AWS customers at no additional cost. It provides basic DDoS protection against common, large-scale Layer 3 (Network) and Layer 4 (Transport) attacks, such as SYN floods, UDP reflection attacks, and IP fragmentation attacks.

- **Key Features**
  - Always-on monitoring for suspicious traffic patterns.
  - Automatic traffic baselining and anomaly detection for DDoS attack identification.
  - Mitigation capabilities integrated into AWS services, such as CloudFront, Route 53, and Application Load Balancer.
  - No additional cost—available by default for all AWS users.

While AWS Shield Standard provides essential defenses, it does not include real-time attack visibility, advanced analytics, or financial protection against attack-related costs. For businesses running mission-critical applications, AWS Shield Advanced may be necessary to ensure enhanced security, faster response, and greater control over attack mitigation.

AWS Shield Advanced: Comprehensive DDoS Protection with Enhanced Features

AWS Shield Advanced is a premium, subscription-based service that provides additional layers of protection against large-scale, sophisticated DDoS attacks. It is designed for high-risk, highly available applications that require advanced threat mitigation, real-time insights, and proactive defense mechanisms.

- **Key Features:**
  - Advanced detection and automated mitigation for Layer 3, Layer 4, and even some Layer 7 (Application) attacks.
  - Real-time visibility into attack details through the Response Team of AWS Shield (AWS SRT).
  - Integration with AWS WAF for more granular, rule-based traffic filtering.
  - DDoS Cost Protection, which provides financial compensation for scaling costs incurred during a DDoS attack.
  - 24/7 access to AWS security experts for guidance and incident response.

Choosing the Right AWS Shield Tier for Your Workloads

Selecting between AWS Shield Standard and AWS Shield Advanced depends on the risk profile, application architecture, and security requirements of an organization.

- **When to Use AWS Shield Standard:**
  - If you need basic, built-in DDoS protection without additional costs.
  - If your applications primarily rely on AWS services like CloudFront, Route 53, and ELB, which have native DDoS defenses.
  - If you do not require real-time attack visibility or AWS support for mitigation strategies.
- **When to Use AWS Shield Advanced:**
  - If your organization operates mission-critical, publicly accessible applications that require high availability.
  - If you need real-time threat intelligence, deeper attack insights, and proactive response capabilities.
  - If your business wants financial protection against unexpected scaling costs due to a DDoS attack.
  - If you require 24/7 security team support to assist in active threat mitigation.

By understanding the capabilities, limitations, and use cases of AWS Shield Standard and Advanced, businesses can make informed decisions about securing their cloud infrastructure. The next section explores how to configure AWS Shield to maximize its DDoS protection capabilities.

AWS Shield: Detects and Mitigates DDoS Attacks

With the increasing frequency and sophistication of Distributed Denial-of-Service (DDoS) attacks, organizations must deploy robust and intelligent defense mechanisms to safeguard their cloud infrastructure. AWS Shield provides real-time detection, automated response, and mitigation strategies to ensure applications remain available and resilient even during large-scale attacks.

Detect → Mitigate → Respond

- Abnormal traffic is detected automatically
- Mitigation controls are applied in real time
- Monitoring and response mechanisms ensure continuity and visibility

By combining continuous detection, automated mitigation, and integrated response mechanisms, AWS Shield enables organizations to defend against DDoS attacks while maintaining high availability and uninterrupted network operations.

This section explores how AWS Shield detects and mitigates DDoS threats, including the key detection mechanisms, mitigation strategies, and integration with AWS services to provide seamless, uninterrupted network operations.

Real-Time Traffic Analysis and Anomaly Detection

The foundation of DDoS protection by AWS Shield lies in its real-time traffic monitoring and anomaly detection systems. AWS Shield continuously analyzes incoming network traffic patterns to identify suspicious activities that may indicate a potential attack.

- **AWS Shield Traffic Monitoring:**
  - It uses machine learning algorithms to establish a baseline of normal traffic patterns.
  - It detects abnormal spikes in request rates, connection attempts, and unusual protocol behaviors.
  - It differentiates between legitimate traffic surges and actual attack patterns using historical data.
  - It integrates with AWS services such as CloudFront, Route 53, and Elastic Load Balancer (ELB) to monitor network requests in real time.

When AWS Shield detects a potential attack, it triggers automated responses to mitigate the threat before it can impact the application.

Automated DDoS Mitigation Techniques

Once an attack is detected, AWS Shield automatically applies mitigation strategies to neutralize the threat. The mitigation process varies depending on the type of attack and the level of AWS Shield protection (Standard versus Advanced).

- **Mitigation Methods for Layer 3 and Layer 4 Attacks (Network and Transport Layers)**
  - **Traffic Rate Limiting:** AWS Shield applies rate-based thresholds to block excessive requests.
  - **Packet Filtering:** It drops malicious packets that do not conform to normal network behavior.
  - **Blackhole Routing:** In extreme cases, AWS may temporarily reroute traffic to a null route to protect the network.
- **Mitigation Methods for Layer 7 Attacks (Application Layer)**
  - **AWS WAF Integration:** AWS Shield works alongside AWS WAF (Web Application Firewall) to filter out malicious requests targeting web applications.
  - **Challenge-Response Mechanisms:** It can enforce CAPTCHAs or JavaScript-based verification to differentiate bots from real users.

- **Traffic Prioritization:** Shield Advanced routes legitimate requests to alternative endpoints while filtering attack traffic.

AWS Shield ensures that mitigation happens instantly, preventing service degradation even during high-intensity DDoS attacks.

Adaptive Threat Intelligence and Attack Signature Analysis

AWS Shield continuously learns and adapts based on global attack trends and previous incidents. This intelligence-driven approach enables Shield to recognize emerging threats and proactively update mitigation strategies.

- **Threat Intelligence in AWS Shield**
  - AWS Shield aggregates threat data from various AWS environments to detect patterns in attacks.
  - It updates attack signatures dynamically to identify and block new attack techniques.
  - AWS Shield works alongside AWS Security Hub to provide detailed reports and insights on attack attempts.

For AWS Shield Advanced customers, this threat intelligence is accessible in real time, allowing organizations to fine-tune security measures and adjust application defenses proactively.

Proactive Response with AWS Shield Advanced and AWS SRT

For high-risk applications that require enhanced security, AWS Shield Advanced provides proactive incident response capabilities through the AWS Shield Response Team (AWS SRT).

- **Benefits of AWS SRT for Attack Mitigation**
  - **24/7 Security Assistance:** Security experts analyze the attack in real time and recommend countermeasures.
  - **Custom Rule Adjustments:** AWS SRT can modify WAF rules or traffic filters to mitigate ongoing attacks.
  - **DDoS Cost Protection:** Organizations receive financial compensation for scaling costs incurred due to attack traffic.

With the human expertise of AWS SRT combined with automated mitigation, organizations can reduce downtime and minimize the business impact of DDoS threats.

Integration with AWS Services for Comprehensive Protection

AWS Shield is most effective when integrated with other AWS security services, creating a multi-layered defense strategy.

- **AWS WAF (Web Application Firewall):** Blocks malicious web requests at the application layer.
- **AWS CloudFront:** Distributes traffic across multiple edge locations, reducing attack surface exposure.
- **AWS Route 53:** Implements DNS-based traffic routing to reroute traffic during an attack.
- **AWS Security Hub:** Provides centralized security monitoring and insights on detected threats.

By combining AWS Shield with these services, businesses can create a resilient and robust security posture against DDoS attacks.

AWS Shield is a powerful, automated DDoS protection service that ensures continuous security, real-time threat detection, and rapid attack mitigation. By leveraging machine learning-driven analysis, automated mitigation, and expert security response, AWS Shield effectively protects applications from network disruptions and cyber threats.

In the next section, we will explore how to configure AWS Shield for optimal protection, ensuring your AWS environment remains secure and resilient against evolving attack vectors.

Configuring AWS Shield Advanced for Enhanced Protection

As cyber threats grow more sophisticated, organizations handling critical workloads require advanced security mechanisms to ensure uninterrupted availability. AWS Shield Advanced provides proactive defense, real-time monitoring, and expert guidance to mitigate even the most complex Distributed Denial-of-Service (DDoS) attacks.

This section walks through the configuration and setup of AWS Shield Advanced, including enabling protection, defining response mechanisms, and integrating with AWS security services for a comprehensive, resilient security strategy.

Activating AWS Shield Advanced for Mission-Critical Applications

To leverage enhanced DDoS protection, organizations must first enable AWS Shield Advanced on their most critical resources. This activation provides additional security measures, such as attack detection intelligence, cost protection, and dedicated AWS Security Response Team (SRT) support.

Steps to Enable AWS Shield Advanced

1. **Navigate to AWS Shield Dashboard**
    a. Sign in to the AWS Management Console and open the AWS Shield service.
2. **Select Protected Resources**
    a. Choose AWS services that need advanced DDoS protection, such as:
        i. Elastic Load Balancers (ELB)
        ii. Amazon CloudFront distributions
        iii. AWS Global Accelerator
        iv. Amazon Route 53 hosted zones
3. **Enable Shield Advanced Protection**
    a. Click **`Enable AWS Shield Advanced`** and configure the resource selection criteria.
4. **Define Response Preferences**
    a. Configure automatic incident notifications for security teams.
    b. Enable AWS SRT access to allow proactive mitigation assistance during attacks.
5. **Review and Confirm**
    a. Review the selected resources, configurations, and estimated costs. Then, confirm activation.

Once AWS Shield Advanced is enabled, it immediately begins monitoring traffic and applying proactive security measures to mitigate attack risks.

Customizing Shield Advanced Detection and Mitigation Settings

AWS Shield Advanced allows security teams to customize detection parameters and fine-tune mitigation settings to align with business requirements.

Key Customization Options

- **Traffic Threshold Configuration**
  - Define baseline traffic patterns to improve anomaly detection.
  - Set custom alert thresholds to notify teams before an attack escalates.
- **Layer 3 and 4 Attack Prevention**
  - Adjust network-layer defense settings for TCP SYN flood protection, volumetric attack filtering, and spoofed IP detection.
- **Layer 7 Application-Layer Protection**
  - Integrate AWS WAF (Web Application Firewall) to block malicious HTTP/S traffic.
  - Apply automated rule-based responses to prevent bot-driven attacks.

These settings ensure real-time attack mitigation while minimizing false positives, allowing legitimate traffic to flow uninterrupted.

Enabling Cost Protection Feature of AWS Shield Advanced

A key advantage of AWS Shield Advanced is DDoS cost protection, which reimburses organizations for unexpected cost spikes caused by a cyberattack.

AWS Cost Protection:

- Monitors abnormal usage patterns during an attack.
- Reimburses increased AWS costs due to scaling or recovery efforts.
- Provides financial relief for bandwidth overuse caused by attack traffic.

Enabling Cost Protection:

1. Go to the AWS Shield Advanced console.
2. Select the resources under protection.
3. Enable Cost Protection for Elastic Load Balancers, CloudFront distributions, and Route 53 zones.
4. Define reporting policies to claim compensation for eligible incidents.

By enabling this feature, businesses can mitigate financial risks while maintaining high network availability.

Setting up Incident Response with AWS Shield Response Team (SRT)

One of the biggest advantages of AWS Shield Advanced is 24/7 access to the AWS Shield Response Team (SRT), a group of cybersecurity experts that assist during ongoing attacks.

Benefits of AWS SRT Support

- Real-time attack diagnostics to analyze DDoS traffic sources.

- Customized mitigation recommendations to enhance security posture.
- Direct AWS support in configuring WAF rules, rate limiting, and traffic rerouting.

Configuring AWS SRT Access

1. Navigate to AWS Shield Advanced settings.
2. Enable AWS SRT engagement for high-priority incidents.
3. Define escalation contacts that who will be notified during an attack.
4. Integrate AWS SRT response into security playbooks for automated handling.

With AWS SRT, businesses can minimize downtime, accelerate mitigation, and maintain service availability even during high-scale DDoS events.

Integrating AWS Shield Advanced with AWS Security Services

To maximize protection, AWS Shield Advanced integrates seamlessly with other AWS security services, creating a multi-layered defense against cyber threats.

Key Integrations

- **AWS WAF (Web Application Firewall):** Automatically blocks malicious traffic from known attack sources.
- **AWS CloudFront (CDN):** Distributes traffic across edge locations, minimizing attack surface.
- **AWS Route 53 (DNS Protection):** Provides DNS-level attack mitigation and automatic failover.
- **AWS Security Hub:** Aggregates threat intelligence and security alerts for centralized monitoring.

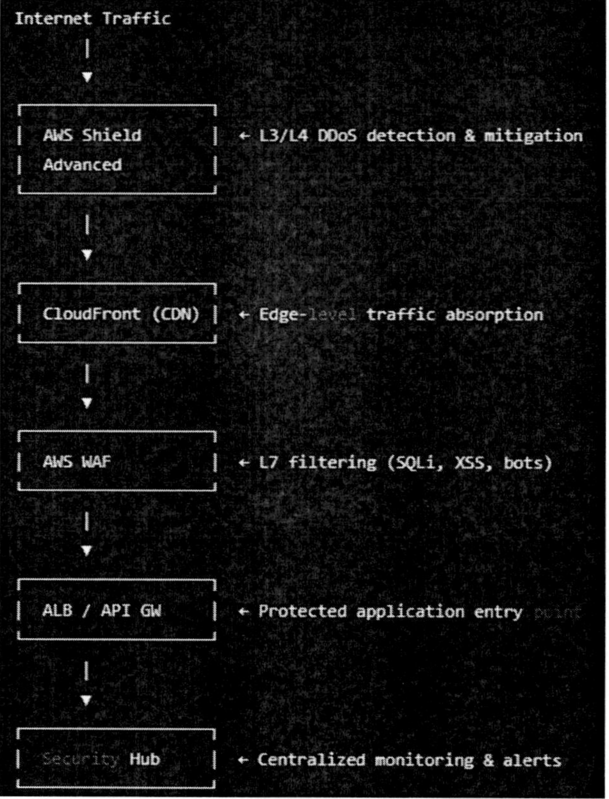

Figure 11.1: *Multi-Layered Defense Flow*

By combining always-on network-layer protection, edge-based traffic distribution, application-layer inspection, and centralized security visibility, AWS Shield Advanced enables organizations to:

- Detect DDoS attacks within seconds
- Automatically mitigate attacks without manual intervention
- Maintain application availability during large-scale events
- Gain real-time insights and expert support via AWS SRT/DRT

AWS Shield Advanced provides next-level DDoS protection for organizations that require continuous availability, automated response, and proactive incident handling. By activating protection, customizing mitigation settings, leveraging AWS SRT support, and integrating with security services, businesses can fortify their network infrastructure against even the most sophisticated cyber threats.

Security Hub

As cloud environments grow more complex, security monitoring becomes a critical challenge. AWS Security Hub provides a centralized security management platform, aggregating security findings from multiple AWS services, third-party tools, and compliance frameworks. By offering a unified view of security alerts, it helps organizations detect, investigate, and respond to threats efficiently.

AWS Security Hub collects security findings from AWS services and third-party tools using the AWS Security Finding Format (ASFF), a standardized JSON schema. All findings are normalized into this format, enabling consistent severity scoring, resource identification, and compliance mapping across accounts and regions. This allows Security Hub to correlate alerts, reduce noise, and provide a unified view of the security posture of an organization.

This section explores how AWS Security Hub enhances security visibility, automates compliance checks, and streamlines threat management to maintain a secure AWS environment. Readers will learn how to configure Security Hub, interpret security findings, and integrate it with AWS security services for proactive risk mitigation.

Key Topics Covered

- Understanding the role in cloud security in AWS Security Hub
- Enabling and configuring Security Hub for security monitoring
- Analyzing security findings from integrated AWS services
- Automating security responses with AWS Lambda and EventBridge

By the end of this section, readers will have a comprehensive understanding of the capabilities of AWS Security Hub and how to leverage it for continuous security monitoring and compliance enforcement.

Overview of AWS Security Hub and Its Benefits

As organizations expand their cloud presence, maintaining a strong security posture requires continuous monitoring and analysis of threats across multiple AWS services. AWS Security Hub provides a centralized security management platform that aggregates, prioritizes, and analyzes security findings from AWS services and third-party security tools. By automating compliance checks and consolidating security insights, Security Hub enables organizations to take proactive security measures before threats escalate.

This section explores how AWS Security Hub works, its core functionalities, and the key benefits it brings to cloud security management.

The Role of AWS Security Hub in Cloud Security

As cyber threats evolve, organizations need a unified security platform that can aggregate security findings, correlate data, and provide actionable insights. Security Hub acts as a Security Operations Center (SOC) tool, enabling teams to detect misconfigurations, monitor vulnerabilities, and track compliance violations across their AWS environments.

Key roles of AWS Security Hub include

- **Consolidating security findings from AWS services** (such as GuardDuty, Inspector, and Macie) ***Operational impact:*** Eliminates the need to manually review alerts across multiple services, saving investigation time and reducing blind spots.
- **Providing a single-pane-of-glass view for security alerts and compliance status**

  Operational impact: Reduces alert fatigue by centralizing and prioritizing findings, allowing security teams to focus on high-risk issues first.
- **Integrating with third-party security solutions**

  Operational impact: Enables broader threat detection by correlating AWS-native and external security signals in one consistent format.
- **Automating security best practices using AWS-native tools**

  Operational impact: Accelerates incident response by triggering automated remediation workflows, minimizing manual intervention and human error.

By offering a centralized dashboard, AWS Security Hub simplifies security management and enables organizations to respond swiftly to potential threats.

Benefits of Using AWS Security Hub for Threat Management

Security Hub delivers multiple advantages to organizations looking to enhance their security visibility and operational efficiency.

Some key benefits include:

- **Centralized Security Monitoring:** Collects and normalizes security findings from multiple sources, reducing the need to manually track security events.
- **Automated Compliance Checks:** Uses AWS Config rules and security standards (including the CIS AWS Foundations Benchmark) to assess compliance continuously.
- **Integrated Threat Intelligence:** Works with services like GuardDuty and third-party tools to detect advanced threats and anomalies.
- **Prioritization of Security Findings:** Uses the AWS Security Finding Format (ASFF) to standardize alerts and help security teams focus on high-risk issues.
- **Automated Security Responses:** Supports integration with AWS Lambda and Amazon EventBridge to trigger automatic remediation actions.

By leveraging AWS Security Hub, organizations can detect, analyze, and respond to security risks efficiently, ensuring a proactive and resilient cloud security strategy.

Integrating AWS Security Hub with Other AWS Services

To maximize its effectiveness, AWS Security Hub seamlessly integrates with various AWS services, enhancing threat detection, compliance monitoring, and automated response capabilities. By leveraging these integrations, organizations can create a unified security framework, correlating security insights from multiple AWS-native tools to identify vulnerabilities, detect intrusions, and enforce security policies proactively.

AWS Service	Primary Focus	What It Sends to Security Hub	Operational Benefit
Amazon GuardDuty	Threat detection	Findings on malicious activity, compromised credentials, unusual API behavior	Enables rapid detection of active security threats
AWS Config	Configuration compliance	Resource configuration changes and compliance violations	Identifies misconfigurations and policy drift
Amazon Inspector	Vulnerability management	EC2 and container vulnerability findings	Highlights exploitable software weaknesses
Amazon Macie	Data security	Sensitive data discovery and exposure alerts	Protects PII and regulated data
AWS WAF	Application-layer security	Blocked and suspicious web request patterns	Improves visibility into application attacks
AWS Shield	DDoS protection	DDoS detection and mitigation events	Centralizes DDoS visibility and response
Third-party tools	Extended security coverage	External security findings (via ASFF)	Unifies AWS and non-AWS security insights

Table 11.1: *AWS Security Hub Integration Overview*

This section explores how AWS Security Hub integrates with key AWS security services, ensuring a comprehensive and automated security management approach.

Integrating Security Hub with AWS GuardDuty for Threat Detection

AWS GuardDuty is a threat detection service that continuously monitors AWS accounts and workloads for malicious activity and unauthorized behavior. When integrated with Security Hub, GuardDuty alerts are automatically ingested and analyzed, providing organizations with a centralized view of security threats across their cloud environment.

Key benefits

- **Automated Threat Analysis:** GuardDuty detects anomalies and potential attacks, while Security Hub correlates findings across multiple accounts and services.
- **Real-Time Threat Alerts:** GuardDuty generates alerts for suspicious activity (for instance, compromised credentials, unusual API calls), which Security Hub prioritizes based on severity.
- **Efficient Incident Response:** Findings can be routed through AWS Lambda or EventBridge, enabling automated remediation workflows.

This integration helps security teams stay ahead of potential security incidents by providing actionable intelligence on cloud-based threats.

Using AWS Config and Security Hub for Compliance Monitoring

AWS Config is a configuration auditing service that tracks changes to AWS resources and ensures compliance with security policies. When combined with Security Hub, AWS Config provides deeper insights into security misconfigurations, helping organizations maintain compliance with industry regulations and best practices.

AWS Security Hub leverages AWS Config rules to assess compliance against recognized security frameworks such as CIS AWS Foundations Benchmark, NIST, and PCI DSS. Each control in these frameworks is mapped to one or more Config rules that evaluate specific resource configurations.

- AWS Config rules perform the technical evaluation (pass/fail).
- Security Hub maps these results to high-level compliance controls.
- Non-compliant resources appear as findings with severity and remediation guidance.

Example: A CIS benchmark requires that Amazon S3 buckets must not allow public read access.

- **AWS Config rule:** s3-bucket-public-read-prohibited.
- **What it checks:** Ensures S3 buckets do not allow public access.
- **Security Hub outcome:** Flags non-compliant buckets under CIS and AWS Foundational Security Best Practices standards.

Key advantages

- **Continuous Compliance Checks:** AWS Config rules are mapped to industry standards (for example, CIS, NIST, PCI DSS) and their compliance status is visible in Security Hub.
- **Automated Risk Identification:** Security Hub aggregates findings from Config to detect misconfigured resources and non-compliant deployments.
- **Remediation Recommendations:** Security teams receive detailed insights and suggested remediation steps directly within the dashboard of the Security Hub.

By integrating AWS Config, organizations can proactively enforce security controls and reduce compliance risks.

Enhancing Incident Response with AWS Lambda and Amazon EventBridge

Automating incident response is a key capability of AWS Security Hub. By integrating with AWS Lambda and Amazon EventBridge, organizations can trigger automated security actions when specific threats or compliance violations are detected.

Working

1. **Event-Driven Automation:** Security Hub findings trigger EventBridge rules, which can invoke Lambda functions to take action.
2. **Automated Remediation:** Lambda scripts can quarantine compromised instances, revoke access keys, or modify security groups based on detected threats.
3. **Real-Time Security Enforcement:** Security teams can define custom workflows to respond instantly to threats, reducing response times and manual intervention.

This integration ensures that security threats are not just detected but actively mitigated, strengthening the incident response strategy of an organization.

Aggregating Insights from AWS Macie and Inspector for Data Protection

AWS Macie and Inspector are powerful security tools that help identify vulnerabilities and protect sensitive data. When integrated with Security Hub, they provide centralized visibility into data security risks.

- **AWS Macie Integration:** Identifies and protects sensitive data in Amazon S3, alerting Security Hub when Personally Identifiable Information (PII) is exposed.
- **AWS Inspector Integration:** Scans EC2 instances and container workloads for known vulnerabilities, reporting findings directly to Security Hub.

Service	Focus Area	Typical Findings in Security Hub	Operational Value
Amazon Macie	Data security	Exposure of PII, financial data, or credentials in S3 buckets	Prevents data leaks and regulatory violations
Amazon Inspector	Vulnerability management	CVEs, missing patches, insecure software versions on EC2 and containers	Reduces exploitability of workloads

Table 11.2: *Type of Findings Contributed to Security Hub*

By consolidating insights from Macie and Inspector, Security Hub helps organizations detect security risks early and implement preventive measures.

Integrating AWS Security Hub with AWS GuardDuty, Config, Lambda, EventBridge, Macie, and Inspector provides a unified security approach that enhances threat detection, compliance enforcement, and automated remediation. By leveraging these integrations, organizations can gain real-time insights, strengthen their security posture, and ensure continuous monitoring of their AWS environments.

Automating Security Monitoring and Incident Response

As cloud environments grow in complexity, manual security monitoring and incident response become inefficient and prone to human error. To ensure rapid threat detection and mitigation, organizations must adopt automation-driven security operations. AWS Security Hub provides powerful automation capabilities that integrate with other AWS services, enabling continuous security monitoring and real-time incident response.

Findings versus Insights (quick clarity)

- **Findings** = Individual security issues reported by services (such as a vulnerable EC2 instance or exposed S3 data).
- **Insights** = Grouped and analyzed findings that show patterns or trends (for instance repeated misconfigurations across accounts).

In short, Findings tell you what is wrong now; Insights show what keeps going wrong.

This section explores how to automate security event detection, alerting, and remediation using AWS Security Hub and its integrations with AWS-native security services.

Automating Threat Detection with AWS Security Hub Insights

AWS Security Hub Insights allow organizations to automatically analyze and prioritize security findings based on risk severity. These insights are generated by correlating threat intelligence across multiple AWS security services, helping security teams focus on the most critical threats.

Key aspects

- **Predefined and Custom Insights:** Security Hub offers prebuilt security insights for common threats while allowing users to create custom rules for specific security concerns.

  Example: "High-severity findings from Amazon GuardDuty in the last 7 days" — highlights recent, critical threat detections requiring immediate investigation.

- **Automated Risk Prioritization:** Security Hub ranks security findings based on severity, allowing organizations to address high-risk vulnerabilities first.

  Operational benefit: Teams can address high-risk issues first instead of manually sifting through large volumes of alerts.

- **Continuous Security Analytics:** Automated insights ensure that security teams always have an up-to-date view of the security posture of the organization.

  Operational benefit: Security teams maintain an always-current view of the security posture of the organization without manual reporting.

By leveraging automated insights, organizations can detect security anomalies quickly and take proactive measures.

Configuring Event-Driven Security Alerts with Amazon EventBridge

Amazon EventBridge enables event-driven automation by triggering security alerts and workflows based on Security Hub findings. This integration ensures that security teams are notified in real time and can take immediate action on potential threats.

Working

1. Security Hub generates a security finding (including an unauthorized access attempt, or a non-compliant configuration).
2. EventBridge detects the finding and routes it to a predefined action, such as sending an alert or executing a remediation task.
3. Security teams receive notifications via Amazon SNS, Slack, or email, ensuring quick response.

By automating security event notifications, organizations can accelerate threat response times and minimize potential damage.

Implementing Auto-Remediation with AWS Lambda and Systems Manager

To further enhance security automation, AWS Security Hub can be integrated with AWS Lambda and AWS Systems Manager to enable automatic incident response. This approach eliminates the need for manual intervention and ensures that security threats are mitigated instantly.

Working

- **Lambda Functions:** Security Hub findings trigger Lambda functions that execute predefined security actions, such as:
  - Revoking compromised IAM credentials.
  - Blocking suspicious IP addresses in security groups.
  - Stopping compromised EC2 instances.

- **AWS Systems Manager Automation:** Provides prebuilt remediation runbooks to handle common security issues without human intervention.

By implementing auto-remediation, organizations can reduce incident response times and prevent security threats from escalating.

Strengthening Incident Response with AWS Security Hub and SOAR Platforms

Security Orchestration, Automation, and Response (SOAR) platforms help security teams streamline their workflows by integrating with AWS Security Hub. These platforms automate investigation, triage, and response to security incidents, ensuring efficient threat management.

Benefits of integrating Security Hub with SOAR platforms

- **Automated Playbooks:** Security Hub findings trigger predefined response actions, eliminating manual processing delays.
- **Incident Correlation:** SOAR platforms aggregate multiple security alerts, reducing noise and helping teams focus on real threats.
- **Collaboration and Case Management:** Security incidents can be tracked and assigned within a centralized dashboard for effective resolution.

By integrating SOAR platforms with AWS Security Hub, organizations can achieve a proactive, automated, and scalable incident response system.

Automating security monitoring and incident response in AWS is essential for maintaining a secure and resilient cloud environment. By leveraging Security Hub Insights, EventBridge, Lambda, AWS Systems Manager, and SOAR platforms, organizations can detect threats in real time, generate automated alerts, and execute remediation actions without manual intervention. This approach enhances cloud security, minimizes response times, and ensures continuous compliance with industry best practices.

Vulnerability Management

Amidst the rapidly evolving cyber landscape of the modern day, organizations must adopt a proactive approach to vulnerability management to protect their applications and networks from potential security threats. Cyber attackers continuously exploit misconfigurations, outdated software, and weak security controls, making vulnerability management a critical aspect of securing AWS environments.

AWS offers a robust suite of security tools to help organizations detect, assess, and mitigate vulnerabilities before they can be exploited. By leveraging AWS security services, automated scanning, and best practices, businesses can significantly reduce their risk exposure and maintain a resilient security posture.

This section explores key vulnerability management strategies, including:

- Identifying and prioritizing security weaknesses using AWS tools.
- Implementing automated vulnerability assessments.
- Applying security patches and updates efficiently.
- Strengthening security postures through continuous monitoring and remediation.

By implementing an effective vulnerability management strategy, organizations can proactively defend against cyber threats, reduce security risks, and ensure compliance with industry standards.

Identifying and Addressing Common Security Vulnerabilities

Security vulnerabilities are one of the most significant threats to cloud environments, making proactive identification and mitigation essential for safeguarding AWS workloads. Attackers frequently exploit weaknesses such as misconfigured access controls, unpatched software, exposed credentials, and weak encryption, leading to data breaches, service disruptions, and financial losses.

To minimize security risks and maintain compliance, organizations must adopt a structured approach to vulnerability management. This involves identifying, prioritizing, and remediating vulnerabilities before they can be exploited. AWS provides a range of security tools and services to help businesses detect weaknesses, enforce security best practices, and automate remediation efforts.

This section explores the most common security vulnerabilities in AWS environments and how organizations can effectively address these using AWS-native security features and best practices.

Common Security Vulnerabilities in AWS

Several security vulnerabilities can impact AWS environments if not properly managed. Understanding these weaknesses is the first step in developing an effective mitigation strategy. Some of the most prevalent security risks include:

- **Misconfigured Identity and Access Management (IAM) Policies:** Overly permissive roles and unprotected credentials can expose critical resources to unauthorized access.

  Mitigation tip: Use IAM Access Analyzer and least-privilege policies; regularly review roles and rotate credentials.

- **Unpatched Software and Outdated Dependencies:** Failure to apply security updates can leave applications vulnerable to known exploits.

  Mitigation tip: Use Amazon Inspector to identify vulnerabilities and automate patching with AWS Systems Manager.

- **Publicly Exposed Data and Services:** Improperly configured Amazon S3 buckets, databases, and APIs can lead to unauthorized data access.

  Mitigation tip: Enable S3 Block Public Access, use VPC endpoints, and continuously monitor exposure with Amazon Macie.

- **Weak or Default Encryption Practices:** Lack of encryption for data at rest or in transit increases the risk of data breaches.

  Mitigation tip: Enforce encryption using AWS KMS, enable TLS for all endpoints, and use service-managed encryption by default.

- **Lack of Network Segmentation:** Overly open network access can expose internal services to external threats.

  Mitigation tip: Implement VPC subnet isolation, restrictive security groups, and network ACLs based on least access.

- **Insufficient Logging and Monitoring:** Missing or incomplete logs can delay detection and response to security incidents.

  Mitigation tip: Enable AWS CloudTrail, VPC Flow Logs, and centralize alerts using AWS Security Hub.

Identifying these vulnerabilities early reduces attack surfaces and enhances cloud security resilience.

AWS Tools for Detecting and Assessing Vulnerabilities

AWS provides powerful security tools to detect, assess, and mitigate vulnerabilities before they become threats. Organizations can leverage these services for continuous monitoring and proactive security assessments:

- **AWS Security Hub:** Aggregates and analyzes security findings across multiple AWS services.
- **Amazon Inspector:** Performs automated security assessments to identify vulnerabilities in AWS workloads.
- **AWS Trusted Advisor:** Scans AWS environments for security misconfigurations and provides best-practice recommendations.
- **AWS Config:** Tracks configuration changes and detects compliance violations.
- **GuardDuty:** Uses AI-based threat intelligence to detect suspicious activities and unauthorized access attempts.

By integrating these tools into their security strategy, businesses can automate vulnerability scanning, enforce compliance policies, and strengthen their AWS security posture.

Best Practices for Addressing Security Vulnerabilities

To effectively address security vulnerabilities in AWS environments, organizations should follow industry best practices for vulnerability management. Key recommendations include:

- **Implement Least Privilege Access:** Restrict IAM permissions to only what is necessary for each role or service.
- **Enforce Regular Patch Management:** Apply software updates and security patches consistently using automation tools like AWS Systems Manager Patch Manager.
- **Enable Data Encryption:** Use AWS Key Management Service (KMS) to encrypt sensitive data at rest and in transit.
- **Audit and Monitor Continuously:** Utilize AWS CloudTrail and AWS Security Hub for security logging and threat detection.
- **Conduct Regular Security Assessments:** Perform penetration testing and vulnerability scans using AWS Inspector and third-party tools.
- **Implement Multi-Factor Authentication (MFA):** Secure IAM users, roles, and applications with MFA to prevent unauthorized access.

By proactively addressing vulnerabilities, organizations can mitigate security risks, maintain compliance, and ensure a robust defense against evolving cyber threats.

Using AWS Inspector for Automated Security Assessments

Earlier documentation may reference Amazon Inspector Classic, which required manual agent installation, assessment templates, and scheduled scans focused mainly on EC2 instances. The new Amazon Inspector is a fully managed, agentless (where supported) service that provides continuous vulnerability scanning for EC2 instances, container images in Amazon ECR, and Lambda functions. It automatically discovers workloads, detects CVEs using up-to-date threat intelligence, assigns severity scores, and integrates natively with AWS Security Hub—making it more scalable, real-time, and operationally simpler than the classic version.

This section explores the capabilities of AWS Inspector, detailing how it works, what vulnerabilities it detects, and how organizations can integrate it into their security workflows for real-time monitoring and threat mitigation.

Overview of AWS Inspector and Its Security Capabilities

AWS Inspector is an automated vulnerability management service that continuously scans AWS workloads for security risks. It uses a combination of threat intelligence, Common Vulnerabilities and Exposures (CVE) databases, and AWS security best practices to identify weaknesses in the cloud environment of an organization.

Key Capabilities of AWS Inspector Include:

- **Continuous and Automated Scanning:** Periodic and real-time assessments to detect security risks.
- **Support for Multiple AWS Services:** Scans Amazon EC2 instances, Amazon Elastic Container Registry (ECR) container images, and AWS Lambda functions.
- **Vulnerability Prioritization:** Assigns risk scores to identified threats, helping teams focus on the most critical issues.
- **Seamless Integration with AWS Security Hub:** Aggregates findings and aligns them with industry security frameworks.
- **Automated Remediation Recommendations:** Provides detailed guidance on how to mitigate identified vulnerabilities.

AWS Inspector acts as a first line of defense, ensuring cloud workloads are regularly scanned and kept secure from evolving threats.

Configuring AWS Inspector for Automated Vulnerability Scanning

To leverage AWS Inspector effectively, organizations must configure it to continuously monitor their workloads and trigger security assessments based on defined policies. Setting up AWS Inspector involves the following steps:

1. **Enabling AWS Inspector**
    a. Navigate to the AWS Management Console and activate AWS Inspector in the desired AWS region.
    b. Assign IAM permissions to allow AWS Inspector to scan resources securely.
2. **Defining Assessment Targets**
    a. Select specific AWS resources, including EC2 instances, container repositories, and Lambda functions.
    b. Group assets based on security policies and compliance needs.
3. **Setting up Assessment Rules**
    a. Define security benchmarks for vulnerability detection, including CVE databases, CIS benchmarks, and AWS best practices.
    b. Configure scan frequency (on-demand or scheduled).
4. **Automating Scan Execution**
    a. Enable event-driven scans triggered by AWS CloudWatch Events, ensuring real-time threat detection.

  b. Use AWS Lambda functions to trigger automatic remediation for detected issues.

By automating vulnerability scanning, organizations can maintain a proactive security posture and prevent security incidents before they occur.

Interpreting AWS Inspector Findings and Taking Action

Once AWS Inspector completes its scans, it generates detailed security findings that organizations must analyze and act upon. Each finding includes:

- **Vulnerability ID (CVE Reference):** Links to known security threats.
- **Risk Score:** Indicates the severity of the vulnerability (Critical, High, Medium, or Low).
- **Affected Resource:** Specifies which EC2 instance, container, or Lambda function is impacted.
- **Recommended Mitigation Steps:** Provides actionable guidance for patching or reconfiguring the affected asset.

Example Inspector Finding (Simplified)

Title: OpenSSL Vulnerability Detected

Severity: HIGH

CVE ID: CVE-2023-0464

Affected Resource: EC2 instance i-0a12bc34def56789

Package: openssl 1.1.1k

Recommendation: Update OpenSSL to version 1.1.1t or later

Steps to Address Inspector Findings

1. **Prioritize High-Severity Issues:** Focus on critical vulnerabilities that could lead to data breaches or system compromise.
2. **Apply Security Patches:** Use AWS Systems Manager Patch Manager to automatically update software packages.
3. **Implement IAM and Network Restrictions:** Restrict unnecessary permissions and secure network access to prevent exploitation.
4. **Automate Remediation:** Integrate AWS Lambda with AWS Inspector to automatically apply fixes based on predefined security rules.
5. **Review and Update Security Policies:** Adjust security configurations based on findings to prevent recurring vulnerabilities.

By interpreting and acting on the security reports of AWS Inspector, organizations can quickly mitigate threats and ensure continuous protection against evolving cyber risks.

Best Practices for Using AWS Inspector in Security Workflows

To maximize the benefits of AWS Inspector, organizations should adopt best practices that enhance security monitoring, automation, and compliance:

- **Enable Continuous Scanning:** Regular assessments help detect vulnerabilities before attackers exploit them.
- **Integrate with AWS Security Hub:** Centralize security findings for better visibility and streamlined incident response.

- **Automate Patching with AWS Systems Manager:** Apply security patches to fix vulnerabilities without manual intervention.
- **Use IAM Policies to Limit AWS Inspector Access:** Ensure only authorized security teams can modify assessment settings.
- **Monitor Findings with Amazon CloudWatch:** Set up alerts for critical vulnerabilities to ensure immediate action.
- **Perform Regular Compliance Audits:** Align AWS Inspector findings with industry standards such as CIS, ISO 27001, and NIST.

By following these best practices, organizations can fortify their cloud infrastructure, minimize security risks, and maintain compliance with industry regulations.

AWS Inspector is a powerful tool for proactive security management, ensuring that vulnerabilities are detected, prioritized, and mitigated efficiently. By automating security assessments, organizations can strengthen their AWS security posture and reduce the risk of cyber threats.

Implementing Best Practices for Continuous Threat Management

Once vulnerabilities are identified through services like Amazon Inspector, continuous threat management ensures those risks are monitored, remediated, and prevented from re-emerging over time.

Cyber threats evolve continuously, making it imperative for organizations to adopt proactive and adaptive security strategies. AWS provides a range of security tools and best practices that help businesses maintain a robust, real-time security posture. Implementing a continuous threat management strategy ensures that vulnerabilities are detected early, security gaps are addressed, and that the organizations do remain compliant with industry standards.

This section explores best practices for threat detection, monitoring, and incident response, leveraging AWS security services to automate, streamline, and strengthen cloud security.

Establishing a Proactive Threat Detection Strategy

A proactive approach to threat management helps organizations detect and mitigate security threats before they escalate. Instead of reacting to incidents after they occur, businesses should focus on real-time monitoring, automated alerts, and continuous assessment to stay ahead of potential threats.

Key Components

- **Continuous Security Monitoring:** Implement AWS Security Hub, AWS GuardDuty, and Amazon Detective to monitor unusual activity in real-time.
- **Automated Threat Intelligence:** Leverage the threat intelligence services of AWS to stay updated on emerging cyber threats and vulnerabilities.
- **Security Baseline Policies:** Define and enforce IAM policies, security group rules, and network segmentation to reduce the attack surface.
- **Regular Vulnerability Assessments:** Use AWS Inspector and AWS Config to identify misconfigurations and security loopholes.
- **Behavioral Analytics for Anomaly Detection:** Utilize Amazon Detective to analyze logs and detect suspicious activities.

Example Proactive Detection Scenario

Amazon GuardDuty detects anomalous API activity, such as repeated AssumeRole calls from an unfamiliar geographic location.

This finding is sent to AWS Security Hub, which triggers an Amazon EventBridge rule.

EventBridge invokes an AWS Lambda function that automatically:

- Disables the compromised IAM credentials.
- Applies a restrictive security group.
- Notifies the security team via SNS.

Outcome:

The threat is contained within minutes—without manual intervention—before any data exfiltration or resource misuse occurs.

By focusing on early detection and real-time monitoring, organizations can mitigate risks before they lead to data breaches.

Leveraging AWS Security Tools for Continuous Monitoring

AWS offers a suite of security tools designed to enhance continuous monitoring and automated threat response. Each tool plays a unique role in identifying, tracking, and mitigating security risks:

- **AWS GuardDuty – Threat Intelligence and Anomaly Detection**
  - Uses machine learning and AI-driven analytics to detect unauthorized access attempts, malware activity, and reconnaissance attacks.
  - Identifies potential compromised EC2 instances, IAM anomalies, and malicious API calls.
  - Provides automated alerts and recommendations for threat mitigation.
- **AWS Security Hub – Centralized Security Management**
  - Aggregates findings from AWS Inspector, GuardDuty, IAM Access Analyzer, and AWS Config.
  - Provides a single-pane view for tracking security vulnerabilities.
  - Aligns security policies with industry standards (CIS, NIST, PCI-DSS).
- **AWS CloudTrail – Logging and Forensic Analysis**
  - Tracks all API activity and user actions within AWS accounts.
  - Provides a detailed audit trail for security investigations.
  - Helps detect unauthorized access and policy violations.
- **Amazon Detective – Threat Investigation and Incident Analysis**
  - Uses machine learning to identify attack patterns and unusual behavior.
  - Provides deep insights into user access history, network traffic, and security events.
  - Helps security teams analyze and respond to incidents faster.

By integrating these tools, organizations can ensure continuous security monitoring and a swift response to potential threats.

Automating Incident Response with AWS Lambda and AWS Systems Manager

Manual incident response can be slow and inefficient, increasing the risk of prolonged security exposure. By automating security responses, organizations can contain threats, isolate compromised resources, and enforce corrective actions in real-time.

AWS Automates Security Incident Response

1. **AWS Lambda for Automated Security Actions**
    a. Trigger automated security workflows based on GuardDuty, Security Hub, or AWS CloudTrail findings.
    b. Automatically quarantine compromised EC2 instances and revoke unauthorized IAM credentials.
2. **AWS Systems Manager for Remediation**
    a. Apply security patches automatically using AWS Systems Manager Patch Manager.
    b. Enforce compliance by correcting misconfigurations in security groups and IAM policies.
    c. Execute scripts to lock down compromised environments instantly.
3. **AWS Step Functions for Coordinated Security Actions**
    a. Orchestrate multi-step security responses, such as scanning, isolating, and notifying administrators.
    b. Ensure seamless incident containment and mitigation workflows.

By automating security workflows, organizations can detect and neutralize threats before they escalate into major security breaches.

Implementing Security Best Practices for Long-Term Protection

Beyond automated threat detection and incident response, businesses must embed security into their cloud architecture. The following best practices help establish a strong security foundation for long-term threat management:

- **Implement the Principle of Least Privilege (PoLP):** Restrict IAM permissions to only what is necessary.
- **Regularly Rotate Access Keys and Credentials:** Use **AWS Secrets Manager** for secure credential storage.
- **Encrypt Data at Rest and in Transit:** Apply **AWS KMS for encryption management**.
- **Use Multi-Factor Authentication (MFA) for IAM Users:** Add an extra layer of security to prevent unauthorized access.
- **Enable AWS Shield and WAF for DDoS Mitigation:** Protect against distributed denial-of-service attacks.
- **Conduct Regular Security Audits and Compliance Checks:** Use **AWS Config and Security Hub** for governance.
- **Monitor Network Traffic with VPC Flow Logs:** Detect suspicious network activity.

By adopting these security best practices, organizations can continuously fortify their AWS environment against emerging cyber threats.

In an era where cyber threats are becoming increasingly sophisticated, organizations must adopt a multi-layered security approach to safeguard their cloud infrastructure. By implementing continuous threat management strategies, leveraging AWS security tools, and automating incident response workflows, businesses can achieve proactive security resilience.

Case Studies

Here are four unique case studies corresponding to AWS WAF Configuration (11.1), AWS Shield (11.2), Security Hub (11.3), and Vulnerability Management (11.4). These case studies illustrate real-world scenarios, challenges, solutions, and outcomes for organizations implementing AWS security services.

Enhancing Web Security with AWS WAF – E-Commerce Platform Protection

Background

An e-commerce company with millions of daily visitors was struggling with bot traffic, SQL injection attacks, and cross-site scripting (XSS) threats targeting their web applications. Their previous security solution lacked granular traffic control, leading to false positives and increased downtime.

Challenges

- Frequent DDoS attempts causing high server loads.
- Malicious requests leading to unauthorized data access.
- Need for custom security rules without affecting legitimate traffic.

Solution: AWS WAF Implementation

The company deployed AWS WAF with the following custom security measures:

1. **Web ACLs:** Configured rules to block suspicious traffic patterns based on geolocation, IP reputation, and request signatures.
2. **Rate-Based Rules:** Mitigated bot traffic by limiting repeated requests from specific IPs.
3. **Managed Rule Groups:** Enabled AWS WAF Managed Rules for real-time SQL injection and XSS protection.
4. **Logging and Insights:** Integrated with AWS CloudWatch for attack pattern analysis.

Results

- 98% reduction in bot traffic without affecting genuine users.
- Zero successful SQL injection/XSS attacks post-implementation.
- Improved website performance due to decreased unwanted traffic.

Preventing DDoS Attacks with AWS Shield – A Financial Services Company

Background

A global financial institution faced frequent volumetric DDoS attacks, causing latency spikes and service outages on their trading platform. The company required an automated, scalable DDoS mitigation solution.

Challenges

- Large-scale DDoS attacks disrupted online transactions.
- High downtime costs and regulatory compliance risks.
- Existing security struggled to differentiate between legitimate and attack traffic.

Solution: AWS Shield Advanced Deployment

1. **AWS Shield Advanced Activation:** Automatically detected and mitigated volumetric, state-exhaustion, and application-layer attacks.
2. **Global Threat Intelligence:** Leveraged real-time threat analysis of AWS Shield to identify emerging attack patterns.
3. **Elastic Load Balancing (ELB) Integration:** Ensured traffic distribution across multiple AWS regions.
4. **Route 53 Health Checks:** Redirected traffic dynamically to healthy endpoints during attacks.

Results

- DDoS attack mitigation within milliseconds, preventing service disruptions.
- Downtime reduced by 95%, ensuring uninterrupted financial transactions.
- Zero customer complaints regarding platform availability after deployment.

Centralized Security Monitoring with AWS Security Hub – Healthcare Sector

Background

A healthcare provider managing sensitive patient data across multiple AWS accounts lacked centralized visibility into security threats. Compliance with HIPAA and GDPR regulations was at risk.

Challenges

- Fragmented security monitoring across different AWS services.
- Slow detection and response to security vulnerabilities.
- Difficulty maintaining compliance with industry standards.

Solution: AWS Security Hub Integration

1. **Security Findings Aggregation:** Collected threat intelligence from GuardDuty, AWS Config, and AWS Inspector in a single dashboard.
2. **Automated Compliance Checks:** Aligned security posture with HIPAA and GDPR benchmarks.
3. **Incident Prioritization:** Used severity scoring of Security Hub to respond to critical threats first.
4. **Event-Driven Response:** Leveraged AWS Lambda for automated remediation when security risks were detected.

Results

- Improved threat detection by 80%, reducing the risk of data breaches.
- Faster incident response times, cutting remediation efforts from hours to minutes.
- Achieved full compliance with HIPAA and GDPR, avoiding legal penalties.

Strengthening Vulnerability Management with AWS Inspector – SaaS Company

Background

A fast-growing SaaS provider offering cloud-based collaboration tools faced security vulnerabilities due to misconfigurations, outdated dependencies, and unpatched systems.

Challenges

- Security gaps leading to increased attack surfaces.
- Manual vulnerability assessments were slow and ineffective.
- Developers lacked visibility into security flaws in application code.

Solution: AWS Inspector Deployment

1. **Automated Vulnerability Scans:** Used AWS Inspector to scan EC2 instances, container workloads, and Lambda functions.
2. **Real-Time Risk Analysis:** Prioritized vulnerabilities based on AWS Common Vulnerability Scoring System (CVSS).
3. **Developer Alerts and Fix Recommendations:** Integrated findings with JIRA and Slack to alert developers immediately.
4. **Continuous Security Posture Monitoring:** Used AWS Config to detect insecure configurations in real time.

Results

- Reduced unpatched vulnerabilities by 70%, strengthening security.
- Faster remediation workflows, cutting resolution time by 50%.
- Zero successful exploitation attempts, improving system resilience.

These case studies highlight how organizations enhance cloud security and resilience using AWS WAF, AWS Shield, Security Hub, and AWS Inspector. By implementing proactive security strategies, businesses can:

- Prevent cyber threats before they impact operations.
- Achieve compliance with industry regulations.
- Improve incident response time through automation.
- Enhance visibility and control over cloud security risks.

Conclusion

In this chapter, we have explored the essential AWS network security services that help organizations fortify their cloud infrastructure against cyber threats. From web traffic filtering by AWS WAF, DDoS mitigation by AWS Shield, centralized monitoring by Security Hub, to automated vulnerability assessments by AWS Inspector, these services play a crucial role in ensuring a secure and compliant AWS environment.

By implementing these tools effectively, businesses can proactively defend against evolving security threats, maintain regulatory compliance, and enhance overall cloud security posture. With automated monitoring, intelligent threat detection, and real-time response mechanisms, AWS security services empower organizations to mitigate risks before they escalate into critical incidents.

In the next chapter, we shall learn how to create disaster recovery plans for AWS infrastructure, covering the key concepts of backup, failover, and recovery. And also we shall explore how to design fault-tolerant systems using multiple Availability Zones (AZs) and Regions, while adhering to Recovery Point (RPO) and Recovery Time (RTO) Objectives.

Points to Remember

- **AWS WAF Enhances Web Security:** Protects applications from SQL injection, XSS, and bot attacks through customizable Web ACLs and managed rules.
- **AWS Shield Provides DDoS Protection:** Automatically detects and mitigates volumetric and application-layer DDoS attacks, ensuring uninterrupted service.
- **AWS Security Hub Enables Centralized Security Management:** Aggregates threat intelligence, compliance status, and security alerts from multiple AWS services into a single pane of glass.
- **AWS Inspector Automates Vulnerability Scanning:** Continuously identifies security weaknesses in EC2 instances, containers, and Lambda functions, helping teams prioritize and remediate critical risks.
- **Proactive Security Measures Reduce Business Risk:** Organizations that adopt automated threat detection, real-time response mechanisms, and compliance frameworks can significantly lower their exposure to cyber threats.

By leveraging these AWS security services, organizations can maintain a resilient, secure, and high-performing cloud environment, ensuring data protection, business continuity, and regulatory compliance in an ever-evolving threat landscape.

CHAPTER 12
Disaster Recovery Strategies

Introduction

An effective disaster recovery strategy not only safeguards business continuity but also optimizes costs by aligning recovery investments with clearly defined RPO and RTO requirements. Disruptions in cloud environments can have serious consequences, ranging from data loss and downtime to financial and reputational damage. To ensure business continuity, organizations must implement robust Disaster Recovery (DR) strategies that enable rapid recovery from failures. AWS provides a comprehensive suite of disaster recovery tools and services, allowing businesses to build resilient architecture that can withstand outages, cyberattacks, and unexpected failures.

This chapter delves into the fundamental principles of disaster recovery in AWS, covering backup and restore mechanisms, failover strategies, and automated recovery processes. We will be exploring key metrics such as Recovery Point Objective (RPO) and Recovery Time Objective (RTO)—which help define acceptable data loss and downtime limits—and, shall further examine how to design fault-tolerant systems using multi-AZ and cross-region deployments.

By the end of this chapter, readers will gain hands-on knowledge of AWS disaster recovery solutions, learning how to create effective failover configurations, test recovery procedures, and automate resilience measures to ensure business continuity even in the face of unexpected failures.

Structure

In this chapter, we will walk through:

- Backup and Restore Process
- RPO and RTO Guidelines
- Failover Configurations
- Testing Disaster Recovery Plans
- Case Studies

Backup and Restore Process

In the current digital landscape, data is one of the most valuable assets for any organization. Ensuring data availability and recoverability is critical to maintaining business continuity, preventing data loss, and mitigating risks associated with system failures, accidental deletions, or cyber threats. AWS provides a comprehensive set of backups and restore solutions that enable organizations to securely store, manage, and recover data efficiently.

This section explores AWS Backup and Amazon S3, two key services that play a pivotal role in disaster recovery strategies. AWS Backup simplifies and automates the backup process across multiple AWS services, ensuring that data is consistently protected without manual intervention. Amazon S3, with its high durability, versioning, and replication capabilities, serves as a reliable storage solution for backup and archival purposes.

Aspect	AWS Backup	Amazon S3
Primary Purpose	Centralized, policy-based backup and restore service	Highly durable object storage for backups, archives, and replication
Backup Frequency	Automated and scheduled (hourly, daily, weekly via backup plans)	Manual or application-driven; lifecycle rules control retention
Supported Services	EBS, RDS, DynamoDB, EFS, FSx, Storage Gateway, more	Any data stored as objects (including exported snapshots and logs)
Durability	Inherits durability of underlying service snapshots	99.999999999% (11 nines) durability
Restore Speed	Faster, service-native restores	Slower for large restores; depends on retrieval tier
Cost Model	Backup storage + restore + cross-region copy costs	Pay for storage tier, requests, retrieval, and replication
Cross-Region DR	Built-in cross-region and cross-account backups	Cross-Region Replication (CRR) configurable per bucket
Compliance and Governance	Backup vaults, encryption, audit via AWS Backup Audit Manager	Object Lock, versioning, lifecycle, encryption
Best Use Case	Operational backups with defined RPO/RTO	Long-term retention, archival, immutable backups

Table 12.1: *AWS Backup versus Amazon S3 – Disaster Recovery Use Cases*

By understanding and implementing effective backup and restore strategies using AWS services, organizations can enhance their resilience, minimize downtime, and meet compliance requirements. This section provides a detailed overview of AWS Backup and S3, best practices for data protection, and step-by-step guidance on restoring data efficiently.

Understanding Backup Strategies – Importance of Regular Data Backups in AWS

Data loss can occur due to system failures, cyberattacks, accidental deletions, or natural disasters, making it essential for organizations to implement a robust backup strategy.

In AWS, backups generally fall into two categories: operational backups and disaster recovery backups. Operational backups focus on day-to-day protection against accidental deletions, application errors, or short-term failures, enabling quick restores within the same Region or Availability Zone. Disaster recovery backups, on the other hand, are designed for large-scale outages or regional failures and typically involve cross-Region replication, longer retention periods, and stricter alignment with business-defined RPO and RTO objectives.

A well-structured backup strategy in AWS helps businesses achieve high availability, prevent service disruptions, and minimize downtime. This section delves into the importance of regular backups, different backup methods, and best practices for ensuring a reliable and efficient backup process within AWS.

Importance of Regular Backups for Business Continuity

For any organization, business continuity depends on data availability. A lack of backups can result in significant financial losses, reputational damage, and operational disruptions. AWS provides various tools and services to automate and simplify regular backups, ensuring that critical data is protected against unforeseen failures.

Regular backups in AWS support business continuity by enabling organizations to:

- Minimize data loss by meeting defined Recovery Point Objectives (RPO) (for example, hourly backups achieving an RPO of ≤1 hour).
- Reduce downtime through faster restores aligned with Recovery Time Objectives (RTO).
- Recover from cyber incidents such as ransomware using immutable or versioned backups.
- Meet regulatory and compliance requirements, such as:
    - **GDPR:** Data retention, recoverability, and the ability to restore personal data after an incident.
    - **ISO 27001:** Backup controls and availability safeguards.
    - **SOC 2:** Evidence of data protection and recovery processes.
- Support audits and governance by maintaining consistent backup policies, retention schedules, and encrypted storage.
- Protect business reputation by ensuring critical services and customer data can be restored quickly after failures.

Key reasons why regular backups are crucial

Let us look into some of the key reasons why the regular backups are crucial.

- **Data Protection:** Prevents accidental data loss due to human errors or software issues.
- **Disaster Recovery Readiness:** Enables quick restoration of systems after failures.
- **Compliance and Security:** Meets legal and industry standards for data retention.
- **Operational Efficiency:** Reduces downtime and maintains productivity.

Types of Backup Strategies in AWS

AWS provides multiple backup strategies tailored to different business needs and workloads. The choice of strategy depends on factors like recovery objectives, data sensitivity, and cost considerations.

- **Full Backup:** Copies the entire dataset, ensuring a complete restoration if needed.
- **Incremental Backup:** Backs up only new or modified data since the last backup, reducing storage costs.
- **Differential Backup:** Captures changes made since the last full backup, offering a balance between speed and storage efficiency.
- **Automated Backup:** Uses AWS Backup to schedule and manage backups seamlessly.
- **Versioned Backups:** Utilizes Amazon S3 versioning to track and restore specific file versions.

Backup Strategy	Pros	Cons	Typical AWS Use Cases
Full Backup	Complete data copy, simplest restore process	High storage cost, longer backup time	EC2 AMIs before major deployments, baseline backups
Incremental Backup	Lowest storage usage, fastest backups	Restore requires full + all incrementals	RDS automated backups, EBS snapshots
Differential Backup	Faster restore than incremental, moderate storage	Grows larger over time until next full backup	File systems with periodic full backups
Automated Backup	Fully managed, policy-based, compliant	Less granular control than custom scripts	Centralized backups using AWS Backup
Versioned Backups	Protects against accidental deletes/overwrites	Higher storage cost if not lifecycle-managed	Amazon S3 object recovery, ransomware protection

Table 12.2: *Comparison of Backup Strategies in AWS*

- **RDS / DynamoDB** → Incremental backups via AWS Backup
- **EC2** → Full backups using AMIs + incremental EBS snapshots
- **S3** → Versioned backups with lifecycle and Object Lock
- **Enterprise workloads** → Automated backups with cross-Region copy

Understanding these strategies helps organizations implement the most effective backup plan based on their reliability, cost, and recovery objectives.

Establishing Backup Policies and Schedules

Having a defined backup policy ensures consistency and compliance with business and regulatory requirements. Organizations should establish backup schedules based on data criticality and recovery needs.

Key Considerations for Backup Policies

Some of the key considerations that are needed to be taken into account for the backup policies are as follows:

- **Frequency:** Define how often backups should be performed (for instance hourly, daily, or weekly).
- **Retention Period:** Determine how long backup copies should be retained before deletion.
- **Storage Location:** Store backups in multiple AWS Regions or Availability Zones for redundancy.
- **Security and Encryption:** Implement encryption and access controls to protect backup data.
- **Testing and Validation:** Periodically test backups to ensure successful recovery.

By following these backup strategies and best practices, organizations can strengthen their disaster recovery posture, minimize risks, and enhance operational resilience.

Example: AWS Backup Policy (JSON)

The following is a simplified **AWS Backup plan snippet** demonstrating frequency, retention, tagging, and cross-account copy—perfect for adding technical depth:

```
{
  "BackupPlanName": "prod-critical-backup-plan",
  "Rules": [
    {
      "RuleName": "daily-backup-rule",
```

```
        "TargetBackupVaultName": "prod-backup-vault",
        "ScheduleExpression": "cron(0 1 * * ? *)",
        "StartWindowMinutes": 60,
        "CompletionWindowMinutes": 180,
        "Lifecycle": {
          "DeleteAfterDays": 35
        },
        "CopyActions": [
          {
            "DestinationBackupVaultArn": "arn:aws:backup:us-west-
2:123456789012:backup-vault:dr-vault",
            "Lifecycle": {
              "DeleteAfterDays": 90
            }
          }
        ],
        "RecoveryPointTags": {
          "Environment": "Production",
          "Compliance": "GDPR",
          "DataClass": "Critical"
        }
      }
    ]
  }
```

What This Policy Demonstrates

- Daily automated backups (1 AM UTC).
- Primary retention of 35 days.
- Cross-Region / cross-account copy with longer retention (90 days).
- Retention tagging for audit traceability and compliance mapping.

AWS Backup – Automating Backup Management for Various AWS Services

Manually managing backups for multiple AWS services can be complex, time-consuming, and prone to human error. AWS Backup is a fully managed service that simplifies the process by automating backup creation, retention, and restoration across AWS resources. It ensures data consistency, security, and compliance while reducing operational overhead.

This section explores how AWS Backup helps in centralized backup management, supports various AWS services, and integrates with organizational policies to enhance disaster recovery preparedness.

Overview of AWS Backup and Its Key Features

AWS Backup provides a unified solution for configuring, scheduling, and monitoring backups across AWS workloads. It eliminates the need for custom scripts and manual interventions, allowing businesses to focus on their core operations.

Key Features of AWS Backup

Some of the key features of AWS Backup are provided as follows.

- **Automated Backup Scheduling:** Enables policy-based backup creation at predefined intervals.

- **Cross-Region and Cross-Account Backups:** Ensures redundancy and disaster recovery readiness.
- **Lifecycle Policies:** Defines retention periods and automates backup deletion.
- **Incremental and Full Backups:** Optimizes storage by backing up only changed data where applicable.
- **Centralized Backup Monitoring:** Provides a dashboard for tracking backup status and health.
- **Compliance and Security:** Offers encryption, access controls, and audit logs for regulatory compliance.

AWS Backup integrates with Amazon RDS, DynamoDB, EFS, EC2, FSx, and other AWS services, ensuring comprehensive coverage for critical business data.

Setting up AWS Backup for Automated Protection

To automate backups effectively, organizations need to configure AWS Backup policies based on their data protection requirements.

Step-by-Step Guide for Setting up AWS Backup

The following is the step-by-step guide to setting up AWS backup:

1. **Access AWS Backup Console.**
   a. Navigate to the AWS Backup service in the AWS Management Console.
   b. Click `Create Backup Plan` to define a new backup strategy.
2. **Define Backup Plan.**
   a. Choose between predefined templates or create a custom backup plan.
   b. Specify backup frequency, retention policies, and vault locations.
3. **Assign Resources to Backup Plan.**
   a. Select AWS resources (some of which includes EC2 instances, RDS databases, S3 buckets).
   b. Apply IAM permissions to grant access for backup operations.
4. **Enable Cross-Region and Cross-Account Backups** *(Optional).*
   a. Store backup copies in different AWS Regions for disaster recovery.
   b. Share backups across multiple AWS accounts for added resilience.
5. **Monitor and Validate Backups**
   a. Use AWS Backup Dashboard to track backup status.
   b. Test backup recovery periodically to ensure reliability and completeness.

Implementing automated backups reduces the risk of data loss, enhances operational efficiency, and aligns with business continuity objectives.

Managing Backup Storage, Encryption, and Security

To ensure data security and compliance, AWS Backup includes advanced storage management, encryption, and access controls.

Key Aspects of Backup Storage Management

The key aspects of backup storage management are provided as follows:

- **Backup Vaults:** AWS Backup stores backups in vaults that support encryption and access policies.
- **Retention Policies:** Automatically delete old backups based on organizational policies to optimize costs.
- **Lifecycle Management:** Move backups to low-cost storage tiers to minimize expenses.

Securing Backups with Encryption and IAM Policies

The following are the few processes to be leveraged to maintain a compliant backup strategy:

- **AWS Key Management Service (KMS) Encryption:** Encrypts backups at rest and in transit.
- **IAM Role-Based Access:** Restricts backup access to authorized users only.
- **Audit Logs and Monitoring:** Tracks backup activities with AWS CloudTrail for compliance reporting.

Example: IAM Policy for Securing AWS Backup Access

The following IAM policy snippet demonstrates **least-privilege access** for backup operations, allowing users to manage backups while preventing deletion of recovery points:

```
{
  "Version": "2012-10-17",
  "Statement": [
    {
      "Sid": "AllowBackupOperations",
      "Effect": "Allow",
      "Action": [
        "backup:StartBackupJob",
        "backup:StartRestoreJob",
        "backup:ListBackupJobs",
        "backup:ListRecoveryPointsByBackupVault",
        "backup:DescribeBackupJob"
      ],
      "Resource": "*"
    },
    {
      "Sid": "DenyBackupDeletion",
      "Effect": "Deny",
      "Action": [
        "backup:DeleteRecoveryPoint"
      ],
      "Resource": "*"
    }
  ]
}
```

- Enforces **separation of duties** (common audit requirement).
- Protects backups from **accidental or malicious deletion.**
- Supports compliance frameworks such as **SOC 2** and **ISO 27001.**

By leveraging the automation, security, and policy-based management of AWS Backup, organizations can maintain a resilient, cost-effective, and compliant backup strategy for all critical workloads.

Amazon S3 for Disaster Recovery – Using Versioning, Replication, and Lifecycle Policies

Amazon Simple Storage Service (Amazon S3) is a highly scalable, durable, and secure cloud storage solution that plays a crucial role in Disaster Recovery (DR) strategies. Organizations rely on S3 for data backup, redundancy, and long-term archival, ensuring business continuity in the event of failures, cyberattacks, or accidental deletions.

This section explores how S3 versioning, cross-region replication (CRR), and lifecycle policies help organizations implement a robust disaster recovery framework, optimize storage costs, and protect mission-critical data.

Enabling Amazon S3 Versioning for Data Protection

Amazon S3 versioning preserves every version of an object, protecting data from accidental deletion, overwrites, and malicious activity such as ransomware. While versioning significantly improves recoverability, it can increase storage consumption if not managed properly—making lifecycle policies essential for cost optimization.

Example: Lifecycle Rule for Versioned Objects (Cost Optimization)

The following example shows how organizations can retain recent versions for fast recovery while reducing costs for older versions:

```
{
  "Rules": [
    {
      "ID": "VersionedObjectLifecycleRule",
      "Status": "Enabled",
      "NoncurrentVersionTransitions": [
        {
          "NoncurrentDays": 60,
          "StorageClass": "STANDARD_IA"
        }
      ],
      "NoncurrentVersionExpiration": {
        "NoncurrentDays": 365
      }
    }
  ]
}
```

What This Rule Achieves

- Keeps current object versions in S3 Standard for quick access.
- Moves noncurrent (older) versions to S3 Standard-IA after 60 days.
- Deletes noncurrent versions after 365 days, aligning with retention policies.

Key Benefits of S3 Versioning

Some of the key benefits of S3 versioning are provided as follows:

- **Recover Accidental Deletions:** Even if a file is deleted, older versions remain accessible.
- **Restore Previous Versions:** Allows rollback to an earlier state of a file in case of corruption.
- **Protect against Overwrites:** Ensures historical versions are preserved for auditing and compliance.

Enabling S3 Versioning

The following are the steps to enable the S3 versioning:

1. **Navigate to the S3 Console.**
   a. Open the AWS Management Console and go to the S3 service.
2. **Select or Create a Bucket.**
   a. Choose an existing bucket or create a new one for storing versioned objects.
3. **Enable Versioning.**
   a. In the Bucket Settings, go to the Versioning tab and click `Enable`.
4. **Monitor and Manage Versions.**
   a. List and restore previous file versions using the AWS CLI, SDKs, or Console.

Although versioning enhances data protection, it can increase storage costs. To optimize costs, organizations can combine versioning with lifecycle policies to automatically delete older versions or move them to cheaper storage tiers.

Implementing Cross-Region Replication (CRR) for Disaster Recovery

Cross-Region Replication (CRR) automatically replicates objects from one Amazon S3 bucket to another in a different AWS Region, ensuring geographically distributed copies of data for rapid recovery during regional outages.

In addition to cross-Region protection, cross-account replication adds a critical security layer by isolating replicated data in a separate AWS account.

Significance of Cross-Account CRR

- **Protection against accidental or malicious deletions:** If objects are deleted or corrupted in the source account, replicas in the destination account remain protected—especially when combined with versioning or Object Lock.
- **Reduced blast radius:** Compromise of the source AWS account does not automatically compromise the replicated data.
- **Stronger governance and compliance:** Supports separation of duties, a common requirement in frameworks such as SOC 2 and ISO 27001.
- **Independent access controls:** Destination buckets enforce their own IAM and bucket policies, preventing unauthorized modifications.

Best Practices for Secure CRR

- Enable versioning on both source and destination buckets.
- Use cross-account IAM roles with least-privilege permissions.
- Store replicas in a separate AWS account and Region.
- Apply lifecycle policies on the destination bucket for cost-efficient long-term retention.

Key Benefits of Cross-Region Replication

Some of the key benefits of Cross-Region Replication are as follows:

- **Ensures Data Redundancy:** Stores multiple copies of data in different locations.
- **Improves Business Continuity:** Reduces downtime in case of regional outages.

- **Compliance with Data Regulations:** Helps organizations meet geo-specific compliance requirements.

Steps to Set Up Cross-Region Replication (CRR)

The steps to set up Cross-Region Replication (CRR) are provided as follows.

1. **Enable Versioning on Both Buckets.**
    a. Ensure that source and destination buckets have versioning enabled.
2. **Create a Replication Rule.**
    a. Define a replication rule in the source bucket settings.
    b. Specify the destination bucket and AWS Region.
3. **Set IAM Permissions for Replication.**
    a. Grant S3 the necessary IAM role permissions to perform replication.
4. **Test the Replication Process.**
    a. Upload a file to the source bucket and verify its replication in the destination bucket.

CRR ensures continuous backup availability in different AWS regions, allowing organizations to recover quickly without data loss.

Optimizing Storage Costs with S3 Lifecycle Policies

While S3 versioning and replication enhance data durability, they can lead to higher storage costs if not managed properly. Lifecycle policies allow organizations to automate the transition and expiration of objects, optimizing storage costs while maintaining disaster recovery readiness.

Key Benefits of Lifecycle Policies

The key benefits of lifecycle policies are provided as follows.

- **Automated Cost Optimization:** Moves older data to lower-cost storage tiers.
- **Efficient Storage Management:** Reduces clutter by deleting obsolete versions.
- **Long-Term Data Retention:** Ensures archived data is preserved for compliance.

Common Lifecycle Policy Rules

The common lifecycle policy rules are provided as follows.

- **Transition to Infrequent Access (IA) Storage:** Move files older than 30 days to S3 Standard-IA for cost savings.
- **Migrate to Glacier or Deep Archive:** Archive data older than 90 days to Glacier for long-term retention.
- **Delete Expired Object Versions:** Automatically remove old versions after 365 days to free up storage.

Steps to Configure Lifecycle Policies

Some of the steps to configure lifecycle policies are provided below:

1. Open the S3 Console and Select a Bucket.
2. Go to the Lifecycle Configuration Tab.
3. Create a New Lifecycle Rule.
    a. Define the object transition timelines and expiration periods.
4. Save and Monitor Policy Execution.

By combining S3 versioning, cross-region replication, and lifecycle policies, organizations can achieve a highly resilient, cost-efficient disaster recovery strategy, ensuring data availability, integrity, and compliance at all times.

Restoring Data from Backups – Recovery Best Practices and Considerations

Creating regular backups is an essential part of a Disaster Recovery (DR) strategy, but having a structured plan for restoring data quickly and efficiently is just as crucial. An ineffective recovery process can lead to extended downtime, data inconsistency, and operational disruptions, negating the benefits of having a backup in the first place.

This section explores the best practices for data restoration using AWS services such as AWS Backup, Amazon S3, and Amazon RDS Snapshots. It also highlights key considerations for minimizing downtime, ensuring data integrity, and aligning with business continuity objectives.

Choosing the Right Backup for Recovery Scenarios

Different types of backups serve different recovery purposes, and choosing the right one depends on business needs, data criticality, and Recovery Time Objectives (RTOs).

Key Types of Backups and Their Uses

- **Full Backups:** Restore entire datasets quickly but require more storage.
- **Incremental Backups:** Restore only the latest changes since the last backup, reducing storage needs.
- **Snapshot-Based Backups:** Faster restoration of Amazon RDS, Amazon EBS, and EC2 instances.
- **Amazon S3 Versioning:** Retrieve older versions of files in case of accidental overwrites or deletions.

Selecting a Backup Strategy Based on Recovery Objectives

- **For mission-critical applications** → Use snapshot-based backups for fast recovery.
- **For large datasets with minimal changes** → Use incremental backups to save costs.
- **For regulatory compliance** → Implement long-term S3 storage with lifecycle policies.

Restoring Data from AWS Backup

AWS Backup provides a centralized backup management system that supports various AWS services. The restoration process varies based on the backup source, but the general workflow remains similar across different AWS resources.

CLI command example like:

```
aws backup start-restore-job --recovery-point-arn <ARN> --resource-type EC2
```

Steps to Restore Data from AWS Backup

The following are the steps to restore data from AWS backup:

1. Navigate to the AWS Backup Console.
    a. Select Backup Vault to locate saved backups.
2. Choose the Backup to Restore.
    a. Identify the backup based on timestamp and data source.

3. Initiate the Restore Process.
   a. Click **`Restore Backup`** and configure the necessary parameters.
4. Monitor the Restoration Progress.
   a. Use AWS CloudWatch Logs to track and verify the restoration.

Best Practices for AWS Backup Recovery

The following are few of the best practices to be followed for better AWS Backup recovery:

- Test recovery procedures regularly to ensure backups function as expected.
- Use IAM policies to restrict unauthorized access to backup data.
- Maintain multiple backup copies in different AWS regions for redundancy.

Recovering Deleted or Corrupted Objects from Amazon S3

Amazon S3 offers multiple built-in mechanisms to recover deleted or corrupted objects, reducing the risk of permanent data loss.

Key Recovery Methods

- **Restoring from S3 Versioning:** Retrieve an earlier version of an object if the latest one is deleted or modified.
- **Recovering from Cross-Region Replication (CRR):** If a primary S3 bucket fails, retrieve data from a replicated bucket in another region.
- **Restoring from S3 Glacier or Deep Archive:** Retrieve archived data for long-term storage compliance.

Steps to Restore an Object from S3 Glacier

The steps to restore an object from S3 glacier are given as follows.

1. Go to the S3 Console and Locate the Object.
2. Initiate the Restore Process.
   a. Choose the restore duration (expedited, standard, or bulk retrieval).
3. Download the Retrieved Object Once Available.

Important Considerations

- **Expedited retrievals:** These are faster but can be more costly.
- **Bulk retrievals:** These take longer (up to 12 hours) but are cost-efficient.

Restoring Amazon RDS, EC2, and EBS Snapshots

For applications running on Amazon RDS, EC2, or EBS, snapshots serve as a quick and efficient method to restore entire environments without manually reinstalling or reconfiguring resources.

Restoring an Amazon RDS Snapshot

1. Go to the RDS Console → Select **`Snapshots`**.
2. Choose the Desired Backup → Click **`Restore Snapshot`**.
3. Define New Database Instance Settings → Modify instance class, storage, and security groups.
4. Launch the Restored Database Instance → Ensure it operates as expected before resuming production workloads.

Recovering EC2 Instances Using EBS Snapshots

1. Identify the Most Recent Snapshot in the EBS console.
2. Create a New Volume from the snapshot.
3. Attach the New Volume to an EC2 instance for data recovery.

Key Considerations

- Automate snapshot creation to ensure recent copies are always available.
- Use encrypted snapshots for securing sensitive workloads.
- Test restored instances before making them live in production.

Best Practices for Ensuring a Smooth Recovery Process

Effective disaster recovery goes beyond simply restoring data—it requires a strategic, well-tested plan to ensure minimum downtime and data integrity.

An AWS disaster recovery–ready environment combines clearly defined recovery objectives, automated backups, cross-Region and cross-account protection, strong security controls, and regularly tested restore procedures.

Essential Best Practices for Recovery

- **Regularly Test Backups:** Schedule periodic recovery drills to verify backup reliability.
- **Automate Recovery Workflows:** Use AWS Lambda or AWS Backup Policies to streamline recovery tasks.
- **Document Recovery Procedures:** Maintain a clear, step-by-step recovery plan to minimize errors.
- **Monitor and Log Restoration Activities:** Use AWS CloudWatch and AWS Security Hub to track anomalies.
- **Ensure Multi-Region Redundancy:** Store backups in geographically separate AWS regions for failover protection.

Common Recovery Pitfalls to Avoid

- **Relying Only on Manual Recovery:** Increases downtime and operational risks.
- **Ignoring Access Control Measures:** Can lead to unauthorized recovery attempts.
- **Skipping Regular Backup Audits:** Can result in outdated or incomplete backups.

By implementing these best practices, organizations can ensure a seamless recovery process that aligns with business continuity goals while minimizing disruptions.

Restoring data from backups is not just about recovering lost files—it is about ensuring business resilience, data integrity, and operational continuity in times of crisis. AWS provides a comprehensive suite of tools, including AWS Backup, S3 versioning, cross-region replication, and snapshots, which organizations can leverage to implement effective recovery strategies.

By following structured recovery procedures, automating failover mechanisms, and regularly testing disaster recovery plans, businesses can achieve faster recovery times and reduce downtime impact in the face of unexpected failures.

RPO and RTO Guidelines

In the realm of Disaster Recovery (DR) and business continuity, two critical metrics determine how effectively an organization can recover from system failures and minimize downtime: Recovery Point

Objective (RPO) and Recovery Time Objective (RTO). These metrics help organizations establish clear expectations for data loss tolerance and system restoration time.

- **RPO (Recovery Point Objective):** It defines how much data loss is acceptable in the event of a disaster.
- **RTO (Recovery Time Objective):** It establishes how quickly systems need to be restored to resume normal operations.

This section explores the importance of RPO and RTO, how to define appropriate targets based on business needs, and how to leverage AWS services to meet these recovery objectives efficiently.

Understanding Recovery Point Objective (RPO) and Recovery Time Objective (RTO)

RPO determines the maximum amount of acceptable data loss measured in time intervals. For example, an RPO of 1 hour means that data backups must occur at least once every hour to ensure that no more than one hour of data is lost in a failure scenario.

Some of the Key Factors Influencing RPO Decisions are as follows:

- **Data criticality:** Highly transactional systems (such as banking) require low RPOs.
- **Backup frequency:** More frequent backups reduce data loss but increase storage costs.
- **Infrastructure limitations:** Network bandwidth and storage performance impact backup intervals.

Some of the AWS Services to Support RPO Goals are provided as follows:

- **Amazon S3 Versioning**: Retains multiple object versions to prevent accidental deletions.
- **AWS Backup**: Automates frequent backups for key AWS services.
- **Amazon RDS Automated Backups**: Ensures that databases can be restored to a precise point in time.

RTO defines the maximum allowable downtime before business operations are severely impacted. For instance, an RTO of 15 minutes means that services must be fully operational within that time after a failure.

Some of the key factors affecting RTO Planning are as follows:

- **System complexity:** More complex architectures require longer recovery times.
- **Automation level:** Automated failover reduces manual recovery efforts.
- **Redundancy setup:** Multi-AZ and multi-region deployments improve recovery speed.

A few of the AWS Services to Achieve Low RTO are given as follows:

- **AWS Elastic Load Balancer (ELB)**: Distributes traffic across healthy instances.
- **Amazon Route 53 Health Checks**: Automates failover based on system availability.
- **AWS Auto Scaling**: Quickly provisions additional resources when needed.

Balancing RPO and RTO for Optimal Disaster Recovery

While RPO and RTO are closely related, achieving both low RPO and low RTO can be expensive. Organizations must find a balanced approach that aligns with business needs and budget constraints.

Some of the Strategies to Optimize RPO and RTO are given as follows.

- **Critical applications**: Low RPO (seconds to minutes) and low RTO (near-instant failover).

- **Moderate-priority workloads**: RPO of a few hours and RTO of 30-60 minutes.
- **Non-essential systems**: Higher RPO and RTO to reduce costs.

By defining clear recovery objectives and using the right AWS tools, businesses can ensure that their disaster recovery strategy is cost-effective, efficient, and resilient against failures.

Defining Business-Specific Recovery Goals – Mapping RPO/RTO to Workloads

Every organization has diverse workloads, each with unique recovery requirements. A one-size-fits-all Disaster Recovery (DR) strategy is inefficient and costly. Instead, businesses must categorize workloads based on criticality and define appropriate RPO and RTO targets for each category.

Automation tools such as **AWS CloudFormation** and **Terraform** help define disaster recovery policies per workload tier as code, ensuring consistent backups, replication, and retention while reducing manual errors and configuration drift.

This section outlines how to classify workloads, align recovery goals with business needs, and choose the right AWS services to achieve an optimal balance between cost and resilience.

Categorizing Workloads by Business Criticality

Workloads should be classified into tiers based on their impact on business operations:

- **Mission-Critical Workloads**
  - Require near-zero downtime (RTO of seconds to minutes).
  - Must have minimal to no data loss (RPO of seconds).
  - **Example:** Financial transactions, healthcare systems, e-commerce checkout services.
  - **Recommended AWS Services:** Multi-Region Active-Active setups, AWS Elastic Disaster Recovery, Amazon Aurora Global Database.
- **High-Priority Workloads**
  - Can tolerate brief outages (RTO of minutes to an hour).
  - Limited data loss is acceptable (RPO of minutes to an hour).
  - **Example:** Internal operational databases, customer service applications.
  - **Recommended AWS Services:** AWS Backup, Amazon RDS Multi-AZ, Amazon Route 53 Failover.
- **Moderate-Priority Workloads**
  - Can sustain moderate downtime (RTO of hours).
  - Some data loss is tolerable (RPO of hours).
  - **Example:** Reporting systems, marketing databases, batch-processing workloads.
  - **Recommended AWS Services:** Amazon S3 Cross-Region Replication, AWS Storage Gateway.
- **Low-Priority Workloads**
  - Can be restored gradually (RTO of a day or more).
  - RPO of 24 hours or longer is acceptable.
  - **Example:** Archived data, historical analytics, compliance logs.
  - **Recommended AWS Services:** Amazon Glacier, AWS Backup Lifecycle Policies.

Aligning RPO and RTO Goals with Business Needs

When defining RPO and RTO, organizations should consider:

- **Regulatory Compliance:** Industries like finance and healthcare often require near-instant recovery.
- **Customer Expectations:** E-commerce and SaaS providers need high availability to prevent revenue loss.
- **Operational Costs:** Lower RTO and RPO require higher investments in replication and failover systems.

AWS Tools for Efficient Recovery Goal Mapping

AWS offers several tools to map business-specific recovery goals effectively:

Business Requirement	AWS Service	Functionality
Zero Downtime and No Data Loss	AWS Elastic Disaster Recovery	Real-time replication with near-instant failover
High Availability	Amazon RDS Multi-AZ	Automatic failover for critical databases
Cost-Effective Backup	AWS Backup	Automated backup across AWS services
Long-Term Archiving	Amazon Glacier	Low-cost, cold storage for compliance data

Table 12.3: *Mapping Business-Specific Recovery Goals*

RPO and RTO targets should be continuously reassessed and adjusted as workloads, data volumes, and business priorities evolve, rather than treated as a one-time configuration. By strategically mapping RPO and RTO to workloads, organizations can ensure that their disaster recovery strategies are both cost-effective and resilient, aligning recovery efforts with business impact and customer expectations.

Optimizing Costs versus Recovery Speed – Balancing Availability, Performance, and Cost-Effectiveness

When designing a disaster recovery strategy, organizations must carefully balance costs, recovery speed, and system availability. While high availability and near-instant recovery are ideal, they often come with higher costs due to increased resource usage, data replication, and failover infrastructure.

This section explores how businesses can optimize their disaster recovery setup by making strategic trade-offs between cost and recovery speed. By leveraging the flexible pricing models, tiered storage, automated scaling, and failover mechanisms of AWS, organizations can design a cost-effective yet resilient disaster recovery plan.

Understanding the Cost Factors in Disaster Recovery

The cost of implementing disaster recovery in AWS depends on multiple factors, including:

- **Storage Costs:** Backup frequency, snapshot retention, and cross-region replication.
- **Compute Costs:** Keeping standby instances running for failover scenarios.
- **Data Transfer Costs:** Replicating data across Availability Zones (AZs) and AWS Regions.
- **Backup Management Costs:** Using AWS Backup features such as cross-Region backup copy, which incur additional storage and transfer costs but provide stronger regional disaster recovery and compliance isolation.

- **Automation and Monitoring:** Using AWS services like CloudWatch and Lambda for failover automation.

Some of the key considerations for Cost versus Performance are given as follows:

- **High Availability versus On-Demand Recovery:** Continuous availability (such as Multi-AZ deployments) is more expensive but ensures minimal downtime, while cold backups are cheaper but increase recovery time.
- **Regional Redundancy versus Single Region:** Storing data across AWS Regions enhances resilience but incurs additional data transfer and replication costs.
- **Backup Frequency versus Storage Costs:** More frequent backups ensure lower data loss (RPO) but increase storage expenses.

Choosing the Right AWS Disaster Recovery Strategy for Cost Optimization

Organizations can select from different disaster recovery approaches based on their budget and recovery requirements:

Strategy	Recovery Speed (RTO)	Cost Level	Description
Backup and Restore	Hours	Low	Periodic backups stored in S3/EBS, restored when needed.
Pilot Light	Minutes to Hours	Moderate	Core infrastructure is preconfigured but scaled down until activated.
Warm Standby	Minutes	High	A smaller version of the production environment is always running.
Multi-Site (Hot Standby)	Near-Zero	Very High	Fully redundant infrastructure running in multiple AWS Regions.

Table 12.4: *Strategic Selection for Cost-Effectiveness*

- For critical applications, a Warm Standby approach balances cost and quick recovery.
- For less critical workloads, the Backup & Restore model is the most cost-efficient.
- Highly regulated industries (like banking) may require Hot Standby for compliance despite high costs.

Cost-Optimization Techniques for Disaster Recovery in AWS

Some of the cost-optimization techniques for Disaster Recovery in AWS are as follows:

- **Reduce Storage Costs with Tiered Data Management**

  AWS offers storage tiers that allow businesses to optimize backup costs:

  - **Frequent backups**: Store in S3 Standard or EBS Snapshots for quick recovery.
  - **Long-term backups**: Move to S3 Glacier or Glacier Deep Archive for lower costs.
  - **Automate lifecycle policies**: Use S3 Lifecycle Rules to transition older backups to cheaper storage.

- **Optimize Compute Costs with Auto Scaling and Spot Instances**
  - **Use Auto Scaling**: Deploy EC2 Auto Scaling to provision instances only when needed.
  - **Leverage Spot Instances**: Use cost-effective Spot Instances for temporary disaster recovery workloads.

  - **Use Lambda for Failover**: Replace always-running standby servers with serverless failover automation.
- **Minimize Data Transfer Costs with Regional Strategies**
  - **Use VPC Peering**: Optimize cross-region replication by using AWS PrivateLink and VPC Peering.
  - **Compress and Deduplicate Data**: Reduce replication bandwidth by using AWS DataSync or third-party tools.

For example, transitioning long-term backups to Glacier Deep Archive can reduce storage costs by up to 70–90%, while scaling DR compute only during failover events can lower standby costs by 50% or more, depending on workload patterns.

Practical Example: Cost versus Recovery Speed Decision-Making

Consider a Scenario regarding an E-Commerce Platform with Budget Constraints.

A global e-commerce company wants a disaster recovery strategy that ensures minimum downtime but remains cost-effective.

Challenge

- The company needs to protect its order processing system but cannot afford a full hot-standby deployment.
- It must meet a 1-hour RTO and a 5-minute RPO.

Optimized Solution

- **Multi-AZ RDS Deployment**: Ensures database resilience without the cost of cross-region failover.
- **S3 Intelligent-Tiering**: Reduces storage costs by automatically moving old backups to Glacier.
- **Lambda-Based Failover**: Uses AWS Lambda to trigger recovery processes only during an outage, reducing standby costs.

This approach balances performance and cost, ensuring resilience while keeping expenses under control.

Result

This design achieves the required 1-hour RTO and 5-minute RPO at a significantly lower cost than a traditional hot-standby approach.

Optimizing disaster recovery costs requires balancing performance, availability, and financial constraints. By leveraging the flexible options of AWS such as tiered storage, auto scaling, and cost-effective failover strategies, organizations can design a resilient yet economic disaster recovery plan.

- **Understand Cost Drivers**: Compute, storage, data transfer, and automation impact DR expenses.
- **Select the Right Strategy**: Backup and Restore (low cost) versus Multi-Site (high performance).
- **Leverage Cost Optimization Tools**: Use S3 Lifecycle Policies, Auto Scaling, and Spot Instances to minimize expenses.
- **Implement Smart Recovery Mechanisms**: Use Lambda and automated failover to reduce standby infrastructure costs.

By following these best practices, organizations can achieve fast disaster recovery while optimizing AWS costs, ensuring business continuity without unnecessary financial burden.

Failover Configurations

Disruptions in cloud environments can occur due to hardware failures, network outages, cyberattacks, or natural disasters. To ensure high availability and minimize downtime, organizations must implement robust failover strategies within their AWS infrastructure.

AWS offers two primary failover configurations to enhance system resilience:

- **Multi-AZ (Availability Zone) Failover**: Provides redundancy within a single AWS Region by replicating resources across multiple Availability Zones.
- **Cross-Region Failover**: Ensures geo-redundancy by replicating resources across multiple AWS Regions, protecting against regional outages.

This section explores how to design, configure, and implement Multi-AZ and Cross-Region failover mechanisms to ensure business continuity, data integrity, and minimal service disruptions.

Understanding Failover Mechanisms in AWS

Failover is a critical component of Disaster Recovery (DR) and High Availability (HA) strategies. It enables AWS workloads to:

- Automatically switch to a backup system when the primary system fails.
- Minimize downtime by quickly redirecting traffic to operational instances.
- Ensure continuous business operations, even in the face of unexpected failures.

In AWS, failover models are implemented using services such as Active-Passive with Amazon Route 53 health checks, Warm Standby with Auto Scaling and Multi-AZ databases, and Active-Active architectures using services like Amazon Aurora Global Database.

Key Failover Concepts

Some of the few key failover concepts are provided as follows:

- **Active-Passive Failover:** A secondary system remains idle until needed. (For example, Pilot Light and Warm Standby models).
- **Active-Active Failover:** All systems run simultaneously across multiple locations, balancing workloads and ensuring instant redundancy.
- **Automated versus Manual Failover:** AWS provides automated failover solutions (including RDS Multi-AZ, and Route 53 failover) but also supports manual intervention if needed.

Multi-AZ Failover Strategies – Ensuring High Availability within a Single AWS Region

Ensuring high availability is a key component of a resilient cloud infrastructure. AWS Multi-AZ (Availability Zone) failover strategies are designed to provide automatic redundancy and failover protection within a single AWS Region. By distributing workloads across multiple Availability Zones (AZs), AWS minimizes downtime and ensures seamless failover in case of an instance or AZ failure.

While Multi-AZ architectures improve availability, proper identity and access management is essential to ensure failover works securely and predictably.

Key security considerations include:

- **IAM Roles for Services:** Ensure AWS services (such as load balancers, Auto Scaling groups, and databases) have the required permissions via AWS Identity and Access Management roles to perform health checks, launch replacement instances, and attach resources during failover.

- **Least-Privilege Permissions:** Grant only the permissions required for failover actions (such as instance replacement, target registration) to reduce security risk.
- **Consistent Security Groups Across AZs:** Use identical security group rules in each AZ to avoid traffic failures during failover.
- **Encrypted Data Replication:** Ensure data replicated across AZs (for databases, storage, or messaging services) is encrypted using managed or customer-managed keys.
- **Audit and Monitoring:** Log failover-related actions to enable visibility and compliance verification.

A secure Multi-AZ failover strategy combines redundancy with tightly controlled permissions to ensure availability without expanding the attack surface.

This section explores how Multi-AZ failover mechanisms work, the AWS services that support them, and best practices for implementing fault-tolerant architectures within a single AWS Region.

Understanding Multi-AZ Failover and Its Importance

Multi-AZ failover is a high availability mechanism where AWS services automatically switch to a standby instance in another Availability Zone when a failure is detected. This ensures uninterrupted service and minimizes downtime.

- **Protection against Localized Failures:** If one AZ experiences a failure, AWS can redirect traffic to healthy instances in another AZ.
- **Automatic Recovery:** Failover happens automatically, reducing manual intervention.
- **Minimal Downtime:** AWS Multi-AZ services are designed for near-instantaneous failover, ensuring business continuity.
- **Regulatory Compliance:** Many industries require high availability and redundancy to meet compliance standards.

Key AWS Services Supporting Multi-AZ Failover

Several AWS services natively support Multi-AZ failover mechanisms, ensuring high availability and automatic recovery within a single AWS Region.

- **Amazon RDS Multi-AZ Deployments**
    - AWS automatically synchronizes the primary database to a standby instance in a different AZ.
    - If a failure occurs, AWS automatically promotes the standby instance to primary.
    - Failover typically happens within 60-120 seconds with zero data loss.
- **Amazon EC2 with Elastic Load Balancer (ELB)**
    - ELB distributes incoming traffic across multiple EC2 instances in different AZs.
    - If one instance becomes unhealthy, ELB reroutes traffic to healthy instances.
- **Amazon EFS (Elastic File System) Multi-AZ Storage**
    - Provides highly available file storage that spans multiple AZs.
    - Ensures persistent data availability even if one AZ goes offline.
- **AWS Auto Scaling Across Multi-AZs**
    - Automatically adjusts the number of EC2 instances to maintain application availability.
    - Ensures instances are evenly distributed across multiple AZs for high resilience.

Configuring Multi-AZ Failover for High Availability

Step 1: Deploy Resources Across Multiple Availability Zones.

1. When launching EC2 instances, select a deployment option that spreads instances across multiple AZs.
2. For databases, enable Multi-AZ deployments in Amazon RDS settings.

Step 2: Use Elastic Load Balancing (ELB) for Traffic Distribution.

1. Configure an Application Load Balancer (ALB) or Network Load Balancer (NLB).
2. Enable health checks to detect failures and redirect traffic automatically.

Step 3: Enable Auto Scaling for Automatic Recovery.

1. Define Auto Scaling policies to launch new instances if one becomes unavailable.
2. Set up policies to balance instances across multiple AZs.

Step 4: Implement Amazon Route 53 for DNS-Based Failover.

1. Configure Route 53 DNS failover policies to redirect traffic between healthy instances.
2. Use health checks to automatically detect and reroute traffic during an outage.

Monitoring and Testing Multi-AZ Failover

In high-availability architecture, Multi-AZ (Availability Zone) deployments are essential to ensuring minimal downtime during infrastructure failure. However, building a resilient system is only part of the equation—proactive monitoring and rigorous failover testing are critical to guarantee that your failover mechanisms actually perform under pressure. This guide dives into the key considerations, tools, and best practices for monitoring the health of Multi-AZ environments and simulating failover scenarios to validate the robustness of disaster recovery strategies.

Key Metrics for Monitoring Multi-AZ Failover

AWS services emit metrics and events that help teams detect failures early and validate that Multi-AZ failover is functioning as expected.

Example: Monitoring RDS Multi-AZ Failover

For Multi-AZ database deployments, AWS publishes failover-related signals to Amazon CloudWatch and service events.

Common metrics and indicators include:

- **DatabaseConnections:** Sudden drops can indicate an AZ-level failure or failover event.
- **ReplicaLag** (for read replicas): Spikes may signal replication delays prior to failover.
- **CPUUtilization / FreeableMemory:** Resource exhaustion that could trigger failover.
- **RDS Events:** Events such as "*Multi-AZ failover started*" and "*Failover completed*" confirm successful transitions.

Practical Monitoring Example

A CloudWatch alarm can be configured to notify operators if database connections drop below a threshold or if a failover event is triggered, enabling immediate validation of recovery behavior.

Monitoring Multi-AZ Deployments

AWS provides monitoring tools to track failover and ensure system resilience:

- **Amazon CloudWatch:** Monitors instance health and failover events.
- **AWS CloudTrail:** Logs changes in failover configurations.
- **AWS Trusted Advisor:** Provides recommendations for high availability improvements.

Testing Failover Mechanisms

To ensure failover mechanisms work effectively, organizations should:

- Conduct regular failover drills by manually shutting down instances.
- Simulate AZ failures to observe AWS automated responses.
- Validate data consistency after failover events.

Best Practices for Multi-AZ Failover Strategies

- **Design for Redundancy:** Always deploy critical resources across multiple AZs.
- **Enable Automatic Failover:** Use AWS-native failover services like RDS Multi-AZ, Auto Scaling, and ELB.
- **Optimize Cost versus Availability:** Balance failover configurations to minimize costs without sacrificing reliability.
- **Perform Regular Failover Tests:** Simulate outages to verify failover mechanisms are working as expected.

By implementing Multi-AZ failover strategies, businesses can enhance the resilience of their AWS infrastructure, reduce downtime risks, and ensure seamless operations during unexpected failures.

Cross-Region Disaster Recovery – Using Route 53, Global Accelerator, and AWS Transit Gateway for Redundancy

While Multi-AZ failover provides redundancy within a single AWS Region, Cross-Region Disaster Recovery (DR) ensures business continuity even if an entire AWS Region experiences a failure. This strategy involves replicating workloads, databases, and network configurations across geographically separated AWS Regions to withstand large-scale disruptions.

AWS offers multiple services to facilitate Cross-Region Disaster Recovery, including Amazon Route 53 for DNS failover, AWS Global Accelerator for low-latency routing, and AWS Transit Gateway for seamless network communication. This section explores how these services work together to ensure global redundancy and high availability.

The importance of Cross-Region Disaster Recovery are as follows:

- **Protection against Regional Failures:** If an AWS Region becomes unavailable due to outages, disasters, or cyberattacks, workloads can fail over to another Region.
- **Global Redundancy:** Organizations with a worldwide presence need distributed architectures to serve customers without disruption.
- **Improved RTO and RPO Compliance:** A well-designed Cross-Region DR strategy helps meet stringent Recovery Time Objectives (RTO) and Recovery Point Objectives (RPO).
- **Minimized Performance Impact:** Ensuring low-latency access even during failover is crucial for customer experience and SLA compliance.

Key AWS Services for Cross-Region Disaster Recovery

AWS provides several services that facilitate Cross-Region Disaster Recovery by ensuring efficient routing, data replication, and seamless network transitions.

- **Amazon Route 53 – DNS Failover for Global Workloads**
  - **Route 53 Traffic Routing:** Enables DNS-based traffic control between primary and secondary Regions.
  - **Health Checks:** Automatically detects failures and redirects users to a backup Region.
  - **Geolocation and Latency-Based Routing:** Ensures users connect to the nearest, most responsive Region.
- **AWS Global Accelerator – Improving Failover Performance**
  - Uses AWS Edge Locations to provide intelligent routing and failover.
  - Reroutes traffic automatically to the closest healthy Region.
  - Reduces failover time compared to standard DNS-based routing.
- **AWS Transit Gateway – Seamless Cross-Region Networking**
  - Creates a unified global network across AWS Regions.
  - Simplifies routing configurations and enhances security.
  - Supports VPN and Direct Connect for hybrid cloud connectivity.

Configuring Cross-Region Disaster Recovery

Step 1: Replicate Resources across AWS Regions.

1. Deploy instances in multiple AWS Regions to ensure redundancy.
2. Use Amazon S3 Cross-Region Replication for object storage.
3. Enable RDS Multi-Region Replication for database availability.

Step 2: Set Up Route 53 for Automated DNS Failover.

1. Configure primary and secondary endpoints for web applications.
2. Enable Route 53 health checks to monitor service availability.
3. Use failover routing policies to redirect users during an outage.

Step 3: Optimize Traffic Routing with AWS Global Accelerator.

1. Set up Global Accelerator endpoints for multiple AWS Regions.
2. Configure automatic traffic rerouting to a secondary Region during failures.
3. Ensure low-latency performance even during disaster recovery scenarios.

Step 4: Establish Secure Network Connectivity with AWS Transit Gateway.

1. Configure AWS Transit Gateway attachments to interconnect multiple VPCs across Regions.
2. Use VPN or Direct Connect for hybrid cloud failover strategies.
3. Implement centralized monitoring to detect and resolve network failures proactively.

Testing and Monitoring Cross-Region DR Strategies

Cross-region Disaster Recovery (DR) strategies play a pivotal role in minimizing downtime and data loss during regional failures. As organizations increasingly operate across cloud platforms and global regions, the ability to shift operations instantly and securely is critical. Yet, having a DR plan on paper isn't enough. Effective DR demands proactive testing routines, real-world failover drills, and continuous monitoring frameworks that can detect anomalies before they escalate. By prioritizing these activities, enterprises not only enhance resilience but also gain confidence that their infrastructure can withstand unplanned disruptions without compromising user experience or business performance.

Testing Disaster Recovery Failover

To validate failover mechanisms, organizations should:

- Perform planned failover drills by manually triggering failovers.
- Monitor RTO and RPO compliance during testing.
- Simulate regional outages and assess system resilience.

Monitoring Cross-Region Failover Readiness

AWS provides several monitoring tools to track the health and availability of disaster recovery setups:

- **Amazon CloudWatch:** Monitors failover performance and traffic patterns.
- **AWS CloudTrail:** Logs failover events and configuration changes.
- **AWS Trusted Advisor:** Provides recommendations for disaster recovery improvements.

Best Practices for Cross-Region Disaster Recovery

- Deploy workloads across at least two AWS Regions to ensure redundancy.
- Use Route 53 failover routing to automate disaster recovery.
- Leverage AWS Global Accelerator for faster traffic rerouting.
- Enable AWS Transit Gateway for seamless cross-region networking.
- Test failover mechanisms regularly to ensure readiness.

By implementing Cross-Region Disaster Recovery strategies, organizations can minimize downtime, enhance system resilience, and ensure business continuity even in the face of regional failures.

Best Practices for Failover Configuration

To ensure a cost-effective, efficient, and reliable failover strategy, organizations should follow these best practices:

- **Test and Validate Failover Mechanisms Regularly**
  - Conduct failover simulations to identify weaknesses in disaster recovery plans.
  - Use AWS Fault Injection Simulator to simulate failures and test response times.
- **Optimize Cost versus Performance in Failover Configurations**
  - Use on-demand or Spot Instances instead of running full standby infrastructure.
  - Implement tiered storage solutions (such as S3 Glacier for less critical data).
- **Automate Failover with AWS Lambda and CloudWatch**
  - Use AWS Lambda functions to trigger failover processes automatically.
  - Configure CloudWatch alarms to detect failures and initiate responses.
- **Ensure Compliance and Security in Failover Setups**
  - Encrypt data at rest and in transit during cross-region replication.
  - Implement IAM policies to restrict failover access to authorized users.

Failover configurations in AWS provide business continuity, data protection, and service resilience against failures. Organizations can choose between Multi-AZ failover for high availability within a region and Cross-Region failover for full-scale disaster recovery. By carefully designing and testing automated failover strategies, businesses can ensure seamless operations with minimal downtime.

Automated Failover Mechanisms – Setting up CloudWatch Alarms and AWS Lambda for Automated Responses

A robust disaster recovery strategy requires not just failover capabilities but also automated mechanisms to ensure rapid response to failures. Manual intervention can delay recovery and increase downtime, making automation a crucial element of a well-designed failover system.

AWS provides multiple automation tools—such as Amazon CloudWatch Alarms, AWS Lambda, and Route 53 health checks—to detect failures and trigger failover actions without human intervention. This section explores how to implement automated failover mechanisms to improve resilience and minimize disruptions.

Some of the challenges with Manual Failover are as follows:

- Slower recovery times due to reliance on human response.
- Inconsistent decision-making leading to errors in failover execution.
- Increased operational complexity, requiring real-time monitoring and intervention.

The benefits of Automated Failover are provided as follows:

- Faster response times by detecting failures in real time and triggering failover instantly.
- Reduced downtime and data loss, improving RTO (Recovery Time Objective) and RPO (Recovery Point Objective).
- Consistent and reliable failover execution without human intervention.
- Cost efficiency by ensuring that resources are only utilized when necessary.

The Key AWS Services for Automated Failover are as follows.

Amazon CloudWatch Alarms – Real-Time Failure Detection

CloudWatch monitors key AWS services and triggers alarms when performance metrics deviate from expected values.

Working:

- Monitors metrics like EC2 instance health, RDS database availability, and latency.
- Triggers alarms when thresholds (namely CPU utilization spikes and server unresponsiveness) are exceeded.
- Integrates with AWS Lambda to automate failover actions.

AWS Lambda – Executing Failover Responses Automatically

AWS Lambda allows you to run serverless scripts that execute failover actions when triggered by CloudWatch alarms.

Use Cases:

- Automatically reroute traffic to a secondary AWS Region using Route 53 API calls.
- Restart failed EC2 instances or switch to a backup instance in another AZ/Region.

- Trigger data replication processes to restore lost data.

Route 53 Health Checks – DNS-Based Failover

Amazon Route 53 continuously monitors the availability of primary resources and redirects traffic when failures occur.

Features:

- Checks application endpoints to determine if the primary service is running.
- Automatically updates DNS records to reroute users to a backup endpoint.
- Works with CloudWatch and Lambda for enhanced automation.

AWS Auto Scaling – Ensuring Infrastructure Availability

AWS Auto Scaling ensures that enough instances are available to handle traffic during a failover event.

Benefits:

- Launches replacement instances automatically when a failure occurs.
- Maintains system availability by scaling resources based on demand.
- Works with CloudWatch metrics to adjust resources dynamically.

Configuring Automated Failover in AWS

Step 1: Define Failure Scenarios and Metrics

1. Identify critical failure points (particularly EC2 instance crashes, database failures).
2. Set performance thresholds for failover triggers (including response time that exceeds 500ms).
3. Choose AWS services that require failover automation.

Step 2: Set up CloudWatch Alarms for Failure Detection

1. Create CloudWatch alarms to track service health.
2. Configure alarm thresholds (like CPU usage over 90% for 5 minutes).
3. Set up alarm actions to trigger AWS Lambda or Route 53 failover.

Step 3: Create an AWS Lambda Function for Failover Response

Write a Lambda function to:

1. Modify Route 53 records to switch traffic.
2. Stop/restart EC2 instances in another AZ or Region.
3. Activate backup databases and redirect application traffic.
    a. Deploy the function and integrate it with CloudWatch alarms.

Step 4: Enable Route 53 Health Checks for DNS Failover

1. Configure primary and secondary application endpoints.
2. Set up health check conditions (such as server unresponsiveness > 30 seconds).
3. Enable automated failover routing policies to switch traffic.

Step 5: Test and Validate Automated Failover

1. Simulate failure scenarios (for instance manually shutting down a primary instance).
2. Monitor how CloudWatch, Lambda, and Route 53 respond to failures.
3. Make improvements to enhance response time and reliability.

Best Practices for Automated Failover

- Use multiple AWS services (CloudWatch, Lambda, or Route 53) for comprehensive failover automation.
- Test failover mechanisms regularly to ensure reliability.
- Optimize thresholds in CloudWatch alarms to avoid false positives.
- Implement security best practices for Lambda functions to prevent unauthorized modifications.
- Monitor and log failover events using AWS CloudTrail and CloudWatch Logs.

By implementing automated failover mechanisms, organizations can achieve resilient, self-healing infrastructure that minimizes downtime and ensures seamless recovery during unexpected failures.

Minimizing Downtime with DNS Failover – Implementing Route 53 Health Checks for Seamless Failover

In a Disaster Recovery plan, minimizing downtime is critical to maintaining business continuity and ensuring user satisfaction. One of the most effective ways to achieve this is by implementing DNS-based failover using Amazon Route 53 health checks. Route 53 continuously monitors the availability of application endpoints and automatically reroutes traffic to backup resources in case of a failure.

By integrating Route 53 with failover routing policies and automated health checks, organizations can ensure seamless transitions between primary and secondary resources, reducing downtime and maintaining high availability.

Record Name	Type	Routing Policy	Target	Health Check
app.example.com	A / Alias	Failover (Primary)	ALB – Region A	Enabled
app.example.com	A / Alias	Failover (Secondary)	ALB – Region B	Not required

Table 12.5: *Simplified DNS Records*

The challenges of Downtime without Automated DNS Failover are as follows:

- **User Experience Impact:** If a primary web server or database goes down, users experience slow response times or complete inaccessibility.
- **Revenue Loss:** For e-commerce and SaaS businesses, even a few minutes of downtime can lead to financial losses.
- **Manual Intervention Delays:** If failover is handled manually, response times increase, worsening downtime effects.

Let us see how Route 53 helps minimize Downtime:

- **Continuous Health Monitoring:** Automatically checks if endpoints are accessible and performing optimally.
- **Instant Traffic Rerouting:** Redirects users to healthy endpoints without manual intervention.
- **Seamless Multi-Region Support:** Supports failover between AWS Availability Zones (AZs) and Regions for global resilience.

Implementing Route 53 DNS Failover

Setting Up Route 53 Health Checks

Amazon Route 53 provides automated health checks to monitor the status of application endpoints such as web servers, databases, or APIs.

Steps to Configure Health Checks:

1. Navigate to the Route 53 console and select Health Checks.
2. Click `Create Health Check` and define:
    a. Target endpoint (IP address or domain).
    b. Monitoring protocol (HTTP, HTTPS, TCP).
    c. Failure conditions (specifically timeout, or failed response).
        i. Configure **notification settings** (CloudWatch alarms, SNS alerts).
        ii. Save and activate the health check.

Configuring Route 53 Failover Routing Policy

Once health checks are in place, the next step is to set up failover routing to reroute traffic during a failure.

Steps to Configure Failover Routing:

1. Go to the Route 53 console and open Hosted Zones.
2. Select your domain name and create a new record set.
3. Choose Failover as the routing policy.
4. Define the Primary Resource (like primary EC2 instance or load balancer).
5. Associate the Primary Resource with its corresponding health check.
6. Create a Secondary Resource (backup instance in another AZ or Region).
7. Route traffic to the Secondary Resource only when the primary fails.

Testing and Validating DNS Failover

Once configured, it is essential to test the failover mechanism to ensure smooth transitions during real-world failures.

Testing Steps:

1. Manually shut down the primary resource and observe the response of Route 53.
2. Monitor traffic logs to ensure users are redirected to the backup server.
3. Verify that failover occurs within the expected timeframe (should be near-instant).
4. Test multi-region failover by simulating a complete AWS Region outage.

Optimizing Route 53 Failover for High Availability

Reducing DNS Propagation Delays

- Lower TTL (Time-To-Live) values in DNS settings to ensure faster updates.
- Default TTL settings can delay failover—set TTL to 60 seconds or less for near-instant DNS updates.

Implementing Weighted Routing for Gradual Traffic Shift

- Instead of an immediate switch, Route 53 allows gradual traffic migration to the backup resource.

- Useful for load balancing failover scenarios (for example shifting 50% of traffic first, then 100%).

Enhancing Multi-Region Resilience

- Combine Route 53 with AWS Global Accelerator to optimize cross-region failover.
- Use Amazon CloudFront for edge-based DNS failover, reducing latency.

Best Practices for Route 53 DNS Failover

- Monitor Route 53 logs to detect unusual failover patterns.
- Use multiple health checkers to avoid false-positive failures.
- Regularly test failover mechanisms to confirm they work under real conditions.
- Enable CloudWatch alarms to receive failure notifications instantly.
- Integrate failover with AWS Lambda to trigger automated recovery actions.

Implementing Route 53 health checks with DNS failover is a powerful strategy to minimize downtime and enhance system availability. By automating traffic rerouting in response to failures, businesses can maintain seamless user experiences even during outages.

With properly configured health checks, optimized routing policies, and periodic failover testing, organizations can achieve high availability, reduced downtime, and improved disaster resilience across AWS environments.

Testing Disaster Recovery Plans

A well-designed Disaster Recovery (DR) plan is only as effective as its ability to function under real-world conditions. Regular testing of disaster recovery strategies ensures that failover mechanisms work as expected, minimizing downtime and preventing unexpected failures. Organizations that do not perform simulated failover tests may face severe disruptions during an actual disaster, leading to data loss, financial impact, and reputational damage.

This section focuses on the importance of testing disaster recovery plans, key methodologies for simulating failover scenarios, and how to validate AWS-based recovery strategies. By incorporating structured testing into operational workflows, businesses can ensure they are prepared for any unforeseen outages or cyber threats.

The reasons that make Testing Disaster Recovery Plans critical are identified as follows:

- **Identifying Gaps and Weaknesses in the Plan**

  Even the most well-documented disaster recovery strategies can have blind spots. Testing allows organizations to:

  - Detects misconfigurations in backup and failover processes.
  - Uncover dependency failures between cloud resources.
  - Validate that Recovery Point Objectives (RPOs) and Recovery Time Objectives (RTOs) are being met.

- **Ensuring Compliance with Regulatory Requirements**

  Many industries, such as finance and healthcare, have strict compliance mandates for data availability and disaster recovery. Testing disaster recovery plans ensures:

  - Compliance with ISO 27001, SOC 2, PCI-DSS, HIPAA, and GDPR regulations.
  - Evidence of preparedness for audits and security assessments.

- **Reducing Downtime and Financial Losses**
    - Without proper testing: Recovery procedures may take hours or days, leading to business losses and reputational damage.
    - With proactive testing: Organizations can ensure rapid recovery within minutes, reducing financial impact.

Types of Disaster Recovery Testing Methods

- **Tabletop Exercises (Theoretical Testing):** A discussion-based review where teams walk through DR scenarios without actual system disruptions.
    - **Purpose:** Ensures that employees understand their roles and responsibilities in a disaster event.
    - **Best for:** Evaluating business continuity plans and improving documentation.
- **Functional Testing (Component-Level Validation):** A small-scale test where individual AWS services (such as database failovers or S3 backup restorations) are tested independently.
    - **Purpose:** Validates that each component works correctly before conducting full-scale recovery tests.
    - **Best for:** Application-level recovery testing with minimal impact on production.

Testing Method	Risk Level	Downtime Impact	Suitable For	Tools / Examples
Tabletop Exercises	Very Low	None	Business continuity planning, role clarity, audits	Runbooks, DR documentation
Functional Testing	Low	Minimal / Controlled	Validating individual components	RDS failover tests, S3 restore, AWS Backup restores
Full-Scale Failover Simulations	High	Significant (planned)	Mission-critical systems with strict RTO/RPO	Route 53 failover, cross-Region recovery
Chaos Engineering	Medium-High	Variable (controlled)	Highly resilient, self-healing architectures	AWS Fault Injection Simulator

***Table 12.6**: Comparison of Disaster Recovery Testing Methods*

- **Full-Scale Failover Simulations (Live Environment Testing):** A complete failover from the primary AWS region to a secondary region or backup site.
    - **Purpose:** Evaluates the ability of the organization to recover from a real disaster.
    - **Best for:** Mission-critical applications requiring high availability.
    - **Risks:** Can impact production workloads if not carefully planned.
- **Chaos Engineering (Randomized Failure Testing):** Intentional injection of random failures into production or staging environments to test resilience.
    - **Purpose:** Helps identify unexpected vulnerabilities and validate self-healing mechanisms.
    - **Tools:** AWS Fault Injection Simulator (FIS) for controlled failure testing.
    - **Best for:** Organizations aiming for high availability and self-healing architectures.

Performing Simulated Failover Scenarios in AWS

Defining the Scope of the Failover Test

- Identify which workloads and AWS services will be tested.
- Decide between partial or full failover simulations.

- Establish clear metrics for success (such as RTO < 15 minutes).

Executing the Failover Test

1. **Step 1:** Shut down the primary AWS environment (or simulate failure using AWS Fault Injection Simulator).
2. **Step 2:** Trigger failover mechanisms (Route 53 DNS failover, RDS Multi-AZ, Elastic Load Balancer, and so on).
3. **Step 3:** Monitor AWS **CloudWatch logs** and alerts to track recovery speed.
4. **Step 4:** Validate that workloads are restored to the backup environment.

Analyzing Test Results and Optimizing DR Strategies

Some of the key metrics to evaluate are as follows.

- Failover time versus defined RTO.
- Data integrity post-recovery (ensuring backups are complete).
- System performance in failover mode.

Post-Test Actions:

- Document findings and update disaster recovery playbooks.
- Train staff on lessons learned from the test.
- Schedule regular failover tests (quarterly or biannually).

Best Practices for Effective Disaster Recovery Testing

- Test in a non-production environment first before applying changes to production.
- Leverage automation (AWS Lambda, Step Functions) to streamline failover execution.
- Use AWS Backup and AWS Elastic Disaster Recovery for automated snapshots and fast recovery.
- Ensure cross-region replication is functioning before disaster strikes.
- Continuously refine disaster recovery policies based on test results.

AWS services such as AWS Resilience Hub and AWS Elastic Disaster Recovery further support disaster recovery testing by continuously assessing application resilience, identifying gaps against RTO/RPO targets, and enabling rapid, automated recovery during real incidents.

Testing disaster recovery plans is not optional—it is a critical process to ensure business continuity and resilience against failures. By conducting regular simulated failover tests, organizations can identify weaknesses, optimize recovery processes, and ensure AWS infrastructure meets RTO and RPO requirements.

With the right combination of tabletop exercises, functional testing, full-scale failover simulations, and chaos engineering, businesses can be fully prepared to recover swiftly from unexpected failures, minimizing downtime and ensuring uninterrupted service availability.

Case Studies

Below are real-world-inspired case studies demonstrating how businesses implement AWS Disaster Recovery (DR) strategies to safeguard their critical systems. Each case study is aligned with the topics covered in this chapter.

Case Study 1: Implementing AWS Backup and Amazon S3 for Data Protection

Industry: Healthcare

Challenge: A healthcare organization managing Electronic Medical Records (EMR) faced strict compliance requirements (HIPAA) for data availability and protection. They needed a scalable backup solution that could automate data protection and enable quick recovery in case of system failures.

Solution

- AWS Backup was implemented to schedule automated backups of Amazon RDS databases and Amazon EBS volumes.
- Amazon S3 with versioning and cross-region replication was used to store patient records securely.
- Lifecycle policies automatically archived old records to Amazon S3 Glacier for cost optimization.

Outcome:

- Reduced risk of data loss with automated backup scheduling.
- Compliance with HIPAA regulations through encrypted storage and access control policies.
- Faster recovery times—data restoration from Amazon S3 Glacier was achieved within minutes.

Recovery Metrics Achieved: The solution met an RPO of 15 minutes for critical EMR databases through automated backups using AWS Backup, and an RTO of less than an hour, with rapid restores from Amazon S3 and Amazon S3 Glacier.

Case Study 2: Meeting RPO and RTO Guidelines with AWS Disaster Recovery Solutions

Industry: E-commerce

Challenge: A global e-commerce platform experienced a database corruption event that caused extended downtime, impacting thousands of users. The company needed a faster recovery strategy with well-defined Recovery Point Objective (RPO) and Recovery Time Objective (RTO) guidelines.

Solution:

- **RPO and RTO Definitions:**
  - **RPO:** Max data loss limited to 5 minutes.
  - **RTO:** Service restoration within 30 minutes.
- **AWS RDS Multi-AZ deployment** was configured to ensure automatic failover for transactional databases.
- **Amazon S3 Cross-Region Replication** was used to maintain real-time backups of business-critical data.
- **AWS Lambda functions** automated the recovery process by restoring backups on failure detection.

Outcome:

- Near-zero data loss achieved through real-time replication.
- RTO goal (30 minutes) met with automated failover mechanisms.
- Business continuity ensured—customer transactions resumed quickly after the failure.

Failover Monitoring and Traffic Management:

Amazon CloudWatch alarms were configured to detect database health and replication issues, triggering automated recovery workflows. Amazon Route 53 failover routing policies ensured user traffic was automatically redirected to healthy application endpoints during the outage.

Case Study 3: Multi-AZ and Cross-Region Failover for High Availability

Industry: Financial Services

Challenge: A fintech startup providing real-time stock trading faced a major risk—downtime during a regional AWS outage could result in millions of dollars in lost transactions.

Solution:

- **Multi-AZ Failover:**
    - Amazon RDS and Elastic Load Balancer (ELB) were deployed with Multi-AZ failover to ensure redundancy within the same AWS region.
- **Cross-Region Disaster Recovery:**
    - Amazon Route 53 and AWS Global Accelerator were used to route traffic dynamically in case of regional failure.
    - AWS Transit Gateway was used to interconnect VPCs across multiple regions.
- **Automated Failover Mechanism:**
    - AWS CloudWatch Alarms detected failures and triggered AWS Lambda functions to redirect traffic to the secondary region.

Outcome:

- 99.99% uptime maintained, even during AWS regional outages.
- Seamless user experience—traders never faced downtime during stock transactions.
- Risk mitigation achieved, reducing potential revenue loss from downtime.

Case Study 4: Simulated Failover Testing and Chaos Engineering with AWS

Industry: SaaS (Software-as-a-Service)

Challenge: A SaaS company running a cloud-based CRM application needed to ensure its Disaster Recovery (DR) plan was fully operational. However, without real failover testing, they could not guarantee its effectiveness.

Solution:

- **Failover Testing Implementation:** A scheduled failover drill was performed where AWS Route 53 traffic routing was redirected to a standby disaster recovery region.
- **Chaos Engineering Approach:** AWS Fault Injection Simulator (FIS) was used to intentionally disrupt services and observe recovery times.
- **Post-Test Analysis & Optimization:** DR configurations were fine-tuned based on test results, ensuring the system met RTO (15 minutes) and RPO (10 minutes) goals.

Outcome:

- Identified and resolved hidden DR flaws before a real incident.
- Reduced manual intervention, making failover 100% automated.

- Achieved full service recovery within 12 minutes, exceeding RTO expectations.

AWS Fault Injection Simulator experiments were initially validated in staging to reduce production impact, ensuring safe and controlled chaos testing.

Key Takeaways from the Case Studies

- Automated backups using AWS Backup and S3 help organizations reduce data loss risks.
- Multi-AZ and cross-region failover ensure high availability during regional AWS outages.
- Defining clear RPO & RTO objectives allows companies to create an effective recovery strategy.
- Simulated failover testing uncovers potential weaknesses before a real disaster occurs.

By applying AWS disaster recovery best practices, businesses can achieve resilience, compliance, and operational continuity, even in the face of major failures or cyber threats.

Conclusion

Disaster Recovery (DR) is not a one-time setup but an evolving strategy. DR is a crucial component of any cloud infrastructure, ensuring business continuity and resilience against unexpected failures. This chapter explored essential AWS disaster recovery strategies, focusing on backup and restore processes, Recovery Objectives (RPO and RTO), failover configurations, and DR testing. Organizations leveraging the robust DR services of AWS—such as AWS Backup, Amazon S3, Route 53, and AWS Global Accelerator—can achieve high availability, minimal downtime, and rapid recovery from failures.

By implementing multi-AZ failover, cross-region replication, and automated response mechanisms, businesses can safeguard their applications and data against hardware failures, cyberattacks, and natural disasters. Additionally, regular failover testing and chaos engineering simulations are vital to validating recovery plans and optimizing response strategies.

A well-defined AWS disaster recovery plan minimizes data loss, ensures compliance with industry regulations, and maintains a seamless user experience—even during unexpected outages.

The next chapter introduces Infrastructure as Code (IaC) and how it can automate network setups. Using AWS CloudFormation, we will learn how to define network resources like VPCs, subnets, security groups, and route tables in templates. The chapter also covers template creation, management, versioning, and testing, ensuring that readers can deploy entire networks automatically.

Points to Remember

- **Regular Backups are Essential:** Implement AWS Backup and Amazon S3 versioning to maintain secure copies of critical data.
- **RPO and RTO Define Recovery Goals:** Recovery Point Objective (RPO) and Recovery Time Objective (RTO) guide backup frequency and system failover speed.
- **Multi-AZ and Cross-Region Failover Minimize Downtime:** Deploy Amazon RDS Multi-AZ, Route 53, and Global Accelerator for automated failover and traffic routing.
- **Automated DR Mechanisms Improve Response Time:** Utilize AWS CloudWatch Alarms, Lambda functions, and AWS Fault Injection Simulator (FIS) for proactive disaster recovery.
- **Testing Disaster Recovery Plans is Critical:** Conduct regular failover simulations to identify weaknesses and improve system resilience.
- **Balancing Cost and Performance is Key:** Optimize DR strategies to ensure cost-effective yet reliable business continuity solutions.

By integrating these best practices, businesses can mitigate risks, protect mission-critical workloads, and ensure continuous service availability—even in the face of major disruptions

Chapter 13
Automating Network Deployments

Introduction

In present-time dynamic cloud environments, manual network configuration can be time-consuming, error-prone, and difficult to scale. As infrastructure complexity increases, the need for automated, consistent, and repeatable network provisioning becomes essential. Infrastructure as Code (IaC) addresses this challenge by enabling developers and system administrators to define and manage infrastructure using code, just like application development. This chapter introduces AWS CloudFormation, a powerful IaC tool that allows for the automatic provisioning of AWS network components through declarative templates.

By learning how to define Virtual Private Clouds (VPCs), subnets, route tables, Internet gateways, and security groups within code templates, you gain the ability to reproduce, test, and scale environments quickly and reliably. This chapter also covers advanced topics like version control, change management, and template testing, ensuring that you not only automate deployments but do so securely and efficiently.

Structure

In this chapter, we will walk through:

- CloudFormation Overview
- Creating CloudFormation Templates
- Automating Security Groups
- Versioning and Template Management
- Case Studies

CloudFormation Overview

As cloud environments scale and evolve, the demand for consistent, repeatable, and error-free infrastructure deployment has never been higher. Gone are the days of manual configurations and point-and-click setups that often lead to inconsistencies and delays. This is where Infrastructure as Code (IaC) emerges as a transformative approach—allowing teams to define and manage their infrastructure using machine-readable configuration files.

AWS CloudFormation is a native IaC service of Amazon that enables users to model and automate the creation of AWS resources. Instead of manually provisioning services like VPCs, subnets, and security groups, CloudFormation lets you define them in templates written in JSON or YAML. These templates serve as blueprints, ensuring that your infrastructure is deployed consistently every time, across all environments.

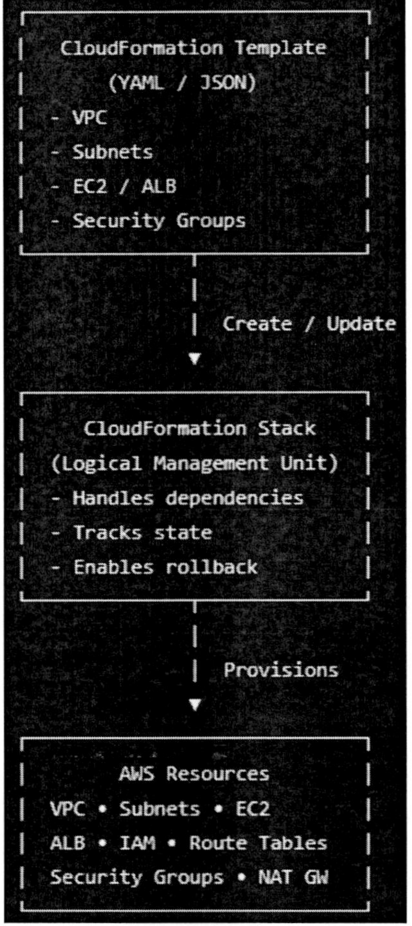

Figure 13.1: *Templates Translate into Stacks and Resources*

This section dives into the core principles of Infrastructure as Code, introduces the architecture and workflow of AWS CloudFormation, and explains why it is a vital tool in any cloud automation strategy. Whether you are managing a single-stack application or a complex multi-tier network, understanding how CloudFormation works is the first step toward mastering infrastructure automation on AWS.

Infrastructure as Code (IaC)

Before diving deep into tools like AWS CloudFormation, it is essential to grasp the underlying philosophy that powers them—**Infrastructure as Code (IaC)**. IaC is not just a buzzword; it is a pivotal practice in modern DevOps and cloud computing that treats infrastructure the same way as application code: versioned, testable, reusable, and automated.

At its core, **Infrastructure as Code** is a method of managing and provisioning infrastructure—such as servers, databases, networks, and security policies—using code rather than manual processes. This approach allows cloud architects and engineers to define the desired state of their infrastructure in files that can be version controlled, tested, and reused across multiple environments.

A Simple IaC Example (VPC in YAML)

The following is a minimal AWS CloudFormation YAML snippet that defines a Virtual Private Cloud (VPC). This file is the infrastructure — versionable, repeatable, and automated.

AWSTemplateFormatVersion: '2010-09-09'

Description: Simple VPC Using Infrastructure as Code

```
Resources:
  MyVPC:
    Type: AWS::EC2::VPC
    Properties:
      CidrBlock: 10.0.0.0/16
      EnableDnsSupport: true
      EnableDnsHostnames: true
      Tags:
        - Key: Name
          Value: My-IaC-VPC
```

What this demonstrates about IaC:

- The infrastructure is declared, not manually configured.
- The desired state is clearly defined in code.
- The same file can be reused for dev, test, or prod.
- Changes are tracked through version control (Git).
- Deployment is fully automated via CloudFormation.

In practice, this single file can be deployed repeatedly to create identical VPCs across regions or accounts—something nearly impossible to guarantee with manual setup.

Key Benefits of IaC in the AWS Ecosystem

Implementing IaC offers a host of benefits that directly address the challenges of manual configurations:

- **Consistency across Environments**: With code-based infrastructure, teams can eliminate discrepancies between development, staging, and production.

  Example: A single CloudFormation template is used to deploy the same VPC, subnet structure, and security groups in dev, test, and prod, eliminating configuration drift.

- **Faster Provisioning**: Automating deployments reduces setup time and eliminates human error.

  Example: A multi-AZ VPC with public and private subnets, NAT Gateways, and route tables can be deployed in minutes using CloudFormation—compared to hours of manual setup.

- **Auditability and Compliance**: All changes to the infrastructure are recorded and can be reviewed like any other source code.

  Example: CloudFormation templates stored in Git provide a full history of infrastructure changes, enabling the teams to trace who changed what and when—a key requirement for audits.

- **Scalability and Reusability**: Infrastructure can be replicated or expanded with minimal effort by reusing templates and parameters.

  Example: Using CloudFormation StackSets, the same VPC template can be deployed across multiple AWS accounts and regions simultaneously to support global expansion.

- **Reduced Human Error:** Declarative templates and dependency management prevent common configuration mistakes.

Example: CloudFormation automatically provisions an Internet Gateway before attaching routes, eliminating ordering errors common in manual setups.

- **Safe Updates and Rollbacks:** Changes are applied in a controlled manner with automatic rollback on failure.

  Example: If a stack update fails while modifying a security group rule, CloudFormation rolls back to the last stable state without manual intervention.

Declarative versus Imperative: Choosing the Right Approach

IaC comes in two primary styles:

- **Declarative Approach**: You define *what* the final state of your infrastructure should look like (such as "I need a VPC with two public subnets"). Tools like AWS CloudFormation and Terraform follow this model.
- **Imperative Approach**: You define *how* to reach that final state step by step (in particular "Create VPC, then create subnets, then attach route table..."). Tools like Ansible and Chef often lean more toward this style.

A **side-by-side micro example** makes this distinction instantly obvious without adding bulk.

Declarative versus Imperative: A Visual Contrast

Declarative (What you want) — CloudFormation / Terraform

```
Resources:
  MyVPC:
    Type: AWS::EC2::VPC
    Properties:
      CidrBlock: 10.0.0.0/16
```

You declare the **desired end state**. The tool figures out *how* to create, update, or fix the infrastructure.

Imperative (How to do it) — Ansible

```
- name: Create VPC
  ec2_vpc_net:
    name: my-vpc
    cidr_block: 10.0.0.0/16
```

You explicitly instruct **each step** required to reach the final state.

- **Declarative tools** handle dependencies, ordering, drift detection, and rollback automatically.
- **Imperative tools** offer fine-grained control but requires you to manage sequencing and state.

Understanding these models helps in selecting the right tool for specific use cases and operational preferences.

Importance of IaC Matters for Network Automation

In AWS networking, Infrastructure as Code enables teams to automate and standardize the creation of complex network environments. Instead of manual setup, entire network architectures are defined and deployed through reusable code.

IaC allows teams to:

- Automate VPC creation and configuration.

- Consistently deploy subnets, route tables, Internet Gateways, and NAT Gateways.
- Enforce repeatable security group and NACL rules.
- Reduce misconfigurations through validation and testing.
- Network Reproducibility across Environments.

A key enterprise benefit of IaC is network reproducibility. The same template can be used to deploy identical network architectures across development, staging, and production—or even across multiple AWS accounts and regions—ensuring consistent behavior and reducing operational risk.

IaC is not just a technical convenience; it is a strategic foundation for building scalable, secure, and reliable AWS network environments.

Key Concepts of AWS CloudFormation

AWS CloudFormation is the cornerstone of Infrastructure as Code within the AWS ecosystem. It empowers developers and cloud engineers to define, provision, and manage AWS resources using declarative templates. Before diving into template authoring and stack deployment, it is crucial to understand the key concepts that make CloudFormation both powerful and efficient.

Templates: The Blueprint of Your Infrastructure

At the heart of every CloudFormation deployment lies a template—a structured JSON or YAML document that defines the desired state of your AWS infrastructure. This template serves as the blueprint for provisioning resources and includes:

- **Resources**: Define the actual AWS services (such as VPCs, EC2 instances, subnets) you want to create.
- **Parameters**: Allow dynamic inputs during deployment, making templates reusable and configurable.
- **Mappings**: Provide static variables that can vary by region or environment.
- **Conditions**: Add logic to create resources only when certain conditions are met.
- **Outputs**: Display important values (like resource IDs or endpoints) after the stack is created.

A template is a YAML or JSON file that describes the desired state of your infrastructure.

Mini YAML Example (VPC)

```
Resources:
  AppVPC:
    Type: AWS::EC2::VPC
    Properties:
      CidrBlock: 10.0.0.0/16
      EnableDnsSupport: true
      EnableDnsHostnames: true
```

This small snippet is enough for CloudFormation to create a fully functional VPC. Templates are modular, reusable, and version-controlled—just like application code.

Stacks: Deploying Your Infrastructure in a Single Operation

A stack is the running instance of a CloudFormation template. It represents the live infrastructure defined by your code and is managed as a single unit. With stacks, you can:

- Deploy an entire environment with a single click or command.

- Track changes to infrastructure over time.
- Easily update or delete resources through controlled operations.

Stacks simplify lifecycle management by treating all components as one coherent deployment package.

Stack Sets: Scaling Infrastructure across Accounts and Regions

When working in a multi-account or multi-region AWS architecture, Stack Sets come into play. They allow you to deploy the same CloudFormation template across multiple AWS accounts and Regions simultaneously. This is particularly valuable for:

- Enforcing standardized networking policies across departments.
- Deploying consistent infrastructure in global environments.
- Simplifying governance and compliance.

Stack Sets are an enterprise-friendly feature that scales the power of IaC beyond a single account.

Change Sets: Previewing Changes before You Deploy

To ensure safe and predictable deployments, CloudFormation offers Change Sets. These are previews that show exactly what changes CloudFormation will make to your existing resources when a template is updated. Change Sets allow you to:

- Review proposed modifications before applying them.
- Avoid unintentional disruptions to live environments.
- Validate the impact of parameter or logic changes.

Using Change Sets reduces deployment risks and increases operational confidence.

Drift Detection: Staying Aligned with Your Template

Drift detection is a diagnostic feature that helps ensure your deployed infrastructure has not been manually altered outside of CloudFormation. It identifies differences (or drifts) between what your stack defines and what actually exists. This is critical for:

- Auditing configuration integrity.
- Troubleshooting unexpected behavior.
- Reinforcing IaC governance.

By catching drift early, teams can enforce consistency and prevent configuration sprawl.

Resources and Resource Types: The Building Blocks of CloudFormation

CloudFormation supports a wide array of resource types, including networking components like:

- AWS::EC2::VPC
- AWS::EC2::Subnet
- AWS::EC2::RouteTable
- AWS::EC2::SecurityGroup

Each resource type maps directly to an AWS service and includes specific properties that can be customized in your template. These resources are the elemental building blocks that bring your network architecture to life.

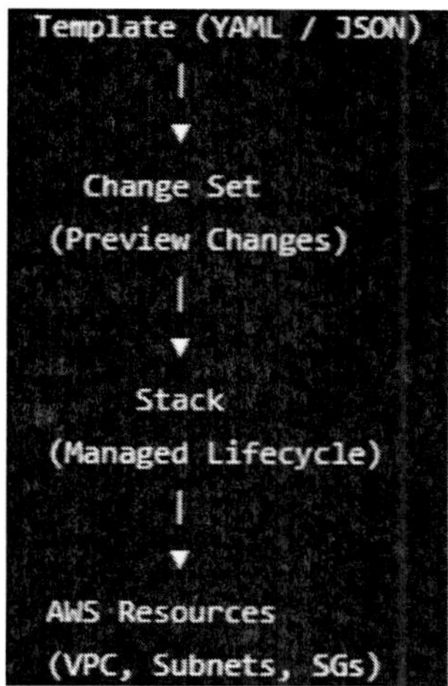

Figure 13.2: *CloudFormation Deployment Flow*

A CloudFormation template defines the desired infrastructure in YAML or JSON. A change set previews exactly what will be created, modified, or deleted before deployment. Once approved, CloudFormation creates or updates a stack, which manages the lifecycle of the actual AWS resources.

Understanding the foundational elements of CloudFormation – templates, stacks, stack sets, change sets, and drift detection–is key to building reliable and automated cloud environments. These components form the backbone of any scalable network deployment strategy and will be your primary tools in creating secure, repeatable infrastructure with minimal manual intervention.

Benefits of Automating Network Setups with Infrastructure as Code (IaC)

Manual network configuration is time-consuming, error-prone, and hard to scale. As modern cloud environments grow in complexity, organizations need a more reliable and agile approach to infrastructure deployment. This is where Infrastructure as Code (IaC) becomes indispensable. By automating network setups through tools like AWS CloudFormation, teams can provision and manage networks with the same discipline and repeatability used in software development.

Speed and Scalability: Deploy Complex Networks in Minutes

Automating network infrastructure with IaC enables rapid and repeatable deployments, turning what once took hours or days into minutes. Whether you are spinning up a single Virtual Private Cloud (VPC) or an entire multi-tier architecture, IaC tools allow you to:

- Launch complete environments using pre-defined templates.
- Scale infrastructure across regions or accounts instantly.
- Eliminate the bottlenecks of manual provisioning.

This speed is especially critical in DevOps workflows and for responding quickly to evolving business needs.

Consistency and Standardization: Eliminate Configuration Drift

Human error is a leading cause of misconfigurations and security vulnerabilities in cloud environments. With IaC, every network component – subnets, route tables, NAT gateways, and more – is defined as code, ensuring:

- Uniform setups across environments (dev, test, production).
- Predictable infrastructure behavior regardless of who deploys it.
- Minimized risk of inconsistencies or undocumented changes.

This level of standardization significantly improves operational integrity.

Version Control and Auditability: Treat Infrastructure like Codes

IaC promotes infrastructure versioning, enabling teams to track every change made to the network configuration. Using version control systems like Git alongside CloudFormation templates allows you to:

- Maintain a detailed history of infrastructure changes.
- Roll back to previous configurations when needed.
- Conduct code reviews for changes to critical network components.

This transparency is especially valuable in regulated industries that require traceability and compliance reporting.

Improved Collaboration: Align DevOps and Infrastructure Teams

With IaC, infrastructure becomes a shared language between developers, operations teams, and security engineers. Network templates can be written, reviewed, and tested just like application code, resulting in:

- Better alignment between teams.
- Fewer handoffs and misunderstandings.
- Enhanced agility through continuous integration and delivery pipelines.

IaC fosters a culture of collaboration where infrastructure decisions are no longer siloed.

Cost Optimization and Resource Efficiency: Reduce Waste and Idle Infrastructure

Automated templates make it easier to define temporary environments that can be spun up and torn down on demand. This approach helps organizations:

- Avoid overprovisioning by right-sizing network resources.
- Automate shutdown of non-production environments after hours.
- Monitor usage through well-defined templates and outputs.

As a result, businesses can control costs without compromising performance.

Disaster Recovery and Testability: Practice Before You Deploy

IaC enables teams to test and simulate network deployments before rolling them out in production. You can:

- Validate templates in isolated environments.
- Use Change Sets to preview the impact of changes.

- Recreate entire environments for testing disaster recovery scenarios.

This ability to test, break, and fix infrastructure safely leads to more resilient deployments.

Security and Compliance: Embed Governance in Code

Security best practices – such as restricting access with security groups, enforcing subnet isolation, or using encrypted traffic – can be codified directly into templates. Automating networks through IaC means:

- Security policies are applied consistently across all environments.
- Infrastructure adheres to compliance standards by design.
- Misconfigurations can be caught early through template validation tools.

This proactive approach shifts security left in the deployment pipeline.

By automating network configurations using IaC, organizations gain not just speed and efficiency, but also control, reliability, and agility. CloudFormation and similar tools empower teams to define cloud networks in a clear, repeatable, and testable way—ushering in a new era where infrastructure is no longer a bottleneck, but a driver of innovation.

Creating CloudFormation Templates

In any AWS cloud environment, the Virtual Private Cloud (VPC) forms the core of the networking layer—enabling users to isolate, organize, and secure their workloads. Within a VPC, subnets further define how resources are distributed and accessed; consequently, making them crucial elements in structuring availability zones and enforcing routing policies.

Traditionally, setting up these foundational components manually through the AWS Management Console can be tedious and error-prone, especially when deploying to multiple environments or accounts. This is where AWS CloudFormation plays a transformative role. By using Infrastructure as Code (IaC) principles, CloudFormation allows users to describe and provision AWS resources, including VPCs and subnets, through declarative JSON or YAML templates.

In this section, we dive into the process of creating CloudFormation templates that automate the design and deployment of VPCs, public and private subnets, route tables, internet gateways, and more. These templates not only save time but also enforce consistency, reusability, and version control across network configurations.

Whether you are building a single-region application or preparing your architecture for multi-AZ high availability, automating your network setup through CloudFormation ensures that your infrastructure is scalable, repeatable, and secure by design.

Writing Basic CloudFormation Templates for Networking

Establishing a foundational network structure in AWS requires configuring a number of critical components, such as VPCs, subnets, route tables, and gateways. Doing this manually can be time-consuming and also becomes difficult to replicate across multiple environments. CloudFormation solves this challenge by allowing you to define these resources programmatically in a single, cohesive template. YAML is more human-readable than JSON and hence widely preferred.

In this section, we shall explore how to write a basic CloudFormation template to automate the creation of a simple network setup. This includes defining the VPC itself, provisioning public and private subnets, and establishing routing mechanisms – all through the code. The focus is on simplicity and clarity, helping you in building a solid foundation for more advanced networking configurations in later sections.

Defining the Template Structure

Every CloudFormation template follows a defined structure, typically written in YAML or JSON. The key sections include:

- **AWSTemplateFormatVersion**: Specifies the version of the CloudFormation template format.
- **Description**: A human-readable explanation of the purpose of the template.
- **Parameters**: Optional inputs that make your template reusable and flexible.
- **Resources**: The heart of the template—this is where you define your entire AWS infrastructure.
- **Outputs**: Used to return values from your stack, like the VPC ID or subnet IDs.

Here is a basic YAML snippet showing the skeleton:

```
AWSTemplateFormatVersion: '2010-09-09'
Description: Basic VPC Setup
Resources:
  # VPC, Subnets, and other components go here
```

Creating a Virtual Private Cloud (VPC)

Enabling DNS support and DNS hostnames allows EC2 instances and other AWS services within the VPC to resolve and communicate using internal DNS names, which is essential for load balancers, service discovery, and many managed AWS services.

The VPC is the starting point of any AWS network. Here an example of how to define one:

```
MyVPC:
   Type: AWS::EC2::VPC
   Properties:
     CidrBlock: 10.0.0.0/16
     EnableDnsSupport: true
     EnableDnsHostnames: true
     Tags:
       - Key: Name
         Value: MyBasicVPC
```

This configuration defines a VPC with a CIDR block large enough to accommodate multiple subnets.

Adding Public and Private Subnets

After the VPC, subnets are added to segment your resources. Each subnet must reside within a specific Availability Zone.

```
  PublicSubnet1:
    Type: AWS::EC2::Subnet
    Properties:
      VpcId: !Ref MyVPC
      CidrBlock: 10.0.1.0/24
      AvailabilityZone: !Select [ 0, !GetAZs '' ]
      MapPublicIpOnLaunch: true  //This setting automatically assigns
a public IPv4 address to instances launched in the subnet, making them
```

```
reachable from the internet when combined with an Internet Gateway and
appropriate route tables.
      Tags:
        - Key: Name
          Value: PublicSubnet1
  PrivateSubnet1:
    Type: AWS::EC2::Subnet
    Properties:
      VpcId: !Ref MyVPC
      CidrBlock: 10.0.2.0/24
      AvailabilityZone: !Select [ 0, !GetAZs '' ]
      Tags:
        - Key: Name
          Value: PrivateSubnet1
```

This setup distinguishes public and private zones for better security and architectural clarity.

Configuring an Internet Gateway and Route Tables

Public subnets require internet access. An Internet Gateway and a route table are needed to route traffic to the outside world.

```
InternetGateway:
    Type: AWS::EC2::InternetGateway
    Properties:
      Tags:
        - Key: Name
          Value: MyInternetGateway
  AttachGateway:
    Type: AWS::EC2::VPCGatewayAttachment
    Properties:
      VpcId: !Ref MyVPC
      InternetGatewayId: !Ref InternetGateway
  PublicRouteTable:
    Type: AWS::EC2::RouteTable
    Properties:
      VpcId: !Ref MyVPC
  PublicRoute:
    Type: AWS::EC2::Route
    DependsOn: AttachGateway
    Properties:
      RouteTableId: !Ref PublicRouteTable
        DestinationCidrBlock: 0.0.0.0/0     //Security note: Only public
subnets should have 0.0.0.0/0 routes to an Internet Gateway.
      GatewayId: !Ref InternetGateway
  RouteTableAssociation:
    Type: AWS::EC2::SubnetRouteTableAssociation
    Properties:
      SubnetId: !Ref PublicSubnet1
      RouteTableId: !Ref PublicRouteTable
```

This block ensures that your public subnet has access to the internet through the specified gateway.

Validating and Deploying the Template

Before launching your template, always validate it using the AWS CLI or CloudFormation console:

```
aws cloudformation validate-template --template-body file://template.yaml
```

Once validated, you can deploy the template with:

```
aws cloudformation create-stack --stack-name MyNetworkStack --template-
body file://template.yaml --capabilities CAPABILITY_NAMED_IAM
```

`CAPABILITY_NAMED_IAM` is required whenever a CloudFormation template creates or updates IAM roles, policies, or instance profiles with explicit names.

Writing basic CloudFormation templates empowers you to automate the foundational layers of your AWS network. By leveraging the declarative power of Infrastructure as Code, you ensure your network resources are reproducible, scalable, and aligned with best practices from the start. As you grow your infrastructure, these templates will evolve into powerful building blocks for complex, multi-tiered architectures.

Automating VPC and Subnet Creation

As cloud environments grow in complexity, manually provisioning networking components like VPCs and subnets becomes error-prone and inefficient. Automation enables teams to eliminate configuration drift, ensure consistency across environments, and accelerate the deployment of repeatable infrastructure. In this section, we will take a deeper dive into how AWS CloudFormation can be used to automate the creation of a Virtual Private Cloud (VPC) and its associated subnets.

Understanding the Value of Automation in Network Design

Before jumping into template creation, it is important to understand *why* automating VPC and subnet provisioning is a game-changer:

- **Consistency**: Ensures that all environments—dev, test, and prod—are identically configured.
- **Speed**: Reduces deployment time from hours to minutes.
- **Auditability**: Provides a transparent, version-controlled record of all infrastructure changes.
- **Scalability**: Easily replicate VPC setups across multiple AWS accounts or regions.

CloudFormation allows this automation through declarative templates that define every element of the network stack.

Creating the VPC: The Core of Your Network

The VPC acts as the foundational container for all AWS networking. Automating its creation begins with defining essential properties:

```
Resources:
  VPC:
    Type: AWS::EC2::VPC
    Properties:
      CidrBlock: 10.20.0.0/16
      EnableDnsSupport: true
      EnableDnsHostnames: true
      Tags:
        - Key: Name
          Value: MyAutoVPC
```

Here, a 16-bit CIDR block is provisioned, supporting thousands of internal IPs—ideal for multi-subnet configurations.

Automating Subnet Creation: Public and Private Zones

Once the VPC is defined, the next step is to configure subnets that segment network traffic. A typical design uses public subnets for internet-facing resources and private subnets for internal applications or databases.

```
PublicSubnet:
   Type: AWS::EC2::Subnet
   Properties:
     VpcId: !Ref VPC
     CidrBlock: 10.20.1.0/24
     AvailabilityZone: !Select [0, !GetAZs '']
     MapPublicIpOnLaunch: true
     Tags:
       - Key: Name
         Value: PublicSubnet-AZ1
 PrivateSubnet:
   Type: AWS::EC2::Subnet
   Properties:
     VpcId: !Ref VPC
     CidrBlock: 10.20.2.0/24
     AvailabilityZone: !Select [1, !GetAZs '']
     Tags:
       - Key: Name
         Value: PrivateSubnet-AZ2
```

With automation, these subnets can be configured for different availability zones to enhance fault tolerance and workload distribution.

Optional: Scaling Subnets with Parameters or Mappings

Instead of hardcoding CIDR blocks, CloudFormation allows you to parameterize or map them—making the template reusable across environments and regions.

Example: Using Parameters for Scalable Subnet Creation

```
Parameters:
  PublicSubnetCidr:
    Type: String
    Default: 10.20.1.0/24
  PrivateSubnetCidr:
    Type: String
    Default: 10.20.2.0/24

Resources:
  PublicSubnet:
    Type: AWS::EC2::Subnet
    Properties:
      VpcId: !Ref VPC
      CidrBlock: !Ref PublicSubnetCidr
      AvailabilityZone: !Select [0, !GetAZs '']
      MapPublicIpOnLaunch: true
```

- The same template can be reused for dev, test, and prod.
- CIDR ranges can be adjusted without editing the template.
- Enables automated, repeatable subnet creation at scale.

Scalability hint: In larger architectures, parameters and mappings are often combined with Stack Sets to deploy identical subnet layouts across multiple accounts and regions.

Enhancing Automation with Template Parameters

Hardcoding CIDR blocks or availability zones are inflexible. Instead, parameters allow templates to be customized at deployment time:

```
Parameters:
  VpcCidr:
    Type: String
    Default: 10.30.0.0/16
  PublicSubnetCidr:
    Type: String
    Default: 10.30.1.0/24
```

These parameters are referenced in the Resources section, making the template reusable across multiple projects and regions.

Making parameters safer with validation:

CloudFormation parameters can include validation rules such as AllowedPattern, AllowedValues, and MinLength to prevent invalid inputs (for example, enforcing valid CIDR formats or restricting environment names).

Automating Subnet Route Table Association

This process can be extended to NAT gateways for private subnet outbound access. Each subnet must be associated with a route table to control outbound and inbound traffic. This step is also automatable:

```
PublicRouteTable:
  Type: AWS::EC2::RouteTable
  Properties:
    VpcId: !Ref VPC
SubnetRouteTableAssociation:
  Type: AWS::EC2::SubnetRouteTableAssociation
  Properties:
    SubnetId: !Ref PublicSubnet
    RouteTableId: !Ref PublicRouteTable
```

This code ensures that all public subnet traffic is properly routed, especially when paired with an Internet Gateway and route definition.

Deployment and Validation Best Practices

Before deploying, validate your template using:

```
aws cloudformation validate-template --template-body file://vpc-template.
yaml
```

Then launch the stack:

```
aws cloudformation create-stack --stack-name MyVPCStack --template-body
file://vpc-template.yaml --capabilities CAPABILITY_NAMED_IAM
```

Always test in a staging environment before promoting to production to ensure behavior aligns with expectations.

Automating the creation of VPCs and subnets with CloudFormation is a powerful way to modernize and standardize network provisioning. This approach not only reduces manual errors but also accelerates deployment times and ensures consistency across your AWS infrastructure. By treating networking as code, teams gain greater control, reliability, and scalability in their cloud environments.

Preview changes with Change Sets: Before updating an existing stack, use CloudFormation Change Sets to review exactly what resources will be added, modified, or removed. This allows teams to catch risky changes early and avoid unintentional outages—especially in production environments.

Managing Route Tables and Internet Gateways in Templates

A well-architected AWS network is not complete without proper routing and internet access configurations. In addition to provisioning subnets and VPCs, it's crucial to define how traffic moves in and out of the cloud environment.

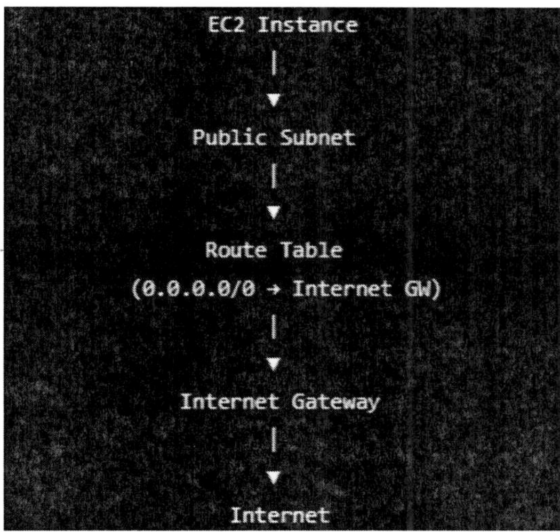

Figure 13.3: *Traffic Flow - Subnet to the Internet*

- Resources inside a public subnet send outbound traffic.
- The route table determines where traffic is forwarded.
- The 0.0.0.0/0 route sends internet-bound traffic to the Internet Gateway.
- The Internet Gateway provides connectivity between the VPC and the public internet.

A subnet becomes public only when it is associated with a route table that has a default route (0.0.0.0/0) pointing to an Internet Gateway.

This section explains how to automate the deployment of route tables and internet gateways using AWS CloudFormation, allowing you to efficiently manage connectivity while ensuring security and consistency across deployments.

Understanding the Role of Route Tables and Internet Gateways

Before diving into the automation process, it is important to understand the two core components involved:

- **Route Tables** define the rules for directing traffic from subnets to other destinations—either within the VPC or to external services like the internet.
- **Internet Gateways (IGWs)** provide a target for VPC traffic that needs to reach the internet and allow responses from the outside world.

For example, a web server in a public subnet uses the IGW to reach the internet, while a database in a private subnet relies only on internal routes.

Automating these components ensures your infrastructure is reproducible, reliable, and capable of supporting internet-bound workloads.

Creating the Internet Gateway with CloudFormation

The first step is to provision the Internet Gateway, which connects your VPC to the internet:

```
Resources:
  MyInternetGateway:
    Type: AWS::EC2::InternetGateway
    Properties:
      Tags:
        - Key: Name
          Value: MyAutoIGW
```

This creates the gateway resource, but it still needs to be attached to the VPC to be functional.

Attaching the Internet Gateway to the VPC

Once the gateway is defined, it must be explicitly attached to your VPC, as it allows for modular template design or separate lifecycle management:

```
AttachGateway:
  Type: AWS::EC2::VPCGatewayAttachment
  Properties:
    VpcId: !Ref VPC
    InternetGatewayId: !Ref MyInternetGateway
```

This association enables internet-bound traffic to pass through the gateway, allowing external communication for public-facing resources.

Defining a Public Route Table and Internet Route

To make the public subnet truly internet-accessible, you must configure a route table and direct all outbound traffic to the gateway:

```
PublicRouteTable:
  Type: AWS::EC2::RouteTable
  Properties:
    VpcId: !Ref VPC
    Tags:
      - Key: Name
        Value: PublicRouteTable

DefaultRoute:
  Type: AWS::EC2::Route
  Properties:
    RouteTableId: !Ref PublicRouteTable
    DestinationCidrBlock: 0.0.0.0/0
    GatewayId: !Ref MyInternetGateway
```

The route with destination 0.0.0.0/0 allows all internet traffic to be directed via the Internet Gateway, giving your subnet outbound internet access.

Security note: *Even with a 0.0.0.0/0 route to an Internet Gateway, only instances that have a public IP or Elastic IP—and are allowed by security group and NACL rules—are actually reachable from the internet.*

Associating the Route Table with a Public Subnet

To activate the route table for a specific subnet, associate the two using the following snippet:

```
PublicSubnetRouteTableAssociation:
  Type: AWS::EC2::SubnetRouteTableAssociation
  Properties:
    SubnetId: !Ref PublicSubnet
    RouteTableId: !Ref PublicRouteTable
```

This binds the routing behavior to the designated subnet, completing the chain for outbound internet traffic.

Parameterizing for Flexibility and Reusability

To make your templates more adaptable for various environments, introduce parameters:

```
Parameters:
  CidrBlock:
    Type: String
    Default: 10.50.0.0/16
  InternetAccess:
    Type: String
    Default: 0.0.0.0/0
```

These can be passed during stack creation, making the templates reusable across different teams or applications.

Best Practices for Managing Route Tables and IGWs

- Separate public and private routing to avoid accidental exposure.
- Use tags consistently to track resources and monitor cost usage.
- Include logical dependencies in templates to ensure resources are created in the right order.

```
PublicRoute:
  Type: AWS::EC2::Route
DependsOn: AttachGateway
  Properties:
    RouteTableId: !Ref PublicRouteTable
    DestinationCidrBlock: 0.0.0.0/0
    GatewayId: !Ref MyInternetGateway
```

This directive ensures routes are not created before the IGW is successfully attached.

Automating the creation and association of route tables and internet gateways using CloudFormation is a foundational step toward achieving scalable, secure, and maintainable AWS networks. It not only simplifies the provisioning process but also enforces consistency in how resources connect to the internet across different environments. As your cloud infrastructure grows, these templates become vital tools for managing complexity while maintaining agility.

Validating and Deploying the Template in AWS Environments

Before a CloudFormation template can bring your network infrastructure to life, it must be validated and deployed correctly. This step ensures your YAML or JSON definitions are error-free and your cloud resources are provisioned exactly as intended. Let us walk through the process of validating, launching, and managing CloudFormation stacks with confidence.

Validating Your CloudFormation Template: Catch Errors Early

Before deployment, validating the syntax and structure of your CloudFormation template is crucial to prevent runtime failures.

- **Using AWS Console for Validation**: The AWS Management Console offers a simple way to validate your template. Navigate to the CloudFormation service, choose "Create Stack," and upload your template. Any structural issues will be flagged during the review step.
- **Command Line Validation with AWS CLI**: For automated workflows, the AWS CloudFormation validate-template command allows for CLI-based syntax checking.

  Example: `aws cloudformation validate-template --template-body file://network-template.yaml`
- **IDE Plugins and Linters**: Extensions for IDEs like VS Code or JetBrains can provide inline linting and suggest corrections in real-time, enhancing the validation process.

Deploying the Template as a CloudFormation Stack

Once validated, the next step is to launch your infrastructure using a CloudFormation stack which is a single unit that deploys all your defined resources.

- **Stack Creation through the Console**

  Choose `Create Stack` in the AWS Console, upload the template, and provide a stack name along with any required parameters. Review the changes and launch the stack to begin provisioning.
- **Automated Deployment via AWS CLI**

  The CLI also supports automated deployments:

  ```
  aws cloudformation create-stack --stack-name my-network-stack --template-body file://network-template.yaml --capabilities CAPABILITY_NAMED_IAM
  ```
- **Monitoring Stack Events**

  As the stack provisions, you can monitor its progress in the CloudFormation dashboard or using the describe-stack-events command in the CLI.

Handling Deployment Errors and Rollbacks

Not all deployments go as planned. If CloudFormation encounters an issue, it may initiate a rollback.

- **Understanding Rollback Events**

  If a resource fails to create (specifically due to permission issues or conflicting settings), then, CloudFormation may reverse all created resources, preserving system integrity.

  Common causes you shall see in practice:

  - **IAM permission errors:** For example, the execution role lacks permission to create an Internet Gateway or modify route tables.

- **CIDR block conflicts:** A subnet CIDR overlaps with another subnet or falls outside the VPC CIDR range.

- **Troubleshooting Common Failures**

  Reviewing the Events tab in the console or running `aws cloudformation describe-stack-events --stack-name my-network-stack` helps identify which resource caused the failure and why.

- **Disabling Rollback for Debugging**

  During troubleshooting, you may want to disable automatic rollback to inspect partially created resources:

```
aws cloudformation create-stack \
  --stack-name MyNetworkStack \
  --template-body file://template.yaml \
  --disable-rollback
```

Best practice: Disable rollback only in non-production environments for debugging. Re-enable it for normal deployments to maintain safety.

Updating and Deleting Stacks

Once deployed, your stack can be updated or safely deleted based on lifecycle needs.

- **Making Safe Updates**

  Use update-stack in the CLI or update through the Console to modify parameters or add resources. Be mindful of replacement actions that may impact availability.

- **Stack Deletion for Cleanup**

  Clean up unused environments by deleting the stack:

```
aws cloudformation delete-stack --stack-name my-network-stack
```

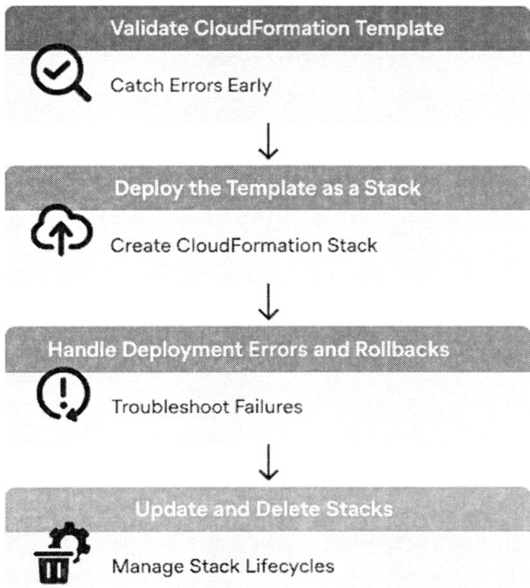

Figure 13.4: *Flowchart for Validating and Deploying AWS CloudFormation Templates*

This unique flowchart visually outlines the step-by-step process for validating and deploying AWS CloudFormation templates in a production or test environment. It begins with the creation of a YAML/JSON template and guides the user through key actions such as syntax validation, template upload via the AWS Management Console or CLI, change set review, and final deployment. The flow also includes error-handling steps and best practice checks, ensuring that infrastructure is safely and efficiently provisioned using Infrastructure as Code (IaC).

Validating and deploying CloudFormation templates is a critical part of automated infrastructure management. By leveraging built-in tools, command-line interfaces, and real-time monitoring, you can ensure your AWS networking environment is provisioned accurately and reliably. The next section will focus on securing these automated deployments by configuring security groups programmatically.

Automating Security Groups

In any cloud-based network architecture, security is a fundamental pillar—and in AWS, Security Groups serve as the virtual firewalls that control inbound and outbound traffic to your resources. Manually configuring these security rules can be error-prone, time-consuming, and inconsistent across environments. This is where automation through Infrastructure as Code (IaC) becomes essential.

This section aims to explore how to automate the creation and management of AWS Security Groups using CloudFormation, ensuring consistent, scalable, and secure access to your resources. From defining rule sets for EC2 instances and load balancers to integrating with VPC configurations, readers will gain a clear understanding of how to codify network access policies. By the end of this section, you'll not only be able to enforce least-privilege principles effectively but also improve deployment speed and auditability across multiple environments.

Now, we will break down the key concepts, walk through examples, and provide best practices for securing network boundaries with automation, reducing the risk of misconfigurations and enhancing operational efficiency.

Defining Security Groups with CloudFormation

Manually configuring security rules for every new instance or environment can be both inefficient and risky. Using AWS CloudFormation to define security groups allows you to maintain standardized, version-controlled, and repeatable access control policies across your entire infrastructure. This sub-section dives into how to define and deploy security groups as part of your infrastructure-as-code strategy.

! *Open SSH access (0.0.0.0/0) - Note that it is acceptable for testing but insecure for production.*

Understanding the Role of Security Groups in AWS

Before jumping into automation, it is important to understand what Security Groups (SGs) are and why they matter. In AWS, a security group acts as a virtual firewall for EC2 instances and other resources, controlling both inbound and outbound traffic based on specified rules. These rules determine which IP addresses, ports, and protocols are permitted or denied access.

Security groups are stateful, meaning that if you allow an incoming request from a source, the response is automatically allowed, regardless of outbound rules. This simplifies configurations but also underscores the importance of clearly defined rules to prevent unauthorized access.

Declaring Security Groups in a CloudFormation Template

The first step in automating your security policies is to declare security groups directly within your CloudFormation templates. Using the AWS::EC2::SecurityGroup resource, you can specify group names, descriptions, VPC IDs, and a list of ingress and egress rules.

Here is a simple example snippet:

```
Resources:
  WebServerSecurityGroup:
```

```
        Type: AWS::EC2::SecurityGroup
        Properties:
          GroupDescription: Allow HTTP and SSH access
          VpcId: !Ref VPC
          SecurityGroupIngress:
            - IpProtocol: tcp
              FromPort: 22
              ToPort: 22
              CidrIp: 0.0.0.0/0
            - IpProtocol: tcp
              FromPort: 80
              ToPort: 80
              CidrIp: 0.0.0.0/0
          Tags:
            - Key: Name
              Value: WebSG
```

This YAML code creates a security group that allows SSH (port 22) and HTTP (port 80) access from any IP address, with tagging for easy identification.

Creating Reusable and Modular Security Group Templates

As your infrastructure scales, managing multiple security groups manually becomes difficult. One of the strengths of CloudFormation is the ability to create modular and reusable templates. You can define parameters to dynamically pass CIDR blocks, port ranges, or protocol types based on the environment (dev, test, prod), making your templates environment-agnostic and easier to maintain.

Example parameterized setup:

```
Parameters:
  SSHLocation:
    Type: String
    Default: 0.0.0.0/0
    Description: IP address range that can SSH to the EC2 instance
```

Linking Security Groups to Resources Programmatically

Once defined, these security groups can be attached to EC2 instances, load balancers, RDS databases, and more—directly from within the same CloudFormation template. This ensures a tightly integrated infrastructure setup where no resource is exposed without predefined rules.

Example EC2 attachment:

```
Resources:
  EC2Instance:
    Type: AWS::EC2::Instance
    Properties:
      SecurityGroupIds:
        - !Ref WebServerSecurityGroup
```

Benefits of Automating Security Groups with CloudFormation

By automating security group creation:

- You ensure consistent policies across environments.

- You reduce human error in complex rule setups.
- You enable faster deployments and updates during scaling.
- You maintain auditable change history through template versioning.

For example: Auto-provisioning web server SGs via pipeline ensures every deployment adheres to compliance standards.

In the next section, we will be diving deeper into managing security group rules dynamically, including rule updates and conditional logic based on environment types. Automating access controls not only strengthens security posture but also streamlines infrastructure deployment pipelines.

Automating Rules for Ingress and Egress Traffic

In cloud environments, controlling how data enters and exits your resources is vital to maintaining a secure network. Ingress and egress rules define the traffic allowed into and out of your AWS infrastructure.

For example: Automating SGs for web apps across multiple environments.

By automating these rules with AWS CloudFormation, you can enforce security standards consistently across deployments, eliminate manual configuration errors, and scale securely.

Clarifying the Difference: Ingress vs. Egress

Before automating traffic rules, it is crucial to distinguish between ingress and egress:

- **Ingress traffic** refers to incoming data, such as HTTP requests to a web server or SSH connections from administrators.
- **Egress traffic** pertains to outgoing data, like application responses to users or API calls made from inside your VPC.

Both directions need carefully designed rules to avoid leaving systems vulnerable to attacks or unauthorized data leaks.

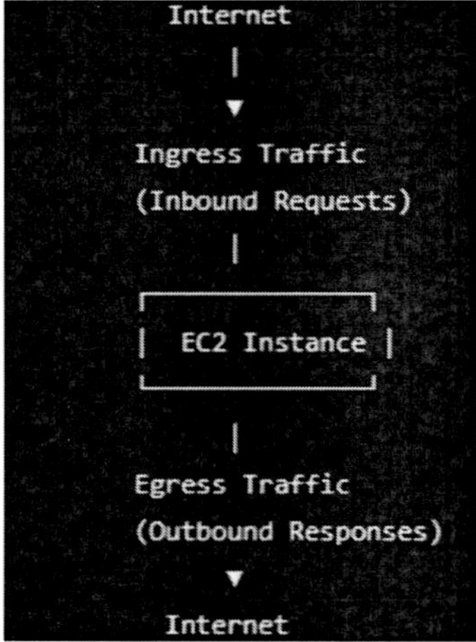

Figure 13.5: *Traffic Direction (Visual Contrast)*

New security groups deny all inbound (ingress) traffic by default but allow all outbound (egress) traffic.

This means inbound access must be explicitly permitted, while outbound traffic should be restricted as needed for security.

Ingress controls who can reach your resources; egress controls where your resources can send data. Both are essential for a secure AWS network design.

Defining Ingress Rules in CloudFormation Templates

Ingress rules control what types of inbound traffic are permitted. These rules are defined using the SecurityGroupIngress property within a CloudFormation template. You can specify allowed IP ranges (CidrIp), specific ports (including 80 for HTTP or 443 for HTTPS), and even the protocols (similar to TCP, UDP, and ICMP).

Example snippet for inbound rules:

```
SecurityGroupIngress:
  - IpProtocol: tcp
    FromPort: 443
    ToPort: 443
    CidrIp: 0.0.0.0/0
  - IpProtocol: tcp
    FromPort: 22
    ToPort: 22
    CidrIp: !Ref SSHLocation
```

This setup ensures that HTTPS is always accessible, while SSH access is configurable during stack deployment via a parameter.

Automating Egress Rules to Control Outbound Traffic

Outbound traffic is often overlooked, but egress rules are equally important for restricting access to external systems. CloudFormation supports automated egress configuration using the SecurityGroupEgress block.

Here is a sample configuration:

SecurityGroupEgress:

```
- IpProtocol: -1  //it means all protocol
  CidrIp: 0.0.0.0/0
```

This rule allows all outbound traffic by default, but you can fine-tune it to restrict certain protocols or destinations. For example, you might want to block access to the public internet in certain environments like staging.

Using Parameters and Mappings for Dynamic Rule Management

To make your templates reusable across different environments (particularly dev, QA, and production), leverage CloudFormation parameters and mappings. This allows you to dynamically adjust traffic permissions depending on region, security level, or application requirements.

Example of a parameterized rule:

```
Parameters:
  WebPort:
    Type: Number
    Default: 80
    Description: Web server port

SecurityGroupIngress:
  - IpProtocol: tcp
    FromPort: !Ref WebPort
```

```
        ToPort: !Ref WebPort
        CidrIp: 0.0.0.0/0
```

This ensures flexibility while avoiding hardcoded values.

Implementing Conditionals for Environment-Specific Access

You can enhance automation by using Conditions in CloudFormation. These enable or disable certain rules depending on variables like deployment stage or compliance requirements.

Condition only evaluates at stack creation/update time, not dynamically afterward.

Example:

```
Conditions:
  IsProd: !Equals [ !Ref Environment, "prod" ]

Resources:
  ProdSSHAccess:
    Type: AWS::EC2::SecurityGroupIngress
    Condition: IsProd
    Properties:
      GroupId: !Ref MySecurityGroup
      IpProtocol: tcp
      FromPort: 22
      ToPort: 22
      CidrIp: 10.0.0.0/16
```

This ensures that only production environments receive strict access controls, while dev/test environments can remain flexible.

Benefits of Automating Traffic Rules

Automating ingress and egress rules offers multiple advantages:

- **Scalability:** Easily apply consistent rules across hundreds of resources.
- **Security:** Avoid ad-hoc permissions that may expose your environment.
- **Auditability:** Clearly documented access policies embedded in code.
- **Version Control:** Easily roll back rule changes or compare configurations over time.

In the next section, we will explore how to continuously manage and update these security rules as part of a larger infrastructure versioning strategy. With automation in place, you ensure that access to your AWS resources is predictable, maintainable, and compliant.

Implementing Least Privilege Network Access

In a cloud-native world where infrastructure is both dynamic and expansive, over-permissive access can quickly turn into a major security liability. Applying the principle of *least privilege* ensures that each resource, user, and service has only the minimum necessary access—no more, no less. In this section, we explore how to enforce least privilege at the network level using AWS security constructs and automation via CloudFormation.

Understanding the Principle of Least Privilege in Networking

The concept of least privilege originates from security architecture but applies seamlessly to network access. It means granting only the exact ports, IP addresses, and protocols that a system or user needs to function. Anything outside that scope is blocked by default.

The "deny all" is the implicit baseline and permissions must be explicitly granted.

In AWS networking, this means:

- Only opening required ports (for instance 443 for HTTPS).
- Limiting access to specific IP ranges (such as company VPNs).
- Avoiding wildcards like 0.0.0.0/0 unless absolutely necessary.

Designing Security Groups with Minimal Permissions

When creating Security Groups in AWS, one should avoid using broad rules. Instead, one can tailor ingress and egress to the specific resource.

22 for SSH should generally be restricted or moved behind a bastion or SSM Session Manager.

Example of overly permissive ingress:

```
CidrIp: 0.0.0.0/0
FromPort: 22
ToPort: 22
This allows global SSH access—a major risk.
Least privilege approach:
CidrIp: 203.0.113.10/32
FromPort: 22
ToPort: 22
This restricts SSH access to a specific admin IP only.
```

Use CloudFormation templates to codify these tight permissions and apply them consistently across environments.

Segmenting Network Access Using Subnet-Level Restrictions

Beyond Security Groups, AWS allows network segmentation via public and private subnets. Placing sensitive resources in private subnets and restricting their outbound access through NAT Gateways or VPC endpoints minimizes exposure.

CloudFormation can define these subnet types along with appropriate route tables and ACLs, ensuring automated enforcement of segmentation policies.

You can reinforce this concept with a small, focused CloudFormation example that shows how a private subnet stays isolated while still allowing outbound access via a NAT Gateway.

Example: Private Subnet with NAT Gateway Routing

```
PrivateSubnet:
  Type: AWS::EC2::Subnet
  Properties:
    VpcId: !Ref VPC
    CidrBlock: 10.40.2.0/24
    AvailabilityZone: !Select [1, !GetAZs '']
    Tags:
      - Key: Name
        Value: PrivateSubnet-AZ2

PrivateRouteTable:
  Type: AWS::EC2::RouteTable
  Properties:
```

```
      VpcId: !Ref VPC

  PrivateRoute:
    Type: AWS::EC2::Route
    Properties:
      RouteTableId: !Ref PrivateRouteTable
      DestinationCidrBlock: 0.0.0.0/0
      NatGatewayId: !Ref NatGateway

  PrivateSubnetRouteAssociation:
    Type: AWS::EC2::SubnetRouteTableAssociation
    Properties:
      SubnetId: !Ref PrivateSubnet
      RouteTableId: !Ref PrivateRouteTable
```

This achieves:

- Instances in the private subnet have no direct internet exposure.
- Outbound traffic is routed through a NAT Gateway.
- Inbound internet traffic is blocked by design.

Private subnets combined with NAT Gateways or VPC endpoints enforce strong network segmentation while still allowing required outbound connectivity.

Tag-Based Policies for Role-Based Access Control

Tagging resources with metadata (like Environment=Production or Role=Database) allows for better organization and policy enforcement.

By combining resource tags with AWS Identity and Access Management (IAM) policies or config rules, you can ensure:

- Only certain teams can modify production networking rules.
- Automated scanners alert or block overly broad configurations.

This enforces least privilege access through both automation and governance.

AWS Resource Access Manager (RAM) and Service Control Policies (SCPs) also support tag-based controls. Also, tagging helps integrate with AWS Config Rules or Security Hub insights for compliance tracking.

Using Conditions in Templates to Control Access Dynamically

CloudFormation supports **Conditions**, which allow you to add logic to templates. For example, you can define access rules only if the stack is deployed in production.

Conditions:

```
IsProduction: !Equals [ !Ref EnvType, "prod" ]
```

This ensures that resources deployed in lower environments do not accidentally receive production-level access rules.

If a condition evaluates to false, CloudFormation simply skips creating or modifying any resources associated with that condition. The stack deployment continues without error, but the conditional resources are not included.

Auditing and Continuous Validation of Network Rules

Automated tools like AWS Config, AWS Security Hub, and third-party scanners can monitor deployed security rules and flag any that violate least privilege principles. CloudFormation can also include AWS Config rule creation, helping to automate compliance enforcement.

Regular validation helps ensure that:

- No accidental changes introduce overly permissive rules.
- Access policies remain aligned with business and compliance needs.

AWS Config rule types:

AWS Config supports both managed rules (prebuilt by AWS for common compliance checks) and custom rules (defined using Lambda for organization-specific policies).

CloudFormation can create and manage AWS Config rules using the resource type AWS::Config::ConfigRule, allowing compliance checks to be defined, versioned, and deployed as code alongside your network infrastructure.

Note: *Continuous validation should be automated via CI/CD for ongoing drift detection.*

Benefits of Least Privilege Network Access

Implementing least privilege network policies offers several critical advantages:

- **Improved Security:** Reduces the attack surface dramatically.
- **Compliance Readiness:** Supports frameworks like PCI-DSS, HIPAA, and ISO 27001.
- **Operational Confidence:** Developers and teams operate safely within well-defined boundaries.
- **Scalability with Control:** Policies grow with infrastructure without compromising security.

In the next section, we will shift our focus to best practices for managing and versioning CloudFormation templates — ensuring that as your network grows, your security posture remains tight and controlled.

Versioning and Template Management

As organizations increasingly rely on Infrastructure as Code (IaC) to automate and manage cloud environments, the ability to version, organize, and maintain CloudFormation templates becomes critical. Just like software code, infrastructure templates need structured management to ensure consistency, traceability, and controlled changes across development, staging, and production environments.

In this section, we explore how to apply version control practices to CloudFormation templates, manage template lifecycles effectively, and use stack policies and change sets to protect production environments from unintentional updates. We will also cover how to integrate template management with modern DevOps workflows, which will ensure infrastructure deployments remain agile, secure, and reproducible.

By mastering versioning and management of CloudFormation stacks, teams can confidently scale their AWS infrastructure while maintaining governance, reducing risk, and supporting continuous delivery pipelines.

Using Git and Code Repositories for Template Versioning

In modern cloud-native development, managing infrastructure templates like application code is essential for consistency, collaboration, and traceability. CloudFormation templates are not static documents—they evolve with your architecture. Introducing version control through Git repositories allows teams to manage changes, collaborate efficiently, and roll back configurations safely if needed. This section explores how Git and repositories like GitHub, GitLab, or AWS CodeCommit can be used to effectively version and organize CloudFormation templates across environments.

As a best practice, keep sensitive parameters (like passwords) in Secrets Manager or SSM Parameter Store instead of templates.

Version Control as a Foundation for IaC

Version Control Systems (VCS) are the backbone of Infrastructure as Code. Just as developers track code changes, infrastructure teams can use Git to maintain a clear record of changes in templates, who made them, and why. This practice promotes accountability and enables collaboration through pull requests, code reviews, and branching strategies.

Setting up Git Repositories for CloudFormation

To begin versioning CloudFormation templates, create a Git repository structured around your AWS environment. Organize templates based on services, projects, or environments (some of which includes `dev/`, `prod/`, `networking/`, and `security/`). A clean directory structure makes it easier to locate, modify, and deploy templates using automation tools.

Example Structure:

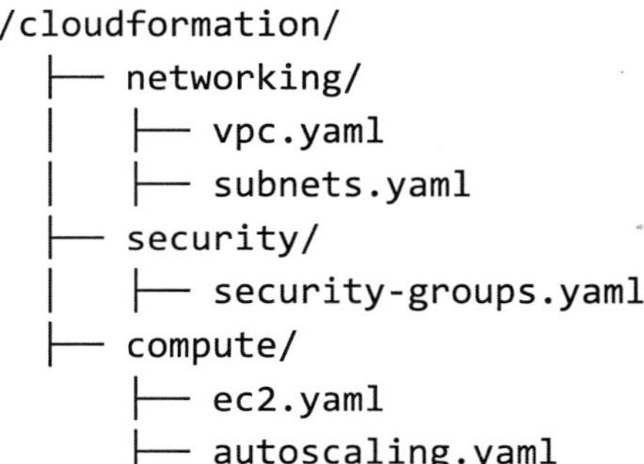

```
/cloudformation/
  ├── networking/
  │   ├── vpc.yaml
  │   ├── subnets.yaml
  ├── security/
  │   ├── security-groups.yaml
  ├── compute/
      ├── ec2.yaml
      ├── autoscaling.yaml
```

Tracking Template Changes with Git Commits

Every modification to a CloudFormation template should be accompanied by a meaningful Git commit. Commit messages should follow a convention such as:

- Feat: Add new subnet configuration.
- Fix: Correct security group ingress rules.
- Refactor: Simplify VPC template structure.

This ensures clarity and auditability of infrastructure changes over time.

Branching Strategies for Infrastructure

Apply branching strategies commonly used in application development:

- **Feature Branches** for new infrastructure capabilities.
- **Development and Production Branches** for staging changes before going live.
- **Hotfix Branches** for immediate production fixes.

Merging changes only after code review helps prevent configuration drift and unintentional errors.

Using Tags and Releases

Tagging specific commits in Git (such as v1.0, networking-v2) allows teams to mark tested and stable versions of templates. This is particularly useful for rollback scenarios or when coordinating deployments across teams.

Tags help CI/CD pipelines deploy specific tested versions, ensuring reproducibility.

Integration with CI/CD for Template Deployment

Pairing version-controlled templates with CI/CD pipelines (particularly GitHub Actions, GitLab CI, or AWS CodePipeline) ensures automated validation, testing, and deployment. This closes the loop from development to deployment, enabling consistent, repeatable infrastructure provisioning.

By treating CloudFormation templates like application code and storing them in version-controlled repositories, organizations gain full visibility into infrastructure changes. This approach enables collaboration, supports rollback, and integrates seamlessly with automation workflows—empowering teams to build robust, scalable, and well-governed AWS environments.

Stack Updates and Change Set Management

As cloud environments evolve, so too must the infrastructure configurations that support them. In AWS, CloudFormation Stacks serve as the foundation for deploying and managing resources. However, updating these stacks requires caution to prevent unintended changes or downtime. This is where Change Sets become invaluable—they offer a safe, reviewable preview of modifications before they are applied. In this section, we shall explore how to manage CloudFormation stack updates effectively using Change Sets, ensuring controlled and predictable infrastructure changes.

Note: *Change Sets are non-destructive until executed. Some updates (like* VPC CIDR) *are irreversible without replacement.*

Understanding Stack Lifecycle in AWS CloudFormation

Every CloudFormation stack represents a deployed instance of infrastructure defined by a template. When you need to modify the infrastructure — whether adding a subnet, updating an EC2 instance type, or changing a security group — you update the stack with a revised template. These updates must be managed carefully to preserve system stability and meet compliance standards.

Change Sets in CloudFormation

A Change Set is essentially a dry run of your stack update. Instead of applying changes immediately, it provides a summary of proposed modifications, allowing you to:

- Review which resources will be added, modified, or deleted.
- Catch unintended deletions or updates before they happen.
- Ensure that no destructive changes are introduced without approval.

This safety net is especially crucial in production environments where even a small misconfiguration can lead to costly outages.

Creating and Executing Change Sets

To use Change Sets effectively:

1. Submit a new or modified template.
2. Create a Change Set for the target stack using AWS Console, CLI, or SDK.

3. Review the Change Set summary, which outlines the impact of the update.
4. Execute the Change Set only after confirming that the proposed changes align with your expectations.

Example CLI Command:

```
aws cloudformation create-change-set \
  --stack-name my-app-stack \
  --template-body file://updated-template.yaml \
  --change-set-name my-change-set
```

Detecting Unintended Resource Replacements

Some changes in a CloudFormation template can trigger resource replacement rather than in-place updates. For example, changing the CIDR block of a VPC requires creating a new one and deleting the old. Change Sets help detect such situations in advance, so you can assess the impact and plan mitigation strategies like data backup or phased deployments.

Using Nested Stacks for Isolated Updates

Nested stacks—CloudFormation stacks within stacks—are a modular way to manage infrastructure. When updates are confined to a specific component, such as a database or networking configuration, nested stacks allow targeted updates without impacting the broader environment. Change Sets can also be created and reviewed at the nested stack level for even finer control.

Best Practices for Managing Stack Updates

- Test changes in a staging environment before applying them to production.
- Always use Change Sets in critical environments to preview and validate updates.
- Track Change Set executions for auditing and rollback planning.
- Automate Change Set generation in CI/CD pipelines for continuous delivery with safety checks.

Stack updates are an inevitable part of managing AWS infrastructure, but they do not have to be risky. By leveraging Change Sets, you gain visibility and control over every change applied to your environment. This methodical approach reduces errors, minimizes downtime, and aligns infrastructure updates with the change management policies of your organization.

Testing, Validating, and Auditing Templates

Before deploying infrastructure using AWS CloudFormation, ensuring the integrity, reliability, and security of your templates is critical. Just as software undergoes testing and code reviews, infrastructure as code (IaC) templates should also be rigorously validated. In this section, we explore the importance of validating CloudFormation templates before deployment, how to test them for logical correctness, and ways to audit changes for governance and compliance purposes.

Note: *Validation should be part of CI/CD rather than manual. Linting tools can be run locally via pre-commit for faster feedback.*

Template Validation in IaC Workflows

Validating CloudFormation templates is not just about syntax—it is about protecting your infrastructure from unexpected errors. Even a minor misconfiguration in a VPC, route table, or security group can cause major outages. Validation acts as the first gatekeeper, ensuring the template is structurally sound and semantically correct before it is applied in an AWS environment.

Using CloudFormation Validate-Template for Syntax Checking

AWS provides a built-in validation command that checks the format of the template and JSON/YAML syntax. While it does not catch logical errors (such as unreachable subnets), it however, helps in identifying missing properties, unsupported parameters, and basic formatting issues.

Example CLI command:

```
aws cloudformation validate-template --template-body file://network-setup.yaml
```

This step should be incorporated into any IaC deployment pipeline as a non-negotiable prerequisite.

Dry Run Deployments with Change Sets

To go beyond syntax, simulate deployments using Change Sets (as discussed in the previous section). This provides a preview of actions the stack will take—create, update, delete—before actually modifying any resources.

Use Change Sets to:

- Test template updates in staging environments.
- Ensure no unexpected deletions or replacements occur.
- Validate dependencies between resources.

Reviewing IAM policy impacts before applying Change Sets.

Unit Testing Infrastructure with Tools like TaskCat and CFN-Lint

For deeper testing, tools such as TaskCat and CFN-Lint are invaluable:

- **TaskCat** allows you to test CloudFormation templates by deploying them in multiple regions simultaneously, verifying deployment success and output.
- **CFN-Lint** (CloudFormation Linter) checks for AWS-specific best practices, catching issues like unsupported values, resource misconfigurations, or typos in logical IDs.

These tools should be integrated into your CI/CD workflow for consistent template health checks.

As a best practice: run these tools per pull request before merging.

Auditing Template Changes with Version Control Systems

Every change to a CloudFormation template should be tracked, reviewed, and approved. Using Git or similar version control systems:

- Maintains a historical log of infrastructure changes.
- Enables code review workflows for templates.
- Helps pinpoint when a faulty configuration was introduced.

Audit trails become particularly important in regulated environments where compliance and traceability are essential.

Leveraging AWS Config and CloudTrail for Post-Deployment Audits

Even after deployment, auditing does not stop. AWS offers services like:

- **AWS Config** to track configuration changes to infrastructure and ensure compliance with desired state definitions.

- **AWS CloudTrail** to log API calls, including CloudFormation stack updates and deletions.

These tools help you verify that the deployed resources match the intended design and detect any drift or unauthorized changes.

Best Practices for Testing and Auditing CloudFormation Templates

- Validate before every deployment to prevent avoidable issues.
- Test templates in isolated environments before pushing to production.
- Use automated linting and testing tools in your pipeline.
- Implement peer reviews for every template change.
- Maintain logs and history of template versions and stack changes.
- Scan embedded IAM policies for least privilege** to catch overly permissive permissions before deployment.

Testing, validating, and auditing CloudFormation templates are foundational practices in any robust infrastructure automation strategy. They ensure that your cloud infrastructure is reliable, secure, and compliant—before, during, and after deployment. By integrating these steps into your workflow, you not only reduce risk but also enable faster and more confident deployments across your AWS environments.

Case Studies

As organizations embrace cloud-native architectures, the ability to automate network deployments becomes a cornerstone of scalable, secure, and reliable infrastructure. While theoretical knowledge of tools like AWS CloudFormation and Infrastructure as Code (IaC) is essential, it is the practical application that truly validates their value.

In this section, we explore real-world case studies that demonstrate how companies across various industries have implemented automated network provisioning, security configurations, and template versioning. These examples illustrate both the challenges and transformative outcomes experienced when shifting from manual processes to automated, codified network infrastructure.

From improving compliance in highly regulated sectors to accelerating customer onboarding in fast-growing startups, these case studies provide insight into the strategic benefits and technical nuances of automating AWS network setups. Each scenario highlights best practices, measurable results, and key lessons that can inspire and inform your own infrastructure automation journey.

CloudFormation Overview (Infrastructure as Code at FinNova Bank)

FinNova Bank, a mid-sized digital banking company, needed to scale its cloud infrastructure quickly while maintaining strict compliance and security standards. Their DevOps team was managing AWS resources manually through the console, which often led to inconsistencies and undocumented changes.

Solution:

The team transitioned to Infrastructure as Code (IaC) using AWS CloudFormation. They began by codifying their VPC structure, subnet allocations, NAT gateways, and routing logic into YAML templates. Every network resource was now version-controlled and documented.

Outcome:

- Reduced provisioning time by 70%.
- Eliminated misconfiguration errors during deployments.
- Enabled traceable and repeatable infrastructure changes.

Automating VPC and Subnet Creation (EduWave Platform)

EduWave, an online learning startup, needed to launch learning environments for new customers in isolated VPCs. Manually creating VPCs and subnets for each new client was slowing down onboarding.

Solution:

EduWave created reusable CloudFormation templates to automate the provisioning of custom VPCs, subnets (public/private), NAT gateways, and route tables. Each time a new client signed up, the system automatically deployed an isolated environment using those templates.

Outcome:

- Client onboarding time dropped from 5 days to under 4 hours.
- VPC configurations became consistent and scalable.
- Engineers could focus on app improvements instead of manual setups.

Automating Security Groups (HealthOne Telemedicine App)

HealthOne, a telemedicine application provider, faced security breaches due to overly permissive manual security group rules created by different teams.

Solution:

They enforced strict network access rules using CloudFormation-defined security groups. All templates followed the least privilege principle, only opening specific ports to known IP ranges. Changes were peer-reviewed through Git pull requests.

Outcome:

- 90% reduction in exposed ports across environments.
- Improved auditability and rollback capabilities for security rules
- Achieved HIPAA compliance more easily during security audits.

Versioning and Template Management (LogiTrack Logistics)

The DevOps team of LogiTrack was struggling to manage multiple versions of CloudFormation templates across environments (dev, test, production). Often, templates would behave differently due to undocumented tweaks.

Solution:

They adopted a Git-based workflow using feature branches, peer reviews, and tagged versions for each template. They also started using CloudFormation change sets to preview impacts before updates, and integrated TaskCat to test templates in CI pipelines.

Outcome:

- Gained full control and traceability over infrastructure changes.
- Eliminated deployment-related outages during template updates.
- Reduced downtime by safely rolling back to previous template versions when needed.

Conclusion

As organizations scale their cloud infrastructure, the need for consistency, speed, and control becomes critical. Manual network configurations are not only time-consuming but also error-prone. This chapter introduced the transformative power of Infrastructure as Code (IaC), especially through AWS CloudFormation, to automate and standardize the deployment of complex network architectures.

From setting up VPCs, subnets, route tables, and internet gateways, to managing security groups and controlling access with least privilege principles—every step of the network design can now be codified, versioned, and deployed repeatedly with confidence. By leveraging Git-based version control, change sets, and automated testing tools like CFN-Lint and TaskCat, organizations can enforce governance while maintaining agility.

Security and operational resilience are also embedded into this automation process. With proper template auditing, validation, and update practices, teams reduce the likelihood of misconfiguration and ensure that changes are predictable, reviewed, and traceable.

Ultimately, automating network deployments with CloudFormation does not just improve efficiency—it lays the foundation for a secure, scalable, and modern cloud infrastructure.

In the next chapter, we shall focus on diagnosing and fixing advanced networking issues within AWS using AWS CLI, VPC Flow Logs, and CloudWatch Logs. Also, it explains common pitfalls like misconfigured route tables, improper security group settings, and connectivity issues between VPCs. Let us also discuss practical troubleshooting scenarios that will guide the reader through diagnosing and resolving complex network problems.

Points to Remember

- Infrastructure as Code (IaC) enables the repeatable, automated deployment of AWS network components, reducing manual errors and configuration drift.
- AWS CloudFormation allows you to define and provision resources like VPCs, subnets, security groups, and route tables using declarative templates in JSON or YAML.
- Security groups can be fully managed through templates, allowing fine-grained control over inbound and outbound traffic using an automated, least-privilege approach.
- Version control and template management with tools like Git ensure every change is auditable, traceable, and reversible.
- Change sets provide a safe mechanism to preview updates before applying them to production environments.
- Validation and testing tools (specifically CloudFormation validate-template, CFN-Lint, and TaskCat) help catch errors early and improve template quality.
- Auditing mechanisms like AWS Config and CloudTrail help track post-deployment changes and maintain governance.

Automation is not just efficiency - it is the foundation of secure, scalable cloud operations.

Chapter 14
Advanced Troubleshooting Techniques

Introduction

In the dynamic landscape of cloud networking, even well-architected infrastructures can encounter performance bottlenecks, connectivity disruptions, or configuration errors. For example, consider a scenario where an application hosted in one VPC suddenly experiences high latency while communicating with a database in another VPC. Upon investigation, the issue could stem from misconfigured route tables or restrictive security group rules silently blocking optimal traffic paths. Such real-world challenges highlight the importance of effective troubleshooting skills in cloud environments.

As businesses increasingly rely on platforms like AWS, the ability to swiftly identify, diagnose, and resolve networking issues becomes a mission-critical capability. This chapter is dedicated to equipping readers with practical, in-depth troubleshooting techniques tailored for advanced AWS networking environments. Moving beyond basic diagnostics, we will explore the powerful capabilities of tools like the AWS Command Line Interface (CLI), VPC Flow Logs, and Amazon CloudWatch Logs to uncover the root causes of complex network challenges.

Readers will learn how to systematically analyze logs, interpret flow data, validate security group and ACL configurations, and resolve issues such as blocked traffic, route misalignments, and cross-VPC communication breakdowns. The chapter also addresses network latency and throughput issues, providing methods to detect, monitor, and optimize traffic patterns for improved performance.

Whether you are an operations engineer, cloud architect, or security analyst, mastering these techniques will enable you to maintain resilient, high-performing AWS networks under any circumstances.

Structure

In this chapter, we will walk through:

- AWS CLI For Networking
- VPC Flow Logs and CloudWatch Logs
- Connectivity Troubleshooting
- Latency and Performance Issues
- Case Studies

AWS CLI for Networking

In modern cloud operations, real-time visibility and control are vital for managing complex networking environments. While the AWS Management Console offers a graphical interface for most configurations, it can be limiting when troubleshooting requires speed, repeatability, or automation. This is where the AWS Command Line Interface (CLI) emerges as a powerful ally.

The AWS CLI enables administrators and engineers to interact with AWS services through a terminal or scripting environment. For networking, this means the ability to query VPC components, inspect route tables, validate subnet associations, and evaluate security group settings—all without leaving the command line. It empowers users to perform swift diagnostics, deploy scripted investigations, and even integrate with monitoring systems or automation workflows.

This section explores how the AWS CLI can be used effectively to troubleshoot network-related issues, validate infrastructure configurations, and streamline diagnostic efforts in real-time. By mastering the CLI, cloud professionals gain not just a tool, but a strategic advantage in maintaining resilient and secure AWS networks.

Common AWS CLI Networking Commands

Before diving into deeper diagnostics, it is crucial to be familiarized with the most commonly used AWS CLI commands for networking. These foundational commands serve as the first line of defense when investigating connectivity or configuration issues across your AWS environment.

Understanding the Role of CLI in Network Management

While AWS Management Console offers a visual interface for managing resources, the CLI provides precise control, faster troubleshooting, and scriptable automation. Whether you're checking VPC associations, route table entries, or the status of security groups, CLI commands give you low-level access to exactly what is happening behind the scenes.

Listing All VPCs in Your Account

To begin, the following command helps you view all VPCs configured in a specific AWS region:

```
aws ec2 describe-vpcs --region us-east-1
```

You can use **`--query`** and **`--output`** to refine the results:

```
aws ec2 describe-vpcs --query 'Vpcs[*].{ID:VpcId, CIDR:CidrBlock}' --output table
```

This displays a neatly formatted table of VPC IDs and their CIDR blocks.

Checking Subnets and Availability Zones

To investigate subnet allocations and their corresponding AZs, use:

```
aws ec2 describe-subnets --region us-east-1
```

Refine output:

```
aws ec2 describe-subnets --query 'Subnets[*].{ID:SubnetId, VPC:VpcId,
AZ:AvailabilityZone, CIDR:CidrBlock}' --output table
```

This is particularly helpful when mapping resources across zones for high availability.

Inspecting Route Tables

Routing issues can silently break communication between components. Use this command to review the routing rules:

```
aws ec2 describe-route-tables --region us-east-1
```

To narrow it down to a specific route table:

```
aws ec2 describe-route-tables --route-table-ids rtb-xxxxxxxx --output json
Sample output:
{
  "RouteTables": [
    {
      "RouteTableId": "rtb-0abcd1234efgh5678",
      "VpcId": "vpc-0abcd1234efgh5678",
      "Routes": [
        {
          "DestinationCidrBlock": "10.0.0.0/16",
          "GatewayId": "local",
          "State": "active"
        },
        {
          "DestinationCidrBlock": "0.0.0.0/0",
          "GatewayId": "igw-0abcd1234efgh5678",
          "State": "active"
        },
        {
          "DestinationCidrBlock": "10.1.0.0/16",
          "VpcPeeringConnectionId": "pcx-0abcd1234efgh5678",
          "State": "blackhole"
        }
      ]
    }
  ]
}
```

You will see destination CIDRs, next hops (like Internet Gateways, NAT Gateways), and their status.

Viewing Security Groups and Their Rules

Security groups control the flow of traffic. To list all security groups and their associated rules:

```
aws ec2 describe-security-groups --region us-east-1
```

Add query filters for better insights:

```
aws ec2 describe-security-groups --query 'SecurityGroups[*].{Name:GroupName,
ID:GroupId, VPC:VpcId}' --output table
```

You can also inspect specific rules using:

```
aws ec2 describe-security-groups --group-ids sg-xxxxxxxx
```

Listing Network Interfaces and IP Addresses

For debugging ENIs and their associations:

```
aws ec2 describe-network-interfaces
```

Look out for associated instances, private IPs, and attached subnets. This is valuable when tracking down connectivity problems at the interface level.

Resource Type	Sample CLI Command
VPCs	aws ec2 describe-vpcs
Subnets	aws ec2 describe-subnets
Route Tables	aws ec2 describe-route-tables
Security Groups	aws ec2 describe-security-groups
Network Interfaces	aws ec2 describe-network-interfaces

Table 14.1: *Summarizing with Quick Reference Commands*

These common CLI commands form the backbone of any diagnostic workflow in AWS networking. Mastering them gives you instant visibility into your environment, enabling faster detection and resolution of issues.

Inspecting VPC Configuration and Subnet Associations

Before tackling complex connectivity issues, it is essential to ensure the foundational network components — your VPCs and subnets — are configured correctly and logically associated. AWS CLI provides a direct, efficient way to inspect these relationships, validate setup integrity, and diagnose configuration mismatches.

Getting a Clear View of VPC Attributes

Start by confirming the properties of your VPC. This includes CIDR blocks, tenancy, DHCP options, and whether DNS support is enabled. Use the following command:

```
aws ec2 describe-vpcs --vpc-ids vpc-xxxxxxxx --region us-west-2
```

To get focused insight into specific attributes like DNS settings:

```
aws ec2 describe-vpc-attribute --vpc-id vpc-xxxxxxxx --attribute enableDnsSupport
```

This helps determine if services relying on DNS resolution (like private hosted zones) will function properly.

Listing Subnets and Their Associations by VPC

Each subnet must be explicitly associated with a VPC and an availability zone. To see all subnets in a given VPC:

```
aws ec2 describe-subnets --filters "Name=vpc-id,Values=vpc-xxxxxxxx"
```

To extract readable details:

```
aws ec2 describe-subnets \
--query 'Subnets[*].{ID:SubnetId, AZ:AvailabilityZone, CIDR:CidrBlock}' \
--output table
```

This output is useful for validating IP space usage and zone distribution, especially in high-availability architecture.

Mapping Subnets to Route Tables

One of the most common misconfigurations involves incorrect subnet-to-route-table mappings. Use this command to find which route table a subnet is associated with:

```
aws ec2 describe-route-tables \
--filters "Name=association.subnet-id,Values=subnet-xxxxxxxx"
```

Look out for route tables that are not explicitly associated with subnets—these inherit the main route table for the VPC, which may cause unintended routing behaviors.

Checking Public and Private Subnet Allocation

To confirm whether a subnet is public (that is associated with a route to an Internet Gateway), you can cross-reference:

1. Route Table (has 0.0.0.0/0 pointing to an IGW)
2. Subnet Auto-assign Public IP Setting

To verify public IP auto-assignment:

```
aws ec2 describe-subnets --subnet-ids subnet-xxxxxxxx \
--query 'Subnets[*].MapPublicIpOnLaunch'
```

If false, even with IGW routing, instances will not be assigned public IPs automatically—resulting in no external access.

Confirming Subnet Availability across AZs

Balanced architecture requires distributing subnets across multiple Availability Zones. To review subnet availability distribution:

```
aws ec2 describe-subnets \
--query 'Subnets[*].{SubnetID:SubnetId, AZ:AvailabilityZone}' \
--output table
```

This helps ensure services like Auto Scaling or ELB span fault domains effectively.

Element	Command Summary
View VPC config	describe-vpcs, describe-vpc-attribute
List subnets by VPC	describe-subnets --filters
Inspect route associations	describe-route-tables --filters
Check public subnet status	MapPublicIpOnLaunch, IGW route table lookup
Availability zone spread	describe-subnets --query AvailabilityZone

Table 14.2: *Putting it All Together – Cross-Checking Configuration*

Inspecting your VPC and subnet associations thoroughly via the AWS CLI allows you to validate the backbone of your network. Misconfigured associations are a silent killer in cloud networking—this step ensures your traffic flows exactly where it should, and your architecture behaves reliably under scale and failover conditions.

Diagnosing Route Table and Internet Gateway Issues

Routing issues in AWS environments often stem from misconfigured route tables or incorrectly attached Internet Gateways (IGWs). These components dictate how traffic flows between subnets, other VPCs, and the outside world. This section outlines how to use the AWS CLI to identify and resolve common routing-related misconfigurations.

Understanding Route Tables: The Backbone of Network Traffic

Every subnet in a VPC is associated with a route table that controls outbound and inbound traffic paths. To inspect your route tables and understand their current state, use:

```
aws ec2 describe-route-tables --region us-west-2
```

This command gives a full overview of your route configurations, including destination CIDR blocks and the associated targets like NAT Gateways, Internet Gateways, or Transit Gateways.

Identifying the Main Route Table for a VPC

When a subnet is not explicitly associated with a route table, it uses the main route table of the VPC by default. To identify the main route table:

```
aws ec2 describe-route-tables \
--filters "Name=vpc-id,Values=vpc-xxxxxxxx" \
--query "RouteTables[?Associations[?Main==\`true\`]]"
```

Confirming which table is set as default can help resolve cases where routing behaves unexpectedly for subnets with no direct associations.

Tracing Route Mismatches or Conflicts

If your instances cannot reach the internet or private subnets are not able to access NAT Gateways, the issue might lie in missing or incorrect routes. Look for:

- Missing 0.0.0.0/0 route to an Internet Gateway for public subnets.
- Routes pointing to the wrong target (for instance NAT Gateway versus IGW).
- Overlapping CIDR blocks or redundant routes.

To inspect specific route targets:

```
aws ec2 describe-route-tables \
--query 'RouteTables[*].Routes[*].{CIDR:DestinationCidrBlock, Target:GatewayId}' \
--output table
```

Verifying Internet Gateway Attachments

Even if a route exists pointing to an IGW, it must be properly attached to the VPC to function. To check for IGW association:

```
aws ec2 describe-internet-gateways \
--filters "Name=attachment.vpc-id,Values=vpc-xxxxxxxx"
```

If no IGW is attached, internet-bound traffic will silently fail.

Troubleshooting Common IGW Problems

Some of the most frequent Internet Gateway-related issues include:

- IGW not attached to the correct VPC.
- Missing 0.0.0.0/0 route to the IGW in the associated route table.
- Subnet not configured to auto-assign public IPs.

Run this to confirm IGW routes are present:

```
aws ec2 describe-route-tables \
--filters "Name=route.gateway-id,Values=igw-xxxxxxxx"
```

This helps ensure that traffic destined for the internet has a path via the IGW.

Testing Network Reachability with AWS CLI

To verify that your route table is functioning as intended, use the aws ec2 reachability-analyzer if enabled for your region:

```
aws ec2 start-network-insights-path \
--source ip-instance-id --destination ip-target-id \
--protocol TCP
```

This diagnostic tool offers simulated insights into the path packets would take, helping you find gaps or blocks in the network flow.

Diagnosing route table and internet gateway issues with the AWS CLI helps ensure seamless traffic flow both within the VPC and to external endpoints. From detecting misrouted subnets to ensuring gateway connectivity, this approach offers an efficient, code-driven way to maintain a reliable network architecture.

Debugging NAT Gateway and Egress Connectivity Problems

In AWS architectures, NAT Gateways play a critical role in allowing private subnets to access the internet without exposing instances to inbound traffic. However, misconfigurations in routing, elastic IP association, or subnet setup can lead to frustrating connectivity issues. This section explores how to diagnose and resolve NAT Gateway and outbound (egress) traffic problems using the AWS Command Line Interface (CLI).

Understanding the Role of a NAT Gateway in Private Subnets

Before diving into diagnostics, it's important to recognize that NAT Gateways are designed for one-way communication — outbound only. They enable instances in private subnets to:

- Download OS updates.
- Access APIs or internet-hosted repositories.
- Communicate securely without public IPs.

Missteps in setup often lead to "silent failures," where outbound requests are made but no response is received.

Step 1: Verifying NAT Gateway Deployment

To begin, ensure your NAT Gateway is deployed correctly and tied to the right subnet and Elastic IP:

```
aws ec2 describe-nat-gateways \
--filter Name=vpc-id,Values=vpc-xxxxxxxx
```

Check that the State is listed as available and that the NAT Gateway is in a public subnet with a route to an Internet Gateway.

Step 2: Confirming Elastic IP Allocation and Association

Each NAT Gateway must have an associated Elastic IP (EIP). If the EIP is missing, the gateway cannot facilitate internet-bound traffic. Use this command to verify:

```
aws ec2 describe-addresses
```

Cross-reference with your NAT Gateway details to ensure that the EIP is both allocated and attached.

Step 3: Inspecting Route Tables for Private Subnets

Ensure that your private subnets have route tables pointing to the NAT Gateway for internet-bound traffic (typically 0.0.0.0/0):

```
aws ec2 describe-route-tables \
--filters Name=route.nat-gateway-id,Values=nat-xxxxxxxx
```

If this route is missing or incorrectly defined, instances will not reach external services.

Step 4: Ensuring that the NAT Gateway is in a Public Subnet

A frequent mistake is placing the NAT Gateway in a private subnet, which will break functionality. To confirm:

```
aws ec2 describe-subnets --subnet-ids subnet-xxxxxxxx \
--query 'Subnets[*].MapPublicIpOnLaunch'
```

The subnet must be configured to auto-assign public IPs and have a route to the Internet Gateway.

Step 5: Testing Outbound Traffic Using EC2 Instance Metadata

You can SSH into a private EC2 instance and use curl or ping to test outbound access, but if you prefer staying on the CLI, use VPC Reachability Analyzer:

```
aws ec2 start-network-insights-path \
--source ec2-instance-id --destination 8.8.8.8 --protocol TCP
```

This helps simulate traffic from the instance to the internet, identifying potential failure points.

Step 6: Diagnosing with VPC Flow Logs

Enable and review VPC Flow Logs for the private subnet:

```
aws ec2 describe-flow-logs \
--filter Name=resource-id,Values=subnet-xxxxxxxx
```

Look for REJECT entries with destination: 0.0.0.0/0, which indicate dropped outbound packets. This often points to routing or NAT misconfigurations.

Step 7: Validating Network ACL Rules

Although often overlooked, overly restrictive network ACLs can block outbound traffic. Use this command to audit current ACL rules:

```
aws ec2 describe-network-acls --region us-west-2
```

Ensure there are matching **allow** rules for ephemeral ports on outbound traffic.

Problem	Root Cause	Resolution
Instances cannot connect to the internet	NAT Gateway not in public subnet	Move NAT Gateway to a correctly configured public subnet
NAT Gateway is unreachable	Missing EIP or incorrect route	Attach Elastic IP and update route table
Flow logs show REJECT status	ACL or SG blocks traffic	Update rules to allow outbound access

***Table 14.3**: Troubleshooting Example: Common Failure Scenarios*

Debugging NAT Gateway and egress issues requires a methodical review of all linked components—NAT Gateway state, Elastic IP, route tables, public subnet settings, and ACLs. The AWS CLI provides a quick and reliable toolkit for uncovering configuration errors, restoring outbound connectivity with precision and speed.

VPC Flow Logs and CloudWatch Logs

In cloud-based network environments, visibility into traffic flow is essential for diagnosing and resolving issues. While AWS provides robust tools for monitoring and alerting, log data serves as the foundational source for in-depth troubleshooting. Two of the most powerful logging services in AWS—VPC Flow Logs and Amazon CloudWatch Logs—enable engineers to trace traffic patterns, identify access anomalies, and detect misconfigurations at the packet or application level.

This section explores how these tools work together to provide granular insight into your network's behavior. Whether you are trying to understand why a service is unreachable, identifying unauthorized access attempts, or pinpointing the root of latency, these logging tools can significantly accelerate your investigation and resolution process.

By the end of this section, readers will gain a strong understanding of how to activate, interpret, and leverage VPC Flow Logs and CloudWatch Logs to troubleshoot connectivity and performance problems in AWS with precision.

Enabling and Configuring VPC Flow Logs for Network Interfaces

To effectively troubleshoot network connectivity issues, it is crucial to have a transparent view of traffic entering and leaving your resources. VPC Flow Logs offer a powerful method to capture detailed information about IP traffic traversing network interfaces within your Virtual Private Cloud (VPC). By enabling these logs, engineers gain insight into traffic patterns, connection attempts, and denied communications—enabling swift identification of misconfigured security groups, network ACLs, or routing rules.

Understanding the Role of Flow Logs in Network Diagnostics

Before setting up VPC Flow Logs, it's important to understand what they capture and why they matter. Flow logs provide visibility into accepted and rejected traffic at the network interface level, including metadata such as source and destination IP addresses, ports, protocols, packet counts, and bytes transferred. This metadata becomes a critical component in diagnosing both routine and complex network issues.

Choosing the Right Resource Scope for Logging

VPC Flow Logs can be created at different levels:

- **VPC Level:** Captures traffic for all ENIs within a VPC.
- **Subnet Level:** Focuses on specific network segments for more targeted analysis.
- **Network Interface Level:** Allows high granularity, helpful when tracing issues tied to individual EC2 instances or endpoints.

Choosing the appropriate scope depends on the level of detail needed for your investigation or monitoring goals.

Steps to Enable VPC Flow Logs

To enable VPC Flow Logs, follow these basic steps:

1. **Navigate to the VPC Console**: Open the Amazon VPC dashboard in the AWS Management Console.
2. **Select the Desired Resource:** Choose the VPC, subnet, or network interface you want to monitor.
3. **Create Flow Log:** Click `Create Flow Log`, define the log format, select the destination (CloudWatch Logs or S3), and assign a role with appropriate permissions.
4. **Set Filtering Options**: You can filter the logs to capture accepted, rejected, or all traffic, depending on your monitoring objectives.
5. **Launch and Monitor**: Once created, the flow log will start capturing traffic and exporting to the specified destination for analysis.

Security and Permissions Considerations

When configuring VPC Flow Logs, you must ensure the IAM role associated with log delivery has the necessary permissions to publish logs to CloudWatch or write to S3. Misconfigured roles are a common reason for flow log delivery failures, so double-check your permissions policy.

Use Case Example: Diagnosing Dropped Traffic

Suppose you have an EC2 instance that cannot communicate with a database hosted in another subnet. By enabling VPC Flow Logs at the ENI level of both instances, you can determine whether the traffic is being dropped and at which point—helping to isolate the issue to a misconfigured security group or route table entry.

Interpreting Flow Log Records: Analyzing Traffic Patterns and Errors

After enabling VPC Flow Logs, the next critical step is making sense of the data they generate. Flow log records provide detailed metadata for each network flow, which can help identify abnormal behavior, troubleshoot failures, and optimize your network configuration. By understanding how to interpret these records, engineers can pinpoint issues quickly and improve operational efficiency.

Breaking Down a Flow Log Record: Understanding Key Fields

Each VPC Flow Log record is a structured entry containing a predefined set of fields. These fields provide insights into the source, destination, nature, and result of each connection attempt. A typical record includes:

- **Version:** Specifies the log format version.
- **Account ID:** AWS account that owns the resource.
- **Interface ID:** Elastic Network Interface (ENI) ID the traffic is associated with.
- **Source/Destination IP and Port:** Indicates where the traffic originated and where it was intended to go.
- **Protocol:** Identifies the transport protocol (which includes TCP and UDP).
- **Packets and Bytes:** Shows the volume of data exchanged.
- **Action:** Whether the traffic was ACCEPTED or REJECTED.
- **Log Status:** Indicates the logging status (such as OK, NODATA, SKIPDATA).

By analyzing these fields, teams can determine whether traffic is flowing as expected or being blocked due to access restrictions.

Identifying Common Patterns in Network Traffic

Patterns often emerge when you observe flow logs over time. For example:

- Consistent REJECTED logs from a specific IP may indicate a misconfigured security group or unauthorized access attempt.
- Sudden spikes in REJECTED logs across multiple interfaces may suggest a misapplied Network ACL.
- Repeated traffic to high-numbered ports from the same source could point to port scanning activity.

Recognizing these patterns is essential in proactive threat detection and debugging.

Correlating Flow Logs with Application Behavior

It is important to tie network log data back to application behavior. For instance:

- If an application fails to connect to a backend service, look at the flow logs for REJECT actions between those ENIs.
- If latency is observed, compare bytes transferred and packet count to determine throughput or packet loss issues.
- If DNS resolution is failing, trace traffic between the EC2 instance and Amazon DNS IP (typically 169.254.169.253) to confirm whether queries are leaving the network.

Correlating flow logs with system logs, CloudWatch metrics, and application logs enables deeper root cause analysis.

Filtering and Querying Logs Efficiently

As flow logs can generate massive volumes of data, using efficient filtering methods is crucial. Within CloudWatch Logs, use CloudWatch Log Insights to run queries like:

```
fields @timestamp, interface_id, srcAddr, dstAddr, action
| filter action = "REJECT"
| sort @timestamp desc
| limit 20
```

These queries help isolate issues quickly without combing through raw logs manually.

Use Case Example: Debugging a Broken Web Application

Imagine a web server is not responding to requests. Flow logs show repeated REJECT actions for TCP traffic on port 443, revealing that the security group isn't allowing HTTPS traffic. By updating the security group to permit inbound traffic on port 443, connectivity is restored—an example of how interpreting flow logs can directly lead to resolution.

Integrating CloudWatch Logs with Flow Logs for Centralized Monitoring

While VPC Flow Logs offer valuable insights into your network traffic, they become significantly more powerful when integrated with AWS CloudWatch Logs. This integration creates a centralized environment for storing, querying, visualizing, and setting alerts on flow data. In this section, we explore how this integration works and how to leverage it for proactive network management.

Centralizing Network Visibility: Why Integration Matters

Manually examining raw flow logs can be cumbersome and time-consuming—especially in large environments. By sending flow log data to Amazon CloudWatch Logs, you centralize visibility and enable structured querying, visualization, and alert automation. This not only streamlines monitoring but also aligns network data with application logs and system metrics for a unified troubleshooting experience.

Setting up the Integration: Configuring Flow Logs to Send Data to CloudWatch

To enable integration, users must specify CloudWatch Logs as the destination when creating or modifying VPC Flow Logs. The process includes:

1. **Log Group Creation**: Define or select a CloudWatch Log Group to store the logs.
2. **IAM Role Assignment**: Provide an IAM role with logs:PutLogEvents permissions, allowing the VPC service to send logs.
3. **Flow Log Creation**: Choose the appropriate VPC, subnet, or network interface, and direct its logs to the designated Log Group.

Once configured, log entries start streaming into CloudWatch within minutes.

Using CloudWatch Log Insights for Intelligent Queries

CloudWatch Log Insights is a powerful feature that enables you to query large volumes of log data using a simple syntax. Sample use cases include:

- **Filtering Rejected Traffic**

```
fields @timestamp, srcAddr, dstAddr, action
| filter action="REJECT"
| sort @timestamp desc
```

- **Monitoring Specific Ports**

```
fields @timestamp, srcPort, dstPort
| filter dstPort = 3306
```

These queries can be used to create dashboards and investigate network issues with precision and speed.

Creating Alarms for Proactive Detection

CloudWatch integration also allows you to set Alarms based on specific patterns, such as:

- A sudden increase in rejected traffic
- Excessive outbound connections from an EC2 instance
- Unexpected traffic from unknown IP ranges

You can use metric filters to extract values from logs and create CloudWatch Alarms that notify you via SNS, Lambda, or other automated workflows.

Visualizing Network Behavior in Dashboards

By combining flow log insights with CloudWatch Dashboards, teams can create visual representations of:

- Traffic volumes over time
- Trends in rejected versus accepted packets
- Port usage distribution
- Top talkers (source IPs generating the most traffic)

This enables quick executive overviews and helps identify anomalies in real time.

Use Case Example: Early Detection of a DDoS Attempt

Suppose a VPC experiences a sudden spike in traffic on high-numbered ports. CloudWatch Insights flags the increase, and an alarm is triggered based on a predefined metric filter. The security team is notified, and traffic is quickly rerouted through AWS Shield or WAF to mitigate the threat. This proactive response is only possible due to the seamless integration of flow logs and CloudWatch.

Connectivity Troubleshooting

In Cloud Networking, connectivity issues can arise from a variety of misconfigurations—often buried within the layers of routing, access controls, and security rules. While AWS offers highly flexible networking capabilities, this very flexibility can lead to complex setups that become difficult to debug when things don't work as expected. This section focuses on troubleshooting connectivity issues specifically tied to three foundational AWS networking components: Route Tables, Network Access Control Lists (ACLs), and Security Groups.

Understanding how each of these elements contributes to network communication—and how missteps in their configuration can silently block traffic—is essential for diagnosing and resolving real-world issues. We shall explore how these layers interact, walk through typical problem scenarios, and offer practical diagnostic techniques to identify and fix the root causes.

Whether you are trying to figure out why an EC2 instance was not able to reach the internet, why communication between subnets is failing, or why your database seems unreachable from an application server—this section provides the framework to dissect and resolve the problem effectively.

Troubleshooting Route Table Misconfigurations

Routing forms the backbone of network traffic flow within AWS. When connections between resources are failing, one of the first places to investigate is the route table. Route tables define the paths that traffic can take, and even a single incorrect entry can disrupt connectivity across entire subnets or VPCs. In this section, we delve into how to detect, diagnose, and resolve issues stemming from misconfigured route tables.

Understanding the Role of Route Tables in AWS Networking

Before troubleshooting, it's essential to revisit how route tables operate. In AWS, each subnet must be associated with a route table that defines where traffic is directed. These routes include entries for local traffic, Internet Gateways (IGWs), Virtual Private Gateways (VGWs), peering connections, NAT gateways, and more.

A missing or incorrect route — for instance, omitting a route to the internet gateway for public subnets — can prevent instances from connecting externally. Similarly, internal traffic between subnets or VPCs may fail if the appropriate peering or transit routes are not defined.

Common Route Table Misconfiguration Scenarios

Even experienced cloud engineers can run into issues caused by subtle mistakes. Some typical scenarios include:

- **Missing Internet Gateway Route**: Public subnet without a route to the IGW results in no internet access.
- **Overlapping CIDR Blocks with Incomplete Peering Routes**: VPC peering exists but traffic doesn't flow due to missing or incorrect routes.
- **Incorrect Target Associations**: Routes pointing to a terminated NAT Gateway or non-existent ENI.
- **Multiple Route Tables with Wrong Subnet Associations**: Subnets inadvertently associated with private route tables.

Each of these misconfigurations can lead to connectivity problems that are not immediately obvious until traffic fails to reach its destination.

Diagnosing Route Table Issues Using AWS CLI and Console

When troubleshooting, a combination of the AWS Console and CLI provides a full picture. Some key steps include:

- **List Associated Route Tables**: `aws ec2 describe-route-tables --filters "Name=association.subnet-id,Values=subnet-xxxxxxxx"`
- **Review Routes for Missing or Invalid Entries**: Use the console to visually inspect route tables and verify targets like NAT Gateways, IGWs, or Transit Gateways exist and are operational.
- **Trace the Path Using VPC Reachability Analyzer**: This AWS tool simulates traffic between resources and pinpoints where it's blocked in the routing path.

Best Practices for Route Table Configuration and Maintenance

To reduce the likelihood of issues:

- **Use Tags Strategically**: Clearly label route tables and their associated subnets for clarity.
- **Separate Public and Private Routes**: Maintain distinct route tables for different subnet types.
- **Document Routing Logic**: Keep architecture diagrams or templates updated with routing decisions.
- **Automate Configuration with IaC Tools**: Use CloudFormation or Terraform to avoid manual missteps.

Route tables are critical to ensuring traffic reaches the right destination in an AWS environment. By understanding their structure, recognizing common pitfalls, and applying diagnostic techniques, engineers can quickly isolate and resolve routing issues. Preventive measures like tagging, documentation, and automation go a long way in maintaining healthy network operations.

Troubleshooting Security Group Settings

Security groups are often the unsung gatekeepers of AWS networking. While they silently protect your workloads, misconfigured rules can lead to frustrating connectivity issues. Whether you are dealing with blocked ports, broken inter-instance communication, or inaccessible services, reviewing security group rules is a crucial part of any troubleshooting process. This section guides you through identifying, interpreting, and fixing common security group misconfigurations.

The Role of Security Groups in AWS Networking

Security groups act as virtual firewalls for EC2 instances, RDS databases, and other AWS services. Unlike traditional firewalls, security groups are *stateful* — if you allow inbound traffic on a port, the corresponding outbound response is automatically permitted.

Each security group defines both ingress rules (what can come in) and egress rules (what can go out). Understanding this dual structure is the key when debugging blocked traffic.

Frequent Security Group Misconfiguration Patterns

Misconfigured security groups are a leading cause of connectivity failures. Some of the most common issues include:

- **Missing Ingress Rules**: An application listening on port 443 might be unreachable if the security group doesn't explicitly allow HTTPS inbound traffic.
- **Incorrect CIDR Ranges**: Using an overly restrictive CIDR block (including 10.0.0.0/32) can block traffic that appears allowed on paper.
- **Omitted Intra-Security Group Access**: If two instances share the same group but are not allowed to communicate with each other, internal calls may fail.
- **Excessive Restrictions on Egress**: Blocking outbound traffic unintentionally can prevent API calls or access to updates.

Diagnosing Security Group Issues Step-by-Step

When a resource is unreachable, validating the security group rules is an important early step. Here is how to investigate:

- **List the Security Groups Attached to an Instance**:

```
aws ec2 describe-instances --instance-ids i-xxxxxxxxxxxx --query "Reservations[*].
Instances[*].SecurityGroups[*].GroupId"
```

- **Inspect Ingress and Egress Rules**:

```
aws ec2 describe-security-groups --group-ids sg-xxxxxxxx
```

- **Use VPC Reachability Analyzer**: This tool will show whether security groups (and other elements) are blocking the flow.
- **Check Network ACLs in Parallel**: Even if security group rules are correct, overly strict NACLs can still block traffic. Always check both.

Best Practices to Avoid Security Group Pitfalls

To maintain healthy and secure access control, follow these practical tips:

- **Use Descriptive Naming Conventions**: "sg-web-https" is more helpful than "sg-123abc".
- **Implement Least Privilege Access**: Avoid broad 0.0.0.0/0 permissions unless absolutely necessary.
- **Group by Functionality**: Assign security groups based on roles (like web-tier, db-tier) to make rules easier to manage.
- **Audit Regularly**: Periodically review rules and remove unused or overly permissive entries.
- **Use Automation and IaC**: Define security groups in CloudFormation or Terraform to maintain consistency and prevent drift.

Security groups serve as the first line of defense in AWS networking. Missteps in rule configuration—often minor and easy to miss—can completely block access between components. By knowing what to look for, leveraging diagnostic tools like the AWS CLI and Reachability Analyzer, and following best practices, you can rapidly identify and resolve these issues while maintaining robust security.

Troubleshooting Network ACL Issues

Network Access Control Lists (NACLs) play a critical yet often misunderstood role in AWS networking. While security groups operate at the instance level, NACLs function at the subnet level, applying an additional layer of stateless control over inbound and outbound traffic. When connectivity issues persist despite properly configured security groups, NACLs may be the hidden culprit. This section explains how to diagnose, interpret, and resolve NACL-related problems to ensure uninterrupted traffic flow.

Understanding the Role of NACLs in VPC Architecture

Network ACLs serve as *stateless* firewalls for controlling traffic in and out of subnets. Unlike security groups, NACLs require explicit rules for both ingress and egress — responses to allowed inbound traffic must also be explicitly allowed in the outbound direction.

Each rule within a NACL is evaluated based on its number, from lowest to highest. Once a match is found, the rule is applied, and no further rules are checked. The default NACL in a VPC allows all traffic, but any custom NACL must be configured manually.

Common Symptoms of NACL Misconfigurations

Misconfigured NACLs often result in symptoms that can be confused with security group or route table issues. Key indicators include:

- **Unidirectional Traffic Flow**: One-way traffic works (such as client sends request), but no response returns.
- **Intermittent Connectivity**: Some users or applications can connect while others are blocked.
- **Unreachable Subnets**: Entire subnets appear isolated despite valid routes and instance configurations.
- **Blocked Logs or Monitoring Tools**: Services like CloudWatch Agent or third-party monitoring tools silently fail due to restricted outbound ports.

Step-by-Step Troubleshooting Approach

To uncover and resolve NACL-related issues, use the following diagnostic steps:

1. **Identify the Subnet and Associated NACL**:

```
aws ec2 describe-subnets --subnet-ids subnet-xxxxxxxx --query "Subnets[*].
NetworkAclId"
```

2. **Review NACL Rules**:

```
aws ec2 describe-network-acls --network-acl-ids acl-xxxxxxxx
```

Look closely at the rule numbers, CIDR ranges, and port ranges. Ensure that return traffic (especially for ephemeral ports: 1024–65535) is permitted.

3. **Check for "DENY" Rules with Lower Rule Numbers**: A DENY rule with a lower rule number than an ALLOW rule will override it. Carefully re-order or renumber rules as needed.
4. **Match Rule Directions with the Right Traffic**:
    a. Inbound traffic must be allowed by inbound rules.
    b. Response traffic must be allowed by outbound rules.
5. **Enable VPC Flow Logs to Confirm Blocked Packets**: Flow logs can reveal if packets are being rejected and whether it is due to NACLs.

Best Practices for Managing NACLs

While NACLs offer granular control, mismanagement can introduce complexity. Follow these guidelines to ensure clarity and performance:

- **Start with Broad Rules, Then Narrow Down**: Begin with permissive rules during testing, then refine as needed.
- **Always Account for Return Traffic**: Many connectivity issues stem from forgetting to open return ports.
- **Avoid Overlapping Rule Numbers**: Maintain consistent numbering to prevent logic conflicts.
- **Document Changes**: Track NACL changes for troubleshooting and rollback purposes.
- **Use Logging**: Keep VPC Flow Logs enabled for subnets governed by strict NACLs.

Although often overlooked, NACLs are powerful tools for subnet-level traffic control. Misconfigured rules can lead to baffling connectivity issues, especially in applications requiring two-way traffic or external communication. By using structured troubleshooting steps and adhering to best practices, you can avoid common mistakes and maintain clean, efficient subnet controls.

Latency and Performance Issues

In modern cloud environments, ensuring fast, reliable network performance is just as important as maintaining connectivity. As applications scale and traffic patterns evolve, even minor network inefficiencies can result in significant latency, packet loss, or degraded user experience. This section explores how to identify, analyze, and resolve network performance issues within AWS by leveraging diagnostic tools, architectural best practices, and traffic optimization techniques.

Latency and performance problems are often elusive, emerging only under specific loads or configurations. They may be rooted in misconfigured resources, uneven traffic distribution, noisy neighbors, or even regional service constraints. This chapter helps bridge the gap between symptom and solution—guiding you through performance troubleshooting using AWS-native tools like CloudWatch, VPC Flow Logs, and Reachability Analyzer.

Whether you're running latency-sensitive applications, experiencing degraded throughput between VPCs, or dealing with bottlenecks across Availability Zones, this section will equip you with practical strategies to isolate and resolve the root causes. It will also offer proactive measures to enhance performance and future-proof your network setup.

Common Causes of Latency in AWS Networks

Before diving into resolution strategies, it's crucial to understand the typical culprits behind latency in AWS environments. Identifying these causes is the first step toward ensuring smooth and responsive applications.

Understanding the Latency Puzzle in Cloud Networks

Latency, simply defined, is the delay between a request and its response. In AWS, latency issues can stem from multiple layers—ranging from the physical distance between services to the misalignment of configurations across VPCs, subnets, and availability zones. Recognizing these layers helps isolate issues effectively.

Cross-AZ and Cross-Region Traffic

While AWS promotes fault tolerance through multi-AZ and multi-region deployments, these configurations can introduce latency if not architected properly.

When traffic travels across Availability Zones (AZs) or AWS regions, it naturally incurs higher latency due to increased network hops and physical distance. Using resources across zones or regions without a clear performance strategy can degrade real-time responsiveness.

Network Address Translation (NAT) Bottlenecks

A single misconfigured NAT Gateway can impact hundreds of workloads behind it.

NAT gateways are essential for providing internet access to private subnets, but they can become a bottleneck if throughput is not adequately planned. High utilization or under-provisioned NAT gateways may lead to increased packet processing delays, affecting outbound traffic latency.

Overutilized Network Interfaces (ENIs)

Not all performance issues originate from application logic—some start at the network interface level.

Elastic Network Interfaces (ENIs) have throughput limits based on instance type. When these limits are reached, packet delays and queueing may occur. This is especially common in high-traffic services or EC2 instances handling multiple roles.

Load Balancer Configuration

Load balancers are designed to enhance performance—but incorrect settings can do the opposite.

AWS Application Load Balancers (ALB) and Network Load Balancers (NLB) must be properly tuned for connection timeout settings, target health checks, and listener rules. Misconfigurations can cause request retries, slow failovers, or excessive hop latency.

DNS Resolution Delays

Sometimes, it is not the connection speed—it is the time taken to resolve the endpoint.

Inefficient DNS resolution—caused by caching issues, misconfigured Route 53 settings, or unoptimized record types—can delay the initiation of requests. Latency-sensitive apps can suffer noticeable performance degradation from these delays.

Instance Resource Contention (Noisy Neighbors)

Sharing is caring—unless it affects network throughput.

In shared tenancy models, your instance may reside on the same hardware as others. If neighboring instances consume excessive network I/O, your application may face degraded performance. This is commonly referred to as the "noisy neighbor" problem.

Security Group and NACL Evaluation Delays

Security checks are vital, but overly complex rules can slow traffic inspection.

Although rare, complex and large-scale Security Group or Network ACL configurations can impact latency by increasing evaluation time, especially in environments with thousands of rules. Simplifying rulesets and optimizing traffic flows can help.

AWS Throttling and Limits

AWS enforces service limits to protect its infrastructure, but they can surprise the unprepared.

Network throughput, API calls, or flow logs can be throttled when limits are exceeded. This may introduce latency or outright drop connections. Monitoring and proactively requesting limit increases is a best practice.

Improper Use of VPN and Direct Connect

Hybrid cloud connectivity is powerful — but needs to be set up with performance in mind.

If a site-to-site VPN tunnel or Direct Connect connection is misconfigured or under-provisioned, it can become a significant source of latency. Ensuring optimal path routing, failover, and bandwidth is essential in hybrid environments.

Pinpointing the cause of latency is a layered process that requires examining infrastructure, resource utilization, security controls, and external dependencies. Each factor discussed here is a potential source of delay—and understanding them sets the foundation for effective optimization in the next sections.

Tools for Measuring and Monitoring Network Performance

Effectively measuring and monitoring network performance requires the right combination of tools, each designed to provide visibility into different layers of the network stack—from infrastructure metrics to traffic flow and configuration changes.

Tool	Primary Use Case	Key Insight Provided	When to Use
Amazon CloudWatch	Real-time monitoring and alerting	Metrics, alarms, dashboards	Detect spikes, latency, resource saturation
VPC Flow Logs	Traffic-level visibility	ACCEPT/REJECT logs, IP traffic flow	Diagnose blocked traffic, packet drops
AWS CloudTrail	Configuration auditing	API activity and changes	Investigate sudden issues due to config changes
EC2 Metrics / Insights	Instance-level performance	Network throughput, packet drops	Identify instance bottlenecks
Reachability Analyzer	Path validation	Connectivity simulation	Debug routing/security issues
Contributor Insights	Traffic pattern analysis	Top contributors to metrics	Identify heavy traffic sources
Third-Party Tools	Advanced observability	End-to-end tracing, synthetic monitoring	Complex, multi-cloud environments

Table 14.4: *Quick Comparison of AWS Monitoring Tools*

Understanding where latency originates is only half the battle—accurately measuring it is the key to solving it. AWS offers several robust tools and services designed specifically to monitor and diagnose network performance issues in real-time and over time.

Gaining Visibility into Network Health

Just like a mechanic uses gauges and sensors to understand the performance of a car, cloud engineers rely on metrics, logs, and visual dashboards to assess how the network is functioning. In AWS, these tools provide vital data points to pinpoint anomalies, measure throughput, and identify potential network bottlenecks before they escalate into critical issues.

Amazon CloudWatch Metrics and Alarms

At the core of AWS monitoring lies CloudWatch—a versatile service for observing trends and reacting in real-time.

CloudWatch tracks performance metrics such as network in/out, CPU usage, and packet drops for EC2 instances, ELBs, and other AWS resources. Custom metrics can also be created to monitor application-specific KPIs. Alarms can be configured to trigger actions or notifications when thresholds are breached, enabling proactive management.

VPC Flow Logs for Traffic Analysis

When it comes to tracing the path of every packet, VPC Flow Logs are an invaluable source of truth.

VPC Flow Logs capture IP traffic going to and from network interfaces in your VPC. By analyzing these logs, administrators can determine if traffic is reaching its destination, if it is being blocked by security groups or ACLs, or if there are unexplained delays in traffic flow. Logs can be pushed to CloudWatch Logs or S3 for long-term analysis and auditing.

AWS CloudTrail for Network-Related Changes

Performance issues aren't always about the traffic—they can be rooted in configuration changes.

CloudTrail provides a record of all API calls made in your AWS account. If network performance drops suddenly, you can check CloudTrail to see if someone recently modified a route table, changed a security group, or deployed an update that impacted the network path. This forensic capability is essential for root cause analysis.

Network Performance Insights in Amazon EC2

For a closer look at what is happening inside an EC2 instance, Performance Insights offers deeper visibility.

EC2 instances provide built-in metrics for monitoring network performance, including packets sent/received, dropped packets, and throughput levels. These insights help determine whether the instance's capacity is being exceeded or if traffic patterns are abnormal.

AWS Reachability Analyzer

Wondering whether two resources should be able to communicate? This tool provides a definitive answer.

Reachability Analyzer helps validate the path between two AWS resources—such as an EC2 instance and an RDS database—by simulating traffic flow and analyzing whether the configurations (security groups, route tables, network ACLs) allow communication. It's especially useful for pinpointing broken paths in complex network architectures.

Third-Party Network Monitoring Tools

While AWS-native tools are powerful, some use cases benefit from external observability platforms.

Tools like Datadog, New Relic, ThousandEyes, and SolarWinds offer advanced network visibility and custom dashboards that integrate with AWS environments. These platforms often support synthetic transaction monitoring, distributed tracing, and more granular latency tracking across services and regions.

CloudWatch Contributor Insights

Finding out *what* is causing the problem is easier when you know *who* or *what* is contributing most.

Contributor Insights identifies the top contributors to a particular metric, such as which IP addresses or source ports are generating the most traffic. This can help isolate rogue services or traffic spikes responsible for performance degradation.

Using These Tools in Tandem

No single tool solves every problem—but when combined, these services provide a comprehensive view of your network's behavior. Whether you're diagnosing slow database queries or unexplained packet loss, the visibility offered by these AWS tools empowers engineers to respond quickly and with precision.

Strategies to Optimize Network Performance

While monitoring and diagnosis are vital for identifying performance issues, optimization is the proactive step that keeps your network fast, scalable, and resilient. In AWS, optimizing network performance involves thoughtful architecture, smart resource placement, and leveraging the right services for the job.

Architecting for Performance: The Foundation Matters

A high-performing network starts with the way it's built. From the ground up, AWS provides tools and best practices to design an efficient, low-latency, and highly available network infrastructure. The goal is to reduce unnecessary hops, avoid single points of failure, and place resources strategically.

Optimize VPC Design and Subnet Placement

Where you place your resources has a big impact on how quickly they can communicate.

Keep resources that need low-latency communication—such as application servers and databases—within the same Availability Zone and subnet when possible. Splitting them across AZs adds resilience but can also add latency. Use public, private, and isolated subnets effectively to segment traffic and improve routing efficiency.

Use AWS Global Accelerator for Global Applications

For applications serving users around the world, AWS Global Accelerator reduces the distance data has to travel.

AWS Global Accelerator routes user traffic to the nearest AWS edge location and uses the AWS global network backbone to reach your resources. This minimizes the latency and jitter associated with the public internet, leading to faster and more consistent user experiences.

Cost-Performance Tradeoff:

Global Accelerator introduces additional cost (hourly charges + data transfer fees), but it provides consistent low latency and improved availability, especially for real-time applications like gaming, financial platforms, or live streaming. It is best justified for latency-sensitive, global workloads where user experience directly impacts revenue.

Leverage Placement Groups for EC2 Instances

When milliseconds matter, bringing computed resources physically closer helps.

Placement Groups let you influence the placement of EC2 instances within the AWS infrastructure. Use cluster placement groups for tightly coupled, latency-sensitive applications that need high-speed connectivity and low network latency between instances.

Minimize Network Hops with VPC Endpoints

Eliminate unnecessary trips across the internet by using direct paths within the AWS network.

Use VPC endpoints to privately connect your VPC to AWS services such as S3 and DynamoDB without using an internet gateway or NAT device. This not only improves security but also reduces latency and increases throughput.

Cost Insight:

While some endpoints (like Gateway Endpoints for S3/DynamoDB) are free, Interface Endpoints incur hourly and data processing charges. However, they often reduce NAT Gateway costs and improve performance, making them cost-efficient in many architectures.

Implement Load Balancing for Traffic Distribution

Don't let one instance bear the brunt of your traffic—spread the load intelligently.

Elastic Load Balancing (ELB) automatically distributes incoming application traffic across multiple targets, such as EC2 instances. This ensures no single resource becomes a bottleneck, improving both performance and fault tolerance.

Monitor and Adjust MTU Settings

Sometimes the smallest settings make the biggest difference.

Incorrect Maximum Transmission Unit (MTU) settings can lead to fragmentation and degraded performance. AWS supports jumbo frames (MTU of 9001) in many networking scenarios. For high-throughput workloads like data transfers between EC2 instances, properly tuning MTU can yield significant gains.

Optimize DNS Resolution with Amazon Route 53

Fast responses begin with fast name resolution.

Amazon Route 53 is a highly available DNS service designed to provide low-latency resolution and health checks. Use geolocation routing, latency-based routing, and weighted routing policies to direct users to the most optimal endpoints based on performance or regional preferences.

Implement Caching and Content Delivery with Amazon CloudFront

Reduce repetitive backend load by bringing content closer to users.

Amazon CloudFront is a Content Delivery Network (CDN) that caches content at edge locations. This reduces the number of requests that hit your backend services, improving overall response times and reducing latency—especially for static content.

Cost-Performance Tradeoff:

CloudFront adds costs based on data transfer and requests, but it can dramatically reduce origin load, lower backend infrastructure costs, and improve user experience globally. For static and cacheable content, it often results in net cost savings, while for dynamic workloads, careful cache tuning is required to balance cost and performance.

Analyze and Fine-Tune Network Pathing with Reachability Analyzer

Never assume the best path — test and validate it.

AWS Reachability Analyzer helps identify suboptimal paths and misconfigurations in routing or security. Use it to simulate traffic flows and validate that your design supports optimal performance.

Prioritize Traffic Using Quality of Service (QoS)

Not all traffic is created equal — treat critical packets accordingly.

While AWS does not currently offer native QoS controls for customer-defined priorities, you can design your architecture to simulate traffic prioritization. For example, use different subnets and routing rules to separate real-time data from batch transfers, ensuring time-sensitive packets are not delayed.

Optimizing network performance is not a one-time task—it is a continuous process of measuring, tuning, and adapting. By designing with performance in mind and leveraging AWS-native tools, services, and architectural best practices, you can create networks that are not just functional but finely tuned for speed, reliability, and growth.

Case Studies

Understanding theory is crucial, but mastering advanced network troubleshooting on AWS truly comes to life when applied to real-world scenarios. In this section, we walk through practical case studies that illustrate how organizations have encountered, diagnosed, and resolved complex networking issues in dynamic cloud environments.

Each case study highlights specific challenges—ranging from latency spikes and misconfigured route tables to unexplained connectivity drops and bottlenecks in cross-region traffic. You'll explore how AWS tools like the CLI, VPC Flow Logs, CloudWatch Logs, and Reachability Analyzer were leveraged to trace symptoms to their root causes, and how strategic remediation restored performance and reliability.

These stories not only validate the tools and techniques discussed throughout this chapter, but also reinforce the importance of methodical troubleshooting, data interpretation, and continuous network auditing in modern cloud operations.

Diagnosing VPC Connectivity Issues Using AWS CLI

FinEdge Analytics, a financial analytics platform, deployed a multi-tier application with separate VPCs for frontend, backend, and data services. Recently, the frontend instances stopped communicating with the backend layer.

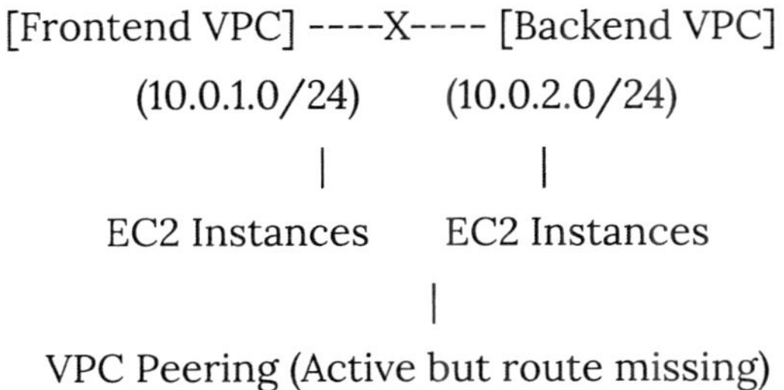

Issue

Users reported failed logins and timeouts. Initial console checks did not reveal any instance issues.

Solution Steps

Using the AWS CLI, the DevOps team ran a series of diagnostics:

- aws ec2 describe-instances confirmed that instances were running and properly tagged.

- aws ec2 describe-route-tables revealed a missing route entry in the route table of the backend VPC pointing to the VPC of the frontend via the peering connection.
- aws ec2 describe-vpc-peering-connections showed the peering status as "active," but no traffic was reaching the backend.

Resolution

The team updated the route table using:

```
aws ec2 create-route \
  --route-table-id rtb-0abcd123 \
  --destination-cidr-block 10.0.1.0/24 \
  --vpc-peering-connection-id pcx-0abcd456
```

Traffic flow was immediately restored.

[Frontend VPC] ---------> [Backend VPC]

✓ Traffic Restored

The CLI provided a fast and scriptable way to trace and resolve route table misconfigurations between VPCs.

Tracing Packet Drops Using VPC Flow Logs and CloudWatch Logs

HealthSync Cloud: A HIPAA-compliant SaaS platform, experienced intermittent API failures from internal applications hosted in different subnets.

```
[App Subnet A] ---> [App Subnet B]
      |                  |
EC2 Instance       EC2 Instance
                         |
        Security Group (Blocking 443)
```

Issue

Support tickets indicated random timeouts. Network engineers suspected packet loss or dropped connections.

Solution Steps

- VPC Flow Logs were enabled on the affected subnets.
- Logs were streamed to Amazon CloudWatch Logs for centralized analysis.
- A CloudWatch Insights query identified repeated REJECT records tied to specific security groups.

Resolution

The logs revealed that ingress traffic on port 443 from a specific internal subnet was being blocked. A missing rule in the security group was quickly added to allow HTTPS traffic.

App A -----> ✓ Allowed (Port 443 Open) -----> App B

Flow Logs combined with CloudWatch Insights gave deep visibility into traffic flows and rejected connections—critical for secure and compliant cloud environments.

Resolving Cross-AZ Latency with Route Table Optimization

MediaNova – A global media delivery company, noticed performance degradation in their video rendering pipeline, especially during peak hours. Their architecture spanned multiple Availability Zones for high availability.

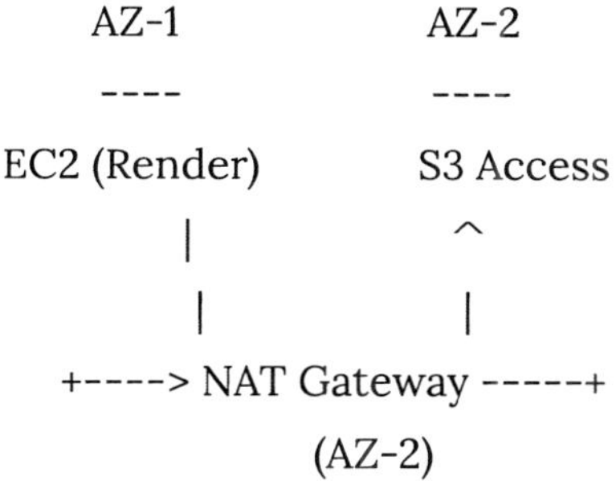

Issue

Latency between EC2 instances processing media and their S3 bucket interface grew consistently during peak traffic.

Solution Steps

- Reachability Analyzer and CloudWatch metrics were used to simulate traffic flow and measure hop counts.
- Network metrics revealed that all rendering traffic was being routed through a NAT Gateway in a different AZ.

Resolution

They restructured subnets and adjusted route tables to use local S3 VPC endpoints within each AZ:

Resources:

S3Endpoint:

```
Type: AWS::EC2::VPCEndpoint
```

Properties:

```
    ServiceName: com.amazonaws.us-east-1.s3
VpcId: vpc-0abcd123
```

RouteTableIds:

```
- rtb-0zone1
- rtb-0zone2
```

Performance improved by over 35%.

```
        AZ-1                AZ-2
        ----                ----
    EC2 (Render)        EC2 (Render)
          |                   |
    +----> S3 VPC Endpoint <----+
```

Proximity and route efficiency are key factors in minimizing latency, especially for large media transfers.

Misconfigured Security Groups Blocking External Integrations

EduCore LMS: A learning management system used by schools, had integrated a third-party content provider. However, after a recent redeployment, video streaming from the third-party broke.

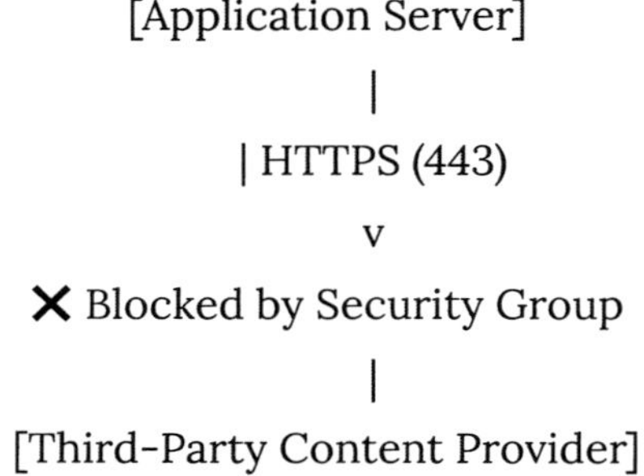

Issue

Content delivery was timing out. No alarms were triggered, and no changes were visible in the application logs.

Solution Steps

- Using Reachability Analyzer, the team discovered the application's outbound requests were blocked.
- The egress rule in the security group had been restricted to only specific IP ranges, omitting the third-party provider's updated IPs.

Resolution

The egress rules were updated to include the new content delivery IPs:

```
aws ec2 authorize-security-group-egress \
  --group-id sg-0abcd123 \
  --protocol tcp \
  --port 443 \
  --cidr 203.0.113.0/24
```

[Application] -----> ✓ Allowed -----> [External Provider]

When working with external integrations, security groups must be flexible enough to accommodate changing IP ranges while still enforcing least privilege.

Optimizing Network Performance for Real-Time Gaming Platform

PixelRush Interactive: A startup delivering multiplayer mobile games. Player complaints were flooding in due to lag and desync during real-time gameplay events.

[Global Users]

|

v

Internet (High latency)

|

v

[AWS Region - Game Servers]

Issue

Performance analytics showed rising Round Trip Time (RTT) for global users, especially those far from the main hosting region.

Solution Steps

- The team deployed AWS Global Accelerator and CloudFront to reduce the number of hops over the public internet.
- Placement groups were used to tightly couple game logic and matchmaking servers.

Resolution

Latency dropped by 40%, user satisfaction soared, and retention improved during live events.

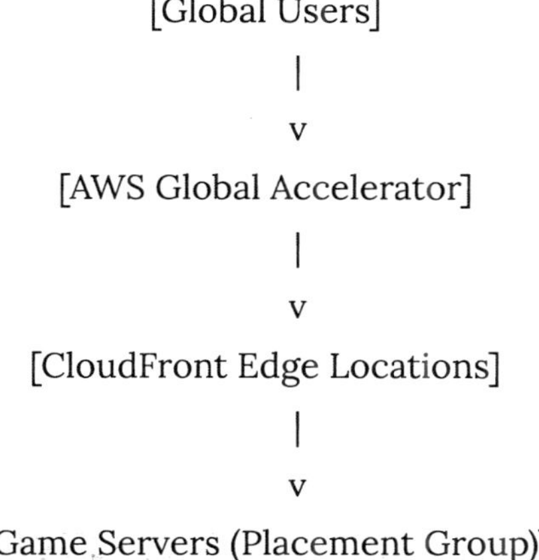

Low-latency architecture demands strategic use of global networking tools and careful server co-location.

Conclusion

As AWS environments become increasingly complex, the ability to troubleshoot and diagnose networking issues with precision has evolved from a nice-to-have skill into a mission-critical capability. This chapter has equipped you with the tools, insights, and methodologies required in uncovering hidden problems, interpreting intricate logs, and resolving connectivity issues that could otherwise derail performance, security, and user experience.

You've explored the power of the AWS Command Line Interface (CLI) for direct, scriptable diagnostics, and how to dive into network telemetry with VPC Flow Logs and CloudWatch Logs to pinpoint failures. You've also stepped through the architecture-level thinking needed to resolve misconfigured route tables, improperly scoped ACLs, and overly restrictive security groups. Finally, you navigated strategies for reducing latency and improving throughput using placement groups, traffic analysis, and advanced AWS services.

By combining data-driven approaches with practical tooling, you can now confidently troubleshoot even the most elusive network issues in production-grade cloud environments.

In the next chapter, we shall focus on strategies and tips for taking the AWS Certified Advanced Networking – Specialty (ANS-C01) exam. Also, the next chapter focuses on time management, understanding the question formats, and tips for solving complex, scenario-based questions.

Points to Remember

- **Command Line Confidence:** The AWS CLI enables deep inspection of network configurations including subnets, route tables, NAT gateways, and VPC peering—allowing for swift issue detection and resolution.
- **Log-Based Diagnostics:** VPC Flow Logs and CloudWatch Logs are invaluable for observing real-time and historical traffic patterns, identifying dropped packets, and tracing unauthorized access attempts.
- **Connectivity Requires Context:** Common pitfalls such as missing routes, mismatched CIDR blocks, or misaligned NACL rules can block traffic even when instances and services are healthy.
- **Security Groups Can be Overprotective:** Security groups, while essential for protection, can inadvertently restrict legitimate traffic if not continuously reviewed and updated—especially in dynamic environments.
- **Performance is Not Just Compute-Based:** Latency and throughput issues often stem from network bottlenecks, inefficient routing, or regional distance. Optimizations may require global services like AWS Global Accelerator or content caching with CloudFront.
- **Tool Synergy Matters:** Using Reachability Analyzer, AWS Trusted Advisor, and log-based observability tools together provides a multi-dimensional view of your network landscape.
- **Prepare for the Unexpected:** Real-world troubleshooting is often messy. Having repeatable diagnostics processes, templates, and automation scripts can drastically reduce MTTR (Mean Time to Resolution).

CHAPTER 15

Exam Strategy and Tips

Introduction

The AWS Certified Advanced Networking - Specialty (ANS-C01) exam is not just a measure of your technical proficiency — it is a test of how well you can apply advanced networking knowledge in high-stakes, scenario-driven environments. While a deep understanding of AWS services is essential, so too is your ability to interpret, analyze, and respond efficiently to complex questions under time pressure.

While Associate and Professional exams test cloud usage and architecture, ANS-C01 tests whether you can think like a network engineer inside AWS — making it one of the most technically demanding AWS certifications.

This chapter is your strategic guide to approaching the exam with clarity and confidence. From understanding the format and structure of the exam to managing your time effectively, and finally, mastering the art of solving scenario-based questions — this section aims to sharpen both your technical edge and your tactical mindset.

We shall also highlight common traps that derail even well-prepared candidates, and how to avoid them through focused reasoning and attention to detail. Whether you are preparing for your first attempt or refining your strategy for a retake, this chapter ensures you walk into the exam room with a plan—not just hope.

Structure

In this chapter, we will walk through:

- Exam Overview: Understanding the Exam Format and Structure
- Time Management: Allocating Time per Question and Section
- Scenario-Based Questions: Analyzing and Solving Real-World Scenarios
- Common Pitfalls: Identifying and Avoiding Exam Traps
- Pre-Exam Strategy: The Final Week Plan
- Exam-Day Execution: From Login to Submission
- Beyond the Exam - Think like a Certified Architect
- Conclusion

Exam Overview: Understanding the Exam Format and Structure

Before diving into preparation, it is essential to know what you are preparing for.

How Scoring and Question Distribution Works

The ANS-C01 exam uses a scaled scoring model (100–1000), meaning not all questions carry equal weight. Scenario-heavy questions that test design decisions, troubleshooting, and hybrid architectures often contribute more to your final score than straightforward definition-based questions. You may also encounter unscored (pilot) questions, which are indistinguishable from scored ones—so every question deserves equal attention.

Approximate domain emphasis (not officially published):

- **Hybrid Connectivity and Network Design:** High weight
- **Routing, Traffic Flow and HA:** High weight
- **Security and Network Protection:** Medium–High
- **Monitoring and Troubleshooting:** Medium–High
- **Basic VPC Concepts:** Lower weight (but easy marks)

Key takeaway: You do not need to get *everything* right—but you must consistently perform well on complex, real-world scenarios, which is exactly what ANS-C01 is designed to evaluate.

The ANS-C01 exam is built to test not just your technical knowledge, but your ability to solve real-world networking problems using AWS services.

Element	Details
Exam Code	ANS-C01
Duration	170 minutes
Questions	65 total (mix of multiple choice & response)
Passing Score	750 (scaled score out of 1000)
Delivery Method	Testing center or online proctored

Table 15.1: *Key Details at a Glance*

The Question Types are as follows:

- **Multiple Choices:** One correct option out of four.
- **Multiple Responses:** Two or more correct options (all must be selected for credit).
- **Scenario-Based:** Descriptive setups testing your analysis and decision-making skills.

Domains and Their Weightage

Understanding what areas are tested—and their weight—helps you focus your study:

Domain	Weight
Design and Implement AWS Networks	29%
Design and Implement Hybrid IT Network Architectures	23%
Network Security, Compliance, and Governance	18%
Network Management, Monitoring, and Troubleshooting	18%
Automation of Network Tasks	12%

***Table 15.2:** Domain and Their Weightage*

Your score is **scaled**, not a simple percentage. Some questions are harder and carry more weight. There's no penalty for wrong answers—so never leave a question blank.

Each domain covers a variety of use cases, and the questions are typically **interconnected**, testing your ability to make decisions based on a complete architectural view.

AWS Question Philosophy

AWS does not test your memory — it tests your ability to think like an AWS network architect. Expect:

- Scenario-based questions with ambiguous information.
- Trade-offs between security, cost, and availability.
- Questions where multiple options seem valid, but only one follows AWS best practices.

Interface Tools

- **Flag for Review:** Mark questions to revisit later.
- **Timer and Navigation Panel:** Helps track progress.
- **Scratchpad:** Digital note tool (for online exams) or physical notepad (in test centers).

Quick Tip: *Know the format inside out before exam day. It reduces anxiety and helps you manage time better under pressure.*

Time Management: Allocating Time per Question and Section

Time is your most valuable resource during the ANS-C01 exam. With 65 questions to answer in 170 minutes, you get about 2.5 minutes per question. While that seems manageable on paper, real-world scenario-based questions can quickly consume more time than expected.

A solid time management strategy helps ensure you finish the exam without rushing or second-guessing.

Stick to the Average: 2–3 Minutes per Question

Aim to complete each question in no more than 3 minutes. Some straightforward questions may take less than a minute — use that saved time for more complex, scenario-heavy items.

Question Type	Target Time
Simple/Direct	~1 minute
Moderate Complexity	~2 minutes
Scenario-Based	~3–4 minutes (max)

***Table 15.3:** Question Type versus Target Time*

If a question takes longer, flag it and come back later.

Use the First-Pass Approach

Do not waste time on tricky questions early on. Instead:

- **First Pass:** Answer only what you are confident about.
- **Second Pass:** Tackle flagged questions that need deeper thinking.
- **Final Pass:** Use leftover time to review and refine.

This helps maintain momentum and prevents you from getting stuck early.

Prioritize Mental Stamina

Three hours is a long time to stay focused. Plan for quick mental resets:

- Take a 5-second break in every 20 questions.
- Close your eyes briefly or stretch your fingers.
- Stay hydrated (if allowed).

Managing your mental energy is just as important as managing time.

Watch the Clock — but do not be Obsessed

Keep an eye on the timer, but do not let it distract you. Use these checkpoints:

- **After 60 minutes:** ~23 questions done
- **After 120 minutes:** ~46 questions done
- **Last 30 minutes:** Reserve for flagged or complex items

Practice Timing before Exam Day

Time management is a skill — build it with practice exams:

- Simulate real exam conditions.
- Use a timer while solving mock tests.
- Review which question types slow you down.

This will train you to instinctively pace yourself without panic.

Quick Tip: *Do not aim for perfection on every question. Focus on answering confidently, moving on when stuck, and returning later with a fresh perspective.*

Scenario-Based Questions: Analyzing and Solving Real-World Scenarios

One of the most defining aspects of the ANS-C01 exam is its heavy reliance on scenario-based questions. These are not your typical "*choose the correct definition*" items—they are built to simulate real-life AWS networking challenges. These questions test your judgment, experience, and ability to choose the best solution based on AWS best practices.

To succeed, you need a structured approach to reading, analyzing, and answering.

Start with the Last Line First

In long questions, jump to the last sentence first. This line usually contains the actual question prompt, such as:

- *"Which solution provides high availability and security?"*
- *"What's the most cost-effective way to connect the on-premises data center?"*

Knowing what is being asked helps you read the rest of the scenario with purpose.

Spot the Keywords

Look for key requirements hidden in the scenario:

Keyword	Implied Focus Area
Low latency	Direct Connect, placement groups
Secure communication	VPNs, private links, encryption
High availability	Multi-AZ, failover, route health checks
Cost optimization	NAT gateways vs. instances, data transfer paths
Hybrid connectivity	Direct Connect, VPN, Transit Gateway

***Table 15.4**: Keywords and Their Implied Focus Area*

These clues help eliminate wrong choices quickly.

Use the Elimination Method

Instead of jumping to the right answer, first rule out the wrong ones. Ask yourself:

- Does this solution meet all requirements?
- Does it follow AWS best practices?
- Is there a hidden drawback (in particular a single point of failure, or an unnecessary complexity)?

Eliminating 1–2 obviously incorrect answers often make the correct choice clearer.

Recognize AWS Service Traps

Many answers include options that are *technically valid*, but not the most recommended. Examples:

- Using EC2-based NAT instead of managed NAT Gateway (when availability is the key).
- Choosing VPC peering where Transit Gateway is more scalable.
- Selecting Route 53 failover when Global Accelerator would be more effective for global routing.

Always ask: "*What would AWS recommend in this scenario?*"

Watch out for Multi-Select Pitfalls

Multi-response questions can be tricky. You're asked to select two or more correct answers, and partial correctness does not earn points. Tips:

- All selected answers must complement each other and form a complete solution.
- Avoid combining answers that overlap or conflict (that might include two different VPN strategies doing the same job).

Stay Calm with Complex Diagrams or Flows

Some questions may describe multi-account or multi-region setups. If it seems overwhelming:

- Break the setup into components: on-prem, edge services, VPC, routing.
- Mentally draw the architecture as you read.
- Focus only on the part relevant to the question asked.

Trust Logic over Instinct

Sometimes, a service you have never used might be the right answer. Do not rely only on familiarity—focus on what fits the scenario best, not what you have personally implemented.

Quick Tip: *Read slowly, think critically, and aim to match the scenario with a well-architected AWS solution. When in doubt, eliminate obviously flawed answers and go with the most scalable, secure, and reliable option.*

Common Pitfalls: Identifying and Avoiding Exam Traps

Even experienced candidates can stumble in the ANS-C01 exam — not due to lack of knowledge, but by falling into carefully designed traps. The exam questions are crafted to test judgment under pressure, and it is easy to make assumptions, overlook details, or choose an answer that sounds right but does not align with AWS best practices.

Pitfall	What Goes Wrong	Prevention Strategy
Ignoring the actual requirement	Answer fits the scenario but not what the question asks (cost, HA, security, latency)	Read the last line first and mentally list 2–3 explicit requirements before evaluating options
Choosing familiar over correct	Picking services you've used before instead of AWS-recommended patterns	Ask: Is this scalable, fault-tolerant, and AWS-preferred at scale?
Overlooking hidden costs	Technically correct design but violates cost optimization goals	Watch for data transfer, cross-AZ traffic, managed vs unmanaged services
Misinterpreting multi-response questions	Selecting partially correct combinations → zero points	Ensure answers work together and form a complete solution, not overlapping ones
Falling for distractor options	Choosing "almost right" answers missing HA, encryption, or scalability	Prefer the most complete and resilient option, not just "works"
Forgetting service limitations	Assuming unsupported behavior (for example, transitive routing in VPC peering)	Remember hard limits & defaults of core services; never assume
Spending too long on one question	Time drain causes rushed guesses later	Flag after ~3 minutes, move on, and protect your final review window

Table 15.5: *Pitfall -> Prevention Strategy*

In this section, we shall highlight the most common mistakes candidates make—and how to avoid them.

Ignoring the Actual Requirement

One of the biggest traps is answering based on what the scenario describes, rather than what the question actually asks. Often, you will be given a detailed setup, but the final question will focus on something very specific, like cost, failover, or encryption.

Avoid it by:

- Always reading the last line first.
- Highlighting or mentally noting key requirements.

Choosing Familiar over Correct

It is natural to pick the service or method you have used before. But in AWS, the "familiar" option is not always the recommended one.

Example: You might default to VPC peering because you have used it before, but Transit Gateway is often the better option for large, multi-account environments.

Avoid it by:

- Asking: *Is this solution scalable, fault-tolerant, and aligned with* AWS *design principles?*
- Thinking like an AWS architect – not just a user.

Overlooking Hidden Costs

Some options may work technically but are not cost-efficient, which is often part of the scenario requirement.

Example: Choosing NAT Gateway for a high-traffic workload in multiple AZs without considering data transfer costs.

Avoid it by:

- Remembering key cost drivers: data transfer, cross-AZ traffic, managed versus unmanaged services.
- Favoring simpler, cost-effective architectures when performance or security is not compromised.

Misinterpreting Multi-Response Questions

In "choose two or more" questions, AWS expects a complete solution. Picking only one correct and one semi-correct option earns no points.

Avoid it by:

- Evaluating whether the selected answers work together, not just independently.
- Avoiding overlap – do not choose two answers that do the same thing.

Falling for Distractor Options

AWS often includes "*almost right*" answers that are technically possible but miss a critical element—like missing encryption, lacking fault tolerance, or using a deprecated approach.

Avoid it by:

- Looking for the most complete, secure, and AWS-aligned option.
- Being wary of answers that include older services or vague wording.

Forgetting Service Limitations or Defaults

Some answers may assume functionality that does not exist or works differently than expected.

Examples:

- Assuming VPC peering supports transitive routing (it does not).
- Thinking Security Groups can span VPCs by default (they cannot).

Avoid it by:

- Brushing up on limitations, regional behaviors, and edge cases for core services.
- Avoiding assumptions — read the question carefully.

Spending Too Long on One Question

Sometimes, the trap is not in the answers—it is in the time sink. A complex question can eat up 10 minutes, causing a rush later on.

Avoid it by:

- Using the first-pass approach: answer what you can confidently, and flag the rest.
- Keeping an eye on the clock and pacing yourself accordingly.

Quick Tip: *The smartest candidates do not just know AWS—they know how AWS expects them to think. Read critically, stay calm, and think in terms of best practices, not just what works.*

Avoiding these common pitfalls can give you the edge you need. Many candidates fail not because they didn't study, but because they did not read carefully, manage their time, or understand the perspective of AWS.

Pre-Exam Strategy: The Final Week Plan

7 Days before Exam

- Review weak domains (such as automation, DNS in hybrid environments).
- Take one full-length practice exam under timed conditions.
  - **Using Practice Tests Effectively**
    - A single practice test can be more powerful than 2 hours of reading—if used strategically.
  - **Do not Just Score — Diagnose**

    After every practice test, categorize questions you got wrong into:
    - Misread the question.
    - Did not know the concept.
    - Eliminated the right answer.

    This helps you pinpoint whether it is a knowledge gap or a thinking gap.
  - **Create Your "Mistake Log"**

    Keep a track of:
    - The topic (such as TGW route propagation)
    - What confused you

    - The correct approach
    - Review this mistake log 48 hours before the exam for maximum retention.
- Revisit explanations—especially for questions you guessed.

5 Days Before

- Focus on domain-specific scenarios.
- Build a personal cheat sheet:
    - DX link speeds
    - TGW route table behavior
    - VPC endpoints vs. NAT
    - Route 53 policies

2–3 Days Before

- Light review only.
- Avoid cramming.
- Walk through high-yield topics like BGP routing, inter-region communication, and security group/NACL behavior.

Day before Exam

- Rest.
- Read a few lightweight questions.
- Reaffirm your strategy: pacing, flagging, and reviewing.

Exam-Day Execution: From Login to Submission

Before the Exam

- Eat something. Hydrate. Avoid caffeine overload.
- Log in 30 minutes early if taking online.
- Prepare your environment—quiet, distraction-free, and a good internet connection.

During the Exam

- Stick to your timing strategy.
- Do not panic at unfamiliar questions.
- Flag liberally, but answer everything—there is no negative marking.

Final 20 Minutes

- Prioritize flagged questions.
- Use logic and elimination if you are stuck.
    - **Strategic Guessing – When You Truly Do not Know**

      When you reach a point where **all options seem unfamiliar**, apply these techniques:

        - **Eliminate Extreme Options**
            - AWS avoids absolute phrasing like:
            - "Only supported by..."
            - "Never compatible with..."

    - Such options are usually incorrect unless you are dealing with strict compliance questions.

  - **Apply Best Practices Filters**
    - **Is it managed or self-hosted?** Prefer managed.
    - **Is it regional or global?** Pick the one matching the scenario scale.
    - **Does it use IAM, tags, or centralized control?** AWS loves centralized management.

- Do not change answers unless you are sure—it often leads to mistakes.

Beyond the Exam – Think like a Certified Architect

Passing the ANS-C01 is a milestone, but the real value is in your transformed thinking process. Here is what sets certified professionals apart:

- They evaluate solutions holistically; always balancing cost, security, availability, and performance.
- They document architectures with modular thinking, using diagrams, Terraform, or CloudFormation — everything reusable and audit-ready.
- They act as bridge-builders, translating business requirements into scalable technical designs using native AWS services.

A Short Example: How the Thinking Differs

Problem: A company wants a highly available outbound internet access path for workloads in private subnets.

Non-architect thinking:

"Let us deploy a NAT Gateway in every AZ for maximum availability."

Certified Architect thinking:

"What is the traffic volume? Is outbound traffic bursty or constant?

Do we need per-AZ isolation, or is a centralized egress with failover acceptable?"

Final design:

- Centralized NAT Gateways with failover routing.
- IaC templates to scale or redesign later.
- Cost modeled upfront to avoid unnecessary cross-AZ data transfer.

Result:

- The required availability is met.
- Significant cost reduction.
- Design remains flexible for future growth.

Conclusion

Chapter 15 has equipped you with the strategic mindset needed to succeed in the ANS-C01 exam. While technical knowledge is essential, this chapter emphasizes on how to apply that knowledge under pressure, manage your time effectively, and make accurate decisions in complex, scenario-driven questions.

The chapter had begun with an overview of the exam structure, question types, and domain weightage, thereby helping you to understand what to expect on test day. It then focused on time management strategies, including pacing techniques, the "first-pass" method, and also how to avoid spending too long on any single question.

A core highlight is the approach to scenario-based questions—how to break them down, identify key terms, eliminate incorrect answers, and align responses with AWS best practices. You have learnt how to handle complex architectures and multi-service solutions through logical deduction and real-world thinking.

Finally, the chapter successfully outlines the common pitfalls that even experienced professionals fall into—like choosing familiar but incorrect options, ignoring cost considerations, or misinterpreting multi-response questions. Practical advice is given on how to avoid these traps and maintain composure throughout the exam.

In the next chapter, let us dive into practice questions designed to simulate real-world AWS networking challenges. These questions are aligned with the exam objectives, focusing on topics such as VPC configurations, security group management, and hybrid network setups. In short, Chapter 15 is your tactical guide—ensuring that you do not just know the material, but know how to think, prioritize, and respond like a certified AWS networking expert.

CHAPTER 16
Practice Questions on Realistic Scenarios

Introduction

Theory alone is not enough to pass the AWS Certified Advanced Networking – Specialty (ANS-C01) exam—you must be able to apply your knowledge to real-world situations. This chapter is designed to help you do exactly that. Through a collection of carefully crafted, scenario-based practice questions, you will experience the types of challenges AWS networking professionals face in production environments—and more importantly, the kinds of questions you will encounter on exam day.

Each scenario has been developed to mirror the depth, complexity, and style of the actual exam, covering areas such as VPC configurations, hybrid networking, network security, and AWS-native routing solutions. Every question is followed by a detailed explanation, helping you understand not just the *correct answer*, but the *why* behind it.

By the end of this chapter, you will have:

- Improved your speed and accuracy in answering multi-faceted questions.
- Strengthened your grasp of AWS networking concepts in a practical context.
- Build confidence to approach the real exam with clarity and strategy.

Use this chapter to test yourself, uncover weak areas, and sharpen your exam readiness through realistic, exam-aligned practice.

Structure

In this chapter, we will cover the following topics:

- Real-World Scenarios: VPC, Direct Connect, and Route 53
- Hybrid Networks: Configuring Hybrid Cloud Solutions
- Security Questions: Evaluating Security Best Practices
- Advanced Networking Solutions: Troubleshooting and Configuration Scenarios

Real-World Scenarios: VPC, Direct Connect, and Route 53

In this section, you will encounter scenario-based questions focused on core AWS networking components—Amazon VPC, AWS Direct Connect, and Amazon Route 53. These services form the backbone of most AWS networking architectures and are heavily tested in the ANS-C01 exam.

Each scenario replicates a real-world use case where you will be asked to analyze the architecture and choose the most appropriate solution based on AWS best practices.

Scenario 1: Multi-VPC Connectivity and Route Management

Scenario:

An enterprise runs multiple business units, each with its own dedicated VPC within the same AWS region. The networking team wants to enable communication between these VPCs while ensuring:

- Centralized route management.
- Ease of scaling as more VPCs are added.
- Minimal configuration overhead.

1. Which of the following is the most suitable solution?
    a. Configure full-mesh VPC peering connections between all VPCs and update route tables manually.
    b. Use AWS Transit Gateway to connect all VPCs through a centralized hub.
    c. Use a shared VPC model and route traffic via NAT Gateways.
    d. Connect the VPCs using VPN tunnels between them.

Correct Answer: b

Explanation:

- Transit Gateway is the recommended solution for connecting multiple VPCs at scale. It simplifies routing, supports centralized management, and easily scales with growing environments.
- Option A (full-mesh peering) becomes unmanageable with more VPCs due to exponential peering connections and complex routing.
- Option C (shared VPC + NAT) is not appropriate for intra-VPC communication; NAT is for outbound internet access.
- Option D (VPN tunnels between VPCs) is not scalable or cost-effective for intra-cloud communication.

Central Route Management with Transit Gateway

- Each VPC attaches to the Transit Gateway via a TGW attachment.
- Transit Gateway uses one or more route tables to control traffic flow.
- Attachments can be associated with different route tables for traffic segmentation.
- Route propagation can be enabled to automatically learn VPC CIDRs.
- All routing decisions are made centrally, not inside individual VPCs.

This is a major exam keyword: centralized routing domain.

Limits and Cost Considerations (Exam-Relevant)

Key Limits

- **Default limit:** 5,000 VPC attachments per Transit Gateway (region-specific, adjustable).
- Supports thousands of routes, far exceeding VPC peering scalability.

Cost Model

- Hourly cost per Transit Gateway.
- Per-attachment hourly cost.
- Data processing charges per GB.

Exam Tip: *Even with added cost, Transit Gateway is still the recommended solution when scale, simplicity, and operational control are the priorities.*

Scenario 2: DNS Failover for Global Services

Scenario:

A SaaS provider runs its application in two AWS regions to support global users. They want to:

- Direct users to the closest region.
- Automatically failover to the secondary region in case of a failure.
- Use DNS-based routing with minimal latency.

1. Which Route 53 configuration best meets this requirement?
    a. Weighted routing policy with health checks enabled
    b. Failover routing policy with primary and secondary endpoints
    c. Geolocation routing policy without health checks
    d. Latency routing policy combined with health checks

Correct Answer: d

Explanation:

- Latency routing ensures users are directed to the closest region with the best response time.
- When combined with health checks, it enables automatic failover if one region becomes unhealthy.
- Option A (weighted routing) can split traffic but is not based on user proximity.
- Option B provides failover but lacks latency optimization.
- Option C does not include health checks and may misroute during outages.

Routing Policy	Traffic Decision Based On	Supports Health Checks	Best Use Case
Latency	Lowest network latency	Yes	Global apps needing performance + failover
Failover	Primary versus secondary	Yes	Active-passive disaster recovery
Weighted	Traffic percentage	Yes	A/B testing, gradual rollouts

Table 16.1: *Comparison Table between Latency, Failover, and Weighted Routing*

Route 53 Health Check Behavior:

- Health checks are performed from multiple AWS edge locations worldwide.
- Endpoint is considered unhealthy only if multiple checkers fail.
- Health check status is evaluated independently of the user's location.
- DNS responses are adjusted automatically—no client-side changes needed.

This distributed checking model prevents false positives caused by regional network issues.

Scenario 3: Secure and Resilient Hybrid Connectivity

Scenario:

A financial institution connects its on-premises data center to AWS using a single Direct Connect connection. Due to compliance and uptime requirements, they want to:

- Ensure resilience if the primary connection fails.
- Encrypt traffic in transit between on-prem and AWS.
- Minimize downtime during failover.

1. What is the best approach?
    a. Set up a second Direct Connect connection in a different location, using BGP for failover
    b. Use a site-to-site VPN over the internet as the primary connection
    c. Replace Direct Connect with AWS Snowball Edge
    d. Enable VPC peering and use NAT Gateway for redundancy

Correct Answer: a

Explanation:

- AWS recommends multiple DX connections in separate locations for high availability.
- BGP allows automatic failover when one path fails.
- Option B is not preferred for primary connectivity due to latency and reliability concerns.
- Option C (Snowball Edge) is a data transfer appliance, not a connectivity solution.
- Option D is irrelevant—VPC peering and NAT have no role in hybrid failover.

AWS best practice for hybrid connectivity—especially in regulated industries—is to deploy multiple Direct Connect connections:

- Provision two DX connections in separate DX locations.
- Use Border Gateway Protocol (BGP) to dynamically advertise routes.
- If one connection fails, traffic automatically reroutes to the healthy path.
- Failover is fast and requires no manual intervention.

This approach directly satisfies:

- High availability
- Low latency
- Minimal downtime

Direct Connect does *not* encrypt traffic by default.

For compliance-sensitive environments (finance, healthcare, government):

- Use Direct Connect for performance and reliability.
- Overlay an IPsec Site-to-Site VPN on top of Direct Connect.
- This provides encryption in transit while retaining DX benefits.

Exam Insight: *When a question mentions encryption + DX, the expected mental model is "DX + VPN overlay", not VPN instead of DX.*

AWS Best Practices and SLA Notes

- AWS recommends at least two DX connections for production workloads.

- Connections should be:
    - In separate DX locations.
    - On separate devices.
- When combined with BGP:
    - Failover is automatic.
    - Route convergence happens without downtime.

Many architectures also include:

- DX as primary.
- Site-to-Site VPN as encrypted backup.

This layered design is frequently referenced in Amazon Web Services hybrid networking guidance.

Scenario 4: Cross-Region VPC Communication

Scenario: Your organization runs two VPCs—one in us-east-1 and another in eu-west-1. You want to enable private communication between them without using public IPs or NAT. The solution must be scalable as more regions are added.

1. What is the best solution?
    a. VPC Peering
    b. VPN tunnels
    c. Transit Gateway Peering
    d. Internet Gateway with routing filters

Correct Answer: c

Explanation:

Transit Gateway peering enables private, scalable cross-region VPC connectivity over the AWS backbone without public IPs or NAT. Unlike VPC peering, it supports centralized routing and scales cleanly as more regions are added.

Note: *TGW peering is non-transitive and requires explicit peerings per region.*

Feature	VPC Peering	TGW Peering
Connectivity Model	Point-to-point	Hub-to-hub
Scalability	Poor at scale	Designed for scale
Route Management	Distributed	Centralized
Cross-Region Support	Yes (manual)	Yes (native)
Cost Pattern	Lower initially	Higher, but predictable
Operational Overhead	High as VPCs grow	Low

Table 16.2: *Cost and Scalability Comparison*

Scenario 5: Direct Connect for Enterprise Applications

Scenario: A healthcare company needs low-latency, high-throughput connectivity between its AWS environment and on-premises infrastructure. The solution must also support BGP routing and maintain dedicated bandwidth.

1. Which service best meets these needs?
    a. AWS Site-to-Site VPN
    b. Internet Gateway
    c. AWS Direct Connect
    d. AWS Snowball Edge

Correct Answer: c

Explanation:

Direct Connect offers dedicated network connections, supports BGP, and is ideal for workloads that require consistent performance.

Key Takeaways:

- Use Transit Gateway for scalable VPC-to-VPC connectivity.
- Combine Route 53 latency routing with health checks for regional failover and low-latency DNS.
- Always implement redundant Direct Connect links with BGP for hybrid resilience and compliance.

Hybrid Networks: Configuring Hybrid Cloud Solutions

Hybrid networking is a critical area in AWS architecture—especially for organizations transitioning from traditional data centers to the cloud or building resilient, multi-environment systems. The ANS-C01 exam evaluates your ability to design, implement, and troubleshoot hybrid connectivity while balancing redundancy, routing behavior, scalability, and security.

From an exam perspective, these scenarios map primarily to Domain 2: Network Connectivity Design, with overlap into network security, routing optimization, and high availability. You are expected to reason through real-world trade-offs rather than rely on single-service knowledge.

Typical enterprise pattern:

- Direct Connect for predictable performance and low latency.
- Site-to-Site VPN as encrypted backup or overlay for compliance.
- Transit Gateway as the central routing hub for VPCs and on-prem connectivity.

This pattern appears frequently in Amazon Web Services reference architectures and ANS-C01 questions.

Exam Tips (Remember These)

Redundancy

- Always assume multiple DX connections in separate locations.
- BGP is expected for automatic failover.

Security

- Direct Connect does not encrypt traffic.
- Use VPN over DX when encryption or compliance is required.

Design Clues

- "Minimal downtime" → BGP + redundant links

- "Centralized routing" → Transit Gateway
- "Compliance / encryption" → VPN overlay

Scenario 1: Building a Redundant Hybrid Architecture

Scenario:

An enterprise customer is building a hybrid network to connect its on-premises data center to AWS. The requirements include:

- Redundancy and automatic failover.
- Encrypted communication over public links.
- Seamless traffic routing between on-prem and multiple VPCs in different regions.

1. Which setup satisfies all the requirements?
   a. Single Direct Connect with static routing to a VPC
   b. Dual Direct Connect connections, each with BGP, connected to a Transit Gateway
   c. Site-to-site VPN over the internet with static routes to each VPC
   d. VPC peering with a single VPN connection and route propagation enabled

Correct Answer: b

Explanation:

- Redundancy is achieved through dual DX connections.
- BGP provides automatic failover and dynamic routing.
- Transit Gateway allows central connection and propagation to multiple VPCs—even across regions (with Transit Gateway peering).
- Options A and C lack resilience and scalability.
- Option D mixes solutions that do not provide full redundancy or centralized routing.

Dual Direct Connect connections provide link redundancy, while BGP enables automatic failover. Transit Gateway centralizes routing to multiple VPCs and supports multi-region expansion via TGW peering. Encryption can be added using a VPN overlay on DX when compliance requires it.

Key Design Notes (High-Yield)

- **DX Location Diversity:** For full fault tolerance, each Direct Connect should terminate in different DX locations / facilities.
- **Encryption Requirement:** Direct Connect itself is not encrypted → use Site-to-Site VPN over DX for compliance-sensitive traffic.
- **Route Propagation:** BGP advertises on-prem routes to the Transit Gateway, which then propagates routes automatically to attached VPCs—eliminating per-VPC route management.

Exam Tip

If a question mentions hybrid + redundancy + multiple VPCs, the mental answer path should be: Redundant DX → BGP → Transit Gateway → (VPN overlay if encryption is mentioned).

This is a canonical enterprise hybrid pattern in Amazon Web Services architectures and shows up frequently in ANS-C01.

Scenario 2: Hybrid Routing and Prefix Advertisement

Scenario: Your organization has an MPLS-based private WAN and wants to connect to AWS using AWS Direct Connect. You are using BGP for dynamic routing. However, you want to control which prefixes are advertised to AWS to avoid leaking internal IP space unnecessarily.

1. Which of the following should you implement?
    a. Use static routes in the on-prem router
    b. Filter BGP prefixes using route filters on the customer-side router
    c. Disable BGP and rely on manual route injection
    d. Use NAT Gateway to hide on-premises IPs

Correct Answer: b

Explanation:

- Route filtering at the customer router level allows you to selectively advertise specific prefixes to AWS via BGP.
- Option A does not scale and lacks dynamic control.
- Option C defeats the purpose of BGP's flexibility.
- Option D is not related to route advertisement—NAT deals with IP translation, not BGP.

BGP route filtering on the customer edge router allows selective prefix advertisement to AWS, preventing internal IP leakage. This preserves the dynamic behavior of BGP while maintaining strict control over routing visibility.

NAT is unrelated to BGP advertisements and does not control routing propagation.

Where Route Filtering is Configured

- Implemented on the customer/on-prem edge router.
- Defined using BGP policies such as prefix-lists, route-maps, or policy statements.
- AWS accepts only the prefixes you explicitly advertise.

Conceptual Example (Vendor-Neutral)

```
PREFIX-LIST ALLOW-AWS-PREFIXES
  permit 10.10.0.0/16
  permit 10.20.0.0/16

ROUTE-POLICY BGP-OUT
  if destination in ALLOW-AWS-PREFIXES then
    advertise
  else
    deny
```

(Syntax varies by vendor; concept is what matters for the exam.)

Exam Alert (Very Common Trap)

- NAT ≠ Route Advertisement.
- NAT translates IP addresses at packet level.
- BGP controls reachability, not IP masking.

If a question mentions "*leaking prefixes*" or "*controlling advertised routes*", the answer is BGP filtering, not NAT.

Scenario 3: Designing Hybrid Connectivity with Regional Resilience

Scenario:

A global retail company is hosting services in two AWS regions. Their goal is to ensure:

- On-premises data center can access workloads in both regions.
- Regional failure does not impact full connectivity.
- Optimized routing through the closest region by default.

1. Which design should be implemented?
    a. Use a single Transit Gateway and attach both VPCs, with Site-to-Site VPN as backup
    b. Use separate Transit Gateways in each region and connect them with Transit Gateway Peering
    c. Configure VPC peering between regions and use Direct Connect to one region
    d. Use NAT Gateway and load balancer to route cross-region traffic

Correct Answer: b

Explanation:

- Multi-region resilience is best achieved with independent Transit Gateways, ensuring regional autonomy.
- Transit Gateway Peering enables low-latency, inter-region routing and resilience.
- Option A creates a single point of failure in one region.
- Option C (VPC peering) lacks central route management and does not scale well.
- Option D is unrelated to hybrid or inter-region connectivity design.

Using independent Transit Gateways per region ensures regional isolation and avoids single points of failure. Transit Gateway peering enables private, low-latency inter-region routing while allowing traffic to default to the closest healthy region.

- **TGW Peering Is Non-Transitive**: Each region maintains its own TGW and connections; traffic does **not hop transitively** across multiple TGWs.
- **Direct Connect for Full Resilience**: For true hybrid resilience, **DX connections should terminate in both regions**, allowing on-prem traffic to enter the nearest region even during failures.
- **Latency Consideration**: TGW peering traffic stays on the **AWS global backbone**, offering predictable latency, but still higher than intra-region paths—hence the preference for **local region first** routing.

If a question mentions multi-region + hybrid + resilience, the expected pattern is:

Regional TGWs + TGW Peering (+ regional DX where possible) — a standard enterprise design in Amazon Web Services architectures.

Scenario 4: Encrypted Backup for Direct Connect

Scenario: You have an active Direct Connect connection to AWS from your data center. Compliance requires an encrypted backup path. You must ensure automatic failover if the Direct Connect connection fails.

1. What should you implement?
    a. A second Direct Connect in another region
    b. A Site-to-Site VPN using the same Virtual Private Gateway
    c. NAT Gateway in each AZ
    d. Route 53 health checks

Correct Answer: b

Explanation:

This setup enables BGP failover and maintains encryption. The VPN tunnel automatically takes over if the Direct Connect link fails. A Site-to-Site VPN on the same VGW provides encrypted connectivity and automatically takes over when the Direct Connect link fails. BGP metrics ensure DX is preferred while VPN remains on standby.

- **Failover Control:** Use BGP attributes (local preference or AS_PATH prepending) so **DX is primary** and **VPN is backup**.
- **Termination Options:** VPN backup can terminate on the **same VGW** (simple setups) or on a **Transit Gateway** for larger, scalable environments.
- **Compliance Tip:** Always **test failover** to validate encryption and recovery behavior—often hinted at in exam scenarios.

If you see Direct Connect + encryption + backup, the expected answer is:

VPN overlay with BGP-based failover, following Amazon Web Services best practices.

Scenario 5: Multi-Region Hybrid Connectivity

Scenario: A multinational company wants to connect its on-prem data center to multiple AWS regions for redundancy. They require simplified routing and regional failover.

1. What is the best solution?
    a. VPC Peering and static routes
    b. VPN tunnel per VPC
    c. Use Transit Gateways in each region with peering
    d. Internet Gateway with NAT

Correct Answer: c

Explanation:

Regional Transit Gateways provide scalable, centralized routing, and peering them enables inter-region communication with simplified route control.

Regional Transit Gateways provide centralized, scalable routing within each region, while TGW peering enables private inter-region connectivity and failover. This design avoids point-to-point complexity and supports clean regional isolation.

Feature	TGW Peering	AWS Cloud WAN
Scope	Region-to-region	Global network
Routing Control	Manual, explicit	Policy-based
Complexity	Lower	Higher
Exam Focus	**High (ANS-C01)**	Low

Table 16.3: *TGW Peering versus Global WAN*

- **Non-Transitive:** TGW peering is **non-transitive** – each region must maintain its own TGW and peering.
- **Route Propagation:** Routes **do not auto-propagate** across peered TGWs; they must be **manually configured**.
- **Cost & Latency:** Inter-region TGW traffic incurs **data processing + inter-region transfer costs** and slightly higher latency than intra-region traffic.

If a question mentions multi-region + hybrid + simplified routing, the expected architecture is:

Regional Transit Gateways + TGW Peering, following Amazon Web Services enterprise best practices.

Scenario 6: BGP Route Advertisement Control

Scenario: You want to limit which on-prem IP prefixes are advertised to AWS over a Direct Connect link using BGP, to avoid exposing unnecessary internal networks.

1. What should you do?
    a. Modify AWS route tables
    b. Use route filters on the customer edge router
    c. Use NAT to translate Ips
    d. Disable BGP and configure static routes

Correct Answer: b

Explanation:

BGP route filtering on the customer edge router allows precise control over which prefixes are advertised to AWS. This prevents internal IP leakage while retaining dynamic routing and failover benefits.

NAT does not affect BGP advertisements and AWS route tables cannot block advertised prefixes.

This is done as follows.

- Configured on the on-prem/customer router.
- Implemented via prefix-lists, route-maps, or BGP policies.
- AWS only learns routes you explicitly advertise.

Verify Advertised Routes

- Check Direct Connect → Virtual Interface → BGP status.
- Validate learned prefixes on:
    - Virtual Private Gateway, or,
    - Transit Gateway route tables.

This confirms only intended prefixes are visible inside AWS.

Best Practice

Advertise the minimum required prefixes only. Limiting route visibility reduces blast radius and supports compliance-driven network segmentation—standard guidance in Amazon Web Services hybrid designs.

Key Takeaways:

- Use BGP prefix filtering to control route advertisement.
- NAT ≠ routing control (very common exam trap).

- Combine DX + BGP + TGW for scalable hybrid networks.
- Always design with least-route exposure in mind.

Security Questions: Evaluating Security Best Practices

Security is foundational in AWS networking, and the ANS-C01 exam evaluates your ability to design, assess, and troubleshoot secure network architectures across complex environments. This includes managing access control, monitoring traffic, enforcing encryption, and meeting governance and compliance requirements.

At its core, AWS security design follows the principle of least privilege and a defense-in-depth strategy — no single control is trusted alone, and every layer enforces security independently.

This section presents real-world scenarios to test your understanding of:

- Security Groups and NACLs
- VPC Flow Logs and traffic visibility
- VPC Endpoints and private service access
- Traffic inspection and centralized enforcement
- Encryption in transit and at rest

Scenario 1: Controlling Inbound Access to a Web Application

Scenario:

Your organization hosts a public web application in a private subnet behind an Application Load Balancer (ALB). You need to:

- Allow access to the ALB from the internet.
- Ensure that only HTTPS (port 443) traffic reaches the backend EC2 instances.
- Block all other inbound connections.

1. Which configuration best meets these requirements?
    a. Security group on EC2 allows port 443 from ALB's security group; NACL allows all traffic
    b. EC2 security group allows inbound 443 from 0.0.0.0/0; ALB forwards HTTP and HTTPS
    c. EC2 security group allows port 443 from ALB; NACL restricts to port 443 inbound
    d. ALB security group allows port 80 and 443; EC2 security group allows all traffic from ALB

Correct Answer: c

Explanation:

- Best practice: Restrict EC2 instance access to only what is required—in this case, HTTPS from the ALB.
- Security groups are stateful; the group of EC2 must allow inbound 443 from the group of ALB.
- NACLs, being stateless, should allow port 443 for both inbound and outbound traffic, blocking other ports for defense-in-depth.

- Options B and D are overly permissive.
- Option A lacks specific port restrictions in NACL.

EC2 instances should accept only HTTPS traffic from the ALB, enforced via security groups. NACLs add a subnet-level restriction by allowing only port 443, providing defense-in-depth. Other options are overly permissive or lack proper port restriction.

- Security Groups → *Stateful*
    - If inbound 443 is allowed, return traffic is automatically allowed.
- NACLs → *Stateless*
    - Must explicitly allow both inbound and outbound traffic for port 443.

Always allow only the minimum required ports and sources at every layer. Combining restrictive security groups with NACL guardrails reflects a least-privilege + layered security design—frequently rewarded in ANS-C01.

If a question mentions ALB + private EC2 + strict access, think: SGs for precise access control, NACLs for coarse subnet protection.

Scenario 2: Monitoring Suspicious Network Activity

Scenario: Your team suspects a misconfigured application is making unexpected outbound connections from a private subnet. You are asked to monitor all network traffic logs for that subnet with minimal impact on performance or cost.

1. Which AWS feature should you use?
    a. Enable VPC Flow Logs on the subnet
    b. Use CloudTrail to log all EC2 outbound requests
    c. Enable traffic mirroring to a third-party appliance
    d. Deploy a NAT Gateway and enable logging

Correct Answer: d

Explanation:

- VPC Flow Logs are the recommended, cost-effective way to capture IP-level traffic metadata.
- They allow filtering by IP, port, protocol, and more — perfect for identifying suspicious flows.
- CloudTrail logs API calls, not actual network traffic.
- Traffic mirroring captures packets but is more resource-intensive and used for deep inspection.
- NAT Gateway logging only tracks traffic passing through the NAT, not full subnet-level visibility.

VPC Flow Logs provide IP-level traffic metadata (source/destination IP, port, protocol, action) at low cost and low overhead, ideal for detecting suspicious outbound flows. CloudTrail logs API calls, and traffic mirroring is heavier and used for deep packet inspection.

Example: Finding Suspicious Traffic

Sample Flow Log fields:

```
srcaddr=10.0.2.15 dstaddr=198.51.100.20 dstport=4444 protocol=6 action=ACCEPT
```

CloudWatch Logs filter idea:

```
dstport = 4444 OR dstaddr NOT LIKE 10.0.0.0/8
```

This quickly surfaces unexpected external destinations or unusual ports.

Feature	What It Captures	Use Case	Cost/Impact
VPC Flow Logs	IP metadata only	Traffic visibility & auditing	Low
Traffic Mirroring	Full packets	Deep inspection/IDS	High
CloudTrail	API calls	Who changed what	Low

Table 16.4: *Quick Comparison Flow Logs versus Traffic Monitoring versus CloudTrail*

- Flow Logs do not capture payloads, keeping overhead minimal.
- You can enable them at VPC, subnet, or ENI level.
- Store in CloudWatch Logs or S3 to control retention and cost.

Scenario 3: Securing Access to S3 from a Private Subnet

Scenario: A team runs a Lambda function inside a private subnet that must access an S3 bucket securely, without traversing the internet. The subnet has no NAT Gateway or internet access.

1. What is the most secure and efficient solution?
    a. Create a NAT Gateway in the public subnet for the Lambda function
    b. Attach an Internet Gateway and route traffic via 0.0.0.0/0
    c. Use a VPC endpoint for S3 in the same region
    d. Enable S3 public access temporarily and revoke it after use

Correct Answer: c

Explanation:

- VPC endpoints enable private connectivity to AWS services (such as S3) without requiring public internet access.
- Gateway endpoints for S3 are free and secure, ideal for private subnets.
- Option A introduces NAT costs and unnecessary internet routing.
- Option B breaks the security model.
- Option D is never recommended—exposing buckets even briefly is a security risk.

An S3 Gateway VPC Endpoint allows private connectivity to S3 over the AWS backbone, eliminating the need for NAT or internet access. It is secure, cost-effective, and designed for private subnets.

Gateway versus Interface Endpoint

- S3 uses a Gateway Endpoint:
    - Route-table based.
    - No hourly cost.
    - Scales automatically.
- Interface Endpoints:
    - ENI-based, used for most other AWS services.
    - Hourly and data processing costs.

If the service is S3 or DynamoDB, think Gateway Endpoint.

Security Best Practice Note

Use endpoint policies to restrict:

- Which S3 buckets can be accessed, and,
- Which actions (GetObject, PutObject, and so on) are allowed.

This enforces least privilege even within private connectivity.

If a question mentions private subnet + S3 + no NAT, the answer is always S3 Gateway VPC Endpoint—a standard secure design in Amazon Web Services architectures.

Scenario 4: Designing East-West Traffic Inspection

Scenario: Your security team wants to inspect all east-west traffic (traffic between EC2 instances in different subnets or VPCs) for malware or unauthorized connections. The solution must be scalable and integrate with third-party firewalls.

1. What is the best approach?
    a. Enable AWS Shield Advanced for internal traffic
    b. Deploy a centralized Transit Gateway with VPC traffic mirroring to a security VPC
    c. Use AWS WAF rules on each EC2 instance
    d. Route all internal traffic through a NAT Gateway

Correct Answer: b

Explanation:

- Traffic mirroring allows capturing packets at the ENI level and sending them to an inspection appliance or security VPC.
- When paired with Transit Gateway, you can inspect traffic from multiple VPCs centrally and at scale.
- AWS WAF and Shield Advanced protect inbound web traffic, not east-west internal traffic.
- NAT Gateway is for internet-bound traffic—not internal inspection.

VPC Traffic Mirroring captures packets at the ENI level and sends them to inspection appliances in a security VPC. Combined with the Transit Gateway, this enables centralized, scalable inspection across multiple VPCs.

WAF and Shield protect north-south traffic; NAT is irrelevant for internal inspection.

Feature	What It Sees	Primary Use Case
Traffic Mirroring	Full packets	IDS/IPS, malware inspection
VPC Flow Logs	IP metadata only	Auditing, traffic analysis
GuardDuty	Analyzed signals	Threat detection (no packets)

Table 16.5: *Know the Difference (High-Yield Table)*

Exam cue: *If the question mentions deep inspection or third-party firewalls, choose Traffic Mirroring.*

Cost and Performance Notes

- Traffic Mirroring increases network throughput and processing costs.
- Best applied selectively (specific ENIs/flows), not everywhere.
- Centralizing inspection via TGW avoids duplicating appliances per VPC.

For east–west inspection at scale, the canonical design is:

Transit Gateway + Traffic Mirroring → Security VPC, as recommended in enterprise architectures by Amazon Web Services.

Scenario 5: Investigating Unusual Outbound Traffic

Scenario: Your security team suspects EC2 instances are sending unauthorized traffic from a private subnet. You need visibility into who is communicating and on what ports.

1. What service should you enable?
    a. AWS CloudTrail
    b. GuardDuty
    c. VPC Flow Logs
    d. AWS Inspector

Correct Answer: c

Explanation:

VPC Flow Logs capture IP-level metadata such as source/destination IPs, ports, protocols, and accept/reject actions—ideal for investigating suspicious outbound traffic. CloudTrail logs API calls; Inspector scans hosts; GuardDuty analyzes signals but does not replace raw traffic visibility.

Alerting and Integration

- Send Flow Logs to CloudWatch Logs or S3.
- Create CloudWatch metric filters and alarms for unusual ports or destinations.
- GuardDuty can consume VPC Flow Logs to detect threats and raise findings automatically.

Targeted Monitoring Tip

Filter Flow Logs by:

- Destination IP (external ranges).
- Destination port (non-standard ports).
- Protocol (unexpected TCP/UDP usage).

This keeps investigations focused and cost-efficient.

Exam Takeaway: *If the question asks "who talked to whom and on what port?" The answer is always* VPC *Flow Logs—a foundational visibility tool in Amazon Web Services security designs.*

Scenario 6: Isolating East-West Traffic

Scenario: A financial application requires deep packet inspection of all east-west (intra-VPC) traffic to detect malware.

1. What is the best approach?
    a. Deploy AWS Shield Advanced
    b. Mirror traffic using VPC Traffic Mirroring
    c. Use GuardDuty
    d. Enable NAT Gateway logging

Correct Answer: b

Explanation:

VPC Traffic Mirroring captures packet-level traffic directly from EC2 network interfaces and forwards it to inspection tools, enabling real-time malware detection.

Shield and GuardDuty do not provide packet inspection, and NAT logging is unrelated to intra-VPC traffic.

- **Instance Support:** Traffic Mirroring works with Nitro-based EC2 instances only.
- **Cost Control:** Use selective mirroring (specific ENIs, subnets, or filters) to reduce data volume and processing cost.

Scaling Best Practices (Multi-VPC / Multi-Subnet)

- Centralize inspection in a security VPC.
- Use Transit Gateway to aggregate traffic sources.
- Mirror only high-risk or sensitive workloads.
- Avoid mirroring all traffic by default—scale selectively.

Key Takeaways:

- Use Security Groups + NACLs for layered access control.
- VPC Flow Logs → lightweight visibility.
- VPC Endpoints → private access to AWS services.
- Traffic Mirroring (+ TGW) → scalable east-west inspection.
- Never rely on temporary exposure or permissive rules.

If a question mentions deep inspection, packet capture, or IDS/IPS, the answer is VPC Traffic Mirroring—a standard pattern in secure enterprise designs on Amazon Web Services.

Advanced Networking Solutions: Troubleshooting and Configuration Scenarios

In real-world AWS environments, networking is not just about initial setup—it is about maintaining performance, diagnosing failures, and optimizing designs under pressure. The ANS-C01 exam mirrors this reality by testing how effectively you can troubleshoot bottlenecks, resolve connectivity issues, and fine-tune complex architectures.

This section focuses on advanced, multi-layered problem-solving scenarios, covering:

- Transit Gateway routing and propagation issues.
- Multi-AZ and multi-VPC traffic paths.
- Elastic Network Interfaces (ENIs) and throughput limits.
- Routing loops, blackhole routes, and asymmetric traffic.
- Performance bottlenecks and scaling constraints.

A key expectation in the exam is methodical troubleshooting: identify the problem → isolate the failing layer → resolve with the least disruptive change.

Typical failure points tested in ANS-C01:

- Subnet route tables (missing or incorrect routes).
- Security Groups versus NACL mismatches.
- Transit Gateway route association/propagation errors.

- ENI limits or bandwidth saturation.
- AZ-specific failures impacting traffic flow.

Scenario 1: Investigating Intermittent Network Latency

Scenario:

A development team reports intermittent latency when accessing a microservices-based application deployed in private subnets across two Availability Zones. The architecture uses:

- ALB in the public subnet.
- Auto Scaling Group for EC2 in private subnets.
- NAT Gateway in a single AZ for outbound internet access.

1. What is the most likely cause of the issue?
    a. Lack of route propagation between the subnets
    b. Load balancer health checks misconfigured
    c. NAT Gateway is located in only one AZ
    d. EC2 instances are using public IPs

Correct Answer: c

Explanation:

- NAT Gateway placed in a single AZ can create cross-AZ traffic, which incurs latency and costs when instances in another AZ send internet-bound requests.
- **AWS best practice:** Create a NAT Gateway in each AZ and update route tables accordingly.
- Option A is irrelevant—route propagation applies to Transit Gateway or VPN, not subnets.
- Option B would cause traffic failure, not latency.
- Option D conflicts with the architecture (private subnets do not use public IPs directly).

A single-AZ NAT Gateway forces instances in the other AZ to send internet-bound traffic cross-AZ, increasing latency and cost. AWS best practice is one NAT Gateway per AZ with AZ-local route tables.

Exam-Relevant Best Practice

- Create a NAT Gateway in each AZ.
- Update each private subnet's route table to use the local NAT.
- Avoid cross-AZ dependencies for egress paths.

Performance Monitoring Tip

Use CloudWatch metrics such as:

- ActiveConnectionCount,
- BytesOutToDestination, and
- ErrorPortAllocation.

This helps in detecting saturation or imbalance—often hinted at in troubleshooting questions.

If you see intermittent latency + private subnets + single NAT, the answer is cross-AZ NAT traffic—a classic ANS-C01 design pitfall in Amazon Web Services architectures.

Scenario 2: Connectivity Failure between VPCs

Scenario: Two VPCs are connected via VPC peering. Instances in VPC A cannot access services in VPC B, although routing tables are configured to allow traffic between them. Security groups are open to each other's CIDRs.

1. What is the most probable cause?
    a. Overlapping CIDR blocks between the two VPCs
    b. VPC peering only allows outbound traffic
    c. Transit Gateway was not used for routing
    d. Security group rules require port translation

Correct Answer: a

Explanation:

- VPC peering does not support overlapping CIDR ranges—it causes routing conflicts and dropped traffic.
- Option B is incorrect—VPC peering supports bi-directional communication.
- Option C is irrelevant—Transit Gateway is not mandatory if peering is correctly configured.
- Option D is incorrect—SGs do not rely on port translation.

VPC peering does not support overlapping CIDR ranges. If CIDRs overlap, AWS cannot determine correct routing paths, causing traffic to be dropped even when routes and security groups appear correct.

Verify CIDR Conflicts

- Check VPC → CIDR block details in the AWS console.
- **Use CLI:** describe-vpcs to compare CIDR ranges.
- Conflicts must be resolved by re-addressing or using NAT / TGW-based designs.

Design Best Practice

Always plan non-overlapping IP address ranges for multi-VPC and hybrid architectures. Poor IP planning is a common root cause tested in ANS-C01 troubleshooting questions.

If peering + routes + SGs all look correct but traffic still fails, CIDR overlap should be your first suspicion—a classic pitfall in Amazon Web Services networking designs.

Scenario 3: Slow Global Access to Application Hosted in One Region

Scenario: A company runs a multi-tenant SaaS platform hosted in US-East-1, but users in Europe report slow performance. The application is accessed via a public-facing ALB with CloudFront distribution.

1. How can you improve global performance without migrating infrastructure?
    a. Add an additional ALB in the EU region
    b. Enable latency-based routing with Route 53
    c. Replace CloudFront with Global Accelerator
    d. Create a second VPC and use VPC peering

Correct Answer: c

Explanation:

- Global Accelerator uses the AWS global network to route TCP/UDP traffic via optimal paths to the application endpoint, significantly improving latency for global users.
- While CloudFront is effective for static content, it is not optimal for dynamic, non-cacheable content.
- Option A requires infrastructure duplication.
- Option B helps only with DNS-based failover when multiple regions exist.
- Option D does not help with global access performance.

Global Accelerator routes TCP/UDP traffic over the AWS global network to the closest edge, then forwards it to the optimal regional endpoint—reducing latency for dynamic, non-cacheable traffic. CloudFront excels at caching static content but offers limited benefit for fully dynamic requests.

When to Use Which

- **CloudFront** → Static or cacheable content (images, JS, video).
- **Global Accelerator** → Dynamic, latency-sensitive apps (APIs, SaaS, gaming).

Cost and Performance Note

Global Accelerator has fixed hourly + data transfer costs, but delivers predictable low latency worldwide—often the correct trade-off when performance is the priority.

Exam Takeaway: *If a question mentions global users + dynamic traffic + single region, then, think Global Accelerator as a standard performance optimization in Amazon Web Services architectures.*

Scenario 4: Debugging Transit Gateway Traffic Issues

Scenario: An organization uses AWS Transit Gateway to connect three VPCs and an on-premises network via VPN. Traffic between the VPCs is working, but the on-prem network cannot reach one of the VPCs (VPC-C). Route tables and security groups appear correct.

1. Which of the following is the first thing to check?
   a. If BGP route propagation to Transit Gateway is enabled
   b. If Transit Gateway attachments are using the same route table
   c. If NAT Gateway exists in VPC-C
   d. If the VPN tunnel has expired

Correct Answer: b

Explanation:

- Transit Gateway attachments can be associated with different route tables.
- If VPC-C's attachment is associated with a route table not shared with the on-prem VPN, traffic will not flow.
- Option A is a possibility but would affect all VPCs, not just one.
- Option C applies only to outbound internet, not private connectivity.
- Option D would likely disrupt all on-prem connectivity.

Transit Gateway attachments can be associated with different TGW route tables. If VPC-C's attachment is not associated with (or does not propagate routes to) the same route table as the VPN attachment, on-prem traffic will not reach VPC-C—even though other VPCs work.

TGW Troubleshooting Checklist

1. Route table association (VPN + VPC attachments).
2. Route propagation (are routes learned/advertised?).
3. Static routes in TGW route tables.
4. Security Groups / NACLs.
5. VPN status and BGP.

ANS-C01 often tests association versus propagation confusion.

TGW is Non-Transitive

- Traffic only flows where routes explicitly exist.
- No implicit "hop-through" behavior.
- Every attachment must be intentionally associated and routed.

If some VPCs work but one does not, suspect TGW route table association first—a classic troubleshooting pattern in Amazon Web Services architectures.

Scenario 5: Transit Gateway Troubleshooting

Scenario: VPC-A is connected to a Transit Gateway. It cannot communicate with VPC-B, also attached to the same Transit Gateway. Both attachments are "available," and security groups are open.

1. What should you check next?
    a. DNS settings
    b. Transit Gateway route table association
    c. Subnet CIDR ranges
    d. VPC Flow Logs

Correct Answer: b

Explanation:

TGW attachments can be associated with different route tables. If VPC-A and VPC-B aren't associated with (or routed via) the same TGW route table, traffic won't flow—even though attachments are "available."

Step	Check	Why
1	Attachment status	Must be Available
2	Route table association	Determines who can talk
3	Route propagation / static routes	Ensures prefixes exist
4	Security Groups / NACLs	Final allow/deny gates
5	Reachability Analyzer	Validate the full path

***Table 16.6:** TGW Troubleshooting Flow*

Validate with Reachability Analyzer

Use VPC Reachability Analyzer to simulate the path VPC-A → TGW → VPC-B and pinpoint where routing breaks—often the fastest way under exam pressure.

Best Practices (Multi-VPC TGW)

- Use clear, minimal TGW route tables (do not over-fragment).
- Be explicit about association versus propagation.

- Document which attachments use which tables.
- Remember: TGW routing is non-transitive.

When TGW attachments are up but traffic fails, check route table association first—a classic pitfall in Amazon Web Services designs.

Scenario 6: NAT Gateway Bottlenecks

Scenario: You observe packet loss and slow response from EC2 instances in a private subnet using a single NAT Gateway. Traffic increases during business hours.

1. How can you improve performance?
    a. Use Elastic IPs
    b. Add more NAT Gateways in other AZs
    c. Use Internet Gateway
    d. Increase EC2 instance size

Correct Answer: b

Explanation:

NAT Gateways have throughput limits. Scaling horizontally across AZs improves performance and redundancy.

A single NAT Gateway can become a throughput bottleneck. Deploying one NAT Gateway per AZ and routing AZ-local traffic to it scales throughput and improves resilience, avoiding cross-AZ contention.

Monitor These CloudWatch Metrics

- ActiveConnectionCount
- BytesOutToDestination / BytesInFromSource
- ErrorPortAllocation
- PacketsDropCount

Spikes here often indicate NAT saturation.

Cost and Throughput Notes

- NAT Gateways scale horizontally; more AZs = more cost.
- You pay per NAT Gateway + data processed.
- The trade-off is higher throughput, lower latency, and HA.

If you see private subnets + single NAT + peak-time slowdowns, the fix is NAT Gateway per AZ with AZ-local routes—a classic ANS-C01 performance pattern.

Scenario 7: Reachability Analysis

Scenario: A new EC2 instance cannot connect to an internal service in another subnet. You have checked security groups and routing. You need to simulate packet flow.

1. What tool should you use?
    a. AWS Config
    b. Reachability Analyzer
    c. GuardDuty
    d. CloudTrail

Correct Answer: b

Explanation:

Reachability Analyzer simulates the network path between AWS resources and identifies exactly where traffic is allowed or blocked (routes, NACLs, SGs, TGW paths). It does this without generating real traffic or changing infrastructure.

Tool	Best For
Reachability Analyzer	Simulating connectivity paths
VPC Flow Logs	Observing actual traffic metadata
Traffic Mirroring	Deep packet inspection
CloudTrail	API activity, not network flow

Table 16.7: *When to Use Which Tool*

Exam cue: *If the question says "simulate" or "analyze path without traffic", the answer is Reachability Analyzer.*

ANS-C01 frequently tests your ability to troubleshoot logically before making changes. Reachability Analyzer is the fastest way to validate assumptions in complex VPC, TGW, or subnet routing scenarios—exactly how Amazon Web Services expects architects to debug connectivity.

Key Takeaways:

- AZ-specific resources (such as NAT Gateways) can introduce cross-AZ latency if not duplicated.
- CIDR overlap breaks peering and must be avoided.
- Use Global Accelerator for dynamic content acceleration across continents.
- Transit Gateway routing tables must be reviewed per attachment to ensure proper path propagation.

Conclusion

This chapter has taken you beyond theoretical concepts and into the realm of real-world AWS networking challenges. Through scenario-driven practice questions, you have explored the most critical areas of the ANS-C01 exam—from VPC architectures and hybrid connectivity to security best practices and advanced troubleshooting techniques.

Each question was carefully crafted to mirror the complexity, depth, and decision-making required in the actual certification exam. More importantly, the accompanying explanations were designed to build your reasoning skills, helping you understand not just *what* the correct answer is, but *why* it is the most appropriate solution in a given context.

You have seen how the Transit Gateway and Direct Connect create scalable, hybrid environments. Also the Route 53 routing policies drive high availability and latency optimization, security controls such as VPC endpoints, NACLs, and traffic mirroring fortify your architecture and also regarding the tools such as Reachability Analyzer and VPC Flow Logs assist in proactive and reactive troubleshooting.

The key to mastering the ANS-C01 exam lies in your ability to think like a cloud network architect—balancing performance, security, cost, and availability across complex, distributed systems. The scenarios in this chapter are not just preparation tools; they are reflections of the problems you may solve as a certified professional.

In the next chapter, let us dive into full-length mock tests designed to reflect the ANS-C01 exam. Each test is followed by a detailed explanation of the answers, clarifying why certain choices are correct or incorrect. This helps reinforce the understanding of key concepts and improves exam-taking strategies.

CHAPTER 17

Mock Tests with Detailed Explanations

Introduction

Success in the AWS Certified Advanced Networking – Specialty (ANS-C01) exam hinges not only on deep conceptual understanding but also on effective exam strategy and time management. While theoretical knowledge builds the foundation, it is rigorous practice that transforms knowledge into skill. This chapter is designed to bridge that gap.

In this chapter, you will find two full-length mock exams, each meticulously crafted to reflect the complexity, format, and pressure of the real ANS-C01 exam. These mock tests cover all core domains, from hybrid networking and network design to automation, security, and cost optimization. Every question is followed by a comprehensive explanation, offering not just the correct answer but also insights into why the other options are incorrect. These explanations are not mere justifications—they are learning opportunities that reinforce key networking concepts and highlight nuances often missed in first-pass learning.

Estimated Time: ~2.5 minutes per question

- Full-length mock (65 questions): ~170 minutes
- Sectional mock (15–18 questions): ~40–45 minutes
- Quick practice (10 questions): ~20–25 minutes

In addition to strengthening technical mastery, this chapter also emphasizes upon certain strategic exam techniques: identifying distractors, eliminating obviously incorrect choices, managing time across question types, and using logical deduction when unsure.

Whether you are taking this as a final rehearsal before your exam or as a targeted diagnostic to identify weak areas, these mock tests aim to build your confidence, sharpen your precision, and help you walk into the testing center with clarity and competence.

Structure

In this chapter, we will walk through:

- Mock Test 1 (65 Questions)
- Answers and Detailed Explanations
- Key Takeaways and Exam Strategy Reinforcement

Mock Test 1 (65 Questions)

In this section, you shall encounter a mock test consisting of multiple-choice questions focused on core AWS networking components—Amazon VPC, AWS Direct Connect, and Amazon Route 53. These services form the backbone of most AWS networking architectures and are heavily tested in the ANS-C01 exam.

1. **You need to enable private connectivity from multiple VPCs across different AWS accounts to a central Amazon S3 bucket without using public IPs or NAT gateways. Which is the best solution?**
   a. Use VPC Peering and configure route tables to point to S3.
   b. Create an interface VPC endpoint for S3 in each VPC.
   c. Use a gateway VPC endpoint for S3 in each VPC.
   d. Use a VPN tunnel from each VPC to a centralized VPC with a gateway endpoint.
2. **Your on-premises network is connected to AWS via Direct Connect. You want to use BGP for dynamic routing and failover with two connections in different locations. Which configuration ensures optimal performance and resiliency?**
   a. Use static routing and manually update routes when one connection fails.
   b. Use BGP with ECMP enabled on your on-premises router.
   c. Use VPN over Direct Connect for dynamic failover.
   d. Deploy two Direct Connect gateways and route based on latency.
3. **You want to enforce a rule that no subnet in any VPC can be created without associated NACLs and route tables meeting specific standards. Which is the most scalable way to enforce this?**
   a. Use AWS CloudTrail to log violations.
   b. Use a Lambda function triggered by EventBridge on subnet creation.
   c. Use VPC Flow Logs to detect misconfigured subnets.
   d. Use Route 53 Resolver with DNS filtering.
4. **An application in a private subnet needs to securely access DynamoDB without public internet access. Which of the following is the best solution?**
   a. Use a NAT Gateway.
   b. Use a gateway VPC endpoint for DynamoDB.
   c. Use an interface endpoint for DynamoDB.
   d. Assign public IPs to the instances.
5. **Your security team needs to log and analyze all DNS queries from workloads in a VPC. Which service combination meets this requirement?**
   a. Enable Route 53 Resolver query logging to CloudWatch Logs.
   b. Enable VPC Flow Logs with DNS filters.
   c. Use CloudTrail to track DNS queries.
   d. Configure interface endpoints for Route 53.
6. **You want to allow secure, low-latency communication between EC2 instances in different VPCs within the same region. Which according to you is the recommended solution?**
   a. Use VPC Peering.
   b. Use Transit Gateway.

c. Use Site-to-Site VPN.

d. Use NAT Gateway and route through public IPs.

7. **A centralized security VPC is used for outbound inspection using AWS Network Firewall. Other VPCs must route traffic through it. Which AWS feature supports this architecture?**

a. VPC Peering with custom routes.

b. PrivateLink endpoints in the security VPC.

c. Transit Gateway with route propagation.

d. Route 53 Resolver outbound rules.

8. **Your hybrid network includes multiple AWS accounts and you need to aggregate VPC Flow Logs for central analysis. Which is the best solution?**

a. Enable VPC Flow Logs and store them in a central S3 bucket using cross-account access.

b. Enable CloudTrail across all accounts.

c. Use GuardDuty and aggregate findings.

d. Configure NAT Gateway to log flow data.

9. **You are using AWS Global Accelerator with multiple ALB endpoints. You want to ensure traffic is routed to the nearest healthy region. Which feature enables this?**

a. Weighted routing with Route 53.

b. Anycast IP and health checks of Global Accelerator.

c. CloudFront origin failover.

d. NAT Gateway with cross-region routing.

10. **A Lambda function inside a VPC is timing out when trying to reach the internet. Which is a likely cause?**

a. Missing NAT Gateway in a public subnet.

b. Missing CloudWatch permissions.

c. Lambda cannot access internet from a VPC.

d. Lambda memory setting is too low.

11. **You want to monitor cross-VPC network latency between applications deployed in different AWS Regions. What should you do?**

a. Enable VPC Flow Logs.

b. Enable Amazon CloudWatch Internet Monitor.

c. Use CloudTrail and Route 53 logs.

d. Enable S3 Transfer Acceleration.

12. **You are designing a scalable solution for interconnecting 50 VPCs in a hub-and-spoke model. Which AWS service is best suited for this use case?**

a. AWS VPC Peering

b. AWS Direct Connect Gateway

c. AWS Site-to-Site VPN

d. AWS Transit Gateway

13. **Your application is hosted in private subnets and must access Amazon S3. You must ensure this communication does not traverse the internet. What do you do?**
    a. Use NAT Gateway for outbound access to S3.
    b. Use a VPC interface endpoint for S3.
    c. Use a VPC gateway endpoint for S3.
    d. Assign public IPs to the EC2 instances.
14. **Your organization wants to restrict egress traffic from VPC workloads to only approved domains. Which AWS feature can help implement this?**
    a. VPC Flow Logs with CloudWatch
    b. Route 53 Resolver DNS Firewall
    c. Direct Connect with BGP filtering
    d. Use AWS Config with Network ACL rules
15. **You need to ensure that Lambda functions accessing AWS services from a VPC do not use public IPs. Which of the following configurations do you require?**
    a. Assign public IPs to Lambda ENIs.
    b. Use NAT Gateway for outbound traffic.
    c. Deploy Lambda in a public subnet.
    d. Use VPC interface endpoints.
16. **You want to establish private connectivity between your on-premises network and AWS using AWS Direct Connect. Which configuration allows access to both public AWS services and private VPC resources?**
    a. Use a public virtual interface only.
    b. Use a private virtual interface only.
    c. Use both public and private virtual interfaces via a Direct Connect gateway.
    d. Use a NAT Gateway and Direct Connect gateway together.
17. **A security team requires that all data transferred over Direct Connect is encrypted. Which approach meets this requirement?**
    a. Enable MACsec on Direct Connect.
    b. Use AWS VPN over Direct Connect.
    c. Use SSL/TLS encryption at the application level.
    d. All of the above.
18. **Your application architecture spans three AWS Regions and requires consistent network policy enforcement across VPCs. Which of these is the best solution?**
    a. Use VPC Peering and configure NACLs manually.
    b. Use AWS Firewall Manager with AWS Network Firewall and Transit Gateway.
    c. Use EC2 Security Groups only.
    d. Use Route 53 Resolver rules to isolate Regions.
19. **How can you reduce the blast radius in shared services of VPC architecture across multiple business units?**
    a. Use a single route table with all subnets.
    b. Use different availability zones for each business unit.

   c. Use Transit Gateway route tables and security domains.
   d. Use VPC endpoints in every subnet.

20. **You need to audit which VPC endpoints are being used in your environment across all accounts. What should you do?**
   a. Use AWS Config to track endpoint configuration changes.
   b. Use Route 53 logs.
   c. Use GuardDuty findings.
   d. Use NAT Gateway logs.

21. **Your organization requires all outbound internet traffic from multiple VPCs to be inspected and logged centrally. Which architecture allows centralized egress control using AWS-native services?**
   a. Deploy NAT Gateways in each VPC and use CloudTrail for logging.
   b. Use VPC Peering with centralized NAT Gateway logging.
   c. Use Transit Gateway to route traffic to a centralized VPC with Network Firewall.
   d. Use S3 VPC Gateway Endpoints for outbound traffic control.

22. **You are designing a multi-account AWS environment where VPCs from different accounts need to communicate securely. Which is the most scalable networking solution?**
   a. VPC Peering between all accounts.
   b. Transit Gateway shared via AWS Resource Access Manager (RAM).
   c. Site-to-Site VPN between each account.
   d. Route 53 Resolver forwarding rules.

23. **An EC2 instance in a private subnet needs to download patches from the internet. How should you configure this setup to maintain network security and cost-efficiency?**
   a. Assign a public IP and route through an Internet Gateway.
   b. Use a NAT Instance in the same subnet.
   c. Use a NAT Gateway in a public subnet and route traffic through it.
   d. Attach an Elastic IP directly to the instance.

24. **You want to allow DNS resolution for AWS resources across multiple VPCs in different accounts. Which solution best supports this requirement?**
   a. Use Route 53 private hosted zones associated with each VPC individually.
   b. Configure Route 53 Resolver endpoints with forwarding rules and shared rules.
   c. Use VPC Peering and rely on default DNS behavior.
   d. Set up custom DHCP options sets for each VPC.

25. **You are using Direct Connect with a private virtual interface. Which of the following is required for a VPC to communicate with your on-premises network over Direct Connect?**
   a. Create a Direct Connect Gateway and associate the VPC.
   b. Attach a public virtual interface to your VPC.
   c. Create a Site-to-Site VPN on top of Direct Connect.
   d. Associate your VPC with AWS Shield Advanced.

26. **Your application accesses Amazon S3 and DynamoDB frequently from a private subnet. Which is the most secure and cost-effective method to ensure access without using NAT?**
    a. Deploy a NAT Gateway and route all traffic through it.
    b. Assign public IPs to the EC2 instances.
    c. Use VPC Gateway Endpoints for S3 and DynamoDB.
    d. Use an Internet Gateway and block all other traffic via NACLs.
27. **How can you secure your VPC against unapproved outbound DNS traffic?**
    a. Disable VPC DNS resolution.
    b. Use Route 53 Resolver DNS Firewall with rule groups.
    c. Use NAT Gateway flow logs for DNS traffic analysis.
    d. Route DNS queries through GuardDuty.
28. **You need to provide private, secure access from on-premises to an internal API hosted in AWS without traversing the public internet. Which solution is most appropriate?**
    a. Expose the API through a public API Gateway endpoint.
    b. Use a VPC endpoint for the API and route traffic over Direct Connect.
    c. Use an Elastic Load Balancer and allow traffic through a NAT Gateway.
    d. Deploy a proxy server in a public subnet.
29. **You want to troubleshoot asymmetric routing issues between two VPCs connected through a Transit Gateway. Which of these tools can you use to investigate traffic flows?**
    a. Amazon Inspector
    b. VPC Traffic Mirroring
    c. AWS Shield Advanced
    d. AWS Systems Manager Session Manager
30. **You need to minimize downtime during updates to a CloudFormation stack that modifies network components like route tables. Which of the following strategy should you use?**
    a. Use a Change Set to preview changes before applying.
    b. Update resources manually before updating the stack.
    c. Delete the existing stack and recreate it.
    d. Run stack updates in parallel for speed.
31. **Your company needs to host a multi-tenant SaaS application where each tenant should access a dedicated network path. Which AWS networking service best supports this requirement?**
    a. VPC Peering
    b. PrivateLink with separate endpoints per tenant
    c. NAT Gateway with multiple route tables
    d. Internet Gateway with firewall rules per tenant
32. **An application in one VPC must frequently call a microservice hosted in another VPC in the same account. Which, according to you, is the best solution for high throughput and low latency?**
    a. Use VPC Peering and update route tables accordingly.
    b. Deploy a NAT Gateway in the source VPC.

   c. Use AWS Site-to-Site VPN.
   d. Create a Direct Connect link between VPCs.

33. **A security team wants to block all outbound access to known malicious domains from within a VPC. Which is the most appropriate AWS-native solution?**
   a. Use Route 53 Resolver DNS Firewall.
   b. Use NACLs to block domain names.
   c. Configure WAF on outbound traffic.
   d. Use GuardDuty to generate alerts.

34. **You are designing connectivity between your AWS environment and multiple on-premises data centers. Each site needs secure, high-bandwidth, and reliable access. Which of these should you recommend?**
   a. Use VPN tunnels from each data center.
   b. Use AWS Direct Connect with a Direct Connect Gateway.
   c. Use NAT Gateways with Internet Gateway fallback.
   d. Use VPC Peering between each data center and AWS.

35. **Your application is deployed across multiple Availability Zones behind a Network Load Balancer. You notice uneven traffic distribution. Which of the following is the most likely cause?**
   a. Mismatch in target group health checks
   b. Improper subnet associations on the NLB
   c. Unbalanced AZ capacity
   d. Cross-zone load balancing disabled

36. **A VPC contains a private subnet where EC2 instances must download OS updates. You want to minimize cost and avoid public IPs. Which is the recommended solution?**
   a. Attach public IPs to each instance.
   b. Use an Internet Gateway directly.
   c. Deploy a NAT Gateway in a public subnet.
   d. Use interface endpoints where supported and NAT Gateway otherwise.

37. **You need to centralize DNS resolution across hundreds of AWS accounts and VPCs. Which scalable solution supports this design?**
   a. Use private hosted zones in each VPC.
   b. Use Route 53 Resolver with shared forwarding rules.
   c. Create DHCP options for all VPCs.
   d. Use VPC Peering with Resolver endpoints.

38. **Your application uses Amazon CloudFront with an S3 origin. You want to restrict access to the origin bucket only from CloudFront. How can you achieve this?**
   a. Enable bucket versioning.
   b. Use an origin access control or Origin Access Identity (OAI).
   c. Enable transfer acceleration.
   d. Use CloudTrail to audit access.

39. **A workload in a private subnet must securely retrieve credentials stored in Secrets Manager. Which is the most secure solution?**
    a. Assign a public IP and access Secrets Manager directly.
    b. Use NAT Gateway to access Secrets Manager.
    c. Use a VPC interface endpoint for Secrets Manager.
    d. Use CloudTrail to retrieve credentials.
40. **You must ensure that all infrastructure created in your organization includes mandatory tags like 'Environment' and 'Owner'. How can this be enforced at creation time?**
    a. Use AWS Config with remediation rules.
    b. Use IAM policies with tag condition keys.
    c. Create manual tagging documentation for developers.
    d. Use GuardDuty to detect untagged resources.
41. **You are deploying an internal application used by employees across three regions. The application must be accessed using a single global IP with low latency. Which of the following services should you use?**
    a. Amazon Route 53 with latency-based routing
    b. AWS Global Accelerator
    c. Amazon CloudFront with geo restriction
    d. Elastic Load Balancer with cross-region DNS failover
42. **Which AWS feature helps detect and prevent configuration drift across networking components in a multi-account environment?**
    a. AWS CloudTrail
    b. AWS Systems Manager Parameter Store
    c. AWS Config Rules
    d. AWS Trusted Advisor
43. **Your VPC has both IPv4 and IPv6 enabled. You want EC2 instances to access the internet using IPv6 but restrict IPv4 egress. Which configuration is required?**
    a. Assign public IPv4 addresses and restrict outbound rules.
    b. Use an egress-only Internet Gateway for IPv6 traffic.
    c. Use NAT Gateway for IPv6 only.
    d. Disable DNS hostnames in the VPC.
44. **How can you ensure that Route 53 only returns healthy endpoints for your application during DNS resolution?**
    a. Use failover routing with Route 53 health checks.
    b. Enable DNSSEC for all Route 53 hosted zones.
    c. Configure alias records without health checks.
    d. Use latency-based routing with static weights.
45. **Your application requires encrypted traffic between EC2 instances across AZs. What is the most efficient AWS-native solution?**
    a. Use security groups to control access.
    b. Enable TLS encryption in the application layer.

c. Use VPC Peering with custom route tables.

d. Enable IPsec on all EC2 instances.

46. Which AWS service allows you to create logical boundaries for route propagation between different business units using Transit Gateway?

a. VPC Peering

b. Transit Gateway Route Tables

c. Site-to-Site VPN Policies

d. Direct Connect Gateways

47. A company uses a shared services VPC that multiple application VPCs connect to. Which of the following should be used to allow secure, private access to the shared services without exposing them publicly?

a. NAT Gateways in each application VPC

b. Public IPs with security groups

c. Interface VPC Endpoints shared via PrivateLink

d. Route 53 public hosted zones

48. You are designing an architecture with multiple applications that require DNS-based failover between primary and backup regions. What should you use?

a. Route 53 with health checks and failover routing.

b. CloudFront with geo-restriction.

c. Global Accelerator with endpoint weighting.

d. Elastic Load Balancer with cross-region routing.

49. Which AWS service enables detailed logging and inspection of DNS queries for VPC resources?

a. AWS CloudTrail

b. VPC Flow Logs

c. Route 53 Resolver Query Logging

d. Amazon Inspector

50. What is the purpose of an egress-only Internet Gateway in a dual-stack (IPv4 + IPv6) VPC?

a. To allow public access to IPv4 endpoints only.

b. To route IPv6 traffic to the internet while preventing inbound IPv6 connections.

c. To enable NAT for IPv6 traffic.

d. To encrypt all IPv6 traffic leaving the VPC.

51. You are designing a scalable multi-account AWS network using AWS Organizations. Which is the best way to apply centralized routing policies and monitor cross-account traffic?

a. Use VPC Peering and centralized CloudTrail logging.

b. Use Transit Gateway with shared access via Resource Access Manager (RAM).

c. Use Route 53 public hosted zones.

d. Use a NAT Gateway in each account.

52. **A new regulation mandates all external traffic logs must be stored for one year and be queryable. Which of these solutions best supports this requirement?**
    a. Enable NAT Gateway metrics and export to S3.
    b. Enable VPC Flow Logs with S3 destination and use Athena for querying.
    c. Enable Route 53 DNS query logging.
    d. Use Systems Manager Inventory.
53. **You need to restrict direct access to EC2 instances from the internet but still allow them to connect to AWS services. What should you do?**
    a. Assign public IPs and block all inbound ports.
    b. Use VPC endpoints and remove the Internet Gateway.
    c. Deploy EC2 in a public subnet and use security groups.
    d. Use a VPN and enable remote desktop.
54. **Which AWS-native tool allows you to define and enforce rules for CloudFormation templates to ensure secure and compliant networking configurations?**
    a. AWS Config
    b. IAM policy conditions
    c. CloudFormation Guard (cfn-guard)
    d. Service Control Policies (SCPs)
55. **You need to ensure applications in different VPCs can access AWS Secrets Manager securely without using the public internet. What is the recommended setup?**
    a. Create VPC peering between all VPCs and route via NAT Gateway.
    b. Use interface VPC endpoints for Secrets Manager in each VPC.
    c. Use VPN tunnels between VPCs and deploy Secrets Manager in one VPC.
    d. Use Transit Gateway with internet routing.
56. **Your network team wants to allow connectivity between hundreds of VPCs while maintaining isolated routing domains for development, staging, and production. Which AWS feature supports this architecture?**
    a. Multiple Internet Gateways
    b. Transit Gateway with route tables per environment
    c. VPC Peering with NACLs
    d. Global Accelerator
57. **Which feature helps reduce latency for users globally when accessing a multi-region application hosted on AWS?**
    a. Route 53 with geolocation routing
    b. Global Accelerator with endpoint health checks
    c. CloudFront with Lambda@Edge
    d. All of the above
58. **Your EC2 instances in a private subnet are unable to resolve domain names. Which configuration should you check?**
    a. Whether NAT Gateway is available.
    b. Whether DNS resolution is enabled in the VPC settings.

   c. Whether the subnet is associated with a public route table.
   d. Whether IAM permissions allow DNS resolution.

59. **Which of the following helps implement zero-trust architecture in AWS networking?**
   a. Security groups with default allow-all rules.
   b. Network ACLs with wide IP ranges.
   c. Micro-segmentation using security groups and IAM policies.
   d. Creating VPCs with overlapping CIDRs.

60. **Your application requires periodic access to S3 from an on-premises data center without using a VPN. Which is a secure way to achieve this?**
   a. Enable public access on the S3 bucket.
   b. Use AWS Direct Connect public virtual interface.
   c. Expose S3 through a public API Gateway endpoint.
   d. Use CloudFront signed URLs.

61. **What feature of Transit Gateway allows for automatic updates to routing tables when new VPCs are added?**
   a. Route propagation
   b. Static routing
   c. Direct Connect Gateway association
   d. NAT translation

62. **Which AWS service allows you to build private connectivity between your VPC and the network of a SaaS?**
   a. Direct Connect
   b. Site-to-Site VPN
   c. AWS PrivateLink
   d. Transit Gateway

63. **How can you restrict certain AWS users from creating internet-facing load balancers in a specific region?**
   a. Use IAM policy with condition on region and scheme type.
   b. Disable Elastic Load Balancing service in the region.
   c. Remove EC2 privileges from all users.
   d. Use Security Groups with deny-all rules.

64. **You are inspecting packets between two EC2 instances for troubleshooting. Which tool should you use?**
   a. CloudTrail
   b. VPC Flow Logs
   c. VPC Traffic Mirroring
   d. AWS Config

65. Which is the best AWS-native solution for a secure and scalable hybrid DNS configuration between on-premises and AWS VPCs?

a. Create custom DNS resolvers on EC2.

b. Use Route 53 Resolver inbound and outbound endpoints.

c. Deploy DNS Forwarders using NAT Gateway.

d. Create multiple DHCP options sets.

Answers and Detailed Explanations

Question 1 – Correct Answer: C

Q: You need to enable private connectivity from multiple VPCs across different AWS accounts to a central Amazon S3 bucket without using public IPs or NAT gateways. Which is the best solution?

Explanation: Gateway endpoints are optimized for services like S3 and DynamoDB to allow private, secure access without NAT.

A: Incorrect – Use VPC Peering and configure route tables to point to S3.

B: Incorrect – Create an interface VPC endpoint for S3 in each VPC.

C: Correct – Use a gateway VPC endpoint for S3 in each VPC.

D: Incorrect – Use a VPN tunnel from each VPC to a centralized VPC with a gateway endpoint.

Note: *Gateway versus Interface VPC Endpoints (Important Distinction)*

- Gateway VPC Endpoints
  - Used only for Amazon S3 and DynamoDB.
  - Added to route tables (no ENIs, no security groups).
  - Free (no hourly cost).
  - Best for private, high-throughput access without NAT or public Ips.
- Interface VPC Endpoints (AWS PrivateLink)
  - Used for most other AWS services.
  - Create ENIs in subnets and require security groups.
  - Hourly + data processing cost.
  - Not recommended for S3 when gateway endpoints are available.

Question 2 – Correct Answer: B

Q: Your on-premises network is connected to AWS via Direct Connect. You want to use BGP for dynamic routing and failover with two connections in different locations. Which configuration ensures optimal performance and resiliency?

Explanation: BGP with ECMP allows resilient and load-balanced routing for multiple Direct Connect connections.

A: Incorrect – Use static routing and manually update routes when one connection fails.

B: Correct – Use BGP with ECMP enabled on your on-premises router.

C: Incorrect – Use VPN over Direct Connect for dynamic failover.

D: Incorrect – Deploy two Direct Connect gateways and route based on latency.

ECMP (Equal-Cost Multi-Path routing) allows BGP to:

- Use multiple paths with the same cost simultaneously.
- Load-balance traffic across both Direct Connect links.
- Automatically fail over if one connection goes down.

In Direct Connect, enabling BGP + ECMP on the on-prem router ensures:

- High availability.
- Better throughput.
- No manual intervention during failures.

Question 3 – Correct Answer: B

Q: You want to enforce a rule that no subnet in any VPC can be created without associated NACLs and route tables meeting specific standards. Which is the most scalable way to enforce this?

Explanation: EventBridge and Lambda offer real-time enforcement of infrastructure compliance upon subnet creation.

A: Incorrect – Use AWS CloudTrail to log violations.

B: Correct – Use a Lambda function triggered by EventBridge on subnet creation.

C: Incorrect – Use VPC Flow Logs to detect misconfigured subnets.

D: Incorrect – Use Route 53 Resolver with DNS filtering.

Note: *EventBridge vs AWS Config (Real-Time versus Audit)*

- **EventBridge + Lambda**
    - Enforces rules immediately at subnet creation.
    - Can auto-remediate (attach NACLs, fix route tables, or block changes).
    - Best for real-time, preventative governance.
- **AWS Config (Alternative)**
    - Evaluates resources after creation.
    - Ideal for compliance auditing, reporting, and drift detection.
    - Can trigger remediation, but not strictly real-time.

Question 4 – Correct Answer: B

Q: An application in a private subnet needs to securely access DynamoDB without public internet access. What of the following is the best solution?

Explanation: Gateway endpoints for DynamoDB ensure private traffic stays inside the AWS network.

A: Incorrect – Use a NAT Gateway.

B: Correct – Use a gateway VPC endpoint for DynamoDB.

C: Incorrect – Use an interface endpoint for DynamoDB.

D: Incorrect – Assign public IPs to the instances.

- **Gateway VPC Endpoints**
    - Designed specifically for DynamoDB and S3.
    - Use route tables (no ENIs, no security groups).
    - No hourly cost.
    - Highest throughput for data-plane access.

- **Interface VPC Endpoints**
  - Used for most other AWS services.
  - Create ENIs in subnets.
  - Extra cost and unnecessary for DynamoDB.

If the service is DynamoDB or S3 and the requirement is *private access without internet*, the answer is Gateway VPC Endpoint — not Interface.

Question 5 – Correct Answer: A

Q: Your security team needs to log and analyze all DNS queries from workloads in a VPC. Which service combination meets this requirement?

Explanation: Route 53 Resolver query logs capture detailed DNS resolution data for VPC workloads.

A: Correct – Enable Route 53 Resolver query logging to CloudWatch Logs.

B: Incorrect – Enable VPC Flow Logs with DNS filters.

C: Incorrect – Use CloudTrail to track DNS queries.

D: Incorrect – Configure interface endpoints for Route 53.

Note: *Route 53 Resolver query logs can be sent to* **CloudWatch Logs** *for near real-time monitoring and analysis, or to* **Amazon S3** *for long-term retention and compliance needs.*

Question 6 – Correct Answer: A

Q: You want to allow secure, low-latency communication between EC2 instances in different VPCs within the same region. Which according to you is the recommended solution?

Explanation: VPC Peering allows fast, secure traffic between VPCs in the same Region.

A: Correct – Use VPC Peering.

B: Incorrect – Use Transit Gateway.

C: Incorrect – Use Site-to-Site VPN.

D: Incorrect – Use NAT Gateway and route through public IPs.

Note: *VPC Peering is* ***non-transitive*** *(VPC A ↔ B ↔ C does* **not** *work), does* **not** *support overlapping CIDR blocks, and requires* ***explicit routing*** *in each VPC. For hub-and-spoke or large-scale connectivity,* ***Transit Gateway*** *is preferred.*

Question 7 – Correct Answer: C

Q: A centralized security VPC is used for outbound inspection using AWS Network Firewall. Other VPCs must route traffic through it. Which AWS feature supports this architecture?

Explanation: Transit Gateway with route propagation enables centralized traffic inspection from other VPCs.

A: Incorrect – VPC Peering with custom routes.

B: Incorrect – PrivateLink endpoints in the security VPC.

C: Correct – Transit Gateway with route propagation.

D: Incorrect – Route 53 Resolver outbound rules.

Question 8 – Correct Answer: A

Q: Your hybrid network includes multiple AWS accounts and you need to aggregate VPC Flow Logs for central analysis. Which is the best solution?

Explanation: Flow logs can be stored centrally in S3 and queried with Athena for cross-account visibility.

A: Correct – Enable VPC Flow Logs and store them in a central S3 bucket using cross-account access.

B: Incorrect – Enable CloudTrail across all accounts.

C: Incorrect – Use GuardDuty and aggregate findings.

D: Incorrect – Configure NAT Gateway to log flow data.

Note: *Centralized VPC Flow Logs stored in Amazon S3 can be queried using Amazon Athena for large-scale analysis or sent to CloudWatch Logs and analyzed with CloudWatch Logs Insights for near real-time visibility.*

Question 9 – Correct Answer: B

Q: You are using AWS Global Accelerator with multiple ALB endpoints. You want to ensure traffic is routed to the nearest healthy region. Which feature enables this?

Explanation: Global Accelerator uses Anycast and health checks for low-latency, region-aware routing.

A: Incorrect – Weighted routing with Route 53.

B: Correct – Anycast IP and health checks of Global Accelerator.

C: Incorrect – CloudFront origin failover.

D: Incorrect – NAT Gateway with cross-region routing.

Global Accelerator versus Route 53 Latency Routing

- **AWS Global Accelerator**
  - Uses **Anycast Ips.**
  - Routes users to the **nearest healthy AWS edge**, then over the **AWS global network.**
  - Reacts **fast** to health check failures (seconds).
  - Best for **TCP/UDP** and latency-sensitive apps.
- **Route 53 Latency-Based Routing**
  - Uses **DNS responses.**
  - Routing depends on **DNS resolver location**, not real-time user location.
  - **Slower failover** (DNS TTL-based).
  - Works for **DNS-aware, HTTP/S apps.**

Exam tip: *If the question emphasizes **real-time health, fastest failover, or Anycast**, the answer is **Global Accelerator** — not Route 53.*

Question 10 – Correct Answer: A

Q: A Lambda function inside a VPC is timing out when trying to reach the internet. Which is a likely cause?

Explanation: Lambda in a private subnet requires NAT Gateway for internet access.

A: Correct – Missing NAT Gateway in a public subnet.

B: Incorrect – Missing CloudWatch permissions.

C: Incorrect – Lambda cannot access internet from a VPC.

D: Incorrect – Lambda memory setting is too low.

Note: A NAT *Gateway is required only for general internet access. If the Lambda function needs to access AWS services only (such as S3 or DynamoDB), a VPC endpoint (Gateway or Interface, depending on the service) can be used instead of a NAT Gateway, avoiding internet access entirely.*

Exam tip:

- Internet access needed → **NAT Gateway**
- Only AWS service access needed → **VPC Endpoint**

Question 11 – Correct Answer: C

Q: You want to monitor cross-VPC network latency between applications deployed in different AWS Regions. What should you do?

Explanation: CloudWatch Internet Monitor is designed to measure latency, availability, and performance of traffic between users, AWS Regions, and AWS endpoints. It uses AWS global network data to provide real latency insights, not just logs.

A: Incorrect – Enable VPC Flow Logs.

B: Correct – Enable Amazon CloudWatch Internet Monitor.

C: Incorrect – Use CloudTrail and Route 53 logs.

D: Incorrect – Enable S3 Transfer Acceleration.

Question 12 – Correct Answer: B

Q: You are designing a scalable solution for interconnecting 50 VPCs in a hub-and-spoke model. Which AWS service is best suited for this use case?

Explanation: AWS Transit Gateway is the recommended and scalable solution for interconnecting dozens (or hundreds) of VPCs in a hub-and-spoke architecture. It provides:

- Centralized routing between VPCs.
- Transitive connectivity (which VPC Peering does not support).
- High scalability (thousands of attachments).
- Multi-account support via AWS RAM.
- Easy integration with firewalls, inspection VPCs, and on-prem networks.

A: Incorrect – AWS VPC Peering

B: Incorrect – AWS Direct Connect Gateway

C: Incorrect – AWS Site-to-Site VPN

D: Correct – AWS Transit Gateway

Why the other options are incorrect

- **AWS VPC Peering** → Not scalable, **no transitive routing.**
- **AWS Direct Connect Gateway** → Used to connect **on-premises networks to AWS**, not to interconnect VPCs.
- **AWS Site-to-Site VPN** → Meant for **on-prem connectivity**, not VPC-to-VPC at scale.

Question 13 – Correct Answer: C

Q: Your application is hosted in private subnets and must access Amazon S3. You must ensure this communication does not traverse the internet. What do you do?

Explanation: A VPC gateway endpoint for Amazon S3 allows resources in private subnets to access S3 privately over the AWS network, without using the internet, NAT Gateway, or public IPs. Traffic is routed through VPC route tables, keeping it fully private and cost-effective.

A: Incorrect – Use NAT Gateway for outbound access to S3.

B: Incorrect – Use a VPC interface endpoint for S3.

C: Correct – Use a VPC gateway endpoint for S3.

D: Incorrect – Assign public IPs to the EC2 instances.

Question 14 – Correct Answer: B

Q: Your organization wants to restrict egress traffic from VPC workloads to only approved domains. Which AWS feature can help implement this?

Explanation: Route 53 Resolver forwarding rules support cross-VPC DNS resolution.

A: Incorrect – VPC Flow Logs with CloudWatch

B: Correct – Route 53 Resolver DNS Firewall

C: Incorrect – Direct Connect with BGP filtering

D: Incorrect – Use AWS Config with Network ACL rules

Here is a simple, concrete example to make it clearer:

Example:

With **Route 53 Resolver DNS Firewall**, you can:

- Allow domains like api.mycompany.com or amazonaws.com
- Block domains like malware-site.com or unapproved-external.com

Any DNS query to a **blocked domain is denied**, preventing workloads from connecting to it—even if routing allows it.

Exam tip: *If the question says **"restrict egress by domain name"**, think **Route 53 Resolver DNS Firewall** (not NACLs or Flow Logs).*

Question 15 – Correct Answer: A

Q: You need to ensure that Lambda functions accessing AWS services from a VPC do not use public IPs. Which of the following configurations do you require?

Explanation: When a Lambda function runs inside a VPC and needs to access AWS services without using public IPs or the internet, you must use VPC interface endpoints (AWS PrivateLink). These endpoints provide private connectivity to AWS services over the AWS network using ENIs inside your VPC.

A: Incorrect – Assign public IPs to Lambda ENIs.

B: Incorrect – Use NAT Gateway for outbound traffic.

C: Incorrect – Deploy Lambda in a public subnet.

D: Correct – Use VPC interface endpoints.

Question 16 – Correct Answer: C

Q: You want to establish private connectivity between your on-premises network and AWS using AWS Direct Connect. Which configuration allows access to both public AWS services and private VPC resources?

Explanation: To access both public AWS services (such as Amazon S3, DynamoDB, or public AWS APIs) and private VPC resources over AWS Direct Connect, you must configure:

- A Public Virtual Interface (Public VIF) → for public AWS services.
- A Private Virtual Interface (Private VIF) → for private VPC access.

Using a Direct Connect Gateway allows:

- Connectivity to multiple VPCs.
- Multi-account support.
- Scalable, centralized on-premises connectivity.

A: Incorrect – Use a public virtual interface only.

B: Incorrect – Use a private virtual interface only.

C: Correct – Use both public and private virtual interfaces via a Direct Connect gateway.

D: Incorrect – Use a NAT Gateway and Direct Connect gateway together.

Question 17 – Correct Answer: B

Q: A security team requires that all data transferred over Direct Connect is encrypted. Which approach meets this requirement?

Explanation: AWS Direct Connect does not encrypt traffic by default. To ensure encryption in transit, you can run an IPsec Site-to-Site VPN over the Direct Connect link. This provides:

- End-to-end encryption.
- Traffic still benefits from the reliability and consistency of Direct Connect.
- A common pattern for regulated or security-sensitive workloads.

A: Incorrect – Enable MACsec on Direct Connect.

B: Correct – Use AWS VPN over Direct Connect.

C: Incorrect – Use SSL/TLS encryption at the application level.

D: Incorrect – All of the above.

Question 18 – Correct Answer: B

Q: Your application architecture spans three AWS Regions and requires consistent network policy enforcement across VPCs. Which of these is the best solution?

Explanation: To enforce consistent network security policies across VPCs in multiple AWS Regions, use AWS Firewall Manager to centrally manage AWS Network Firewall policies. When combined with Transit Gateway, traffic from multiple VPCs can be routed through centralized inspection points.

This approach provides:

- Centralized policy management across accounts and Regions.
- Consistent firewall rules applied automatically.
- Scalable inspection architecture using Transit Gateway.
- Reduced operational overhead compared to manual configuration.

A: Incorrect – Use VPC Peering and configure NACLs manually.

B: Correct – Use AWS Firewall Manager with AWS Network Firewall and Transit Gateway.

C: Incorrect – Use EC2 Security Groups only.

D: Incorrect – Use Route 53 Resolver rules to isolate Regions.

Question 19 – Correct Answer: B

Q: How can you reduce the blast radius in shared services of VPC architecture across multiple business units?

Explanation: Using Transit Gateway route tables and security domains allows you to logically segment traffic between business units in the shared services architecture. This limits lateral movement and ensures an issue in one unit does not impact others, effectively reducing the blast radius.

A: Incorrect – Use a single route table with all subnets.

B: Correct – Use different availability zones for each business unit.

C: Incorrect – Use Transit Gateway route tables and security domains.

D: Incorrect – Use VPC endpoints in every subnet.

Question 20 – Correct Answer: A

Q: You need to audit which VPC endpoints are being used in your environment across all accounts. What should you do?

Explanation: AWS Config records and tracks VPC endpoint resources and configuration changes across accounts and Regions. This enables centralized auditing, historical visibility, and compliance reporting for which VPC endpoints are in use.

A: Correct – Use AWS Config to track endpoint configuration changes.

B: Incorrect – Use Route 53 logs.

C: Incorrect – Use GuardDuty findings.

D: Incorrect – Use NAT Gateway logs.

Question 21 – Correct Answer: C

Q: Your organization requires all outbound internet traffic from multiple VPCs to be inspected and logged centrally. Which architecture allows centralized egress control using AWS-native services?

Explanation: Using a centralized inspection VPC with Network Firewall via Transit Gateway is the best practice for outbound control.

A: Incorrect – Deploy NAT Gateways in each VPC and use CloudTrail for logging.

B: Incorrect – Use VPC Peering with centralized NAT Gateway logging.

C: Correct – Use Transit Gateway to route traffic to a centralized VPC with Network Firewall.

D: Incorrect – Use S3 VPC Gateway Endpoints for outbound traffic control.

Note: *In this architecture, all VPCs attach to a Transit Gateway, which routes outbound traffic to a central inspection VPC running AWS Network Firewall. Firewall logs (alert, flow, and TLS logs) can be centrally stored in CloudWatch Logs or Amazon S3 for monitoring, auditing, and compliance.*

Exam tip: *If the question says centralized egress inspection + logging across multiple VPCs, think Transit Gateway + inspection VPC + Network Firewall.*

Question 22 – Correct Answer: B

Q: You are designing a multi-account AWS environment where VPCs from different accounts need to communicate securely. Which is the most scalable networking solution?

Explanation: Transit Gateway shared through RAM is scalable and efficient for multi-account VPC communication.

A: Incorrect – VPC Peering between all accounts.

B: Correct – Transit Gateway shared via AWS Resource Access Manager (RAM).

C: Incorrect – Site-to-Site VPN between each account.

D: Incorrect – Route 53 Resolver forwarding rules.

Question 23 – Correct Answer: C

Q: An EC2 instance in a private subnet needs to download patches from the internet. How should you configure this setup to maintain network security and cost-efficiency?

Explanation: A NAT Gateway in a public subnet is the recommended secure solution for internet access from private subnets.

A: Incorrect – Assign a public IP and route through an Internet Gateway.

B: Incorrect – Use a NAT Instance in the same subnet.

C: Correct – Use a NAT Gateway in a public subnet and route traffic through it.

D: Incorrect – Attach an Elastic IP directly to the instance.

Note: *NAT Gateway incurs hourly + data processing cost; mention Gateway endpoints as cheaper for S3/DynamoDB.*

Question 24 – Correct Answer: B

Q: You want to allow DNS resolution for AWS resources across multiple VPCs in different accounts. Which solution best supports this requirement?

Explanation: Route 53 Resolver with forwarding rules and sharing allows centralized DNS resolution across accounts.

A: Incorrect – Use Route 53 private hosted zones associated with each VPC individually.

B: Correct – Configure Route 53 Resolver endpoints with forwarding rules and shared rules.

C: Incorrect – Use VPC Peering and rely on default DNS behavior.

D: Incorrect – Set up custom DHCP options sets for each VPC.

Note: *Resolver endpoints + forwarding rules work across accounts when shared via RAM.*

Question 25 – Correct Answer: A

Q: You are using Direct Connect with a private virtual interface. Which of the following is required for a VPC to communicate with your on-premises network over Direct Connect?

Explanation: Associating a VPC with a Direct Connect Gateway using a private VIF enables private communication. Direct Connect Gateway allows association with multiple VPCs across regions for scalability.

A: Correct – Create a Direct Connect Gateway and associate the VPC.

B: Incorrect – Attach a public virtual interface to your VPC.

C: Incorrect – Create a Site-to-Site VPN on top of Direct Connect.

D: Incorrect – Associate your VPC with AWS Shield Advanced.

Question 26 – Correct Answer: C

Q: Your application accesses Amazon S3 and DynamoDB frequently from a private subnet. Which is the most secure and cost-effective method to ensure access without using NAT?

Explanation: Gateway endpoints are the optimal, cost-effective way to access S3/DynamoDB without NAT.

Gateway Endpoints do not support all AWS services, only S3/DynamoDB.

A: Incorrect – Deploy a NAT Gateway and route all traffic through it.

B: Incorrect – Assign public IPs to the EC2 instances.

C: Correct – Use VPC Gateway Endpoints for S3 and DynamoDB.

D: Incorrect – Use an Internet Gateway and block all other traffic via NACLs.

Question 27 – Correct Answer: B

Q: How can you secure your VPC against unapproved outbound DNS traffic?

Explanation: Route 53 Resolver DNS Firewall lets you block or allow DNS requests based on rules.

DNS Firewall operates at the VPC DNS Resolver level, not for public DNS queries via Internet Gateway.

A: Incorrect – Disable VPC DNS resolution.

B: Correct – Use Route 53 Resolver DNS Firewall with rule groups.

C: Incorrect – Use NAT Gateway flow logs for DNS traffic analysis.

D: Incorrect – Route DNS queries through GuardDuty.

Question 28 – Correct Answer: B

Q: You need to provide private, secure access from on-premises to an internal API hosted in AWS without traversing the public internet. Which solution is most appropriate?

Explanation: PrivateLink endpoints, combined with Direct Connect routing, ensure secure access to private services.

PrivateLink endpoints use interface endpoints (ENIs) within subnets and can integrate with Direct Connect or VPN.

A: Incorrect – Expose the API through a public API Gateway endpoint.

B: Correct – Use a VPC endpoint for the API and route traffic over Direct Connect.

C: Incorrect – Use an Elastic Load Balancer and allow traffic through a NAT Gateway.

D: Incorrect – Deploy a proxy server in a public subnet.

Question 29 – Correct Answer: B

Q: You want to troubleshoot asymmetric routing issues between two VPCs connected through a Transit Gateway. Which of these tools can you use to investigate traffic flows?

Explanation: Traffic Mirroring allows real-time visibility into network traffic, useful for diagnosing asymmetry.

Traffic Mirroring operates only on ENIs attached to EC2 instances (not all traffic types).

A: Incorrect – Amazon Inspector

B: Correct – VPC Traffic Mirroring

C: Incorrect – AWS Shield Advanced

D: Incorrect – AWS Systems Manager Session Manager

Question 30 – Correct Answer: A

Q: You need to minimize downtime during updates to a CloudFormation stack that modifies network components like route tables. Which of the following strategy should you use?

Explanation: CloudFormation Change Sets enable validation of proposed changes before execution, reducing risk.

A: Correct – Use a Change Set to preview changes before applying.

B: Incorrect – Update resources manually before updating the stack.

C: Incorrect – Delete the existing stack and recreate it.

D: Incorrect – Run stack updates in parallel for speed.

Question 31 – Correct Answer: B

Q: Your company needs to host a multi-tenant SaaS application where each tenant should access a dedicated network path. Which AWS networking service best supports this requirement?

Explanation: Using PrivateLink allows per-tenant access control via endpoints while maintaining privacy and isolation.

PrivateLink allows per-tenant isolation via endpoint policies.

A: Incorrect – VPC Peering

B: Correct – PrivateLink with separate endpoints per tenant

C: Incorrect – NAT Gateway with multiple route tables

D: Incorrect – Internet Gateway with firewall rules per tenant

Question 32 – Correct Answer: A

Q: An application in one VPC must frequently call a microservice hosted in another VPC in the same account. Which, according to you, is the best solution for high throughput and low latency?

Explanation: VPC Peering is efficient and provides high throughput and low latency for intra-account connectivity.

VPC Peering is non-transitive.

A: Correct – Use VPC Peering and update route tables accordingly.

B: Incorrect – Deploy a NAT Gateway in the source VPC.

C: Incorrect – Use AWS Site-to-Site VPN.

D: Incorrect – Create a Direct Connect link between VPCs.

Question 33 – Correct Answer: A

Q: A security team wants to block all outbound access to known malicious domains from within a VPC. Which is the most appropriate AWS-native solution?

Explanation: Route 53 Resolver DNS Firewall enables DNS-level threat prevention using managed domain lists.

A: Correct – Use Route 53 Resolver DNS Firewall.

B: Incorrect – Use NACLs to block domain names.

C: Incorrect – Configure WAF on outbound traffic.

D: Incorrect – Use GuardDuty to generate alerts.

Note: *Route 53 Resolver DNS Firewall supports AWS-managed threat intelligence domain lists as well as custom allow/block lists, enabling automatic blocking of known malicious domains at the DNS layer without managing IP addresses.*

Question 34 – Correct Answer: B

Q: You are designing connectivity between your AWS environment and multiple on-premises data centers. Each site needs secure, high-bandwidth, and reliable access. Which of these should you recommend?

Explanation: Direct Connect with a Direct Connect Gateway is most scalable for multi-site hybrid access.

DX + DX Gateway offers up to 100 Gbps, unlike VPN limits.

A: Incorrect – Use VPN tunnels from each data center.

B: Correct – Use AWS Direct Connect with a Direct Connect Gateway.

C: Incorrect – Use NAT Gateways with Internet Gateway fallback.

D: Incorrect – Use VPC Peering between each data center and AWS.

Question 35 – Correct Answer: D

Q: Your application is deployed across multiple Availability Zones behind a Network Load Balancer. You notice uneven traffic distribution. Which of the following is the most likely cause?

Explanation: Disabling cross-zone load balancing can cause traffic to remain in a single AZ even if targets are healthy elsewhere.

Cross-zone load balancing is disabled by default on NLBs and incurs extra data transfer costs when enabled.

A: Incorrect – Mismatch in target group health checks

B: Incorrect – Improper subnet associations on the NLB

C: Incorrect – Unbalanced AZ capacity

D: Correct – Cross-zone load balancing disabled

Question 36 – Correct Answer: D

Q: A VPC contains a private subnet where EC2 instances must download OS updates. You want to minimize cost and avoid public IPs. Which is the recommended solution?

Explanation: Interface endpoints allow direct, private connectivity; fallback to NAT Gateway when not available. Interface endpoints are billed hourly and per GB, so hybrid usage (interface + NAT fallback) balances cost vs coverage

A: Incorrect – Attach public IPs to each instance.

B: Incorrect – Use an Internet Gateway directly.

C: Incorrect – Deploy a NAT Gateway in a public subnet.

D: Correct – Use interface endpoints where supported and NAT Gateway otherwise.

Question 37 – Correct Answer: B

Q: You need to centralize DNS resolution across hundreds of AWS accounts and VPCs. Which scalable solution supports this design?

Explanation: Route 53 Resolver forwarding rules work across accounts and VPCs only when they are shared using AWS Resource Access Manager (RAM). Once shared, multiple VPCs in different accounts can use the same centralized DNS resolution setup.

A: Incorrect – Use private hosted zones in each VPC.

B: Correct – Use Route 53 Resolver with shared forwarding rules.

C: Incorrect – Create DHCP options for all VPCs.

D: Incorrect – Use VPC Peering with Resolver endpoints.

Question 38 – Correct Answer: B

Q: Your application uses Amazon CloudFront with an S3 origin. You want to restrict access to the origin bucket only from CloudFront. How can you achieve this?

Explanation: Origin Access Control (OAC) is the recommended and preferred way to restrict Amazon S3 access so that only CloudFront can read objects. OAC uses SigV4 signing, supports all S3 features, and replaces Origin Access Identity (OAI), which is now legacy/deprecated.

A: Incorrect – Enable bucket versioning.

B: Correct – Use an origin access control or Origin Access Identity (OAI).

C: Incorrect – Enable transfer acceleration.

D: Incorrect – Use CloudTrail to audit access.

Question 39 – Correct Answer: C

Q: A workload in a private subnet must securely retrieve credentials stored in Secrets Manager. Which is the most secure solution?

Explanation: Interface endpoints provide secure private connectivity to services like Secrets Manager.

A: Incorrect – Assign a public IP and access Secrets Manager directly.

B: Incorrect – Use NAT Gateway to access Secrets Manager.

C: Correct – Use a VPC interface endpoint for Secrets Manager.

D: Incorrect – Use CloudTrail to retrieve credentials.

Note: *Interface Endpoint for Secrets Manager also restricts access via endpoint policy for least privilege.*

Question 40 – Correct Answer: B

Q: You must ensure that the entire infrastructure created in your organization includes mandatory tags like 'Environment' and 'Owner'. How can this be enforced at creation time?

Explanation: IAM policy conditions can enforce tagging rules during provisioning, ensuring compliance from the start.

A: Incorrect – Use AWS Config with remediation rules.

B: Correct – Use IAM policies with tag condition keys.

C: Incorrect – Create manual tagging documentation for developers.

D: Incorrect – Use GuardDuty to detect untagged resources.

Question 41 – Correct Answer: B

Q: You are deploying an internal application used by employees across three regions. The application must be accessed using a single global IP with low latency. Which of the following services should you use?

Explanation: Global Accelerator provides a static IP and routes users to the nearest AWS Region with low latency.

A: Incorrect – Amazon Route 53 with latency-based routing

B: Correct – AWS Global Accelerator

C: Incorrect – Amazon CloudFront with geo restriction

D: Incorrect – Elastic Load Balancer with cross-region DNS failover

Question 42 – Correct Answer: C

Q: Which AWS feature helps detect and prevent configuration drift across networking components in a multi-account environment?

Explanation: AWS Config continuously monitors changes and helps enforce compliance and detect configuration drift.

A: Incorrect – AWS CloudTrail

B: Incorrect – AWS Systems Manager Parameter Store

C: Correct – AWS Config Rules

D: Incorrect – AWS Trusted Advisor

Question 43 – Correct Answer: B

Q: Your VPC has both IPv4 and IPv6 enabled. You want EC2 instances to access the internet using IPv6 but restrict IPv4 egress. Which configuration is required?

Explanation: An egress-only internet gateway enables outbound-only IPv6 traffic, securing inbound connections.

A: Incorrect – Assign public IPv4 addresses and restrict outbound rules.

B: Correct – Use an egress-only Internet Gateway for IPv6 traffic.

C: Incorrect – Use NAT Gateway for IPv6 only.

D: Incorrect – Disable DNS hostnames in the VPC.

Question 44 – Correct Answer: A

Q: How can you ensure that Route 53 only returns healthy endpoints for your application during DNS resolution?

Explanation: Route 53 health checks enable automatic DNS failover to healthy endpoints.

A: Correct – Use failover routing with Route 53 health checks.

B: Incorrect – Enable DNSSEC for all Route 53 hosted zones.

C: Incorrect – Configure alias records without health checks.

D: Incorrect – Use latency-based routing with static weights.

Question 45 – Correct Answer: B

Q: Your application requires encrypted traffic between EC2 instances across AZs. What is the most efficient AWS-native solution?

Explanation: Application-level TLS ensures encryption in-transit and offers flexibility across protocols.

A: Incorrect – Use security groups to control access.

B: Correct – Enable TLS encryption in the application layer.

C: Incorrect – Use VPC Peering with custom route tables.

D: Incorrect – Enable IPsec on all EC2 instances.

Question 46 – Correct Answer: B

Q: Which AWS service allows you to create logical boundaries for route propagation between different business units using Transit Gateway?

Explanation: Transit Gateway route tables allow segmentation and controlled route propagation between business units.

A: Incorrect – VPC Peering

B: Correct – Transit Gateway Route Tables

C: Incorrect – Site-to-Site VPN Policies

D: Incorrect – Direct Connect Gateways

Question 47 – Correct Answer: C

Q: A company uses a shared services VPC that multiple application VPCs connect to. Which of the following should be used to allow secure, private access to the shared services without exposing them publicly?

Explanation: PrivateLink provides private connectivity without requiring public IPs, ideal for shared services access.

A: Incorrect – NAT Gateways in each application VPC

B: Incorrect – Public IPs with security groups

C: Correct – Interface VPC Endpoints shared via PrivateLink

D: Incorrect – Route 53 public hosted zones

Question 48 – Correct Answer: A

Q: You are designing an architecture with multiple applications that require DNS-based failover between primary and backup regions. What should you use?

Explanation: Route 53 failover routing ensures DNS directs users to healthy endpoints during failure.

A: Correct – Route 53 with health checks and failover routing.

B: Incorrect – CloudFront with geo-restriction.

C: Incorrect – Global Accelerator with endpoint weighting.

D: Incorrect – Elastic Load Balancer with cross-region routing.

Question 49 – Correct Answer: C

Q: Which AWS service enables detailed logging and inspection of DNS queries for VPC resources?

Explanation: Route 53 Resolver Query Logging allows deep DNS query analysis within your VPC.

A: Incorrect – AWS CloudTrail

B: Incorrect – VPC Flow Logs

C: Correct – Route 53 Resolver Query Logging

D: Incorrect – Amazon Inspector

Question 50 – Correct Answer: B

Q: What is the purpose of an egress-only Internet Gateway in a dual-stack (IPv4 + IPv6) VPC?

Explanation: Egress-only internet gateways are required to route IPv6 traffic securely while blocking inbound.

A: Incorrect – To allow public access to IPv4 endpoints only.

B: Correct – To route IPv6 traffic to the internet while preventing inbound IPv6 connections.

C: Incorrect – To enable NAT for IPv6 traffic.

D: Incorrect – To encrypt all IPv6 traffic leaving the VPC.

Question 51 – Correct Answer: B

Q: You are designing a scalable multi-account AWS network using AWS Organizations. Which is the best way to apply centralized routing policies and monitor cross-account traffic?

Explanation: Transit Gateway with RAM enables shared routing and monitoring across AWS accounts.

A: Incorrect – Use VPC Peering and centralized CloudTrail logging.

B: Correct – Use Transit Gateway with shared access via Resource Access Manager (RAM).

C: Incorrect – Use Route 53 public hosted zones.

D: Incorrect – Use a NAT Gateway in each account.

Question 52 – Correct Answer: B

Q: A new regulation mandates all external traffic logs must be stored for one year and be queryable. Which of these solutions best supports this requirement?

Explanation: VPC Flow Logs to S3 and Athena support long-term storage and querying of traffic data.

A: Incorrect – Enable NAT Gateway metrics and export to S3.

B: Correct – Enable VPC Flow Logs with S3 destination and use Athena for querying.

C: Incorrect – Enable Route 53 DNS query logging.

D: Incorrect – Use Systems Manager Inventory.

Question 53 – Correct Answer: B

Q: You need to restrict direct access to EC2 instances from the internet but still allow them to connect to AWS services. What should you do?

Explanation: VPC endpoints allow secure access to AWS services while blocking public traffic.

A: Incorrect – Assign public IPs and block all inbound ports.

B: Correct – Use VPC endpoints and remove the Internet Gateway.

C: Incorrect – Deploy EC2 in a public subnet and use security groups.

D: Incorrect – Use a VPN and enable remote desktop.

Question 54 – Correct Answer: C

Q: Which AWS-native tool allows you to define and enforce rules for CloudFormation templates to ensure secure and compliant networking configurations?

Explanation: CloudFormation Guard validates infrastructure definitions against compliance policies.

A: Incorrect – AWS Config

B: Incorrect – IAM policy conditions

C: Correct – CloudFormation Guard (cfn-guard)

D: Incorrect – Service Control Policies (SCPs)

Question 55 – Correct Answer: B

Q: You need to ensure applications in different VPCs can access AWS Secrets Manager securely without using the public internet. What is the recommended setup?

Explanation: Interface endpoints provide secure, private access to Secrets Manager.

A: Incorrect – Create VPC peering between all VPCs and route via NAT Gateway.

B: Correct – Use interface VPC endpoints for Secrets Manager in each VPC.

C: Incorrect – Use VPN tunnels between VPCs and deploy Secrets Manager in one VPC.

D: Incorrect – Use Transit Gateway with internet routing.

Question 56 – Correct Answer: B

Q: Your network team wants to allow connectivity between hundreds of VPCs while maintaining isolated routing domains for development, staging, and production. Which AWS feature supports this architecture?

Explanation: Transit Gateway route tables allow segmented routing policies by environment.

A: Incorrect – Multiple Internet Gateways

B: Correct – Transit Gateway with route tables per environment

C: Incorrect – VPC Peering with NACLs

D: Incorrect – Global Accelerator

Question 57 – Correct Answer: D

Q: Which feature helps reduce latency for users globally when accessing a multi-region application hosted on AWS?

Explanation: All listed options help improve latency and delivery for global applications.

A: Incorrect – Route 53 with geolocation routing.

B: Incorrect – Global Accelerator with endpoint health checks.

C: Incorrect – CloudFront with Lambda@Edge.

D: Correct – All of the above.

Question 58 – Correct Answer: B

Q: Your EC2 instances in a private subnet are unable to resolve domain names. Which configuration should you check?

Explanation: DNS resolution failures in private subnets are usually caused by DNS settings in VPC configuration.

A: Incorrect – Whether NAT Gateway is available.

B: Correct – Whether DNS resolution is enabled in the VPC settings.

C: Incorrect – Whether the subnet is associated with a public route table.

D: Incorrect – Whether IAM permissions allow DNS resolution.

Question 59 – Correct Answer: C

Q: Which of the following helps implement zero-trust architecture in AWS networking?

Explanation: Security groups and IAM enable fine-grained access control aligned with zero-trust architecture.

A: Incorrect – Security groups with default allow-all rules.

B: Incorrect – Network ACLs with wide IP ranges.

C: Correct – Micro-segmentation using security groups and IAM policies.

D: Incorrect – Creating VPCs with overlapping CIDRs.

Question 60 – Correct Answer: B

Q: Your application requires periodic access to S3 from an on-premises data center without using a VPN. Which is a secure way to achieve this?

Explanation: Direct Connect public virtual interface allows access to AWS public services from on-premises.

A: Incorrect – Enable public access on the S3 bucket.

B: Correct – Use AWS Direct Connect public virtual interface.

C: Incorrect – Expose S3 through a public API Gateway endpoint.

D: Incorrect – Use CloudFront signed URLs.

Question 61 – Correct Answer: A

Q: What feature of Transit Gateway allows for automatic updates to routing tables when new VPCs are added?

Explanation: Route propagation automatically updates Transit Gateway route tables as attachments change.

A: Correct – Route propagation

B: Incorrect – Static routing

C: Incorrect – Direct Connect Gateway association

D: Incorrect – NAT translation

Question 62 – Correct Answer: C

Q: Which AWS service allows you to build private connectivity between your VPC and the network of a SaaS provider?

Explanation: PrivateLink establishes private connections to partner and SaaS services.

A: Incorrect – Direct Connect

B: Incorrect – Site-to-Site VPN

C: Correct – AWS PrivateLink

D: Incorrect – Transit Gateway

Question 63 – Correct Answer: A

Q: How can you restrict certain AWS users from creating internet-facing load balancers in a specific region?

Explanation: IAM policy conditions can block creation of internet-facing resources in restricted regions.

A: Correct – Use IAM policy with condition on region and scheme type.

B: Incorrect – Disable Elastic Load Balancing service in the region.

C: Incorrect – Remove EC2 privileges from all users.

D: Incorrect – Use Security Groups with deny-all rules.

Question 64 – Correct Answer: C

Q: You are inspecting packets between two EC2 instances for troubleshooting. Which tool should you use?

Explanation: Traffic Mirroring is used to inspect packets in real-time between EC2 instances.

A: Incorrect – CloudTrail

B: Incorrect – VPC Flow Logs

C: Correct – VPC Traffic Mirroring

D: Incorrect – AWS Config

Question 65 – Correct Answer: B

Q: What is the best AWS-native solution for a secure and scalable hybrid DNS configuration between on-premises and AWS VPCs?

Explanation: Route 53 Resolver endpoints allow hybrid DNS resolution between AWS and on-premises.

A: Incorrect – Create custom DNS resolvers on EC2.

B: Correct – Use Route 53 Resolver inbound and outbound endpoints.

C: Incorrect – Deploy DNS Forwarders using NAT Gateway.

D: Incorrect – Create multiple DHCP options sets.

Key Takeaways and Exam Strategies Reinforcement

Key Concept Summary

Here is the summary of some of the key concept that needs to be taken into consideration before taking the examination.

- Understand the difference between Gateway and Interface VPC endpoints.
- Use Transit Gateway for scalable hub-and-spoke network topologies.
- Implement Route 53 Resolver DNS Firewall for domain-based filtering.
- Utilize VPC Flow Logs and Traffic Mirroring for network monitoring and troubleshooting.
- Enable BGP with Direct Connect for resilient hybrid connections.
- Use CloudFormation Guard to enforce secure infrastructure patterns.
- Apply IAM policies to restrict creation of public-facing resources.
- Leverage Route 53 for DNS failover and latency-based routing.
- Use PrivateLink to expose services securely within and across VPCs.
- Implement zero-trust architecture with granular Security Groups and IAM conditions.

Exam Strategy Tips

Here are some of the Exam strategy tips that needs to be taken into consideration before taking the examination.

- Read each question carefully and identify keywords like 'secure', 'cost-effective', or 'high availability'.
- Eliminate obviously incorrect answers first to improve your odds.
- Expect scenario-based questions with multiple services; think in terms of architecture, not individual components.
- Time management is crucial – don't spend too long on a single question.
- Use AWS-provided whitepapers, especially the Advanced Networking whitepaper, for deep conceptual knowledge.
- Practice questions by domain (hybrid, security, automation, and the like) to identify weak areas.
- Be cautious with answers involving public exposure unless explicitly required.
- Check if a NAT Gateway is really necessary – in many cases, VPC endpoints are better.
- Understand service limits and regional features; they may affect design choices.
- Don't memorize – aim to understand how services interact under different scenarios.

Final Review Checklist before Exam

Here are some of the Final Review Checklist that needs to be verified before taking the examination.

- Transit Gateway versus VPC Peering versus PrivateLink – when to use each.

- NAT Gateway versus Interface Endpoint versus Gateway Endpoint.
- Route 53 Resolver rules and DNS forwarding.
- CloudFormation deployment controls and drift detection.
- Direct Connect versus VPN - use cases and encryption.
- IAM policies with tag conditions and SCPs for control.
- Traffic Mirroring and Flow Logs for packet inspection.
- Regional failover strategies using Route 53 and Global Accelerator.
- Resource sharing via AWS RAM and cross-account access.
- Route table isolation using Transit Gateway route domains.

Conclusion

This chapter provided a critical opportunity to reinforce your knowledge and test your readiness for the AWS Certified Advanced Networking - Specialty (ANS-C01) exam through a series of 65 high-quality, scenario-based mock questions. Each question was designed not only to reflect the real exam environment but also to push your understanding of core AWS networking services and architectural best practices.

Through detailed explanations in Section 17.3, we did not just tell you what the correct answer was — we showed you why it was correct and why the other options were not, helping you train your mind to think like an AWS networking architect. This chapter encouraged logical elimination, contextual thinking, and real-world AWS implementation awareness.

In Section 17.4, we distilled this vast domain into key takeaways, actionable exam strategies, and a final review checklist that should serve as your last-mile revision resource. Whether it's understanding VPC design patterns, securing hybrid connections, choosing between PrivateLink, Peering, and Transit Gateway, or evaluating the nuances of DNS, NAT, or firewall controls — you have now had the chance to face the same kind of decisions that certified AWS professionals make every day.

The next chapter is a concluding chapter that provides a comprehensive review of key concepts, followed by a question-and-answer section to consolidate knowledge. It also offers career guidance on advancing in AWS networking roles, highlighting job opportunities, certifications, and networking with industry professionals. The chapter includes additional resources like study groups, online forums, and AWS communities.

CHAPTER 18
Final Q&A and Career Guidance

Introduction

As you approach the final stretch of your journey toward becoming an AWS Certified Advanced Networking Specialist, this chapter serves as both a comprehensive recap and a strategic launchpad for your future. The ANS-C01 exam is not merely a test of knowledge — it is a measure of how effectively you can apply advanced networking principles to real-world AWS environments.

While Associate and Professional exams test cloud usage and architecture, ANS-C01 tests whether you can think like a network engineer inside AWS — making it one of the most technically demanding AWS certifications.

In this concluding chapter, we will revisit the essential networking concepts that form the backbone of AWS networking architecture. You will engage with a curated Final Q&A section that challenges your understanding, consolidates your knowledge, and prepares you for success on exam day.

Beyond certification, we shall explore the career paths available in AWS networking, provide actionable advice for advancing in cloud networking roles, and highlight valuable communities, resources, and strategies to stay current in this fast-evolving field. Whether you're aspiring to become a Network Cloud Engineer, Solutions Architect, or Cloud Security Specialist, this chapter is your gateway to turning certification into career momentum.

Structure

In this chapter, we will walk through:

- Key Networking Concepts: Final Recap
- Final Q&A: Consolidating Your Knowledge
- Career Path in AWS Networking
- Study Resources and Continued Learning
- Real-World Applications of AWS Networking Expertise
- Final Words: From Certification to Cloud Leadership
- Key Takeaways and Exam Strategies Reinforcement

Key Networking Concepts: Final Recap

In this section, we will be revisiting the key networking principles essential for success in the ANS-C01 exam.

- **Amazon VPC**

  Scenario: Design a VPC with public subnets for ALBs and private subnets for app servers accessing the internet via a NAT Gateway.

- **AWS Transit Gateway**

  Scenario: Centrally connect 30 VPCs and an on-prem data center while controlling traffic flow using route propagation and TGW route tables.

- **PrivateLink**

  Scenario: Expose a shared internal service to multiple AWS accounts without using public IPs or VPC peering.

- **AWS Global Accelerator**

  Scenario: Route global users to the nearest healthy regional endpoint to reduce latency and improve availability for a worldwide application.

- **Hybrid Networking (Direct Connect + VPN)**

  Scenario: Use Direct Connect for primary traffic and VPN as failover to ensure resilient on-prem to AWS connectivity.

- **Security Controls (NACLs, Security Groups, Network Firewall)**

  Scenario: Block a malicious IP range at the subnet level with NACLs while allowing only application-specific ports via Security Groups.

- **VPC Traffic Mirroring**

  Scenario: Mirror EC2 traffic to a third-party IDS appliance to analyze suspicious packet-level behavior.

- **Monitoring (Flow Logs, CloudWatch, GuardDuty)**

  Scenario: Use VPC Flow Logs to identify rejected traffic patterns and GuardDuty to detect anomalous network activity.

- **High Availability & Resilience**

  Scenario: Deploy workloads across multiple AZs with health-check-based failover and replicate critical data across regions.

Final tip: *Understand how these services integrate within multi-account architectures using* AWS *Organizations and Service Control Policies* (SCPs).

Final Q&A: Consolidating Your Knowledge

Sample Question 1:

Your company has a hybrid environment with AWS and an on-premises data center. They require low-latency, highly available connectivity. Which of the following should you recommend?

a. AWS Site-to-Site VPN only.

b. Direct Connect with VPN backup.

c. Internet Gateway with IPsec VPN.

d. AWS Global Accelerator.

Correct Answer: **b**

Explanation: Direct Connect provides low-latency, high-bandwidth connectivity. Adding VPN as backup increases resiliency, aligning with HA principles.

Sample Question 2:

Which AWS service allows private connectivity between VPCs in different accounts without traversing the internet?

a. VPC Peering

b. Transit Gateway

c. PrivateLink

d. NAT Gateway

Correct Answer: c

Explanation: PrivateLink provides private connectivity to services across VPCs/accounts without public IPs or traffic over the Internet.

...And so on up to 30+ questions, each mapped to real-world scenarios from the ANS-C01 exam blueprint.

Career Path in AWS Networking

With the ANS-C01 certification, doors open across several roles:

- **Cloud Network Engineer:** Focuses on designing, implementing, and maintaining AWS-based network infrastructure.
- **Cloud Security Engineer:** Combines networking expertise with security controls, such as AWS WAF, Shield, and Network Firewall.
- **Solutions Architect (Networking Focus):** Provides guidance on scalable network designs.
- **Cloud Consultant or DevOps Engineer:** Implements hybrid cloud strategies, CI/CD integration with networking requirements.
- **Network Automation Engineer (Highly recommended pairing with ANS-C01):** Automates network provisioning, configuration, and compliance using Infrastructure as Code (Terraform, CloudFormation), Python, and APIs.

  Why it matters: Manual networking is fading—automation is becoming the default.
- **Cloud Platform Engineer (Networking-heavy):** Builds reusable networking platforms (landing zones, shared VPCs, centralized TGW, firewall hubs) for internal teams.
- **SRE / Reliability Engineer (Network-centric):** Focuses on latency, fault tolerance, traffic flow, and failure recovery at scale—especially in multi-region systems.
- **Multi-Cloud Network Architect:** Designs and manages networking across AWS, Azure, and GCP, handling inter-cloud routing, identity, and security.

Salary Expectations (varies by region):

- Entry-level (1-3 years): $90,000 - $120,000/year

- Mid-level (4-6 years): $120,000 - $150,000/year

- Senior (7+ years): $150,000 - $200,000+/year

Certifications to pair with ANS-C01:

- AWS Certified Security – Specialty

- AWS Certified Solutions Architect – Professional

- Cisco CCNP or CCNA Cloud

- Certified Kubernetes Administrator (CKA)

Study Resources and Continued Learning

Preparing for advanced AWS networking certifications requires a combination of official documentation, hands-on practice, and community-driven insights to build both theoretical knowledge and real-world problem-solving skills.

Free Resources

Free learning resources provide an excellent starting point for building foundational knowledge and staying updated with AWS networking concepts without financial investment.

Official AWS Learning

AWS offers a wide range of authoritative learning materials that align closely with real-world architectures and certification requirements.

- **AWS Skill Builder:** Free digital courses, exam readiness modules, and selected hands-on labs straight from AWS.
- **AWS Documentation and What is New:** Essential for understanding *current* behavior of services like Transit Gateway, PrivateLink, and Direct Connect.

Community and Peer Learning

Engaging with the AWS community helps you gain practical insights, learn from real-world experiences, and stay informed about evolving best practices.

- **Reddit - r/AWSCertifications:** Real exam feedback, last-minute tips, and scenario discussions.
- **Discord / Slack AWS Communities:** Live troubleshooting discussions and architecture debates (very ANS-C01-style thinking).
- **LinkedIn (AWS Heroes and Networking Specialists):** Follow practitioners who share real-world architectures, failures, and lessons learned.

Paid Resources

Paid platforms offer structured, in-depth learning paths and high-quality practice materials designed to accelerate certification readiness.

Structured Learning & Practice

- **A Cloud Guru / Pluralsight:** Deep video courses, scenario walkthroughs, and visual explanations of complex routing and hybrid setups.
- **Tutorials Dojo:** Industry-best practice questions with explanations that mirror ANS-C01 exam logic, not just answers.

Must-Read AWS Whitepapers and Guides (High-Yield)

These are gold for scenario-based questions:

- **AWS Well-Architected Framework - Reliability & Security Pillars:**

  → Directly maps to HA, failover, and defense-in-depth questions.
- **AWS Hybrid Connectivity Whitepaper:**

  → Covers Direct Connect, VPN, resiliency models, and BGP behavior (exam favorite).

- **Amazon VPC Connectivity Options:**
  → Helps choose between Peering, Transit Gateway, PrivateLink, and endpoints.
- **AWS Best Practices for DDoS Resiliency:**
  → Critical for WAF, Shield, and edge protection scenarios.
- **AWS Networking & Content Delivery Blog:**
  → Real examples of TGW scaling, Global Accelerator, and multi-region traffic patterns.

Events and Ongoing Learning

- **AWS re:Invent:**
  Deep-dive sessions on networking internals, failures, and new service behavior.
- **AWS Summits (Regional):**
  Practical architecture sessions and hands-on demos.
- **Local AWS User Groups:**
  Great for real-world stories that mirror exam scenarios.

Real-World Applications of AWS Networking Expertise

Companies are constantly shifting to hybrid and cloud-native architectures. Here is how your skills apply:

- **Multi-Region App Deployment:**

How it is done:

- Centralized routing using Transit Gateway.
- Global traffic distribution via Route 53 latency-based routing.
- Automated provisioning with Terraform / CloudFormation.

Result / Impact:

- 30–60% latency reduction for global users.
- Seamless regional failover with minimal downtime.
- Faster environment rollout through IaC.

Industries: Media, SaaS, e-commerce (performance-driven).

- **Zero Trust Networking:**

How it is done:

- Service exposure via PrivateLink (no public IPs).
- Fine-grained access using IAM policies & SCPs.
- Network rules enforced through automated security baselines (IaC).

Result / Impact:

- Eliminates public attack surface.
- Reduced lateral movement risk inside the network.

- Easier compliance audits through consistent, codified controls.

Industries: Finance, healthcare, enterprise IT (compliance-driven).

- Disaster Recovery & Business Continuity:

How it is done:

- Route 53 health checks with DNS failover.
- Cross-region data replication (such as S3 replication).
- DR infrastructure deployed on-demand using Terraform.

Result / Impact:

- RTO reduced from hours to minutes.
- Lower DR costs by avoiding always-on secondary stacks.
- Predictable recovery via repeatable IaC workflows.

Industries: Banking, insurance, healthcare (mission-critical systems).

- Security Monitoring and Threat Detection:

How it is done:

- VPC Traffic Mirroring for packet-level visibility.
- Stream traffic via Amazon Kinesis to SIEM tools.
- Monitoring pipelines deployed and version-controlled using IaC.

Result / Impact:

- Faster threat detection and response.
- Deep visibility into east-west traffic.
- Easier integration with enterprise SOC tools.

Industries: Finance, regulated enterprises, large platforms.

Significance of Automation (across All Scenarios)

Using Infrastructure as Code:

- Ensures consistent network configurations.
- Reduces human error in complex routing and security setups.
- Enables rapid scaling and rollback.
- Makes networking auditable, testable, and repeatable.

Final Words: From Certification to Cloud Leadership

Congratulations on making it this far! ANS-C01 is a testament to your networking expertise.

Next Steps:

- **Stay certified:** Plan your recertification every 3 years.
- **Mentor and contribute:** Write blogs, publish solutions on Medium or Dev.to, speak at webinars.
- **Build a 1-Year Plan:** Master container networking, edge networking, and advanced automation.

- **Build a 5-Year Vision:** Transition into cloud network architecture leadership or consulting.

The cloud journey is ever-evolving. Your success lies not just in mastering AWS networking but in continuously adapting and innovating.

After earning ANS-C01, many professionals face a common gap: the knowledge is there, but production environments are messier than exam scenarios. Real systems involve legacy IP overlaps, undocumented routes, organizational silos, and security constraints that don't appear in whitepapers. Another frequent challenge is translating deep networking insight into influence—convincing teams why a design choice matters, not just how it works. Finally, keeping skills current requires ongoing effort, as AWS networking services evolve rapidly.

The upside: those who pair certification knowledge with hands-on labs, automation (IaC), and real incident analysis quickly move from "certified" to trusted expert.

ANS-C01 opens the door — but real growth happens when theory meets imperfect reality.

Key Takeaways and Exam Strategies Reinforcement

- Mastering core AWS networking services like VPC, Transit Gateway, PrivateLink, and Route 53 is essential for the ANS-C01 exam.
- Hybrid connectivity, security layers, and real-world architectural decisions play a significant role in both the exam and daily work.
- The Final Q&A section mimics the depth and scenario-driven nature of the actual certification, enhancing your critical thinking.
- Certification opens doors to various career paths including Network Engineer, Cloud Architect, and Security Consultant.
- Active participation in AWS communities, conferences, and ongoing learning is crucial for long-term success in cloud networking.

Conclusion

Chapter 18, *Final Q&A and Career Guidance*, is more than just a final review—it is a gateway to your transition from certification candidate to cloud networking professional. As you step beyond the ANS-C01 exam, remember that your value lies not only in your technical expertise but also in your adaptability and contribution to the broader tech community.

The cloud is ever-evolving, and networking is at its heart. So, keep building, keep learning, and keep sharing. Your journey does not end with this certification — it begins.

Index

A

B

C

D

E

F

G

H

I

O

P

Q

R

S

T